AN INTRODUCTION TO
THEORIES
OF
PERSONALITY
Fourth Edition

Robert B. Ewen

AN INTRODUCTION TO

THEORIES
OF
PERSONALITY

Fourth Edition

LEA LAWRENCE ERLBAUM ASSOCIATES, PUBLISHERS
1993   Hillsdale, New Jersey   Hove and London

Lawrence Erlbaum Associates, Inc., Publishers
365 Broadway
Hillsdale, New Jersey 07642

Library of Congress Cataloging-in-Publication Data

Ewen, Robert B., 1940–
    An introduction to theories of personality / Robert B. Ewen.
        p.   cm.
    Bibliography: p.
    Includes index.
    ISBN 0-8058-0109-X
    1. Personality   I. Title.
BF698.E87   1988
155.2–dc19
                                                                        88-1075
                                                                        CIP

Printed in the United States of America
10   9   8   7   6   5   4   3   2   1

CONTENTS

PART IV
HUMANISTIC AND EXISTENTIAL PSYCHOLOGY

CHAPTER 12
CARL R. ROGERS
Self-Actualization Theory (I)   *373*

CHAPTER 13
ABRAHAM H. MASLOW
Self-Actualization Theory (II)   *397*

CHAPTER 14
ROLLO MAY
Existential Psychology   *423*

PREFACE

This book is intended as an introduction to the field of personality theory. The major goals are to provide a solid foundation for further study, to stimulate enthusiasm for this important and provocative area, and to promote interest in the primary sources on which this secondary one is based. I have sought to implement these objectives in the following ways:

First-hand Quotations. The student of personality theory is undoubtedly eager to examine the writings of the famous theorists themselves, rather than relying wholly on the interpretations of the textbook's author. Therefore, numerous quotations have been integrated within the text. Also, paperback reprints are cited as well as more standard editions. Paperbacks make it possible to acquire a comprehensive scholarly library at moderate cost, and my hope is that the somewhat awkward referencing system will justify its existence by facilitating comparisons with (and promoting interest in) the original sources.

Capsule Summaries. Most personality theorists are fond (perhaps too fond) of neologisms. To help the student learn the many definitions presented in each chapter, Capsule Summaries of these concepts are included throughout the text.

Theoretical Applications. In my opinion, some knowledge of the major applications of a personality theory helps to clarify its more abstruse concepts. I have therefore included an introduction to such applications as dream interpretation, psychopathology, psychotherapy, work, religion, education, literature, and any area of importance to a particular psychologist (e.g., Allport and prejudice). Most chapters also contain some discussion of research designed to evaluate the theory in question, and/or the theorist's views about psychological research in general.

Common Framework. To facilitate comparisons among the various theories, each chapter follows a common framework (described in Chapter 1). In addition, mention is made at times of important similarities and differences among the various theories. Each chapter and subchapter stands on its own, however, so that the instructor may select virtually any combination for inclusion in a given course.

Coverage. In addition to my own personal preferences, the coverage of the present text was influenced by two polls of those who teach theories of personality. According to the first poll, conducted in 1980 (N = 17), this text includes the thirteen most important theorists plus four of the following six. The second poll, taken in 1987 (N = 21), produced similar results: the theorists discussed herein represent the eleven most important plus five of the following six. Thus the present edition includes 16 of the top 17 theorists plus Murray, who ranked 19th.

Interest and Readability. I have sought to maintain a readable and interesting style, without sacrificing accuracy or scholarliness. In most cases I have begun each chapter with a significant anecdote from the theorist's life, and used this to lead into his or her theory.

This book is divided into five parts. Each section is preceded by a brief prologue, designed to preview and promote interest in what lies ahead. (It may be stretching a point to include Kelly in the section on research-oriented theories, because he was a clinician; but his theory does contend that we all behave much like the research scientist.)

I have avoided the use of "he" to refer to people in general. But I do not feel justified in rewriting history, so I have left such pronouns intact in the firsthand quotations. At times I have made minor changes in the quotations, such as adding or deleting a comma or interchanging a capital and a small letter, without inserting an ellipsis or brackets. However, any more major alterations have been so denoted.

Study Questions. Study questions are presented at the end of each chapter dealing with a personality theory (that is, Chapters 2-16). These questions have been designed to encourage critical thinking about the material, and to stimulate discussion and debate about important issues. Comments, hints, case histories, and practical examples concerning these questions are given in an appendix at the end of this book.

General Approach. Each chapter in this text is based on the work of a specific theorist (or theorists). Although quite popular, this approach has been subjected to some sharp criticism. (See for example the chapter on personality in the 1987 *Annual Review of Psychology.*) These dissenters state that all other psychology courses are organized by content area, rather than by what they cynically refer to as "a tour through the graveyard" of noted but (in most cases) deceased psychologists. They argue that personality theory must be a rather backward area to be explicated in this fashion. And they regard the texts that use this approach as similar, "copy-cat" versions of one another.

Needless to say, I emphatically disagree with this point of view. Different courses cover different types of material, so different pedagogical approaches may therefore be desirable. Of course, there is an underlying reason for the insistence on organization by content: this facilitates an emphasis on empirical research. Specific, narrow content areas can easily be organized around research findings. There is no need to bother with grand theories that attempt to explain a much wider segment of human behavior, or to grapple with abstract and/or unconscious processes that are quite difficult to study in the psychological laboratory.

The scientific method has well-known and important advantages. But as many noted theorists have pointed out, there is also a negative side to empirical psychological research: the tendency to focus on trivial but easily investigated issues. Maslow put it this way: "The besetting sin of the academicians [is] that they prefer to do what they are easily able rather than what they ought, like the not-so-bright kitchen helper I knew who opened every can in the hotel one day because he was so *very* good at opening cans. . . . The journals of science are full of instances that illustrate [this] point, that what is not worth doing, is not worth doing well." Rogers, Allport, and Murray also conclude that psychologists are far too fearful and defensive about appearing unscientific, and therefore focus on methodologically precise but trivial research topics. None of these theorists is anti-research; they are warning that the pro-research emphasis can go too far.

To study grand theories is to study the work of truly brilliant and creative thinkers. Thus the study of personality theory, as presented herein, is educational in the truest sense of the word. The student must adopt a different outlook in each chapter: first thinking like a Freudian, then like a Jungian, and so forth. This is likely to provide valuable training in open-mindedness, because all of these diverse and often contradictory theories have made important contributions to our knowledge. It will also enable students to acquire a breadth of concepts and principles that they can use to unravel the mysteries of human behavior. To be sure, many profound discoveries made by personality theorists were derived from clinical observation. This source of knowledge is anathematic to all too many research-oriented psychologists, but it is nevertheless extremely important. As Dollard and Miller observe, "Outside of psychotherapy, how many subjects have been studied for an hour a day, for five days a week, [and] for from one to three years . . . [and in a] life situation [which] is vital, [where] the alternatives are years of misery or years of relative peace and success?"

The prejudice of those who insist on organization by content is most apparent in their view that all theorist-organized textbooks are copy-cat versions of one another. In other areas of psychology, those who see an existing situation and try to improve on it are praised for their initiative. Not so to these critics, for textbook writing is a form of teaching—and as we all know, undergraduate teaching ranks a poor third to research and to graduate teaching in the hierarchy of higher education. Shocking though it may be to these critics, there are those of us who perceive the possibility of significant improvements in theorist-organized personality textbooks, just as some psychologists perceive better ways to design and execute research studies. If undergraduate teaching were accorded greater priority in higher education, and if efforts to produce better textbooks were not so readily denigrated, perhaps this respect would filter down to secondary education, and perhaps we would not have so many serious problems in that area. But all too many academic psychologists believe that by regarding themselves as "scientists," they are laying claim to a far higher and more worthwhile calling than "teacher." And they promote their prejudice by requiring all other academic psychologists to carry out research, even though much of psychological research is trivial, and even though some excellent teachers have no interest in conducting research.

There are important differences among the various theorist-organized personality texts. Whether or not I have succeeded in making significant improvements isn't for me to say, although reviews of previous editions have been reassuring. This I do know: I have learned a great deal from writing a book organized as is this one, and I have found that students also learn much from this approach.

Thanks are due once again to those who helped in various ways with the preparation of previous editions of this book: Dr. Eugene Sachs, Dr. Olaf W. Millert, Dr. Ronald Tikofsky, Joan Goldstein, Jack Burton, and James Anker. And a special vote of thanks goes to Larry Erlbaum for making the present edition possible.

AN INTRODUCTION TO
THEORIES
OF
PERSONALITY
Fourth Edition

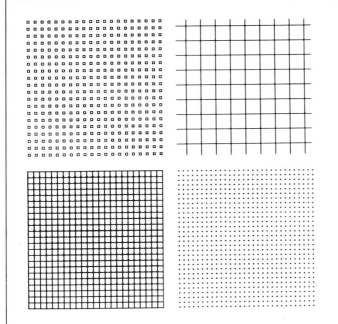

1

INTRODUCTION
Theories of Personality

This book is about one of the most fascinating of all topics: the human personality, how it is formed, how it develops, and how it influences behavior. There is as yet no one best theory of personality, and the great psychologists whose views we will examine frequently disagree with one another, so the reader seeking a unified and noncontradictory subject will be disappointed. But if you are intrigued by the challenge of trying to understand human nature, by comparing and evaluating different and thought-provoking ideas, and by watching a science that began only some 100 years ago grow slowly toward maturity, you should find this field to be highly rewarding.

THE MEANING OF PERSONALITY

Most of us have an intuitive understanding of the meaning of "personality." However, formally defining this multifaceted term is considerably more difficult.

One possibility is to highlight the visible and social aspects of personality, or the way a person appears to others (aggressive, shy, friendly, immature, and so forth). In fact, some theorists insist that personality can be studied only through its interpersonal manifestations. However, this approach overlooks some important considerations: personality may exist even in the absence of other people, and may have aspects that are not visible. Therefore, perhaps the most common approach is to define personality in terms of *characteristics or qualities within an individual.* Such definitions typically include virtually everything about a person (mental, emotional, social, and physical). Yet some of these definitions stress those characteristics that all human beings have in common, while others emphasize the uniqueness of every human personality.

Such disagreements reflect the current status of psychology, where limited knowledge makes possible many different theories of personality—and where different theorists define personality in different ways. However, most psychologists do agree on certain general considerations. In particular, personality is regarded as relatively *stable.* It may change over a long period of time, and a person may well behave differently in different situations. Nevertheless, personality refers to long-lasting and *important* characteristics of an individual, ones that continue to exert a strong influence on behavior.

3

Some aspects of personality are *unobservable,* such as thoughts, memories, and dreams; while others are *observable,* as is the case with overt actions. Personality also includes aspects that are concealed from oneself, or *unconscious,* as well as those that are *conscious* and well within one's awareness.

THEORIES OF PERSONALITY

Theories and Constructs

Insofar as the term "theory" is concerned, there is less controversy and greater agreement. First of all, a theory is an *unproved speculation* about reality, one not known to be either true or false. Established facts are often lacking in scientific work, and a theory offers guidelines that will serve us in the absence of more precise information. Second, a theory consists of *a set of terms and principles constructed or applied by the theorist,* which are referred to as **constructs.** Like the author or inventor, the theorist is a creator (of constructs); and like creators in other disciplines, the theorist borrows from and builds upon the work of his or her predecessors. Third, the constructs must be *interrelated* so that the theory is logically consistent. In addition to defining and explaining the terms and principles, the theorist must show how they fit together into a coherent whole.

Dimensions for Comparing Theories of Personality

Ideally, there are four criteria that a theory of personality should satisfy: description, explanation, prediction, and control.

Human behavior can be bewilderingly complicated, and a useful theory helps bring order out of chaos. It provides convenient *descriptions,* establishes a framework for organizing substantial amounts of data, and focuses attention on those matters that are of greater importance. In addition, a good personality theory *explains* the phenomena under study. It offers answers to such significant questions as the causes of individual differences in personality, why some people are more pathological than others, how personality is formed, and so forth. A theory should also generate *predictions,* so that it may be evaluated and improved (or discarded). To many psychologists, the acid test of any theory is its ability to predict future events. Finally, a valuable theory usually leads to important practical applications. It facilitates *control* and change of the environment—for example, by bringing about better techniques of parenting, education, or psychotherapy.

These criteria may seem unambiguous, yet there is often considerable disagreement about how to apply them. Some psychologists emphasize that a scientific theory should generate formal, objective predictions that can be tested under the controlled conditions of the research laboratory. By these lights, a theory with many constructs that are difficult to evaluate empirically (such as the Freudian id, ego, and superego), or one that does not stimulate a considerable amount of research, would be regarded as inferior. Other psychologists view the research laboratory as inevitably artificial. They prefer to derive their theories of personality from informal clinical observations, an approach they regard as respectably and sufficiently scientific:

> In point of fact psychoanalysis is a method of research, an impartial instrument, like the infinitesimal calculus. . . . The use of analysis for the treatment of the neuroses is only one of its applications; the future will perhaps show that it is not the most important one. . . . It is only by carrying on our analytic pastoral work that we can deepen our dawning comprehension of the human mind. This prospect of scientific gain has been the proudest and happiest feature of analytic work. (Freud, 1927/1961c, p. 36; 1926/1969b, pp. 97, 109–110.)[1]

If laboratory research methods in psychology were as effective as those of other sciences, such an approach might well be superior. Clinical observation is subjective and uncontrolled, and the power of suggestion may influence the patient's behavior in ways that support the therapist's theory of personality. Or the therapist may more readily perceive evidence that supports the theory, and disregard contradictory data. Therefore, the prospect of objective validation through laboratory research is highly appealing.

Unfortunately, psychology is a much younger science than physics or chemistry, its subject matter is quite different, and its techniques are less well refined. Practical and financial limitations often require the use of small and/or atypical samples, such as college students, laboratory animals, or volunteers. Experimental procedures are often too insensitive to measure unobservable or unconscious processes with any accuracy, or even to ensure that the effects intended by the experimenter are created within the minds of the subjects. And human beings differ rather significantly from chemical elements or inert physical objects. For these reasons, the insights available from experiences of real importance to people (such as psychotherapy) are extremely valuable, and both approaches are essential to present-day psychology. (For a further discussion of these and related issues, see Dunnette, 1966; Oppenheimer, 1956; Sechrest, 1976; Silverman, 1975; Wachtel, 1980).

Since psychological theorizing is not yet advanced enough for the usual criteria to be applied in a universally acceptable way, we will compare the theories along the following content-oriented dimensions:

The Basic Nature of Human Beings. Personality is a comprehensive construct, and motivation is a fundamental aspect of behavior. Therefore, theo-

---

[1]Where two dates appear separated by a slash (such as 1927/1961c), the first is that of the original publication, while the second refers to a widely available paperback reprint of the same work. Although awkward, this notation should prove helpful to readers who do not have ready access to the standard edition (or who would like to build an inexpensive library of their own).

ries of personality are in large part theories of motivation, and must (directly or indirectly) make some crucial assumptions about the basic nature of human beings. Are we selfish and willful? Socially oriented and considerate of others? Devoted to maximizing our innate positive potentials in constructive ways? Or have we no basic nature at all, being wholly influenced by the effects of our behavior on the environment? Are we motivated primarily by prior causes, or by our intentions for the future? By conscious or unconscious aspects of personality? Such important issues provide a useful basis for comparing the various theories.

The Structure of Personality. The constructs that are used to explain the structure of personality also facilitate comparisons among the theories. Thus Freudian theory is well known for its concepts of id, ego, and superego; Jungian theory is denoted by such ideas as the collective unconscious and archetypes; and so forth.

The Development of Personality. Some theories posit specific stages of growth that delineate the development of personality. The characteristics and essential nature of such stages (e.g., sexual in Freudian theory), and of any corresponding character types (e.g., oral, anal, phallic, and genital), also highlight important theoretical similarities and differences.

Further Applications. A theory of personality can be better understood by examining its important applications. These may include such areas as dream interpretation, psychopathology, psychotherapy, education, work, religion, and literature.

Evaluation. Although it is difficult to evaluate a theory of personality, it would be remiss not to make some educated guesses about the usefulness of its major constructs.

THE PRE-FREUDIAN ERA

While personality theory proper begins with Sigmund Freud, we must first back up a bit in order to set the stage—and to avoid some potentially serious misconceptions.

Freud versus Wundt

In the year 1879, Wilhelm Wundt founded the first psychological laboratory at Leipzig, Germany. Psychology grew out of two well-established fields, philosophy and experimental physiology; and so the early efforts of the fledgling science dealt with such objective issues as measuring the speed of the nerve impulse, and searching for specific locations of the brain that controlled various organic functions.

At about this time, Freud was viewing his medical training with some skepticism and beginning to study human beings from a different direction—the treatment of people suffering from disorders that could *not* be traced to physical causes. Academic Wundtian psychology had little to say about such matters, and Freud and his followers were understandably loath to wait. Their patients needed immediate help, and their own thirst for knowledge demanded satisfaction. Thus they organized their research in ways more suitable to the study of psychopathology. They dealt with the whole person (symptoms, childhood causes, underlying intrapsychic processes, dreams, and so forth), rather than with physiological details. They evolved techniques to help their suffering patients, and theories to explain the origin and dynamics of the psychological disorders that they confronted. They disdained the psychological laboratory in favor of natural observation in the clinical setting, provoking a controversy that persists even today (as we have seen). And they even extended their findings to people in general, arguing that the intensive searchlight provided by psychotherapy illuminated universal truths:

> The source of our findings [i.e., sick people] does not seem to me to deprive them of their value. . . . If we throw a crystal to the floor, it breaks; but not into haphazard pieces. It comes apart along its lines of cleavage into fragments whose boundaries, though they were invisible, were predetermined by the crystal's structure. Mental patients are split and broken structures of this same kind. Even we cannot withhold from them something of the reverential awe which peoples of the past felt for the insane. They have turned away from external reality, but for that very reason they know more about internal, psychical reality and can reveal a number of things to us that would otherwise be inaccessible to us. . . . Pathology has always done us the service of making discernible by isolation and exaggeration conditions which would remain concealed in a normal state. (Freud, 1933/1965b, pp. 59, 121; 1926/1969b, p. 14.)

The perspective of history thus explains the emphasis of early personality theories on psychopathology. It also accounts for their complexity, since a theory that deals with the totality of human behavior will be more involved than one that concentrates on specific details. It was not until some years later that psychologists raised the question of approaching personality theory through the study of particularly healthy and well-adjusted individuals, or tried to extend the applications of academic laboratory research to such functional issues as psychopathology and dreams.

The Unconscious Before Freud

A common misconception is that Freud invented such ideas as the unconscious and dream analysis out of a clear sky, filling in what had theretofore been a complete void in our knowledge. In actuality, not even a genius operates in a vacuum; he or she draws on the work of those who have gone before. The quest to understand the basic nature of human beings is as old as time, and many of Freud's theories existed in some form well before he appeared on the scene.

The idea of unconscious determinants of behavior was clearly in evidence some 100 years prior to Freud (Ellenberger, 1970). Hypnotism was used to gain access to the unknown mind as early as 1784, starting with such pioneers as Franz Anton Mesmer and James Braid and continuing with Jean-Martin Charcot, with whom Freud studied briefly. Certain German philosophers of the early nineteenth century, notably Gotthilf Heinrich von Schubert, Carl Gustav Carus, and Arthur Schopenhauer, anticipated many of Freud's theories. Von Schubert developed a tripartite theory somewhat similar to the Freudian id, ego, and superego, as well as concepts much like narcissism and the death instinct. Carus argued that the key to knowledge of conscious life lay in the realm of the unconscious. Schopenhauer's statement, "The Will's opposition to let what is repellent to it come to the knowledge of the intellect is the spot through which insanity can break through the spirit," closely parallels Freud's later ideas of the id (Will), ego (intellect), and repression.

Toward the latter half of the nineteenth century, the philosopher Friedrich Nietzsche discussed the self-deceiving and self-destructive nature of human beings, the active inhibition of threatening thoughts, and the need to unmask unconscious materials so as to remove self-deceptions. Nietzsche was also the first to use the term "id," and is regarded by some as the true founder of modern psychology. A noted French contemporary of Freud's, Pierre Janet, theorized that traumatic events caused ideas to become fixed in the subconscious (a word that he coined) and to be replaced by neurotic symptoms. And Gustav Theodor Fechner, the "father of experimental psychology" and Wundt's immediate predecessor, recognized the possibility of unconscious perception and supplied Freud with such principles as mental energy and pleasure-unpleasure. (Despite his reservations about academic psychology, Freud [1920/1961a, p. 2; 1900/1965a, p. 574] was quite complimentary about Fechner.)

Similarly, attempts to interpret the meaning of dreams can be traced back even to medieval times (Ellenberger, 1970; Freud, 1900/1965a). Some ancient theories were quite farfetched, such as the belief that a person's soul left the body and performed the actions of the dream. Others contained elements of truth, as with Plato's claim that there are strong impulses within us that emerge more readily during sleep. According to Plato, these impulses include desires for "intercourse with a mother or anyone else," and they emerge in our dreams "when the reasonable and humane part of us is asleep and its control relaxed, and our bestial nature . . . wakes and has its fling"— ideas which are remarkably similar to Freud's concepts of Oedipal conflicts, the id, and the relaxing of the ego's defenses during sleep.

By the nineteenth century, there was increasingly accurate knowledge about dreams. Von Schubert emphasized the symbolic nature of dream language, and observed that dream symbols may combine many concepts in a single picture (what Freud later called condensation). Karl Albert Scherner designated elongated objects (towers, the mouthpiece of a pipe) as symbols of the male genitals, and a slippery courtyard footpath as symbolic of the female genitals. Alfred Maury studied the effects of sensory stimulation on dreams, and drew attention to the role of forgotten memories in dream formation. The Marquis Hervey de Saint-Denis, who developed the remarkable technique of learning to become aware that he was dreaming and then waking himself at will in order to make appropriate notes, published an extremely thorough study of his own dreams and anticipated the Freudian concepts of condensation and displacement. Yves Delage concluded that dreams originate from unfinished acts or thoughts, primarily those of the preceding day. And still other investigators were adding important theories and insights.

It should also be noted that Freud was by no means the first theorist to concentrate on sexuality, or to relate it to psychopathology. To cite just two illustrations, Schopenhauer argued strongly that sexuality was the most important of all instincts; while Richard von Krafft-Ebing published his famous *Psychopathia Sexualis* in 1886, coined the terms "sadism" and "masochism," and even used the term "libido" six years prior to Freud in an 1889 article.

This brief sketch hardly does justice to a long and painstaking search for knowledge, and the interested reader will want to consult Ellenberger (1970) for additional information. It does support the contention made previously that theorists do not work in isolation, but rather draw on the contributions of others. However, this in no way argues against Freud's genius. He made many original and important contributions, and he is the first person identified as a psychologist to develop a theory of personality. Therefore, we will begin our investigation of personality theories with a study of his work.

■ SUMMARY

1. PERSONALITY. There is as yet no one universally accepted definition of personality. In general, personality refers to long-lasting and important characteristics within an individual, ones that continue to exert a strong influence on behavior. Aspects of personality may be observable or unobservable, and conscious or unconscious.

2. THEORIES AND CONSTRUCTS. A theory is an unproved speculation about reality. It consists of a set of interrelated terms and principles, called *constructs,* that are created or applied by the theorist. Ideally, a useful theory should provide accurate descriptions, comprehensive explanations, predictions that allow us to verify or

discard the theory, and applications that enable us to control and change our environment. Both formal laboratory research and informal clinical observation have important advantages and serious drawbacks, and both are essential sources of information for present-day psychology.

3. THE PRE-FREUDIAN ERA. The first academic psychology dealt primarily with physiological and organic issues. Therefore Freud and his followers, who were concerned with the treatment of psychopathology, developed clinically oriented theories of personality to explain the phenomena that they encountered. While Freud is properly regarded as the first psychologist to develop a theory of personality, many of his ideas (the unconscious, dream analysis, the id, repression, the sexual nature of psychopathology, and so forth) can be traced back to philosophers and other theorists who preceded him by many years.

PART I

FOUNDATIONS OF PERSONALITY THEORY

PROLOGUE

In Part I of this book, you will meet the three theorists whose work forms the foundation of personality theory: Sigmund Freud, Carl Jung, and Alfred Adler.

These seminal theorists sought to explore a relatively new and unknown world: the human psyche. To explain their discoveries, therefore, they were forced to develop many new concepts and terms—so many, in fact, that becoming acquainted with these theories can at times be as challenging as learning a new language. In the pages that follow, you may well find it somewhat disconcerting to encounter cathexes, introjections, libido, parapraxes, repressions, resistances, transferences, animas, archetypes, enantiodromia, et al.

Nevertheless, the study of personality theory is well worth the effort required. Freud, Jung, and Adler (and the theorists to be discussed in subsequent sections) made profoundly important discoveries, yet their work is all too often misunderstood. For example, if your knowledge of Freud's theory is limited to such generalities as the use of the well-known therapeutic couch and the fact that material is unearthed from the unconscious, you are likely to be surprised and intrigued by the intricate, meticulous way in which he analyzes the human personality.

Thus our goal will be to understand the theories and constructs devised by these brilliant and creative thinkers. In Chapter 2, for example, you will look through Freud's eyes at such issues as human nature, the structure and development of personality, dream interpretation, and the causes and treatment of neurosis. In Chapter 3, you will shift gears and become a Jungian. And in Chapter 4, you will focus on the realm of personality from an Adlerian perspective.

As the preceding discussion implies, the course in theories of personality is *not* specifically intended to promote self-insight. Exploring your inner psychological world requires considerable courage, for it is all too easy to deceive yourself about the more undesirable and painful aspects of your personality. Therefore, this task is usually best accomplished within the framework of formal counseling or psychotherapy. But if you do wish to learn more about your own personality, and if you can be sufficiently honest, you may well find valuable food for thought in the following pages. After all, we all use Freudian defense mechanisms to some degree; we all fall somewhere along the Jungian dimension of introversion—extraversion; we are all capable of developing an Adlerian inferiority complex if the relationship with our parents during childhood is sufficiently pathogenic.

Keep in mind, however, that our primary objective in this book is scholarly rather than therapeutic. Freud, Jung, Adler, and the others whose theories we will examine are among the greatest names in psychology. Although some of their ideas have been subject to criticism (and at times deservedly so, as we will see), their work is also widely admired, quoted, and discussed. If you are interested in the study of human behavior, you cannot afford to be without a knowledge of the material presented herein.

A Suggested Approach to the Study of Personality Theory

You will probably find that some of the theories presented in this book are more to your liking than others. Possibly, one particular theory will seem clearly superior to the rest. There are indeed modern psychologists who consider themselves to be strict Freudians, or Jungians, or Adlerians, and who adamantly reject the ideas and constructs of any other theorist. So you are within your rights if you choose to follow in their footsteps.

Nevertheless, I urge you *not* to adopt such a rigid point of view. Theoretical constructs (e.g., the Freudian id, ego, and superego) are not undeniable truths, nor are they concrete entities. They are concepts that have been created (or adopted) by the theorist better to describe, explain, predict, and control human behavior. Thus any theory of personality represents but one possible way of interpreting psychological phenomena. No one of these alternative conceptions has proved to be completely without fault; each one has its own significant virtues and defects. Therefore, if you understand and make use of constructs from a variety of personality theories, you will have at your disposal more useful tools (and a more flexible approach) for unraveling the mysteries of human behavior (Ewen, 1984).

When you study any of the theories in this book, then, I recommend doing so with a wholly accepting attitude—at least at first. For example, when you read Chapter 2, become a Freudian (if only for the moment) and try to see the functioning of personality strictly from his point of view. As we observed in Chapter 1, personality theorists must interrelate their constructs and fit them together into a coherent whole. So if you are too quick to criticize and discard certain aspects of a theory, this may make it impossible for you to appreciate both the overall design of the theory and those concepts that are more palatable. If you do find some aspect of a theory that you simply cannot accept, make a note of this and put it aside. When you complete the evaluation section, *then* decide on your opinions about the theory.

By following this approach, you may well find (as I did) that some theories which at first glance seem absurdly complicated (or even far-fetched) actually contain quite a few pearls of genuine wisdom about human behavior. At the very least, you will better appreciate what the theorists were trying to accomplish with their constructs and principles. And you are much more likely to avoid the trap of becoming what I call a "constructual tyrant" (Chapter 17)—namely, rejecting (or even ridiculing) good and useful ideas and constructs simply because they were devised by a theorist other than your particular favorite.

Preview: Freud, Jung, and Adler

In Freudian theory, you will find that much of personality is unconscious and cannot be called to consciousness on demand; we are driven by many wishes, fears, beliefs, conflicts, and memories of which we are totally unaware. You will encounter Freud's belief that humans are motivated solely by sexual and destructive instincts, and that human nature is inherently malignant (including such innate illicit impulses as incest and the lust for killing). You will discover that nothing in the psyche happens by chance; all mental behavior is determined by prior causes. You will learn about "Freudian slips" and what they reveal about personality. You will examine the structural constructs of id, ego, and superego, and the workings of the various defense mechanisms. You will follow the development of personality through various psychosexual stages, including the occurrence of the all-important Oedipus complex. And you will see how Freud applied his theories and constructs to the interpretation of dreams, understanding and treating neurosis, religion, and other areas.

Jungian theory also posits that unconscious processes are extremely important. But here you will find considerably less emphasis on sexuality and a more extensive list of human instincts, including power and individuation or self-realization (the forerunner of the modern concept of self-actualization). You will also encounter a more optimistic view of human nature, and the belief that we are influenced by our goals and plans for the future as well as by prior causes. You will find an entirely different view of the structure and development of personality, including such controversial concepts as the collective unconscious and archetypes. You will examine the dimension of introversion—extraversion, which is more complicated than is commonly believed. You will learn about the perils of an overly one-sided personality. And you will see how Jung's theoretical differences with Freud led him to different conclusions concerning the interpretation of dreams, the causes and treatment of psychopathology, and the value of religion.

Adlerian theory does *not* agree that instincts and unconscious processes have a strong effect on the human personality. Here you will find that personality is influenced primarily by social determinants, such as the relationships with our parents during childhood, and by the life goals that we consciously select for ourselves and how we choose to achieve them. You will discover a view of human nature that is far more optimistic than Freud's or even Jung's, one that includes an innate potential for relating to other people in a positive way. You will also encounter the belief that striving for superiority (self-perfection) is a more important human motive than sexuality. You will learn how inferiority complexes are caused by pathogenic parental behaviors, and about the effects of birth order on personality. And you will see how Adler's theoretical differences with Freud and Jung are reflected in a markedly different approach to dream interpretation, psychopathology, psychotherapy, and other important areas.

Let us now begin our exploration through the realm of personality theory. In fairness, it must be said that this will not be an easy journey. But for those of you who share my fascination with the world within us—that is, with the human personality—it will be a richly rewarding one.

2

SIGMUND FREUD
Psychoanalysis

Throughout the course of history, scientists have dealt three great shocks to our feelings of self-importance. Nicolaus Copernicus demonstrated that the Earth is not the center of all creation, but merely one of several planets that rotate around the sun. Charles Darwin showed that humans are not a unique and privileged life form, but just one of many animal species that have evolved over millions of years. Sigmund Freud emphasized that we are not even the masters of our own minds, but are driven by many powerful unconscious processes (wishes, fears, beliefs, conflicts, emotions, memories) of which we are totally unaware. (See Freud, 1917a; 1916–1917/1966, pp. 284–285.)

Theories that minimize our role in the general scheme of things, and attack widely held beliefs, will not find ready acceptance. Galileo, a follower of Copernicus, was forced to recant his beliefs about the solar system in order to avoid being burned at the stake; while John Thomas Scopes was fired in 1925 for daring to teach evolutionary theory in an American high school, precipitating the famous "Monkey Trial." Freud's theory of personality has also provoked strong resistance, but here there are additional reasons for controversy. Early in Freud's career, three men whom he admired gave him similar (and startling) bits of information. Josef Breuer, with whom Freud later coauthored the landmark *Studies on Hysteria* (Freud & Breuer, 1895/1966), remarked that neurotic behaviors were always concerned with secrets of the marital bed. Jean-Martin Charcot emphatically proclaimed to an assistant that certain nervous disorders were "always a question of the genitals," a conversation Freud overheard. And the distinguished gynecologist Rudolf Chrobak advised Freud that the only cure for a female patient with severe anxiety and an impotent husband could not be prescribed: "Rx: A normal penis, dose to be repeated" (Freud, 1914/1967, pp. 13–15; E. Jones, 1953/1963a, p. 158). Although Freud was somewhat shocked by these radical notions and dismissed them from his mind, they later emerged from his preconscious to form the cornerstone of his theory—one that attributes virtually all human behavior to the erotic instinct.

BIOGRAPHICAL SKETCH

Sigmund Freud was born on May 6, 1856, at Freiberg, Moravia (now Czechoslovakia). His father was a wool merchant, his parents Jewish. Freud spent nearly all of his life in Vienna, where his family moved in 1860, and gradually rose from the lower middle class to the heights of society and world fame—though not without considerable physical and psychological suffering.

Freud was an excellent student throughout his academic career, receiving his medical degree from the University of Vienna in 1881. He was not overly enthusiastic about becoming a practicing physician, a slow route to economic security in those days, and longed for the brilliant discovery that would bring rapid fame. After graduation he continued to work in the physiology laboratory of his teacher, Ernst Brücke, and performed some high-quality research in microscopic neuroanatomy. Ironically, Freud narrowly missed out on the renown that he sought by failing to appreciate the full significance of some of his findings.

Freud's future at this time was highly uncertain. His finances were meager, his job was not well paying, and two senior assistants blocked his chances for advancement. When he became engaged to Martha Bernays in 1882, he accepted Brücke's friendly advice to seek his fortune elsewhere. He spent the next three years as an assistant to two noted medical scientists, Hermann Nothnagel and Theodor Meynert, won a travel grant to study for a few months with Charcot in Paris, and at last ended a four-year courtship by marrying Martha on September 30, 1886. Freud's letters to his betrothed show him to have been an ardent and devoted lover, if at times jealous and possessive, and the marriage was for some time a happy one. The Freuds had six children, three boys and three girls, with the youngest (Anna) becoming a prominent child psychoanalyst and ultimately assuming the leadership of the Freudian movement. Interestingly, the man who emphasized sexuality so heavily in his theories was in all probability celibate until his marriage at age 30. Also, while Freud normally declined to practice his psychological ideas on his own wife and children, he did create a rather bizarre Oedipal situation by psychoanalyzing Anna himself; and no doubt due in part to this unusual emotional involvement with her father, she never married, devoted her life to the cause of psychoanalysis, and eventually replaced Martha as the most important woman in Sigmund's life (Roazen, 1975/1976b, pp. 58–59, 63, 439–440).

Freud's own life provided him with a great deal of psychological data. He was himself Oedipal, had powerful unconscious hostility toward his father, and was quite close to his mother (who was some nineteen years younger than her husband and devoted to her "golden Sigi"). Freud suffered from a severe neurosis during the 1890s yet did strikingly original work during this time, as though the pressure of his own emerging psychopathology drove him to new heights (E. Jones, 1953/1963a, p. 194). Ellenberger (1970, pp. 447ff.) has described this syndrome as a "creative illness." The sufferer undergoes agonizing symptoms that alternately worsen and improve, exaggerated feelings of isolation, and intense self-absorption, and ultimately emerges from this ordeal with a permanently transformed personality and the conviction of having discovered profound new truths. During this period Freud also began his self-analysis (1897), probing the inner depths of his own mind with the psychological techniques that he developed. Though his creative illness ended by 1900, he continued the self-analysis for the remainder of his life and reserved the last half-hour of each day for this purpose.

Personally, Freud was highly moral and ethical—even puritanical. Some found him cold, bitter, rejecting, the kind of man who does not suffer fools gladly, and more interested in the discoveries to be made from his patients than in themselves. Others depicted him as warm, humorous, profoundly understanding, and extremely kind. (See, for example, Clark, 1980; Ellenberger, 1970, pp. 457–469; E. Jones, 1953/1963a; 1955/1963b; 1957/1963c; Reik, 1948/1964, p. 258; Rieff, 1959/1961; Roazen, 1975/1976b; Schur, 1972.) Some colleagues remained devotedly loyal to Freud throughout their lives, while others (including Josef Breuer, Wilhelm Fliess, Carl Jung, and Alfred Adler) engaged in acrimonious partings because of Freud's adamant emphasis on sexuality as the prime mover of human behavior.

Freud's professional life had many interesting highlights, and also a few major blunders. In 1884, his friend Ernst Fleischl von Marxow suffered an extremely painful illness and became addicted to morphine, which he took as medication. Freud recommended a "harmless" substitute—cocaine—and even published an article praising the new drug. Unfortunately, cocaine also proved to be highly addictive, and Freud was justifiably criticized. In 1896, Freud announced that most of his psychoanalytic patients had been seduced by immoral adults during their childhood. A year later he concluded to his chagrin that these incidents were actually imaginary, and that the unconscious cannot distinguish between memory and fantasy.

However, successes far outnumbered failures. Freud and Breuer culminated a decade of work by publishing *Studies on Hysteria* in 1895, which described the psychological treatment of behavior disorders (paralyses, headaches, loss of speech, and so forth) that had no physical cause. *The Interpretation of Dreams,* the cornerstone of Freud's theory, appeared in 1900. Fame was far from instant, and this classic took eight years to sell all of six hundred copies. By now Freud had completed his break with official medicine, however, and was more self-assured as the leader of an established movement. There were some vitriolic accusations that psychoanalysts were obscene sexual perverts, and Freud clearly identified with the role of the lonely hero struggling against insuperable odds, but the belief that he was ostracized by Vienna is one of the unfounded legends that surround his life. Rather, his position and fame continued to improve. (See Ellenberger, 1970, p. 450; Freud, 1927/1961c, p. 36; 1925/1963a, pp. 44, 91; 1933/1965b, pp. 8, 60, 137; E. Jones, 1955/1963b, pp. 237, 291.)

In 1909, Freud received an invitation to visit the United States and deliver a series of lectures at Clark University. They were well received, but he left with the impression that "America is a mistake; a gigantic mistake, it is true, but none the less a mistake" (E. Jones, 1955/1963b, p. 263). World War I impressed upon him the importance of aggression as a basic human drive, and the ensuing runaway inflation cost him his life savings (about

$30,000). Fortunately his reputation was sufficient to attract English and American patients, who paid in a more stable currency, but his hardships were not over.

During the last sixteen years of his life, Freud was afflicted with an extremely serious cancer of the mouth and jaw. This required no fewer than thirty-three operations, forced him to wear an awkward prosthesis to fill the resulting gap between what had been the nasal and oral cavities, and prevented him at times from speaking and swallowing, yet he bore this ordeal with his customary stoic courage. Nor did he curtail his prolific and literate writings, which fill twenty-three volumes and won the Goethe Prize in 1930. Still one more trial was in store: the Nazi invasion of Vienna in 1938, during which Anna was detained by the Gestapo but eventually released. Freud and his family successfully escaped to London, where he was received with great honor. There he finally succumbed to the cancer on September 23, 1939.

THE BASIC NATURE OF HUMAN BEINGS

Freud named his theory **psycho-analysis.** (Most modern writers omit the hyphen.) This term is also widely used to denote the particular form of psychotherapy that Freud originated, but the clinical practice of psycho-analysis is only one of its many applications.

Instincts and Psychic Energy

Freud concludes that human beings are motivated by powerful innate forces, to which he gives the name *Triebe* (**instincts,** or **drives**[1]). These instincts energize and direct all human mental (and physical) activity.

An instinct becomes activated when some aspect of the body requires sustenance, as when you need food, water, or sexual consummation. The activated instinct (need) then produces a psychological state of increased tension or excitation (wish), which you experience as unpleasant. According to Freud, the basic objective of all human behavior is to achieve pleasure and avoid unpleasure or pain (the *pleasure principle,* to be discussed in more detail later in this chapter). So you take action designed to reduce the unpleasant mental tension, which in turn satisfies the underlying instinctual need (drive). Thus the primary human goal of pleasure is realized by means of *drive reduction,* and the instincts serve to restore the body to a previous state of equilibrium. (See Freud, 1911/1963c, p. 22; 1916–1917/1966, p. 356; 1926/1969b, pp. 25–26.) Freud does concede that drive *increases*

---

[1]Freud's native language was German, and translating his constructs and ideas into English has caused more than a few difficulties. Brenner (1973/1974, p. 16) has suggested that *instinct* be used to signify a complete cycle involving a stimulus, central excitation, and motor response (for example, the knee jerk reflex), with *drive* being reserved for the state of central excitation alone (such as hunger). Other writers use the two terms more or less interchangeably.

may sometimes be pleasurable, as in the case of excitement during sexual intercourse, but he regards this as an awkward contradiction that cannot readily be reconciled with his theory (1924/1963h, p. 191).

Insofar as the specific nature of instincts is concerned, Freud changed his mind several times throughout the course of his life. At one point he distinguished between sexuality, on the one hand, and those instincts that serve the goal of self-preservation (such as hunger and thirst) on the other. However, the ultimate version of his theory states that we are motivated by two major instincts: sexual and destructive (aggressive).

The Sexual Instinct (Eros). In Freudian theory, sexuality has an unusually wide meaning: it signifies the whole range of erotic, pleasurable experience. In addition to the genitals, the body has many parts capable of producing sexual gratification (**erotogenic zones**); "in fact, the whole body is an erotogenic zone" (Freud, 1940/1969a, p. 8; see also Freud, 1905/1965d, pp. 58ff).

To emphasize the fact that sexuality refers to far more than just intercourse and reproduction, Freud frequently uses the name **Eros** (the ancient Greek god of love) as a synonym for this instinct. Such self-preservative behavior as eating and drinking involves the sexual instinct because the mouth is one of the major erotogenic zones, and because we preserve ourselves out of self-love (**narcissism**) and the wish to continue gaining erotic pleasure from our bodies.

The Destructive Instinct. One of Freud's more radical conclusions (reached toward the latter part of his career) is that life itself aims at returning to its prior state of nonexistence, with all human beings driven by a "death instinct" (Freud, 1920/1961a, pp. 30ff; see also Freud, 1923/1962, pp. 30–37). According to this formulation, the death instinct constantly opposes the erotic (life) instincts.

As supporting evidence, Freud cites the **compulsion to repeat.** He finds that children pursue the same activity over and over, patients in psychoanalytic therapy repeatedly relive unconscious conflicts, dreams and fantasies often recur, and even history has a tendency to repeat itself. Thus the drive to recreate our original inanimate state would be the ultimate repetition compulsion.

The concept of a death instinct remains highly controversial even among psychoanalysts, since it is incompatible with the accepted evolutionary principle of survival of the fittest. A more widely accepted interpretation of Freud's later ideas is that there are two primary human drives, sexual (Eros) and destructive or aggressive (e.g., Brenner, 1973/1974). These two types of instincts are regularly fused together, though not necessarily in equal amounts. Thus any erotic act, even sexual intercourse, is also at least partly aggressive; while any aggressive act, even murder, contains some erotic components. Similarly, we often have feelings of both love and hate (**ambivalence**) toward important people in our lives. And eating is aggressive as well as erotic, since it involves biting and the destruction of an object in order to incorporate it. (See Freud, 1923/1962, pp. 31–32; 1940/1969a, p. 37).

All instincts, sexual and destructive, are present at birth. Freud (1927/1961c, p. 10) is quite pessimistic about human nature: we are inherently uncivilized and driven by such illicit impulses as incest, cannibalism, and the lust for killing. Since other people will not tolerate such behavior, conflict between the individual and society is inevitable. And this also implies that intrapsychic conflict is unavoidable, for we must reluctantly learn to channel these strong but forbidden impulses into compromise activities that are socially acceptable (**sublimate** them). For example, destructive and sadistic impulses may be sublimated by becoming a surgeon.

Although we may try to make these compromises and substitutes as close to the original goal as society will permit, they are invariably not as satisfying. Thus we are all left with some degree of unpleasant psychological tension, which is the price we must pay for living in a civilized society (Freud, 1908b; 1930/1961b).

Psychic Energy (Libido) and Cathexis. Just as overt behavior is powered by physical energy, mental activity is a highly dynamic process that involves constant expenditures of **psychic energy.** Psychic energy is entirely unobservable and has no known physical correlates, despite Freud's belief that underlying neurological functions would ultimately be discovered. It should be considered a hypothetical construct, rather than an actual entity.

Each individual possesses a more or less fixed supply of psychic energy. If a relatively large amount is usurped by one component of personality, or is expended in pathological forms of behavior, less will be available for other components or for the pursuit of healthy activities.

Freud refers to the psychic energy associated with the sexual instinct as **libido,** but offers no corresponding name for aggressive energy. Since virtually all behavior involves a fusion of sexuality and destructiveness, however, libido may often be considered to refer to both varieties of psychic energy (Brenner, 1973/1974, p. 30). Libido is wholly intrapsychic, and never flows out of the mind into the outside world. It attaches itself to mental representations of objects that will satisfy instinctual needs, a process known as **cathexis** (plural, *cathexes*).

For example, a very young child quickly learns that its mother is an important source of such instinctual satisfactions as feeding, oral stimulation, and physical contact. Therefore it develops a strong desire for her and invests a great deal of psychic energy (libido) in thoughts, images, and fantasies of her. In Freudian terminology, the child forms a strong cathexis for its mother. An unimportant stranger who happens to drop in for a visit, on the other hand, is not greatly desired and is only weakly (if at all) cathected with libido. Similarly, a hungrier person devotes more libido to thoughts of food. And narcissism involves the investment of libido in mental representations of one's own being, or the cathexis of the self (Freud, 1914/1963d.)[2]

Libido is often **displaced** to a substitute object-choice. Thus a person may strongly cathect one kind of food but switch to an alternative because the first choice is not available, childhood thumb sucking may yield to adult cigarette smoking, or an incestuous instinct may unconsciously be sublimated and lead to the cathexis of one's spouse (or even one's favorite dessert).

Psychic Determinism and Parapraxes

Psychoanalytic theory states that nothing in the psyche happens by chance; *all* mental (and physical) behavior is determined by prior causes. Apparently random thoughts, the inability to recall a familiar word or idea, saying or writing the wrong words, self-inflicted injuries, bungled actions, dreams, and neurotic symptoms all have underlying reasons, which are usually unconscious. This principle is known as **psychic determinism,** and Freud (1901/1965c) presents many examples of such **parapraxes** (erroneous actions; singular, *parapraxis*).

One famous illustration of motivated forgetting (**repression**) occurred when a friend tried to convince Freud that their generation was doomed to ultimate dissatisfaction. The friend wished to conclude his argument by quoting a phrase from Virgil that he knew well, "Exoriar(e) aliquis nostris ex ossibus ultor" ("Let someone arise from my bones as an avenger"), but could not recall the word "aliquis" and became hopelessly confused. After supplying the correct quotation, Freud advised his friend to think freely and uninhibitedly about the "forgotten" word (the technique of **free association**). This led to the discovery of numerous unconscious connections—the division of the word into "a" and "liquis," liquidity and fluid, blood and ritual sacrifices, the names of several saints, and a miracle of flowing blood alleged to take place at Naples—and eventually to the friend's fear that a woman with whom he had enjoyed a romantic affair in Naples had become pregnant (that is, her menstrual blood had stopped flowing). Thus the word "aliquis" was deliberately forgotten (repressed) because it was a threatening reminder of an important inner conflict: a wish for (avenging) descendants, as indicated by the Virgil quotation, and a stronger opposing desire not to be embarrassed just then by any out-of-wedlock offspring (Freud, 1901–1965c, pp. 9–11, 14).

Similarly, forgetting (or arriving late at) an appointment or college examination happens for definite reasons. The explanation of these parapraxes may be fairly simple, such as anger at the person to be met or fear of

---

[2]Technically, *primary narcissism* refers to the infant's all-consuming wish for attention at a time when object-cathexes have not yet been formed, and the entire quota of libido relates to the newly developing ego. *Secondary narcissism* involves exaggerated feelings of self-importance and self-love that occur later in life, if at all. (See Fenichel, 1945.)

failing the exam. The causes of important psychic phenomena, however, are usually numerous (**overdetermined**) and more complicated. For example, the forgetful student may also be motivated by an unconscious wish to punish parents who are applying too much pressure to excel and to punish herself because she feels guilty about her strong hostility toward them, and by still other reasons as well.

Slips of the tongue or pen are also parapraxes that reflect unconscious motivation. A politician who secretly expected little good from a meeting began it with the statement, "Gentlemen: I take notice that a full quorum of members is present and herewith declare the sitting *closed!*" Only when the audience burst into laughter did he become aware of his error. A German professor, intending a modest observation that he was not *geeignet* (qualified) to describe an illustrious rival, exposed his true jealousy by declaring that he was not *geneigt* (inclined) to talk about him. Another expert with an exaggerated sense of self-importance declaimed that the number of real authorities in his field could be "counted *on one finger*—I mean on the fingers of one hand." A young man who wished to escort (*begleiten*) a lady acquaintance, but feared that she would regard his offer as an insult (*beleidigen*), revealed his true feelings by unconsciously condensing the two words and offering to "insort" (*begleit-digen*) her (Freud, 1901/1965c, pp. 59, 68–69, 78). Many more examples of spoken and written parapraxes could be cited, including ones created by famous authors (such as Shakespeare) for their fictitious characters.

Self-inflicted injuries are likely to be caused by unconscious guilt that creates a need for punishment. A member of Freud's family who bit a tongue or pinched a finger did not get sympathy, but instead the question: "Why did you do that?" (Freud, 1901/1965c, p. 180). Brenner (1973/1974, p. 139) relates the instance of a female patient who was driving her husband's car in heavy traffic, and stopped so suddenly that the car behind crashed into and crumpled one of the rear fenders. Her free associations indicated that this parapraxis was due to three related, unconscious motives: anger toward her husband because he mistreated her (expressed by smashing up his car), a desire to be punished for such unwifely hostility (which was certain to be satisfied once her husband learned of the accident), and powerful repressed sexual desires that her husband was unable to satisfy (which were symbolically gratified by having someone "bang into her tail"). Thus apparently bungled actions may prove to be quite skillful displays of unconscious motivation.

The Unconscious

The common occurrence of parapraxes implies that much of personality is beyond our immediate awareness. Freud does in fact conclude that the vast majority of mental activity is unconscious, and cannot be called to mind even with strenuous effort. Information that is not conscious at a given moment, but which can readily become so, is described as **preconscious.**

The preconscious is much closer to the conscious than to the unconscious because it is largely within our control, and unconscious material must first become verbalized at the preconscious level before it can become conscious. (See Freud, 1923/1962, pp. 5, 10; 1915/1963g, pp. 116–150.)

THE STRUCTURE OF PERSONALITY

Freud originally defined the structure of personality in terms of the unconscious, preconscious, and conscious (the **topographic** model), but his researches eventually unearthed some damaging contradictions. This model specifies that all emotions are located in the organ of consciousness. It also states that the *act* of repression originates from the preconscious or conscious, and should therefore be accessible to awareness. Yet Freud found that it is not unusual to suffer from feelings of guilt, or to maintain a repression, without having any conscious knowledge of doing so. Since the repressing mechanism itself proved to be unconscious, Freud was forced to conclude that "all that is repressed is unconscious, but not all that is unconscious is repressed" (1923/1962, p. 8; see also Freud, 1915/1963f, pp. 104–115; 1916–1917/1966, pp. 294ff).

To overcome these difficulties, Freud developed a revised theory (the **structural** model) that describes personality in terms of three constructs: the **id,** the **ego,** and the **superego** (Freud, 1923/1962). These concepts, and their relationship to the topographic model, are illustrated in Figure 2.1. ("Pcpt.-cs." refers to the "perceptual-conscious," which is the outermost layer of consciousness.) Freud emphasizes that the id, ego, and superego are not separate compartments within the mind, but blend together like sections of a telescope or colors in a painting. For purposes of discussion, however, it is necessary to treat these interrelated constructs one at a time.

The Id

The **id** (*das Es;* literally, the "it") comprises the whole of the psyche that is present at birth, including the instincts and the total supply of psychic energy. It is entirely unconscious, being "the dark, inaccessible part of our personality . . . a chaos, a cauldron full of seething excitations" (Freud, 1933/1965b, p. 73).

The id transforms biological needs into psychological tension (wishes). Its sole motivation is to gain pleasure by discharging these instinctual cathexes, and to avoid the unpleasure that results from increases in tension (the aforementioned **pleasure principle**). It is totally illogical and amoral, however, and has no conception of reality or self-preservation. Its only resource is to form mental images of objects that will provide satisfaction, a process called **wish-fulfillment.** The id is like an impulsive child that wants pleasure right away, so cathexes are readily displaced onto substitute object-

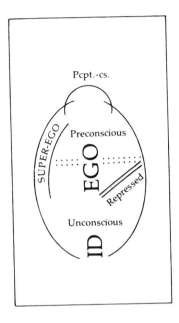

FIGURE 2.1. Freud's structural model of personality. "The space occupied by the unconscious id ought to have been incomparably greater than that of the ego or the preconscious. I must ask you to correct it in your thoughts." (Freud, 1933/1965b, pp. 78–79.)

images if the initial choice is frustrated. For example, the infant deprived of its bottle may instead cathect its thumb (and perhaps some quite fantastic images as well) in order to discharge instinctual tension by sucking.

The irrational, impulsive, and image-producing mode of thought representative of the id is known as the **primary process** (Freud, 1911/1963c). The primary process permits opposites to coexist side by side, represents ideas by parts that stand for the whole, and condenses related concepts into a single entity. It has no sense of time and is not affected by experience, so childhood instinctual impulses and repressions exist in the adult id as strongly as though they had just occurred.

The primary process plays a prominent role in parapraxes, such as the word "insort" produced by condensation or the association of opposites by the chairman who began a meeting by declaring it "closed." It is also evident in some everyday behaviors (as when an adult is childishly impulsive), neurotic symptoms, certain varieties of psychosis, and during the "psychosis" that all of us experience every night—our dreams. (See Freud, 1933/1965b, pp. 15–16; 1940/1969a, p. 29.)

The Ego

Starting at about age 6–8 months, the **ego** (*das Ich;* literally, the "I") begins to develop out of the id. The formation of the ego is aided by experiences that help the infant to differentiate between self and not-self, notably those concerning its own body. When the infant touches itself, it also experiences the sensation of being touched, which does not happen with other objects.

And the infant's body is a source of pleasure (and pain) that cannot be taken away, unlike the bottle or the mother's breast.

The images produced by the id cannot reduce any psychological tension or satisfy any biological needs, since these images are only mental pictures of what the infant wants. However, the maturing child makes an important discovery: the environment contains objects that can satisfy the demands of the id. Thus the child learns to distinguish the id images from objects in the environment, a process called **reality testing,** and to match up an image with a need-satisfying object. At first the infant wants to be like (**identifies** with) these important objects, such as the mother who provides milk; only later does the child's goal become to possess the milk itself (Freud, 1921/1959, pp. 38–39). Ultimately, mental representations of need-satisfying objects are incorporated in the ego, the only component of personality that is able to interact with the environment. In turn, the growth of the ego increases the capacity to deal with reality.

The ego is "a kind of facade of the id . . . like an external, cortical, layer of it" (Freud, 1926/1969b, pp. 18-19). Unlike the id, however, the ego spans the conscious, preconscious, and unconscious. The ego is sane and rational, and forms realistic plans of action designed to satisfy the needs of the id. Therefore, while the ego is also interested in pleasure, it suspends the pleasure principle in favor of the **reality principle** and delays the discharge of tension until a suitable object can be found. This makes it possible to avoid errors, such as eating a pleasurable substance that is actually indigestible or poisonous; to avoid punishment, like a parental slap for trying to eat a forbidden object; and to increase pleasure, as by rejecting an edible but unappetizing object and waiting for a tastier one. The rational, pleasure-delaying, problem-solving, and self-preservative mode of thought representative of the ego is known as the **secondary process** (Freud, 1911/1963c; see also Freud, 1940/1969a, p. 55).

The relationship between the ego and the id is intimate and complex. The ego may be servile, try at all costs to remain on good terms with the id, conceal the id's irrationalities and obstinacies, and behave like a sycophantic and dishonest politician who sees the truth but prefers to keep the favor of the public. Alternatively, the ego's concern with self-preservation may cause it to contest the impulsive id:

> . . . in its relation to the id [the ego] is like a man on horseback, who has to hold in check the superior strength of the horse; with this difference, that the rider tries to do so with his own strength while the ego uses borrowed forces. The analogy may be carried a little further. Often a rider, if he is not to be parted from his horse, is obliged to guide it where it wants to go; so in the same way the ego is in the habit of transforming the id's will into action as if it were its own. (Freud, 1923/1962, p. 15. See also Freud, 1923/1962, p. 46; 1933/1965b, p. 77.)

Freud regards decisions about when to bridle the id's passions and bow before reality, and when to side with them and take arms against the external world, as "the ego's highest function . . . . such decisions make up the whole essence of worldly wisdom" (1926/1969b, p. 27).

Since the id begins with all of the psychic energy, how does its "rider" manage to gain any control at all? Freud theorizes that the growth of the ego weakens the id by drawing psychic energy from it. The ego also has at its disposal various mechanisms of defense, discussed below.

Anxiety. The ego's task is a particularly difficult one because it is "a poor creature owing service to three masters and consequently menaced by three dangers: from the external world, from the libido of the id, and from the severity of the superego" (Freud, 1923/1962, p. 46; see also Freud, 1933/1965b, p. 77). The ego responds to such threats with **anxiety,** a highly unpleasant emotion similar to intense nervousness. Anxiety does serve a self-preservative function, however: it readies the individual for appropriate action, so a limited amount is both normal and desirable.

Freud identifies anxiety by its source, or which of the ego's three masters is responsible. **Realistic** (or **objective**) **anxiety** is caused by danger in the environment, as when one is walking down a deserted street and encounters an ominous-looking individual wielding a knife. In addition to such immediate threats, the ego's memories of previous traumatic experiences may enable it to respond with anxiety as a signal of future danger. Thus a knowledgeable sailor may react with signal anxiety to an apparently trivial cloud on the horizon because it indicates the approach of a hurricane, or a satiated infant may grow upset at the mother's departure because it has learned that becoming hungry in her absence will mean frustration and discomfort (Freud, 1926/1963j, pp. 76-77; 1916-1917/1966, p. 394). Such realistic anxiety may cause the pedestrian to flee or call for help, the sailor to batten down the hatches, and the child to try to get mother to stay by crying.

Neurotic anxiety concerns the harm that will result from yielding to a powerful and dangerous id impulse, often one that has been associated with punishment during childhood. **Moral anxiety** is caused by acts or wishes that violate one's standards of right and wrong (the superego, discussed below) and includes feelings of shame and guilt. These latter two sources of anxiety are more difficult to deal with because they are intrapsychic, and cannot be escaped by such simple physical actions as running away.

The Defense Mechanisms. To cope with severe threats from the id (or from the superego or external world) and with the associated anxiety, the ego may resort to various **defense mechanisms.** Perhaps the most important of these is **repression** (Freud, 1915/1963f), which (as we have seen) consists of unconsciously eliminating threatening material from awareness and being unable to recall it on demand. We are not cognizant of using repression because it originates from the unconscious part of the ego, which expends psychic energy in order to prevent a dangerous object-choice from taking place (a process called **anticathexis** or **countercathexis,** since it opposes a cathexis of the id). So long as the ego's anticathexis is stronger than the id's

■ CAPSULE SUMMARY
Some Important Psychoanalytic Terminology (I)

Ambivalence	Simultaneously holding opposite feelings, such as love and hate, toward the same object.
Anticathexis (countercathexis)	A quantity of psychic energy used by the ego to oppose a dangerous or immoral cathexis.
Anxiety	A highly unpleasant emotion similar to intense nervousness. The three types are realistic or objective anxiety (related to threats in the external world), neurotic anxiety (related to powerful id impulses), and moral anxiety (related to the superego's restrictions).
Castration anxiety	The boy's fears that his sexual organ will be removed as punishment for his Oedipal wishes.
Cathexis	A quantity of psychic energy invested in a mental representation of an object. The stronger the cathexis, the greater the amount of psychic energy and the more the object is desired.
Compulsion to repeat (repetition compulsion)	An innate, unconscious tendency to repeat previous experiences.
Conscious	The part of the psyche that includes material of which one is fully aware.
Conservative nature of instincts	The tendency of instincts to strive for the restoration of a previous state of existence.
Drive	A term sometimes used as a synonym for instinct.
Eros	A synonym for the sexual instinct.
Erotogenic zone	An area of the body that is capable of producing erotic gratification when stimulated.
Instinct	An innate motivating force that reflects a biological need. The two types are sexual and destructive (aggressive).
Libido	The psychic energy associated with the sexual instinct; sometimes used to refer to both sexual and destructive energy.
Narcissism	Self-love; the investment of one's own self with libido.
Object	Whatever will satisfy an instinctual impulse. May be an inanimate entity, a person, or even something fanciful and irrational.
Oedipus complex	Powerful feelings of love for the parent of the opposite sex and hostile jealousy for the parent of the same sex, together with powerful feelings of love for the parent of the same sex and hostile jealousy for the parent of the opposite sex. The former set of attitudes is usually, but not always, the stronger.
Overdetermination	A term referring to the numerous, complicated causes of most behavior.

continued

Parapraxis	An apparent accident or slip that is actually caused by unconscious psychic processes, and therefore indicates one's real feelings and beliefs.
Penis envy	The girl's jealousy of the boy's protruding sexual organ.
Pleasure principle	The principle or goal underlying all human behavior, to achieve pleasure and avoid unpleasure (pain).
Preconscious	The part of the psyche that includes material that is not at the moment within one's awareness, but that can readily be brought to mind.
Primal scene	Observing one's parents' sexual intercourse.
Primary process	The chaotic, irrational mode of thought representative of the id.
Psychic determinism	The principle that nothing in the psyche happens by chance; all mental activity has a prior cause.
Psychic energy	The "fuel" that powers all mental activity; an unobservable, abstract construct.
Psychoanalysis	(1) The name Freud gave to his theory of personality. (2) A term frequently used to refer to the method of psychotherapy devised by Freud.
Reality principle	Delaying the discharge of psychic tension until a suitable object has been found; a function of the ego.
Reality testing	Determining the difference between id images and objects in the real world.
Secondary process	The logical, self-preservative, problem-solving mode of thought representative of the ego.
Unconscious	The part of the psyche that includes material not within one's awareness and that cannot readily be brought to mind. To Freud, the vast majority of mental activity is unconscious.
Wish-fulfillment	Forming a mental image of an object that will satisfy a need; a function of the id.

cathexis, the repression succeeds and the dangerous material does not reach consciousness. During sleep, however, anticathexes weaken and allow repressed material to emerge (in the form of dreams). This may also happen during such waking states as alcohol intoxication, intense deprivation, or extreme temptation.

All important repressions occur during early childhood, when the immature and relatively powerless ego needs special methods to cope with danger. Repression enables an individual to check the irrational primary process and avoid succumbing to psychosis. However, it is more often an inefficient method that resembles running away from a problem instead of solving it (Freud, 1926/1963j, pp. 97–99; 1940/1969a, pp. 18, 42; 1926/1969b, pp. 30–31). Fleeing from an external threat can be a wise choice, but there is no good way to escape one's own psyche. The id im-

■ CAPSULE SUMMARY
The Structure of Personality (Freud)

Id	*Ego*	*Superego*
Present at birth.	Develops out of the id at about age 6–8 months. Results from experience with one's own body and with the outside world.	Develops out of the ego at about age 3–5 years. Results from introjections of parental standards and the resolution of the Oedipus complex.
Entirely unconscious.	Partly conscious, partly preconscious, partly unconscious.	Partly conscious, partly unconscious.
Operates by the primary process: Is chaotic, irrational, amoral, has no sense of time or logic, is capable only of producing wish-fulfilling images.	Operates by the secondary process: Is logical, self-preservative, problem-solving.	Operates by introjected moral imperatives. May or may not be realistic and self-preservative.
Motivated entirely by the pleasure principle. Transforms biological needs into psychological tensions.	Motivated by the reality principle. Delays the discharge of tension until a suitable object is found in order to avoid errors, dangers, punishment.	Motivated by the energy bound in its formation. Enforces its standards by stimulating the ego's feelings of guilt or pride.
Contains innate inherited instincts, which differ in strength from person to person.	The locus of all emotions, including anxiety. Uses defense mechanisms.	Includes the ego ideal (standards of what is right) and the conscience (standards of what is wrong.)
May be too powerful and cruel (or too weak), resulting in psychopathology.	The stronger the ego, the healthier the personality.	May be too powerful and cruel (or too weak), resulting in psychopathology.
In a sense, the biological component of personality.	In a sense, the psychological executive of personality.	In a sense, the social component of personality.

pulses continue to press for satisfaction, forcing the ego to use some of its limited supply of psychic energy in order to maintain the anticathexis. Repressed material is not affected by experience, since it is under the aegis of the id, and remains at a childish and immature level. Thus repression weakens the capacity to deal with reality. Furthermore, repressions usually cannot be undone when they are no longer needed. Self-deception provides relief, but at a price: an inability to perceive that the danger has disappeared, or that one is now old enough to deal with it effectively. Childhood repressions therefore persist into adolescence and adulthood, where they prevent true self-knowledge, help bring about self-defeating behavior, and may even lead to the development of troublesome neurotic symptoms.

Repression often occurs in combination with other defense mechanisms. One of these is **reaction formation** (Freud, 1926/1963j, p. 30; 1905/1965d, pp. 72–73), where threatening impulses are unconsciously replaced by diametrically opposed beliefs. Thus a child who is afraid to confront an abusive but all-powerful parent may repress his or her intense rage, and feel only constant affection. Or a person may repress strong feelings of self-hate and adopt an attitude of showy self-approval, as by behaving arrogantly and dressing unusually well. In either case, overemphasis of the opposite attitude (love) helps maintain the repression of the true one (hate). Conversely, intense narcissism may lurk behind a self-effacing exterior and unusually modest dress. A withdrawn and suspicious patient may repress frightening feelings of love for the psychotherapist and be constantly hostile and resentful. Or an extremist may crusade against sexual immorality or alcohol abuse in order to conceal his or her own powerful desires for sex or liquor. Reaction formations seem sincere, but can usually be distinguished from true beliefs by their excessive and compulsive nature. This defense mechanism also originates from the unconscious part of the ego and occurs without one's awareness, making possible the primary goal of self-deception.

The defense mechanism of **projection** hides dangerous impulses by unconsciously attributing them to other people or things (Freud, 1912–1913/1950, pp. 61ff.; 1922/1963m). For example, projected anger leads to the belief that one is hated or persecuted by other people (or perhaps even by mythical demons). By transforming illicit impulses into external dangers, projection converts neurotic or moral anxiety into less threatening realistic anxiety. (Realistic anxiety is less threatening because you can run away from external danger, but not from your own id or superego.) In addition, drive-reducing aggression can now be plausibly excused (**rationalized**) as a way of dealing with one's enemies. (See E. Jones, 1908.) Projection is also evident when a poorly prepared student complains about the method of grading (or bad luck), an inferior teacher concludes that the students lack ability, and a careless child blames a painful burn on the hot stove. Although projection plays a significant role in the etiology of paranoia, it is a normal way for very young children to dispose of their faults and illicit wishes (A. Freud, 1936/1966, p. 123).

■ CAPSULE SUMMARY
Some Important Psychoanalytic Terminology (II)

Defense mechanism	A mechanism used by the ego to ward off threats from the id, superego, or external world, and to reduce the corresponding anxiety.
Denial of reality	Refusing to believe, or even to perceive, some threat outside the realm of one's own psyche; a defense mechanism.
Displacement	(1) A defense mechanism whereby feelings or behaviors are transferred, usually unconsciously, from one object to another that is less threatening. (2) Any shift of psychic energy to a substitute object-cathexis.
Fantasy (daydreaming)	Gratifying unfulfilled needs by imagining situations in which they are satisfied; a defense mechanism.
Identification	(1) A defense mechanism whereby feelings of painful self-contempt are reduced by becoming like objects that are illustrious and admired, such as idols, aggressors, or lost loves; may be partly or wholly unconscious. (2) The normal, healthy desire to become like one's parents or other need-satisfying objects.
Introjection	A term roughly equivalent to identification, which refers to the incorporation of others' viewpoints or personal qualities within one's own personality.
Isolation (isolation of affect, intellectualization)	Unconsciously separating threatening emotions from the associated thoughts or events and reacting on only an intellectual level, or separating contradictory and dangerous thoughts from each other; a defense mechanism.
Projection	Unconsciously attributing one's own threatening impulses, emotions, or beliefs to other people or things; a defense mechanism.
Rationalization	Using and believing superficially plausible explanations in order to justify illicit behavior and reduce feelings of guilt; a defense mechanism.
Reaction formation	Repressing threatening beliefs, emotions, or impulses and unconsciously replacing them with their opposites; a defense mechanism.
Regression	(1) A defense mechanism whereby one unconsciously adopts behavior typical of an earlier and safer time in one's life. (2) A reverse flow of libido to an object previously abandoned, or to an earlier psychosexual stage.
Repression	Unconsciously eliminating threatening material from consciousness and using anticathexes to prevent it from regaining consciousness, thus being unable to recall it on demand; a defense mechanism.

continued

35

Sublimation	Unconsciously diverting illicit instinctual impulses to socially acceptable outlets. A form of displacement, but one that represents ideal normal behavior.
Turning against the self	Unconsciously displacing aggressiveness from other, more threatening objects onto oneself; a defense mechanism.
Undoing	Unconsciously adopting ritualistic behaviors that symbolically negate previous actions or thoughts about which a person feels guilty; a defense mechanism.

The ego may also protect itself by refusing to face an unpleasant truth (**denial of reality**). Denial differs from repression in that the source of danger is the external world, rather than id impulses (A. Freud, 1936/1966, p. 109). Thus a person may observe storm clouds approaching yet start off on a long walk, reject justified criticism, or even be unable to perceive disparaging looks on the faces of other people. The terrifying specter of death is a frequent cause of denial (Becker, 1973), with most of us not really accepting the fact that we and our loved ones will someday be gone. Denial is often accompanied by another defense mechanism, **fantasy,** where unsatisfied needs are gratified in one's imagination. A child may deny weakness not only by playing with reassuring symbols of strength like toy guns or dolls, but also by daydreaming about being a famous general or worthy parent. (See A. Freud, 1936/1966, pp. 69ff.) While denial achieves some measure of defense, an excessive amount prevents the ego from fulfilling its main function—perceiving and dealing with reality.

Threatening emotions may unconsciously be separated from the related thoughts, memories, or fantasies, a defense mechanism known as both **isolation of affect** and **intellectualization.** Some patients in psychotherapy seek relief by repressing their pain and discussing important problems in a dry and intellectual way, a defense that hinders their progress. Alternatively, contradictory and dangerous thoughts may be isolated from each other. Another defense mechanism, **undoing,** involves rituals that symbolically and unconsciously negate a previous illicit act or thought. (See Freud, 1926/1963j, pp. 53ff.) A well-known literary example is that of Lady Macbeth, who murders the king and later tries to undo this heinous act ("get the blood off her hands") with compulsive handwashing gestures.

The ego can also draw upon any of its usual processes for defensive purposes. Dangerous impulses may undergo **displacement,** as when an adult who is angry with the boss yells at a spouse or pounds on the table. In one form of displacement, **turning against the self,** aggressive impulses are diverted from a frightening object-choice to oneself. This process is primarily unconscious, and may lead to self-inflicted injuries or even to suicide. Anxiety may also be displaced, as when a child victimized by abusive parents shies away from people in general.

Identification is another normal function that may be used as a defense.[3] The ego may incorporate aspects of a deceased or departed parent, thereby reducing the pain of loss by becoming like the missing object (**object-loss identification**). Or the ego may identify with someone hostile to it (**identification with the aggressor**), thereby achieving some feelings of strength in an otherwise humiliating situation. In either case, the identification may be partly or wholly unconscious. Thus a child upset by the death of a pet kitten may claim to be a cat and crawl about on all fours, or a student reproved by a domineering instructor may unconsciously adopt facial expressions similar to those of the antagonist (A. Freud, 1936/1966, p. 110; S. Freud, 1921/1959, p. 41).

A third normal process which may be used as a defense is **regression,** which operates unconsciously and involves the return to behavior typical of an earlier (and safer) period in one's life. The birth of a sibling may cause a child to resume actions long since discarded, like thumb sucking or bed wetting, as a reassuring reminder of a time when no threatening rivals were present.

Finally, as we have seen, **sublimation** serves defensive purposes by unconsciously diverting illicit impulses (such as murder) into more socially acceptable behavior (like contact sports). However, sublimation differs from the other defense mechanisms in that it cannot be used to excess, for it represents ideal normal behavior—the true solution to our having illicit and antisocial instincts, yet also needing the benefits of society.

The defensive capacities of the ego are fortunate in view of the substantial dangers that it faces. But since self-deception is mostly beyond one's conscious control, defense mechanisms can all too easily become excessive and self-defeating:

> . . . the news that reaches your consciousness is incomplete and often not to be relied on. . . . Even if you are not ill, who can tell all that is stirring in your mind of which you know nothing or are falsely informed? You behave like an absolute ruler who is content with the information supplied him by his highest officials and never goes among the people to hear their voice. Turn your eyes inward, look into your own depths, learn first to know yourself! (Freud, 1917a, p. 143.)

The Superego

According to psychoanalytic theory, infants have no sense of right and wrong. (Recall that only the amoral id is present at birth.) At first this function is carried out by the parents, on whom the helpless child must depend for many years. They reward certain behaviors, a gratifying reassurance of their presence and affection; but they also punish other actions, a

---

[3]Another semantic issue: some writers describe the imitation of a highly cathected object as *identification,* with *introjection* referring to the incorporation of another's attributes into one's own personality. Others use the two terms more or less interchangeably.

highly threatening sign that the child has lost their love and is now at the mercy of an awesome and dangerous environment.

Partly to protect itself from such disasters, and partly because it strongly identifies with the all-powerful parents, the ego begins to internalize (**introject**) their standards. This leads to the formation of the **superego** (*das Überich;* literally, the "over I"), a special part of the ego that observes and sits in judgment above the rest. The superego starts to develop out of the ego during the third to fifth year of life and continues to introject characteristics of teachers, teenage idols, and other authority figures, though these usually remain of secondary importance. Since the parents indirectly reflect the demands of society, the superego helps perpetuate the status quo (Freud, 1923/1962, p. 25; 1940/1969a, p. 3).

The superego is the vehicle for the **conscience,** which delineates and punishes illicit thoughts and actions. The superego also provides the ideals by which the ego measures itself, and rewards desirable behaviors. (Freud originally referred to the superego as the **ego ideal,** but eventually came to regard this as only one of its functions.) A person who refuses to cheat, steal, or kill even though no one else is watching, or who strives to do the best possible job without being supervised, is responding to the dictates of the superego. For behaving in such acceptable ways, the superego rewards the ego with feelings of self-praise and virtue.

Unfortunately, psychic life is rarely this pleasant. Much of the super-ego lies in the unconscious, where it is intimately related to the id. It condemns the id's illicit impulses as severely as actual misdeeds, but can directly influence only the ego. Therefore, both forbidden impulses and behaviors cause tension to be generated between the superego and the ego, and this is experienced by the ego as guilt or moral anxiety. (Thus Freudian theory regards the idea of a "guilty conscience" as a misnomer. Emotions occur only in the ego, so the conscience causes the ego to feel guilty.)

Even though the much-put-upon ego may be unaware of the reasons for these unpleasant feelings, it is still obliged to do something about them. It can obtain relief by substituting more acceptable thoughts or actions, or by resorting to defense mechanisms. The superego does enable the ego to exert necessary self-control and identify with the parents' power, but these benefits are obtained at a price: the ego remains forever subject, at least in part, to the introjected parental regulations. Thus the ego's creation ulti-mately proves to be only a sometime ally. It can also be a harsh master—and yet another source of potential danger.

It is possible for the superego to be underdeveloped, leaving the individual without an effective conscience or ego ideal. Children brought up without love do not introject proper standards, lack appropriate tension between the ego and superego, and have few qualms about aggressing against others (Freud, 1930/1961b, p. 77n). More often, however, the super-ego (like the id) is rigid and unyielding. The ego ideal demands ever greater perfection from the ego, and may become so exaggerated and unrealistic that genuine achievements seem worthless. For example, a student who gives an excellent speech before a large group may feel little or no satisfaction because he or she made a few minor errors. Alternatively, the ever-critical conscience may overstep its bounds and punish legitimate behavior:

> . . . the superego . . . can be supermoral and then become as cruel as only the id can be. . . . [It then] becomes over-severe, abuses the poor ego, humiliates it and ill-treats it, threatens it with the direst punishments, [and] reproaches it for actions in the remotest past which had been taken lightly at the time. . . . (Freud, 1923/1962, p. 44; 1933/1965b, p. 61.)

Intense unconscious guilt can be the cause of illicit or self-destructive behavior, rather than the result. Thus a person may commit a crime, suffer an injurious parapraxis, fail at work or school, or take a turn for the worse when praised by the psychoanalyst in order to gain relief by being punished (Freud, 1923/1962, pp. 39ff). Surprisingly, the superego may become relentless even though the parental upbringing was relatively mild and kindly. One reason is that an overly lenient and indulgent parent is a poor target for hostility, increasing the chances that the child will turn its anger against itself. More importantly, the formation of the superego is a complicated process. It involves not only the introjection of parental standards, but also the resolution of the child's Oedipus complex—a major Freudian concept that will be discussed in the following section.

THE DEVELOPMENT OF PERSONALITY

Psychosexual Stages

From the moment of birth, the id's supply of libido is like a pool of energy that constantly seeks an outlet. The growing child proceeds through a series of **psychosexual stages,** with each one characterized by a particular erotogenic zone that serves as the primary source of pleasure.

The Oral Stage. During the first 12 to 18 months of life, the infant's sexual desires center around the oral region (mouth, tongue, and lips). Sucking at the breast or bottle provides not only nourishment, but erotic pleasure as well:

> Primarily, of course, [oral] satisfaction serves the purpose of self-preservation by means of nourishment; but physiology should not be confused with psychology. The baby's obstinate persistence in sucking gives evidence at an early stage of a need for satisfaction which . . . strives to obtain pleasure independently of nourishment and for that reason may and should be termed *sexual.* . . . The most striking feature of this sexual activity is that the instinct is not directed towards other people, but obtains satisfaction from the subject's own body. It is *autoerotic.* . . . No one who has seen a baby sinking back satiated from the breast and falling asleep with flushed cheeks and a blissful smile can escape the

reflection that this picture persists as a prototype of the expression of sexual satisfaction in later life. (Freud, 1905/1965d, pp. 76–77; 1940/1969a, p. 11.)

Pleasure is only part of the story, however. Frustration and conflict are inevitable because food does not always appear at the moment of hunger, and because the child must eventually be weaned from the breast and taught to stop sucking its thumb. These are the first of many lessons about the need to sublimate instinctual urges and satisfy the demands of society.

One main feature of the oral stage, the incorporation of food and other objects, provides a model for the later psychological processes of introjection and identification. Orality also takes an aggressive turn when the teeth emerge and biting becomes possible, with these impulses becoming stronger in the psychosexual stage that follows.

The Anal Stage. At about age 1–1½ years, the infant gains some control over its anal expulsions. Most of the libido detaches from the oral zone and cathects the anus, with the child gaining particular erotic gratification from the bodily sensations involved in excretion. In addition, the child can now exert control over the environment by contributing or withholding the feces. The former becomes an expression of compliance, similar to the giving of a gift, while the latter is a form of disobedience. Frustration and conflict center about the issue of toilet training, a difficult exercise in self-control that is likely to cause considerable hostility. Freud often refers to this stage as "sadistic-anal," in contrast to the more passive oral stage. (See Freud, 1908a; 1917b; 1933/1965b, pp. 99–102; 1905/1965d, pp. 81–83, 96.)

The Urethral Stage. The urethral stage is not clearly distinct from the anal stage, and Freud has relatively little to say about it. The canal carrying urine from the bladder now becomes an erotogenic zone, the child must learn to control urinary urges, and conflict arises from the problem of bed wetting. (See Freud, 1908a; 1905/1965d, pp. 104 n. 2, 144 n. 1.)

The Phallic Stage. At about age 2–3 years, the boy's powerful cathexis for his mother acquires genital properties. He learns to produce pleasurable sensations by manually stimulating his sexual organ, whereupon

he becomes his mother's lover. He wishes to possess her physically in such ways as he has divined from his observations and intuitions about sexual life, and he tries to seduce her by showing her the male organ which he is proud to own. In a word, his early awakened masculinity seeks to take his father's place with her; his father has hitherto in any case been an envied model to the boy, owing to the physical strength he perceives in him and the authority with which he finds him clothed. His father now becomes a rival who stands in his way and whom he would like to get rid of. (Freud, 1940/1969a, p. 46.)

All human beings are inherently bisexual, so the boy also behaves like a girl and displays affection for his father together with jealousy toward his mother. This double set of attitudes toward both parents constitutes the **Oedipus complex,** named after the legendary Greek king who unknowingly killed his father and married his mother.

Oedipal feelings are extremely powerful, and may well be the most intense emotional experience of one's life. They include all the aspects of a true love affair: heights of passion, jealous rages, and desperate yearnings. However, the Oedipus complex ultimately leads to severe conflicts. The boy fears that his illicit wishes will cost him his father's love and protection, a child's strongest need (Freud, 1930/1961b, p. 19; see also Freud, 1909; 1924/1963o; 1905/1965d, p. 92.) He also inevitably learns of the physical differences between the sexes, and draws a terrifying conclusion: that girls originally possessed a penis but had it taken away as punishment, and the same fate will befall his own prized organ if he persists in his Oedipal wishes. To alleviate this intense **castration anxiety,** the boy abandons his Oedipal strivings and replaces them with a complicated set of attitudes. He intensifies his identification with his father, wishing to be like him rather than replace him. And the boy develops a powerful reaction formation, recognizes that he may not do certain things that his father does (such as enjoy special privileges with the mother), and learns to defer to authority. This reduces castration anxiety by eliminating the need for punishment, while identifying with the father also provides some vicarious gratification of the incestuous wishes for the mother.

These identifications and prohibitions are incorporated into the superego and help bring about its formation, with the prevention of Oedipal sexuality and hostility becoming its primary function (albeit an unconscious one). Thus a severe superego may result from an unusually strong Oedipus complex, one that requires powerful countermeasures. The whole issue is so frightening that it is thoroughly repressed, making it impossible to recall Oedipal experiences without the aid of psychoanalytic therapy. The effects of the Oedipus complex are frequently obvious, however, as when a man chooses a wife who strongly resembles his mother.

The fear of castration cannot apply to girls, so Freud must explain their Oedipus complex in different terms.[4] Like the boy, the girl first forms a strong cathexis for the nurturing mother. The girl is also bisexual, and has twofold attitudes (love and jealousy) for both parents. However, the discovery that she does not have a penis causes intense feelings of inferiority and jealousy (**penis envy**). This may lead to neurotic sexual inhibitions, or to strong wishes to become a boy and masculine behavior. More commonly, however, the girl responds by resenting the mother who shares her apparent defect. She intensifies the envious attachment to her father, regards her

---

[4]Some writers refer to this as the Electra complex, but Freud rejected this term (1920/1963l, p. 141n; 1931/1963q, p. 198).

mother as a rival, and develops an unconscious desire to compensate for her supposed physical deficiency by having her father's baby:

> In males . . . the threat of castration brings the Oedipus complex to an end; in females we find that, on the contrary, it is their lack of a penis that forces them into their Oedipus complex. . . . Not until the emergence of the wish for a penis does the doll-baby [that the girl plays with] become a baby from the girl's father, and thereafter the aim of the most powerful feminine wish. Her happiness is great if later on this wish for a baby finds fulfillment in reality, and quite especially so if the baby is a little boy who brings the longed-for penis with him. (Freud, 1933/1965b, p. 128; 1940/1969a, p. 51. See also Freud, 1923/1963n, pp. 171–175; 1924/1963o, p. 181; 1925/1963p, p. 191.)

Thus the girl lacks the vital and immediate threat of castration anxiety, which causes her to have a weaker superego. The result is that women have greater difficulty forming effective sublimations, and remain narcissistically vain and bitter about their sexual equipment. In fact, Freud regards the clitoris as an inferior possession that has permanent negative effects on a woman's character. He also believes that women are more likely to become neurotic, and that their place is in the home (Freud, 1930/1961b, p. 50; 1926/1963j, p. 83; 1933/1965b, p. 65; 1940/1969a, pp. 12, 50; see also Rieff, 1959/1961, pp. 191ff). Freud does admit to great difficulty in understanding the feminine psyche, and ruefully concedes an inability to answer the "great question" of what a woman wants (E. Jones, 1955/1963b, p. 368). However, he has no doubts about the importance of the Oedipal theory:

> I venture to say that if psychoanalysis could boast of no other achievement than the discovery of the repressed Oedipus complex, that alone would give it claim to be included among the precious new acquisitions of mankind. (Freud, 1940/1969a, pp. 49–50.)

The Latency Period. By age 5–6, personality is firmly established. From this time until puberty (age 12 or later), the child's erotic drives become de-emphasized. Oedipal storms subside, sexuality yields to safer forms of expression (such as affection and identification), and amnesia clouds unsettling memories of infantile sexuality. Reaction formation is evident when the child spurns members of the opposite sex, while the preference for playmates of the same sex is a disguised form of autoerotism made possible by (unconscious) displacement from self to others. The latency period is not a true psychosexual stage, however, and may even be largely or entirely absent in some instances.

The Genital Stage. The genital stage is the goal of normal development, and represents true maturity. (The prior oral, anal, urethral, and phallic stages are therefore referred to as **pregenital.**) Narcissism now yields to a more sincere interest in other people, and the woman's primary erotogenic zone shifts from the (pregenital) clitoris to the vagina. Thus "the female genital

■ CAPSULE SUMMARY
The Psychosexual Stages, Fixation, and Regression

Stage	Erotogenic Zone	Duration; Description	Source of Conflict	Personality Characteristics
Oral	Mouth, lips, tongue	About age 0–1-1/2 years. Primarily involves passive incorporation, but becomes aggressive when the teeth emerge and biting is possible.	Feeding	Oral behavior such as smoking and eating; passivity and gullibility (and the ambivalent opposites).
Anal	Anus	About age 1–3 years. Some control over the environment is provided by expelling or withholding the feces. Associated with hostile, sadistic behavior.	Toilet training	Orderliness, parsimoniousness, obstinacy (and the opposites).
Urethral	Urethra (canal carrying urine from the bladder)	Not clearly distinct from the anal stage.	Bed wetting	Ambition (and the opposite).
Phallic	Penis Clitoris	About age 2–5 years.	Oedipus complex	Vanity, recklessness (and the opposites).

[Sexual impulses become deemphasized during the latency period, which occurs at about age 5–12+ years and is not a true psychosexual stage.]

Genital	Penis Vagina	Adulthood; the goal of normal development.	The inevitable difficulties of life	A more sincere interest in others, effective sublimations, realistic enjoyments.

Fixation: Occurs when libido remains attached to pregenital psychosexual stages. A certain amount is inevitable, but too much will result in psychopathology.

Regression: The reverse flow of libido back to an earlier psychosexual stage or object-choice. As with fixation, a certain amount is normal. The most likely objects of regression are ones that were strongly fixated.

organ for the first time meets with the recognition which the male one acquired long before" (Freud, 1933/1965b, p. 99).

So long as the majority of libido successfully reaches this last stage, there is sufficient psychic energy to cathect appropriate heterosexual objects and form satisfactory relationships. Freud's emphasis on sexuality does not blind him to the importance of love and affection, however, and he regards an attachment based solely on lust as doomed to eventual failure because there is little to keep the parties together once instinctual cathexes have been discharged.

The preceding age limits cannot be specified precisely because the psychosexual stages blend together, with no clear-cut point at which one gives way to the next. These stages deal primarily with the erotic drive, and there are no corresponding "psychodestructive stages" (just as there is no destructive analogue of libido). The emphasis on infantile and childhood sexuality may seem radical, but psychoanalysts regard this as a fact that is both obvious and proven (e.g., Brenner, 1973/1974, p. 22; Fenichel, 1945, p. 56; Freud, 1926/1969b, p. 39).

Fixation and Character Typology

Since instincts are conservative, and the living entity has no innate wish to change, parents must pressure the reluctant child to progress through the various stages of development. This task is fraught with difficulties, and some libido inevitably remains attached (**fixated**) to the pregenital erotogenic zones.

So long as these pregenital zones ultimately become subordinated to the genital, no great harm is done. However, it is possible for excessive amounts of libido to become fixated. This may be caused by traumatic events during a given stage, such as rejection by the mother or father, harsh attempts at weaning, or overly severe toilet training. Such severe frustration causes the child to reject further development and demand the withheld satisfactions, so some pleasure must be allowed at each stage. Yet excessive fixations may also be caused by overindulgence, as by allowing the child to enjoy excessive pleasure from thumb sucking or anal incontinence. Such intense gratification is also undesirable, since it is renounced only with considerable reluctance and remains a source of yearning. Thus the parents must be careful not to allow either too little or too much gratification during any pregenital stage (Fenichel, 1945, pp. 65–66).

Fixation may leave too little libido available for mature heterosexuality and result in serious psychological disturbances. However, it is also possible for a personality to be marked by characteristics of a pregenital stage without being classified as pathological.

Oral Characteristics. The oral stage is primarily passive, so the fixation of excessive libido at this stage is likely to cause dependency on others. The oral individual is also prone to overdo such pleasures as eating or smoking, and to be highly gullible (liable to "swallow anything"). Frustration and overindulgence may well have contradictory effects, however, or the defense mechanism of reaction formation may convert a characteristic into its opposite. Therefore, psychoanalytic theory often describes behavioral patterns in terms of polarities, such as gullible-suspicious and passive-manipulative, with the ideal falling somewhere between the two extremes.

If fixation occurs during the latter part of the oral period, when biting is common, the resulting behavior will instead be of a more sadistic nature (such as sarcasm and ridicule). Oral aggression tends to be more ambivalent than destructive, however, because the dependent orientation creates fears about alienating other people.

Anal Characteristics. Three traits consistently result from an excess of anal erotism: orderliness, parsimoniousness, and obstinacy (Freud, 1908a; 1933/1965b, p. 102). In bipolar terms, anal characteristics include miserliness-overgenerosity, stubbornness-acquiescence, and orderliness-sloppiness. Miserliness derives from an autoerotic desire to hoard one's feces, stubbornness is related to a rebellion against toilet training, and orderliness represents obedient cleanliness following evacuation. These characteristics are sometimes referred to as *anal-retentive,* and the opposite extremes (including sadistic behavior and temper tantrums) as *anal-expulsive.*

Urethral Characteristics. Urethral eroticism is related to ambition, which represents a reaction formation against the shame of childhood urinary incontinence. Ambition may have other causes, however, such as parental pressures (Fenichel, 1945, pp. 69, 493).

Phallic Characteristics. The characteristics of phallic fixation depend on how the Oedipus complex is resolved. An excessive concern with sexual activity and self-love may lead to promiscuity, or to a chaste preoccupation with one's own attractiveness. Other common phallic characteristics include vanity-self-contempt and recklessness-timidity.

The concept of fixation does not apply to the latency period (which is not a psychosexual stage), or to the genital stage (which is the ideal and is denoted by effective sublimations, realistic enjoyments, and mature sexuality). However, it is possible to become fixated on an object as well as a stage of development. Thus one may experience considerable grief over the death of a loved one, a fixation of emotion on something that is past (Freud, 1916–1917/1966, p. 276). Or a neurotic may be unable to develop rewarding heterosexual relationships because of a fixation on the parent of the opposite sex.

Regression

Instincts constantly seek to restore a previous state of existence. The ego tries to maintain adult behavior by controlling these powerful pulls, but may weaken in the face of severe frustration or stress and permit **regression** to take place. As we have seen, this involves a return to behavior that is typical of an earlier and safer time in one's life. More precisely, regression refers to a reverse flow of libido—that is, back to an object-choice long since abandoned or to an earlier psychosexual stage. Thus a child in the phallic stage may regress to thumb sucking or bed wetting at the birth of a sibling, with large quantities of libido returning to a cathexis of the oral or urethral zone. Or an adult or adolescent may become childishly stubborn at moments of stress, thereby regressing to the anal stage.

Regression is significantly related to fixation. Both are normal functions of mental life, and the most likely objects of regression are ones that were strongly fixated. The more powerful the fixation, the less frustration that is needed to trigger a response:

> . . . if a people which is in movement has left strong detachments behind at the stopping-places on its migration, it is likely that the more advanced parties will be inclined to retreat to these stopping-places if they have been defeated or have come up against a superior enemy. But they will also be in the greater danger of being defeated, the more of their number they have left behind on their migration. (Freud, 1916–1917/1966, p. 341.)

FURTHER APPLICATIONS OF PSYCHOANALYTIC THEORY

Dream Interpretation

Psychoanalytic theory presents a formidable difficulty: the most important part of personality, the unconscious, is also the most inaccessible. During sleep, however, the ego relaxes its defenses and allows repressed material to emerge; and libidinal impulses and cathexes that were frustrated during waking hours find gratification in the form of dreams. It is as though the ego says to the id, "It's all right, no great harm can happen now, so enjoy yourself." However, the ego recognizes that an overly threatening dream will cause the sleeper to awaken prematurely. Therefore, it censors the repressed material in various ways and limits the id to only partial fulfillment, and the resulting compromise between the pleasure-seeking id and the sleep-preserving ego is what the dreamer experiences.

In accordance with the principle of psychic determinism, no dream is accidental or trivial. But to understand the true meaning, it is necessary to unravel the disguises imposed by the ego and reveal the unconscious thoughts that lie beneath (**interpret** the dream). This is likely to be a difficult task, partly because the language of dreams is an unusual one and partly because repression returns to full force immediately upon awakening. Nevertheless, having analyzed hundreds of dreams (including many of his own), Freud concludes that "the interpretation of dreams is the royal road to a knowledge of the unconscious activities of the mind" (1900/1965a, p. 647).

Manifest Content, Latent Dream-thoughts, and the Dream-work. The part of a dream that one remembers (or could remember) upon awakening is called the **manifest** content. The unconscious impulses, beliefs, emotions, conflicts, and memories concealed behind the façade of manifest content are known as the **latent** dream-thoughts. And the **dream-work** is the process that converts latent thoughts into manifest content (Freud, 1901/1952, p. 27; 1900/1965a, pp. 168, 211, 311ff; 1933/1965b, pp. 9–10; 1916–1917/1966, pp. 120, 170; 1940/1969a, p. 22).

Thus the dream-work may change latent Oedipal thoughts into manifest content wherein the dreamer enjoys a romantic affair with an attractive stranger, defeating a serious rival in the process. If the ego decides that greater concealment is necessary, perhaps because the Oedipus complex is still a source of considerable conflict, the dream-work may turn love into anger and alter the sex (or even the species) of the romantic object. Now the manifest content will have the dreamer fighting with a person of the same sex. Alternatively, the dream-work may attribute the romantic or aggressive impulses to someone else. If these possibilities are still too frightening, the manifest content may reflect only a vague plan to meet some unspecified person for an unknown purpose. And countless other distortions are possible.

Dreams as Wish-fulfillments. Dreams are triggered by memories of the preceding day's events that call important frustrations to mind (**day's residues**). According to Freud, the purpose of dreams is to fulfill the dreamer's wishes. Thus a child forbidden to eat a delectable dish of cherries gained some satisfaction by dreaming of consuming them all, a woman who was pregnant but didn't want to be dreamed of having her period, and a group of explorers in the icy wilderness had frequent dreams of tempting meals and the comforts of home. Adult dreams are usually quite complicated, however, and involve repressed childhood impulses that are frequently (though not always) of a sexual nature. (See Freud, 1901/1952, pp. 32–37; 105ff; 1925/1963a, p. 88; 1900/1965a, pp. 159–164, 431–435; 1933/1965b, p. 8; 1916–1917/1966, pp. 126ff.)

Although some dreams are disappointing, frightening, or self-punishing, closer analysis invariably reveals some form of (or attempt at) wish-fulfillment. (Freud [1920/1961a, pp. 26–27] does recognize one exception: the tendency to have repeated dreams about a previous traumatic physical injury.) A lawyer once heard Freud lecture about dream interpretation, and then dreamed about losing every case. This man had been a former classmate of Freud's, with grades that were quite inferior. Apparently he had developed powerful unconscious feelings of jealousy and wanted to see wish-fulfillment theory (and Freud) look ridiculous, a wish that the dream fulfilled admirably! Similarly, a woman dreamed that she was unable to give a supper party because all the stores were closed. During the preceding day a female friend, whom the dreamer's husband greatly admired but considered much too skinny, had expressed a desire to be invited to dinner. Thus the dream satisfied a wish to prevent a dangerous rival from becoming more attractive (Freud, 1900/1965a, pp. 180–185).

Frightening dreams indicate that the ego's disguises are about to fail and allow dangerous material to emerge. Awakening the dreamer now becomes the lesser of two evils, and the dream-work behaves

> like a conscientious night watchman, who first carries out his duty by suppressing disturbances so that the townsmen may not be waked up, but afterward continues to do his duty by himself waking the townsmen up, if the causes of the disturbance seem to him serious and of a kind that he cannot cope with alone. (Freud, 1901/1952, p. 102. See also Freud, 1900/1965a, p. 267; 1933/1965b, p. 17; 1916–1917/1966, p. 217; 1940/1969a, p. 28.)

Self-punishment dreams satisfy a wish of the superego. An illicit id impulse strives for gratification, and the superego responds by causing the ego to feel guilty. The punishment dream alleviates this unpleasant emotion, thereby serving as an extraordinary sort of compromise between the three components of personality (Freud, 1900/1965a, pp. 514 n. 1, 596 ff; 1933/1965b, pp. 27–28).

The Language of Dreams. Dreams are expressed in **symbols,** a device also found in myths, legends, jokes, and literature. For example, a stranger who appears in the manifest content may actually represent a parent, spouse, or even the dreamer. Freud attributes a sexual meaning to most symbols, with the male organ represented by elongated and potent objects (sticks, rifles, knives, umbrellas, neckties, snakes, plows) and the female organ denoted by containers (cupboards, caves, bottles, rooms, jewel cases). Staircases, going upstairs or downstairs, and being run over stand for the sexual act, while decapitation or the loss of teeth reflects castration (Freud, 1901/1952, pp. 107ff; 1900/1965a, pp. 385ff; 1916–1917/1966, pp. 149ff).

However, dream interpretation requires far more than a list of symbols and their meanings. Some symbols are used in an idiosyncratic way known only to the dreamer, and some elements are just what they seem and not symbolic at all. Therefore, as was the case with parapraxes, free association must be used to reveal the underlying thoughts:

> . . . we ask the dreamer . . . to free himself from the impression of the manifest dream, to divert his attention from the dream as a whole on to the separate portions of its content and to report to us in succession everything that occurs to him in relation to each of these portions—what associations present themselves to him if he focuses on each of them separately. . . . A knowledge of dream symbolism will never do more than enable us to translate certain constituents of the dream content. . . . It will, however, afford the most

valuable assistance to interpretation precisely at points at which the dreamer's associations are insufficient or fail altogether. (Freud, 1901/1952, pp. 110–111; 1933/1965b, pp. 10–11.)

Manifest content that can be described in a few paragraphs often leads to many pages of latent thoughts. The dream-work eliminates many of the connections between the latent thoughts, and even some of the latent material as well. It separates causes from effects. And it takes different symbols or words that share an important characteristic, and combines them into a single entity that reflects a multiplicity of meanings (the process of **condensation**). Thus dream symbols, like behavior, are usually overdetermined. A man dreamed that his dead father had been exhumed, and subsequently associated this with an aching tooth that he wished to have extracted. The common factor underlying the condensation of father-exhumation and tooth-extraction was that the father's lengthy illness had also caused the dreamer considerable annoyance, a fact repressed during waking hours because it aroused strong feelings of guilt. In addition, the dreamer's hostility toward his father involved childhood sexual impulses and fears of castration (Freud, 1916–1917/1966, pp. 188–190).

The dream-work also makes use of displacement, whereby a major element in the latent dream-thoughts may become a minor aspect of the manifest content (or vice versa). Yet another characteristic of the dream-work is "reversal," which is similar to reaction formation and projection. Love may be transformed into hate (or vice versa), or a hostile latent thought toward the dreamer's father may result in manifest content wherein the father scolds the dreamer (Freud, 1900/1965a, pp. 363–364). Reversal may also be chronological, with the end of a series of latent thoughts occurring at the beginning of the manifest content (or vice versa). These aspects are typical of the primary process, which recognizes no sense of time and no contradictions, and give some indication of the chaotic nature of the thoughts typical of the id.

Finally, after the dream-work has been completed, the process of **secondary revision** (or **secondary elaboration**) fills in gaps in the manifest content and produces a consistent whole (Freud, 1901/1952, pp. 73ff; 1900/1965a, pp. 526ff; 1933/1965b, p. 21; 1916–1917/1966, p. 182; 1940/1969a, p. 24). It is possible for this step to be omitted, however, resulting in manifest content that is highly confused.

Because of these complexities, and because the dreamer's free associations are likely to grind to a halt as they get closer to threatening material, not every dream can be interpreted (Freud, 1933/1965b, p. 13). Nevertheless, in the preface to the 1932 English edition of *The Interpretation of Dreams,* Freud concluded that

> this book . . . contains, even according to my present-day judgment, the most valuable of all the discoveries it has been my good fortune to make. Insight such as this falls to one's lot but once in a lifetime.

Psychopathology

The components of a well-adjusted adult personality work together in relative harmony, under the leadership of the ego, to achieve pleasurable yet safe discharges of tension. The majority of libido successfully reaches the genital stage, enabling the ego to deal with the many demands that it must face. It sublimates or blocks dangerous id impulses, but not those of a healthy nature. It heeds the moral dictates of the superego, but checks a conscience that speaks too loudly or an ego ideal that becomes overly perfectionistic. And it takes the frustrations and restrictions of reality more or less in stride, forming appropriate plans and revising them as necessary. Though life is difficult and some unhappiness inevitable, the healthy individual is able to do two things well: love and work (Freud, cited by Erikson, 1963, pp. 264–265).

In maladjustment, on the other hand, the capacity of the ego is impaired. Weakened by the loss of libido to strong childhood fixations, the ego cannot cope with the inevitable frustrations of reality, or with the pressures of the id and superego. Thus the ego may respond to external frustration by allowing still more libido to regress to the earlier points of fixation, resulting in childishness or narcissism. It may be dominated by a stern and unyielding superego, enforce various defense mechanisms far too rigidly, and deprive the individual of even those pleasures that are realizable and socially acceptable. The inability to form effective sublimations results in a damming up of libido, with limited discharge achieved only after tortuous difficulty. Alternatively, if the superego is also weak, illicit id impulses may emerge unchecked in the form of immorality and destructiveness.

Although psychopathology may cause behavior that seems extreme or bizarre, there is no sharp borderline between the normal and abnormal personality. The distinction involves a difference in degree, not in kind. The painful difficulties of childhood can never be entirely avoided, with the result that "we are all a little neurotic" (Freud, 1901/1965c, p. 278).

Causes of Neurosis. Neurosis invariably begins in infancy and childhood, though it may not become clearly evident until much later. It is possible for the innate sexual constitution to be so defective that neurosis is virtually inevitable, or so healthy that neurosis will occur only if life imposes unusually heavy burdens. Usually, however, environmental factors play a significant role in the etiology of neurosis. (See Freud, 1916–1917/1966, pp. 346–348, 362–364; 1926/1969b, p. 88.)

One such factor is a lack of physical affection, which makes it difficult for the infant to distinguish self from not-self and seriously hinders the development of the ego. Overindulgence or too much frustration during a psychosexual stage will result in excessive fixations, as we have seen. The child may suffer such traumatic events as observing the parents' sexual intercourse (the **primal scene**), being seduced by an adult, or (in the case of the boy) being threatened with castration. This overwhelms the immature

CAPSULE SUMMARY
Some Important Psychoanalytic Terminology (III)

Condensation	The unconscious combination of various symbols or words into a single entity with a multiplicity of meanings.
Countertransference	An unconscious displacement of emotion or behavior, by the psychoanalyst, from some other person to the patient.
Day's residues	Memories of events during the preceding day that trigger a dream because they are somehow related to important unconscious issues.
Dream-work	The unconscious process that converts latent dream-thoughts into manifest content, using such methods as condensation and displacement.
Free association	Saying whatever comes to mind, no matter how silly or embarrassing it may seem. The "fundamental rule" of psychoanalytic therapy, used to bring unconscious material to consciousness.
Insight	An emotional and intellectual understanding of the causes and dynamics of one's behavior, achieved by bringing unconscious material to consciousness.
Interpretation	The psychoanalyst's explanation of the true meaning of the patient's free associations, resistances, dreams, or other behaviors.
Latent dream-thoughts	The true unconscious impulses, beliefs, emotions, conflicts, and memories that are concealed behind the manifest content of a dream; usually related to Oedipal issues.
Manifest content	The part of a dream that one remembers, or could remember, upon awakening.
Primary gain	The partial discharge of libido provided by neurotic symptoms.
Resistance	The patient's unconscious attempts to defeat the purpose of psychoanalytic therapy and preserve illicit id wishes. May take any form that violates the fundamental rule, such as long silences, refusing to talk about certain topics, and so forth.
Secondary gain	An incidental advantage provided by neurotic symptoms, such as avoiding unpleasant tasks or receiving sympathy from others.
Secondary revision (Secondary elaboration)	An unconscious process that fills gaps in the manifest content of a dream and produces a coherent whole. May be omitted in some instances.
Symbol	An entity, usually pictorial, which conveys a meaning that is not immediately apparent; the "language" in which dreams occur. According to Freud, most dream symbols have a sexual connotation.

continued

Transference	An unconscious displacement of emotion or behavior, by the patient, from some other person to the psychoanalyst. Produces the attachment that makes positive therapeutic change possible, but may defeat the therapy if it becomes overly negative.
Transference neurosis	A major intensification of transference, wherein the relationship to the analyst becomes even more important than the problems that originally brought the patient into psychoanalytic therapy.
Working through	The process by which the patient in psychoanalytic therapy becomes convinced about formerly unconscious material, learns to avoid repressing it, and gradually refines the new knowledge into appropriate and effective behavior.

ego with more excitement than it can discharge, a painful condition, and creates the impression that sexuality is dangerous. During the phallic stage, lack of love may prevent the superego from introjecting proper standards. Or the superego may become overly severe, either because of introjects from stern parents or the need to overcome unusually powerful Oedipal conflicts.

The child who succumbs to neurosis enters the latency period with the Oedipus complex unsuccessfully resolved. For awhile, the immature ego is able to achieve a state of balance by resorting to repression and other defense mechanisms. At puberty, however, when sexual activity heightens, this complicated and basically unstable adjustment begins to collapse. The unconscious fantasies, memories, and instinctual impulses are now reinforced by an increased supply of libido, so they surge forth with renewed vigor.

A more healthy individual who had renounced Oedipal strivings could form cathexes for nonfamilial objects of the opposite sex, but the more neurotic person remains fixated on Oedipal desires and conflicts. The ego, influenced by the superego, regards these renascent drives as dangerous and tries to ward them off by the usual methods of anticathexes and defense mechanisms. But since the psyche is not functioning properly, the ego's attempt at repression is only partly successful. (If repression were total, there would be no symptoms.)

The libido is thus deprived of both Oedipal objects and reasonable substitutes. Instead, it finds a devious route to success. It regresses to cathexes fixated during infancy and childhood, passes through the realm of the unconscious, and undergoes the processes of condensation and displacement. This disguise proves acceptable to the ego and superego, and the instinctual impulses finally gain a measure of discharge by emerging in the form of a neurotic symptom. (See Fenichel, 1945, p. 20; Freud, 1915/1963f, pp. 111–112.)

Neurotic Symptoms. Neurotic symptoms are markedly similar to dreams. They communicate important facts about the unconscious, using a symbolic language. And they represent a compromise among the three components of personality, one that reflects both an unconscious attempt at wish-fulfillment and the influence of the opposing defenses. Thus the symptom is "an ingeniously chosen piece of ambiguity with two meanings in complete mutual contradiction" (Freud, 1916–1917/1966, p. 360; see also Freud, 1900/1965a, p. 608 n. 1).

Like dream symbols, neurotic symptoms are usually overdetermined and have a variety of meanings. Unlike dreams, however, symptoms are always caused by sexual impulses (Freud, 1905/1963b, p. 136; 1906/1963k). And more powerful defensive measures are necessary, since the waking state is indeed a source of potential danger to the individual.

As an illustration, let us consider one of Freud's less successful (but more instructive) cases. In *hysteria,* psychological difficulties are unconsciously converted into physical symptoms. An 18-year-old girl, given the pseudonym of Dora, suffered from hysterical nervous coughing and the occasional loss of her voice. Dora's unresolved Oedipal conflicts stemmed in part from an overindulgent father, who tried to compensate for an unhappy marriage by making her his confidante at an early age. Aided by two detailed dream interpretations, Freud discovered that Dora's symptoms communicated a number of meanings. They reflected a clash between an id impulse for oral sex and the defenses of a horrified ego, with the coughing providing some disguised wish-fulfillment in the appropriate erotogenic zone. It also served as punishment for such an illicit wish. Dora had experienced a traumatic seductive embrace with an older married man when she was 14, and she unconsciously displaced this threatening genital stimulation to the oral zone. She spent some time in the company of this man, whose wife was having an affair with her father, and formed strong unconscious desires for him. Her vocal difficulties often occurred during his absenses, expressing a disguised wish not to talk at all unless she could speak to him. The coughing also resulted from an identification with her father, who had a similar mannerism (Freud, 1905/1963b; 1921/1959, p. 38).[5]

One patient successfully treated by Freud, the "Rat Man," was ob-

---

[5]Dora terminated treatment prematurely. As is common in psychotherapy, she unconsciously displaced the hostility that she felt for her aloof parents and elderly seductor onto the therapist (the phenomenon of transference, to be discussed later in this chapter). Freud felt that he blundered by not realizing the strength of these feelings in time, allowing Dora to act out her anger by depriving him of the chance to cure her. However, others have attributed the error to an excessive emphasis on sexuality. Freud apparently ignored the possibility that Dora's conscious distaste for her seductor was not so much a reaction formation against her own unconscious sexual desires, but justified resentment at being "a pawn in her elders' pathetic little end-games, her cooperation necessary in order for them to salvage something erotic for themselves in a loveless world" (Rieff, 1963, p. 16; see also Rieff, 1959/1961, pp. 88–92; Singer, 1970, p. 389).

sessed by horrifying (yet also unconsciously pleasing) thoughts that a pot containing hungry rats would be attached to the buttocks of his father and girl friend. These symptoms were due in part to a powerful conflict between love and hate for his father, a former "gambling rat" who once ran up a gambling debt that he could not afford to pay, and involved a regression to anal erotism (Freud, 1909/ 1963y). Perhaps Freud's most famous case was that of the "Wolf Man," who suffered from a severe animal phobia. (A *phobia* is an intense fear of a specific object or situation that is actually not dangerous.) Through a detailed analysis of the patient's free associations and dreams, these symptoms were traced to various traumatic childhood events: seeing a frightening picture of a wolf during his early childhood, observing either a primal scene or intercourse between animals that was similar to this picture, and threats of castration from a beloved nurse when his sister engaged him in sex play at the age of three (Freud, 1918/ 1963aa). Another well-known case involved the horse phobia of the child known as "Little Hans," who often played horse-and-rider with his father and had once seen a horse fall. Freud attributed this phobia to Oedipal wishes that Hans' father would suffer a painful fall and displaced castration fears, expressed as regressed oral anxiety about the horse biting him. This case is atypical, however, being analyzed primarily through correspondence with Hans's father (Freud, 1909; 1926/ 1963j, pp. 29–41, 59–68).

Freud actually reports very few case histories, opting instead to preserve the anonymity of his patients by presenting his findings in the form of theoretical arguments. He also has relatively little to say about the problems caused by an overly lenient supergo, preferring not to treat such "worthless" people as juvenile delinquents and criminals (Roazen, 1975/ 1976b, pp. 145–153). Among the other areas of interest to Freud are homosexuality and sexual perversions (1920/ 1963l; 1905/ 1965d). In a letter to the mother of a homosexual son, he wrote:

> Homosexuality is assuredly no advantage, but it is nothing to be ashamed of, no vice, no degradation, it cannot be classified as an illness; we consider it to be a variation of the sexual function produced by a certain arrest of sexual development. . . . It is a great injustice to persecute homosexuality as a crime, and cruelty too. (Jones, 1957/ 1963c, p. 502.)

Whatever the form, neurotic symptoms can be remarkably persistent. They represent a compromise between the id, ego, and superego, and are thus actively maintained by all three parties to the conflict. In addition, discovering just one or two meanings of an overdetermined symptom will not be sufficient to eliminate it. Neurosis often involves powerful feelings of guilt, with the symptoms fulfilling an unconscious wish for relief through punishment. As in the case of Dora, not getting well may also be a (primarily unconscious) way of punishing other people. Finally, in addition to the **primary gain** provided by the partial discharge of libido, symptoms may be supported by **secondary gains** as well. The sufferer may receive outpourings of sympathy from others, or be relieved of such onerous tasks as working or going to war, with these fringe benefits making it still more difficult to relinquish the symptoms. (See Freud, 1923/1962, p. 39; 1905/1963b, pp. 60–61; 1933/1965b, pp. 109–110.) These strong reasons for *not* wanting to be cured conflict with the sufferer's wish for relief, making the task of psychotherapy an extremely challenging one.

Psychosis. In psychosis, the patient's severe withdrawal from reality is likely to make hospitalization necessary. Repressed material becomes so powerful that it overwhelms the ego, or the conflict between the ego and reality proves to be so traumatic that the ego surrenders and throws itself into the fantasy world of the id.

Freud's view of psychopathology as a difference in degree does extend to psychosis, but he regards a moderately well-functioning ego as essential for treatment and rejects the use of psychoanalytic therapy with psychotics. (See Freud, 1933/1965b, pp. 16, 154; 1916–1917/1966, p. 447; 1940/1969a, pp. 30, 58; 1926/1969b, pp. 31–32.) This view may well reflect some defensiveness on his part, and has been successfully challenged by later theorists (e.g., Fromm-Reichmann, 1950; Searles, 1965; Sullivan, 1962/1974).

Freud did analyze the autobiography of a psychotic named Daniel Schreber. He concluded that paranoia is inevitably related to underlying homosexuality: love for people of the same sex is converted into hate by reaction formation, and then projected onto others (Freud, 1922/1963m; 1911/1963z). However, modern theory also regards this idea as only partially correct at best (e.g., Arieti, 1974, p. 118).

Psychotherapy

During the years 1880–1882, Freud's noted friend Josef Breuer treated the 21-year-old hysterical patient known as "Anna O." Severe sexual and intellectual deprivation during her childhood and adolescence, followed by the fatal illness of her beloved father, produced a veritable museum of neurotic and psychotic symptoms: paralyzed limbs, hallucinations, an occasional inability to eat, a second personality that lived exactly one year in the past, nervous coughing, sleepwalking, and various speech disorders—and perhaps a hysterical pregnancy as well, although this has been disputed.

Breuer discovered a most unusual way to alleviate these formidable difficulties. He hypnotized Anna O., and had her relive each previous occurrence of a symptom in reverse chronological order! This procedure enabled her to release powerful emotions that she had been afraid to express at the time (the process of "catharsis"). Unfortunately, Breuer's sympathetic care aroused such powerful displaced love from his attractive patient that he became upset, his wife became even more upset, and he dropped the case with considerable embarrassment. But he had shown that the forces causing psychopathology were unconscious, and could be brought to light with words and ideas alone. (See Ellenberger, 1970, pp. 480–484; Ellenberger, 1972; Freud & Breuer, 1895/1966, pp. 55–82; E. Jones, 1953/1963a, pp. 142ff; Rieff, 1959/1961, pp. 10, 41.)

Freud was so impressed by this demonstration that he adopted the hypnotic method with his own patients. However, he soon found that it left much to be desired. Cures were likely to be only temporary, with the patient becoming dependent on the therapist and suffering a relapse as soon as treatment was discontinued. The cathartic removal of a symptom left the underlying causes and conflicts unresolved, free to create new difficulties. Thus hypnotic therapy acted more like a cosmetic cover-up than successful surgery. (The reason, according to Freud, is that hypnosis immobilizes the ego. Since the ego is the rational and problem-solving part of personality, it must remain active and functioning for therapy to succeed.) And some of Freud's patients were unable to achieve a trance state, partly because he wasn't a particularly good hypnotist (Freud, 1916–1917/1966, pp. 450–451; Freud & Breuer, 1895/1966, pp. 145ff). For these reasons, Freud abandoned hypnosis (and catharsis) and gradually developed the form of psychotherapy that has become known as psychoanalysis.

Theoretical Foundation. Simply telling the patient about the causes and dynamics of neurotic symptoms will not produce a cure, for the information will be deflected by the ego's defenses and appear to be irrelevant or incorrect (Freud, 1916–1917/1966, p. 281). A psyche dominated by unknown forces from the past can be liberated in only one way: by bringing crucial unconscious material to consciousness, where it can be experienced by one part of the ego while another (more rational) part looks on. This provides intellectual and emotional understanding (**insight**) about such issues as unresolved Oedipal conflicts, distorted beliefs, irrational loves and hates, and childhood fixations.

These insights reeducate the ego so that it can apply the secondary process to problems that were approached impulsively, and self-destructively, with an excess of primary process thinking. As Freud puts it, "where id was, there ego shall be" (1933/1965b, p. 80; see also Freud, 1900/1965a, p. 617). The patient also learns to abandon excessive self-punishment, guilt, and wishes for vengeance against others, so that "where superego was, there ego shall be" (Fenichel, 1945, p. 589). Thus psychoanalytic therapy undertakes the difficult task of reconstructing one's entire personality, strengthening the ego so that it may assume its proper role of leadership.

Since the origin of neurosis lies in infancy and childhood, psychoanalysis deliberately strives to bring about a certain amount of regression. This regression is therapeutic because it occurs in a favorable atmosphere of introspection and self-understanding, though there may well be a temporary turn for the worse as defense mechanisms and pretenses at normality are stripped away. The process is somewhat similar to removing an embedded fishhook, which must first be pushed further in and the barb cut off before the hook can be extracted (Menninger & Holzman, 1973, p. 45).

Therapeutic regression is induced by carefully applied frustration, with the psychoanalyst remaining essentially silent for considerable periods of time. This also avoids the error of excessive sympathy, which would add to the secondary gains of neurosis and make it still harder for the patient to get well. Freud views the analyst's role as similar to the gardener, who removes weeds that impede growth but does not provide a direct cure (Ellenberger, 1970, p. 461). Yet the analyst must also give enough gratification to prevent excessive frustration and regression, which would lead to infantile behavior. Unlike some modern psychoanalysts, who refuse even a small Christmas present and then try to deduce the patient's unconscious motives for offering it, Freud would accept the gift of a book and might even respond in kind (Roazen, 1975/1976b, p. 125). The psychoanalyst also places great emphasis on the information provided by dreams, which usually involve a regression to the wishes of infantile and childhood sexuality.

Therapeutic Procedures: Free Association, Resistance, Transference, and Others. Treatment normally begins with a series of preliminary interviews, which are used to determine the sufferer's suitability for psychoanalysis. The patient in standard psychoanalytic therapy reclines on a couch while the analyst sits to the rear, out of view. This procedure, which has become a popular symbol of psychoanalysis, enables the patient to relax physically and devote all energies to the demanding mental tasks that are required. It also prevents the patient's regressions from being disrupted by the analyst's facial expressions and gestures. Finally, it allowed Freud to avoid the unpleasant experience of being stared at for hours on end (1913/1963t, p. 146). The patient attends therapy from four to six times per week, for approximately fifty minutes (and up to 100 dollars or more) per session, and usually for several years. The heavy expense in money and time is a definite disadvantage that makes psychoanalysis inaccessible to most people, but an appropriately high fee is claimed to benefit the analysis (as well as the analyst) by providing an additional incentive to tear down one's psychological defenses and enter the frightening world of one's own unconscious (Menninger & Holzman, 1973, pp. 31–32).

While reclining on the couch, the patient is required to say whatever comes to mind (the aforementioned technique of **free association**). Nothing may be held back, no matter how silly, embarrassing, or trivial it may seem:

> Your talk with me must differ in one respect from an ordinary conversation. Whereas usually you rightly try to keep the threads of your story together and to exclude all intruding associations and side issues, so as not to wander too far from the point, here you must proceed differently. You will notice that as you relate things various ideas will occur to you which you feel inclined to put aside with certain criticisms and objections. You will be tempted to say to yourself: "This or that has no connection here, or it is quite unimportant, or it is nonsensical, so it cannot be necessary to mention it." Never give in to these objections, but mention it even if you feel a disinclination against it, or indeed

just because of this. . . . Never forget that you have promised absolute honesty, and never leave anything unsaid because for any reason it is unpleasant to say it. (Freud, 1913/1963t, p. 147.)

This "fundamental rule" of psychoanalysis was actually suggested by one of Freud's patients ("Emmy von N."), who asked that he refrain from interrupting so that she could say what was on her mind (Freud & Breuer, 1895/1966, pp. 97–98). The goal is to minimize the effects of conscious intentions, external stimuli, and internal physical stimuli (such as hunger), while emphasizing those behaviors that derive from unconscious intrapsychic conflicts. While the patient free associates (or tries to), the analyst gives full attention and (in most cases) avoids such distractions as taking written notes.

Free association is much more difficult than might be imagined. The patient's conscious wishes to be cured by psychoanalysis conflict with strong unconscious drives to repress threatening material, not be in analysis, and remain ill. The ego's defenses cannot be eliminated just by an instruction to tell everything, and they intrude upon the free associations in the form of **resistances.** These may include long silences, refusing to say something that seems silly or embarrassing, telling carefully structured stories, avoiding important topics, "forgetting" (i.e., repressing) insights or issues discussed previously, hiding emotion behind a façade of intellectualization, concealing thought behind an excess of emotion, being late or absent from therapy, or a myriad of other devices that violate the fundamental rule and prevent the patient from producing material from the unconscious. (See Fenichel, 1945, p. 27; Freud, 1900/1965a, p. 555.) The analyst must then help the patient become aware that a resistance is taking place, the form in which it occurs, and (lastly) the underlying reason, ultimately eliminating it so that free association can continue. Thus it is necessary to analyze not only the threatening Oedipal impulses and other unconscious residues from childhood, but also the obstacles unconsciously placed in the path of therapy by powerful anticathexes and defense mechanisms.

During those periods when free association is not impeded by resistances, the compulsion to repeat drives the patient to relive childhood conflicts in the analytic situation. Behaviors and emotions are thus unconsciously displaced from the past to the present, and from other important people in the patient's life to the analyst. This process is known as **transference.** (See Freud, 1920/1961a, pp. 12–13; 1905/1963b, p. 138; 1914–1963u, pp. 160, 165; 1916–1917/1966, p. 455.)

Transference provides the analyst with first-hand evidence about the patient's neurosis. It also usually involves some degree of childhood love for the parents, and it is this transferred emotional attachment that makes the patient receptive to the analyst's influence. The analyst therefore tries to intensify this process and make the transference, rather than the original neurotic symptoms, the main focus of treatment (**transference neurosis**). However, this essential procedure is not without potential pitfalls. It is possible for the transference to become extremely negative, as when power-ful distrust or obstinacy is displaced from a castrating parent to the analyst. In fact, "there are cases in which one cannot master the unleashed transfer-ence and the analysis has to be broken off" (Freud, 1937/1963w, p. 270; 1926/1969b, p. 66). The analyst must also be careful not to provoke de-served love or hate, which would give the patient a valid excuse for refusing to recognize (and learn from) transferential love and hate. Thus managing the transference is the most crucial aspect of psychoanalytic therapy, and Freud succeeded where Breuer failed partly because he was able to accept and deal with this important phenomenon. (See Fenichel, 1945, pp. 29–31; Freud, 1925/1963a, pp. 79–81; 1915/1963v.)

Since free association is distorted by resistances and transferences, the psychoanalyst is obliged to deduce the true meaning of the patient's words and actions. For example, such an **interpretation** might relate a patient's present heterosexual difficulties to unresolved childhood Oedipal conflicts. However, interpretations must be withheld until the patient is only a few steps away from the repressed material, and the related ego defenses are ready to crumble. Otherwise, even a correct interpretation is likely to pro-duce resistance and rejection because it is too far beyond the patient's conscious knowledge. (See Freud, 1913/1963t, pp. 152–153; 1937/1963x; 1926/1969b, p. 56.)

As is the case with most learning, the insights gained through psycho-analytic therapy must be practiced in order to integrate them effectively into one's life (the process of **working through**). Learning for the first time about an unconscious conflict, resistance, or self-defeating behavior is usually not sufficient to produce change. The patient only gradually becomes convinced about the truth of formerly unconscious material, learns to avoid repressing it again, and refines the new knowledge into appropriate and effective be-havior (Freud, 1914/1963u).

A final aspect of Freudian psychotherapy concerns the analyst's unconscious tendency to displace emotions and behaviors from other impor-tant people, such as a parent or spouse, onto the patient. Such **countertrans-ferences** may well prevent the analyst from perceiving the patient accurately and responding appropriately (Freud, 1910–1963s, pp. 86–87). For exam-ple, a nagging patient might trigger the therapist's unresolved unconscious resentment toward a parent who behaved in the same way. Or the therapist might overlook some important symptoms because they are frighteningly similar to his or her own serious problems. To help avoid such errors, and to provide a true understanding of psychoanalysis, psychoanalysts must under-go analysis themselves as part of their training. Many do not even begin private practice until they are in their forties (Fenichel, 1945, pp. 30–31; Fine, 1973, p. 6; Freud, 1937/1963w, pp. 267/268).

Although Freud regards psychoanalysis as the premier method of psy-chotherapy, he does not recommend it for everyone or regard it as infallible, nor does he reject other approaches so long as they work (Freud, 1905/1963r, pp. 65–66, 69–72; 1937/1963w; 1933/1965b, p. 157). Psychoanalytic therapy strives to gain the best possible psychological conditions for the functioning of the ego, thereby enabling it to accept the challenge of living and loving. In a sense, the patient is freed from the extreme misery of neurosis in order to face the normal misery of everyday life. More optimistically, the successful patient leaves analysis with feelings similar to those of an anonymous poet (cited by Menninger & Holzman, 1973, p. 182):

> I asked for all things, that I might enjoy life;
> I was given life, that I might enjoy all things.

Work

According to psychoanalytic theory, human behavior is governed by the pleasure principle. People seek to avoid the unpleasure of increased drives, and to obtain pleasure by discharging psychic tension. If every instinctual impulse were satisfied, no drives would need to be reduced—and no one would choose to work. However, this ideal is impossible to achieve. Nature is uncaring and often cruel, creating powerful obstacles and frustrations; and society rules out the greatest sources of pleasure by imposing numerous restrictions against the wild and untamed instincts, such as incest and murder. A certain amount of gratification must be sacrificed in order to survive, and work offers a good outlet for such sublimations.

A few gifted individuals achieve the "finer and higher" pleasures of artistic creation or scientific discovery. Others gain special satisfaction by choosing work that conforms with their innate abilities and channels their instinctual impulses into socially acceptable outlets. For example, a young boy developed intense curiosity about the births of his brothers and sisters. These dramatic events took place in his farmhouse home, yet he was not allowed to watch. As an adult, he satisfied his longstanding wish to know about such matters by becoming an obstetrician. This profession also required him to be kind and considerate toward the babies and mothers whom he treated, thereby strengthening his unconscious defenses against the murderous rage he had felt at the birth of each new sibling. And it enabled him to sublimate hostile Oedipal wishes by identifying with his mother's doctor, a superior figure treated with great deference by his father (Brenner, 1973/1974, p. 200).

Alternatively, a person may become a surgeon partly in order to sublimate sadistic impulses by cutting people up in a socially approved way. Or powerful Oedipal conflicts might help influence one to become a photographer or painter of the opposite sex. Unfortunately, "the great majority of people only work under the stress of necessity [and have a] natural human aversion to work," thus overlooking an important source of potential satisfaction (Freud, 1930/1961b, p. 27 n. 1; see also Freud, 1927/1961c, p. 8).

Religion

Not even modern civilization can conquer the crushingly superior forces of nature and fate. Earthquakes, floods, storms, and diseases exact their inevitable toll in lives and property, while the relentless specter of death awaits us all.

To alleviate such threatening reminders of human helplessness, certain religions preach a reassuring message: Life continues even after death, brings the perfection that may have been missed while on earth, and ensures that all good is inevitably rewarded and all evil punished. Fate and nature only appear to be cruel, for the omnipotent and omniscient Providence that governs all creation is beneficient as well. The difficulties of life actually serve some higher purpose, so there is no reason to despair. Those who successfully subject their thinking to religion receive comfort in return; while those who may be skeptical are advised that these tenets have been handed down from the beginning of time, and that one does not question the highest Authority of all.

Freud regards such beliefs as extremely harmful to the individual and to society, and has authored some of the sharpest and most profound attacks on religion ever published (Freud, 1939; 1930/1961b, pp. 21–22, 28–32, 56–58; 1933/1965b, pp. 160–175; 1927/1961c.) He views religion as a regression to infancy, when the helpless organism lacked sufficient ability to deal with a threatening environment and desperately needed the protection of an all-powerful father. These childhood wishes are unconsciously projected onto reality, creating the image of an exalted deity who also must be blindly obeyed:

> The whole thing is so patently infantile, so foreign to reality, that to anyone with a friendly attitude to humanity it is painful to think that the great majority of mortals will never be able to rise above this view of life. (Freud, 1930/1961b, p. 21.)

Thus religion is in fact a collective neurosis, a shared fixation at a very early stage of development. It is an illusion that tries to master the real world with fantasized wish-fulfillments. This surrender to the magical primary process may spare some people the task of constructing an individual neurosis (Freud, 1930/1961b, p. 32; 1927/1961c, p. 44), but it must ultimately fall before the onslaught of reason and intellect. The more intelligent must eventually realize that our ancestors were wrong about a great many things, and perhaps religion as well; that the prohibitions against questioning religious doctrines are a clear sign of weakness, designed to protect these ideas from critical examination; that tales of miracles contradict everything learned from sober observation; that earthquakes, floods, and diseases do not distinguish between believer and nonbeliever; that human evolution follows Darwinian principles rather than a divine plan; that scoundrels often capture the good things in life while the pious come up empty-handed; and that the promised afterlife of perfect justice is most unlikely ever to be delivered.

In addition to hindering the individual, religion offers a poor foundation on which to base social morality. "Thou shalt not kill," a commandment frequently violated even during those times when the influence of religion was strongest, becomes completely empty if people do not believe that a God will enforce it. And it hardly pays to "love thy neighbor" if the neighbor returns love with hate, and no omnipotent being is on hand to keep score and redress the injustice.[6] Civilization does require prohibitions against killing, but should base them on rational grounds: if one person may kill, so may everyone else. Ultimately all will be wiped out, for even the strongest cannot withstand the attack of a sufficient number of weaker people. If refusing to kill were properly recognized as a self-serving human principle, rather than a commandment of God, people would understand how such rules work to their own interests and strive to preserve rather than abolish them (Freud, 1930/1961b, pp. 56–58; 1927/1961c, pp. 37–44).

Freud concedes that his arguments will encounter powerful and emotional opposition. Since people are indoctrinated with religion during childhood, before they are able to apply reason to the whole issue, they become dependent on its narcotizing effects. Therefore, he recommends bringing children up without religion. This would force us to face the full extent of our insignificance in the universe, abandon the security blankets of childhood, learn to rely on our own resources, and grow from infantilism to maturity (Freud, 1927/1961c, pp. 49–50). Just as Freud took no more than an occasional aspirin during sixteen painful years with cancer, he allows us no narcotics and no rationalizations. We must forgo the illusions of ideal justice and happiness in the hereafter, and be content merely to relieve the inevitable burdens of life. This will enable us to make the most of our innate capacities, and to deal most effectively with reality:

> No belittlement of science can in any way alter the fact that it is attempting to take account of our dependence on the real external world, while religion is an illusion and it derives its strength from its readiness to fit in with our instinctual wishful impulses. . . . Our science is no illusion. But an illusion it would be to suppose that what science cannot give us we can get elsewhere. (Freud, 1927/1961c, p. 56; 1933/1965b, pp. 174–175).

Education

Primary education must teach children to control their illicit instincts and get along with others. But if it is too harsh, and interferes too greatly with the discharge of libido, neurosis is likely to result. "Thus education has to

---

[6]Freud did take a more positive approach to loving one's neighbor in a subsequent publication (1933).

find its way between the Scylla of non-interference and the Charybdis of frustration" (Freud, 1933/1965b, p. 149).

Unfortunately, this challenging goal is rarely achieved. Children vary considerably in their innate constitutional dispositions, so teaching methods helpful to some are harmful to others. Subtle indications of important psychic events are likely to be overlooked by educators not trained in psychoanalysis. Education unwisely conceals the major role that sexuality plays in life, and fails to prepare children for the destructiveness that they will encounter in others. To Freud, preparing a child for life by teaching that every adult is virtuous is like starting out on an expedition to the North Pole with summer clothing and a map of southern Europe. It would be far better to state honestly that while people ought to be virtuous, so as to make themselves and others happy, they often will not be (Freud, 1930/1961b, p. 81n).

To remedy these serious defects, Freud recommends that educators undergo psychoanalysis as part of their training (Freud, 1933/1965b, p. 150). And some modern analysts also argue that all who teach psychology and the social sciences should be psychoanalyzed (Menninger & Holzman, 1973, p. xii).

Literature

According to psychoanalytic theory, Oedipal themes can be found throughout literature and the arts. The young hero who slays the fearsome giant in "Jack and the Beanstalk" is actually scoring a symbolic Oedipal triumph over a castration-threatening father, while Cinderella achieves a similar victory over her horrid mother and sisters by winning the heart of a handsome father-figure (the prince). To minimize the listener's guilt feelings about fulfilling such illicit wishes, the hero(ine) with whom the child identifies is invariably depicted as honest and in the right, while the rivals are portrayed as evil villains or monsters. In adult literature, Shakespeare's Hamlet cannot bring himself to avenge his father's murder because the behavior of his dastardly uncle is an all-too-threatening reminder of his own longstanding forbidden wish: to take his father's place with his mother. Parricide also plays a major role in many novels (e.g., Dostoevski's *Brothers Karamazov*) and in various myths and legends, notably the story of Oedipus that formed the basis for Freud's theories. Even in tales where the characters are loving or submissive, the manifest content can be interpreted as a defense against underlying illicit impulses. For example, the Homeric myth of immortal gods and goddesses disguises the issue of parricide by having a father-figure (Zeus) who cannot be killed (Brenner, 1973/1974, p. 206).

Freud regards jokes as of considerable psychological importance, and has devoted a monograph to this topic (1905/1963i). Many jokes allow the discharge of sexual or aggressive tension in a socially acceptable way, with a "joke-work" (similar to the dream-work) concealing the true meaning by using condensation and displacement. Freud's analysis presents considerable difficulties for the modern American reader, however, and is probably the least read of all his works. Jokes that are obviously funny in Freud's native German often require a lengthy explanation in English or involve a play on words that cannot be translated at all, while others are amusing only to those who are also familiar with life in Vienna at the turn of the century.

Social Psychology

Freud rejects the possibility of an autonomous human social instinct. Groups form when people identify with a leader, and introject the leader's standards in place of their own superegos. (See Freud, 1921/1959. Freud did not introduce the superego construct until 1923, so the term *ego ideal* is used in this monograph.)

Like dependent children, group members seek to resolve mutual jealousy by believing that the leader loves them all equally. Thus libido is the psychic cement that binds the group together, with the group (and its all-powerful parental figure, the leader) satisfying unconscious erotic longings for protection that persist from childhood.

Groups often reflect such primary process characteristics as impulsiveness, immorality, unquestioning acceptance of contradictions, and frequent displacements caused by the inability to tolerate delays in gratification. If the leader's standards are particularly righteous, however, the group may actually be more moral than the individuals who comprise it.

EVALUATION

Sigmund Freud was a true genius, with many brilliant insights about the nature of human personality. There are some errors in his theory, however, as well as aspects that remain highly controversial. To complicate matters, Freud changed his mind often and left more than a few loose ends. Conceding and correcting an error is in the best spirit of scientific integrity, but his many revisions have caused considerable difficulties for those trying to evaluate his theory.

Criticisms and Controversies

Female Sexuality. Freud's belief that women are inferior creatures with defective sexual organs, weaker superegos, and a greater predisposition to neurosis is regarded by virtually all modern psychologists as absurd—a truly major blunder. Freud's own attitudes apparently contained built-in sexist prejudices (as was common in his era), which made it difficult even for such a sensible and rational man to take seriously the humiliations suffered by women. Today, of course, theorists tend to stress the equality or even superiority of women (such as greater longevity and the ability to bear children).

The psychoanalytic belief that clitoral orgasm is an inferior and pregenital form of sexuality, and that vaginal orgasm is the only mature version, has also been contradicted by modern research. Although sexual response is probably too complex to be attributed to any single factor, studies have indicated that women who experience orgasm through clitoral stimulation are as normal and well-adjusted as those who obtain it from vaginal penetration. To many observers, therefore, Freudian theory represents yet another expression of an age-old cultural bias against women. (See for example Breger, 1981; Fromm, 1973; 1980; Horney, 1923–1937/1967; Lewis, 1981; Masters & Johnson, 1966.)

Sexuality and Rigidity. Freudian theory has been strongly attacked for its heavy emphasis on sexuality: the universality of the Oedipus complex, libido, the psychosexual stages, attributing all psychopathology to malfunctions of the sexual drive, regarding most dream symbols as sexual, and so forth. Even today, when sexuality is no longer so shocking, many find it hard to believe that this one drive explains nearly all human behavior. Psychoanalysts would argue that we have not yet come far enough along the path of freeing ourselves from our repressions, but there is also the possibility that Freud's personal life affected his theorizing to an excessive degree. For example, his frequent allusions to Oedipal parricide wishes may be related to an unusual degree of resentment toward his father (Ellenberger, 1970, pp. 451–452; Roazen, 1975/1976b, pp. 36–37). And although Freud was in many respects a fearless and objective investigator, he appears to have had an intense personal commitment to the issue of sexuality:

> There was no mistaking the fact that Freud was emotionally involved in his sexual theory to an extraordinary degree. When he spoke of it, his tone became urgent, almost anxious, and all signs of his normally critical and skeptical manner vanished. A strange, deeply moved expression came over his face, the cause of which I was at a loss to understand. I had a strong intuition that for him sexuality was a sort of *numinosum.* (Jung, 1961/1965, p. 150.)

Freud was in the extremely difficult position of having the intelligence and sensitivity to fear death very strongly, yet not believing in religion. He hated helplessness and passivity, particularly the inevitable nonexistence and insignificance of death. Thus psychoanalysis may well have become the religion that would provide him with the immortality of lasting recognition. In fact, his harsh rejection of former colleagues who criticized libido theory (such as Jung and Adler) reflects an intolerance more suited to religion than to scientific controversy. (See Becker, 1973, pp. 100–101; Roazen, 1975/1976b, pp. 188, 209). Interestingly, Freud himself recognized this potential characteristic of a science:

> . . . every religion is . . . a religion of love for all those whom it embraces; while cruelty and intolerance towards those who do not belong to it are natural to every religion. . . . If another group tie takes the place of the

religious one . . . then there will be the same intolerance towards outsiders . . . and if differences between scientific opinions could ever attain a
similar significance for groups, the same result would again be repeated with
this new motivation. (Freud, 1921/1959, pp. 30–31.)

Some modern analysts do act like members of an exclusive ingroup,
invoking scathing criticisms against even the most respected psychologists of
other persuasions. Fine (1973, pp. 8–10), for example, characterizes Adler's
contributions to psychological theory as "negligible" and dismisses behavior
therapy as a "gimmick." Challenging psychoanalytic theory, on the other
hand, can be as difficult and frustrating as attacking a religion. If one cannot
recall any Oedipal trauma, the analyst would reply that these events have
been cloaked by repression. Similarly, a novel or dream that affords no
obvious evidence of sexuality would usually be explained as the result of
various defenses. Disagreement with a psychoanalyst's interpretation is almost always seen as a resistance, rather than an error by the analyst. When
Freud told Dora that a jewel case in her dream symbolized the female
genitals, and she replied with "I knew you would say that," Freud promptly
rejected the obvious conclusion (that she knew his theories well enough by
then to predict his responses) and regarded her answer as a typical way of
resisting the truth of his interpretation (Freud, 1905/1963b, p. 87). In fact,
there is virtually no way to have a legitimate argument about sexuality with a
Freudian.

To be sure, Freud's beliefs did derive from a deep and passionate
commitment to what he regarded as the truth. He spent a lifetime of hard
work sharing his patients' deepest thoughts and most intimate feelings, and
he could hardly be expected to accept points of view with which he disagreed just to appear openminded. And he was well aware that psychoanalysis has serious limitations. (See Freud, 1937/1963w; 1933/1965b, p.
144; 1916–1917/1966, p. 245.) Nor is professional arrogance limited to
psychoanalysis, or even to psychology. Yet psychoanalysis would appear to
suffer from an excessive rigidity, one that provokes public and professional
disillusionment and risks losing the more valuable of Freud's hard-won
insights (Strupp, 1971).

Pessimism and Drive Reduction. Freud's picture of the dark side of personality has also provoked strong criticism. No one can deny that people are
capable of highly destructive and illicit acts, but can we really be inherently
murderous and incestuous? Is adult pleasure limited to watered-down sublimations of our forbidden childhood desires? Is the belief in the goodness
of human nature "one of those evil illusions by which mankind expect their
lives to be beautified and made easier, while in reality they only cause
damage?" (Freud, 1933/1965b, p. 104). Rather than accept such somber
conclusions, some theorists have tried to recast Freudian psychoanalysis in
more optimistic terms (e.g., Horney, Fromm, Erikson). Others have chosen
to opt for Freud's "illusion" (e.g., Rogers, Maslow).

Freud's emphasis on drive reduction has also come under heavy fire. A wealth of everyday experience suggests that people are also motivated by desires for increases in tension, and actively seek out excitation and stimulation. Children display an incessant and lively curiosity, some adults continue to work despite being financially secure, and many people take up a challenging project or hobby instead of remaining idle. This issue is deceptively complex, however, and some of these criticisms seem to be based on misunderstandings of psychoanalytic theory. If the id is as chaotic as Freud believed, a child's apparently aimless exploration may serve to reduce drives that are incomprehensible to a rational adult. Work that appears to be unnecessary and stimulus-seeking may actually be due to the lash of an overdeveloped and demanding superego, or it may provide an opportunity for effective sublimations. Psychoanalytic theory does regard boredom as an unpleasant state, where some tension whose aim is unconscious is blocked from discharge (Fenichel, 1945, p. 15). Some gratifying drive increases, such as sexual forepleasure, depend on the expectation of subsequent drive reduction and lose their appeal if this belief is shattered. And Freud himself conceded the existence of pleasurable drive increases (1924/1963h, p. 191), as we have seen. It is probably true, however, that he did not give this factor sufficient attention.

Psychic Energy. According to Freud, excessive fixation or regression will lead to neurosis. But just how much is excessive? It is impossible to measure the quantity of psychic energy that is invested in any given cathexis, nor is there any way to determine the minimum amount of discharge needed to prevent libido from becoming blocked. Therefore, some psychologists include the energy model among Freud's dramatic failures. (See for example Bieber, 1980; Carlson, 1975.)

Internal Consistency. Despite the fact that Freud's constructs are carefully and intricately interrelated, psychoanalytic theory does not quite hold together. Serious contradictions tear at the foundation and threaten to bring down the entire structure.

As an example, let us consider once again the nature of the instincts. Freud originally regarded the sexual and self-preservative instincts as two separate categories. He also maintained that all instincts have the conservative function of restoring matter to a previous state of existence (e.g., returning from hunger to satiation). In 1920, however, Freud made some significant theoretical changes. Partly because aggressive behavior was becoming increasingly difficult to explain in terms of his theory, he redefined the two major types of instincts as sexual and destructive, with self-preservation included as part of Eros. However, tinkering with one part of a theory is likely to affect other aspects as well. Freud continued to argue that all instincts are conservative, yet this now became a new source of difficulty. If nonexistence was our original condition, it is easy to see how the death instinct is conservative: it tries to bring us back to the inanimate state from which we started. But how, then, can the self-preserving Eros be conservative? If, on the other hand, our earliest condition was that of existence, then the death instinct cannot be conservative. And if no instincts are conservative, all sorts of horrible complications set in. (For example, such all-important concepts as drive reduction and the pleasure principle are destroyed.)

Freud finally indicated that perhaps Eros is not conservative (1940/1969a, p. 6), yet this creates a whole host of new difficulties. One gets the distinct impression of a man approaching the twilight of his life, confronting a majestic but weakening theoretical dam, and creating new leaks with every attempt to patch up old ones. These inconsistencies by no means vitiate psychoanalytic theory, but they do indicate that it is undoubtedly not the last word in theories of personality.

Methodology. Some critics regard psychoanalysis as too subjective and uncontrolled. The psychoanalyst may be biased by preconceived theoretical notions and disregard contradictory evidence, or the patient may be influenced to behave in ways that support the analyst's beliefs. The analyst exerts a powerful effect on the patient despite the apparent passivity of the procedure (e.g., Strupp, 1972), and Freud's assertion (1937/1963x, pp. 278–279) that he never led a patient astray by suggestion seems highly improbable.

It has even been argued that Freud exaggerated the success of some of his cases, and distorted some of the facts in ways that would support his theory. According to these critics, Freud paid too little attention to the crucial issue of transference during his treatment of the "Rat Man," he tried to force interpretations on the patient that were favorable to his theory by using the power of his intellect and personality, and he fictitiously lengthened the case report and changed the order of events to create a false impression of greater treatment orderliness and effectiveness. Although these issues are very troublesome, they do not necessarily mean that Freud was seriously lacking in integrity; they do suggest that he was considerably more prone to human failings than his legend allows. And there are historians of psychoanalysis who regard these criticisms as unfair, and as unlikely to have much effect on the prevailing view of Freud's work. (For a further discussion of these and related issues, see Eagle, 1988; the *New York Times* article by Goleman, 1990; Mahony, 1986.)

Freud's refusal to take notes during the analytic session, so that he could respond unconsciously and empathically to the patient, is questioned by those who distrust the vagaries of memory (Wallerstein & Sampson, 1971). Despite Freud's protestations, concentrating on neurotic people may have limited his understanding of the healthy and fulfilled personality. And there are no statistical analyses or differential hypothesis tests in Freud's writings, in contrast to the usual scientific emphasis on quantification and control. For example, his analysis of the "aliquis" parapraxis may not prove that it was motivated by the unconscious fear of having impregnated a woman, since free associations beginning with any other word might also have led to this all-important personal issue.

Other Issues. Such psychoanalytically oriented theorists as Erikson, Fromm, Horney, and Sullivan believe that Freud overemphasized the biological determinants of personality, and underestimated social and environmental factors (as we will see in subsequent chapters). Jung, Sullivan, and Erikson are among those who contend that personality development continues during adolescence and adulthood, rather than concluding at age 5–6 years. It has been argued that Freud gave too much stress to the consoling aspects of religion, overlooked some of its advantages (and some of the disadvantages of science), and had a personal bias regarding the whole issue (Rieff, 1959/1961, pp. 325–328; Roazen, 1975/1976b, pp. 250–251).

It now appears that dreams are *not* the guardians of sleep, as Freud contended. It is sleep that serves to protect dreaming, a process that is apparently essential to our well-being. It is also doubtful that dreams are as sexually oriented as Freud thought, and it may well be that dream symbols are used more to reveal and express complicated ideas than to conceal illicit wishes. (See Dement, 1964; 1974; Fisher & Greenberg, 1977, pp. 21–79; Fromm, 1951/1957; C. S. Hall, 1966.)

Behaviorists claim that Little Hans's horse phobia was caused by learning and external stimuli, rather than by internal Oedipal conflicts (Bandura, 1969; Wolpe & Rachman, 1960). Those who are optimistic about our innate nature do not agree that people have a natural aversion to work.

Empirical Research

As would be expected of a science, psychology has tried to resolve the aforementioned controversies by turning to empirical research. Unfortunately, the results have been little better than equivocal.

Psychoanalytic Theory. A number of studies carried out between 1950 and 1970 focused on the defense mechanisms. Some investigators tried to induce adolescent or adult subjects to repress previously learned material by persuading them that they had failed on an important task, such as a test of intelligence or a measure of sexual deviation. Other researchers studied the ability to remember fairly recent life events, hypothesizing that traumatic incidents should be more readily repressed than pleasurable ones. Still others concentrated on the perceptual aspects of defense, using a tachistoscope (a high-speed projection device) to flash a series of individual words on a screen for brief instants. These investigators hypothesized that taboo words (e.g., "penis," "rape") should be more readily repressed, and hence more difficult to perceive, than neutral words (e.g., "apple," "stove").

Taken as a whole, the results appear to indicate little support for the existence of repression. That is, the experimental group (which underwent the unpleasant experience) usually did *not* demonstrate poorer recall than the control group (which did not). However, since Freud states that the decisive repressions all take place during early childhood, it is difficult to see how an experimenter can justifiably claim to have refuted psychoanalytic theory merely by failing to trigger this mechanism in older subjects. Even though the taboo words in the perceptual defense experiments were sometimes readily identified, the existence of some people who do not deny this particular aspect of reality is hardly a major blow to psychoanalytic theory. Thus the clinical evidence in favor of repression and the defense mechanisms would appear to outweigh these negative, but flawed, research findings. The studies in question may be of interest in other respects; but their relevance to Freudian theory is at best doubtful, and they will not be discussed further herein. (For specific references, see the first edition of this book [Ewen, 1980, p. 65] and Hilgard & Bower [1975, pp. 362–369].)

Silverman (1976) also concludes that research on psychoanalytic theory prior to the 1970s has been poorly designed, in part because it is difficult to study unconscious material without allowing it to become conscious. As a result, there has been a lack of convincing research support for the major propositions of psychoanalysis. To help remedy this defect, he reports on two independent research programs conducted over a ten-year period. Both programs dispensed with the metaphysical aspects of psychoanalysis (e.g., psychic energy and cathexes), and concentrated instead on basic clinical propositions. One program used subliminal tachistoscopic presentations of stimuli designed to intensify the subjects' wishes, feelings, and conflicts about sex and aggression (and *not* to induce repression, as in the studies criticized above). The other program employed hypnotic suggestion to induce conflict, as by suggesting that the subject strongly desired a member of the opposite sex who was married, more experienced, and likely to treat any advances with ridicule. The results supported a fundamental contention of psychoanalytic theory, namely that psychopathology is causally related to unconscious conflicts about sex and aggression.

Fisher and Greenberg (1977) have reviewed a substantial amount of research dealing with psychoanalytic theory. The evidence indicates that dreams do *not* serve to preserve sleep, as noted in a previous section. Nor is the manifest content of a dream merely a meaningless conglomeration of camouflage devices. It may at times function defensively, but it also provides important information about the dreamer's personality and success in coping with important life issues. However, Freud was correct when he concluded that dreams provide an outlet for our internal, unconscious tensions. With regard to personality types, such oral characteristics as dependency, pessimism, and passivity do frequently cluster together. The same is true for the anal characteristics of orderliness, parsimoniousness, and obstinacy. Research on Oedipal issues supports Freud's belief that both sexes begin life with a closer attachment to the mother, that castration anxiety is a common occurrence among men, and that the boy does go through a phase of rivalry with his father. But the studies also indicate that Freud was fundamentally wrong about female Oedipality: there is no evidence that women believe their bodies to be inferior because they possess a vagina instead of a penis, or that women have less severe superegos than men. The research findings also suggest that the boy resolves his Oedipus complex *not* to reduce castration anxiety, but because the father's friendliness and nurturance invite the boy to become like him. That is, the resolution of the boy's Oedipus complex is due to trust rather than fear.

Hunt (1979) reviewed literature dealing with the psychosexual stages, and concluded that Freudian theory is incorrect in certain respects. Although some support does exist for the anal character, there is no evidence that it derives from the management of toilet training. Also questionable is the Oedipal hypothesis that children regularly compete with the parent of the same sex for the attention and love of the parent of the opposite sex. However, the research results do support Freud's general emphasis on experiences during early life as determinants of personality.

Some critics of psychoanalytic theory cite animal studies that purportedly demonstrate the existence of pleasurable tension increases. Animals will explore the environment, learn to solve mechanical puzzles, and learn to open a door in an opaque cage just to see outside, without any biological drive reduction taking place. Thus, insofar as learning theory is concerned, it has been concluded that the drive-reduction hypothesis is very probably inadequate (Bower & Hilgard, 1981, p. 113). On the other hand, Freud's original theory about the seduction of children by adults may not have been as incorrect as he ultimately concluded. It has been suggested that incest is considerably more prevalent than is generally believed, but is not publicized because of (understandable) feelings of shame and guilt. The continuing interest in such Freudian issues is evidenced by the prominent coverage in such popular periodicals as *The New York Times* (Blumenthal, 1981a; 1981b; Goleman, 1990) and *Newsweek* (Gelman, 1981; 1991).

Finally, Shevrin and Dickman (1980) surveyed diverse fields of empirical research dealing with the unconscious. Although the results by no means always agree with Freudian theory, the authors conclude that no psychological model that seeks to explain human knowledge, learning, or behavior can afford to ignore the concept of unconscious processes.

Psychoanalytic Therapy. Psychoanalytic therapy has also been subjected to the rigors of formal research, though there are serious methodological problems here also. (See for example Bergin & Suinn, 1975; Fisher & Greenberg, 1977; Gomes-Schwartz et al., 1978; VandenBos, 1986; VandenBos & Pino, 1980; Williams & Spitzer, 1984.)

There is increasing evidence that newer forms of psychotherapy may be more efficient and effective than psychoanalysis, at least for certain types of pathology (e.g., Corsini, 1973; Sloane et al., 1975). Even Eysenck's polemical attacks on psychoanalysis (1952; 1965; 1966), which at one time appeared to have been convincingly refuted (Bergin, 1971; Meltzoff &

Kornreich, 1970), have since met with some support (Erwin, 1980; Garfield, 1981). Nevertheless, a study of twenty behavior therapists who were themselves in personal therapy revealed that ten opted for psychoanalysis (and none for behavior therapy!), with some freely conceding that analysis is the treatment of choice if one can afford it (Lazarus, 1971). And some analysts have sought to update their procedures by having the patient attend only once or twice per week, and by dispensing with the couch in favor of face-to-face interviews, while retaining many of the fundamental aspects of Freudian theory (e.g., Bieber, 1980).

Some theorists emphasize the common factors among the various forms of psychotherapy, arguing that the differences are more apparent than real (e.g., Bergin & Strupp, 1972; Luborsky, Singer, & Luborsky, 1975; Strupp, 1973). Others argue that those differences that do exist can and should be reconciled, so that psychologists can concentrate on advancing our knowledge rather than debating the merits of particular delimited schools of thought. (See Goldfried, 1980; Marmor & Woods, 1980; Wachtel, 1977; 1987). At present, then, there are no simple answers regarding the relative effectiveness of psychoanalytic therapy.

Contributions

Despite the controversies that beset psychoanalysis, Freud fully deserves his lasting place in history. Although there are modern psychologists who would disagree, the following almost certainly represent major progress in our attempts to understand the human personality.

Freud emphasized the importance of the unconscious so accurately, and so vividly, that many people think of it as his own private discovery. Instead of naively assuming that behavior is what it seems on the surface, it is now widely accepted that a part of human personality—and probably a very significant part—is below the level of awareness. The term *Freudian slip* has become part of our everyday language, and there is increasing recognition that apparently accidental behavior may well be purposeful (and that one must accept the responsibility for it). Freud and his daughter Anna identified the defense mechanisms, which are also now part of common speech. He devised valuable techniques for interpreting dreams, and was the first to incorporate dream analysis as a formal part of psychotherapy.

Freud developed the first thorough method of psychotherapy, including procedures for bringing unconscious material to consciousness. He formally identified such fundamental issues as resistance and transference, and showed that many difficulties in adult life relate to childhood conflicts with one's parents. Thus he pointed out the importance of early childhood on personality development and attacked the myth of the "happy child," demonstrating that our earliest years are often a time of considerable trial and frustration. He also stressed that psychopathology represents a difference in degree rather than kind, and showed that apparently incomprehensible neurotic symptoms have a definite meaning.

Freud called attention to the importance of anxiety, and emphasized that psychic pain can be as or more troublesome than physical pain. He showed that psychopathology may involve self-imposed commands and restrictions that are relentless and cruel, a concept accepted by many other theorists (albeit often presented using their own terminology rather than the superego). He analyzed himself without the aid of another analyst, because there were no others, and probed the terrors of his own unconscious with no one else to lean on. And his theories about infantile sexuality and the inevitable conflict between the individual and society, while controversial, have triggered valuable discussions and rethinkings of these issues.

Despite many sharp attacks and incredulous critics, Freud is accorded great esteem throughout psychology and psychiatry. Textbooks in all areas of psychology pay him due respect, while many of the noted personality theorists whose views we will examine in subsequent chapters have used psychoanalytic theory as the foundation for their own work. Whatever Freud's errors may have been, this extraordinary and brilliant man opened new psychological vistas for all humanity. The ultimate personality theory must surely include, at the very least, the best of his ideas; and no one who claims an interest in human behavior can afford to be without a first-hand knowledge of his works.

Suggested Reading

The best way to approach Freud is by starting with his latest writings, which express his theory in its final form. *The Question of Lay Analysis* (1926/1969b) is a highly readable short monograph that summarizes many of the main points of psychoanalysis. The *New Introductory Lectures on Psychoanalysis* (1933/1965b), which was designed as a sequel to the *Introductory Lectures on Psychoanalysis* (1916–1917/1966), can stand in its own right as a well-written guide to various aspects of Freudian theory. *An Outline of Psychoanalysis* (1940/1969a) is a brief and highly condensed survey, while *The Ego and the Id* (1923/1962) is the seminal work that introduced the structural model of personality. Many of Freud's views on religion and society will be found in *The Future of an Illusion* (1927/1961c) and *Civilization and its Discontents* (1930/1961b).

Among Freud's earlier works, *The Interpretation of Dreams* (1900/1965a) is probably his single most important effort. *The Psychopathology of Everyday Life* (1901/1965c) is the definitive work on parapraxes. *Beyond the Pleasure Principle* (1920/1961a), a difficult and challenging monograph, brought forth the concept of the death instinct. Freud's description of his treatment of Dora (1905/1963b), the Rat Man (1909/1963y), and the Wolf Man (1918/1963aa) are also readily available, as are many of his theoretical papers. Of the various alternatives, the standard edition of Freud's works (edited by James Strachey) is the most accurate.

The classic biography of Freud is by Ernest Jones (1953–1957/1963), though there are those who feel that it affords too favorable a picture of its subject. Other valuable sources of biographical information and critical evaluation are Ellenberger (1970), Rieff (1959/1961), Roazen (1975/1976b), and Schur (1972). Interest in Freud remains high, and biographies continue to appear (e.g., Clark, 1980; Gay, 1988; Kauffman, 1980; Sulloway, 1979). Freud also wrote a brief autobiographical sketch (1925/1963a). Useful secondary sources include Brenner (1973/1974) on psychoanalytic theory, Menninger and Holzman (1973) on psychoanalytic therapy, and Fenichel (1945) on both areas.

■ SUMMARY

1. THE BASIC NATURE OF HUMAN BEINGS. *The Instincts:* People are motivated by innate instincts that convert bodily needs into psychological tensions. We seek to gain pleasure by reducing these drives and to avoid unpleasure (the pleasure principle). The two basic types of instincts are sexual, which includes the whole range of pleasurable and self-preserving behavior, and destructive. These two kinds are fused together, though not necessarily in equal amounts, so that any behavior is at least partly erotic and partly aggressive. Our inherent nature is murderous, incestuous, and cannibalistic; so to enjoy the benefits of a civilized society, we must accept some frustration and sublimate our true illicit desires into socially acceptable outlets. *Psychic Energy:* All mental activity is powered by psychic energy. The energy associated with the sexual instincts is called libido, while that related to the destructive instincts has no name. Mental representations of objects are cathected with varying quantities of psychic energy; the greater the amount, the stronger the cathexis and the more the object is desired. *Psychic Determinism:* All mental activity has underlying causes; nothing in the psyche happens by chance. Apparent accidents (parapraxes), dreams, seemingly irrelevant thoughts, and so forth provide evidence about one's unconscious feelings and beliefs, which may well be quite different from their conscious counterparts. *The Unconscious:* The vast majority of mental activity is unconscious, and cannot be called to mind without the aid of such psychoanalytic techniques as free association and dream interpretation.

2. THE STRUCTURE OF PERSONALITY. *The Id:* The id is present at birth, is entirely unconscious, and includes all innate instincts. It operates in accordance with the irrational primary process, and is motivated entirely by the pleasure principle. It has no sense of logic, time, or self-preservation, and its only resource is to form wish-fulfilling mental images of desired objects. *The Ego:* The ego begins to develop out of the id at about age 6–8 months. The ego results from experience with one's own body and with the outside world, and spans the conscious, preconscious, and unconscious. It operates in accordance with the logical and self-preservative secondary process and is motivated by the reality principle, delaying pleasure until a suitable and safe object has been found. The ego is the locus of all emotions, including anxiety, and tries to keep the id under control by using

various defense mechanisms. *The Superego:* The superego begins to develop out of the ego at about age 3–5 years. It is partly conscious and partly unconscious, and includes the ego ideal and the conscience. The superego results from introjected parental standards and from the resolution of the Oedipus complex.

3. THE DEVELOPMENT OF PERSONALITY. *Psychosexual Stages:* Personality is determined primarily during the first five years of life. We proceed through a series of psychosexual stages: oral, anal, urethral, phallic, a latency period (usually), and genital. A different part of the body serves as the primary erotogenic zone during each stage, providing the main source of pleasure (and conflict). The Oedipus complex occurs during the phallic stage and consists of a double set of attitudes toward both parents, with love for the parent of the opposite sex and jealousy toward the parent of the same sex usually stronger than the reverse feelings. The boy eventually abandons his Oedipal strivings because of castration fears, while the girl ultimately seeks resolution by having children. *Fixation and Regression:* Normally, most libido eventually reaches the genital stage. The fixation of excessive amounts of libido at pregenital stages results in various character patterns, and perhaps in psychopathology. Libido may also regress to a previous psychosexual stage or to an earlier object choice long since abandoned, usually one that was strongly fixated.

4. FURTHER APPLICATIONS: *Dream Interpretation:* Dreams serve as "the royal road to the unconscious." But they are expressed in a symbolic language that is difficult to understand, with the dream-work condensing and displacing threatening latent dream-thoughts into more acceptable manifest content. Most dreams involve childhood sexual impulses, though some (especially those of children) are obvious and nonsexual. Virtually all dreams seek to fulfill some wish. *Psychopathology:* Neurosis invariably begins in infancy and childhood, though it may not become evident until much later. Failure to resolve the Oedipus complex results in a damming up of libido, which gains discharge only through a tortuous process that leads to the formation of neurotic symptoms. Like dreams, neurotic symptoms represent a compromise among the id, ego, and superego; and they have important underlying meanings, however strange they may appear on the surface. *Psychotherapy:* Psychoanalytic therapy strives to bring unconscious material to consciousness, where it can be examined and corrected by the ego. These insights strengthen the ego, increase its control over the id and superego, and improve its ability to deal with the difficulties of everyday life. Psychoanalytic therapy is extremely expensive and time-consuming, uses the well-known couch, has the patient free-associate by saying whatever comes to mind, pays special attention to the patient's resistances and transferences, and emphasizes carefully timed interpretations by the analyst. *Other Applications:* Psychoanalysis has been applied to such areas as work, religion (of which Freud was extremely critical), education, literature, and social psychology.

5. EVALUATION. Psychoanalysis has both devoted admirers and strong critics. Among its weaknesses are male chauvinism, internal inconsistencies, meth-

odological problems, severe difficulties with the metaphysical energy model, a resilience to attack that borders on evasiveness, a lack of tolerance for other ideas and modern innovations, and (perhaps) an overemphasis on sexuality, drive reduction, and the biological determinants of personality. It has proved difficult to subject the propositions of psychoanalytic theory to empirical research, and the results have been equivocal. Nevertheless, Freud's contributions are monumental: the importance of the unconscious, dream interpretation, psychoanalytic therapy, resistance and transference, repression and the defense mechanisms, parapraxes, anxiety, the meaning of neurotic symptoms, and more.

STUDY QUESTIONS

Note. A set of study questions appears at the end of each chapter dealing with a theory of personality. It is important to understand that many of these questions do *not* have a single "right" answer. The questions are designed to encourage critical thinking about the material you have read, and to stimulate discussion and debate about important issues.

For those who wish some guidance, some comments and suggestions are provided in an Appendix at the end of this book. However, try to formulate your own ideas before you consult the Appendix.

1. It has been argued that the content of any theory of personality is strongly influenced by the theorist's own personality (e.g., Mindess, 1988). Why might a personality theorist want to believe that aspects of his or her personality are shared by everyone?

2. How might Freud's personality and life experiences have influenced his conclusions regarding: (a) the Oedipus complex? (b) the extent of the unconscious (i.e., that nearly all of personality is unconscious)?

3. (a) To what extent did Freud's own neurosis contribute to his desire to study and understand personality? (b) Would a person who is psychologically healthy have Freud's intense desire to probe deeply within his or her own psyche?

4. (a) Did Freud regard at least some of his ideas and constructs as truths that deserved to remain unchallenged for a long time? (b) What is the difference between a construct and a fact? (See Chapter 1.) (c) Given this difference, is it likely that Freud's constructs would survive unchallenged for a long time?

5. Provide an original example of a parapraxis from your own life, and suggest how Freud might interpret it. How would you interpret it?

6. Provide an example from your own life, or from the life of someone you know well, to show that anxiety can be just as painful as (or even more painful than) a physical injury.

7. (a) Provide examples from your own life of the use of one or more defense mechanisms. (b) What purpose did the defense mechanism(s)

serve? (c) Were there any harmful effects? (d) Since many of these mechanisms are used unconsciously, how can you (or anyone) know that they actually exist?

8. Give an example from your own life of an undesirable id impulse overcoming the ego's restrictions and defenses.

9. Give an example from your own life of the superego being overly demanding and cruel to the ego.

10. A person smokes three packs of cigarettes per day. How might this relate to Freud's concept of fixation?

11. By today's standards, Freud's views of women were clearly biased. To what extent (if any) should criticism of Freud take into account the era in which he lived?

12. A young woman dreams that she rushes to catch a train but gets to the station too late, the train leaves without her, and there are no more trains to her destination for several weeks. On the surface, it appears that the dreamer has been disappointed. How might this dream be interpreted to support Freud's belief that virtually every dream fulfills some wish of the dreamer?

13. Consider the following quotes from Chapter 1: (a) "Psychoanalysis is a method of research, an impartial instrument, like the infinitesimal calculus." Do you agree? Why or why not? (b) "[Mental patients] have turned away from external reality, but for that very reason they know more about internal, psychical reality and can reveal a number of things to us that would otherwise be inaccessible to us." Do you agree that studies of mental patients can provide important information about personality in general? Why or why not?

14. Explain how the concept of resistance can be viewed both as a major contribution to our knowledge and as a way for Freud to protect his theory against attack.

15. Do you agree or disagree with Freud's negative views about religion? If you disagree, how would you counter Freud's arguments?

3

CARL GUSTAV JUNG
Analytical Psychology

Early in 1909 Carl Jung, then a colleague and close friend of Freud's, expressed a keen interest in precognition and parapsychology. To Jung's dismay and irritation, Freud strongly denounced such beliefs as nonsensical. The rejection made Jung feel as though his diaphragm were made of red-hot iron, whereupon a strange loud noise issued from a nearby bookcase.

"There," Jung argued, "that is an example of a so-called catalytic exteriorization phenomenon."

"Bosh," retorted Freud.

"It is not," Jung replied. "And to prove my point I now predict that in a moment there will be another such loud report!"

Surely enough, no sooner had these words been spoken than a second inexplicable detonation went off in the bookcase. "To this day I do not know what gave me this certainty," Jung was to reflect years later, "but I knew beyond all doubt that the report would come again. Freud only stared aghast at me. . . ." (Jung, 1961/1965, pp. 155–156.)[1]

Jung's quest for information about the human psyche led him to sources that many would regard as farfetched—the occult, studies of extrasensory perception, alchemy, the myth of flying saucers. The result is a theory of personality more controversial than Freud's, one easy to dismiss as absurd and unscientific. Yet Jung regarded himself first and foremost as an empirical researcher, possessed a fine mind, read voraciously and acquired an immense store of knowledge, traveled widely in order to study various races and classes, and was an esteemed psychotherapist; and some of his ideas have become part of the everyday language of psychology and life.

BIOGRAPHICAL SKETCH

Carl Gustav Jung was born on July 26, 1875, in Kesswil, a small village in Switzerland. His father was a Protestant country minister who was tormented by a lack of faith, and unable to answer Jung's penetrating questions about religion and life. Jung's skepticism about the Oedipus complex may have been due in part to a mother who was a "kindly, fat old woman"

---

[1]No doubt due in part to Jung's influence, Freud later took a more positive approach to the occult. (See for example Freud, 1933/1965b, pp. 31–56; Roazen, 1975/1976b, pp. 232–241.)

troubled by marital difficulties (Jung, 1961/1965, p. 48), an influence quite different from that of Freud's beautiful, young doting mother. Like Freud, Jung rose from austere middle-class origins to the heights of world fame.

Jung was an introverted and lonely child, deeply preoccupied with his inner psychic world. He would talk and write messages in secret code to a manikin he had carved, or sit on a stone for hours while pondering: "Am I the one who is sitting on the stone, or am I the stone on which *he* is sitting?" Yet he also responded to the golden sunlight and blue sky of a warm summer day, or the vast expanse of a majestic lake, as wonderful and splendid. From an early age he experienced visions of the supernatural, such as a faintly luminous figure with a detached head that appeared to emanate from his mother's bedroom. He soon came to regard himself as "a solitary, because I know things and must hint at things which other people do not know, and usually do not even want to know. . . . Loneliness does not come from having no people about one, but from being unable to communicate the things that seem important to oneself, or from holding certain views which others find inadmissible" (Jung, 1961/1965, pp. 20, 42, 356; see also pp. 18, 21–23, 41).

One day a schoolmate threw Jung to the ground. Dazed, he pretended to remain unconscious in order to make his antagonist feel guilty. Thereafter Jung would faint in order to avoid such onerous chores as schoolwork, until he overheard his father express grave concern about Carl's future if the boy could not earn his own living. Jung was thunderstruck, recognized that life was a serious matter, and successfully overcame the fainting spells. Thus his childhood neurosis was cured by being brought back to reality, a principle he was later to use effectively with his patients.

Jung became attracted to the fledgling field of psychiatry during his medical studies at the University of Basel, where he received his degree in 1900. Some of his professors were amazed and disappointed by his choice, but Jung was convinced that he had found his true calling. He became absorbed with the occult, participated in experiments with mediums, and devoured books on parapsychology. In addition to his visions, various experiences appeared to confirm the existence of the supernatural: A solid table and a steel knife in his parents' home inexplicably shattered into pieces by themselves. He made up a supposedly imaginary story to entertain a group, only to find that he was clairvoyantly revealing true and intimate secrets about a man he did not know. And the morning after being awakened by an extremely sharp headache, he discovered that one of his patients had that night shot himself in the back of the skull (Jung, 1961/1965, pp. 51, 105–106, 109, 137, 206).

Jung first worked at the famed Burghölzli Psychiatric Hospital in Zurich under the direction of Eugen Bleuler, who coined the term *schizophrenia* and was well known for his work on this disorder. After taking a few months leave of absence to study with Pierre Janet in Paris during 1902–1903, Jung returned to the Burghölzli and developed the word association test. He was to remain there until 1909, when he departed to concentrate on his growing private practice. In 1903 he married Emma Rauschenbach, who also became his collaborator and learned to apply his psychotherapeutic methods. The marriage was basically successful, with the Jungs having four daughters and a son. But no one woman could make up for the emotional deprivations of Carl's childhood. During middle age he entered into a lengthy affair with a young, attractive, and well-educated former patient, Toni Wolff. He even drew Toni into his family life, making her a regular guest for Sunday dinner. Emma ultimately decided to accept this triangular situation, and Carl kept both his mistress and his family. (See Stern, 1976/1977.)

Jung had read *The Interpretation of Dreams* upon its publication in 1900, and began what proved to be a lengthy correspondence with Freud in 1906. The two men met a year later, and were so captivated with each other that they talked continuously for thirteen hours. Unfortunately, the union of the two giants was based on a fundamental misconception that was ultimately to destroy the relationship. Freud was seeking disciples who would carry forth the psychoanalytic banner, and saw Jung as his crown prince and successor. Jung, on the other hand, regarded his association with Freud as a collaboration that left both sides free to pursue their own inclinations. Thus it was inevitable that Jung would come to view Freud's insistence on the universality of the Oedipus complex and the sexual nature of libido as evidence of dogmatism, whereas Freud would see Jung's attempts to develop his own theory as a betrayal.

For some years, Jung did follow in Freud's footsteps. Jung defended Freud's ideas, accompanied him to the United States as an invited lecturer at Clark University in 1909, became a psychoanalyst and taught this subject at the University of Zurich, and served as the first president of the International Psychoanalytic Association. But Jung had to be his own man. His analysis of the delusions and hallucinations of psychotic patients at the Burghölzli had persuaded him of the frequent occurrence of universal archetypes. He therefore came to view the human personality quite differently from Freud. When Jung continued to argue for his own version of psychology, the breach with Freud became irreparable—a trying experience that occasioned two fainting spells on Freud's part, and more than a little anguish on Jung's. The formal parting came in 1913, with Jung also resigning from the International Psychoanalytic Association in 1914.

Jung now turned to the solitude of his home, a large and beautiful edifice of his own design in Küsnacht (a suburb of Zurich) where he was to live for the rest of his life. Here he spent the years from 1913 to 1919 in relative isolation, probing the depths of his own unconscious. He conversed with voices from within his psyche, including a female that he interpreted as his anima, a wise old man, and a group of ghosts that he believed to be souls returning from the dead (Jung, 1961/1965, pp. 170–199). He observed representations of many archetypes emerging into his consciousness, and felt that he was going through the process of individuation and discovering his self. He also suffered some symptoms of emotional disturbance, suggesting that this experience was similar to the "creative illness" undergone by Freud (Ellenberger, 1970, p. 672). To avoid succumbing to psychosis, Jung forced himself to retain close ties with his family and patients and scrupulously fulfilled his commitments to the external world. He emerged from this period of introspection in 1919, with a firm belief in the universal validity of the constructs that he developed.

Jung was now widely admired as an unusually skilled psychotherapist, attracting patients from England and the United States. He also continued his study of the occult. His approach was always that of the scientist in search of empirical evidence, however, and he impressed people as a practical man with a firm grip on reality. He was active, vigorous, and jovial, over six feet tall and broad-shouldered, interested in sailing and mountain climbing as well as scholarly pursuits, a good listener and fine conversationalist, and a democratic man at ease with all types of people. Like Freud, however, Jung's personality was complex and multifaceted. Some saw him as wise, sensitive, and caring; while others viewed him as cantankerous, womanizing, sarcastic (even brutal), and highly critical and condescending toward others—especially those who failed to meet his high standards of scholarship. (See Brome, 1978; Stern, 1976/1977, pp. 181–182.)

In 1923, Jung built a primitive, towerlike house in nearby Bollingen, which served as a place for reflection and meditation. He also traveled extensively and observed a variety of peoples and cultures, including the Pueblo Indians of New Mexico and tribes in Tunis, Kenya, Uganda, and India. World War II sharpened his interest in world politics and mass psychoses and also brought charges that he was pro-Nazi and anti-Semitic, which ultimately proved to be unjustified. In 1944, Jung nearly died from a heart attack, had a vision of his soul leaving his body, and at first felt bitter disappointment upon returning to life. He also predicted that his doctor would die in his place, which actually happened shortly thereafter. Jung now became the "wise old man of Küsnacht," with people coming from all over the world to visit him. His many honors include the City of Zurich Award for literature and honorary doctorates from Harvard and Oxford, and his prolific writings fill some twenty volumes. Jung died in his Küsnacht home on June 6, 1961.

THE BASIC NATURE OF HUMAN BEINGS

Jung called his theory **analytical psychology.** Despite the similarity of names (and of some of the constructs), analytical psychology is substantially different from Freudian psychoanalysis.

Instincts and Psychic Energy

Libido and Value. Jung agrees with Freud that humans are motivated by innate physiological urges (**instincts**), which he defines as inborn, uniform, and regularly recurring modes of action and reaction (Jung, 1919/1971c, p. 54; 1921/1976, p. 376). He also concurs that mental activity is powered by psychic energy (**libido**). But Jung, while not unsympathetic to certain aspects of psychoanalytic theory, emphatically rejects the heavy emphasis on sexuality:

> I am no opponent of Freud's; I am merely presented in that light by his own short-sightedness and that of his pupils. No experienced psychiatrist can deny having met with dozens of cases whose psychology answers in all essentials to that of Freud. . . . I do not mean to deny the importance of sexuality in psychic life, though Freud stubbornly maintains that I do deny it. What I seek is to set bounds to the rampant terminology of sex which vitiates all discussion of the human psyche, and to put sexuality itself in its proper place. . . . Eros is certainly always and everywhere present . . . but the psyche is not *just* [that]. . . [Therefore] I do not connect any specifically sexual definition with the word "libido." . . . [This term] is used by me in much wider sense. (Jung, 1928/1969a, p. 30; 1917/1972d, pp. 46, 52n.6; 1929/1975c, pp. 226, 230. See also Jung, 1911–1912; 1961/1965, pp. 168, 209.)

Jungian libido refers to the total psychic energy invested in a mental event or activity, regardless of the instinct(s) involved. The greater the amount of libido (**value**), the more the event is desired. Even a child readily begins to form different values, as by weighing whether the mother or the father is more preferred, what objects in the environment are liked or disliked more than others, and so forth. Jung's construct of "value" is therefore somewhat similar to Freud's concept of "cathexis," except that cathexes are invariably sexual (in one sense or another) while values need not be.

For example, in an extremely competitive society like our own, some people may value power so highly that they direct most of their psychic energy toward professional success and become sexually impotent. Freud would take an extremely dim view of this sort of behavior, since (sexual) libido is denied its most satisfactory outlet. But Jungian libido includes energy from many sources, including the sexual and power instincts, so its expression solely in the quest for power is neither more or less pathological than its expression solely in the form of sexuality. Or in a primitive society where food is scarce but sex is readily available, considerably more psychic energy will be devoted to thoughts of eating than to thoughts of sex. Jung would regard this as a most understandable difference in values, rather than as a sublimation of some inherently sexual instinct. "The shoe that fits one person pinches another; there is no universal recipe for living" (Jung, 1931/1933b, p. 41; see also Jung, cited by Evans, 1976, p. 46). This refusal to force all people into a single theoretical mold is one of the hallmarks of analytical psychology, although it must also be noted that Jung could be just as dogmatic as Freud about the truth of his theoretical constructs. (See Ellenberger, 1970, p. 673; Roazen, 1975/1976b, p. 288.)

According to Jung (1919/1971c, p. 53), instinctual behavior is easily confused with conscious motives. This makes it difficult to identify all of the human instincts, or to ascertain the exact nature of libido. A partial list of instincts includes nutrition (hunger and thirst), sexuality, power, activity (including the love of change, the urge to travel, and play), becoming whole or one's true self (individuation), and creativity (Jung, 1917/1972d; 1937). Jung also differs sharply with Freud by concluding that human beings have an inborn moral nature and innate religious need, and that the idea of God is an absolutely necessary psychological function:

> Man positively needs general ideas and convictions that will give a meaning to his life and enable him to find a place for himself in the universe. He can stand the most incredible hardships when he is convinced that they make sense; he is crushed when, on top of all his misfortunes, he has to admit that he is taking part in a "tale told by an idiot." (Jung, 1964/1968, p. 76. See also Jung, 1957/1958b, p. 36; 1917/1972d, pp. 27, 71; 1929/1975c, p. 227.)

Complexes. Psychic energy attracts constellations of related and emotionally charged ideas, and these **complexes** are the characteristic way in which the psyche expresses itself.[2] (See Jung, 1934a; 1938/1970a, pp. 19ff.) For example, the group of thoughts and feelings that concern "mother" cluster together to form the mother-complex, while the complex relating to "I" or "myself" constitutes the component of personality known as the ego.

The constellating power of a complex, or its capacity to engage psychic material, depends on the amount of libido at its disposal (its value). A weak mother-complex possesses little psychic energy (low value), includes only a small quantity of associated ideas, and has relatively little influence on the individual's behavior. Alternatively, a mother-complex may be so powerful that it dominates the psyche like a large electromagnet, attracting ideas that actually belong elsewhere. Such highly valued complexes can exert considerable control over the personality. For example, a man ruled by his mother-complex may be unable to form satisfying heterosexual relationships because he is far more concerned about her wishes and opinions. He may also talk about his mother at length, make her the subject of various slips of the tongue, and constantly dream of mother-symbols. Similarly, a person in the grip of an intense power-complex will be preoccupied with the idea of attaining a position of authority. Complexes may be wholly or partly conscious, or they may be entirely within either of the two realms of the unconscious (personal and collective, to be discussed below). (See Jung, 1928/1969a, p. 11; Fordham, 1966, pp. 22–23.)

The Word Association Test. Jung cautions that the construct of libido is useful only if quantitative differences in values can be estimated. Otherwise the energic approach could never become scientific, and would have to be abandoned.

---

[2]The term *complex* also appears in the theories of Freud and Adler, since these men were at one time colleagues of Jung, but Jung was its originator.

For a time Jung measured the constellating power of a complex by using the **word association test,** wherein a list of single words is read one at a time and the subject must reply with the first word that comes to mind. (See Jung, 1910; 1928/1969a, p. 9; 1905/1974e). For example, the stimulus word "mother" might well evoke the response of "father." After the list has been completed, the subject goes through it once again and tries to recall the previous responses. If a series of related words in the list should cause such signs of disturbance as significant hesitations, unusual responses (e.g. "mother"— "anger"), becoming pale or having a markedly increased pulse rate, or failing to recall the original responses during the retest, this would indicate the existence of an important (and probably troublesome) complex. On occasion Jung even used the word association test as a sort of verbal lie detector, and successfully identified a thief from among a group of suspects. However, he ultimately realized that the test could easily mistake subjective feelings of imagined guilt for actual wrongdoing. Eventually he abandoned this technique, concluding that

> anyone who wants to know the human psyche will learn next to nothing from experimental psychology. He would be better advised to abandon exact science, put away his scholar's gown, bid farewell to his study, and wander with human heart through the world. There, in the horrors of prisons, lunatic asylums and hospitals, in drab suburban pubs . . . he would reap richer stores of knowledge than textbooks a foot thick could give him, and he will know how to doctor the sick with real knowledge of the human soul. (Jung, 1912/1972f, pp. 246–247. See also Ellenberger, 1970, pp. 691–694; Jung, 1957/1958b, pp. 61–62.)

The Principle of Opposites

To Jung, life consists of "a complex of inexorable opposites": day and night, birth and death, happiness and misery, good and evil, introversion (inner-directedness) and extraversion (outer-directedness), consciousness and unconsciousness, thinking and feeling, love and hate, cynicism and belief, haughtiness and inferiority, and so forth. Such contradictory ideas, emotions, and instincts exist simultaneously within the psyche, producing a tension that creates psychic energy and enables life to exist. "There is no energy unless there is a tension of opposites. . . . Life is born only of the spark of opposites" (Jung, 1917/1972d, pp. 53–54; see also Jung, 1964/1968, p. 75; 1928/1972e, p. 142).

When any one extreme is primarily conscious, the unconscious **compensates** by emphasizing the other extreme. The psyche is for the most part a closed system, so libido withdrawn from one aspect of personality normally reappears somewhere else (the principle of **equivalence**). The psyche is also a self-regulating system wherein libido flows from a more intense to a less intense component, just as heat flows from a warmer to a colder body (the principle of **entropy**). Sooner or later, therefore, any overvalued component will yield psychic energy to its undervalued counterpart. Thus the (unconscious) opposite is likely to emerge in the course of time, a tendency Jung refers to as **enantiodromia.** For example, intense love may well eventually give way to profound hate, or an extremely rationalistic and skeptical scientist may turn to mysticism and the occult. Values are particularly likely to undergo radical changes as one grows from the morning of youth to the afternoon of middle age, with religious and cultural needs gaining ascendance while material and sexual urges become less important (Jung, 1917/1972d, pp. 74–75; see also Jung, 1928/1969a, pp. 18, 25; 1934/1974c, p. 101).

The principle of opposites and the phenomenon of enantiodromia imply that no personality is ever truly one-sided. Even an individual who appears to be entirely cold and lacking in sentiment will have warm and emotional characteristics, though these compensating tendencies may be unconscious and unobservable. "Extremes always arouse suspicion of their opposite" (Jung, 1917/1972d, p. 21). Furthermore, any extreme (introversion, extraversion, emotionality, rationality, or whatever) is harmful because it prevents the simultaneously existing contradictory tendency from gaining satisfactory expression. The opposites must then waste libido in conflict with each other, as when the apparently unfeeling individual uses up psychic energy in a misguided attempt to suppress innate emotional instincts and repeal the principle of entropy.

In a mature and well-adjusted personality, on the other hand, the various opposites are united through some middle path. This concept is common in Eastern philosophies, as with the Taoist symbols of Yin and Yang; but it is a difficult one for our Western culture, which has never even devised a name for it. Jung proposes the term **transcendent function** for the process that unites the various opposing aspects of personality, particularly consciousness and unconsciousness, into a coherent middle ground. The transcendent function also provides us with guidelines for personal development that enable us to become our true selves—guidelines that cannot be found in the external world or opinions of other people. (See Jung, 1916/1971e, pp. 298, 300; 1921/1976, p. 449; 1928/1972e, p. 205.)

Teleology

Whereas Freud stressed the childhood determinants of personality (**causality**), Jung argues that behavior must also be understood in terms of its purpose or goal (**teleology**).

> A man is only half understood when we know how everything in him came into being. . . . Life does not have only a yesterday, nor is it explained by reducing today to yesterday. Life has also a tomorrow, and today is understood only when we can add to our knowledge of what was yesterday the beginnings of tomorrow. (Jung, 1917/1972d, p. 46. See also Jung, 1921/1976, p. 431.)

Personality (including everyday behaviors, dreams, symbols, and even neurotic symptoms) is not shaped only by the past; it is also strongly influenced by our intentions and plans for the future. A complex also develops for some purpose, one that might well be contrary to the goals of other parts of the personality.

In addition to his emphasis on teleology, Jung rejects Freud's contention that psychic events can be reduced to physiological causes. Instincts do have an organic aspect, but mental life follows "a specific law of its own which cannot be deduced from the known physical laws of nature" (Jung, 1947/1969b, p. 91; see also p. 90).

The Unconscious

Jung readily accepts the existence of parapraxes, even contributing some specimens to Freud's collection. (See Freud, 1901/1965c, p. 84; Jung, 1927/1971b, p. 28; 1916/1971e, p. 276; 1917/1972d, p. 115; 1928/1972e, pp. 177, 180.) In marked contrast to Freud, however, Jung views the unconscious as relatively autonomous. According to Jung, the messages and wishes that emanate from the unconscious are events that happen to us. They are formulated by the autonomous unconscious, and *not* by any actions of our own. Some people hear their unconscious as a voice within themselves and actually carry on a conversation with it, "as if a dialogue were taking place between two human beings with equal rights, each of whom gives the other credit for a valid argument." But most of us do not allow this invisible partner of ours to make itself heard, for "we are so in the habit of identifying ourselves with the thoughts that come to us that we invariably assume we have made them" (Jung, 1916/1971e, p. 297; 1928/1972e, p. 201).

Jung does agree with Freud about the importance of bringing unconscious material to consciousness, and about our reluctance to experience the dark side of our personality. So long as unconscious factors influence our behaviors and evoke emotions that we are unable to control, we are not the masters of our own personality. Yet we turn away in fear from investigating our shadow-side, for it consists not just of minor weaknesses but of a "positively demonic dynamism" (Jung, 1917/1972d, p. 30; see also Jung, 1964/1968, p. 72; 1917/1972d, p. 26).

Unlike Freud, however, Jung does not regard the unconscious as a purely demoniacal monster. The unconscious includes wellsprings of creativity and sources of guidance that can suggest solutions when the conscious mind becomes hopelessly bogged down. "[The unconscious] has at its disposal . . . all those things which have been forgotten or overlooked, as well as the wisdom and experience of uncounted centuries" (Jung, 1917/1972d, p. 116; see also Jung, 1931/1933b, pp. 61–62; Jung, 1934/1974c, p. 100). A substantial part of the unconscious is collective, and contains predispositions and guidelines inherited from past generations.

Only a smaller part results from repressions and other personal experiences unique to the individual.

THE STRUCTURE OF PERSONALITY

Jung's model of the psyche is considerably more chaotic than Freud's. For example, complexes originating in the unconscious can gravitate to consciousness and exert control over the personality for purposes of their own. And unconscious components may fuse together, rather than remaining separate and distinct.

Consciousness

Consciousness in psychoanalytic theory is often depicted as the tip of a huge iceberg, with the unconscious represented by the vast subaqueous portion. Similarly, consciousness in analytical psychology resembles a small island rising from the midst of a vast sea (Jung, 1928/1969d, p. 41).

The Ego. The **ego** is a complex of conscious ideas that constitutes the center of one's awareness. It appears to possess a high degree of continuity and identity, and begins to develop at about the fourth year of life. The growth of the ego is aided by bodily sensations that promote a differentiation between "I" and "not-I," and by experiences (such as success) that are readily attributed to one's subjective sense of identity, but it never becomes a truly finished product. (See Jung, 1951; 1928/1972e, p. 196; 1921/1976, p. 425; Jung, cited by Evans, 1976, pp. 60–61.)

Jung conceives of the ego as a relatively weak entity that is often at the mercy of more powerful forces, tossed like a shuttlecock between the demands of reality and those of the unconscious. However, it can consign threatening material to the (personal) unconscious by means of **repression.**

The Persona. We usually cannot afford to confront the world with our true inner feelings. Instead, we must fashion an outward appearance that will satisfy the demands of society. This protective façade is known as the **persona,** after the masks worn by ancient actors to signify the roles that they played.

The persona helps us to deal with other people by indicating what may be expected from them. The doctor's professional role is validated in the patient's eyes by an appropriately reassuring manner, while the college professor is supposed to display a persona of expertise. If instead the doctor or professor violates these expectations by behaving in an anxious and uncertain way, this will undoubtedly provoke substantial suspicion and resistance. In general, people with underdeveloped personas appear to be incompetent, boring, tactless, gauche, eternally misunderstood, and blind to the realities of the world. (See Jung, 1928/1972e, pp. 198–199; Jung, cited by Evans, 1976, p. 79.)

In addition to the demands of society, the persona also reflects one's aspirations and fantasies. This aspect of the persona gives it some apparently personal qualities, but can also cause it to become overdeveloped and intrude upon the ego. For example, a mediocre doctor with false visions of greatness may present a pompous persona of excellence. In such instances the ego misguidedly identifies with the persona, mistakes this formal mask for the true personality, and becomes **inflated** with a sense of excess importance:

> *L'état c'est moi* is the motto for such people. . . . In vain would one look for a personality behind the husk. Underneath all the padding one would find a very pitiable little creature. That is why the office—or whatever this outer husk may be—is so attractive: it offers easy compensation for personal deficiencies. (Jung, 1928/1972e, pp. 143, 145; see also p. 156 n.1.)

As would be expected from the principle of opposites, this conscious arrogance is compensated for by unconscious feelings of inferiority that cannot find satisfactory expression. In addition to wasting libido that could better be used elsewhere, the conflict between these extreme aspects of personality is likely to result in pronounced irritability.

The persona is a complex of conscious material whose content is determined primarily by experience. However, we do inherit from our ancestors an innate tendency to conceive of and develop this component of personality (the persona archetype, discussed later in this chapter).

The Personal Unconscious

The **personal unconscious** begins to form at birth, and contains material derived from personal experience that is no longer (or is not yet) at the level of awareness. Some memories are simply forgotten because they are no longer important, many of which can easily be recalled to consciousness on demand (such as a familiar telephone number, or the contents of last night's dinner). Other material in the personal unconscious is repressed because of its painful nature. For example, a secretary who is jealous of one of her employer's associates may habitually "forget" to invite this individual to meetings and never admit—not even to herself—the true reason for her omission. (See Jung, 1964/1968, p. 22; 1927/1971b, p. 38; 1917/1972d, pp. 64ff, 77; 1928/1972e, pp. 135ff.)

Still other aspects of mental life remain in the personal unconscious because they lack sufficient psychic energy to enter awareness. We often see, hear, taste, and smell things without noticing them because the sensory impressions are not strong enough to impinge upon our consciousness ("subliminal perceptions"). For example, a professor who was walking in the country with a student suddenly noticed that his thoughts were invaded by memories of his early childhood. He could not account for this distraction until he retraced his steps and realized that they had recently passed some geese, whose odor provided a subliminal reminder of a farm where he had lived as a youth. Similarly, a young woman once suddenly developed a blinding headache. Without consciously noticing it, she had heard the foghorn of a distant ship, which reminded her of an unhappy parting with a loved one (Jung, 1964/1968, pp. 21–22).

The Shadow. The **shadow** is the primitive and unwelcome side of personality that derives from our animal forebears. (See Jung, 1951.) It consists of material repressed into the personal unconscious because it is shameful and unpleasant, and plays a compensatory role to the more favorably oriented persona and ego. (There are some exceptional cases, however, where the positive aspects of personality are repressed and the ego is essentially negative.) The shadow's power is evident when one is overcome by a period of violent and uncontrollable rage, a theme exemplified in literature by the dangerous Mr. Hyde underlying the implacable Dr. Jekyll.

As with any construct in analytical psychology, the shadow must be at least somewhat beneficial in order to have survived generations of evolution. Like the Freudian id, it provides a necessary ingredient of vitality and creativity. "Too much of the animal distorts the civilized man, [but] too much civilization makes sick animals" (Jung, 1917/1972d, p. 28). Just as it is impossible to have sunshine without shadow, the light of consciousness must always be accompanied by the dark side of our personality. Rather than turn away in disgust from our shadow, we must open this Pandora's box and accept its contents. Jung does not regard repression as an actively maintained process, so a person who honestly wishes to examine the shadow can do so, but this is a highly threatening task that most prefer to avoid.

The shadow, like all that is unconscious, is **projected** onto other people. We normally experience it in this indirect fashion, with the characteristics that we find most objectionable in others very likely to be just those aspects of ourselves that we most dislike. Thus another unfortunate effect of denying our shadow is that the resulting deeper repressions will trigger more powerful projections of our undesirable characteristics, producing greater dislike of other people—and, quite possibly, culminating in the sick system of social relationships that constitutes neurosis. (See Jung, 1931/1933c, p. 142; 1935b, p. 24; 1951; 1957/1958b, pp. 109–114; 1964/1968, p. 73; 1917/1972d, p. 26.)

The shadow reflects not only individual weaknesses, but also aspects common to all people. It therefore has representation in the collective unconscious as well.

The Collective Unconscious

Although the personal unconscious and the ego originate only after birth, the newborn infant is far from a *tabula rasa.* Its psyche is a tremendously

Some Important Jungian Terminology (I)

Analytical psychology	The name given by Jung to his theory of personality.
Anima	The female archetype in man. Predisposes man to understand the nature of woman, serves as the compensatory sentimental inner face of the rational male persona, and is experienced as a feminine voice within the psyche.
Animus	The male archetype in woman. Predisposes woman to understand the nature of man, serves as the compensatory rational inner face of the sentimental female persona, and is experienced as a masculine voice within the psyche.
Archetype (imago, primordial image)	A universal thought form, inherited from past generations, that predisposes one to apprehend the world in particular ways; *not* a specific idea or belief. Results from the deposits of the oft-repeated experiences of humanity, and is in the collective unconscious. Archetypes include the anima, animus, shadow, persona, mother, father, and many others.
Compensation	The tendency of one component of personality to balance or adjust for another component. For example, the unconscious will compensate for pronounced conscious introversion by emphasizing the quality of extraversion.
Complex	A constellation of related and emotionally charged thoughts, feelings, or ideas. A complex varies in strength according to the amount of psychic energy at its disposal (its value), and may be conscious or unconscious (or both).
Enantiodromia	The tendency of any characteristic to turn into its opposite in the course of time.
Inflation	Expansion of the ego beyond its proper limits, resulting in feelings of exaggerated self-importance. Usually compensated for by unconscious feelings of inferiority.
Instinct	An inborn physiological urge that produces uniform and regularly recurring modes of action and reaction. The instincts include hunger, thirst, sexuality, power, individuation, activity, creativity, morality, and religious needs.
Libido	A synonym for psychic energy; *not* necessarily sexual.
Numinosum	A profound experience with spiritual, mystical, and religious connotations.
Principle of entropy	The tendency for psychic energy to flow from a more highly valued to a less highly valued component of personality, just as heat flows from a warmer to a colder body.
Principle of equivalence	The tendency for psychic energy withdrawn from one component of personality to reappear elsewhere within the psyche. Thus the psyche is for the most part a closed system.

continued

93

Projection	Unconsciously attributing one's own feelings, beliefs, or impulses to other people or things; the expulsion of subjective content onto an object. Similar to Freud's use of the term.
Psychic energy	The "fuel" that powers mental activity; an unobservable, abstract construct.
Repression	Unconsciously eliminating threatening material from consciousness and relegating it to the personal unconscious. *Not* actively maintained (as in Freudian theory), so repressed material may be recovered fairly easily.
Symbol	A representation of something vague and unknown, such as an archetype; differs from "signs," which denote known concepts, such as a badge of office.
Transcendent function	A process that joins various opposing forces into a coherent middle ground, and furthers the course of individuation by providing personal lines of development that could not be reached by adhering to collective norms.
Value	The amount of psychic energy invested in a mental event or activity. The greater the value, the more the event is preferred or desired.
Word association test	A procedure for determining the strength of a complex. The tester reads a list of single words, one at a time, and the respondent answers with the first single word that comes to mind. The stronger the complex, the more likely are unusual responses, hesitations, and physiological changes.

complicated, sharply defined entity consisting of the **collective** (or **transpersonal**) **unconscious,** a storehouse of archaic remnants ("primordial images" or **archetypes**) inherited from our ancestral past. (See Jung, 1938/1970a, p. 11; 1919/1971c, p. 52; 1917/1972d, pp. 65–66; 1921/1976, p. 376.)

Characteristics of Archetypes. Archetypes are universal thought forms and emotions that result from the "deposits of the constantly repeated experiences of humanity" (Jung, 1917/1972d, p. 69). They differ from instincts in that they are modes of perception, rather than of action and reaction. That is, archetypes predispose an individual to apprehend the world in particular ways.

Archetypes resemble poorly formed channels in the psyche that may predispose libido to follow a certain course, but are too roughly hewn to ensure that it will actually do so. They are only potentialities, *not* specific memories or facts, and will remain dormant unless strengthened by appropriate experiences. "I do not by any means assert the inheritance of ideas, but only of the possibility of such ideas, which is something very different" (Jung, 1917/1972d, p. 65; see also Jung, 1938/1970a, pp. 13–17). Thus everyone inherits a tendency to fear objects that our ancestors found to be potentially dangerous (such as darkness), but an individual who grows up enjoying only pleasant encounters with the dark will develop mental images and behaviors that are quite different from the inherent archetype. Similarly, the child's perception of its mother is influenced partly by her true characteristics and partly by the unconscious projection of such archetypal maternal qualities as solicitude, nurturance, and fertility.

The Persona and Shadow Archetypes. The aforementioned persona and shadow have existed in the human psyche throughout countless generations. This is reflected by corresponding archetypes in the collective unconscious, so that we all inherit tendencies to form these components of personality.

The Anima and Animus. Analytical psychology agrees that humans are inherently bisexual, but differs from other theories by attributing this phenomenon to archetypes. Man's unconscious feminine disposition is due to the archetype known as the **anima,** while the male archetype in women is called the **animus.** The anima and animus develop from generations of exposure to the opposite sex, and imbue each sex with an innate understanding of the other. "The whole nature of man presupposes woman, both physically and spiritually. His system is tuned in to woman from the start" (Jung, 1928/1972e, p. 190; see also Jung, 1925/1971d; 1951).

Typically, the inner femininity of the anima compensates for the outward masculine persona of power and effectiveness. Trying to deny this aspect of personality will result in a one-sided and conflicted individual, as when a man who prides himself on an overly virile persona is beset by inner feelings of weakness and moodiness. The masculine animus, on the other hand, produces unshakable and arbitrary convictions. The woman who suppresses her animus in a misguided attempt to appear extremely feminine will be troubled by spells of stubbornness and blind conviction, with these characteristics likely to be projected onto males who seem godlike or heroic (Jung, 1928/1972e, p. 206). The well-adjusted personality integrates the male and female attributes by means of the transcendent function, allowing both to find satisfactory expression.

Other Archetypes. Other archetypes include the wise old man, the mother, the father, the child, the parents, the wife, the husband, God, the hero, various animals, energy, the self (the ultimate goal of personality development), the trickster, rebirth or reincarnation, the spirit, the prophet, the disciple, and an indefinite number of archetypes representative of situations. (See Jung, 1934b; 1940; 1938/1970a; 1940/1970b; 1945/1970c; 1954/1970d; 1917/1972d, pp. 68, 95, 110; 1928/1972e, pp. 171, 178, 190.) However, Jung advises against trying to comprehend the nature of archetypes simply by memorizing such a list. Archetypes are autonomous events that come upon us like fate, and must be experienced first-hand in order to be understood.

Unfortunately, Jung has no simple remedy for those who remain skeptical about analytical psychology because they have never enjoyed such enriching encounters with the collective unconscious. "You can only say that you have never had such an experience, and your opponent will say: 'Sorry, I have.' And there your discussion will come to an end" (Jung, 1938, p. 113). He does recommend learning more about one's personal unconscious, thereby diminishing the layer above the collective unconscious and making archetypal images more accessible to consciousness.

Archetypal Symbols. We never become aware of archetypes themselves, which always remain within the inaccessible collective unconscious. But the collective unconscious is like the base of a volcano that extends to the core of personality and occasionally erupts, shooting archetypal images, motifs, or **symbols** up to the surface.

Unlike such common signs as words and pictures, which merely denote the objects to which they are attached, archetypal symbols imply something vague or hidden from us. Since they are produced entirely by the unconscious psyche, not by personal experience or intellectual thought, they have a powerful numinous or fascinating effect that clearly identifies them as something out of the ordinary. (See Jaffé, 1971/1975, p. 16; Jung, 1964/1968, pp. 3, 41; 1917–1972d, p. 70; Progoff, 1953/1973, p. 56.)

Symbols derived from the same archetype may differ in form and content, especially to the extent that they are influenced by racial, cultural, and even family differences. "There is also a collective psyche limited to race, tribe, and family over and above the 'universal' collective psyche" (Jung, 1928/1972e, pp. 147–148).[3] But such symbols all point back to one basic form, the underlying universal archetype. For this reason, the unconscious processes of widely separated races show a remarkable correspondence. Thus the archetype of the universal creative mother is expressed in such varied cultural myths as Mother Nature, Greek and Roman goddesses, and the "Grandmother" of the American Indians. Similarly, the shadow archetype is often symbolized by some form of devil. Jung was once advised by a psychotic patient that the sun possesses a phallus, whose movement creates the wind; and when he later encountered the same unusual symbology in an ancient Greek papyrus, which the patient could never have seen, he attributed the similar imagery to an unconscious universal archetype. He also cites the production of archetypal symbols by children as further support for his theory, since it often seems clear that they could not have had access to the relevant facts and must therefore have produced the images from their own psyche. (See Jung, 1964/1968, p. 61; 1938/1970a; 1927/1917b, pp. 36–37; 1917/1972d, p. 96; Progoff, 1953/1973, pp. 59–60.)

---

[3]And therefore "it is a quite unpardonable mistake to accept the conclusions of a Jewish psychology [i.e., Freud's] as generally valid" (Jung, 1928/1972e, p. 152 n.8).

	PERSONAL	COLLECTIVE
CONSCIOUS	*The ego:* a complex of conscious ideas that constitutes the center of one's awareness, and provides feelings of identity and continuity. Begins to form at about the fourth year of life, resulting from bodily sensations and experiences that are attributed to one's subjective sense of identity. The only part of the self of which one is consciously aware. Also referred to as the *ego-complex.*	*The persona:* the outward face of personality; a protective façade designed to meet the demands of society while concealing one's true inner nature. Facilitates contacts with people by indicating what may be expected from them.
UNCONSCIOUS	*The personal unconscious:* includes material not within one's awareness because it has been forgotten, repressed, or perceived subliminally. The layer between the collective unconscious and consciousness; begins to form at birth. Includes the primitive, guilt-laden, unwelcome aspects of personality (the *shadow*), plus any positive characteristics that may be incompatible with the persona (and therefore with consciousness).	*The collective (transpersonal) unconscious:* a storehouse of latent predispositions to apprehend the world in particular ways (*archetypes*), inherited from our ancestral past; thus, present at birth. The deepest, most inaccessible layer of the psyche. Includes the persona and shadow arechetypes (among others), which facilitate the development of the corresponding representations elsewhere in the personality.

The collective unconscious is widely regarded as an extremely controversial theory. Yet even Freud, a staunch opponent of analytical psychology, accepted the idea of an *"archaic heritage* which a child brings with him into the world, before any experiences of his own, influenced by the experiences of his ancestors." He criticized Jung's construct not so much as incorrect, but as unnecessary because the unconscious is collective anyway (Freud, 1940/1969a, p. 24; see also Freud, 1916–1917/1966, p. 371; 1939; Rieff, 1959/1961, p. 220).

THE DEVELOPMENT OF PERSONALITY

Individuation and the Self

Jung rejects the psychoanalytic concept of infantile sexuality, arguing instead that this drive begins after the so-called latency period. He also declines to posit any formal stages of development, but does draw a sharp distinction between youth and middle age.

During childhood the ego, personal unconscious, and other components of personality gradually develop into separate entities. This process of differentiation continues through puberty and beyond. Our early years are therefore like the rising sun, which "gains continually in strength until it reaches the zenith-heat of high noon. Then comes the enantiodromia: the steady forward movement no longer denotes an increase, but a decrease, in strength" (Jung, 1917/1972d, p. 74; see also Jung, 1930–1931/1971a, pp. 14–15; 1913/1975a, pp. 35, 83). This "second puberty" occurs at about age thirty-five to forty and serves as the gateway to the latter half of life, which is a time of considerable importance:

> A human being would certainly not grow to be seventy or eighty years old if this longevity had no meaning for the species. The afternoon of human life must also have a significance of its own, and cannot be merely a pitiful appendage to life's morning. (Jung, 1930–1931/1971a, p. 17.)

Middle age is highlighted by a shift from materialism, sexuality, and propagation to more spiritual and cultural values; by radical reversals in one's strongest convictions and emotions, often leading to changes of profession, divorces, and religious upheavals; and by the reconciliation of the various opposing forces of personality through the transcendent function. This gradual, lifelong unfolding of one's inherent and unique personality is known as **individuation.**

Individuation is a difficult and complicated journey of self-discovery, and many hazards along the way are likely to prevent a successful outcome. First of all, the formidable and often terrifying contents of the shadow must be brought to consciousness and experienced both intellectually and emotionally. The persona must also be torn down, for this collectively-oriented façade impedes true individuality. The libido freed by the destruction of these superstructures gravitates downward to the collective unconscious, and this additional energy enables archetypal symbols to rise to consciousness. In particular, the collapse of the persona allows the anima (animus) to gain eminence and express itself as a feminine (masculine) voice within the psyche. If one is able to comprehend and learn from this elusive and unfamiliar aspect of personality, the archetypal images that next emerge from the depths of the collective unconscious are those of the wise old man and great mother. This creates yet another pitfall: these alluring archetypes may prove to be overwhelming, causing the individual to succumb to megalomanic beliefs of omniscience and omnipotence. Jung refers to such an intense state of inflation as the **mana-personality,** after a Melanesian word for extraordinary or supernatural power (1928/1972e, pp. 227–241).

If the individuation process successfully avoids the various dangers, the increased knowledge of the collective unconscious liberates substantial amounts of libido that had been associated with the aforementioned archetypes. This libido comes to rest in a twilight zone between consciousness and unconsciousness and forms an entity known as the **self,** which represents the ultimate goal of personality development and serves as the new center of personality. Thus individuation is the process by which the self becomes differentiated from the other components of personality:

> The . . . purpose of [individuation] is the realization, in all its aspects, of the personality originally hidden away in the embryonic germplasm; the production and unfolding of the original, potential wholeness. . . . Individuation means becoming an "in-dividual," and, insofar as "individuality" embraces our innermost, last, and incomparable uniqueness, it also implies becoming one's own self. We could therefore translate individuation as "coming to selfhood" or "self-realization." (Jung, 1917/1972d, p. 110; 1928/1972e, p. 173. See also Jung, 1929; Fordham, 1966, pp. 49–62, 77; Progoff, 1953/1973, pp. 124–132.)

The emergence of the self is signaled by archetypal symbols that express wholeness, completeness, and perfection. Such a symbol often takes the form of a circle (**mandala,** after the Sanskrit word for "magic circle"), and may appear in dreams or in one's conscious drawings and paintings. (See Fordham, 1966, pp. 65–68; Jung, 1955/1972a; 1934/1972b; 1950/1972c.)

Although the self lies between consciousness and unconsciousness, it is beyond the realm of awareness. The only aspect of selfhood that we know is the ego, the conscious conception of our individuality. Furthermore, while every personality possesses the innate tendency to individuate and develop selfhood and stability, this ideal is rarely if ever achieved to the fullest. For some people, it remains totally out of reach; and so they resort to imitating peers or eminent personages, a specious and sterile way of seeking individuation. "To find out what is truly individual in ourselves, profound reflection is needed; and suddenly we realize how uncommonly difficult the discovery of individuality is" (Jung, 1928/1972e, p. 155).

Progression and Regression

Libido normally proceeds in a forward direction, furthering the development of personality and facilitating one's adjustment to reality. But if this **progression** is blocked by frustrations in the external world, or by the internal barrier of repression, libido turns back to early memories and archetypal images that reside within the depths of the psyche (**regression**).

In contrast to Freud, who conceptualized regression as a stubborn return to childhood fixations, Jung regards the backward flow of libido as a potentially creative process that can awaken neglected aspects of one's personality. "The patient's regressive tendency . . . is not just a relapse into infantilism, but a genuine attempt to get at something necessary. . . . His development was one-sided; it left important items of character and personality behind, and thus it ended in failure. That is why he has to go back" (Jung, 1930, pp. 32–33; see also Jung, 1935a, pp. 8–9). However, regression does involve one significant danger: the unconscious may use the additional psychic energy to overwhelm consciousness, producing neurotic or even psychotic behavior.

Character Typology: Functions and Attitudes

Having rejected the concept of fixation, Jung attributes individual differences in personality to two other processes: the typical way in which a person apprehends internal and external stimuli, and the characteristic direction (inward or outward) of libido movement. (See Jung, 1937; 1921/1976.)

The first dimension, which involves the apprehension of stimuli, consists of four **functions:** merely establishing the fact of what is there (**sensation**), interpreting and understanding the meaning of what is perceived (**thinking**), evaluating the desirability or pleasantness of what is perceived (**feeling**), and forming apparently inexplicable hunches or conclusions without using any of the other functions (**intuition**). "*Sensation* tells you that something exists; *thinking* tells you what it is; *feeling* tells you whether it is agreeable or not; and *intuition* tells you whence it comes and where it is going" (Jung, 1964/1968, p. 49). Thinking and feeling are opposites, and are called "rational" functions because they involve purposive acts of cognition. Sensation and intuition also oppose each other, and these more reflexive functions are referred to as "irrational" (meaning nonrational, *not* pathological). Everyone possesses the capacity to use all four functions, but one becomes more highly differentiated than the others. This "dominant" or "superior" function serves not only as a mode of experience, but also as a major basis for organizing one's personality.

The second dimension, which concerns the direction of libido movement, consists of two **attitudes.** The outward turning of libido toward the external world is known as **extraversion,** while the inward flow of libido toward the depths of the psyche is referred to as **introversion.** Extraversion is denoted by habitual outgoingness, venturing forth with careless confidence into the unknown, adapting easily to a given situation, and being particularly influenced by objects and events in the external world. Introversion, on the other hand, is reflected by a keen interest in one's own psyche, shyness, and inscrutability. (See Jung, 1917/1972d, p. 44; 1921/1976, p. 330.) As with the functions, there is an innate tendency for one attitude to predominate over the other; and the dominant attitude combines with the superior function to form the conscious personality. This schema yields a total of eight possible character types, which are shown in the accompanying Capsule Summary.

Jung's typology is often misunderstood and oversimplified. There are no pure introverts or extraverts, nor can human nature be classified into a mere eight categories. The type theory is a framework for understanding the psyche and the movement of its libido, and people actually reflect the given characteristics to varying degrees. In addition, the unconscious compensates for the superior function and attitude by stressing the opposite tendencies. The remaining two functions waver between consciousness and unconsciousness, and serve as potential auxiliaries to the dominant function. "No function [or attitude] can be entirely eliminated—it can only be greatly distorted" (Jung, 1921/1976, p. 349).

For example, a person with a dominant thinking function will place a particularly high value on rational rules and intellectual conclusions. If introversion becomes the superior attitude, the thoughts will focus on ideas within his or her psyche (as with a philosopher like Kant, or an absentminded professor). If extraversion predominates, thinking will be directed to facts in the external world (as with a scientist like Darwin or Einstein). In either case, the opposite function (feeling) and the opposite attitude become "inferior" and are repressed into the personal unconscious. The remaining two functions (here, sensation and intuition) may serve as conscious or unconscious auxiliaries, as when the scientist's attempts to think out new research hypotheses are aided by intuitive hunches. Thus the typological model for the extraverted—thinking type actually looks like this:

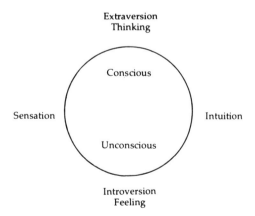

Similar reasoning applies to the remaining categories. (See also Progoff, 1953/1973, p. 90). For example, an introverted-sensation type is unconsciously extraverted and intuitive, and may use thinking or feeling as conscious or unconscious auxiliaries:

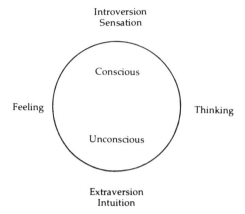

The function and attitude favored by one's innate constitution must become dominant in order for personality development to be successful. Since America strongly favors extraversion, parents and teachers in our society are likely to treat an introverted child with excessive concern and criticism. But extraversion and introversion are equally normal and healthy, and misguided attempts to alter a person's inherent nature will lead to later neurosis. (See Jung, 1921/1976, pp. 332, 375; Jung, cited by Evans, 1976, p. 94.)

Even if the pitfall of denying one's true nature is avoided, maladjustment may occur because the inferior tendencies are repressed too strongly. The natural extravert may blindly ignore internal warnings and follow a self-destructive course, as when a "workaholic" develops an ulcer or suffers a heart attack. The natural introvert may make inept attempts to relate to people, as by rattling on at length about topics that bore others to distraction. The inherent sensation or intuition type may try to tackle a problem that requires thinking, and commit egregious errors. Such behaviors are ineffective and self-defeating because they are governed by inferior processes that have not been sufficiently developed.

The remedy for an overly one-sided personality is a regression to the unconscious, possibly with the aid of Jungian psychotherapy. Ideally, this will enable any undervalued function or attitude to emerge in its own right. Some people do develop a second or even a third function, or strike a balance between introversion and extraversion. But individuation is a difficult process, the goal of a fully differentiated self is never completely achieved, and very few are able to integrate all of the attitudes and functions into a coherent whole and allow each one its due expression.

Psychological Types (Jung)

FUNCTIONS	ATTITUDES	
	EXTRAVERSION	INTROVERSION
THINKING	Emphasizes interpreting and understanding facts about the external world; rational rules, intellectual conclusions, "oughts," "musts." May be a discoverer or problem-solver (Darwin, Einstein), social reformer, public prosecutor; dogmatic or fanatic. More common among men. Unconscious is strongly introverted, feeling.	Emphasizes interpreting and understanding subjective ideas. May be a philosopher (Kant), existential psychologist, absent-minded professor; impractical, stubborn, overly sensitive to criticism. If male, may fear women. Unconscious is strongly extraverted, feeling.
FEELING	Emphasizes judgments that conform to external values. Conservative; genuinely accepts popular standards of all kinds. Sociable, but may seem flighty, capricious, ostentatious. More common among women. Unconscious is strongly introverted, thinking.	Emphasizes judgments related to internal, subjective conditions. Nonconformist; views often contrary to popular opinion. Outwardly cold, reserved, inscrutable; often has powerful hidden emotions. More common among women. Unconscious is strongly extraverted, thinking.
SENSATION	Emphasizes perceiving the external world as it actually is. Realistic, unimaginative, sensual, pleasure-seeking. More common among men. Unconscious is strongly introverted, intuitive.	Emphasizes the subjective result of what is perceived. Regards the external world as banal, trite. May be modern artist, musician. Unconscious is strongly extraverted, intuitive.
INTUITION	Emphasizes seeking new possibilities in the external world. May be speculator, entrepreneur, social climber, unable to persist in one job or activity; lacks good judgment. More common among women. Unconscious is strongly introverted, sensing.	Emphasizes seeking new possibilities in the subjective psyche. May develop brilliant new insights, or be a mystical dreamer, prophet, crank, or "misunderstood genius." Impractical. Unconscious is strongly extraverted, sensing.

FURTHER APPLICATIONS
OF ANALYTICAL PSYCHOLOGY

Dream Interpretation

In analytical psychology, as in psychoanalysis, dreams provide important clues about the hidden realm of the unconscious. However, Jung's approach to dream interpretation differs significantly from that of Freud.

Personal and Collective Dreams. Dreams about one's family, friends, and everyday life arise from the personal unconscious. In contrast, the collective unconscious triggers archetypal dreams of a numinous and fascinating nature. Jung relates that this distinction is prominent among the Elgonyi natives of central Africa: a "little" (i.e., personal) dream is regarded as unimportant, but anyone who has a "big" (i.e., collective) dream summons the whole tribe and tells it to everybody (Jung, 1928/1972e, p. 178; see also Fordham, 1966, pp. 97ff).

The Purpose of Dreams. To Jung, a dream can serve many purposes other than wish-fulfillment. It may express a person's fears, mirror actual situations in the dreamer's life, anticipate the future (as by providing a warning of impending trouble), propose solutions to the dreamer's problems, or even result from telepathy. (See Ellenberger, 1970, p. 716; Jung, 1964/1968, p. 34; 1916/1974a.)

The majority of dreams are compensatory, and aim at restoring a state of psychological balance. For example, Jung once dreamed of bending his head far back in order to see a patient in a high tower. He concluded that he must be looking down on her in reality, and this insight enabled a previously unsuccessful treatment to progress at a rapid pace. Similarly, a man with an inflated ego may dream of himself as a drunken tramp rolling in a ditch, or a person suffering from feelings of inferiority may dream of encountering such famous personages as Napoleon or Alexander the Great (Jung, 1961/1965, p. 133; 1964/1968, pp. 51–52; 1917/1972d, p. 112; 1928/1972e, p. 179; 1934/1974c, pp. 102–103). Although it is possible to detect wish-fulfillments in some of these dreams, the primary goal is to compensate for a one-sided aspect of personality by emphasizing the opposite view.

Dream Symbols. Whereas Freud believed that dream symbols disguise unpleasant truths in order to preserve sleep, Jung regards the manifest content as the true dream. The language of dreams is confusing only because it reflects the natural illogic of the unconscious:

> To me dreams are a part of nature, which harbors no intention to deceive, but expresses something as best it can. . . . What [Freud] called "disguise" is actually the shape all impulses naturally take in the unconscious. (Jung,

1961/1965, p. 161; 1964/1968, p. 53. See also Jung, 1930, p. 32; 1917/1972d, p. 100.)

Jung agrees that some dream symbols have sexual connotations, but emphasizes that there are many other possibilities. Inserting a key in a lock might symbolize sexual intercourse, or it could describe the hopeful opening of new possibilities in one's life. A passive female patient's dream of her energetic father's sword could be caused by childhood sexual fantasies and unconscious wishes for his "weapon" (phallus), or it might signify the need for some new source of strength that would enable her future dealings with the world to be more aggressive and effective.

According to Jung, every dream symbol has at least two meanings. Also, the identical symbol can mean different things to different people. Two of Jung's patients once dreamed of leading a group of horsemen across a wide field and barely managing to jump a ditch, into which the other riders fell. To the first patient, a cautious introvert, the dream indicated that he ought to take more chances. The second patient was a pronounced extravert, however, and his dream warned that he was far too daring. Similarly, a mother-symbol may mean love and nurturance to one dreamer but signify overprotection, frustration, and anger to another. Thus accurate interpretation requires the active cooperation of the dreamer, and "it is plain foolishness to believe in ready-made systematic guides to dream interpretation, as if one could simply buy a reference book and look up a particular symbol" (Jung, 1964/1968, p. 38). Instead Jung favors Freud's technique of free association, though he prefers to restrict the dreamer's train of thought to the context of the dream. (See Fordham, 1966, pp. 97–98; Jung, 1964/1968, pp. 12–15, 18, 42, 56; 1916/1971e, pp. 281–282; 1917/1972d, p. 25; 1945/1974b, pp. 69, 71–72; 1913/1975b, pp. 155–156).

Dream Series. When possible, Jung bases his interpretations on a series of dreams from the same individual. Important themes and issues tend to recur in various dreams, so this approach facilitates accurate interpretations by providing more substantial data.

Jung's writings on dreams are often difficult and controversial, teeming with allusions to obscure ancient references and to such abstruse fields as alchemy. (See for example Jung, 1936/1974d.) Yet certain of his ideas, such as the use of dream series and the nondeceptive nature of dream symbols, have been adopted by some modern theorists in preference to Freudian theory (e.g., C. S. Hall, 1966).

Psychopathology

Jung shares Freud's view of psychopathology as a difference in degree, rather than in kind. The ideal of normality is rarely reached, and virtually every personality is at least somewhat one-sided.

Neurotic phenomena are by no means the products exclusively of disease. They are in fact no more than pathological exaggerations of normal occurrences; it is only because they are exaggerations that they are more obvious than their normal counterparts. . . . At bottom we discover nothing new and unknown in the mentally ill; rather, we encounter the substratum of our own natures. (Jung, 1961/1965, p. 127; 1964/1968, p. 20. See also Jung, 1917/1972d, p. 55; 1928/1972e, pp. 143–144.)

Causes of Neurosis. As we have seen, the collective unconscious predisposes one's personality in various ways: to introversion or extraversion, to one of the four functions, and so forth. The goal of individuation is to develop these innate predispositions. The favored function and attitude must become dominant, and they must be brought into harmony with the inferior opposites.

If this goal is frustrated by the external world, or if the person misguidedly tries to make some other function or attitude dominant, the unconscious will come into conflict with consciousness. This inner cleavage may eventually become so severe as to constitute a neurosis, with the attempt to deny one's true nature causing the normal intrapsychic polarities to erupt into open warfare. Neurotic conflicts may occur between various components of personality, such as the ego versus the shadow, the dominant versus the inferior function or attitude, the persona versus the anima or animus, or the persona versus the shadow. (See Jung, 1932/1933d, p. 236; 1935a, p. 20; 1917/1972d, p. 19.)

To illustrate, suppose that an inherently introverted child is pressured into becoming a pronounced extravert by the parents (or by society). This unwelcome external influence disrupts the individuation process, and causes the child's psyche to resemble a house divided against itself. The conscious mind now seeks conformity with the parental dictates by emphasizing extraverted behavior, and by banishing introverted wishes from awareness. But the introverted tendencies, which must remain within the closed system of the psyche, flourish within the unconscious and strongly oppose the conscious processes. Alternatively, a neurosis might result from the child's own decision to reject the introverted promptings of the unconscious in favor of extraversion. Or it could be caused by overemphasizing the inherent introversion and trying to exclude all traces of extraversion, for not even the inferior aspects of personality can or should be totally eliminated.

In contrast to psychoanalysis, analytical psychology prefers to concentrate on the neurotic's present attempts to maintain a pathological state of one-sidedness. To Jung, dwelling upon childhood memories is an evasion that may well do more harm than good:

> *The cause of the pathogenic conflict lies mainly in the present moment.* . . . We ask: . . . What is the task which the patient does not want to fulfill? What difficulty is he trying to avoid? . . . The task of psychotherapy is to correct the conscious attitude and not go chasing after infantile memories. Naturally you

■ CAPSULE SUMMARY
Some Important Jungian Terminology (II)

Attitude	Introversion or extraversion.
Differentiation	The development of the separate parts of personality from the original, undifferentiated whole.
Extraversion	An outward flow of libido toward the external world. Characterized by habitual outgoingness, venturing forth with confidence into the unknown, adapting easily to different situations, being particularly influenced by objects and events in the environment, and conformity.
Function	A way of experiencing internal or external stimuli. *Sensation* establishes the fact that something is there, *thinking* interprets what is perceived, *feeling* establishes the desirability of what is perceived, and *intuition* forms hunches or conclusions without the aid of the other functions. Thinking and feeling are "rational" functions, while sensation and intuition are "irrational" functions.
Individuation	The unfolding of one's inherent and unique personality, aided by the transcendent function and leading to the differentiation of the self. A lifelong task that is rarely if ever completed.
Introversion	An inward flow of libido toward the depths of the psyche. Characterized by shyness, inscrutability, a particular interest in one's own subjective world, and idiosyncratic behavior.
Mana-personality	An intense state of inflation or megalomania, resulting from the emergence of such alluring archetypes as the wise old man and great mother.
Mandala	A circular symbol of wholeness and perfection, and therefore of the self.
Progression	A forward movement of libido, favoring personal growth and development.
Regression	A backward movement of libido to earlier memories or periods of development. Contrary to Freudian theory, Jungian regression may be a creative process that liberates neglected aspects of personality.
Self	The new center of personality that results from individuation, unifies the various opposites, and lies between consciousness and unconsciousness. There is also a self archetype within the collective unconscious.
Synchronicity	A relationship between events that is based on meaningful coincidence, rather than cause and effect.

cannot do the one without paying attention to the other, but the main emphasis should be upon the attitude of the patient. There are extremely practical
reasons for this, because there is scarcely a neurotic who does not love to dwell
upon the evils of the past and to wallow in self-commiserating memories. Very
often his neurosis consists precisely in his hanging back and constantly excus-
ing himself on account of the past. (Jung, 1930, pp. 31–32; 1913/1975a, pp.
84, 100.)

Neurotic Symptoms. The libido involved in neurotic conflicts cannot move
in a forward direction, since the normal course of progression is disrupted
by the inner war. Instead, the dammed-up libido regresses toward the unconscious. This regression is not necessarily harmful (as we have seen), since
it may help to awaken the neglected and undervalued aspects of personality.
But it is all too easy to maintain the one-sided behaviors that caused the
neurotic conflict, and to ignore the warnings sent by the collective unconscious in the form of dream symbols. (For example, a person who overuses
the thinking function may keep trying to reason out solutions to his or her
problems, instead of allowing the undervalued feeling function to emerge.)
The regressing libido, deprived of a satisfactory outlet, will then constellate
powerful unconscious complexes that express themselves in the form of
neurotic symptoms. Thus a man may be attracted only to mutilated or
undesirable women because he stifled his anima in order to overemphasize a
persona of power and authority; the conflict between the persona and the
anima caused libido to regress to the unconscious, where it constellated
complexes that indicate a damaged anima; and he projects these complexes
onto women in general. (See Jung, 1934c.)

The neuroses of young adults usually concern power and sexuality. In
marked contrast to Freud, however, Jung concludes that the neurotic symptoms of older adults often result from the denial of their inherent religious
needs. Some two-thirds of the patients seeking his services were past middle
age, and the primary problem facing each one was that of finding a religious
outlook on life. Only those who succeeded in this quest were truly healed
(Jung, 1931/1933b, p. 61; 1932/1933d, p. 229). Jung also takes exception to
Freud's literal interpretation of incestuous wishes, arguing instead that these
are symbolic desires to achieve psychological rebirth and bring forth the
undervalued aspects of personality from one's unconscious. Finally, while
Jung does draw some distinctions among the various kinds of neurosis, he is
not overly enthusiastic about using such terms as phobia and hysteria. He
prefers to stress the need for understanding patients, rather than merely
assigning them to preconceived categories. (See Jung, 1961/1965, p. 124;
1964/1968, p. 82; 1913/1975a, p. 86; Progoff, 1953/1973, pp. 110–114.)

Psychosis. Unlike the neurotic, the psychotic is totally inundated by archetypal images. (See Jung, 1907/1974f; 1939/1974g, p. 160.) This gives psychosis a numinous and spellbinding quality, similar to a "big" dream. For
this reason, exploring the depths of one's psyche requires a firm attachment

to reality (as through work or marriage) and the guidance of a competent psychotherapist. In fact, if disinterring a neurosis will allow a latent psychosis to emerge, it may well be best to leave the neurosis alone.

> We are greatly mistaken if we think that [analyzing] the unconscious is something harmless that could be made into an object of entertainment, a parlor game. . . . Something deeply buried and invisible may thereby be set in motion . . . as if one were digging an artesian well and ran the risk of stumbling on a volcano. (Jung, 1917/1972d, p. 114; see also Jung, 1961/1965, pp. 135–136.)

Jung's early psychological training included considerable experience with schizophrenia (then called "dementia praecox"), making him far more comfortable about dealing with this bizarre form of behavior than was Freud. He soon recognized that psychotic symptoms, like those of neurosis, have important meanings. Thus one of his schizophrenic patients who made the apparently senseless statement, "I am the Lorelei," was actually referring to the poor prognosis of her case. Her doctors often discussed her symptomatology with the words "I know not what it means," which is the first line of Heine's famous poem "Die Lorelei" (Jung, 1961/1965, p. 126; 1907/1974f, p. 116). Jung was the first to apply psychoanalytic concepts to schizophrenia, and to recognize the possibility of psychosomatic mechanisms in this disorder (Arieti, 1974, pp. 22–25).

Psychotherapy

Jung's early attempts to explore the unconscious involved the use of hypnosis, but this technique soon proved to be unsatisfactory. At a demonstration before a group of twenty students, he informed a middle-aged woman patient suffering from paralysis of her left leg that he was going to hypnotize her. She obligingly fell into an immediate deep trance without any hypnosis whatsoever and talked at length for half an hour, resisting Jung's attempts to awaken her. Upon finally being brought out of the trance she cried out that she was cured, threw away her crutches, and was able to walk! To cover his embarrassment, Jung announced: "Now you've seen what can be done with hypnosis!" Actually he had not the slightest idea what had happened (Jung, 1961/1965, pp. 118–120).

Such experiences led Jung to seek out more comprehensible and dependable methods, as by obtaining the patient's unconscious projections from dreams and drawings. The latter is generally credited as the forerunner of modern art therapy, while another suggestion of Jung's led indirectly to the establishment of Alcoholics Anonymous (Ellenberger, 1970, pp. 732–733; Roazen, 1975/1976b, p. 284).

Theoretical Foundation. Jungian psychotherapy strives to eliminate the sufferer's inner conflicts and bring the conscious and unconscious opposites into harmonious unity, thereby restoring the normal course of individuation. Through a confrontation or conversation with the unconscious, the patient learns that life is not a matter of being either introverted or extraverted, thinking or feeling, sensing or intuiting, good or evil. Rather, wholeness and development require that the undervalued components of personality be accepted by the ego. Harmful projections also wane as greater knowledge of the unconscious is achieved, enabling the patient to perceive others more accurately and respond more appropriately. The therapist must be careful to avoid proceeding too quickly, however, lest an onslaught of archetypal material result in a psychosis. (See Ellenberger, 1970, pp. 713–719; Jung, 1961/1965, p. 135; 1917/1972d, pp. 111, 114.)

Therapeutic Procedures. Jung advocates a wide variety of therapeutic procedures. "There is no therapeutic technique or doctrine that is of general application, since every case that one receives for treatment is an individual in a specific condition" (Jung, 1964/1968, p. 54). For example, such activities as painting, modeling with clay, singing, and acting are not uncommon in Jungian therapy. When faced with a patient who had not slept for some time, Jung sang her a lullabye. In the case of a woman who was unable to tap her inner religiosity, he taught her the Scriptures and assigned regular homework (Whitmont & Kaufmann, 1973, p. 99). Upon being threatened with a slap by an imposing and arrogant female patient, Jung promptly jumped up to his full six-foot stature. "Very well, you are the lady," he said. "You hit first—ladies first! But then I hit back!" The deflated patient fell back into her chair, and from that moment the treatment began to succeed (Jung, 1961/1965, p. 142). Nor was Jung averse to using psychoanalytic methods, even giving some of his more educated patients books by Freud and Adler and discovering from their reaction the approach that would be more suitable. (See Jung, 1935a, p. 20; 1961/1965, p. 131.)

In the early phase of treatment, the Jungian therapist sees the patient four times a week. The initial stage is one of catharsis and emotional cleansing, wherein the patient's pathogenic secrets are brought to the surface—a period that often requires the utmost in confidentiality and compassion from the therapist. Jung once inferred from the word association test of an apparently psychotic woman patient that she had deliberately allowed one of her children to drink tainted water, which proved fatal. Her pathology dated from the moment she discovered that her true love, whose seeming disinterest had been the occasion of her marrying someone else, had actually cared for her all along. Jung confronted her with his conclusions, which he carefully concealed even from his colleagues, and two weeks later the patient was well enough to be discharged and never again required hospitalization (Jung, 1929/1933a, pp. 55, 57; 1961/1965, pp. 115–116).

The heart-felt outpourings of the cathartic stage tend to bind the patient emotionally to the therapist, leading to the next stage of treatment. The patient now examines the threatening contents of the shadow, while the therapist's interpretations deal with the childhood origins of the neurosis or psychosis and the patient's behaviors and symptoms. The patient learns to abandon immature and unrealistic fantasies, such as the transferential wish for an all-powerful provider, and "the road to a normally disillusioned life is now open" (Jung, 1929/1933a, p. 68). After this comes a stage of education about various aspects of life, designed to overcome the inevitable gaps in knowledge caused by the patient's pathology.

Finally, some patients (particularly those with above-average potentials) require a fourth stage of treatment. This uniquely Jungian approach is referred to as transformation, or as the synthetic-hermeneutic method (after Hermes, the god of revelation). It occurs after the persona, personal unconscious, and shadow have been elucidated, making the deeper layer of the collective unconscious more accessible and allowing archetypal symbols to emerge more readily. These symbols offer clues and guidelines for further individuation, and promote the differentiation of the self. Normally the anima or animus is first to appear, followed by such archetypes as the wise old man and great mother. (See Ellenberger, 1970, pp. 717–718; Fordham, 1966, pp. 59–60, 84–96.)

During the latter stages of therapy (or earlier in less severe cases), the patient is seen only once or twice a week. The patient and therapist sit face to face, and specific tasks and reading matter are often assigned. "In my experience the absolute period of cure is not shortened by too many sittings. It lasts a fair time in all cases requiring thorough treatment. . . . The patient must learn to go his own way" (Jung, 1935a, p. 20; 1935b, p. 27). This approach helps the patient develop independence, is less financially demanding, and allows the therapist more time for other cases.

Resistance, Transference, and Countertransference. Jung does not regard transference as a necessary part of psychotherapy, though its emergence is almost inevitable. He criticizes the transference neurosis of psychoanalysis as a therapeutic blunder that encourages the patient to wallow in infantile fantasies, creating an extreme dependence that can prove most difficult to terminate:

> Apparently we are to fall back on some nebulous trust in fate: somehow or other the matter will settle itself. "The transference stops automatically when the patient runs out of money," as a slightly cynical colleague once remarked to me. (Jung, 1928/1972e, p. 131. See also Jung, 1946/1969f, pp. 8–9; 1917/1972d, pp. 62, n. 13, 66–67; 1913/1975a, pp. 112–118.)

Jung therefore prefers to limit transference to a mild and almost unnoticeable level, which has the additional advantage of freeing more libido for the task of activating unconscious archetypes. He also argues that the patient's rejection of an interpretation is not necessarily a resistance. "Either the patient has not yet reached the point where he understands, or the interpretation does not fit" (Jung, 1964/1968, p. 50). And Jung stresses that the personality and adjustment of the therapist are more important than technique, for it is impossible to lead someone else further than one has gone oneself. The therapist must demonstrate living wholeness to the patient, while avoiding the temptation to feel smug and superior in knowledge. Jung was the first to advocate that all analysts be analyzed themselves so as to reduce the likelihood of harmful countertransferences, a suggestion Freud readily accepted. (See Jung, 1934c, pp. 158–159; 1935a, pp. 5, 8; 1961/1965, p. 132; 1964/1968, p. 48.)

Jung does not regard the effects of psychotherapy as necessarily permanent. The difficulties and contradictions of life cannot be eliminated—nor should they be, since they provide an essential challenge—and periodic returns to therapy may well prove helpful (Jung, 1916/1971e, p. 278).

Work

Jung's prolific writings include relatively little about the psychology of work. As we have seen, his character typology can readily be applied to this area: an extraverted-thinking type would appear well suited for a career in the physical sciences, an extraverted-intuitive type would undoubtedly prefer an entrepreneurial profession, an introvert should probably be dissuaded from becoming a salesperson, and so forth. Such categorizations tend to be oversimplifications, since the inferior and auxiliary processes also affect personality to a significant degree. But in work, as elsewhere, successful adjustment requires that one follow the innate predispositions of the collective unconscious.

Religion

Although Jung takes an emphatically positive approach to religion, as discussed previously, he does not advocate any particular denomination. Having extensively studied Eastern and Western religions, he concludes that people should follow their own cultural path to individuation.

Jung is highly critical of religions that emphasize blind faith and minimize the importance of reason, for this devaluing of the thinking function is merely another form of pathological one-sidedness. He does concede that people need to form some conception of life after death, even though there is at most some probability that aspects of the psyche continue beyond our physical demise. Nevertheless, the literal teaching of religious mythology is likely to present people with a most unpleasant choice: either to believe in impossibilities, or to reject religion entirely. (See Jung, 1957/1958b, pp. 49, 76; 1961–1965, pp. 94, 302, 322; 1964/1968, p. 84.)

Jung therefore recommends an analytical approach to religion. He postulates the existence of a God archetype, which can trigger intense religious feelings. He attributes contradictory aspects even to God, including kindness and cruelty. And he treats religious myths as symbolic representations of the human unconscious. For example, Christ dying for others epitomizes the internal crucifixion of an ego suspended between hostile forces (Jung, 1938; 1952/1973a; Progoff, 1953/1973, p. 115). Jung's ideas have generated more than a little controversy, yet many theologians regard them as major contributions to the development of religious thought (Ellenberger, 1970, pp. 688–689, 734–735).

Education

In education, as in psychotherapy, the wholeness and adjustment of the teacher are all-important. A maladjusted educator is likely to project inner faults onto the students and believe that it is they who are in need of correction, as well as offering a poor model for the child's inevitable identifications. A well-adjusted teacher, on the other hand, facilitates the child's introduction to the world at large. (See Jung, 1928/1969d.)

Because their function is so important, Jung strongly recommends continuing education for educators—and for other adults as well, since the complicated problems of life do not end upon one's graduation from high school or college. He also advises teachers to respect the inclinations of the inherently introverted child, rather than overvaluing extraversion. And he concludes that all too many children are taught to parrot back what they have learned, but not to explore the inner world of their own psyche. Educators must also be prepared to meet the considerable demands involved in teaching the gifted child, and should have some understanding of the common varieties of childhood psychopathology (Jung, 1926/1969c; 1928/1969d, p. 47; 1943/1969e, p. 130; 1921/1976, p. 404).

Insofar as the training of psychologists is concerned, Jung recommends a wide background in the humanities, history, literature, and mythology. He considers such knowledge essential in order to interpret correctly a patient's dreams, fantasies, and other symbolic productions (Jung, 1961/1965, p. 200; Jung, 1964/1968, p. 57; Jung, cited by Evans, 1976, p. 153).

Literature and Mythology

According to Jung, literature that has a clear and asymbolic meaning is determined primarily by the author's conscious intentions. Included in this category are novels about love, crime, and the family; didactic poetry; and many dramas. Other creative impulses are triggered by autonomous unconscious complexes and archetypal images, which use the author as a nutrient medium to fulfill their own particular purpose. A work of this sort, typified by Wagner's *Ring* and the second part of *Faust,* has an obscure and enthralling quality that compels us to seek out its hidden significance. "Sublime, pregnant with meaning, yet chilling the blood with its strangeness, it arises from timeless depths: glamorous, daemonic, and grotesque, it bursts asunder our human standards of value and aesthetic form" (Jung,

1930/1971g, p. 90; see also Jung, 1922/1971f, pp. 72, 83; 1930/1971 g, p. 104). In either case, literature and art exert a broadening effect that helps society to compensate for its faulty, one-sided development.

Analytical psychology offers an interesting interpretation of the common fascination with flying saucers. We are increasingly threatened with disaster from such sources as nuclear weapons and prodigious increases in population, and the earth may well be becoming an overcrowded prison from which humanity would like to escape. Such unpleasant issues tend to be repressed, and to create an unconscious desire for heavenly beings who will resolve our collective distress; and we project the aliens' mode of transportation in the form of a circle or mandala, which symbolizes the order and stability that we so urgently seek (Jung, 1958a).

Alchemy

Jung ascribes a symbolic meaning to the work of ancient alchemists, whose manifest concern was the transmutation of less valuable elements into gold. (See Fordham, 1966, p. 80–82; Jaffé, 1971/1975, pp. 50–52; Jung, 1944; 1955–1956; Rieff, 1959/1961, p. 16.) He argues that alchemical writings represent unconscious projections of inner experience, particularly the need to "transmute" the various components of personality into a new spiritual wholeness. "The secret of alchemy was in fact the transcendent function, the transformation of personality through the blending and fusion of the noble with the base components, of the differentiated with the inferior functions, of the conscious with the unconscious" (Jung, 1928/1972e, p. 220).

Synchronicity

Toward the end of his life, Jung developed the principle of **synchronicity,** which refers to events that are related to each other by meaningful coincidence rather than by cause and effect. When a clock stops at the moment of its owner's death, one event does not cause the other; the malfunction serves no known purpose; yet neither can Jung attribute this coincidence to pure chance. Similarly, one may dream of an unlikely event that shortly thereafter comes true, such as a chance meeting with a friend one has not seen for years. (See Jung, 1964/1968, p. 41; 1952/1973b; 1951/1973c.)

EVALUATION

Criticisms and Controversies

The Autonomy of the Psyche. If sexuality was the "numen" that drove Freud to dogmatism, psychic autonomy may well have done the same to Jung. He regards our thoughts and fantasies as autonomous events that happen to us, triggered by complexes that have a purpose of their own. (See for example Jung, 1928/1972e, p. 201). Not only is it perfectly normal to hear voices originating from within one's head, but this is *necessary* in order to learn from the collective unconscious and further the process of individuation! This unusual position differs radically from modern psychological standards, for a statement about hearing inner voices is in and of itself sufficient for an (actually healthy) individual to be admitted to a mental institution (Rosenhan, 1973).

This aspect of Jung's theory may well have been influenced by a personal bias. His autobiography reveals that at an early age, he was besieged with thoughts so terrible that he developed intense anxiety. "Don't think of it, just don't think of it!" he would tell himself. Ultimately he resolved his inner anguish by deciding that "God Himself had placed me in this situation. . . . God had also created Adam and Eve in such a way that they had to think what they did not at all want to think" (Jung, 1961/1965, pp. 36–40). Thus he attributed his own distressing thoughts to an external, supernatural source, which would seem to be an unconscious projection designed to alleviate the accompanying guilt. Jung did regard it as ironical "that I, a psychiatrist, should at almost every step of my [self-analysis] have run into the same psychic material which is the stuff of psychosis and is found in the insane" (1961/1965, p. 188). Yet he may well have underestimated his need to disavow the creation of his own unpleasant thoughts, and the extent to which this personal consideration influenced the development of his psychology.

Whatever the cause, the concept of psychic autonomy provides dangerous fodder for those who may border on neurosis or psychosis while lacking Jung's basic integrity. The idea that one's thoughts are not one's own offers vast possibilities for harmful rationalizations, and for failures to own up to one's behaviors. To be sure, Jung himself would emphatically reject such distortions of his theory. Nevertheless, Freud's more demanding view that we are primarily responsible for our psyche and our actions would seem far preferable, at least for most people in our present society.

Literary and Conceptual Confusion. Although Jung's writing is at times strikingly clear and insightful, his usual literary style has been described as dreadful, confused, and lacking any semblance of logical order. His readers must frequently struggle through numerous pages of abstruse and free-flowing ideas, often including lengthy citations from obscure and complex references. Nor was Jung overly fond of rigorous definitions, and his terminology is at times a source of potential confusion. For example, his definition of *instinct* includes habitual or learned responses as well as innate determinants of behavior, and *feeling* actually signifies something closer to *evaluating.* To the extent that a theorist is responsible for presenting new ideas clearly and defining original terms precisely, Jung himself has brought on much of the rejections and misunderstandings that surround his work.

Lack of Scientific Rigor. Jung's construct of the collective unconscious has been criticized as mystical and unscientific, as has his belief in parapsychology. His metaphysical model of libido is just as vulnerable to attack as is Freud's, despite the differences in definition. The transcendent function hardly explains the process to which it applies, just as synchronicity seems little more than a name for coincidences to which Jung arbitrarily assigns some grand design. In the latter instance, Jung's manifest dislike of statistics may well have caused him to exaggerate the importance of subjectively unusual events. The so-called law of averages does not necessarily apply in the short run, and even a fair coin or pair of dice is likely to yield some exceptional and apparently noteworthy series. Also, one characteristic of the mathematics of rare events is that the clustering of large frequencies among a small number of cases is to be expected purely by chance. Therefore, a coincidence that seems meaningful or "synchronistic" may only reflect the fact that the laws of statistics do not always operate in accordance with common sense.

Psychology and Religion. Jung's emphasis of our spiritual and religious longings has provoked considerable controversy. Proponents claim that Jung has justifiably extended the scope of psychology by calling attention to a vital area of human functioning. Critics argue that a scientific psychology cannot deal with such arcane issues as the nature of God and the existence of the supernatural, or that Jung's synthesis is shallow and unsuccessful (e.g., Stern, 1976/1977).

Empirical Research

Research on analytical psychology has been relatively sparse, and has tended to concentrate on the psychological types. Some of these studies have over-simplified Jung's position by dealing only with the attitudes, but others have given due attention to the full complexity of Jung's typology.

The Myers-Briggs Type Indicator(Myers, 1962) is a well-standardized pencil-and-paper inventory that measures four bipolar dimensions: introversion versus extraversion, thinking versus feeling, sensation versus intuition, and perception (simply experiencing events) versus judgment (evaluating these events in terms of a set of standards). Studies using this instrument have found that extraverts were more likely (and introverts less likely) to accept a group learning situation, as would be expected, and that social service volunteers tended to be extraverted—intuitive (Carlson & Levy, 1973; Kilmann & Taylor, 1974). Considerable attention has also been given to introversion—extraversion by Eysenck (e.g., 1947; 1967; 1970–1971), who has studied its relationship to sensitive cortical excitation processes. Studies of this dimension of personality have become less frequent, however, due in part to methodological difficulties (Jackson & Paunonen, 1980).

Contributions

In contrast to Freud's pronounced pessimism, Jung's concept of an inherent positive tendency for self-realization anticipates the general outlook of such theorists as Horney, Allport, Rogers, and Maslow. Jung also departed from Freud by taking an active interest in psychosis, and made significant contributions to our understanding of schizophrenia. He emphasized that dream symbols may be neither sexual nor deceptive, and promulgated the dream series method. Introversion and extraversion have become part of our everyday language, if in a more simplified way than Jung intended.

Jung's implicit or explicit suggestions led to such modern forms of treatment as art therapy and Alcoholics Anonymous. Certain of his approaches to psychotherapy have gained widespread acceptance, such as the use of fewer than four sessions per week, face-to-face interviews, procedural eclecticism, and required training analyses for psychoanalysts. His emphasis on the therapist's "living wholeness" anticipates Rogers's "genuineness." Jung's belief in the importance of unconscious projections is accepted by many modern theorists. In a sense, the word association test is the forerunner of the modern lie detector.

The concept of a collective unconscious gives a sense of history to life by suggesting that something of us continues after death. Jung was acutely aware of people's need for meaning in their lives, and his effect on religious thought has been mentioned previously. Finally, many of Jung's practical guidelines make excellent sense: to follow one's true inner nature yet not use this as an excuse to trample on the rights of others, to bring the shadow to light and accept even the unpleasant aspects of one's personality, to avoid the dangers of an excessive and stifling persona or one that is underdeveloped, and—above all—to beware of the extreme one-sidedness that constitutes pathology. To Jung as to Freud, extremism is surely a vice, while true self-knowledge is indeed a virtue.

Freud once tartly characterized Jung as crazy (Roazen, 1975/1976b, p. 261), and there are undoubtedly modern psychologists who would agree. Yet, at the very least, Jung was an insightful psychotherapist and highly imaginative thinker who possessed unusually extensive knowledge about a wide variety of subjects. Many of the criticisms of Jungian theory are cogent and serious, but his writings offer considerable riches as well.

Suggested Reading

Perhaps the best place to begin a first-hand study of Jung is with his autobiography, *Memories, Dreams, Reflections* (1961/1965). Although there are apparently some contradictions and inaccuracies in his retrospections (Ellenberger, 1970, pp. 663, 667), this work provides a strikingly personal glimpse of the man and his theories. Jung's chapter in *Man and His Symbols* (1964/1968) ranks among his clearest expositions, and includes substantial material on dream interpretation. Two of Jung's most important articles appear in *Two Essays on Analytical Psychology* (1917/1972d, 1928/1972e), while the basic introduction to the attitudes and functions is given in Chapter Ten of *Psychological Types* (1921/1976). The latter is also included in *The Portable Jung* (Viking Press, 1971), a collection of significant articles. The standard edition of Jung's work, translated or revised by R. F. C. Hull, is the definitive version.

Among the helpful secondary sources on Jung are those by Ellenberger (1970), Fordham (1966), Progoff (1953/1973), and a critical biography by Stern (1976/1977). Evans (1976) reports an interesting interview with Jung that took place toward the end of the latter's life. The extensive correspondence between Freud and Jung is also readily available (McGuire, 1974).

■ SUMMARY

1. THE BASIC NATURE OF HUMAN BEINGS. *The Instincts:* People are motivated by such innate instincts as hunger, thirst, sexuality, individuation, power, activity, and creativity. Moral tendencies and a need for religion are also inborn. *Psychic Energy:* All mental activity is powered by psychic energy, which is called libido regardless of the instinct(s) involved. The greater the amount of libido (value) that is invested in a mental event or activity, the more the event is desired. Psychic energy attracts constellations or complexes of related and emotionally charged ideas. Powerful conscious or unconscious complexes can exert considerable control over one's thoughts and behaviors. *The Principle of Opposites:* Psychic energy is created by the tension between such opposites as introversion-extraversion, thinking-feeling, sensation-intuition, good-evil, consciousness-unconsciousness, love-hate, and many others. When one extreme is primarily conscious, the unconscious compensates by emphasizing the opposite tendency. Successful adjustment requires uniting the various opposing forces through some middle ground. *Teleology:* Behavior is not only motivated by prior causes, but is also oriented toward a future purpose or goal. *The Unconscious:* The vast majority of the psyche is unconscious, and includes both destructive forces and positive wellsprings of creativity and guidance. The unconscious is divided into two parts, personal and collective.

2. THE STRUCTURE OF PERSONALITY. *The Ego:* The ego is an entirely conscious complex that constitutes the center of one's awareness. It begins to develop at about the fourth year of life, and results from experiences that promote a distinction between "I" and "not-I." The Jungian ego is a relatively weak component of personality. *The Persona:* The (conscious) persona is a protective façade, or social mask, that facilitates contacts with other people. An overdeveloped persona results in a state of pomposity or inflation, while an underdeveloped persona gives one the appearance of being incompetent, tactless, boring, or eternally misunderstood. *The Personal Unconscious:* The personal unconscious begins to form at

birth. It includes material derived from personal experience that is no longer (or not yet) conscious, such as forgotten and unimportant memories, significant repressions, and stimuli that have been perceived subliminally. *The Shadow:* The shadow, located in the personal unconscious, is the primitive and unwelcome side of one's personality. However, it also provides a necessary ingredient of vitality. Like all that is unconscious, the shadow is commonly projected onto other people and experienced in this indirect fashion. *The Collective Unconscious:* The collective unconscious is a storehouse of archetypes inherited from our ancestral past. Archetypes are universal thought forms and emotions that result from the repeated experiences of past generations, and predispose an individual to apprehend the world in particular ways. Included among the many archetypes are the shadow, persona, anima, animus, self, wise old man, and great mother. One never becomes aware of the archetypes themselves, but experiences them through the images or symbols that they produce and transmit to consciousness.

3. THE DEVELOPMENT OF PERSONALITY. *Individuation and the Self:* There are no formal stages of development in analytical psychology. During childhood the various components of personality become differentiated from the whole, with sexuality not appearing until puberty. A "second puberty" occurs at about age thirty-five to forty, at which time interests in sexuality and power yield to more spiritual and cultural values. The lifelong unfolding of one's inherent potential, or individuation, results in the formation of a new center of personality (the self) that unifies the many opposites. Individuation can never be fully achieved, however, and may well be beyond the reach of many people. *Progression and Regression:* Libido normally proceeds in a forward direction, furthering the development of personality. If this progression is blocked by frustrations in the external world, or by internal repressions, libido turns back to earlier memories and archetypal images. Such regressions may result in infantile or pathological behavior, but they may also awaken undervalued and neglected aspects of one's personality. *Character Typology:* Individual differences in personality result from the characteristic direction of libido movement (introversion or extraversion), and from the typical way in which a person apprehends the world (thinking, feeling, sensation, or intuition). The dominant or superior attitude and function are conscious, while the opposite (inferior) processes are primarily unconscious. A predisposition toward one attitude and function is inborn, and these are the ones that should become dominant for the personality to be well-adjusted. However, the inferior processes must also be afforded satisfactory expression.

4. FURTHER APPLICATIONS. *Dream Interpretation:* Dreams provide important information about the personal and collective unconscious. They may serve as wish-fulfillments, express one's fears, mirror actual situations, anticipate the future, provide a warning, synthesize solutions to one's waking problems, or even result from telepathy. A dream symbol has at least two meanings, is not an attempt at deception, and often does not concern sexuality. *Psychopathology:* Psychopathology consists of an excessively one-sided personality, which results in a painful self-division and brings the unconscious into conflict with consciousness.

It may be caused by trying to go against one's true inner nature, or by rejecting essential aspects of one's personality. The neuroses of the young usually concern sexuality and power, while those of older people are more likely to involve the denial of their inherent religious needs. Psychosis is also understandable and amenable to treatment, although the prognosis is poorer than for neurosis. *Psychotherapy:* Jungian psychotherapy uses a wide variety of procedures, often including face-to-face interviews and only one or two weekly sessions. The goal is to eliminate painful inner conflicts and pathological one-sidedness through a regression to the unconscious, thereby bringing the conscious and unconscious opposites into harmonious unity and allowing individuation to continue. The stages of treatment include catharsis, elucidation, education, and perhaps transformation, with transference kept to a much lower level than in psychoanalysis. *Other Applications:* Other applications of analytical psychology include work, religion (to which Jung is highly favorable, but critical of many religious practices), education, literature, mythology, and the analysis of alchemical writings.

5. EVALUATION. Analytical psychology is highly controversial. It has been deservedly criticized for literary and conceptual confusions, a lack of scientific rigor, and overemphasizing the autonomy of the psyche. It is all too easy to misconstrue Jung's words as permission to be neurotic or psychotic, or to disavow the responsibility for one's thoughts and actions. Jungian theory has failed to stimulate a great deal of research, or to attract widespread interest. Nevertheless, Jung has made substantial contributions to the understanding and treatment of psychosis, to dream interpretation, to the development of psychotherapy, to more positive views of human nature, to religious thought, and to our understanding of such characteristics as introversion and extraversion.

STUDY QUESTIONS

1. How might Jung's personality and life experiences have influenced his belief that our thoughts and fantasies are autonomous events that happen to us, rather than our own creations?

2. What differences between the personalities of Jung and Freud might help to explain Jung's greater tolerance for and interest in psychosis?

3. "I know things and must hint at things which other people do not know, and usually do not even want to know. . . . Loneliness does not come from having no people about one, but from being unable to communicate the things that seem important to oneself, or from holding certain views which others find inadmissible." Do you think that this statement by Jung could just as easily have been made by Freud? Why or why not?

4. Compare Jung's list of human instincts with Freud's. Which better explains our behavior?

5. Give a real-life example to support Jung's contention that "extremes [in personality] always arouse suspicion of their [unconscious] opposite."

6. Give an example from your own life, or from the life of someone you know well or have read about, to illustrate: (a) enantiodromia; (b) an inflated persona.

7. Give an example from your own life, or from the life of someone you know well, to support Jung's contention that the characteristics we detest in other people are likely to be what we most dislike about ourselves.

8. "To find out what is truly individual in ourselves, profound reflection is needed; and suddenly we realize how uncommonly difficult the discovery of individuality is." Do you agree? Why or why not?

9. (a) Which attitude is dominant in your personality? How do you know? (b) Which function is dominant in your personality? How do you know? (c) Are the opposite attitude and function underdeveloped and difficult for you to express, as Jung would expect? (d) Based on the preceding answers, what job might you be well suited for?

10. If possible, provide an example from your own life of an archetypal symbol emerging into consciousness or of a "big dream."

11. Why might it be harmful for a patient to try and excuse neurotic behavior by dwelling on childhood events (such as serious mistakes by the parents), even if this neurosis did originate in early childhood?

12. (a) How might Freud criticize such Jungian therapeutic procedures as singing a lullabye to a woman who could not sleep, or teaching Scriptures to a patient who could not tap her inner religious feelings? (b) How might Jung reply?

13. Do you prefer Jung's approach to religion or Freud's? Why?

14. At the moment someone dies, the person's favorite picture falls off a wall and is shattered. How might this be understood as a mere coincidence, rather than as an example of synchronicity?

4

ALFRED ADLER
Individual Psychology

Scientific inquiry is normally rational and objective, yet there are times when it resembles a bitter family feud. One such monumental uproar occurred in 1911, when it became apparent that the theories of Freud's colleague Alfred Adler were irreconcilably different from those of psychoanalysis. An irate Freud "forced the whole Adler gang" to resign from psychoanalytic circles, and even forbade his followers to attend any of Adler's conferences. Long-standing friendships broke up, wives of the combatants stopped speaking to each other, and members of opposing factions refused to sit near each other at dinner parties. Psychoanalysts charged Adler with plagiarism, and were accused in turn of retaining his ideas while expunging his name from their writings. And even Jung, a man known for his tolerance of all races and peoples, was moved to describe Adler's group as an "insolent gang" of "impudent puppies." (See Ellenberger, 1970, pp. 638–645; McGuire, 1974, pp. 447, 534; Roazen, 1975/1976b, pp. 184–193.)

Although Freud's pungent attacks were undoubtedly excessive, it would seem that he better understood the way to lasting fame. Today Freud is clearly recognized as the originator of psychoanalysis; while Adler's significant ideas have been widely subsumed, without credit, into the theories of other psychologists.

BIOGRAPHICAL SKETCH

Alfred Adler was born on February 7, 1870, in Rudolfsheim, a suburb of Vienna. His father was a Jewish grain merchant with a cheerful disposition and a particular fondness for Alfred, while his mother has been described as rather gloomy, rejecting, and self-sacrificing. Like Freud and Jung, Adler rose from lower middle-class origins to world fame; but unlike his illustrious counterparts, he remained emotionally attached to the lower classes and keenly concerned with social problems. Adler was a second-born (Ellenberger, 1970, p. 576) who grew up in the shadow of a gifted and successful older brother, with his family constellation including an envious younger brother and three other siblings. Alfred never developed strong ties to his Jewish heritage, perhaps because his childhood was spent in liberal and heterogeneous surroundings, and he converted to Protestantism in 1904.

Adler pursued his medical studies at the University of Vienna. Ironically, he never did attend any of the lectures on hysteria being given there by a relatively unknown psychologist, Sigmund Freud. He received his degree in 1895, though not with outstanding marks, and soon thereafter began private practice. In 1897 he married Raissa Epstein, an ardent socialist and independent thinker whom he met at a political convention. The Adlers were to have four children (three daughters and a son), two of whom became individual psychologists. His first publication, which appeared in 1898, stressed the pathogenic working conditions of independent tailors and the need of the poor for socialized medicine.

Adler first met Freud in 1902 under circumstances that are shrouded in legend, and still essentially unknown (Ellenberger, 1970, p. 583). He remained active in psychoanalytic circles for some ten years, becoming the first president of the Viennese Psychoanalytic Society in 1910. Like Jung, however, Adler insisted on the freedom to pursue his own ideas. As he once remarked to Freud, "do you think it gives me such great pleasure to stand in your shadow my whole life long?" (Freud, 1914/1967, p. 51; Roazen, 1975/1976b, pp. 179–184.) Eventually Adler's theories became so divergent from psychoanalysis as to precipitate an acrimonious parting of the ways, with Freud accusing him of heresy and imposing the penalty of excommunication. Thus Adler resigned from the Psychoanalytic Society in 1911 and founded his own organization, known first as the Society for Free Psychoanalysis and later as the Society for Individual Psychology.

Adler suffered a particularly painful rebuff in 1915, when he was denied a teaching position at the University of Vienna because his work was regarded as unscientific. During World War I, he engaged in psychiatric work with the Viennese Army. The postwar period was a most difficult one, with the defeated Austria-Hungary suffering from poverty, famine, and epidemics. These trying times undoubtedly reinforced Adler's socialistic leanings, though he rejected any involvement with militant political activities.

Adler was a short and sturdy man. He was less handsome and charismatic than either Freud or Jung, and he often presented an almost sloppy appearance. His style of life was unusually simple and unpretentious, quite unlike the typical man of distinction. He possessed strong emotions that at times yielded to hypersensitivity, as well as the ability to make quick and accurate guesses about a patient's clinical disturbances, life problems, and birth order. He also impressed people as a witty and inspiring lecturer. Unfortunately, he could be highly impractical as well. Whereas psychoanalytic conferences were conducted in a formal and proper manner, Adler unwisely acquired a reputation for superficiality by meeting with both followers and patients in various Viennese coffeehouses.

Adler's most significant achievements came during the years 1920–1933. He published numerous important books, and founded a series of child guidance clinics in Vienna. Adler visited the United States frequently from 1926 onward, participating in a symposium at Wittenberg College and teaching extension courses at Columbia University. In 1930 he was honored with the title of Citizen of Vienna, but the mayor unwittingly earned Adler's deep resentment by introducing him as "a deserving pupil of Freud." Adler foresaw the Nazi menace at an early date and moved permanently to the United States in 1934, where he taught at the Long Island College of Medicine and continued to strive for the establishment of individual psychology. There is no official standard edition of his works, which number perhaps a dozen volumes.

During his later years Adler developed a heart condition, but he enjoyed working too much to lead a limited life. While on a lecture tour in Aberdeen, Scotland, he suffered a fatal heart attack on May 28, 1937.

THE BASIC NATURE OF HUMAN BEINGS

Adler called his theory **individual psychology,** a name that is unfortunately somewhat misleading. The term *individual* expresses his belief in the uniqueness and indivisibility of every human personality. It by no means precludes the social element, a factor he actually considers "all-important. . . . The individual becomes an individual only in a social context. Other systems of psychology make a distinction between what they call individual psychology and social psychology, but for us there is no such distinction" (Adler, 1929/1969, p. 95).

Individual psychology pays relatively little attention to abstruse metaphysical constructs, or to speculations about the deepest layers of the psyche. Instead, Adler prefers to emphasize practical recommendations for dealing with our problems, bringing up children, getting along with others, and upgrading the quality of life in general. (See Adler, 1927/1957, p. 1; 1929/1969, p. 1.)

Social Interest

Whereas psychoanalysis views life as an inevitable struggle between our selfish drives and the demands of society, Adler argues that we have an innate potential for relating to others. This **social interest** or **community feeling** (*Gemeinschaftsgefühl*) involves much more than membership in a particular group. It refers to a sense of kinship with humanity, and it enables our physically weak species to survive through cooperation:

> Imagine a man alone, and without an instrument of culture, in a primitive forest! He would be more inadequate than any other living organism. . . . The community is the best guarantee of the continued existence of human beings . . . [and social interest] is the true and inevitable compensation for all [of their] natural weaknesses. . . . (Adler, 1927/1957, pp. 35–36; 1929/1964a, p. 31. See also Adler, 1933/1964b, pp. 98–99; 1931–1979e, pp. 210–211.)

Thus it is social interest, rather than a superego or collective unconscious, that establishes the guidelines for proper personality development.

The well-adjusted person learns at an early age to develop this inherent potential, and to assist the common good of present and future generations. Maladjustment is defined not as the failure to sublimate or individuate, as Freud or Jung would argue, but as the denial of one's community feeling. A major task of psychology, therefore, is to understand and alleviate deficiencies in cooperation. "Society has no place for deserters" (Adler, 1927/1957, p. 194; see also Adler, 1933/1964b, p. 283; 1933/1979g).

Teleology, Feelings of Inferiority, and Striving for Superiority (Self-Perfection)

Life Goals and Teleology. Adler's early theories included the idea of an aggressive drive, a position he adopted some twelve years prior to Freud, but he eventually abandoned this approach. Instead, Adler differs sharply from Freud and Jung by regarding the idea of inherited personality components as a "superstition" (1931/1958, p. 168). According to Adler, we are not mere pawns of innate instinctual urges. We actively select our fundamental life goals, and also the means of achieving them. Even social interest is only a predisposition, and it is all too possible to deny this tendency and choose to be neurotically self-centered.

> *The psychic life of man is determined by his goal.* No human being can think, feel, will, dream, without all these activities being determined, continued, modified, and directed toward an ever-present objective. . . . A real understanding of the behavior of any human being is impossible without a clear comprehension of the secret goal which he is pursuing. . . . (Adler, 1927/ 1957, pp. 29, 49. See also Adler, 1933/1979a, p. 52; 1932/1979i, p. 87.)

While Adler (like Jung) subordinates causal factors in favor of teleology, he does regard infancy and childhood as a time of considerable importance. Our major goals are usually formed during the first few years of life, and they can be deviated from during adulthood only with great difficulty. Therefore, "no one can understand the grown–up who does not learn to understand the child" (Adler, 1931/1958, p. 65; see also Adler, 1927/1957, pp. 18, 31; 1933/1964b, pp. 81–82).

To illustrate, a young girl who craves attention from her parents may decide to fulfill this goal by becoming ill frequently, so that they will spend a great deal of time taking care of her. She is very likely to behave in similar ways as an adult, as by suffering from persistent migraine headaches because they bring welcome concern from her husband. Freud would regard such rewards as only secondary gains, but to Adler they represent fundamental clues for understanding human nature. "We do not suffer from the shock of [traumatic experiences;] we make out of them just what suits our purposes" (Adler, 1931/1958, p. 14).

Life goals need not be realistic to be important, for we often act "as if" certain **fictions** were actually true. A person's behavior will be significantly affected by the belief that virtue is rewarded with an afterlife in heaven, or by neurotic fantasies of exaggerated self-importance, even though these ideas may not correspond very well with reality. Thus Adler conceives of personality as essentially self-created: we select and pursue our goals according to our subjective conceptions of self, others, and the world in general.

Feelings of Inferiority and the Striving for Superiority. To Adler, the primary goal underlying all human behavior is that of self-perfection. Everyone begins life as a weak and helpless child, and we all possess the innate drive to overcome this inferiority by mastering our formidable environment:

> *To be a human being means the possession of a feeling of inferiority that is constantly pressing on towards its own conquest. . . . The goal of the human soul is conquest, perfection, security, superiority. . . .* Every child is faced with so many obstacles in life that no child ever grows up without striving for some form of significance. . . . Every voluntary act begins with a feeling of inadequacy. . . . (Adler, 1927/1957, pp. 38, 135; 1933/1964b, pp. 73, 145. See also Adler, 1920/1973, pp. 1–15; 1933/1979g, pp. 32–33.)

Healthy **striving for superiority** (or **perfection,** or **significance**) is guided by social interest, and gives due consideration to the welfare of others. Contrariwise, the selfish striving for dominance and personal glory is distorted and pathological (Adler, 1931/1958, p. 8).

The feelings of inferiority that underlie the striving for superiority are by no means abnormal or undesirable. If a child faces its weaknesses with optimism and courage, and strives for superiority by making the necessary effort to **compensate** for them, a satisfactory or even superior level of adjustment may be achieved. A famous example is that of Demosthenes, an apparently incurable stutterer, who practiced speaking with pebbles in his mouth and eventually became the greatest orator in ancient Greece (Adler, 1929/1964a, p. 35; Orgler, 1963/1972, p. 67). Or a physically unattractive person may compensate for the resulting feelings of inferiority, and win numerous friends and admirers, by becoming genuinely warm and compassionate. The feeling of inferiority "becomes a pathological condition only when the sense of inadequacy overwhelms the individual, and . . . makes him depressed and incapable of development." Such a shattering **inferiority complex** can occur as early as the second year of life and is actually "more than a complex, it is almost a disease whose ravages vary under different circumstances" (Adler, 1929/1969, pp. 25, 31; see also Adler, 1927/1957, p. 69). And it is possible to feel vastly inferior without actually being so, since this belief (like any Adlerian personality characteristic) is primarily a matter of self-judgment.

The child who surrenders to an inferiority complex sees only the possibility of evading difficulties, instead of trying to overcome them. "Imagine the goal of the child who is not confident of being able to solve his problems! How dismal the world must appear to such a child! Here we find timidity, introspectiveness, distrust, and all those other characteristics and traits with which the weakling seeks to defend himself" (Adler, 1927/1957, p. 33). Adler devotes considerable attention to those developmental factors that can turn normal feelings of inferiority (and healthy strivings for self-perfection) into a pathological inferiority complex (and distorted, selfish strivings), as we will see in a subsequent section.

THE STRUCTURE OF PERSONALITY

Since Adler regards personality as an indivisible unity, he makes no assumptions about its structure. He does agree with Freud and Jung that much of personality is beyond our awareness, and that "the hardest thing for human beings to do is to know themselves and to change themselves," but he attributes this lack of self-knowledge to holistic and teleological forces. We deceive ourselves in order to fulfill our chosen goals, and the unconscious is whatever we do not wish to understand:

> There can be no question here of anything like a repressed unconscious; it is rather a question of something not understood, of something withheld from the understanding. . . . Consciousness and unconsciousness move together in the same direction and are not contradictions, as is so often believed. What is more, there is no definite line of demarcation between them. It is merely a question of discovering the purpose of their joint movement. . . . Every memory is dominated by the goal idea which directs the personality-as-a-whole. . . . That which is helpful we are conscious of; whatever can disturb our arguments we push into the unconscious. (Adler, 1927/1957, pp. 21, 50, 90–91; 1933/1964b, p. 16; 1929/1969, p. 15.)

Such socially undesirable traits as vanity, stubbornness, cowardice, and hostility are likely to be deliberately misunderstood (i.e., unconscious) so as to preclude the necessity for changing them. Thus a person who requires considerable coaxing from the host before agreeing to attend a party, always arrives late, or dresses unusually poorly is likely to be concealing powerful (unconscious) arrogance behind a façade of excessive modesty. Socrates is said to have once addressed a speaker who mounted the podium wearing old and bedraggled clothes, "Young man of Athens, your vanity peeps out through every hole in your robe!" Similarly, disguised hostility may be expressed by apparently forgetting the instructions of a domineering spouse or employer. (See Adler, 1927/1957, p. 158; 1933/1964b, pp. 206–208.) To Adler, therefore, conscious and unconscious are inextricably intertwined; and human behavior must be interpreted as a holistic and unified quest toward those goals, understood or not, that the individual has selected.

■ CAPSULE SUMMARY
Some Important Adlerian Terminology

Birth order	One's position in the family constellation (first-born, second-born, etc.). Strongly affects the child's perception of self and others, and the treatment accorded by the parents, and is therefore a major factor in the development of personality.
Community feeling	A synonym for social interest.
Compensation	The process of overcoming real or imagined inferiority through effort and practice, or by developing one's abilities in a different area. Physical inferiorities are often compensated for in psychological ways, while social interest enables the human race to compensate for its marked inferiority to the overwhelming forces of nature.
Early recollections	Memories of one's infancy and childhood. Even if inaccurate, these recollections provide important clues about the style of life because they are strongly influenced by one's self-selected goals.
Fictions	Unrealistic life goals that significantly influence behavior because the person acts "as if" they were true.
Individual psychology	The name Adler gave to his theory of personality.
Inferiority complex	Exaggerated and pathological feelings of weakness, including the belief that one cannot overcome one's difficulties through appropriate effort. Usually accompanied by a conscious or unconscious superiority complex.
Inferiority feelings	Normal and inevitable feelings of weakness, which result from our helplessness during childhood. May well stimulate healthy strivings for superiority and compensations, and so are not necessarily pathological or undesirable.
Masculine protest	Behavior motivated by objections to the belief that society regards men as superior to women. May involve the adoption of play, work, dress, or a name typical of the opposite sex, or the failure to form satisfying heterosexual relationships. May occur in males or females.
Neglect	Failing to give a child sufficient care and attention, thereby creating the belief that the world is a cold and unfriendly place. One of the three major reasons why a child selects mistaken, pathogenic goals.
Organ inferiority	A significant physiological defect, usually of unknown cause, that can trigger strong feelings of inferiority. Need not result in pathology if effectively compensated, but often becomes one of the three major reasons why a child selects mistaken and pathogenic goals.

continued

Pampering ("spoiling")	Giving a child excessive attention and protection. Pampering inhibits the development of initiative and independence, and creates the impression that the world owes one a living. One of the three major reasons why a child selects mistaken, pathogenic goals.
Social interest (social feeling)	An innate sense of kinship with all humanity. Everyone possesses the potential for social interest, but it must be consciously developed through appropriate training for personality to become well adjusted.
Striving for superiority (perfection, significance)	A universal, innate drive to achieve a satisfactory level of adaptation and become sufficiently superior to one's environment. Healthy strivings are guided by social interest, whereas pathological strivings ignore the welfare of others.
Style of life	The unique mode of adjustment to life that characterizes a particular personality, notably the individual's self-selected goals and means of achieving them.
Superiority complex	A pathological, false feeling of power and security that invariably conceals an underlying inferiority complex. A misguided attempt at compensation that represents a lack of social interest, and an attempt to evade one's problems rather than resolve them.

THE DEVELOPMENT OF PERSONALITY

Adler shares Freud's belief that personality is formed during the first five years of life, and he agrees that there is sexuality in childhood. To Adler, however, sexual behavior is merely another form of striving for superiority. He also rejects the idea of specific developmental stages, preferring to stress practical guidelines for promoting social interest and avoiding a disastrous inferiority complex. (See Adler, 1931/1958, pp. 12, 34, 200; 1929/1969, pp. 83, 123–130.)

Pathogenic Factors in Personality Development

Ideally, the child's potential for social interest is brought to fruition by the mother. She administers the initial lesson in cooperation by nursing the baby at her breast, thereby serving as the child's first bridge to social life. *"We probably owe to the maternal sense of contact the largest part of human social feeling, and along with it the essential continuance of human civilization"* (Adler, 1933/1964b, p. 221; see also Adler, 1927/1957, p. 220; 1931/1958, pp. 17–18, 120, 125–126). Later she must also help the child extend its relationships to the father, and to others. If the mother is markedly clumsy, uncooperative, or untrustworthy, however, the child will learn to resist social interest instead of striving to develop it.

The father's role is to provide feelings of courage and self-reliance, and to stress the need for choosing a satisfying and worthwhile occupation. To Adler, all too many parents are poorly prepared for the difficult and challenging task of raising their children:

> The first cooperation among other people which [the child] experiences is [that] of his parents; and if their cooperation is poor, they cannot hope to teach him to be cooperative himself. . . . Unfortunately, however, parents are neither good psychologists nor good teachers. . . . Few [of them] are inclined to learn and to avoid mistakes . . . [and those] who most need advice are the [ones] who never come for it. (Adler, 1927/1957, p. 219; 1931/1958, pp. 133, 178; 1929/1969, p. 103. See also Adler, 1931/1958, pp. 134–138.)

Pampering. Perhaps the most serious of all parental errors is that of showering the child with excessive attention, protection, and assistance. Such **pampering** (or "spoiling") robs children of their independence and initiative, shatters their self-confidence, and creates the parasitic impression that the world owes them a living.

Under the misguided belief that they suffer from a lack of ability, rather than from a lack of training, pampered children develop an intense inferiority complex. This pathological condition tends to remain concealed so long as matters proceed favorably, but becomes all too evident when life presents its inevitable stress and disappointments. Having never learned self-reliance, and having been taught to expect but not to give, pampered children try to resolve their problems by making unrealistic demands on other people. Thus they may use enuresis, nightmares, anxiety, or temper tantrums as manipulative (albeit unconscious) devices for obtaining sympathy and attention. They may expect everyone to treat their wishes as laws, crave prominence and acclaim without having to put forth the necessary effort, rebel against parental authority through active opposition or sulking, and act depressed or even suicidal if unable to get everything they want. As adults they tend to approach work and marriage with a selfish orientation, rather than in the spirit of cooperation. Such behavior naturally provokes sharp criticism and rejections, which intensifies the inferiority complex and strengthens the need for more pampering. "Every pampered child becomes a hated child. . . . There is no greater evil than the pampering of children. . . . Grown-up pampered children are perhaps the most dangerous class in our community" (Adler, 1931/1958, p. 16; 1933/1964b, p. 154; 1929/1969, p. 10; see also Adler, 1931/1958, pp. 128, 151, 240, 282–283; 1929/1969, p. 33; Orgler, 1963/1972, pp. 72–75).

Pampering may also result in an apparent Oedipus complex, a phenomenon Adler regards as neither universal nor sexual. "[The] so-called Oedipus complex is not a 'fundamental fact,' but is simply a vicious unnatural result of maternal overindulgence. . . . The victims of the Oedipus complex are children who were pampered by their mothers . . . [and whose fathers were] comparatively indifferent or cold" (Adler, 1931/1958, p. 54; 1933/1964b, p. 21).[1] That is, only a pampered boy wants to eliminate his father and subjugate his mother, and the underlying motive is to preserve the mother's overindulgence. Adler charges psychoanalysis with the error of restricting its study primarily to pampered children, who do in fact follow the pleasure principle and become enraged and defensive if their selfish wishes are not fulfilled, and then overgeneralizing its findings to all of humanity. "The striving for gratification is only one of the million varieties of the striving for superiority; and we cannot take it as the central motive of all expressions of personality" (Adler, 1931/1958, p. 98; see also Adler, 1933/1964b, pp. 36, 51, 154, 213–214).

Neglect. The opposite extreme, failing to provide sufficient care and attention (**neglect**), creates the mistaken impression that the world is totally cold and unsympathetic. The neglected child "has never known what love and cooperation can be: he makes up an interpretation of life which does not include these friendly forces. . . . He will overrate [the difficulties of life] and underrate his own capacity to meet them . . . [and] will not see that he can *win* affection and esteem by actions which are useful to others" (Adler, 1931/1958, p. 17; see also Orgler, 1963/1972, pp. 76–79). Such children regard life as an enemy, expressing their inferiority complex through suspiciousness, isolation, stubbornness, and maliciousness. In the words of Shakespeare's *Richard III,* "since I cannot prove a lover . . . I am determined to prove a villain."

Other Parental Factors. Parents who fail to show a normal amount of tenderness and sentimentality impair the child's ability to recognize and demonstrate love. Establishing unattainable standards or resorting to punishment overemphasizes the child's helplessness, and is therefore likely to bring about an inferiority complex. "Punishment, especially corporal punishment, is always harmful to children. Any teaching which cannot be given in friendship is wrong teaching. . . . Praise or blame should be given to success or failure in the training and not to the personality of the child" (Adler, 1931/1958, p. 135; 1933/1964b, p. 226). Ridiculing a child is "well-nigh criminal," resulting in the constant dread of being laughed at. Excessive criticism of other people will prejudice the child against sociability and cooperation. So too will a father who adopts the role of family ruler, and who acts superior to the mother because he is the primary breadwinner. (See Adler, 1927/1957, p. 66; 1931/1958, pp. 135, 222.)

---

[1]Not so coincidentally, this was the situation in Freud's own family.

Organ Inferiority. In addition to parental errors, a significant physical deficiency or severe illness may trigger strong psychological feelings of helplessness (Adler, 1907/1917b). However, **organ inferiority** need not necessarily result in psychopathology. "Imperfect organs offer many handicaps, but these handicaps are by no means an inescapable fate. If the mind . . . trains hard to overcome the difficulties, the individual may very well succeed in being as successful as those who were originally less burdened" (Adler, 1931/1958, p. 35). One such example is that of Demosthenes, discussed previously. Or a child born with an eye imperfection may strive diligently to see (or hear, or touch) as much as possible and become unusually perceptive. But since organ inferiorities do present substantial difficulties, and since the concerned parents are likely to make matters worse by pampering the invalid, the most likely result is a destructive inferiority complex:

> Children who come into the world with organ inferiorities become involved at an early age in a bitter struggle for existence which results only too often in the strangulation of their social feelings. Instead of interesting themselves in an adjustment to their fellows, they are continually preoccupied with themselves, and with the impression which they make on others. (Adler, 1927/1957, p. 65; see also Adler, 1920/1973, p. 81.)

For example, one boy retained his childish soprano and lack of body hair into his late teens. He reacted so adversely to these organic inferiorities that, as an adult, he constantly tried to prove that he was supremely important. As could be expected, this lack of social interest ultimately resulted in the destruction of his marriage (Adler, 1927/1957, p. 72).

Birth Order

Adler attributes considerable importance to a child's position in the family constellation. "Above all we must rid ourselves of the superstition that the situation within the family is the same for each individual child" (Adler, 1933/1964b, p. 229; see also Adler, 1927/1957, pp. 123–129; 1931/1958, pp. 144–155; 1929/1964a, pp. 96–120; 1933/1964b, pp. 228–241; 1929/1969, pp. 12–13, 90–94).

The oldest child enjoys a temporary period as the unchallenged center of attention. This pleasurable position is likely to involve considerable pampering, however, and it comes to an abrupt and shocking end with the arrival of a younger sibling. Unless the parents carefully prepare the oldest child to cooperate with the newcomer, and continue to provide sufficient care and attention after the second child is born, this painful dethronement may well precipitate an inferiority complex. For this reason, first-born children are the ones most likely to become neurotics, criminals, alcoholics, and perverts (Adler, 1931/1958, pp. 144, 147–148). They also tend to express the fragility of their childhood superiority by having frequent dreams of falling. And they are likely to opt for conservatism, as by following in the footsteps of the parent's occupation. "Oldest children . . . often . . . have the feeling that those in power should remain in power. It is only an accident that they have lost their power, and they have great admiration for it" (Adler, 1929/1969, p. 91).

The middle child experiences pressure from both sides. "He behaves as if he were in a race, as if someone were a step or two in front and he had to hurry to get ahead of him" (Adler, 1931/1958, p. 148). Second-born children therefore tend to be competitive or even revolutionary, prefer to see power change hands, and have dreams of racing. They are the ones most likely to develop favorably, however, since they never occupy the pathogenic position of pampered only child.

The youngest child, confronted with the presence of several older rivals, tends to be highly ambitious. Such children often follow a unique path, as by becoming the only musician or merchant in a family of scientists (or vice versa). Although they avoid the trauma of being dethroned by a younger sibling, their position as the baby of the family makes them the most likely target of pampering. Therefore "the second largest proportion of problem children comes from among the youngest" (Adler, 1931/1958, p. 151; see also Adler, 1927/1957, pp. 123–125; 1929/1969, pp. 91–92). For example, they may turn away from the challenge of competition and resort to chronic evasions, excuses, and laziness.

Other positions in the family constellation may also present formidable problems. Only children are usually pampered, develop unrealistic expectations of always being the center of attention, and form exaggerated opinions of their own importance. They also tend to be timid and dependent, since parents who refuse to have more than one child are typically anxious or neurotic and cannot help communicating their fears to the child. The only child often appears fairly normal while within the context of the family, with pathology and a lack of social interest first becoming evident upon entering school and having to share attention with others. (See Adler, 1927/1957, p. 127; 1931/1958, pp. 152–153; 1933/1964b, p. 230.)

The sole boy in a family with several girls, or a lone girl with numerous brothers, is also in a difficult position. Such children may rebel against the prevailing family atmosphere by overemphasizing the characteristics of their own sex, or they may succumb and become too much like the opposite sex. The third of three boys or girls often faces a most unenviable situation, namely parents who longed to have a child of the opposite sex. And a first-born boy who is closely followed by a girl will probably suffer the embarrassment of being overtaken in maturity by his younger sister, since the girl's physiological development proceeds at a faster rate. (See Adler, 1931/1958, pp. 149–150, 153–154; 1933/1964b, p. 241; 1929/1969, pp. 92–94.)

Adler emphasizes that the effect of birth order is only a tendency, not a certainty. "Individual psychology is opposed to fixed rules" (Adler, 1933/

1964b, p. 233). A bright first-born child may defeat a younger one and not suffer much of a dethronement, a weak-minded oldest child may lose the mantle of leadership to the second-born, or parents may pamper a sickly middle child even more than the youngest or oldest. A child born many years after the older sibling(s) will be treated more like an only child—or, if there are younger siblings as well, an oldest child. Individual psychology advises that the best distance between the births of siblings is approximately three years, by which time the older child has matured sufficiently to accept the parents' preparation for an addition to the family. (See Adler, 1931/1958, pp. 149, 153; 1929/1969, p. 92.)

Character Typology: The Style of Life

The child responds to its feelings of inferiority, birth order, and the parents' behaviors by developing its own **style of life.** (See for example Adler, 1927/1957, pp. 17, 133ff; 1931/1958, pp. 12, 200; 1929/1969, pp. 38–47, 83.) The style of life, which is well formed by age four or five, consists of the child's chosen life goals and the methods used to strive for them. It also includes the perceptions, memories, and other mental activities that are shaped by these objectives.

For example, a pampered child may select the goal of receiving constant attention, try to achieve this aim through sulking and temper tantrums, and perceive others only as potential providers. Or a neglected child may choose the goal of revenge, become hostile and dominating, and cast others in the role of probable enemies. Or a child given proper care and attention may adopt a style of life that ultimately includes a useful and rewarding occupation, a mutually satisfying marriage, and a sincere and sympathetic concern for other people. As always in individual psychology, however, the determinants of personality are primarily subjective. "It is not the child's experiences which dictate his actions; it is the conclusions which he draws from his experiences" (Adler, 1931/1958, p. 123). If a child who is actually pampered should feel neglected, the probable result will be a neglected life style (and vice versa).

Adler emphasizes that every style of life, and therefore every personality, is at least somewhat unique. He concedes that some mention of personality types is probably unavoidable, since our language lacks sufficient precision to describe all of the subtle nuances that distinguish one human being from another. Nevertheless, "we do not consider human beings types, because every human being has an individual style of life. Just as one cannot find two leaves of a tree absolutely identical, so one cannot find two human beings absolutely alike" (Adler, 1929/1969, p. 40; see also Adler, 1933/1964b, pp. 27, 127, 148). According to Adler, there are three valuable sources of information about a person's life style: character traits, physical movements, and early recollections.

Character Traits. Undesirable traits of character indicate that the striving for superiority has become selfish and distorted. Some of these characteristics take an aggressive form, as with vain and arrogant individuals who try to appear more important than everyone else. "No other vice is so well designed to stunt the free development of a human being as that personal vanity which forces an individual to approach every event and every fellow with the query: 'What do I get out of this?' " (Adler, 1927/1957, p. 155). Since arrogance clashes so sharply with social interest, it often takes on the more acceptable guise of keen ambition, false modesty, or a pedantic emphasis on meticulous accuracy and detail.

Other aggressive character traits include jealousy, avarice, and hostility. Jealousy is often expressed by blaming other people for one's own errors and shortcomings, criticizing others excessively, and by a constant fear of being neglected. The avaricious individual rejects social interest and "builds a wall around himself [so as] to be secure in the possession of his wretched treasures." Powerful hostility poisons one's interpersonal relationships, and may well lead to a criminal style of life. These misguided forms of striving for superiority are little more than "cheap tricks by which anyone can imagine whatever he wishes to believe. . . . [and] whereby the personal evaluation is raised at the cost of another's misfortune" (Adler, 1927/1957, pp. 168, 181, 212; see also pp. 155–184).

Some undesirable character traits are primarily nonaggressive. Shy people seek superiority and safety by turning away from society, and excluding close friendships. Some individuals try to gain pity and attention by appearing helpless and anxious, while other life styles are characterized by laziness and pessimism. Thus a student who becomes extremely nervous about a forthcoming examination and refuses to prepare for it has a ready-made excuse in case of failure, and avoids the real pain and disappointment of trying hard but still not succeeding. (See Adler, 1927/1957, pp. 167, 185–198; 1935/1979b, 1935/1979j).

For the most part, a healthy style of life avoids the "cheap tricks" discussed above. It is typified by such desirable character traits and emotions as social interest, cheerfulness, optimism, sympathy, and genuine modesty:

> One can sense that [cheerful people] are good human beings. . . . Joy is an affect which most clearly bridges the distance from man to man. Joy does not brook isolation. . . . Sympathy is the purest expression of the social feeling. Whenever we find sympathy in a human being, we can in general be sure that his social feeling is mature. . . . (Adler, 1927/1957, pp. 199, 216–217.)

Physical Movements. The style of life is also revealed by a person's physical movements. For example, constantly leaning on something may reflect dependency and the need for protection. Persistent slouching, trembling, remaining a great distance from other people, avoiding eye contact, or even sleeping in a fetal position may indicate cowardly tendencies. Or enuresis may be a way of soliciting attention, as we have seen. Thus postures always have their meanings and organs their "dialect," though such tentative clues should be checked against other evidence about the individual before any firm conclusions are drawn. (See Adler, 1931/1958, pp. 28, 34, 41, 72; 1933/1964b, p. 208; 1929/1969, pp. 35, 58–62.)

Early Recollections. The best way to identify someone's style of life is by obtaining the person's **early recollections** of infancy and childhood. Even inaccurate memories provide vital information, for any distortion in our recollections is deliberately (if unconsciously) designed to serve our chosen life goals. Thus memories can never be contrary to one's style of life (Adler, 1931/1958, p. 74).

The earliest recollection is particularly noteworthy because it reveals the person's fundamental view of life. For example, a man's first memory was that of being held in the arms of his mother, only to be summarily deposited on the ground so that she could pick up his younger brother. His adult life style involved persistent fears that others would be preferred to him, including extreme and unwarranted jealousy of his fiancée. Another man, whose style of life was marked by fear and discouragement, recalled falling out of his baby carriage. A woman, still unmarried at age thirty-five, remembered being led down in fear into the cellar to meet a boy cousin. Another woman, who developed a life style that emphasized the distrust of others and the fear of being held back by them, recalled that her parents prevented her from attending school until her younger sister was old enough to accompany her. And the earliest recollection of a person leading a pampered style of life was that of taking a trip with the mother. (See Adler, 1927/1957, pp. 30–31; 1931/1958, pp. 19–22, 71–92; 1929/1964a, pp. 121–127; 1929/1969, pp. 44, 48–57.)

In each of these cases, Adler attributes the sufferer's problems to the faulty goals chosen in childhood and maintained in adulthood, rather than to the childhood incidents themselves. Here again, however, such fragmentary evidence should be verified against other expressions of personality (Adler, 1931/1958, p. 76).

FURTHER APPLICATIONS
OF INDIVIDUAL PSYCHOLOGY

Dream Interpretation

To Adler, dreams are merely another expression of a person's style of life. Conscious and unconscious are united in the service of one's life goals, rather than in opposition (as Freud would have it), so there is no need for a special key to the unconscious. In fact, the information provided by dreams can usually be obtained just as well from early recollections, character traits, and physical movements.

Adler also rejects Freud's contention that virtually all dreams deal with sexuality and wish-fulfillment; this is typical only in the case of the pampered individual. And he denies that dreams are the guardians of sleep, arguing instead that they often awaken the dreamer. However, he does agree with Jung and Freud that dream theory cannot be reduced to a handbook of procedures or symbols. Every dream is at least somewhat unique because every style of life is different, so a first-hand knowledge of the dreamer is essential for accurate interpretation. "One individual's symbols are never the same as another's" (Adler, 1931/1958, p. 108; see also Adler, 1927/1957, pp. 92–100; 1931/1958, pp. 93–119; 1929/1964a, pp. 162–168; 1933/1964b, pp. 242–268; 1929/1969, pp. 69–79; 1931/1979e, pp. 214–216).

If dreams do not reveal some unique and all-important message, their existence must be justified in some other way. Accordingly, Adler holds that virtually every dream serves the purpose of evasion and self-deception. That is, an individual who protects a misguided life style during waking hours by relegating undesirable character traits to the unconscious usually supports this objective by having appropriate dreams. These dreams create an emotional state that remains present upon awakening, and furthers those life goals that the dreamer does not want to understand.

For example, suppose that a student's style of life is highlighted by cowardice and pessimism. On the eve of an important examination, the student may dream of being chased by assailants (or fighting a difficult and losing war, or standing at the edge of a terrifying abyss). This dream enables the student to awaken with feelings of discouragement and fright, emotions that support the secret goal of delaying or avoiding the examination. The student may therefore take an unexcused absence on the grounds that failure was inevitable anyway, without having to recognize the distasteful personality characteristics that underlie this behavior. Or a person who wishes to escape an unpleasant task without incurring blame may dream of failing to catch a train, or of being paralyzed (Adler, 1931/1958, pp. 103–104, 108; 1929/1969, p. 70).

However, this line of theorizing leads Adler to the dubious conclusion that some people do not dream. Included in this category are neurotic individuals who have reached a point of psychological equilibrium and do not wish to change, and healthy people whose realistic life style involves little need for self-deception and irrational emotional support. "Very courageous people dream rarely, for they deal adequately with their situation in the daytime. . . . [I myself] stopped dreaming as soon as [I] realized what dreaming meant" (Adler, 1929/1964a, p. 164; 1929/1969, p. 76). Modern research has essentially refuted this contention by showing that everyone does dream, and people differ only in the extent to which they forget their dreams. (See for example Foulkes, 1966.) Furthermore, Adler seems unable to maintain his conviction that all dreams are unique. He concludes that dreams of falling, "certainly the commonest of all," indicate that the dreamer enjoys the delusion of being superior to other people but feels in imminent danger of losing this exaggerated sense of worth. Dreams of flying reflect a desire to become superior to others, and are often accompanied by warning dreams of falling. And dreams about being improperly clothed express the fear of being caught in an error or imperfection (Adler, 1933/1964b, pp. 263–264).

Adler does make a relevant point about the teleological nature of dreams. To the extent that dreams do prepare one for the future, it is not at all surprising (or prophetic, or "synchronistic") if they correspond with subsequent reality. For example, the ancient Greek poet Simonides dreamed that the ghost of a dead man warned him against taking an impending sea journey. He therefore remained home and, surely enough, the ship sank in a storm and all hands were lost. Adler argues that Simonides probably did not want to make the trip at all, since he knew that travel by sea was quite dangerous in those days, and the dream created the emotional state that made it easier for him to follow his true (but unconscious) wishes. The actual disaster was hardly unusual, if somewhat coincidental, and merely indicated that Simonides's assessment of the situation was an accurate one (Adler, 1927/1957, pp. 98–99; 1929/1969, pp. 73–74).

Psychopathology

Adler's criterion of mental health is similar to Freud's, except that he adds the all-important category of social interest. The well-adjusted individual fulfills his or her obligations to present and future generations by successfully meeting the three major challenges of life: society, occupation, and love and marriage. (See Adler, 1931/1958, pp. 239–286; 1933/1964b, pp. 13–14, 42–67, 147, 167; 1929/1969, pp. 87, 100.)

Perfection is most unlikely, however, and even relatively healthy people possess some undesirable and selfish character traits. Thus Adler agrees with Freud and Jung that psychopathology represents a difference in degree, rather than in kind:

> The psychic anomalies, complexes, [and] mistakes which are found in nervous diseases are fundamentally not different in structure from the activity of normal individuals. The same elements, the same premises, the same movements are under consideration. The sole difference is that in the nervous patient they appear more marked, and are more easily recognized. . . . [Therefore,] we can learn from the abnormal cases. . . . (Adler, 1927/1957, p. 16.)

For the most part, however, Adler's theoretical differences with psychoanalysis and analytical psychology are reflected in his approach to abnormal behavior. Freud and Jung attribute psychopathology to a divisive intrapsychic conflict, but Adler's holistic and unified conception of personality rules out this possibility. Nor can Adler accept Freud's idea of pathogenic fixations and regressions, since he argues that all behavior is primarily designed to serve some future purpose. *"Neurosis is a creative act, and not a reversion to infantile and atavistic forms"* (Adler, 1933/1964b, p. 131; see also pp. 158, 172). Instead, Adler explains psychopathology as the result of a misguided style of life. "I should compare [the pathological individual] to a man who tries to put a horse's collar on from the tail end. It is not a sin, but it is a mistaken method" (Adler, 1931/1958, p. 272).

Origins and Characteristics of Neurosis. Neurosis invariably originates in the first few years of life. Influenced by such factors as pampering, neglect, birth order, and organ inferiorities, the child selects a style of life that suffers from two serious flaws: a pronounced deficiency in social interest, and exaggerated feelings of inadequacy. To make matters worse, this mistaken image of self and the world inevitably clashes with harsh reality. For example, instead of receiving constant attention, pampered children find that they are expected to be cooperative and helpful—behaviors for which they have not been prepared. This unwelcome discovery acts like an "electric shock," intensifying the child's pathology and resulting in the two conditions typical of all neuroses: an inferiority complex and a lack of social interest. (See Adler, 1912/1917a; 1931/1958, pp. 8, 49; 1930/1963; 1933/1964b, pp. 30–31, 106–107, 162–180; 1932/1979i, p. 91.)

Since the neurotic feels unable to cope with the inevitable difficulties and conflicts of everyday life, he or she resorts to the various "cheap tricks" (or "arrangements") for gaining superiority. These include relegating unpleasant character traits to the unconscious, evading responsibilities, attempting only the easiest of tasks, imposing unrealistic demands or expectations on other people, blaming errors or shortcomings on others, avoiding others, anxiety, or any other strategy that appears to turn the apparently inescapable inferiority into an advantage. Such people often become "virtuosos of neurosis, continually extending their repertory, . . . [dropping] symptoms with astonishing rapidity and [taking] on new ones without a moment's hesitation" (Adler, 1931/1958, p. 63). Even the suffering caused by their pathology is preferable to the crushing defeat of trying but failing to achieve superiority more legitimately, and having to recognize their deep-rooted inferiority complex; and so they arrange to have their neurosis justify their evasive style of life. Thus they may argue: "If I weren't so lazy, I could be president." "If not for my stage fright, I'd be a great thespian." "Yes, I need to get a job (or work harder at school, or make more friends), but I can't because I'm too troubled." The implicit or explicit "yes" in these examples reflects the remnants of social interest that still exist, while the more powerful "but" rejects this guideline in favor of making excuses and maintaining the pathological life style. "The easy way of escape is neurosis" (Adler, 1931/1958, p. 186; see also Adler, 1927/1957, pp. 133–218; 1933/1964b, pp. 111, 164, 171–174; 1929/1969, pp. 105–106; 1936/1979d, pp. 239–247; 1936/1979f, pp. 102–105).

Inferiority and Superiority Complexes. One common form of neurotic evasion is to disguise the painful inferiority complex behind a **superiority complex,** which involves the deluded belief of being better than other people. "It is as if a man feared that he was too small, and walked on tiptoe to make himself seem larger" (Adler, 1931/1958, p. 50; see also Adler, 1933/1964b, pp. 40, 120–122, 173; 1929/1969, pp. 27–37, 84, 104). Alternatively, a superiority complex may be more or less hidden by manifestations of weakness.

Whereas useful feelings of superiority are reflected in socially interested abilities and achievements, the superiority complex is only another cheap trick. It establishes grandiose and unreachable goals that cannot help but result in failure, intensifying the underlying inferiority complex and leading to still greater reliance on the pathological sense of superiority. "It is as if [the sufferer] were in a trap: the more he struggles, the worse his position becomes" (Adler, 1931/1958, p. 146; see also p. 51).

Masculine Protest. Adler also attributes psychopathology to inequalities in the structure of society, notably those concerning men and women. In contrast to Freud, who argues that a woman's place is in the home, Adler emphasizes her right to pursue an occupation. He criticizes those boys or men who contend that helping with the housework is beneath their dignity. He regards motherhood as perhaps the highest of all forms of social interest. And he relates many unhappy marriages and personal miseries to the myth of sexual inequality:

> All our institutions, our traditional attitudes, our laws, our morals, our customs, give evidence of the fact that they are determined and maintained by privileged males for the glory of male domination. . . . Nobody can bear a position of inferiority without anger and disgust. . . . That woman must be submissive is . . . [a] superstition. . . . (Adler, 1927/1957, pp. 104, 202–203; 1931/1958, p. 267. See also Adler, 1927/1957, pp. 111–122; 1931/1958, pp. 122, 241; 1929/1969, pp. 66–68.)

When a girl perceives that men are favored, she may misguidedly reject her feminine role and develop the form of superiority complex known as the **masculine protest.** This may include dressing like a boy, insisting upon being called by a boy's name, pursuing more masculine forms of work or play, or eventually turning away from heterosexual relationships and marriage. Or a boy may dress and behave like a girl because he doubts his ability to fulfill his supposedly superior role, thus also falling victim to society's irrational stereotype of males. (See Adler, 1931/1958, pp. 191–192, 276; 1929/1964a, pp. 41–45; 1929/1969, p. 68.)

Adler strongly condemns all varieties of social prejudice. He warns that serious inequalities can lead not only to inferiority complexes and psychopathology, but also to such disastrous attempts at compensation as war and revolution.

Varieties of Psychopathology. Although Adler draws some distinctions among the various kinds of psychopathology, he views them all in much the same way: as serious errors in living, designed to achieve an easy and distorted form of superiority.

For example, depression is an attempt to dominate others through inferiority and complaints. Suicide conveys the reproaches and revenge of a pampered individual who expects too much of life, and is therefore easily disappointed. Compulsions may also express hostility, as when an unhappily married woman successfully irritated her husband (and proclaimed her own virtue) by spending entire days washing her home. Phobias may serve to control others, as with the woman whose fear of going out into the street alone required her errant husband to remain safely by her side. Paranoid behavior preserves an exaggerated self-image by blaming one's errors and defeats on other people or things. Hallucinations and alcoholism enable an individual to boast about being a great drunkard or having unique visions, as well as furnishing a ready excuse for not trying to achieve superiority in more socially interested ways. Homosexuality represents the masculine protest of a fearful individual not properly prepared for heterosexuality during childhood, rather than an innate biological condition. Finally, as we have seen, such psychosomatic symptoms as headaches may support a pampered style of life. (See Adler, 1927/1957, pp. 55, 115–119; 1931/1958, pp. 53, 90, 274–275; 1933/1964b, p. 186; 1929/1969, pp. 47, 117–118; 1920/1973, pp. 51–58, 184–207, 255–260; 1931/1979c).

Adler is unique among the early personality theorists in devoting considerable attention to the problem of criminality. He regards the criminal as a coward hiding behind a weapon, thereby gaining the only triumph that the underlying inferiority complex will allow. There are no "born criminals," but only individuals who have developed a superiority complex so lacking in social interest that they have little or no concern about the consequences of their behavior. "Crime is [another] one of the easy escapes before the problems of life, and especially before the problem of economics and livelihood. . . . Crime is a coward's imitation of heroism" (Adler, 1931/1958, pp. 185, 205; see also Adler, 1931/1958, pp. 197–238; 1933/1964b, pp. 136–140; 1929/1969, pp. 8–9, 37, 107). Adler strongly opposes the use of corporal punishment, arguing that this only increases the criminal's feelings of resentment and bravery. Unlike Freud, who preferred not to have criminals as patients, Adler willingly accepted them as suitable for psychotherapy—and achieved some significant successes.

Psychosis. Adler attempts to cast psychosis in much the same framework as neurosis. He depicts the psychotic as extremely fearful and almost devoid of social interest, lacking even the minimal "yes" of the neurotic and attending only to the evasive "but." This picture may have some validity, but interpreting psychosis only as a more severe expression of discouragement and inferiority would appear to be a serious oversimplification. (See for example Arieti, 1974; Fromm-Reichmann, 1950; Searles, 1965; Sullivan, 1962/1974.)

Psychotherapy

Theoretical Foundation. Whereas psychoanalysis aims toward a strength-ened ego, and Jungian therapy seeks to unite the various intrapsychic op-posites, Adler's objective is to promote a new and more socially interested style of life. To this end, the painful inferiority complex that underlies the patient's selfish and cowardly mode of striving for superiority must be brought to light. "The important thing is to decrease the patient's feeling of inferiority. . . . The method of individual psychology—we have no hesita-tion in confessing it—begins and ends with the problem of inferiority" (Adler, 1929/1969, pp. 45, 131).

The all–important inferiority complex is unearthed by examining the patient's misguided life goals, and the childhood factors that influenced their selection. The patient thus makes an important and encouraging discovery: that his or her problems result from a deficiency in training and social interest that can be overcome with effort, rather than from an incorrigible lack of ability. The therapist facilitates this reeducation by serving as a model of healthy behavior, and by providing a ready target for the patient's fledg-ling attempts at social interest and cooperation.

Therapeutic Procedures. A healthy style of life cannot be imposed by coer-cion, punishment, criticism, blame, or authoritarian displays of omniscience by the therapist, for such tactics are all too likely to reinforce the patient's exaggerated sense of inferiority. Instead, individual psychology attempts to awaken the patient's latent social interest through encouragement and equal-ity. Therapist and patient sit face to face, in chairs of similar size and style. The therapist takes appropriate opportunities to be informal and good-humored, while the patient is free to get up and move around the consultation room. Except for the early stages, the patient attends therapy only once or twice per week. And Adlerian therapy rarely lasts more than a single year, with every correctly handled case expected to show at least partial improvement by the third month of treatment. (See Adler, 1929/1964a, pp. 73, 88; 1933/1964b, pp. 286–298; Ellenberger, 1970, p. 620.)

Like Freud and Jung, Adler is not overly fond of hypnosis. (See Adler, 1929/1969, p. 79.) His techniques for unveiling a disordered life style in-clude an analysis of the patient's dreams, early recollections, and bodily movements, as well as certain key questions and verbal ploys. Often he would ask a patient: "If you did not have this ailment, what would you do?" The answer usually pointed to the life task that the patient feared, such as getting married (or divorced), making more friends, becoming more ag-gressive, finding a job, and so forth.

Adlerian therapy normally consists of three stages. The first task of the therapist is to establish rapport and gain an understanding of the patient's problems and style of life, which may take from one day to two weeks. Early recollections, dream interpretation, and "The Question" play a prominent role during this period. In the second stage of treatment, the therapist gently and gradually helps the patient become aware of his or her pathogenic life style, secret goals, and inferiority complex. Here the therapist must proceed fairly slowly, for the patient is actually (albeit unconsciously) much more afraid of being proved worthless than of remaining ill. The third and final stage occurs if and when the patient decides to expend considerable effort and adopt a new and more cooperative life style, with the therapist providing both emotional support and appropriate factual information. (See Adler, 1929/1964a, p. 73; 1933/1964b, pp. 165–166; Ellenberger, 1970, pp. 620–621.)

In any of these stages, the therapist may elect to use carefully chosen verbal stratagems. Thus Adler might advise a depressed patient, "Only do what is agreeable to you." If the patient replied that nothing was agreeable, Adler would counter with: "Then at least do not exert yourself to do what is disagreeable." These tactics are designed to reduce the patient's hostility and desperation, and therefore the possibility of suicide. Or Adler might tell a patient, "You can be cured in two weeks if you follow this prescription, but it is difficult and I do not know if you can." At this point he would look doubtfully at the patient, whose curiosity and attention were thereby ensured. Then he would add, "Try to think every day how you can please someone." If the patient objected that this task was impossible, or that others were not worth pleasing, Adler would respond with his "strongest move in the game" by saying: "Then you will need four weeks. . . . Perhaps you had better train yourself a little thus: do not actually *do* anything to please someone else, but just think out how you *could* do it." If this also proved to be too difficult, Adler would suggest that at least the patient could please him by paying particular attention to dreams or early recollections and reporting them at the next session. (See Adler, 1931/1958, pp. 256–260; 1929/1964a, pp. 8, 25–26.)

Adler also developed therapeutic techniques for use with children, including treating them in the natural setting of the home and seeing the parents during at least part of each session, and he is credited as one of the originators of family and group psychotherapy. However, he stresses that prevention (in the form of proper parenting and training of children) is far easier and less costly than waiting to cure a full-fledged psychopathology. (See Adler, 1933/1964b, pp. 153, 299–304; Mosak & Dreikurs, 1973, p. 37.)

Resistance and Transference. For the most part, Adler rejects Freud's approach to resistance and transference. Patients do attempt to resist and frustrate their therapist; but this only reflects their inability to cooperate and lack of courage to change, and/or a protest against the therapist's misguided and threatening aura of superiority. Adler regards transference as the result of a therapeutic error, one that triggers a pampered individual's childish wishes for excessive love and overindulgence. He even concludes that transference should not occur in properly conducted Adlerian therapy, a contention that appears rather dubious in view of the established tendency to generalize behavior from one authority figure (such as a parent) to another (such as a therapist or teacher). (See Adler, 1931/1958, p. 72; 1933/1964b, pp. 288–290; 1920/1973, pp. 46, 144–152.)

Ideally, the patient in Adlerian therapy learns to replace major errors in living with less harmful small ones. This involves turning away from the pursuit of a fantastic, imaginary, and selfish superiority, and seeking through courage and cooperation those rewards that the real world can indeed provide.

Work

Adler expressed keen interest in both the sociological and psychological aspects of work, becoming a strong early advocate of humane working conditions and protective labor legislation. He also advises that the choice of vocation should be consistent with one's style of life and early recollections. For example, a neurotic patient's first memory was that of watching through a window while others worked. This man ultimately found satisfaction as an art dealer, a career which enabled him to continue the desired role of onlooker in a socially interested way. Similarly, the earliest recollection of many doctors is that of a death in the family. (See Adler, 1931/1958, pp. 79, 85–86; 1929/1969, p. 52.)

Pathology is indicated when a person tries to escape an unhappy marriage or social life by becoming a "workaholic," or when a pampered individual is unable to accept a subordinate position. The inability to select any prospective occupation during childhood and adolescence also indicates the existence of an underlying inferiority complex, and all schoolchildren should be required to write compositions on "what I want to be later in life" to make them confront this important issue (Adler, 1931/1958, pp. 239–251; 1929/1969, pp. 100–101, 121).

Religion

Adler's approach to religion is one of relative indifference. He regards "loving thy neighbor" and preferring giving to receiving as desirable expressions of social interest, and characterizes Freud's cynical rejection of these precepts as the selfishness of the pampered individual. But he stops well short of embracing Jung's belief in an innate religious need, preferring to stress the practical reasons for cooperating with other human beings. Thus the primary purpose of religion is to sanctify communal living and increase social interest, God symbolizes the goal of self-perfection to which we all aspire, and reincarnation symbolizes the belief that one can indeed change a disordered life style to a healthy one.

Adler does regard the Bible as a wonderful work, but warns that teaching its contents to undiscerning children may lead to fanciful and misguided strivings for superiority. For example, a psychotic may misuse religion by developing a superiority complex that involves hearing the voice of God. Or a neurotic may choose to evade the difficulties of present-day living by concentrating on an existence in the hereafter. (See Adler, 1927/1957, pp. 81, 169, 172–174, 187, 207–208; 1931/1958, pp. 60–61, 253; 1933/1979g, p. 33; 1933/1979h.)

Education

Adler devotes considerable attention to the effect of education on personality development. School provides the acid test of a child's readiness for social living, and offers perhaps the only possibility for correcting whatever parental errors may have occurred. "The school is the prolonged arm of the family. . . . It would be our hope, if all the teachers could be [well] trained, that psychologists would become unnecessary" (Adler, 1931/1958, pp. 156, 180; see also Adler, 1927/1957, p. 222). A truly competent teacher would be able to understand a child's disordered life style in a very short time, and take appropriate corrective action. Unfortunately, few educators are sufficiently well prepared to help each child's personality develop along proper lines. And classes are often far too large, making it difficult for even a skilled teacher to do much more than merely impart the prescribed curriculum.

Adler sees the educator as facing the difficult and challenging task of preparing the child for cooperation, and inculcating the social ideals that enable civilization to continue. "The true purpose of a school is to build character . . . [and] the principal aim of education is social adjustment" (Adler, 1929/1969, pp. 82, 103). The role of heredity in character formation must be minimized by the teacher, lest the child evade responsibility (and the educator excuse poor teaching) by blaming failures on genetic factors. "It may ease [the teacher's] position if he can say to a child, 'You have no gift for mathematics,' but it can do nothing but discourage the child" (Adler, 1931/1958, p. 170). The importance of individual ambition and competition must also be downplayed, so as to avoid inhibiting the development of social interest.

To Adler, coeducation is an excellent way to prepare the child for subsequent cooperation between the sexes. On the other hand, special classes for "slow" children should be avoided because they are all too likely to produce discouragement and inferiority complexes. "Where there are brilliant children in a class, the progress of the whole class can be accelerated and heightened; and it is unfair to the other members to deprive them of such a stimulus" (Adler, 1931/1958, p. 171). It is also a serious error to teach the nature of evil too quickly, for this can intensify the development of a pessimistic style of life. As always, Adler regards encouragement and love as far superior to punishment and threats. Finally, teachers must be sufficiently well-adjusted and experienced in living so that they serve as effective models of social interest, treat their pupils with respect, and genuinely wish to contribute to the welfare of humankind. (See Adler, 1927/1957, pp. 31, 122,

137; 1931/1958, pp. 59, 156–181; 1933/1964, p. 55; 1929/1969, pp. 80–94.)

Literature

Individual psychology has relatively little to say about literature and the arts. Fairy tales may express the desirability of optimism and hope, or they may convey appropriate lessons about the perils of vanity and selfishness. Shakespeare's *Hamlet* portrays the futility of seeking superiority through murder. And the Bible contains various indications of the importance of birth order, as when Jacob (a second-born) or Joseph (a youngest child) develops a strong sense of rivalry and competitiveness. (See Adler, 1927/1957, pp. 81, 126, 172; 1931/1958, pp. 148–151; 1933/1964b, pp. 106, 236–240; 1929/1969, p. 91.)

EVALUATION

Criticisms and Controversies

Oversimplification. Parsimony is an appealing attribute of any theory, and Adler's practical prescriptions for living offer a refreshing contrast to Jung's abstruse metaphysics. However, it would seem that individual psychology seriously underestimates the complexity of human behavior.

Adler frequently implies that the choice of a disordered life style is often triggered by just one or two key incidents in childhood, such as the birth of a sibling or single organ inferiority. This contention is rejected by most modern psychologists, who have found that the causes of psychopathology are more likely to be overdetermined. Adler's holistic model also leads to some questionable implications, particularly a conception of anxiety that is at best a partial truth and at worst astonishingly naive. Neurotic anxiety typically involves intense suffering and personal anguish, and it is hardly likely that this emotional turmoil serves merely as a manipulative attempt to gain the attention of other people. Adler also has difficulty reconciling holism with his acceptance of some sort of unconscious. He rejects the psychoanalytic construct of repression, for this would imply the existence of a subdivided personality. Yet he fails to suggest any alternative way in which undesirable thoughts and emotions are eliminated from one's awareness, other than deliberate intention.

For these reasons, and because of its emphasis on the self-determined aspects of personality, Adlerian theory has been criticized for overemphasizing the capacities of the ego. Psychoanalysts would argue that even if a patient consciously selects new life goals, works diligently to achieve them, and reduces the secondary gains that result from the pathology, these efforts may still be undermined by powerful opposing unconscious forces that have not been sufficiently analyzed:

> The ego is [in Adler's doctrine] playing the ludicrous part of the clown in a circus who by his gestures tries to convince the audience that every change in the circus ring is being carried out under his orders. But only the youngest of the spectators are deceived by him. (Freud, 1914/1967, p. 53.)

Adler's refusal to allow for any hereditary influences on personality seems particularly dubious, as does his contention that transference should not occur in properly conducted psychotherapy. Finally, Adler's claims that healthy people do not dream and that psychosis is simply a more severe version of neurotic discouragement must be regarded as major errors.

Overemphasis on Social Factors. Adler defines personality wholly in terms of interpersonal relationships. Social psychology is indeed an important discipline, but it represents only one facet of modern psychology. Most current theorists would agree that personality exists, and can be studied, in isolation from other human beings.

Overemphasis on Inferiority. Yet another source of controversy concerns Adler's contention that every neurotic, criminal, and psychotic suffers from an inferiority complex. Exaggerated feelings of powerlessness do play an important role in many disorders, but it is questionable whether the myriad varieties of psychopathology can be explained in similar terms. Adler even detects an underlying inferiority complex from such behaviors as sleeping in a curved position and craving strong black coffee, leading one to conclude that "inferiority" is to individual psychology as "sexuality" is to psychoanalysis—a construct so pervasive as to be in danger of losing its explanatory power.

Excessive Optimism. Whereas Freudian theory has been taken to task for being overly pessimistic, individual psychology may well err toward the opposite extreme. If human beings do not have any inherent destructive or illicit traits, and do possess the innate potential for social interest, how then can one explain the occurrence of so many wars, murders, crimes, and other human-made disasters? The psychological and sociological influences on growing children would have to be virulent indeed to bring about so much carnage. For this reason, the less sanguine views of Freud or Jung impress some observers as more consistent with the evidence of recorded history.

Other Criticisms. Adler's work (like that of Freud and Jung) reflects a total lack of statistical analysis, with all of his conclusions being justified solely by his own subjective observations. Nor does he establish any quantitative guidelines for distinguishing between substantial but healthy parental love and pampering, or between minimal but sufficient nurturing and neglect. In addition, Adler fails to maintain his professed belief in the uniqueness of every human personality. He makes frequent mention of character traits, types of dreams, and other similarities among human beings, and he implies that pampered (or neglected) children have life styles that include many common factors.

Like Freud, Adler is vulnerable to criticism by those theorists who believe that personality continues to develop after the fifth or sixth year of life. While modern psychologists have often failed to give Adler sufficient credit, he himself seems to overlook his significant agreements with Jung. Self-realization, teleology, pathology as a sick system of social relationships, and the idea that people establish much of the meaning of their own lives are all prominent in analytical psychology as well, yet there is almost no reference to Jung in Adler's writings. Finally, although Adler's literary style is clear and understandable, it is also extremely repetitious. Many of his books consist of unedited lectures, and suffer from an irritating verbosity and lack of organization.

Empirical Research

A considerable amount of research has been devoted to the effects of birth order on various personality and behavioral variables. These variables range from fundamental concerns like success in school and work, peer relationships, dependency, self-confidence, and competitiveness to more singular issues like hypnotizability and handedness. The results have led some to conclude that there is a tendency for first-born children to be more prominently successful, more dependent, more fearful, more readily influenced by authority, and less likely to participate in dangerous sports; that later-born children tend to be more readily accepted by their peers; and that, contrary to Adlerian expectations, middle children may well represent the highest proportion of delinquents. (A review of this extensive literature is beyond the scope of the present text. The interested reader is referred to such surveys and listings as American Psychological Association [1984, p. 269], Hetherington & McIntyre [1975, pp. 124–125], and Manaster & Corsini [1982, pp. 81–88, 288–300].)

These research findings are by no means clear-cut, however. Numerous studies indicate that birth order is of significant importance, yet there are others that do not. Some studies support Adlerian hypotheses, while others do not. One possible reason for the conflicting results is the problem stated previously: a person's nominal birth order need not correspond to the psychological position in the family constellation. For example, consider the second of two children born six years apart. This child is likely to be treated differently from the younger of two siblings whose birth is separated by only a single year—i.e., more like an only or oldest child. Perhaps the most warranted conclusion is that a child's position in the family constellation probably does have some general influence on its personality (as Adler contended), but that specific predictions about a given person's behavior based solely on this one rather unsophisticated variable are unlikely to be very accurate.

Other research concerning Adlerian theory has dealt with such issues as developing written scales to measure social interest and life styles, the relationship of social interest to cooperative behavior and to interpersonal attraction, and the relationship of early recollections to vocational choice and to college achievement. Much of this research has been published in the *Journal of Individual Psychology* and tends to support Adlerian theory, with some exceptions. (See for example Manaster & Corsini, 1982, pp. 288–300.)

With regard to psychotherapy, a well-known study by Fiedler (1950) compared the procedures used by psychoanalytic, nondirective, and Adlerian therapists. He found that skilled therapists tended to employ similar methods regardless of their professed theoretical orientation, and had significantly more in common than did expert and inexpert therapists of the same psychological persuasion. Several studies have proclaimed positive results for Adlerian therapy, including those of Heine (1953) and Shlien, Mosak, and Dreikurs (1962). Also available is a collection of papers dealing with the use of early recollections in psychotherapy (Olson, 1979).

Contributions

The most striking indication of Adler's importance is the extent to which his ideas are reflected in more recent psychological theories. For example:

Adlerian Theory and Practice	*Modern Counterparts*
Emphasis on social aspects of personality	Socially oriented theories of Fromm, Horney, Sullivan
The neurotic tendency to rule, lean on, or avoid others (see especially Adler, 1935/1979j, p. 68); the misguided quest for personal aggrandizement	Horney's three neurotic solutions, "glory" syndrome
The individual who "guards his wretched treasures"	Fromm's hoarding orientation
The child who determines to prove a villain, or who rejects tenderness	Sullivan's malevolent transformation
Emphasis on the ego	Ego psychology (Erikson and others)
Importance of personal choices and courage in living	"Being-in-the-world," and facing the fear of nothingness, in existential psychology

Adlerian Theory and Practice	*Modern Counterparts*
Importance of self-esteem, of empathy and equality in therapy, and of blaming a child's deeds rather than its personality	Rogers's emphasis on self-esteem, empathy, genuineness, and unconditional positive regard
Use of physical movements to reveal a style of life	"Body language"; Allport's study of expressive behavior
Equality of women	Feminist movement
Self-created style of life	Kelly's psychology of personal constructs; Allport's proprium
Social interest	One criterion of mental health in Maslow's theory
Treating children in the company of their parents; establishing child guidance centers in Vienna	Family therapy; group therapy; community psychiatry
Face-to-face interviews in psychotherapy; patient attending only once or twice per week	Many modern forms of psychotherapy

Adler was the first psychologist to stress the social determinants of personality, an important factor that may well have been underestimated by Freud and Jung. He was also unique among the early personality theorists in devoting considerable attention to criminality, education, and child guidance. Unlike Freud, Adler studied children directly; and his practical suggestions for child rearing contain much of value.

Like Jung, Adler helped emphasize the importance of teleology, purposive decisions, and self-selected goals as determinants of human behavior. The terms *inferiority complex* and *life style* have become part of our everyday language. The importance of exaggerated inferiority feelings in many varieties of psychopathology, and of healthy and distorted attempts at compensation, are also widely accepted by modern psychologists. The relative simplicity of individual psychology offers advantages as well as disadvantages, for at least some patients may find it easier to grasp and utilize Adler's teachings than those of Freud or Jung. Finally, like Freud, Adler allows us no evasions or rationalizations. We ourselves are primarily responsible for our behavior, rather than heredity or some unconscious force.

Despite these significant contributions, Adler has often been denied his due credit. A noteworthy (and typical) example concerns the Swiss psychoanalyst who once publicly declared that Adler's ideas were pure nonsense, only to spend the next few moments characterizing a patient as suffering from grievous inferiority feelings compensated by arrogant manners. Similarly, an obituary in the venerable *New York Times* credited Jung as the discoverer of the inferiority complex. (See Ellenberger, 1970, pp. 641–648.) While Adler's influence on modern psychological thought has been subtle and unobtrusive, there are those who would argue that it has also been extensive—so much so that despite his significant errors, virtually all current psychologists must be regarded as at least to some extent Adlerians.

Suggested Reading

In view of the repetitiousness of Adler's writings, any one of his more recent works should serve as a sufficient introduction. These include *Understanding Human Nature* (1927/1957), *The Science of Living* (1929/1969), *Problems of Neurosis* (1929/1964a), *What Life Should Mean to You* (1931/1958), and *Social Interest: A Challenge to Mankind* (1933/1964b). Among the useful secondary sources are those by Bottome (1957), Dinkmeyer et al. (1987), Ellenberger (1970), Furtmüller (1946/1979), Manaster and Corsini (1982), and Orgler (1963/1972).

■ SUMMARY

1. THE BASIC NATURE OF HUMAN BEINGS. *Social Interest:* Every human being has the innate potential for social interest, which involves a sense of kinship with all humanity. Social interest establishes the guidelines for proper personality development, and enables people to tame the superior forces of nature through cooperation. It is only a tendency, however, and it is all too possible to reject one's inherent social interest and become pathologically self-centered. According to Adler, heredity exerts virtually no influence on personality. *Life Goals and Teleology:* People select their own life goals and the means of achieving them, usually by the fifth year of life. It is these future aspirations, rather than prior causes, that primarily determine one's personality. *Feelings of Inferiority and the Striving for Superiority:* The primary goal underlying all human behavior is that of striving for superiority (or self-perfection), which is motivated in large part by the child's feelings of inferiority relative to the formidable environment. Healthy strivings for superiority are guided by social interest, whereas pathological strivings are characterized by selfishness and a lack of concern for others. Everyone grows up with at least some feelings of inferiority, which may well serve to stimulate beneficial and socially interested forms of compensation. If the child is exposed to pathogenic conditions, however, the feelings of helplessness may become overwhelming and result in a shattering inferiority complex.

2. THE STRUCTURE OF PERSONALITY. Adler's holistic theory treats personality as an indivisible unity, and he makes no assumptions about its structure. He does accept the existence of some sort of unconscious, which includes those unpleasant character traits that one does not wish to understand. However, he views con-

scious and unconscious as united in the service of the individual's chosen life goals, rather than as engaged in conflict.

3. THE DEVELOPMENT OF PERSONALITY. The mother serves as the child's bridge to social life, and proper maternal contact is greatly responsible for the child's development of social interest. The father's role is to provide feelings of courage and self-reliance, and to stress the need for choosing an appropriate occupation. *Pathogenic Developmental Factors:* Personality development is strongly influenced by such potentially pathogenic factors as pampering, neglect, ridicule, and organ inferiorities. It is not so much the child's experiences that determine personality, however, but rather the conclusions drawn from them. *Birth Order:* The child's position in the family constellation is significantly related to personality development. *The Style of Life:* The child responds to the various developmental factors by choosing its major life goals and the means of achieving them. These goals and methods, and the corresponding mental activities (perceptions, memories), are known as the style of life. According to Adler, every life style is unique and is reflected by a person's character traits, physical movements, and early recollections.

4. FURTHER APPLICATIONS. *Dream Interpretation:* Dreams are merely another expression of an individual's style of life. They create a self-deceptive emotional state that remains present upon awakening, and furthers the chosen life goals. *Psychopathology:* Psychopathology always involves an underlying inferiority complex and lack of courage, and misguided attempts to compensate by striving for superiority in ways that are severely lacking in social interest. Common symptoms include the superiority complex and masculine protest. Abnormality invariably originates in childhood, when the various pathogenic factors lead to the selection of a misguided style of life. *Psychotherapy:* The goal of Adlerian psychotherapy is to facilitate the development of a new and more socially interested style of life. To this end, the painful inferiority complex that underlies the patient's selfish and distorted mode of striving for superiority must be brought to light. The therapist is encouraging rather than stern or omniscient, and strives to appear as an equal. *Other Applications:* Adler expressed a keen interest in work, education, and child guidance, preferring prevention (in the form of proper training of children) to cure. He took a relatively indifferent stance with regard to religion and literature.

5. EVALUATION. Individual psychology has been criticized for presenting an oversimplified picture of human behavior, placing too much emphasis on social factors and inferiority feelings, expressing an inordinate optimism about human nature, and relying on an unscientific methodology. On the other hand, many of Adler's ideas have been incorporated into the theories of modern psychologists (including most of the theories discussed in the following pages). He is credited with calling attention to the social determinants of personality, originating the well-known terms *inferiority complex* and *life style,* championing the equality of the sexes, emphasizing the role of self-selected goals on personality development, helping to originate group and family therapy, and furthering our understanding of criminality and child rearing.

STUDY QUESTIONS

1. How might Adler's personality and life experiences have influenced his belief that: (a) conscious and unconscious act together to serve a person's chosen goals, and personality is *not* torn by painful inner conflicts? (b) introspectiveness is one of the characteristics with which the "weakling" seeks to defend himself? (c) inherited instincts are a "superstition" and have no effect on personality? (d) unhealthy character traits (such as arrogance and shyness) and anxiety are "cheap tricks" for avoiding life's difficulties, while neurosis is also an "easy way of escape?"

2. Do you agree or disagree with each of Adler's ideas in the preceding question? Why?

3. Adler argues that social interest should establish the guidelines for proper personality development, rather than a superego. (a) Is this idea likely to be readily accepted in this country? (b) Give a real-life example of a person, or group of people, whose striving for superiority is lacking in social interest and harmful to society.

4. Give an example from real life, or from a well-known novel, to show how "fictions" can strongly influence behavior.

5. "Timidity, introspectiveness, [and] distrust [are] characteristics and traits with which the weakling seeks to defend himself." (a) Why does a person become what Adler calls a "weakling?" (b) What positive reasons might Adler have had for using a derogatory term like "weakling?" (c) How do traits such as timidity and distrust enable a person to defend himself or herself, and from what?

6. Give an example from your own life, from the life of someone you know well, or from fiction to illustrate: (a) how pampering leads to a painful inferiority complex. (b) how neglect leads to a painful inferiority complex. (c) how an inferiority complex may be concealed beneath a superiority complex. (d) a person who rejects social interest by "[building] a wall around himself [so as] to be secure in the possession of his wretched treasures." (e) a healthy style of life.

7. What is the difference between praising or blaming a child's success or failure and blaming the personality of the child? Illustrate with an example.

8. Based on your own life, do you agree with Adler's conclusions regarding birth order? Why or why not?

9. What unconscious wish of Adler's own might have been fulfilled by his belief that he "stopped dreaming as soon as [I] realized what dreaming meant?"

10. How would Adler interpret the following dreams? (a) The "train" dream described in Chapter 2, study question 12. (b) A young man dreams that he is flying in a jet plane. Suddenly the plane goes into a steep descent and seems about to crash. He is afraid, but wakes up before it hits the ground.

11. Give two examples to illustrate views of Adler that were more equalitarian than the corresponding views of Freud.

12. Adler argues that brilliant children should be placed in regular school classes, and *not* in gifted classes, so they can accelerate the progress of less capable students. (a) What personal reasons might Adler have had for such a belief? (b) Do you agree? Why or why not?

PART II

CLINICALLY-BASED NEOANALYTIC THEORIES

PROLOGUE

Foundations are meant to be built upon. The personality theorists whose work we examined in Part I knew that they had made many important contributions to our knowledge. In fact, each of them had fond hopes of leaving a permanent legacy to humanity: a set of constructs so complete as to need no more than minor tinkering. But this was not to be. Because of the criticisms and controversies discussed previously, some of the more creative and insightful psychologists who followed found that major revisions were necessary in order to explain their clinical findings.

The theories that we will examine in Part II are based on the work of Freud, Jung, and Adler. Here you will encounter four famous names: Karen Horney, Erich Fromm, Harry Stack Sullivan, and Erik Erikson. As in Part I, all of these theories are derived from clinical observation rather than from empirical research.

The Libido Controversy

Horney, Fromm, and Sullivan emphatically reject Freud's emphasis on the biological aspects of personality. In none of these theories will you find the construct of libido, or any kind of psychic energy. Given the cogent criticisms of the libidinal model, this would seem to be an important step in the right direction. Yet as we will see, this "heresy" provoked much the same sort of wrath from the psychoanalytic establishment as befell Jung and Adler.

Instead, Horney, Fromm, and Sullivan follow an Adlerian course by stressing the social determinants of personality. Yet each of these theorists also regards Adler's views as an oversimplification, and opts for alternatives that often lead in a distinctly Freudian direction. Despite this common underlying theme, the ideas and constructs of these three psychologists differ in many important respects—so much so that they, too, engaged in highly acrimonious feuds about the relative merits of their theories.

Erik Erikson also devotes considerable attention to the social determinants of personality. However, he seeks to rectify the main faults of Freudian theory while retaining the controversial construct of libido. This approach enabled Erikson to remain on good terms with the psychoanalytic establishment, and it has evoked considerable praise from some psychologists. Yet the desirability of trying to reconcile the metaphysical libidinal model with a greatly increased emphasis on social factors, and the success of Erikson's attempted merger, are open to question (as we will see).

Preview: Horney, Fromm, Sullivan, and Erikson

Karen Horney is highly optimistic about human nature. She argues that pathological behavior occurs only if our innate tendency toward positive growth is blocked by external social forces, such as pathogenic parenting. Unlike Adler, however, Horney concludes that neurosis is characterized by extremely painful and divisive inner conflicts. Thus you will find in Horney's theory a far more insightful explanation of anxiety. You will see how those who suffer from such anxiety seek relief by moving toward, against, or away from people. You will learn about the problem of self-contempt, and the dangers of trying to conceal these threatening feelings by building up an idealized self-image and by embarking on the neurotic quest for glory. You will encounter the "tyranny of the should." You will see how the torments of neurosis can be resolved through appropriate psychotherapy. And you will examine Horney's views on female sexuality, which differ markedly from those of Freud.

In Erich Fromm's theory, you will see how the need for others and for a sense of identity can conflict with selfishness and the desire to depend on a powerful protector. You will learn about the art of loving, which involves a relationship to all humanity rather than to a single individual. You will focus on the mechanisms that we use to defend ourselves against painful feelings of isolation in a frightening world, and to escape from the threatening state of freedom. You will see how psychopathology is caused by pathogenic relationships with the parents, and with society as well. You will discover an important approach to dream interpretation quite different from that of Freud. And you will find that Fromm's psychological prescriptions are more concerned with society than with the individual. Although a noted psychotherapist, he prefers to focus on sweeping suggestions for social change and reform.

Harry Stack Sullivan's theory is the most conceptually difficult in this section, yet also one of the most important. Here you will find an emphasis on the need for others combined with a Freudian model of drive reduction. You will encounter an extensive discussion of anxiety, and the role that it plays in both normal personality development and psychopathology. You will see how personality is organized according to the self system, and how we defend against unpleasant information about ourselves through selective inattention. Sullivan is among those theorists who argue that personality continues to develop through adolescence and beyond; so here you will examine seven stages of personality development, ranging from infancy through adulthood. And you will see how Sullivan applies his theory to psychopathology, notably obsessive-compulsive neurosis and schizophrenia, and to psychotherapy.

Erik Erikson's theory is best known for the "Eight Ages of Man," a series of eight stages through which every human personality presumably develops. These stages cover the entire life span and represent a recasting of Freud's psychosexual stages in social terms, with each stage highlighted by a developmental crisis that represents a crucial turning point for better or worse. You will see how Erikson tries to reconcile Freud's stress on biological, libidinal processes with an emphasis on the social determinants of personality. You will find that Erikson is much more optimistic about the relationship between the individual and society than Freud, and that he seeks to extend the scope of psychoanalysis by emphasizing the healthy and adaptive aspects of personality. You will learn about the occurrence of the identity crisis during adolescence. You will discover that different cultures exert different effects on personality. And you will examine Erikson's approach to dream interpretation, psychopathology, psychotherapy, religion, and psychohistory.

5

KAREN HORNEY
Neurosis and
Human Growth

For Karen Horney, as for Jung and Adler, scientific debate involved some painful moments of professional rejection. Horney's time of trial occurred in 1941, when it became apparent that her approach to psychoanalysis deviated significantly from the traditional Freudian concepts being taught at the New York Psychoanalytic Institute. A vociferous staff meeting ensued, culminating in a vote tantamount to her dismissal. (See Rubins, 1978, pp. 239–240.) In the dead silence of an unforgettably dramatic moment, she arose and slowly walked out with her head held high—and went on to establish her own important theory, one that combines an Adlerian emphasis on social factors and an optimistic view of human nature with the intrapsychic conflict model that Adler specifically rejected.

BIOGRAPHICAL SKETCH

Karen Danielsen Horney was born in a small village (Blankenese) near Hamburg, Germany on September 16, 1885. Her father was a tall, dashing, sternly religious sea captain—and a pronounced male chauvinist, who frequently clashed with her proud, beautiful, intelligent, and free-thinking mother. Her family also included an older brother, several stepsisters and stepbrothers from her father's two other marriages, and a notably warm and loving stepgrandmother. (See Kelman, 1967; Rubins, 1978.)

Karen decided at age twelve to study medicine, and persevered toward this goal despite initial opposition from her father. She was an excellent student throughout her academic career, ultimately receiving her medical doctorate degree from the University of Berlin in 1915. Karen was originally trained as a psychoanalyst, joining the Berlin Psychoanalytic Institute in 1918 and beginning her own private practice one year later, but she ultimately split with Freudian circles over the issue of female sexuality. Karen married Oskar Horney, a businessman, on October 31, 1909. The union produced three daughters; but a near-fatal bout with meningitis and the runaway postwar inflation in Germany left the formerly successful Oskar bankrupt, morose, and withdrawn. The Horneys separated during the 1920s, and were formally divorced in 1939.

Like Freud, Horney has been described as a complicated person who elicited various contradictory impressions: strong and weak, empathic and aloof, motherly and uncaring, dominating and self-effacing, leader and follower, fair and petty. She was a private person who confided primarily in a diary until her early twenties, kept much of herself hidden from public view, and formed few intimate relationships. Yet she also possessed an evident charisma, capable of captivating individuals and large audiences alike. (See Rubins, 1978, pp. xii–xiv, 1–4, 239, 302, 338.)

Horney emigrated from Berlin to Chicago in 1932, and joined the New York Psychoanalytic Institute in 1934. However, the differences between her theoretical views and those of orthodox psychoanalysis soon led to acrimonious disputes. Her students' final theses were summarily rejected by the institute because they did not conform sufficiently to standard doctrine, and she herself suffered the aforementioned fate of being formally disqualified as an instructor and training analyst in 1941. Horney thereupon resigned from the New York Psychoanalytic Society and founded her own American Institute for Psychoanalysis, whose members for a time included Fromm and Sullivan. (They, too, ultimately resigned to pursue their own theoretical predilections.) From then on her writings (in all, six books) were destined to be stubbornly ignored by strict Freudians, but to gain widespread recognition and acclaim elsewhere. Karen Horney died in New York of cancer on December 4, 1952.

THE BASIC NATURE OF HUMAN BEINGS

Horney (pronounced "horn-eye") agrees with Adler that our inherent nature is constructive, and that personality is strongly influenced by cultural factors. We all strive to develop our unique potentialities, and pathological behavior occurs only if this innate force toward positive growth (**self-realization**) is blocked by external, social forces:

> Freud's pessimism as regards neuroses and their treatment arose from the depths of his disbelief in human goodness and human growth. Man, he postulated, is doomed to suffer or to destroy. The instincts which drive him can only be controlled, or at best "sublimated." My own belief is that man has the capacity as well as the desire to develop his potentialities and become a decent human being, and that these deteriorate if his relationship to others and hence to himself is, and continues to be, disturbed. (Horney, 1945, p. 19. See also Horney, 1942, p. 175.)

THE STRUCTURE AND DEVELOPMENT OF PERSONALITY

Horney shares Freud's views about psychic determinism and the importance of unconscious processes, with emphasis on powerful and actively maintained repressions. Thus she rejects Adler's holism in favor of the contention that neurotics are "torn by inner conflicts. . . . Every neurotic . . . is at war with himself" (Horney, 1945, p. 11; 1950, p. 112; see also Horney, 1939, pp. 20–22; 1945, p. 56). However, Horney has little to say about the structure and development of personality. "I do not consider it feasible to localize neurotic conflicts in a schematic way, as Freud does" (Horney, 1939, p. 191). She prefers to devote the majority of her writings to three major applications: neurosis, psychotherapy, and female sexuality.

FURTHER APPLICATIONS
OF HORNEYAN THEORY

Neurosis

Horney agrees with Freud, Jung, and Adler that neurosis is always a matter of degree. However, she cautions that neurotic conflicts are strikingly different from those of more normal people. The latter can be entirely conscious and offer relatively feasible choices, as when one must decide between spending some time in quiet contemplation or being with a friend. Neurotic conflicts are considerably more severe, involve a dilemma that appears to be insoluble, and are always deeply repressed, so that "only slight bubbles of the battle raging within reach the surface" (Horney, 1945, p. 30; see also Horney, 1945, p. 27; 1950, p. 37).

Basic Anxiety. Horney argues that neurosis results from disturbed interpersonal relationships during childhood, rather than from some instinctual or libidinal drive. In particular, the parents may behave in such pathogenic ways as domination, overprotectiveness, overindulgence, humiliation and derision, brutality, perfectionism, hypocrisy, inconsistency, partiality to other siblings, blind adoration, or neglect:

> [These errors] all boil down to the fact that the people in the environment are too wrapped up in their own neuroses to be able to love the child, or even to conceive of him as the particular individual he is; their attitudes toward him are determined by their own neurotic needs and responses. . . . As a result, the child does not develop a feeling of belonging, of "we," but instead a profound insecurity and vague apprehensiveness, for which I use the term *basic anxiety*. (Horney, 1950, p. 18; see also Horney, 1945, p. 41; 1950, pp. 202, 221–222, 275.)

This feeling of being alone in an unfriendly and frightening world prevents the child from relating to others in a normal way. "His first attempts to relate himself to others are determined not by his real feelings, but by strategic necessities. He cannot simply like or dislike, trust or distrust, express his wishes or protest against those of others, but has automatically to devise ways to cope with people and to manipulate them with minimum damage to himself" (Horney, 1945, p. 219). The result is that the healthy quest for self-realization is replaced by an all-out drive for safety. According to Horney, this is accomplished by exaggerating one of the three main characteristics of basic anxiety: helplessness, aggressiveness, or detachment. The neurotic solution of helplessness results in excessive desires for protection (**moving toward people**), the aggressive orientation leads to pronounced wishes for domination and mastery (**moving against people**), and the detached solution emphasizes the avoidance of others (**moving away from people**).

Each of these three neurotic solutions is compulsive and inflexible. Unlike the healthy individual, who can move toward, against, or away from people as circumstances dictate, the neurotic rarely deviates from the chosen orientation. At times, however, exceptions do occur. The two orientations that are consciously underemphasized remain powerful in the unconscious, and they occasionally break through to influence overt behavior.

Moving Toward People. The neurotic who overemphasizes moving toward people seeks safety through the protection and affection of others (Horney, 1945, pp. 48–62; 1950, pp. 214–258). The sufferer tries to convert the apparently inescapable inner weaknesses into an advantage by acting as though others "must love me, protect me, forgive me, not desert me, *because* I am so weak and helpless." This feeling of "poor little me" is rather like "Cinderella bereft of her fairy godmother" (Horney, 1945, p. 53).

Such individuals consciously profess a sincere interest in others and readily comply with their wishes, while repressing their own hostility, selfishness, and healthy self-assertiveness. "Where [this] patient errs is in claiming that all his frantic beating about for affection and approval is genuine, while in reality the genuine portion is heavily overshadowed by his insatiable urge to feel safe. . . . In decided contrast to the apparent oversolicitude, we come upon a [strongly repressed] callous lack of interest in others, attitudes of defiance, unconscious parasitic or exploiting tendencies, propensities to control and manipulate others, [and] relentless needs to excel or to enjoy vindictive triumphs" (Horney, 1945, pp. 51, 55).

Moving Against People. The neurotic who exaggerates moving against people regards life as a Darwinian jungle where only the fittest survive, and seeks security through mastery and domination (Horney, 1945, pp. 63–72; 1950, pp. 187–213). Whereas the compliant individual tends to misperceive others as potential providers, and often comes to grief as a result, the aggressive neurotic regards most people as hostile and hypocritical. Like the neglected child in Adlerian theory, the sufferer is likely to conclude that genuine affection is unattainable or even nonexistent. Therefore, "any situation or relationship is looked at from the standpoint of 'what can I get out of it?' . . . To [this individual] ruthlessness is strength, lack of consideration for others [is] honesty, and a callous pursuit of one's own ends [is] realism" (Horney, 1945, pp. 65, 68).

This attempted solution to the problem of basic anxiety conflicts with the sufferer's pathological sense of helplessness and healthy need for love, with these characteristics being repressed because they threaten the basic orientation. Therefore, aggressive neurotics may also behave sadistically toward those who are weak and helpless because such behaviors provide a highly unpleasant reminder of what they most dislike about themselves. Horney (1945, pp. 115–130) refers to this as the **externalization** of unconscious material, a construct essentially similar to Freudian and Jungian projection (and one that occurs in all forms of neurosis).

Moving Away from People. The neurotic who emphasizes moving away from people tries to resolve basic anxiety, and obtain security, by avoiding contact with others (Horney, 1945, pp. 73–95; 1950, pp. 259–290). Such individuals strive to become completely self-sufficient, and never allow anyone or anything to become indispensable. They achieve this dubious goal by unconsciously limiting their needs, numbing their emotions, and overestimating their uniqueness and superiority. Thus the detached neurotic may refuse to ask for directions when in a strange city, resort to fantasies of glorious success, or consistently behave in offhand and distant ways. "He is like a person in a hotel room who rarely removes the 'Do Not Disturb' sign from his door" (Horney, 1945, p. 76).

Even the physical pressure of a tight collar or necktie, a shelf full of books as yet unread, the need to be on time for an appointment or to give a birthday gift, or the slightest possibility of an emotional attachment to another person may be seen as an unwarranted and hostile intrusion from the outside world. Yet no person is an island, and so the detached orientation causes severe conflicts with the sufferer's (repressed) pathological wishes for extreme dependency and healthy desires for affiliation and love.

The Idealized Image. In most instances, the despised aspects of the neurotic's personality and the painful inner conflicts are further concealed through the development of a glorious **idealized image** (Horney, 1945, pp. 96–114, 139; 1950, pp. 22–23, 86–109). This flattering self-concept may involve the misguided belief that a manipulative compliant neurotic is so unselfish, helpful, and attractive as to deserve undying love. Or an inherently weak and selfish aggressive neurotic may think that he is vastly superior, friendly, and fair. Or a detached neurotic who actually craves affection may believe that she is so capable and self-sufficient as never to need anything from anyone.

Despite its implausible aspects, the idealized image appears quite realistic to its creator. The result is a vicious circle. The idealized image establishes unattainable standards that either bring about eventual defeat, or cause the sufferer to shrink from the acid test of reality. Such failures increase the hate for and alienation from the fallible true self (**self-contempt**), and this intensifies the inner conflicts and the dependence on the idealized image. (See Figure 5.1.) Furthermore, as this image becomes increasingly unrealistic, the individual feels compelled to bolster it with still greater

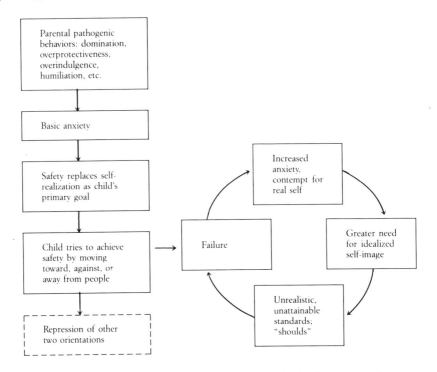

FIGURE 5.1. The vicious circle produced by the idealized image, and its antecedents.

triumphs (**glory**). Thus, like Faust, neurotics "sell their soul to the devil" by abandoning their real desires and capacities in favor of the idealized image; and like Frankenstein, their creation arises to destroy them. (See Horney, 1945, p. 98; 1950, pp. 39, 118, 154–155, 367.)

Horney originally argued that inner conflicts occur only between contradictory neurotic tendencies, such as powerful hostility and an intense desire for dependency. However, she ultimately concluded that "a neurotic conflict can operate either between two neurotic forces, or between healthy and neurotic ones" (Horney, 1950, p. 113; See also Horney, 1945, pp. 37–38). In fact, the battle between the pathological idealized image and the healthy but apparently weak and humiliating real self proves to be the most serious inner conflict of all:

> Roughly speaking, a person builds up an idealized image of himself because he cannot tolerate himself as he actually is. The image apparently counteracts this calamity; but having placed himself on a pedestal, he can tolerate his real self still less and starts to rage against it, to despise himself and to chafe under the yoke of his own unattainable demands upon himself. He wavers then between self-adoration and self-contempt, between his idealized image and his despised image, with no solid middle ground to fall back on. . . . [Neurotic] pride and self-hate belong inseparably together; they are two expressions of

■ CAPSULE SUMMARY
Some Important Horneyan Terminology

Analyst (psychoanalyst)	One who practices either Freudian psychoanalysis or some modified version, such as Horney's.
Basic anxiety	The feeling of being alone in an unfriendly and threatening world. Includes three major components: helplessness, aggressiveness, and detachment. Results from pathogenic social influences during childhood, notably parental errors, and is therefore wholly evitable.
Claims	Unrealistic demands and expectations that the neurotic typically imposes on others, believing them to be justified because they accord with the idealized image.
Externalization	Experiencing intrapsychic processes as occurring outside oneself; essentially similar to projection.
Glory	A feeling of grandiose triumph that fulfills the demands of the idealized image. The neurotic quest for glory is compulsive, insatiable, inflexible, and often unenjoyable. Even achieving the chosen goals is likely to be disappointing, because the idealized image does not reflect one's true values and preferences.
Idealized image (neurotic pride)	A grandiose misconception of one's personality, created to conceal both the despised real self and the painful inner conflicts.
Moving against people (mastery)	A neurotic attempt to gain security through domination and the exploitation of others, while repressing pathological feelings of helplessness and detachment and healthy needs for love. One of the three neurotic solutions to the problem of basic anxiety.
Moving away from people (detachment)	A neurotic attempt to gain security through the avoidance of others, while repressing pathological feelings of helplessness and aggressiveness and healthy needs for affiliation and love. One of the three neurotic solutions to the problem of basic anxiety.
Moving toward people (compliance, morbid dependency)	A neurotic attempt to gain security through protection by others, while repressing pathological feelings of aggressiveness and detachment and healthy self-assertiveness. One of the three neurotic solutions to the problem of basic anxiety.
Neurotic conflict (inner conflict)	A severe intrapsychic rift between contradictory neurotic trends, or between healthy and neurotic drives. Horney originally regarded the former as primary, but ultimately concluded that the latter is more important.
Self-contempt (self-hate)	Intense hate for one's true capacities and wishes, because they are so discrepant from the glorious idealized image.

continued

173

Self-realization	Developing one's true innate capacities, feelings, and interests. Actualizing one's "real self," in contrast to neurosis which involves the attempt to actualize the idealized image.
Shoulds	Inner commands to conform to the dictates of the idealized image. May be externalized, and thus appear (incorrectly) to be imposed from without.

one process. . . . *The godlike [self] is bound to hate his actual [self]. . . . [and this is] the central inner conflict.* (Horney, 1945, p. 112; 1950, pp. 109, 112, 368.)

Thus Horney agrees with Adler that unconscious feelings of weakness are often obscured by a grandiose front, and that powerful unconscious arrogance is frequently concealed behind excessive modesty. But while the idealized image bears some similarity to the superiority complex, it masks unconscious trends that are opposing and divisive rather than unified and holistic. "It was Adler's great contribution to realize the importance for neuroses of drives for power and superiority. Adler, however . . . stayed too much on the surface of the problems involved. . . . [and] is in fact a good example of how even a productive insight into psychological processes can become sterile if pursued onesidedly and without foundation in the basic discoveries of Freud" (Horney, 1950, p. 372; 1937, p. x; see also Horney, 1937, pp. 186–187; 1939, p. 268).

Horney's theory of intrapsychic opposites also differs from that of Jung, for she conceives of introversion as neurotic (i.e., detachment) rather than as an innate and healthy tendency. And she departs from Freud by attributing self-contempt to the impossibility of satisfying the self-created idealized image, rather than to the introjected parental standards of the superego. (See Horney, 1945, pp. 39–40, 71–72, 167–168; 1950, pp. 373–374.)

Claims, Shoulds, and Defense Mechanisms. The idealized image often converts normal wishes into unrealistic **claims,** which supposedly entitle the sufferer to triumph and glory. Thus a lonely individual who unconsciously feels unlovable may make no effort to alleviate this painful situation, expecting instead to be invited out by someone else. A neurotic with repressed feelings of professional incompetence may claim to deserve a better job without earning it, or even asking for it. Or patients may expect great gains from psychotherapy without having to work at their problems (Horney, 1950, pp. 40–63).

The neurotic is also driven by self-imposed inner commands that aim toward the actualization of the idealized image, which Horney calls "the tyranny of the **should.**" This may involve the belief that one should be world famous, totally unselfish, able to avoid ever making a mistake, the winner of every game that one plays, always courageous and never afraid, a perfect lover or spouse, and so forth. Alternatively, the shoulds may be externalized and appear (incorrectly) to be imposed from without. Unlike the Freudian superego, shoulds are always a neurotic force "exactly like political tyranny in a police state" (Horney, 1950, p. 67; see also pp. 64–85, 123).

Such defense mechanisms as isolation, externalization, rationalization, fantasy, and an insistence on always being right may also be used to conceal inner conflicts and restore a sense of personal unity. Cynicism can also serve a defensive purpose by depicting all moral values as false, thereby precluding the painful task of examining just what it is that one really believes in. (See Horney, 1939, pp. 25–31; 1945, pp. 131–140; 1950, pp. 32–37, 46.)

Other Neurotic Symptoms. Although the neurotic's painful inner conflicts are repressed, the disturbance is reflected in various indirect ways. These may include: (1) Inconsistent behavior, as with the person who professes a strong desire for marriage or friendship yet shrinks from contacts with others. (2) Extreme hopelessness, caused by the impossibility of satisfying the idealized image and despair about ever being oneself. (3) Fears of changing, of suffering ridicule and humiliation from others, or of becoming insane. (4) Pronounced indecisiveness, with the conflict between one's dimly perceived true wishes and shoulds turning even minor decisions into major and exhausting crises. (5) Ineffectual behavior, somewhat like a car being driven with one foot on the gas pedal and the other foot on the brake. (6) A cramped and restricted life, with the sufferer preferring not to try at all rather than to strive for something important and fail. (7) Shyness, wherein a desire for contact with others conflicts with a fear of rejection. (8) Vindictive or sadistic behavior. (9) Considerable fatigue, which results from wasting substantial energy on the severe inner turmoil. Like Adler, Horney regards the Oedipus complex as a culturally determined neurotic symptom that results from improper child rearing, rather than as a universal phenomenon. (See Horney, 1937, pp. 79–84, 159–161; 1939, pp. 79–87; 1945, pp. 143–190; 1950, p. 143.)

Neurosis and Work. Not surprisingly, neurosis is often reflected in disturbances at work. The idealized image may drive the sufferer to slave away at unpleasant jobs because they appear to offer the prospect of future triumphs. But achieving these goals invariably proves to be empty and unrewarding, since they do not represent the individual's real wishes and preferences, whereupon the compulsive and misdirected striving for glory begins all over again.

Neurotics who move toward people usually undervalue themselves and their work, feel overwhelmed by difficult tasks, dislike working independently, and avoid the threatening possibility of superiority by modestly minimizing their successes. Neurotics who move against people usually overvalue themselves and their work, are perfectionistic, deny their errors, seek vindictive triumphs over others, and have great difficulty giving credit where it is due. Neurotics who move away from people usually prefer to work alone, and have an intense dislike for schedules and taking orders. (See Horney, 1950, pp. 309–332.)

Neurosis and Literature. According to Horney, various aspects of neurosis have been symbolically expressed in literature. George Orwell's *Nineteen Eighty-Four* depicts the tyranny of the should in externalized form, as a rigid and demoralizing dictatorship. Kafka's *The Trial* reflects the confusion and (externalized) self-condemnation experienced by the neurotic. Stevenson's *Dr. Jekyll and Mr. Hyde* illustrates the conflict between a glorified saintly self and a despised evil self, with the sufferer's true personality lost in the struggle. And Captain Ahab in Melville's *Moby Dick* offers an excellent example of the neurotic need for vindictive triumphs (Horney, 1950, pp. 129–130, 152, 189–190, 198).

Psychotherapy

Theoretical Foundation. The goal of Horneyan psychotherapy is to unearth and resolve the patient's deeply repressed inner conflicts, thereby freeing the innate constructive forces to grow and develop. (See Horney, 1939, pp. 276–305; 1945, pp. 217–243; 1950, pp. 333–365.)

Ideally, the patient makes two important discoveries about the supposedly lifesaving neurotic solution: it actually produces increased frustration and self–contempt, and it conceals powerful opposing forces. Thus the neurotic who moves toward people discovers the hostility and selfishness that underlie the excessive desires to please others. The neurotic who moves against people becomes aware of the formerly repressed feelings of helplessness. And the neurotic who moves away from people recognizes the strong dependency needs that conflict with the desire to avoid others. The patient must then probe still further and bring the central inner conflict to light, relinquish the alluring idealized image, and opt for the substantial satisfaction (and challenge) of actualizing the real self. To be effective, however, such insights must be apprehended emotionally as well as intellectually:

> [The patient's] knowledge of himself must not remain an intellectual knowledge, though it may start this way, but must become an *emotional experience.* . . . The mere intellectual realization is in the strict sense of the word no "realization" at all: it does not become real to him; it does not become his personal property; it does not take roots in him. (Horney, 1950, pp. 342–343.)

Therapeutic Procedures. Like Freud, Horney makes extensive use of free association and interpretation. However, she is more active than the typical Freudian analyst. Also, like Adler, Horney seeks to change the patient's chosen objectives and expectations. For example, in response to a patient's profound feelings of hopelessness, the therapist may say: "Of course the situation is difficult. But what makes it hopeless is your own attitude toward it. If you would consider changing your claims on life, there would be no need to feel hopeless" (Horney, 1945, p. 186). Or, if a patient suffers from powerful fears of being humiliated by others, the therapist may interpret this as an externalization of intense self-contempt. "It is a long and hard lesson for anybody to learn that others can neither hurt nor establish self-esteem" (Horney, 1950, p. 136).

Most patients enter therapy with a highly misguided goal: they want to improve the consequences of their neurotic behavior without having to change, or even recognize, their inner conflicts. Therefore, the therapist must first help the patient discover that the predominant neurotic solution is actually self-defeating, while postponing any interpretation of the repressed opposing tendencies. Horney warns that it is useless to propose major changes in behavior while the patient still insists on moving toward, against, or away from people. The repressed intrapsychic conflicts, the harmful nature of the idealized image, and the true underlying desires begin to surface (and can be analyzed) only after the patient has to some extent abandoned the chosen neurotic solution. (See Horney, 1945, pp. 19, 61–62, 220–224.)

Unlike Freud, Horney often encourages patients to engage in self-analysis. She warns that an overemphasis on childhood events may encourage patients to wallow in the memory of past hurts instead of working at the arduous task of therapy. And Horney stresses that therapy must not ignore the patient's moral values, for inner stability can only be achieved if one has an established set of moral principles. (See Horney, 1942; 1945, pp. 8, 14, 127–129, 177–178; 1950, p. 351.)

Dream Interpretation. As with the other theorists discussed thus far, Horney derives valuable information from a patient's dreams. Unlike Adler, Horney regards dreams as indicative of our true feelings, rather than as an attempt at self-deception.

Dreaming of misplacing one's passport, or of a picture frame that encloses an empty canvas, expresses the loss of the dreamer's real self. As in individual psychology, dreams of falling reveal the insecurity that underlies the patient's conscious conceit; and as in analytical psychology, dreaming of being a tramp or idiot may serve as compensation for an exaggerated self-image. A nightmare of being trapped in a room with a murderer reflects intense self-contempt, while dreaming of tenderly cultivating a growing plant suggests self-concern and sympathy. A dream of making a long-distance telephone call to the therapist indicates the wish to maintain a detached orientation, and dreaming of the analyst as a jailer reveals a desire to blame one's difficulties on others through externalization. (See Horney, 1939, pp. 31–32; 1945, pp. 87, 129; 1950, pp. 31, 152–153, 188, 318, 349–350.)

Resistance and Transference. Horney shares Freud's belief that patients have powerful unconscious resistances to psychotherapy. But Horney argues that patients actively defend their neurotic solutions and deny the existence of their inner conflicts in order to preserve a sense of personal unity, avoid the frightening prospect of change, and cling to the only apparently successful mode of adjustment that they have ever known. However, resistances are not entirely harmful. They provide useful clues about important unconscious issues that the patient wishes to avoid, and they afford invaluable protection when the therapist inadvertently offers interpretations that are highly threatening. (See Horney, 1942, pp. 267–285; 1945, pp. 187–189; 1950, pp. 201, 334, 340; Singer, 1970, pp. 223–248.)

In marked contrast to Adler, Horney regards transference as Freud's greatest discovery. However, she argues that transference occurs because the therapist becomes a ready target for the patient's habitual attempts to move toward, against, or away from people. Thus the aggressive neurotic tries to dominate the therapist, the detached neurotic waits like a patient bystander for the therapist to provide miraculous cures, and the compliant neurotic uses pain and suffering to justify expectations of instant help (Horney, 1939, pp. 154–167; 1950, p. 338).

Horney cautions that the goals of therapy are never wholly attained, nor is it possible to escape the difficulties of everyday living. "It does not lie within the power of the analyst to turn the patient into a flawless human being. He can only help him to become free to strive toward an approximation of these ideals. . . . The aim of analysis is not to render life devoid of risks and conflicts, but to enable an individual eventually to solve his problems himself" (Horney, 1939, p. 305; 1945, p. 243).

Female Sexuality

Although Horney regarded herself primarily as a neo-Freudian, her theory of female sexuality hews more closely to Adler. Her early writings do concede the existence of penis envy; but she emphatically rejects Freud's contention that healthy women crave a boy baby as a disguised penis substitute, and that the lack of a penis produces greater self-contempt and a weaker superego. According to Horney, an organism biologically built for female functions cannot be ruled psychologically by a wish for masculine attributes. She points out that Freudian psychoanalysis is based primarily on studies by male therapists of male patients, which may well have obscured the joys of motherhood and other uniquely feminine superiorities. (See Horney, 1939, pp. 104–105; 1923–1937/1967, pp. 38, 53–55, 60, 63.)

Instead, Horney emphasizes the role of cultural influences on female behavior. If society regards strength, courage, independence, and sexual freedom as masculine characteristics, while depicting frailty and dependence as inherently feminine, women will tend to believe that they deserve a subordinate position. "The view that women are infantile and emotional creatures, and as such, incapable of responsibility and independence is the work of the masculine tendency to lower women's self-respect" (Horney, 1923–1937/1967, p. 146). Horney argues that envy actually works both ways, with men unconsciously jealous of women's breasts, passivity, and ability to bear children. She also warns that the concept of penis envy may encourage female patients to externalize their problems by blaming them on nature, rather than on their own neurotic behavior. "Every person belonging to a minority group or to a less privileged group tends to use that status as a cover for inferiority feelings of various sources" (Horney, 1939, p. 109).

EVALUATION

Criticisms and Controversies

Horney has been criticized for borrowing too freely from individual psychology and/or Freudian psychoanalysis, and for failing to introduce many new and important constructs. Despite her protestations, externalization is virtually indistinguishable from projection; the idealized image is hardly a radical departure from the superiority complex; shoulds operate much like an overly severe superego; and the idea of intrapsychic conflicts between such opposites as aggressiveness and helplessness closely resembles the defense mechanism of reaction formation. In addition, self-realization is a concept of Jungian origin. Scientific judgment can be unkind to those who merely revise the ideas of others, as Horney herself has observed. "[Many successors] fail to give Freud sufficient credit for pioneering work. It is easy enough to modify, but it takes genius to be the first to visualize the possibilities" (Horney, 1939, p. 154). Nor has her theory stimulated much empirical research.

Perhaps most importantly, Horney's emphasis on neurosis causes her to neglect normal personality development and structure. Since she regards neurosis as a matter of degree, and uses the term *neurotic* only in the sense of "a person to the extent that he is neurotic" (Horney, 1945, p. 27), her theory is by no means inapplicable to more healthy individuals as well. Yet all too many critics have taken her writings at surface value and characterized her primarily as a clinician, seriously underestimating her importance as a personality theorist.

Contributions

Horney's writings represent the views of a skilled and experienced psychotherapist, and are presented clearly enough to facilitate self-analysis and understanding. Her attempt to modify Freudian psychoanalysis in an Adlerian direction is sufficiently original to be worthy of serious consideration; and it offers a viable alternative for those who accept some of Adler's tenets and reject Freud's libido theory, yet wish to retain the idea of intrapsychic conflict. Her approach to such important phenomena as anxiety and transference is considerably more insightful than Adler's, while her equalitarian view of women accords well with modern opinion. Such ideas as the "tyranny of the should" and self-realization occupy a prominent place in the work of more recent psychologists, such as Albert Ellis and Carl Rogers. And Horney provides valuable and well-reasoned insights into the meaning and dynamics of the most common form of psychopathology, neurosis. Although there are those who would regard Horney as outdated, her major works should be required reading for anyone who wishes to acquire a better understanding of the human personality.

Suggested Reading

Horney's most important books are her last two, *Our Inner Conflicts* (1945) and *Neurosis and Human Growth* (1950), which present her theory in its final form. *The Neurotic Personality of Our Time* (1937) is also well-regarded, and *Feminine Psychology* (1923–1937/1967) is of interest because it presents her early work on female sexuality, but neither of these captures the true spirit of her ultimate ideas. For a biography of Horney, see Rubins (1978).

■ SUMMARY

1. THE BASIC NATURE OF HUMAN BEINGS. Karen Horney is highly optimistic about human nature, concluding that we have the capacity as well as the desire to develop our potentialities and become decent individuals. Pathological behavior occurs only if this innate tendency toward self-realization is blocked by external, social forces.

2. THE STRUCTURE OF PERSONALITY. Horney stresses the importance of unconscious processes, powerful and actively maintained repressions, and painful intrapsychic conflicts. However, she prefers not to use specific structural constructs.

3. THE DEVELOPMENT OF PERSONALITY. Horney has little to say about normal personality development. She attributes neurosis to disturbed interpersonal relationships with the parents during childhood. Parents who are too wrapped up in their own neuroses to respond to the child's needs engage instead in such pathogenic behaviors as domination, overprotectiveness, overindulgence, humiliation, neglect, and others. The child therefore develops profound insecurity and a sense of being alone in an unfriendly and frightening world (basic anxiety).

4. FURTHER APPLICATIONS. *Neurosis:* The child tries to alleviate the painful basic anxiety by exaggerating one of its three main characteristics: helplessness, aggressiveness, or detachment. This results in a pathological overemphasis on mov-

ing toward, against, or away from people. The sufferer also forms an idealized image that conflicts with the real self, conceals the true wishes and feelings, and establishes unrealistic and unattainable standards. These standards ensure subsequent failure, which increases the hate for the real self (self-contempt) and dependence on the idealized image. Neurosis is also typified by claims, shoulds, the quest for glory, and other symptoms indicative of severe inner conflicts. *Psychotherapy:* Horneyan psychotherapy strives to unearth and resolve the patient's deeply repressed inner conflicts. The patient must learn that the supposedly lifesaving neurotic solution is actually self-defeating, and that it conceals both powerful opposing forces and the sufferer's true desires and wishes. Typical procedures include free association, interpretation, more active participation by the therapist than in Freudian psychoanalysis, and dream interpretation. *Female sexuality:* Horney rejects Freud's contention that women have greater self-contempt and a weaker superego because they lack the male genital organ. Instead she argues that cultural influences cause women to see themselves as inferior and subordinate, and that men actually envy certain characteristics of women.

5. EVALUATION. Horney has been criticized for adhering too closely to the ideas of Freud and Adler, and for failing to develop a comprehensive theory of her own. But since neurosis represents a difference in degree, rather than in kind, her profound insights into this disorder contribute significantly to a better understanding of the human personality. In particular, her attempt to modify Freudian psychoanalysis in an Adlerian direction is sufficiently original to be worthy of serious study.

STUDY QUESTIONS

1. Give an example from your own life, from the life of someone you know well, or from fiction to illustrate painful inner conflicts and one of the three neurotic "solutions" (moving toward, against, or away from people). Explain how the idealized image in this case produces a vicious circle where matters keep getting worse, and why there is a conflict between the idealized image and this person's real self and wishes. Summarize the key points of this case in a diagram similar to Figure 5.1.

2. Give a real-life example of a person who becomes angry toward someone who is weak because this weakness is a threatening reminder of what the person most dislikes about himself or herself.

3. In Figure 5.1, why do "unrealistic, unattainable standards" lead only to failure? Might they not sometimes lead to success?

4. Give an example from your own life, or from the life of someone you know well, to illustrate: (a) neurotic claims. (b) the "tyranny of the should."

5. Give a real-life example of the following neurotic symptoms described by Horney, and explain why the person behaves this way. The same example may be used to illustrate some or all of the symptoms. (a) Inconsistent

behavior. (b) Pronounced indecisiveness. (c) Ineffectual behavior. (d) Preferring not to try something, rather than try and fail.

6. Give an example from your own life, or from the life of someone you know well, to support Horney's view that "it is a long and hard lesson for anybody to learn that others can neither hurt nor establish self-esteem."

7. What is the first step in Horneyan psychotherapy? Why?

8. How would Horney interpret each of the following dreams? (a) The dreamer looks in a mirror, but doesn't see any reflection. (b) The dreamer sends a long telegram to his or her psychotherapist. (c) The airplane dream described in Chapter 4, study question 10b. (d) The "train" dream described in Chapter 2, study question 12, assuming that the dreamer got to the station too late because the taxi driver insisted on going much too slowly.

9. With regard to women, Horney argues that an organism biologically built for female functions cannot be ruled psychologically by a wish for masculine attributes. Do you agree or disagree? Why?

10. Give a real-life example to support Horney's argument that "Every person belonging to a minority group or to a less privileged group tends to use that status as a cover for inferiority feelings of various sources."

6

ERICH FROMM
The Escape from Freedom

From 1941 to 1943, Karen Horney's American Institute for Psychoanalysis proceeded in an amicable fashion. In April of 1943, however, yet another furor shook the psychiatric community. Her institute summarily withdrew Erich Fromm's privilege to conduct training analyses because he lacked a medical degree, and it was feared that his presence would jeopardize plans to develop a relationship with the New York Medical College (Perry, 1982).

Some colleagues thought it unfair that Fromm should have to suffer the same kind of arbitrary expulsion that Horney herself had encountered previously. In any case, Fromm recovered quite well from this painful professional setback: he went on to become a renowned figure in the realm of personality theory.

BIOGRAPHICAL SKETCH

Erich Fromm was born on March 23, 1900, in Frankfurt, Germany. He was the only child of parents he describes as very neurotic; his father was a wine merchant. Fromm's childhood included a strong Jewish influence, but he eventually rejected organized religion at the age of twenty-six because "I just didn't want to participate in any division of the human race, whether religious or political" (Fromm, 1962b; see also Fromm, cited by Evans, 1966, p. 56).

Unlike Freud, Jung, Adler, and Horney, Fromm had no medical training. He received his Ph.D. from the University of Heidelberg in 1922, and later studied at the internationally renowned Berlin Psychoanalytic Institute. As with Adler, the ravages of World War I came as a profound shock and influenced Fromm toward socialism. Fromm married Frieda Reichmann in 1926, a noted psychoanalyst in her own right and the therapist of Joanne Greenberg ("Hannah Green"), author of the well-known autobiographical novel *I Never Promised You a Rose Garden*. The marriage ultimately ended in divorce. Fromm married Henny Garland in 1944 and, after her death, Annis Freeman in 1953.

Fromm visited the Chicago Psychoanalytic Institute in 1933 as guest lecturer, and emigrated to the United States one year later. His first book, the landmark *Escape From Freedom*, appeared in 1941 (1941/1965). Because it departed from standard Freudian theory by stressing the effect of social factors on personality, Fromm was summarily dropped as a direct member of the International Psychoanalytic Association (Roazen, 1973, p. 12). He also suffered the aforementioned split with Horney at about this time.

In 1945, Fromm joined the prestigious William Alanson White Institute of Psychiatry. He also taught at Columbia University, Bennington College, Yale University, Michigan State University, New York University, and the New School for Social Research. Fromm maintained an active interest in social problems and political philosophy, helping to organize SANE (the National Committee for a Sane Nuclear Policy) in 1957. His published works include some twenty volumes, many of which have proved popular with the general public.

Fromm served as professor of psychiatry at the National University in Mexico for 16 years. He died of a heart attack at his home in Muralto, Switzerland, on March 18, 1980.

THE BASIC NATURE OF HUMAN BEINGS

As with Horney, Fromm's theory of personality is an admixture of Freudian and Adlerian constructs. However, Fromm devotes considerably more attention to the role of societal forces. His work strongly reflects the theories of Karl Marx, whom he regards as an even more profound thinker than Freud. (See for example Fromm, 1961; 1962a; 1970/1971a.)

Organic versus Nonorganic Drives: Isolation and Contradiction

To Fromm (1955/1976b, p. 30), "man [is] an anomaly, . . . the freak of the universe." Our fundamental motive is self-preservation, so we are inextricably tied to nature and the animal kingdom by our **organic (instinctual) drives:** hunger, thirst, sex, and defense through fight or flight. Yet our superior intellect also sets us apart from nature, producing a sense of isolation and anxiety not found in lower organisms.

Human behavior cannot simply follow some preordained instinctual course, for we possess such unique characteristics as self-awareness, reason, and imagination. Instead, we must struggle to ascertain the reasons for our existence and create our own place in the world. We must confront the distinctively human problems of boredom and discontentment. And we must face the threatening realization that death will deprive us of sufficient time to fulfill our potentials, so that "it is the tragic fate of most individuals to die before they are [truly] born" (Fromm, 1955/1976b, p. 32; see also Fromm, 1964/1971b, pp. 147–148; 1968/1974b, p. 62; 1973, pp. 4–8, 72–73, 225–226; 1947/1976a, pp. 48–58, 98).

To Fromm, then, innate instincts are only part of the motivational story. In marked contrast to lower organisms, many crucial human motives consist of learned **nonorganic drives** (or **character-rooted passions**).

Nonorganic Drives

Since our nonorganic drives are not instinctual, they are difficult to satisfy. We have no innate program that ensures their fulfillment; so it is all too easy to opt instead for goals that are more alluring, but that ultimately result in unhappiness—or even in psychopathology.

The Need for Others. Because of our painful and uniquely human feelings of isolation, and because we are woefully weak in comparison with the vast forces of nature, we must cooperate with others in order to survive.[1] *"Man's biological weakness is the condition of human culture. . . .* Man is *primarily* a social being . . . [and] individual psychology is fundamentally social psychology" (Fromm, 1941/1965, pp. 48, 317–318; see also Fromm, 1976c, pp. 104–105).

The best way to secure firm social roots in the world is through the development of mature **love,** which resembles the Adlerian construct of social interest. The art of loving involves a genuine caring for and giving to others, an objective and accurate knowledge as to their true feelings and wishes, a respect for their right to develop in their own particular way, and a sense of responsibility toward all humanity:

> Love is not primarily a relationship to a specific person; it is . . . an *orientation* of *character* which determines the relatedness of a person to the world as a whole. . . . If I truly love one person I love all persons, I love the world, I love life. (Fromm, 1956/1974a, pp. 38–39. See also Fromm, 1956/1974a, pp. 18–25; 1968/1974b, pp. 81–83; 1947/1976a, pp. 104–107, 134; 1955/1976b, p. 38; 1976c, p. 103.)

Every human being has the capacity for love, but fulfilling this potential is extremely difficult. We all begin life as wholly self-centered infants, unable even to differentiate between ourselves and others ("primary **narcissism,**" as in Freudian theory). Pathogenic experiences during subsequent years can all too easily cause us to revert to this immature state ("secondary narcissism"). The resulting behavior is like that of an author who meets a friend and talks incessantly about himself for some time, only to conclude with: "Let us now talk about *you.* How did you like my latest book?" (Fromm, 1964/1971b, p. 81. See also Fromm, 1964/1971b, pp. 71–116; 1973, pp. 201–202; 1947/1976a, pp. 132–137; 1955/1976b, pp. 39–41; 1980, pp. 43–54).

Primary narcissism is not without some value, for we would be unlikely to survive the challenges of life if we regarded ourselves as totally unimportant. As a result, most of us remain at least somewhat narcissistic

---

[1]Fromm originally distinguished between the human needs for "relatedness" to others and "rootedness" in the world, but the distinction between these similar terms is not emphasized in his later works. (See for example Fromm, 1973; 1955/1976b, pp. 35–61; 1976c.)

(Fromm, cited by Evans, 1966. p. 69). Nevertheless, perhaps the most important of all human goals is to overcome and minimize this innate tendency. An exaggerated self-interest rules out a true concern for others, and this has disastrous consequences. For the only way to obtain some measure of reassuring social rootedness, yet still preserve the integrity of one's own personality, is by relating to others with mature and genuine love.

Transcendence. Unlike other species, human beings are not satisfied with the role of creature. We need to **transcend** the helpless animal state and exert a significant effect on our environment, and Fromm (like Adler and Horney) believes that we have an innate tendency to achieve such superiority in constructive ways. "Strivings for happiness and health . . . are part of the natural equipment of man. . . . All organisms have an inherent tendency to actualize their specific potentialities" (Fromm, 1947/1976a, pp. vii, 29; see also Fromm, 1973, pp. 235–237; 1955/1976b, pp. 41–42).

Here again, fulfilling our positive potentials is no easy task. In addition to a phylogenetically programmed impulse to preserve ourselves against threat by attacking (**benign aggression**), we also possess the secondary capacity for nonorganically motivated destructiveness that serves no rational defensive purpose (**malignant aggression**). If one's normal development should be blocked, as for example by pathogenic parental behaviors, transcendence may well be sought through malignant aggression instead of healthy creativity:

> The more the drive toward life is thwarted, the stronger is the drive toward destruction; the more life is realized, the less is the strength of destructiveness. *Destructiveness is the outcome of unlived life.* (Fromm, 1941/1965, p. 207. See also Fromm, 1964/1971b, pp. 35–69; 1973; 1947/1976a, p. 218.)

Identity. Lower animals have no sense of **identity,** but humans need to feel: "I am I" (Fromm, 1955/1976b, pp. 62–64). In addition to relating to others, therefore, the growing child must learn to surrender its primary ties with the parents and accept its separateness from other organisms.

As with the other nonorganic drives, identity is not easily achieved. Life has many dangers, and it is tempting to gain some measure of safety by becoming symbiotically involved with an all-powerful protector. Even the growing child's so-called Oedipal strivings are due solely to this desire for security:

> [The maturing individual is] more aware than the infant of the dangers and risks of life; he knows of the natural and social forces he cannot control, the accidents he cannot foresee, the sickness and death he cannot elude. What could be more natural, under the circumstances, than man's frantic longing for a power which gives him certainty, protection, and love? . . . Thus he is torn between two tendencies since the moment of his birth: one, to emerge to the light and the other to regress to the womb; one for adventure and the other for certainty; one for the risk of independence and the other for protection and dependence.

(Fromm, 1964/1971b, pp. 120–121. See also Fromm, 1941/1965, pp. 208–230; 1950/1967, pp. 76–80; 1973, pp. 358–362; 1947/1976a pp. 43–44, 159–161; 1955/1976b, pp. 44–47; 1980, pp. 27–38.)

Thus the desire to be an independent individual conflicts with the wish to escape from this threatening freedom. Dependence is undeniably alluring, since it offers protection from the dangers of nature and society. But it is also unhealthy, since it precludes the development of the needed sense of identity. To Fromm, therefore, people are not truly fulfilled as cogs in a machine—even so elegant a one as our modern technological society.

Frames of Orientation. Like Jung, Fromm concludes that life must have a sense of meaning and purpose. We all need a personal philosophy that establishes our values and goals in life, guides our behavior, and delineates our place in the world (a **frame of orientation,** or **frame of devotion**). " 'Man does not live by bread alone.' . . . [He needs] an answer to the human quest for meaning, and to [the] attempt to make sense of his own existence" (Fromm, 1947/1976a, pp. 55–56; see also Fromm, 1950/1967, pp. 25–26; 1968/1974b, pp. 65–70; 1973, pp. 230–231; 1955/1976b, pp. 64–66; 1976c, pp. 135–139).

Primarily healthy frames of orientation emphasize love, competence, productivity, reason, and the love of life (**biophilia**). But the need for a unifying personal philosophy is so powerful that even an irrational framework, appropriately rationalized, is preferable to none at all. (This is why people can so easily fall under the spell of a warmonger, dictator, or religious zealot.) Among the irrational and unhealthy frames of orientation are the love of death (**necrophilia**), destruction, power, wealth, symbiotic dependence, and narcissism. In addition, healthy and unhealthy frames of orientation may blend together in varying degrees. Thus a biophilic and loving person may also be somewhat narcissistic or power-oriented, or a conscious and charitable frame of orientation may conceal one that is unconscious and rapacious. Yet regardless of the form, "we do not find any culture in which there does not exist [some] frame of orientation. Or any individual either" (Fromm, 1973, p. 230).

THE STRUCTURE OF PERSONALITY

For the most part, Fromm devotes relatively little attention to the structure of personality. He initially accepted the concept of a potentially cruel and relentless superego, characterized this aspect as paternalistic, and added the notion of a maternal conscience that is unquestioningly accepting and tolerant. However, his ultimate conclusion is that psychology is better off "free from the restrictive influence of the libido theory, and particularly the concepts of *id, ego,* and *superego*" (Fromm, 1973, p. 84; see also Fromm, 1956/1974a, pp. 33–38; 1947/1976a, pp. 145–175; 1955/1976b, pp. 50–51).

Mechanisms of Defense and Escape

Fromm does regard unconscious processes as extremely important. He also emphasizes such defense mechanisms as projection, reaction formation, rationalization, regression, identification with the aggressor, fantasy, and repression.

> A person, even if he is subjectively sincere, may frequently be driven unconsciously by a motive that is different from the one he believes himself to be driven by. . . . Freud's revolution was to make us recognize the unconscious aspect of man's mind and the energy which man uses to repress the awareness of undesirable desires. He showed that good intentions mean nothing if they cover up the unconscious intentions; he unmasked "honest" dishonesty by demonstrating that it is not enough to have "meant" well *consciously*. . . . [Therefore,] only a psychology which utilizes the concept of unconscious forces can penetrate the confusing rationalizations we are confronted with in analyzing either an individual or a culture. (Fromm, 1941/1965, pp. 85, 158; 1973, p. 79. See also Fromm, 1950/1967, pp. 58–59, 74–75; 1947/1976a, pp. 228–230; 1980, pp. 23–26.)

The most likely subjects of repression are such unpleasant passions and beliefs as destructiveness, necrophilia, hate, envy, hypocrisy, revenge, and the fear of death. As in Jungian theory, however, even positive characteristics may be repressed if they threaten to contradict one's frames of orientation (Fromm, 1941/1965, p. 229 n. 14).

Fromm also describes three other devices that we use to alleviate the painful human condition of isolation, and to escape the threatening freedom from preordained instinctual behaviors. One such **mechanism of escape** is **authoritarianism,** a symbiotic emotional attachment to another individual. This mechanism consists of two opposing tendencies: an admiration for authority and desire to submit to powerful others ("masochism"), together with a wish to be the authority and dominate other people ("sadism"). Examples include marriages characterized by excessive submission and domination, often with both partners reflecting both tendencies at different times, and fanatical followers of tyrants such as Hitler. **Malignant aggression** is also an escape mechanism, one that seeks to eliminate external threats rather than incorporate them. The most common mechanism of escape in our modern society is **automaton conformity,** a chameleonlike immersion in a socially acceptable role. Automaton conformity is also essentially undesirable because it conflicts with the need for identity—and because whole societies as well as individuals can be "sick," making the common mode of behavior pathological. (See Fromm, 1941/1965, pp. 163–230; 1964/1971b, pp. 117–134; 1955/1976b, pp. 21–28.)

THE DEVELOPMENT OF PERSONALITY

Unlike Freud, Fromm does not posit any specific developmental stages. He also departs from standard psychoanalysis by arguing that personality can

■ CAPSULE SUMMARY
Some Important Frommian Terminology

Authoritarianism	A symbiotic, nonproductive frame of orientation that involves powerful desires for both submission (masochism) and domination (sadism). One of the three mechanisms of escape.
Automaton conformity	Total immersion in a socially acceptable role, at the cost of one's need for identity. One of the three mechanisms of escape.
Benign aggression	An organic, healthy drive to defend oneself against threat by attacking.
Biophilia	Love of life; a productive frame of orientation.
Exploitative orientation	A nonproductive frame of orientation that attributes all good to sources outside oneself, and seeks to take it by force or cunning.
Frame of orientation (frame of devotion)	A set of principles or personal philosophy that gives meaning to one's life, establishes one's values and goals, and delineates one's place in the world; a nonorganic drive. May be productive and rational, nonproductive and irrational, or a combination thereof.
Hoarding orientation	A nonproductive frame of orientation that involves miserliness, compulsive orderliness, obstinacy, and little faith in external rewards. Similar to the Freudian anal character, but without the sexual implications.
Identity	A sense of oneself as a distinct and separate entity; a nonorganic drive.
Love	A genuine sense of responsibility toward humanity that includes giving, caring, a knowledge of how others feel, and a respect for their right to develop in their own way. Similar to Adler's concept of social interest.
Malignant aggression (destructiveness)	Destructive behavior that serves no rational defensive purpose; a nonorganic drive. One of the three mechanisms of escape.
Marketing orientation	A nonproductive frame of orientation wherein one characterizes oneself as a commodity, and seeks the best "rate of exchange" by becoming what others want one to be.
Mechanism of escape	An essentially undesirable method for resolving threatening feelings of isolation and freedom; similar to nonproductive orientation. Includes authoritarianism, automaton conformity, and destructiveness.
Narcissism	An innate tendency toward self-centeredness ("primary narcissism"), which may become a nonproductive frame of orientation later in life ("secondary narcissism"). Similar to Freud's use of the term, but without the sexual implications.

continued

Necrophilia	Love of death; the most pathological and dangerous of all the nonproductive frames of orientation. Often occurs in combination with narcissism and malignant aggression.
Nonorganic drive (character-rooted passion)	A noninstinctual, learned motive. Includes such needs as relatedness, transcendence, identity, and the need for a frame of orientation.
Nonproductive orientation	A frame of orientation that is undesirable because it involves the surrender of one's innate potentials for healthy growth and self-realization.
Organic drive (instinctual drive)	An instinctual, biological motive. Includes hunger, thirst, sex, and defense through fight (benign aggression) or flight.
Productive orientation	A healthy frame of orientation that involves the fulfillment of one's positive innate potentials. Characterized by love, biophilia, work that benefits oneself and others, and rational thought. Similar to the Freudian genital character, but without the sexual implications.
Receptive orientation	A nonproductive frame of orientation that attributes all good to sources outside oneself, and seeks to obtain it by being loved and cared for. Similar to the Freudian oral character, but without the sexual implications.
Relatedness, rootedness	Terms sometimes used by Fromm to refer to the nonorganic drive for interpersonal relationships, which results from the feelings of isolation and physical weakness of the human species.
Symbiotic orientation	A nonproductive frame of orientation that involves intense emotional ties with another individual, at the cost of one's need for identity.
Symbolic language	A mode of expression wherein one entity stands for another; found in dreams, fairy tales, and myths.
Transcendence (effectiveness)	Rising above the helpless animal state, and exerting a significant effect on one's environment; a nonorganic drive. Healthy transcendence is characterized by creativity and love, while pathological transcendence includes hate and malignant aggression. Similar to Adler's concept of striving for superiority.

continue to develop during adulthood, although external influences must be quite intense to affect an older and less impressionable individual (Fromm, 1973, p. 370; 1976c, p. 106). Fromm does share Freud's belief as to the existence of childhood sexuality, however. And he agrees that personality is primarily determined during the early years of life, with the unusually long period of human dependency serving as a powerful lesson about the need to relate to others.

Fromm has relatively little to say about personality development. The growing child slowly learns to distinguish between "I" and "not-I" through its contacts with the environment. notably those involving the all-important parents. This increasing sense of identity and separation from the parents is essential to healthy development, but it also intensifies the child's feelings of isolation and doubts about its true place in the universe. The freedom to do what one wishes is accompanied not only by freedom from the hindrance of authority, but also from the comforts of security and protection. Thus, as humanity has gained greater independence throughout the course of history, we have also become more isolated and anxious. "When one has become an individual, one stands alone and faces the world in all its perilous and overpowering aspects" (Fromm, 1941/1965, p. 45).

If the child's belief in its own ability keeps pace with the increasing feelings of isolation, anxiety is minimal and personality development proceeds normally. Such positive growth is facilitated by parents who are biophilous, warm, affectionate, and nonthreatening. But if the sense of self-reliance should be damaged by pathogenic parental behaviors, the child is likely to sacrifice its innate healthy potentials and seek to escape from the threatening human state of isolation in misguided ways. For example, authoritarian parents may use the child to fulfill their own frustrated ambition for professional success, or to enjoy a sense of personal power. Such parents may well repress their true intentions (and lack of love) by stressing their concern for the child and lavishing it with attention, advice, or gifts—everything but genuine warmth, and the right to be independent:

> The child is put into a golden cage, it can have everything provided it does not want to leave the cage. The result of this is often a profound fear of love on the part of the child when he grows up, as "love" to him implies being caught and blocked in his own quest for freedom. (Fromm, 1941/1965, p. 168. See also Fromm, 1941/1965, pp. 216–217, 268; 1956/1974a, pp. 51–52; 1947/1976a, pp. 136, 157–158.)

Other pathogenic parental behaviors include pessimism, joylessness, narcissism, necrophilia, and physical abuse. To Fromm, such forms of maltreatment are so prevalent that "one must believe that loving parents are the exception, rather than the rule" (1976c, p. 45).

Character Typology

The healthy personality is typified by biophilia, love, creativity, and reason. These characteristics comprise the **productive** frame of orientation (Fromm, 1964/1971b; 1947/1976a, pp. 89–113). This personality type corresponds roughly to the Freudian genital character, albeit without the sexual implications. That is, it results from social and environmental influences (such as parental behaviors), rather than from libidinal instincts.

As we have seen, the undesirable or **nonproductive** frames of orientation include symbiotic attachments, narcissism, necrophilia, compulsive strivings for power or wealth, and the mechanisms of escape (authoritarianism, automaton conformity, and destructiveness). In addition, Fromm (1947/1976a, pp. 70–89) has described four other nonproductive orientations. The **receptive** orientation is similar to the oral-dependent character in Freudian theory (again, without the sexual implications), and to Horney's conception of "moving toward people." This type believes that the source of everything desirable is external, and consistently seeks to be loved and nurtured by others. The person with an **exploitative** orientation also regards the source of all good as external, but strives to obtain it through force or cunning. Such individuals resemble the Freudian oral-sadistic character (Fromm, 1973, p. 80), and Horney's construct of "moving against people." The **hoarding** orientation is denoted by miserliness, compulsive orderliness, and obstinacy, and resembles the Freudian anal character and Horney's "moving away from people." Like Adler's (1927/1957, p. 181) description of people who are determined to guard their wretched treasures, "the hoarding character experiences himself like a beleaguered fortress; he must prevent anything from going out and save what is inside" (Fromm, 1973, p. 293). The **marketing** orientation does not correspond to any of the Freudian character types, though it bears some similarities to the overdeveloped persona in Jungian theory. Marketing types regard themselves as commodities and try to fashion a salable exterior, one that will be coveted on the social market. While some social expertise and polish is desirable, these individuals tend to repress their own needs for identity and self-realization in order to become what others want them to be.

More recently, Fromm (1973, pp. 294–296) has also referred to a "bureaucratic character." In this nonproductive orientation, an individual is controlled from above in a power structure while having authority over one or more subordinates. Often, such people use red tape as an expression of sadistic power and hostility. Thus a clerk may welcome the opportunity to infuriate others by shutting the customer's window at the prescribed time of 5:30 P.M. exactly, forcing one or two people who have been waiting in line for some time to depart empty-handed.

Fromm (1976c) also emphasizes the differences between the nonproductive "having" orientation, and the productive characteristics of "being." "Having" is an amalgam of the hoarding and marketing orientations and tends to result in greed, with one's personality defined by such formulas as "I am [i.e., exist] because I have X" or "I am = what I have and what I consume." Contrariwise, "being" is denoted by a spontaneous and creative state of existence that is independent of one's possessions. Fortunately, "having" is learned and thus evitable, though a society based on maximum production and consumption may well find it advantageous to teach that greed is innate. (See Fromm, 1976c, pp. 7, 27, 77, 112.)

Fromm cautions that the various nonproductive orientations vary in degree as well as type, since they may blend with the productive orientation (or with each other). For example, a receptive person may be polite and adaptable (more productive) or spineless and unprincipled (more nonproductive). Or a hoarding type may be practical and economical (more productive) or unimaginative and stingy (more nonproductive). (See Fromm, 1947/1976a, pp. 118–122.)

FURTHER APPLICATIONS OF FROMMIAN THEORY

Dream Interpretation

Like Freud, Fromm regards dreams as the royal road to the unconscious. He concludes that dream interpretation is probably the most important and revealing technique in psychotherapy, although he by no means restricts its use to this realm. The language of dreams is one that we are all advised to learn, for "[as] the Talmud says, 'dreams which are not interpreted are like letters which have not been opened.' . . . [Dreams] are important communications from ourselves to ourselves" (Fromm, 1951/1957, p. 10; see also Fromm, cited by Evans, 1966, p. 36).

The Purpose of Dreams. Fromm agrees with Freud that dreams can serve the purpose of wish-fulfillment, that they are invariably triggered by day's residues, and that threatening truths may be concealed in various ways. For example, a young lawyer was criticized at work by a superior, but consciously dismissed this incident as trivial. That night, he dreamed of riding a white charger before a cadre of cheering soldiers. Thus he alleviated his fears of failure and restored his self-esteem, which had in fact been shaken by the events of the preceding day. The dream fulfilled these wishes in an irrational and disguised manner, similar to military daydreams he had sought comfort from as a child when rejected and taunted by his peers (Fromm, 1951/1957, pp. 150–157).

Fromm also shares Jung's belief that dreams can have obvious and undisguised meanings, and that they need not necessarily involve childhood conflicts. A dream may express current anxieties and misgivings, as when a man who is unconsciously afraid of domination by females dreams of being murdered by a woman. Alternatively, a dream may serve some teleological or problem-solving function. A writer was offered a tempting position that would compromise his integrity for a great deal of money. He resolved this dilemma by dreaming that two opportunists advised him to drive up a peak, whereupon he was killed in a crash and awoke in terror—a clear indication that accepting the job would destroy him psychologically. Similarly, the discoverer of the Benzine ring first visualized the correct chemical structure in a dream of snakes biting each others' tails.

Dreams may also afford accurate and crucial insights about oneself or others. For example, frequent dreams of corpses and skulls suggest an unconscious necrophilous orientation. Or one may meet supposedly kind and generous persons during waking hours, unconsciously sense that they are not nearly so wonderful as everyone believes, dream of them as cruel or dishonest, and subsequently find that they have proved guilty of embezzlement or ruthlessness. Thus we are able to heed in our dreams important stimuli that were perceived only subliminally during the day. *"We are not only less reasonable and less decent in our dreams but . . . also more intelligent, wiser, and capable of better judgment when we are asleep than when we are awake"* (Fromm, 1951/1957, p. 33; see also Fromm, 1951/1957, pp. 36–45; 1964/1971b, pp. 42, 127–128; 1947/1976a, pp. 168–169; 1980, pp. 100–101).

Regardless of its specific content, every dream is a deliberate creation of the dreamer. "Whatever the role we play in the dream, *we* are the author, it is *our* dream, *we* have invented the plot" (Fromm, 1951/1957, p. 4). Nor is a dream ever unimportant, although its true significance may be concealed by a trivial façade. Thus a young woman once claimed that a dream of hers was meaningless because it consisted only of serving her husband a dish of strawberries, whereupon he pointed out with a laugh: "You seem to forget that strawberries are the one fruit which I do not eat" (Fromm, 1951/1957, p. 149; see also p. 24). Whether this dream expresses a severe marital conflict or only mild annoyance is not clear; but, like all dreams, it deals with issues of demonstrable importance.

Dream Symbols. Fromm agrees that dreams are expressed in **symbolic language,** an important mode of communication also found in fairy tales and myths. Unlike Freud, however, Fromm regards many dream symbols as asexual. For example, a person who feels lost and confused may dream of arriving at the outskirts of a city where the streets are empty, the surroundings are unfamiliar, and there is no transportation to where the dreamer wishes to go. Or, since symbolic language has its own syntax and can be quite unrealistic, the dreamer may depict a cowardly human being in the form of a chicken. (See Fromm, 1951/1957, pp. 11–23, 28.)

Some dream symbols have universal meanings because they are intrinsically related to what they represent, such as the power and vitality of fire, the slow and steady quality of moving water, and the security of a valley enclosed by mountains. In contrast to Jungian archetypes, universal symbols result from these intrinsic meanings rather than from racial inheritances (Fromm, 1951/1957, p. 18). Other dream elements possess only an accidental, learned relationship to the concepts that they express. For example, the street or city where one falls in love is likely to symbolize happiness, whereas the identical scene may represent sorrow to an individual who suffered a painful parting in that location. Thus the meaning of accidental symbols must be supplied by the dreamer, and Fromm (like Freud) makes use of free association to bring information to consciousness.

The Dreams of Freud and Jung. Interpreting one's own dreams is no easy task, and Fromm argues that even Freud and Jung showed a tendency to shy away from threatening truths. Thus Freud once dreamed of having written a botanical monograph, with each copy containing a dried specimen of the plant in question. Based on extensive free associations, Freud interpreted this dream as an expression of pride in his professional achievements. However, Fromm concludes that the dream actually reflects profound self-reproach over Freud's puritanical and lifeless treatment of sexuality. "He has dried the flower, made sex and love the object of scientific inspection and speculation, rather than leave it alive" (Fromm, 1951/1957, p. 93).

Jung once dreamed of killing someone named Siegfried with a rifle, became horror-stricken, and awakened with the thought that he must kill himself unless he could understand the dream. He eventually decided that he had symbolically murdered the hero within himself, thereby expressing a sense of humility. Fromm suggests that Jung was at this time angry with his esteemed mentor Freud, even to the extent of harboring powerful unconscious death wishes (which Freud had in fact commented upon, but which Jung indignantly denied). Therefore, the dream-victim was actually Freud himself, with Jung unable to recognize the truth because he was intensely repressing a rather necrophilous orientation. "The slight change from *Sigmund* to *Siegfried* was enough to enable a man whose greatest skill was the interpretation of dreams, to hide the real meaning of this dream from himself" (Fromm, 1964/1971b, p. 44; see also Fromm, 1951/1957, pp. 47–108; 1980, pp. 73–89).

Psychopathology

In essence, Fromm accepts Freud's definition of mental health as the capacity for love and productive work. He also agrees that psychopathology represents a difference in degree, rather than in kind:

> The phenomena which we observe in the neurotic person are in principle not different from those we find in the normal. They are only more accentuated, clear-cut, and frequently more accessible to the awareness of the neurotic person than they are in the normal. . . . (Fromm, 1941/1965, p. 159; see also p. 46.)

Causes of Neurosis. In addition to the aforementioned pathogenic parental behaviors, Fromm stresses that neurosis is often caused by the culture in which one lives. He argues that society seeks to make people *wish* to do what they *have* to do, which presents "a difficult problem: *How to break a person's will without his being aware of it?* Yet by a complicated process of indoctrination, rewards, punishments, and fitting ideology, [society] solves this task by and large so well that most people believe they are following their own will and are unaware that their will itself is conditioned and manipulated" (Fromm, 1976c, p. 78; see also p. 133). Thus we are pressured into automaton conformity by the very society we have created to serve our ends.

To make matters worse, we are constantly bombarded by a huge variety of pathogenic stimuli. These include the "rationalizing lies" used by modern advertising that play upon our sexual desires, threaten us with social ostracism unless we use the appropriate deodorants, promise revolutionary changes in our love life if we purchase a particular brand of toothpaste, or urge us to buy products simply because they are endorsed by famous or attractive individuals. "All these methods are essentially irrational; they have nothing to do with the qualities of the merchandise, and they smother and kill the critical capacities of the customer like an opiate or outright hypnosis" (Fromm, 1951/1957, p. 35; 1941/1965, p. 149; 1976c, p. 188).

Also adding to our sense of alienation and insignificance are elected politicians whom one hardly ever sees in person, and who cunningly hide their true intentions behind jargonistic double-talk; huge bureaucracies and businesses that regard individual customers as unimportant; repetitive jobs that transform workers into machinelike cogs, and eliminate the pride of producing a complete product; vast and overcrowded cities; conflicting societal prescriptions that advise us to be self-centered winners on the one hand, and charitably selfless on the other; and the ominous threat of nuclear war. And since parents serve as *"the psychological agent[s] of society,"* we are all exposed to these influences (at least indirectly) from the moment of birth. In fact, "the real problem of mental life is not why some people become insane, but rather why most avoid insanity" (Fromm, 1941/1965, p. 315; 1955/1976b, p. 34; see also Fromm, 1947/1976a, p. 132; 1981).

Dynamics of Neurosis. According to Fromm, neurosis always consists of a conflict between two opposing forces. It occurs when our healthy innate drives toward self-realization and independence are blocked by parental or societal influences. The individual may then opt for narcissism instead of love, malignant aggression instead of transcendence, symbiotic dependence instead of identity and independence, or any of the other nonproductive frames of orientation. Thus the goal of the psychologist is not to define and treat a set of symptoms, but to understand the neurotic character and the resulting difficulties in living. (See Fromm, 1941/1965, pp. 162, 176, 201; 1950/1967, p. 65; 1947/1976a, p. 222.)

Psychotherapy and Social Reform

Fromm accepts many of the tenets and procedures of Freudian psychoanalysis, including the need to bring unconscious material to consciousness, free association, resistance, transference, countertransference, working through, and the importance of dream interpretation. He also shares Freud's belief that psychoanalysis is not suitable for everyone, nor can it guarantee improvement. Fromm prefers to dispense with transference neurosis, however, and to have the patient perceive the analyst as a rational authority and genuine human being. He favors the Adlerian technique of early recollections, and he shares Horney's view that insights must be achieved on both an intellectual and emotional level in order to be effective. In particular, analytic therapy strives to help the patient replace the chosen nonproductive frame(s) of orientation with the productive orientation, as by abandoning narcissism in favor of love. (See Fromm, 1950/1967, p. 84; 1973, pp. 205–207; 1947/1976a, p. 225; 1976c, pp. 31, 169–170; Fromm, cited by Evans, 1976, pp. 30–55, 82).

For the most part, Fromm's psychological prescriptions refer to society in general rather than to the individual. He warns that the diminishing worldwide supply of food, the environmental deterioration resulting from such influences as the automobile and pesticides, and the proliferation of nuclear weapons have brought us to a crisis that threatens the very survival of our species:

> Some 10–20 million people are starving to death annually now. . . . [while] population growth increases the probability of a lethal worldwide plague and of a thermonuclear war. . . . [Thus] for the first time in history, the *physical survival of the human race depends on a radical change of the human heart.* . . . [a] change [that] is the only alternative to economic catastrophe. . . . [Yet] we go on plundering the raw materials of the earth, poisoning the earth, and preparing nuclear war. We hesitate not at all leaving our own descendants this plundered earth as their heritage. (Fromm, 1976c, pp. 10, 164, 166, 189.)

To Fromm, the only alternative to disaster is a radical remodeling of society. Most importantly, unlimited growth must be replaced by selective, planned expansion. We must abandon the "having" orientation that is characterized by conspicuous and excessive consumption, such as the purchase of an oversized new car every year. In its place we must substitute the "being" orientation, which minimizes the importance of material possessions and emphasizes the goal of consumption based on actual necessity.

Fromm also recommends that the "brainwashing" techniques of modern industrial and political advertising be prohibited, so that we can wean ourselves from such propaganda and learn to make better use of our powers of reason. Consumer strikes should be used to impress our will on industry, since a boycott of (say) private automobiles by even 20 percent of the buying public would have a profound impact. The reestablishment of the town meeting would enable people to exert a more meaningful effect on the process of government. Education should enable students to fulfill their innate potentials and experience what they learn, rather than merely memorizing a vast number of unrelated facts. The gap between rich and poor nations must be closed by appropriate foreign aid, so as to decrease the probability of epidemics and nuclear wars instigated by the "have-nots." A guaranteed annual income must be established, ensuring everyone of the right to subsist. Women must be freed from patriarchal domination. Movies should foster pride in the whole human race, rather than one particular national or ethnic group. A Supreme Cultural Council, neither elected by popular vote nor appointed by the government, should be established to advise both political leaders and the citizenry. Finally, atomic disarmament is essential (Fromm, 1976c, pp. 173–196; see also Fromm, 1941/1965, p. 273; 1964/1971b, p. 112 n. 14; 1968/1974b, pp. 119–120; 1955/1976b, pp. 291–298; 1981).

Fromm recognizes that many individuals may be too accustomed to our present society to accept such drastic alterations, even at the cost of possible future catastrophes. Nor is he optimistic about the possibility that academic psychology will provide effective answers, concluding that researchers all too often prefer to deal with problems that are insignificant but capable of rigorous measurement. Yet despite the difficulties and limited chances of success, Fromm argues that the attempt to change must be made:

> If a sick person has even the barest chance for survival, no responsible physician will say "Let's give up the effort," or will use only palliatives. On the contrary, everything conceivable is done to save the sick person's life. Certainly, a sick society cannot expect anything less. (Fromm, 1976c, p. 197; see also Fromm, 1976c, p. 11; Fromm, cited by Evans, 1966, p. 74, 84.)

Religion

Fromm regards religion as one of the various possible frames of orientation. As would be expected from his definition of love, he differs from Freud by praising "loving thy neighbor as thyself" as the most important standard for living (Fromm, 1950/1967, p. 84). However, Fromm also cautions that religion may well have harmful effects. Misguided and dated principles, such as prohibitions against birth control, may stifle healthy personal growth and development. Or religious tenets may be used in the service of destruction and warfare. In particular, Fromm criticizes the concept of "original sin" as typical of the authoritarian and undesirable aspects of religion. He also objects to the divisiveness that results from the existence of many different religions, preferring to emphasize the commonness of all humanity. (See Fromm, 1941/1965, pp. 81–122, 193, 271; 1950/1967; 1947/1976a, pp. 23–24; 1976c, pp. 41–44, 79.)

Literature and Mythology

In addition to dreams, Fromm devotes considerable attention to the symbolic nature of literature and mythology. For example, the myth of Jonah symbolizes the futility of trying to escape from one's obligations to others. It also illustrates how neurotic defenses like seclusiveness, denoted by being thrown into the ocean and swallowed by the whale, exceed their original function and become extremely self-destructive. Little Red Riding Hood symbolically describes a young girl facing the problem of sexuality and the issue of male-female conflicts, with the heroine's red cap representing menstruation and men depicted in the form of dangerous wolves. And Walt Disney's Mickey Mouse serves a psychological function by enabling people who suffer from feelings of insignificance to identify with a small, persecuted entity who overcomes a powerful and hostile enemy. (See Fromm, 1951/1957, pp. 20–23, 195–263; 1941/1965, pp. 153–154; 1947/1976a, pp. 104–105, 171–175.)

EVALUATION

Criticisms and Controversies

Not surprisingly, Fromm's sweeping recommendations for social reform have proved to be highly controversial. His socialistic approach is unacceptable to those who believe that capitalism, with its faults, is still the best method for meeting the needs of the people. Some of his proposals are vague and lacking in detail, while others would be extremely difficult to implement (as he himself concedes). Furthermore, many modern psychologists regard Fromm's ideas as little more than unsupported philosophical speculations. His writings lack the quantitative analyses commonly expected of a scientist (especially one who proposes such profound social changes). In contrast to Freud, it is even difficult to detect much correspondence between Fromm's conclusions and evidence from his psychoanalytic practice. This absence of hard data gives his books a distinctly sermonic tone, which he justifies with the subjective argument that he finds in psychology that which proves him to be right (Fromm, cited by Evans, 1966, p. 80).

Some noted philosophers have seriously questioned Fromm's interpretation of Marxist socialism as humanistic. Unlike Freud, Fromm does not always clarify the relationships among terms used in his earlier works and those in his later writings. Fromm's theory has generated little empirical research. And while he does at times cite such predecessors as Jung and Adler, he often appears to ignore important similarities between their constructs and his own.

Contributions

Fromm's warnings about the dangers of abusing our environment, world famine, and nuclear war are timely and important. He has made major contributions to our understanding of dream interpretation, and of freedom and totalitarianism. His inclusion of organic drives appears superior to Adler's rejection of innate determinants of behavior, while his view of feminine equality accords more closely with modern opinion than that of Freud. Fromm's emphasis on narcissism also seems well justified when applied to our affluent, "spoiled" society. And as a colleague of such noted psychologists as Horney and Sullivan, Fromm has exerted some influence on theories other than his own.

Like Horney, Fromm does not pretend to offer a complete theory of personality. But Horney's crucial insights into neurotic behavior make her writings of considerable value to psychology, while Fromm's sweeping yet unsubstantiated social criticisms would seem to belong more in the realm of philosophy. Psychologists and personality theorists are expected to follow a more scientific course, where recommendations are clearly linked to clinical and/or research data. By devoting so much of his attention to apparently unsupported speculations, Fromm himself has limited the impact of his work on modern psychological thought.

Suggested Reading

Among Fromm's many titles, two stand out: *Escape From Freedom* (1941/1965), which has been praised as a landmark in psychological, political, and philosophical thought, and his classic work on dream interpretation, *The Forgotten Language* (1951/1957). *The Art of Loving* (1956/1974a) has also achieved wide popularity, while *The Anatomy of Human Destructiveness* (1973) offers interesting insights into this important area.

■ SUMMARY

1. THE BASIC NATURE OF HUMAN BEINGS. Fromm emphasizes the conflict between our innate, organic animal side and the uniquely human characteristics of self-awareness, reason, and imagination. He also stresses the importance of such nonorganic drives as the need for others, transcendence, identity, and frames of orientation. Fromm is optimistic about human nature, but he is more pessimistic than Horney about our secondary capacity for learned pathological behavior. Nonorganic drives are difficult to satisfy, since there is no innate program that ensures their fulfillment. Thus love may surrender to narcissism, transcendence to destructiveness, and identity to dependence.

2. THE STRUCTURE OF PERSONALITY. Fromm accepts the importance of unconscious processes, repression, and defense mechanisms. But he rejects the Freudian constructs of id, ego, and superego, nor does he favor any alternative structural model. He does posit three mechanisms that we use to escape the threatening freedom from preordained instinctual behaviors: a symbiotic emotional attachment to another person (authoritarianism), eliminating external threats (malignant aggression), and a chameleonlike immersion in a socially acceptable role (automaton conformity).

3. THE DEVELOPMENT OF PERSONALITY. Fromm concludes that personality may continue to develop into adulthood, but he posits no specific developmental stages. He warns against such pathogenic parental behaviors as necrophilia, narcissism, pessimism, and lack of warmth. He also devotes considerable attention to such character types or frames of orientation as receptive, exploitative, and hoarding (which correspond roughly to the Freudian oral-dependent, oral-sadistic, and anal character, albeit without the sexual implications), bureaucratic, and "having." All of these are nonproductive frames of orientation. In contrast, the healthy productive orientation stresses biophilia, love, and reason.

4. FURTHER APPLICATIONS. Fromm is noted for his major work on dream interpretation, *The Forgotten Language*. He argues that dreams may well be relatively obvious as well as disguised, and that we are often wiser and more reasonable in our dreams than when we are awake. Fromm is also a social philosopher who offers numerous criticisms of our hypocritical, alienating, and destructive

society. He therefore proposes sweeping (and highly controversial) changes in the basic structure of society.

5. EVALUATION. Fromm's radical and sermonistic proposals for social change strike many modern observers as unscientific and excessive. Yet his works have also been praised as landmarks in psychological, political, and philosophical thought, and it is by no means clear that his recommendations can be safely ignored.

STUDY QUESTIONS

1. Fromm argues that "destructiveness is the outcome of unlived life." Freud contends that destructiveness occurs because we fail to sublimate our illicit instincts. Since both theorists agree that we are destructive, why is this theoretical difference important?

2. According to Adler, it is all too possible to deny our predisposition for social interest and become neurotically self-centered. Fromm argues that we must overcome our innate narcissistic tendencies in order to develop healthy and mature love. Does the difference in terminology between Adler and Fromm reflect important theoretical differences?

3. Explain how each of the following is related to Fromm's conception of "escape from freedom:" (a) The conflict between the healthy need for identity and the desire for a powerful protector. (b) A growing child gets increasing freedom to do what he or she wants, which involves both freedom from the hindrance of parental authority and freedom from the comforts of security and protection. (c) Unlike lower animals, humans have nonorganic drives. (d) The case history described in the Appendix, Chapter 5, question 4b.

4. Give a real-life example of a child who grows up with a profound fear of being loved. Why might this happen?

5. Give an example from your own life, from the life of someone you know well, or from fiction to illustrate: (a) the receptive orientation. (b) the exploitative orientation. (c) the hoarding orientation. (d) the productive orientation.

6. A young woman dreams that she is having breakfast with her husband and hands him the comics section of the newspaper. To her, this seems meaningless and unimportant. How would Fromm interpret this dream?

7. Fromm takes a negative view of many aspects of our society, including: (a) advertising by businesses and politicians; (b) politicians; (c) inadequate foreign aid; (d) the lack of a guaranteed annual income; (e) the existence of so many different religions; (f) the threat of nuclear war; (g) plundering our environment and poisoning the earth. Do you agree or disagree? Why?

7

HARRY STACK SULLIVAN
The Interpersonal
Theory of Psychiatry

For approximately two years, Harry Stack Sullivan was an honorary member of Karen Horney's new psychoanalytic institute. However, he was one of those angered by the seemingly arbitrary expulsion of Erich Fromm (Chapter 6). Sullivan therefore resigned from the institute in April 1943, arguing that it is wrong to attack the integrity and judgment of gifted colleagues just because they prefer the path of innovator and critic.

In the course of defending Fromm, Sullivan also evoked the wrath of the Freudians. He took exception to a scathing review of Fromm's classic *Escape from Freedom* by the psychoanalyst Otto Fenichel, which concluded with the claim that only the true faith—Freudian psychoanalysis—was "pure gold." Sullivan contended that this review was designed primarily for political purposes, and that it was a pro-Freudian diatribe that lacked any substantive quality.

Once again, orthodox psychoanalysis responded to challenge by imposing the penalty of excommunication. Many analysts were asked (in effect) to choose between Freud's beliefs and associating with Sullivan, and those who selected the latter alternative were subjected to various forms of professional intimidation. This political rivalry grew so intense that even today, there are psychoanalysts who have adopted important Sullivanian theories yet who steadfastly refuse to credit him accordingly. (See Perry, 1982, pp. 386–389.) Nevertheless, Sullivan ultimately emerged from these professional difficulties as one of the leading figures in the realm of personality theory.

BIOGRAPHICAL SKETCH

Harry Stack Sullivan was born on February 21, 1892, in Norwich, New York. He was the only surviving child of a taciturn father, a farmer and skilled workman, and a mother who "never troubled to notice the characteristics of the child she had brought forth. . . . 'Her son' was so different from me that I felt she had no use for me, except as a clotheshorse on which to hang an elaborate pattern of illusions" (Sullivan, 1942).

Partly because the Sullivans were the only Catholic family in a Protestant community, Harry had a lonely childhood. This undoubtedly helped him develop an unusual empathy for the intense isolation of the schizophrenic, together with a rather withdrawn personality of his own.

Sullivan encountered significant personal problems during his freshman year at Cornell University. He became the cat's-paw for a gang of boys in the dormitory, and shouldered the blame for some illegalities engineered by the group. He is also believed to have undergone a schizophrenic breakdown of his own at about this time. (See Perry, 1982, pp. 3, 143–146, 151.)

Sullivan never returned to Cornell after his one-semester suspension. In 1911 he entered the Chicago College of Medicine and Surgery, the medical branch of Valparaiso University of Indiana. His grades were erratic; but he completed his course work in 1915, and ultimately received the M.D. degree from Valparaiso in 1917 (Perry, 1982, pp. 156–159, 165).

Sullivan demonstrated considerable skill as an internist, but he preferred a career in psychiatry. He therefore entered psychoanalytic therapy as a patient during 1916–1917. After serving in World War I as a first lieutenant in the Medical Corps, Sullivan worked at government and private hospitals in Maryland and Washington, D.C. Here he began his intensive studies of schizophrenia; came under the influence of William Alanson White, who later founded a prestigious psychiatric foundation and named Sullivan its president in 1933; and gradually modified Freudian psychoanalysis to suit his own theoretical predilections.

In 1931, Sullivan moved to New York City and pursued further psychoanalytic training. He suffered financial problems that forced him to file for bankruptcy, but ultimately established a lucrative private practice. During World War II, he served as consultant to the newly formed Selective Service System, and subsequently participated in UNESCO and other world health projects.

Sullivan was a lifelong bachelor. In 1927 he began a close relationship with a young man he describes as a former patient, James Inscoe. "Jimmie" lived with Sullivan for some twenty years as a "beloved foster son . . . friend and ward," though he was never legally adopted. (See Perry, 1982, pp. 209–210; Sullivan, 1942).

Sullivan's writings fill seven volumes, only one of which he completed himself (1932–1933/1972). Five were published posthumously, and consist of edited lectures. Harry Stack Sullivan died of a cerebral hemorrhage in Paris on January 14, 1949, while returning home from a mental health conference in Amsterdam.

THE BASIC NATURE OF HUMAN BEINGS

Like Horney and Fromm, Sullivan emphasizes the interpersonal nature of personality. But whereas Horney concentrates on neurosis, and Fromm stresses the pathogenic role of society, Sullivan is primarily concerned with two other important areas: the development of personality, and the dynamics and treatment of schizophrenia. In fact, he regards the developmental approach as the only good way to communicate his theoretical constructs. "If we go with almost microscopic care over how everybody comes to be what he is at chronologic adulthood, then perhaps we can learn a good deal of what is highly probable about living and difficulties in living" (Sullivan, 1953/1968, p. 4).

The One-Genus Postulate

Like Fromm, Sullivan makes some allowances for the effects of heredity on personality. Every human being is influenced by such physiological motives as hunger, thirst, respiration, sexuality, and the maintenance of body temperature. This animalistic aspect of personality accounts for individual differences in physical characteristics, sensory abilities, intelligence, and the rate at which we mature.

However, Sullivan also concludes that the similarities among human personalities far exceed the differences(the **One-Genus Postulate**). Even the most retarded individual differs far less from the greatest genius than from any member of any other species. Thus Sullivan (unlike Adler) prefers to minimize the importance of individual differences, and to devote his theoretical attention to those phenomena that humans have in common. (See Sullivan, 1947/1953, p. 16; 1953/1968, pp. 32–33.)

The Need for Others

Sullivan shares Fromm's and Horney's distaste for Freudian libido theory, arguing that it is "completely preposterous" to assume that our behavior is rigidly determined by instincts. In fact, except for such hereditary disasters as congenital idiocy, human nature is extremely pliable and adaptive. "[Even] the most fantastic social rules and regulations [could] be lived up to, if they were properly inculcated in the young, [and] they would seem very natural and proper ways of life" (Sullivan, 1953/1968, pp. 6, 21).

Sullivan concludes that personality is shaped primarily by social forces, with the child's lengthy period of dependence making it particularly vulnerable to influence by others. He posits a powerful human need for interpersonal relationships, so that "it is a rare person who can cut himself off from . . . relations with others for long spaces of time without undergoing a deterioration of personality." And he insists that personality exists, and can be studied, only through its interpersonal manifestations:

> *Personality is the relatively enduring pattern of recurrent interpersonal situations which characterize a human life. . . . A personality* can never be isolated from the complex of interpersonal relationships in which the person lives . . . [Therefore,] psychiatry is the study of the phenomena that occur in interpersonal situations, in configurations made up of two or more people, all but one of whom may be more or less completely illusory. (Sullivan, 1947/1953, p. 10; 1953/1968, pp. 32, 110–111; 1964/1971, p. 33. See also Sullivan, 1953/1968, pp. 18–20, 367–368.)

Since Sullivan's definition of interpersonal relationships includes those that are illusory, even a recluse or psychotic does not lack a personality. Such individuals have memories and/or fantasies of relationships with real or fictitious others, so they too are strongly influenced by interpersonal situations.

Tension Reduction

In accordance with Horney and Fromm, Sullivan concludes that human beings have a tendency or drive toward mental health. Nevertheless, he also shares Freud's belief that we are motivated by the desire to reduce inner tensions. The ideal human condition is that of total equilibrium (absolute **euphoria**), a state of utter well-being characterized by the absence of any internal deficiencies or noxious external stimuli. The opposite extreme, absolute **tension,** is reciprocally related to euphoria and is similar to a state of terror. Like mathematical limits, however, absolute euphoria and absolute tension can only be approached and do not exist in nature. (See Sullivan, 1947/1953, p. 97; 1953/1968, p. 35; 1954/1970, p. 106; 1956/1973, p. 265.)

According to Sullivan, there are four major causes of tension: the so-called physicochemical needs, the need for sleep, anxiety, and the need to express tenderness.

Physicochemical Needs and Sleep. A state of inner disequilibrium is created by such important "physicochemical" needs as sexual desire, the necessity of eliminating bodily wastes, and deficiencies in food, water, oxygen, or body heat. This is accompanied by tension that is often (but not always) conscious, thereby motivating us to expend energy and satisfy the need. Tension also arises from the need to sleep, which Sullivan regards as significantly different from the physicochemical needs.

Anxiety. Perhaps the most important cause of tension is **anxiety.** This unpleasant emotion varies considerably in intensity. At its most extreme, anxiety resembles the **uncanny emotions** of awe, dread, horror, and loathing:

> Uncanny emotions have a sort of shuddery, not-of-this-earth component . . . [somewhat like one's] first glimpse into the Grand Canyon. . . . If you try to analyze the experience, you may talk about your skin crawling . . . [and] if there were a great deal more of such emotion, you would be very far from a going concern as long as you had it. That is the nearest I can come to hinting at what I surmise infants undergo when they are severely anxious. (Sullivan, 1953/1968, p. 10; see also pp. 4, 8–11, 41–45, 59.)

Anxiety can be provoked by disturbances in the environment, such as a sudden loud noise or pronounced threat. But its major source concerns the child's relationship to its mother, or whichever person fulfills the mothering function. "The basic vulnerabilities to anxiety [are] in interpersonal relations. . . . *The tension of anxiety, when present in the mothering one, induces anxiety in the infant"* (Sullivan, 1953/1968, pp. 11, 41; see also pp. 9, 113–

117, 144, 204). Thus anxiety differs from the tension of **fear,** which occurs when the satisfaction of a general need is substantially delayed.

The means by which anxiety is communicated from the mothering one to the baby is uncertain, perhaps including some sort of empathy on the part of the latter. In any case, its effects are extremely troublesome. Unlike the physicochemical needs, which are readily satisfied through such actions as eating or drinking, anxiety is best alleviated by safe relationships with non-anxious others (**interpersonal security**). No specific action by the infant is involved, which makes the relief of anxiety significantly different from all other needs—and notably more difficult to achieve.

To make matters worse, anxiety opposes the satisfaction of other needs. It can interfere with the ability to swallow when hungry or thirsty, or to fall asleep when tired. It can disrupt the capacity for rational thought, much like a severe blow on the head. And it can sabotage potentially gratifying interpersonal relationships, as when the hungry but anxious infant rejects the proffered nipple. For these reasons, we devote much of our lifetimes (and a great deal of energy) to reducing or avoiding the wholly unwanted tension of anxiety—as by ignoring that with which we cannot cope (**selective inattention**), or by unconsciously converting anxiety into the more palatable emotion of anger. "It is anxiety which is responsible for a great part of the inadequate, inefficient, unduly rigid, or otherwise unfortunate performances of people. . . . [and] for a great deal of what comes to a psychiatrist for attention" (Sullivan, 1953/1968, p. 160; see also Sullivan, 1953/1968, pp. 42, 53, 92–96, 152, 319, 353; 1954/1970, pp. 100, 135; 1956/1973, pp. 38–76).

Tenderness. Tension also occurs when the mothering one observes activity by the infant that indicates the existence of a need, such as crying. This tension *"is experienced as tenderness, and as an impulsion to activities toward the relief of the infant's needs"* (Sullivan, 1953/1968, p. 39). Thus the infant's need for the tender cooperation of the mothering one stimulates her need to give it, and produces the baby's first significant interpersonal relationship. If the mothering one should respond to the infant's distress with anxiety, however, her capacity for tenderness will be inhibited. Therefore, "there isn't any right thing to do with infantile anxiety, except for the mother to cease to be anxious" (Sullivan, 1953/1968, p. 54).

Dynamisms

Although Sullivan espouses a tension-reduction model of personality, he rejects the concept of psychic energy. "Energy, when I mention it, is energy as conceived in physics . . . There is no need to add adjectives such as 'mental.' . . . Physical energy . . . is the only kind of energy I know" (Sullivan, 1953/1968, pp. 35–36, 97, 101–102). Thus the human organism transforms physical energy, rather than libido, into behaviors designed to satisfy its needs.

To emphasize that personality is a dynamic process, and constantly in a state of flux, Sullivan refers to such energy transformations as **dynamisms.** This capacity is inborn, and is more or less common to all individuals. A dynamism may take various forms: overt moving or talking, covert reveries and fantasies, or partly or wholly unconscious processes.

For example, the hate dynamism involves the transformation of (physical) energy into behavior that will reduce tension through hostility. The individual may therefore strike or insult someone, have murderous fantasies, and/or form powerful unconscious destructive wishes. The dynamism of lust concerns the use of energy to satisfy sexual needs, as by making love or having erotic daydreams. (See Sullivan, 1953/1968, pp. 102–107; 1964/1971, p. 35 n. 3.)

Dynamisms are modified to some extent by learning and maturation. For this reason, the resulting behaviors are often not identical on different occasions, or as expressed by different individuals. Hate may vary in intensity from mild anger to severe rage, or in its specific form (e.g., blows versus insults). Yet these behaviors still represent the same dynamism, just as two oranges may differ somewhat in size and shape yet belong to the same class of fruit. Hate and lust are inherently different dynamisms, however, like oranges and lemons.

Types of Dynamisms. Some dynamisms reduce euphoria-disturbing tensions that occur in our interpersonal relationships, including lust, fear, anger, hate, guilt, and pride. (See Sullivan, 1953/1968, pp. 98–109; 1956/1973, pp. 91–127.) Also included in this category are the "safety" dynamisms of apathy and somnolent detachment, which prevent tension from reaching dangerous levels. For example, if a hungry infant is not fed for some time, the increasing tension and fear is likely to produce such self-destructive behavior as spasms and cyanosis. So the dynamism of apathy intervenes by acting like a damper, enabling the infant to end the spiraling tension by falling asleep. Similarly, the dynamism of somnolent detachment attenuates excessive anxiety. (Too much apathy or detachment will prove to be injurious or even fatal, however. See Sullivan, 1953/1968, pp. 55–57, 61, 71.)

A second class of dynamisms consists of those energy transformations that occur in specific "bodily end-stations" for dealing with the world (**zones of interaction**), such as the mouth, anus, urethra, genitals, and maternal mammary glands. For example, the oral zone does not serve only the needs of hunger and thirst. "As a dynamism it [also] manifests the need to suck, just as the hands manifest needs to feel and to manipulate, and so on" (Sullivan, 1953/1968, p. 125; see also Sullivan, 1947/1953, pp. 64–67).

Sullivan actually regards the total human organism (and even the entire universe!) as a dynamism made up of various subdynamisms, such as cells and organs. To support this contention, he points out that the cornea of the eye or the heart can go on living (and be successfully transplanted) after an individual has died. Therefore, they must have some dynamic character of their own.

One other particularly important dynamism is the self-system, which serves our need to be free from the tension of anxiety. Since this comes as close as Sullivan ever does to some sort of personality structure, it will be discussed in a subsequent section.

Modes of Experiencing

According to Sullivan, human experience consists entirely of tensions, dynamisms, and need satisfactions. He also argues that this experience occurs in one or more of three modalities: prototaxic, parataxic, and syntaxic.

The Prototaxic Mode. The primitive **prototaxic** mode is the newborn infant's only way of apprehending the environment. This limited form of experience is like a succession of momentary discrete states, and is incapable of such distinctions as before and after or self and others. It does include some indication of the zone of interaction where stimuli impinge on the infant, however, such as the oral zone during nursing. Prototaxic experience cannot be communicated in any kind of symbols, so it is only an educated guess by Sullivan as to the inner processes of the very young infant. (See Sullivan, 1953/1968, pp. xiv, 28–29, 35–36, 100.)

The Parataxic Mode. The prototaxic mode is not unique to early infancy, for it continues (to a lesser extent) throughout one's life. As the infant develops, however, it also becomes capable of the **parataxic** mode. This mode is characterized by the use of private or "autistic" symbols (such as nonsense words whose meaning is known only to the user), and by the ability to distinguish differences in time. Parataxic experience is illogical, however, and reflects a lack of understanding about causality. Examples include the superstitious belief that misfortune will result from walking under a ladder, or in front of a black cat; and the psychotic who thinks about rain on a clear day, and subsequently concludes that these ruminations actually caused the downpour that occurred some time thereafter.

The Syntaxic Mode. The most elaborate form of experience is the **syntaxic** mode, which begins to appear as early as the twelfth to eighteenth month of life. Syntaxic experience can be communicated through the use of symbols that are socially accepted and understood, such as "that fantastic evolutionary development, language." It also includes an understanding of conventional concepts of cause and effect (Sullivan, 1953/1968, p. 20).

Teleology

To Sullivan, as to Jung and Adler, human behavior must be understood in terms of both causality and teleology. Our capacity for foresight develops in early infancy, and represents one of the striking characteristics of the human species (Sullivan, 1953/1968, pp. 38–39; see also pp. 51, 64, 82). Unlike Jung, however, Sullivan concludes that psychological phenomena can ultimately be translated into physiological events; and his writings include numerous allusions to the anatomical and organic aspects of human functioning.

THE STRUCTURE OF PERSONALITY

Sullivan shares Fromm's and Horney's distaste for the Freudian structural model. According to Sullivan, we organize our experiences by forming mental conceptions of ourselves and others. These **personifications** consist of learned feelings and beliefs, which often do not correspond well with reality.

For example, a mother is likely to misperceive her child to at least some extent. She may form a personification that is more like the way she wants the child to be, or one that is influenced by her experiences with previous offspring. The infant gradually develops a personficiation of the good mother from her tender and need-satisfying behaviors, and also forms a personification of the bad mother from her frustrating and anxiety-producing behaviors. These personifications are also somewhat inaccurate, partly because the baby's ability to perceive and interpret the environment is limited. In fact, the infant does not realize at first that the personifications of good and bad mother refer to the same person, although significant portions of each do ultimately fuse into a complicated whole. (See Sullivan, 1953/1968, pp. 110–124, 167, 188–189.)

The irrational aspect of personifications is evident in the case of **stereotypes,** or beliefs that are applied rigidly and equally to a group of people and thus obscure the true differences among them. Young children commonly form a stereotype of the opposite sex as undesirable, while prejudiced individuals incorrectly personify members of a particular group as having certain negative characteristics in common. (See Sullivan, 1953/1968, pp. 236–238, 302–304.) Furthermore, such irrationality is also apparent in the personification that one forms of oneself.

The Self-System

The growing infant begins to conceive of itself as a separate and distinct entity at about age six months, and it organizes this information by forming appropriate personifications. These are so important that Sullivan tends to divide personality into two major categories, the **self-system** (or **self-dynamism**) and everything else. (See Sullivan, 1947/1953, pp. 19–29; 1953/1968, pp. 135–141, 158–171, 198–202; 1954/1970, pp. 101–112, 138.)

The self-system results partly from experiences with one's own body. For example, thumb sucking helps the infant differentiate between self and others because it produces unique feelings of both sucking and being

Anxiety	A harmful, unpleasant emotion similar to intense nervousness or (at its most extreme) to the uncanny emotions. Caused primarily by anxiety in the mothering one, and the corresponding loss of interpersonal security and self-esteem. To Sullivan, the avoidance or reduction of anxiety is one of the major objectives of human behavior.
Dissociation	Unconsciously disowning threatening aspects of one's personality, and associating them with the not-me personification.
Dynamism	The transformation of physical energy into behavior (overt or covert, conscious or unconscious) that will satisfy a need. Common dynamisms include lust, fear, anger, hate, guilt, pride, apathy, somnolent detachment, the self-system, and dynamisms associated with particular zones of interaction.
Euphoria	A state of well-being characterized by the absence of any internal needs or noxious external stimuli; the converse of tension.
Fear	An unpleasant but potentially constructive tension that feels similar to anxiety, but is caused by a substantial delay in the satisfaction of a need.
Interpersonal security	A feeling of safety achieved through one's relationships with others; the best way to reduce anxiety.
Malevolent transformation	A distortion or warp in personality development, resulting in the irrational belief that other people are enemies and have no tenderness or love to give. Caused by insufficient maternal tenderness and excessive parental hostility, irritability, and anxiety during the childhood stage.
Need	A physiological deficiency that creates a state of inner disequilibrium. Includes hunger, thirst, anoxia, sexuality, the maintenance of body temperature, and the necessity of eliminating bodily wastes (the "physicochemical" needs), and sleep.
"Not-me" personification	A normally unconscious component of personality, whose emergence produces uncanny emotions and the feeling of not being oneself. Results from extreme anxiety during childhood, too intense even to be dealt with by the "bad-me" personification.
One-Genus Postulate	The postulate that the similarities among human personalities far exceed the differences.
Parataxic mode	A mode of experiencing internal and external stimuli that is characterized by the use of private symbols, and a lack of understanding of conventional concepts of cause and effect.
Personification	An organized perception of a real or fictitious person, which need not (and often does not) correspond well with reality.

continued

215

Prototaxic mode	The primitive mode of experiencing internal and external stimuli that is most prominent in early infancy, consists of a succession of momentary discrete states, is incapable of such distinctions as before and after or self and others, and cannot be communicated to others.
Selective inattention	Deliberately, albeit unconsciously, not noticing certain (threatening) stimuli; a process used by the self-system to reduce anxiety and preserve self-esteem.
Self-system (self, self dynamism)	The organized perception (personification) of one's own self, including the desirable "good-me" and undesirable "bad-me." Results from experiences with one's body and the reflected opinions of significant others, and has the primary goal of reducing anxiety.
Stereotype	A personification (often irrational) that is rigidly and equally applied to a group of people, and thus obscures the true differences among them.
Sublimation	The unconscious substitution of a partially satisfying behavior for one that would be more gratifying, but would arouse greater anxiety.
Syntaxic mode	The most highly developed form of experiencing internal and external stimuli, characterized by the use of socially understood symbols (such as words and numbers) and by an understanding of conventional concepts of cause and effect.
Tension	A potentiality for action or change resulting from the inner disequilibrium caused by a physicochemical need, the need for sleep, anxiety, or the need to express maternal tenderness; often (but not always) conscious.
Uncanny emotions	Extremely unpleasant emotions, including awe, dread, horror, and loathing, which involve intense anxiety and often indicate the emergence of the "not-me" personification.
Zone of interaction	A bodily end-station that engages in contact with the external environment. Includes the oral, anal, urethral, and genital zones, and the maternal mammary glands.

sucked. For the most part, however, the self-system originates from the appraisals of significant others (such as the parents). We all must learn to transcend our animal origins and get along with others, so the unconditional maternal tenderness of early infancy must eventually be replaced by a system of rewards and punishments that will prepare the child for its place in society.

During later infancy and childhood, therefore, tenderness is used as an anxiety-reducing reward for desirable behaviors (such as achieving success at toilet-training, or abandoning the cherished but socially unacceptable activity of thumb sucking). Forbidding gestures, maternal anxiety, punishment, and even just the absence of tenderness serve as anxiety-inducing responses to the infant's errors and misdeeds. This leads to the development of the two personifications that eventually comprise the self-system: the desirable self or obedient "good-me" is associated with experiences that are rewarded by a decrease in anxiety, while the undesirable self or rebellious "bad-me" results from experiences that are punished by an increase in anxiety.

As with the infant's conceptions of good and bad mother, the good-me and bad-me personifications ultimately fuse into a single entity. The more intense the early experiences of anxiety, the more rigid and extensive this self-system will be. To Sullivan, therefore, self-centered behavior is a learned response to anxiety, rather than the result of innate narcissism. (See Sullivan, 1947/1953, p. 127 n. 41; 1953/1968, pp. 5, 126–134, 151–202.)

Selective Inattention. The primary goal of the self-system is the desirable one of reducing anxiety, thereby enabling the child to get along with its parents and satisfy its needs. However, it accomplishes this objective through such dubious "security operations" as **selective inattention.** That is, if the self-system should encounter information that threatens its stability, it simply ignores or rejects the incongruous data and goes on functioning as before.

Selective inattention may occasionally have beneficial aspects, as when a person avoids costly distractions by concentrating on the task at hand. But it is primarily disadvantageous, for it impedes our ability to learn from our failures and weaknesses; these sources of information are threatening to the self-system, so it is likely to pay no attention to them. (See Sullivan, 1953/1968, p. 319.) Selective inattention is so pervasive that most of our mental processes occur outside the realm of consciousness.

Because the self-system uses selective inattention to combat anxiety, it differs from other dynamisms by being extraordinarily resistant to change. This rigidity helps us to avoid undesirable personality changes, but it also represents the principal stumbling block to constructive growth as well. "We are being perfectly irrational and simply unpleasant if we expect another person to profit quickly from his experience, as long as his self-system is involved—although this is a very reasonable anticipation in all fields in which the self-system is not involved." The security operations of the self-system also create the impression that we differ more from others than is actually the case (a "delusion of unique individuality"), and may even result in a grandiose self-personification somewhat like the Adlerian superiority complex (Sullivan, 1953/1968, pp. 140, 192; see also Sullivan, 1953/1968, pp. 168–170, 247–248, 319, 346, 374; 1964/1971, pp. 198–226; 1956/1973, pp. 38–76.)

The "Not-Me" Personification

Intense anxiety during childhood ("a very poor method of education") leads to the development of the "not-me" personification, a shadowy and dreadful aspect of personality that is usually unconscious. The not-me personification involves material so threatening that even the bad-me personification cannot cope with it, so it is unconsciously divorced (**dissociated**) from one's self-personification. Dissociation is an extreme form of security operation that resembles "[flinging] something of you into outer darkness, where it reposes for years, quite peacefully," although the process is actually more complex because it requires constant (if unconscious) vigilance to maintain it (Sullivan, 1953/1968, pp. 163, 318; see also Sullivan, 1947/1953, p. 71; 1953/1968, pp. 201, 314–328; 1964/1971, pp. 248–249).

For example, a young child or schizophrenic may seek to avoid punishment by arguing and believing, "Oh, I didn't do that, it was my hand." The emergence into consciousness of the not-me personification produces uncanny emotions and the feeling of not being oneself, a terrifying experience that is common in schizophrenia—and in some nightmares and walking states of shock that befall more normal individuals.[1]

Other Defensive Behaviors

Sullivan differs from Freud by interpreting sublimation solely as a device for reducing anxiety, wherein one behavior is unconsciously substituted for another that would be more satisfying but also more threatening. This conception implies that sublimation is not always advantageous, for it may cause us to accept a less satisfying substitute on those occasions when anxiety has mistakenly become associated with acceptable activities. Sullivan also argues that fantasy can help us to make useful, realistic plans for the future.

In addition, Sullivan is highly (and wryly) skeptical about various other Freudian constructs. He regards introjection as "a great magic verbal gesture, the meaning of which cannot be made explicit." Projection is a "nice [topic] for certain late-evening-alcoholic psychiatric discussions." And regression is merely something which happens every twenty-four hours when a child goes to sleep and complicated, recently acquired patterns of behavior collapse, rather than "some great abstruse whatnot" that "psychiatrists often use . . . to brush aside mysteries which they do not grasp at all" (Sullivan, 1953/1968, pp. 166, 197, 359; see also Sullivan, 1947/1953, p. 54 n. 20; 1953/1968, pp. 113, 191–196, 348–350; 1964/1971, pp. 209–210; 1956/1973, pp. 14–20, 232).

---

[1]Since the not-me personification represents a more extreme defense against more intense anxiety than does the bad-me personification, some theorists might regard it as a third aspect of the self-system. Thus the continuum would be: good-me (resulting from minimal childhood anxiety, and most desirable), bad-me, not-me (resulting from maximal childhood anxiety, and least desirable). Because of its dissociated nature, however, it seems more a converse than an adjunct to the self-personification.

THE DEVELOPMENT OF PERSONALITY

Sullivan regards developmental psychology as the key to understanding human behavior, as we have seen. Unlike Freud, Sullivan concludes that significant changes in personality often occur during late childhood and adolescence. He posits seven specific epochs through which personality may develop, each of which represents an optimal time for certain innate capacities to reach fruition.

Infancy

The stage of infancy begins a few minutes after birth, and continues until the appearance of articulate speech (however meaningless). It is highlighted by the influence of maternal tenderness and anxiety. (See Sullivan, 1953/1968, pp. 49–187.) The oral zone is of greatest importance during this period (although not in the Freudian erotogenic sense), being intimately involved with such vital functions as breathing, nursing, crying, and thumb sucking.

Nursing provides the first, prototaxic experience in interpersonal relationships. The infant learns to identify and distinguish among such important external cues as the "good and satisfactory nipple," which is provided by a tender mother and gives milk when the infant is hungry; the "good but unsatisfactory nipple," which is offered by a tender mother when the infant is not hungry; and the "evil nipple" of the anxious mother, which is so unpleasant that it is rejected even if the infant is hungry. (See Sullivan, 1953/1968, pp. 49–50, 73, 79–81, 88, 122.)

Crying is for some time the infant's most effective method of satisfying needs and reducing anxiety, and varies according to its intent ("crying-when-hungry," "crying-when-afraid," "crying-when-cold," and so forth). For example, crying-when-hungry represents the infant's crude, prototaxic way of expressing the idea "come, nipple, into my mouth," and "has no necessary relatedness, in the infant's experience, with crying-when-cold, crying-when-pained, or crying-under-any-other-circumstances" (Sullivan, 1953/1968, p. 67; see also pp. 52–53, 62, 66–75). If satisfaction should be substantially delayed, the dynamisms of apathy and somnolent detachment intervene to reduce the spiraling tension. But crying usually does bring the desired relief, and such successes help the infant to develop foresight and an understanding of cause and effect. That is, the infant (in some primitive prototaxic fashion) concludes that "I cry when I suffer a certain distress, and that produces something different which is connected with the relief of the distress" (Sullivan, 1953/1968, p. 72).

The self-system begins to develop during mid-infancy. As we have seen, this is due primarily to two factors: bodily explorations such as thumb sucking, and the shift from unconditional maternal tenderness to training through rewards and punishments. Such training must be geared to the child's level of maturation, since different capacities emerge during each developmental epoch. Thus the mothering one must be careful not to impose unrealistic restrictions or goals, such as trying to prohibit thumb sucking too soon or striving for a record speed in toilet training.

Sullivan also warns against various other pathogenic parental behaviors. These include excessive anxiety, shattering the infant's will through domination and overly severe punishment, encouraging the baby to remain dependent and infantile, reacting with horror to the infant's manipulations of its genitals or anus, establishing inconsistent standards of reward and punishment, or forming erroneous personifications to which the infant is expected to conform (e.g., following in the footsteps of some physically similar relative). In addition, sublimation originates during this stage. (See Sullivan, 1953/1968, pp. 135–149, 171–175.)

During the twelfth to eighteenth month of life, the use of language begins with the imitation of sounds in the environment. This represents the appearance of the parataxic mode (or syntaxic mode, if the infant's utterances happen to correpond to actual words), and ushers in the second stage of personality development.

Childhood

During childhood, parental punishments further the growth of the bad-me aspect of the self-system. (See Sullivan, 1953/1968, pp. 188–226.) So long as the parents also assist the development of the good-me personification by providing sufficient rewards and tenderness, no great harm should result. But if the child's need for tenderness is consistently rebuffed by parental anxiety, irritability, or hostility, the bad-me component will eventually dominate the self-system. As with the neglected child in Adlerian theory, this **malevolent transformation** results in the misguided belief that other people are hostile and unloving:

> [The malevolent transformation] is perhaps the greatest disaster that [could happen] in the childhood phase of personality development. . . . [Such a child learns] that it is highly disadvantageous to show any need for tender cooperation from the authoritative figures around him. [Instead] he shows . . . the basic malevolent attitude, the attitude that one really lives among enemies. . . . This distortion, this malevolence . . . runs something like this: Once upon a time everything was lovely, but that was before I had to deal with people. (Sullivan, 1953/1968, pp. 214, 216.)

The malevolent child may be mischievous, behave like a bully, or express resentment more passively by stubbornly failing to do whatever is required. This transformation also impairs the sufferer's relationships with others, notably authority figures outside the immediate family.

Another potential problem during childhood is loneliness, which is caused by the parents' failure to join in the child's play. The lonely child

The Developmental Epochs (Sullivan)

	_____ A few minutes after birth
Infancy _____	
	_____ Appearance of articulate speech, even if meaningless
Childhood _____	
	_____ Appearance of the need for playmates
The Juvenile Era _____	
	_____ Appearance of the need for an intimate relationship with a person of the same sex (chum)
Preadolescence _____	
	_____ Puberty; appearance of the need for an intimate relationship with a person of the opposite sex
Early adolescence _____	
	_____ Satisfaction of the lust dynamism.
Late Adolescence _____	
	_____ Completion of personality development; ability for genuine love
Adulthood _____	

resorts to excessive daydreaming, which inhibits the ability to distinguish between reality and fantasy and to substitute syntaxic communication for parataxic symbology. Other serious parental errors include yielding to the child's every whim (similar to the Adlerian concept of pampering), excessive "oughts" (like Horney's "shoulds"), and breaking the child's spirit by creating a state of excessive obedience. (See Sullivan, 1953/1968, pp. 206, 223, 228.)

The personifications of good and bad mother begin to fuse into a single entity during childhood, aided by the fact that our language has only a single word for this important person. The father now joins the mother as an authority to be reckoned with, leading to the child's formation of a father personification. A knowledge of gender also begins to develop, with the boy or girl wishing to be like the parent of the same sex. To Sullivan, however, such identifications are not due to some sort of Oedipus complex. They occur because most parents are more comfortable with the child of the same sex, and reward behavior typical of that sex with approval and tenderness (Sullivan, 1953/1968, pp. 218–219).

The Juvenile Era

The juvenile era originates with the appearance of the need for playmates, which occurs at about the time of entry into school. (See Sullivan, 1953/1968, pp. 227–244.) Like Adler, Sullivan concludes that the educational system can remedy serious parental errors that occurred during infancy and childhood. Such favorable alterations in personality are possible because the normally rigid self-system is more amenable to change at the inception of each developmental stage, when newly maturing abilities increase the probability of significant changes in behavior.

The juvenile learns to adjust to the demands, rewards, and punishments of such new authority figures as teachers. He or she observes how other juveniles are treated by these authorities (and by each other), continues to develop sublimations that reduce anxiety and preserve self-esteem, learns to deal with peers (including the malevolent bully), and is introduced to the social processes of competition and compromise. School also involves the formation of social in-groups and out-groups, bringing the painful possibility of ostracism by one's peers. Thus the juvenile era is the time when the world begins to be complicated by the presence of other people, and is typified by inexperienced attempts at interpersonal relationships that often reflect a shocking insensitivity to other people's feelings of personal worth. (See Sullivan, 1947/1953, pp. 38–41; 1953/1968, pp. 227–232.)

The syntaxic model becomes prominent during the juvenile era. In addition, the parents begin to lose their godlike attributes and take on more human, fallible personifications. "[If one] comes out of the juvenile era with [the feeling that the parents] still have to be sacrosanct, the most perfect people on earth, then one of the most striking and important of the juvenile contributions to socialization has sadly miscarried" (Sullivan, 1953/1968, p. 231). Another potential source of pathology involves parents who frequently move from city to city, thereby preventing the juvenile from establishing relationships with a specific group of peers. Or the parents may constantly disparage other people, which causes the juvenile to feel incapable of knowing what is good:

> If you have to maintain self-esteem by pulling down the standing of others, you are extraordinarily unfortunate. . . . The doctrine that if you are a molehill then, by God, there shall be no mountains . . . is probably the most vicious of the inadequate, inappropriate, and ineffectual performances of parents with juveniles. . . . (Sullivan, 1953/1968, pp. 242–243, 309.)

Ideally, an adequate orientation for living with other people is achieved by the end of the juvenile era. This includes reasonably accurate insights into the nature of one's interpersonal needs and appropriate techniques for satisfying them, notably sublimations. Since these are formed unconsciously, "most of us come into adult life with a great many firmly entrenched ways of dealing with our fellow man which we cannot explain adequately" (Sullivan, 1953/1968, p. 235).

Preadolescence

The preadolescent stage is highlighted by the need for an intimate relationship with a particular individual of the same sex, or chum. (See Sullivan, 1953/1968, pp. 245–262.) This relatively brief period tends to occur between the ages of eight-and-a-half and ten, though it may be delayed by as much as a few years if maturation is relatively slow.

The preadolescent chumship is particularly crucial because it represents the first appearance of an emotion similar to love, or a sincere interest in the welfare of another person. In fact, the influence of this important individual may be sufficient to modify the otherwise rigid self-system and correct any warps in personality carried over from preceding stages. "Because one draws so close to another, because one is newly capable of seeing oneself through the other's eyes, the preadolescent phase of personality development is especially significant in correcting autistic, fantastic ideas about oneself or others" (Sullivan, 1953/1968, p. 248; see also Sullivan, 1947/1953, pp. 41–44). Thus an effective chumship may help alter such misguided views as arrogance, overdependence, or the belief that one should be liked by everyone. It may even reverse or cure a malevolent transformation. Contrariwise, difficulties in dealing with others of the same sex are invariably due (at least in the case of males) to the failure to develop this essential preadolescent relationship, and to the resulting feelings of intense loneliness.

Early Adolescence

The period of early adolescence begins with puberty and the appearance of the powerful lust dynamism, which leads to the desire for a close relationship with a member of the opposite sex. (See Sullivan, 1953/1968, pp. 263–296.) In contrast to the intimacy of the preadolescent stage, which is by no means necessarily sexual, lust is expressed primarily through the genital zone and culminates in the experience of orgasm.

Sullivan warns that early adolescence is rife with possibilities for serious maladjustment, notably because our culture confronts us with singular handicaps in our pursuit of lustful activity. Essential information and guidance may well be totally lacking at this important time, and the parents may even add to the problem by providing ridicule and sarcasm instead of emotional support. Thus the adolescent's fledgling attempts at heterosexuality may lead to such embarrassing outcomes as impotence, frigidity, or premature ejaculation, causing a sharp decrease in self-esteem; and "customarily low self-esteem makes it difficult indeed for the carrier person . . . to mainfest good feeling toward another person" (Sullivan, 1953/1968, p. 351; see also Sullivan, 1947/1953, p. 63; 1954/1970, p. 9).

The unfortunate individual may therefore rush headlong into marriage with the first member of the opposite sex who inspires any feelings akin to love, a relationship that is usually far from satisfying. The adolescent may develop a strong dislike and fear of the opposite sex, possibly resulting in celibacy, excessive fantasizing, or homosexuality. Or the adolescent may conduct an endless quest for the ideal member of the opposite sex, and blame the inevitable failures on apparent defects in every candidate rather than on the unconscious fears about heterosexuality. An adolescent who has not emotionally outgrown the juvenile era may form numerous superficial sexual liaisons ("Don Juanism"). Whereas occasional masturbation is not harmful (and is virtually universal), an anxious adolescent may rely so heavily on self-stimulation that healthy heterosexuality becomes impossible. Some adolescents mature at an unusually slow rate, which retards the desire for heterosexual relationships and is likely to provoke considerable pressure from more socially advanced friends.

Despite the seriousness of such problems, Sullivan does not regard sexual dysfunction as the most important aspect of psychiatry. Instead he prefers to emphasize the inability to form satisfying interpersonal relationships, which invariably lies at the root of the more manifest sexual difficulties (Sullivan, 1953/1968, pp. 295–296; 1954/1970, p. 13).

Late Adolescence

The latter part of adolescence originates with the achievement of satisfying sexual activity. (See Sullivan, 1953/1968, pp. 297–310). The adolescent must now contend with increasing social responsibilities, such as working and paying income tax. Socioeconomic status also affects this stage of personality development, for those who are able to attend college have several years of extraordinary opportunity for observation and learning that others do not. Previously extant warps in personality may now be evidenced by a pronounced tendency to avoid others, or by such pseudosocial rituals as impersonal card games that provide only the most superficial of contacts.

Adulthood

Sullivan has relatively little to say about the stage of adulthood, which represents maturity and the completion of personality development, because psychiatrists do not get many opportunities to observe well-adjusted behavior. Adulthood is denoted by a mature repertory of interpersonal behaviors and the capacity for genuine love, a state wherein "the other person is as significant, or nearly as significant, as one's self" (Sullivan, 1953/1968, p. 34; see also Sullivan, 1947/1953, p. 42; 1953/1968, pp. 297, 309–310). This final epoch is somewhat similar to the Freudian genital stage (without the sexual implications) and to Fromm's productive orientation. However, Sullivan is not overly optimistic about our chances to attain it. "I believe that for a great majority of our people, preadolescence is the nearest that they come to untroubled human life—that from then on, the stresses of life distort them to inferior caricatures of what they might have been" (Sullivan, 1947/1953, p. 56).

FURTHER APPLICATIONS
OF SULLIVANIAN THEORY

Psychopathology

In accordance with all of the theorists discussed thus far, Sullivan regards psychopathology as a difference in degree rather than in kind. Every patient "is *mostly* a person like the psychiatrist," and even the bizarre behavior of the psychotic is related to processes that occur in relatively normal individuals (Sullivan, 1947/1953, p. 96; see also Sullivan, 1953/1968, pp. 208, 223; 1954/1970, pp. 18, 183).

Causes of Psychopathology. To Sullivan, all nonorganic forms of mental disorder (including the neuroses and schizophrenia) are caused by pathogenic interpersonal relationships.[2] These include excessive maternal anxiety during infancy; loneliness, inconsistent punishment, or the lack of sufficient tenderness during childhood; the failure to find a satisfactory juvenile peer group or preadolescent chum; problems in early adolescence with heterosexual relationships and the lust dynamism, a particularly difficult one to sublimate; and so forth. The result is a significant decrease in self-esteem, and an exceptionally rigid and distorted self-system. This prevents the sufferer from establishing a mature repertory of interpersonal behaviors.

For example, the malevolent individual's exaggerated bad-me personification produces an excessive reliance on the hate dynamism and the derogation of self and others. This limited repertoire of social behaviors makes it extremely difficult, if not impossible, to develop satisfying interpersonal relationships. Or chronically low self-esteem may lead to pronounced dependency, exploitativeness, or seclusiveness, like Horney's conception of moving toward, against, or away from people. But whatever the specific cause and form, all mental disorders are to be understood as patterns of inadequate and inappropriate behavior in interpersonal relations. (See Sullivan, 1953/1968, pp. 313–328, 344–363; 1954/1970, pp. 183–208; 1956/1973, pp. 200–202.)

Like Adler, Sullivan warns that ethnic and religious prejudice may well have destructive effects on one's personality. He also shares Fromm's concern about pathogenic societal forces, partly because of the devastation he observed during World War II. "The Western world is a profoundly sick society in which each denizen, each person, is sick to the extent that he is *of it*" (Sullivan, 1964/1971, p. 155; see also pp. 76–84, 100–107).

Varieties of Psychopathology. Sullivan is critical of the standard psychiatric nomenclature, which he regards as a source of potential confusion. "These

---

[2]Sullivan did posit an organic form of schizophrenia as well, but this (erroneous) idea was clearly secondary to his interest in nonorganic disorders. (See Arieti, 1974, p. 29; Sullivan, 1947/1953, pp. 148–149.)

trick words, so far as I can discover, merely make one a member of a somewhat esoteric union made up of people who certainly can't talk to anybody outside the union and who only have the illusion that they are talking to one another" (Sullivan, 1953/1968, p. 7). Nevertheless, Sullivan does make use of such formal diagnostic categories as manic-depressive psychosis, hysteria, hypochrondria, paranoia, and psychopathy. His major clinical interests concern two of the standard classifications, obsessive-compulsive neurosis and schizophrenia.

Obsessive-compulsive neurosis reflects an abnormal vulnerability to anxiety and a profound loss of self-esteem, caused by never having had outstanding success in one's interpersonal relations. The resulting security operations consist of ritualistic thoughts and actions, which are (unconsciously) substituted for behaviors that would provoke greater anxiety. For example, hate may replace the threatening need for others. Or the fear of syntaxically revealing one's true feelings may lead to conversation denoted by so many hairsplitting qualifications, bordering on the parataxic, that other people feel as though they are helplessly entangled in a sheet of flypaper. Secondary gains also play a significant role in this disorder, as with the patient of Sullivan's who could not leave the second floor of his home because of an obsession about committing suicide by jumping from a flight of stairs. He not only achieved some security against a threatening external world, but also enjoyed the constant sympathy and attention of his wife—at least until she grew weary of his neurotic demands, and divorced him a few years later. (See Sullivan, 1953/1968, pp. 210–211, 318–319; 1964/1971, pp. 231–232; 1956/1973, pp. 229–283.)

Obsessive-compulsive neurosis is similar in many respects to schizophrenia, and is often a prelude or postlude to this form of psychosis. Schizophrenia is caused by the occurrence of uncanny emotions early in life, notably extreme anxiety, or by disastrous blows to one's self-esteem during the latter stages of development (particularly adolescence). For example, if a parent has irrational fears about the infant's sexuality and becomes horrified when the baby toys with its genitals, the resulting extreme anxiety is likely to prove as numbing and incomprehensible as a severe blow on the head. Rather than associating the genitals with the bad-me personification, as would be the case with less traumatic punishment, the child may instead dissociate this highly threatening issue from its self-system. Thus sexual impulses and behaviors become associated with the unconscious not-me personification and are attributed to external sources, producing a gap in this area of personality that will create serious difficulties during early adolescence. The schizophrenic's quest for security also involves a regression to parataxic speech that has meaning to the patient, but appears incomprehensible and bizarre to others. To Sullivan, therefore, schizophrenia represents a return to an early form of mental functioning in an attempt to ward off intense anxiety and restore a shattered sense of self-esteem. (See for example Arieti, 1974, pp. 25–29; Sullivan, 1953/1968, pp. 313–328, 360–361; 1956/1973; 1962/1974.)

Psychotherapy

Theoretical Foundation. To Sullivan, psychotherapy is first and foremost a learning process. "There is no *essential* difference between psychotherapeutic achievement and achievements in other forms of education. . . [all of which are] in the end reducible to the common denominator of *experience incorporated into the self. . . .* [Thus] *I am avoiding the term 'cure,' since I do not think it applies in the realm of personality*" (Sullivan, 1956/1973, p. 228; 1962/1974, p. 281; see also Sullivan, 1954/1970, p. 238).

Ideally, therapy enables the patient to gain valuable insights into issues that were selectively inattended, reintegrate dissociated aspects of personality, and establish a proper balance between the good-me and bad-me personifications. This expansion of the self-system facilitates the development of a wider, more effective repertory of interpersonal behaviors. Thus therapy may help a patient suffering from dissociated sexual impulses to accept the existence of inner lustful drives, recognize and eliminate the accompanying shame and guilt, and develop appropriate behaviors for satisfying this need. Or a malevolent patient may learn to reduce an exaggerated bad-me personification, establish some love of self, develop more accurate interpersonal perceptions, and (ultimately) express tenderness and love to others.

Although therapy is aided by the patient's inherent drive toward mental health, surrendering the various security operations and facing up to one's weaknesses is a difficult and threatening task. Therefore, the therapist must be an expert in interpersonal relations—one who knows more than the patient about any aspect of this field that may be brought up for discussion, and who is able to alleviate the patient's doubts and anxieties by demonstrating that therapy will have important benefits (Sullivan, 1954/1970, pp. 11–19, 29, 120, 242).

Therapeutic Procedures. Sullivanian psychotherapy focuses on the interpersonal relationship between the patient and therapist. The therapist is an active participant as well as an observer, focusing on what the patient is saying "with me and to me" and preventing lengthy forays into inconsequential territory. "The expert [therapist] does not permit people to tell him things so beside the point that only God could guess how they happened to get into the account" (Sullivan, 1954/1970, pp. 34, 58; see also Sullivan, 1953/1968, pp. 13–14; 1954/1970, pp. 3–6, 19–25, 82–85, 113).

Sullivanians eschew the use of a couch and sit at a ninety-degree angle to the patient, enabling them to detect sudden changes of posture without being distracted by facial expressions. They also reject the use of free association with schizophrenics as too anxiety-provoking, and limit its use with other disorders to times when the patient is blocked and therefore more ready to recognize its value. Sullivan dislikes taking written notes during the therapeutic session, arguing that this method is distracting and cannot register subtle nuances in behavior, but does advocate the use of tape recordings.

He also favors relatively brief and simple interpretations, so as to avoid causing excessive anxiety and intensifying the defenses of the patient's self-system. The goal of such interpretations is to help the patient realize that the present way of life is unsatisfactory and discover viable new alternatives, whereupon modifying the self-system (even at the cost of some anxiety) becomes preferable to maintaining the status quo. (See Singer, 1970, pp. 196–199; Sullivan, 1953/1968, p. 302; 1954/1970, p. 90; White, 1952, pp. 132–133.)

Psychotherapy begins with the stage of "formal inception," during which the patient first meets the psychiatrist and provides some explanation for entering therapy. Sullivan warns that the therapist's initial behavior is of considerable importance, for even such apparently minor errors as an overly limp handshake, an excessively warm or cool greeting, or somewhat too much arrogance or diffidence can significantly affect the patient's perceptions and distort the subsequent course of treatment. (See Sullivan, 1954.)

The second stage of therapy, or "reconnaissance," occurs when the psychiatrist has formed a fairly good idea as to why the patient is in need of professional assistance. This period generally takes from seven-and-a-half to fifteen hours and consists of an unstructured inquiry into such details as the patient's age, birthplace, birth order, marital status, educational background, occupational history, professions of the parents, and the existence of any other significant adults in the home during infancy and childhood. The reconnaissance concludes with a summary statement of what the therapist has learned about the patient, whereupon the patient usually agrees that some significant problems have emerged that are worthy of further study.

The third stage, or "detailed inquiry," represents the "long haul" of psychotherapy. No matter how skilled the therapist may be, the preceding brief stages are unlikely to provide a wholly accurate picture. Many patients try to reduce anxiety by making statements designed to please or impress the therapist, by rationalizing or ignoring their failures and embarrassments, or by exaggerating their successes. Or a patient's communications may be deceptively difficult to understand because they include a substantial quantity of parataxic symbols. During the detailed inquiry, therefore, the impressions gained from the formal inception and reconnaissance are checked against more substantial data provided by the patient. Thus the therapist probes into important aspects of the patient's developmental history, including such issues as toilet-training, learning speech, attitudes toward competition and compromise, school experiences, the preadolescent chum, puberty, attitudes toward risqué talk and sex, and vocational and marital history. The patient's anxiety and security operations for avoiding it, as demonstrated in the relationship with the therapist, are also of particular importance.

The final stage of therapy ("termination") includes four major steps: a succinct formal statement of what the therapist has learned during the course of treatment, a prescription for actions that the patient should take or avoid, a formal assessment of the patient's probable future course in life, and a clear-cut leave-taking that is neither too indecisive nor too abrupt. Pessimistic prognoses are avoided, however, since they may well become self-fulfilling prophecies. "I try never to close all doors to a person; the person should go away with hope and with an improved grasp on what has been the trouble" (Sullivan, 1954/1970, p. 211).

Unlike Freud, Sullivan devoted the majority of his attention to the treatment of schizophrenia. During his life he was sharply critical of the inferior methods and conditions of most mental hospitals, and any ward under his supervision was conducted according to his own unique regulations. For example, he prohibited female nurses from appearing in all-male wards because the patients were all too likely to regard them as threatening symbols of authoritarianism. Instead he trained his own (male) assistants, and emphasized upon them his belief that the patients' daily life and social contacts on the ward were even more important than the hourly sessions with the psychiatrist. (See Arieti, 1974, p. 541; Sullivan, 1954/1970, pp. xx, 50; 1962/1974, pp. xvi–xix.) Although capable of pronounced sarcasm with colleagues, Sullivan was unfailingly kind and gentle with schizophrenics. Even when an upset patient would slap him in the face, he would strictly prohibit any reprisals and only ask quietly, "Well, do you feel better now?" Nor was he afraid to be somewhat unorthodox, and would compensate for the lack of modern drug techniques by using alcoholic beverages to relax a rigid self-system and make the patient more amenable to change (Sullivan, 1947/1953, p. 219).

Dream Interpretation. As in psychoanalytic theory, Sullivan concludes that the defenses of the self-system relax to some extent during deep sleep. This provides an opportunity to discharge any tensions that were unsatisfied during waking hours, or only partially satisfied through sublimation, because they occasioned too much anxiety. Unlike Freud, however, Sullivan does not regard dreams as particularly rich sources of information about the human personality. He argues that our recall upon awakening is hopelessly distorted by the resurgent self-system, and he criticizes interpretations designed to unearth some sort of latent content as futile efforts to translate the dreamer's private (parataxic) symbology into communicable (syntaxic) experience.

Sullivan limits dream interpretation to reflecting back important aspects, with the goal of stimulating the patient's train of thought. For example, a patient of Sullivan's once dreamed of approaching a highly attractive Dutch windmill, only to find upon entering that it was ruined and inches deep in dust. Sullivan's reply was, "that is, beautiful, active on the outside—utterly dead and decayed within. Does it provoke anything?" Whereupon the patient responded, "my God, my mother," recognizing with astonishment that he actually regarded her as a "sort of zombie . . . [or] weary phonograph offering cultural platitudes" (Sullivan, 1953/1968, pp. 338–339; see also Sullivan, 1947/1953, pp. 69–72; 1953/1968, pp. 329–337; 1956/1973, pp. 19–20).

Resistance, Transference, and Countertransference. Like Horney, Sullivan prefers to redefine the Freudian concept of resistance. He agrees that the self-system constantly opposes the goals of therapy. But he interprets this as an attempt to reduce anxiety, rather than as an effort to preserve illicit impulses. Sullivan is also opposed to the use of transference, which he regards as another erroneous interpersonal perception that the patient must learn to abandon. Nor does he mention countertransference, although he does warn therapists about the dangers of forming stereotypes and concludes that undergoing a personal analysis is essential. (See Sullivan, 1947/1953, p. 212 n. 69; 1953/1968, pp. 237–238; 1954/1970, pp. 26, 104, 139, 219, 231.)

Above all, Sullivan emphasizes the difficulty of doing effective psychotherapy. The psychiatrist's primary obligation is to ensure that therapy benefits the patient, rather than striving for his or her own enjoyment. Psychiatry is "far . . . from being scientific," so the practitioner may well lack essential theoretical and methodological guidelines. And cultural standards may stress that people ought not to need professional help even for the most difficult personal problems, making those who do enter therapy still more defensive. Thus "there is no fun in psychiatry. . . . It is work—work the like of which I do not know" (Sullivan, 1953/1968, p. 14; 1954/1970, p. 10).

Psychotherapy and Social Reform. Like Fromm, Sullivan (1964/1971) discusses such social applications of personality theory as world tensions, national defense, and propaganda and censorship. However, his untimely death prevented him from devoting more than a few articles to this area.

EVALUATION

Criticisms and Controversies

For one who claims to dislike psychiatric jargon, Sullivan is not averse to introducing some formidable terminology of his own. His writings are probably more difficult than any of the theorists discussed thus far except Jung (and perhaps some parts of Freudian theory), and his language poses a considerable barrier to the prospective reader (Mullahy, 1945/1953, p. 291).

Although based on a different premise, Sullivan's tension-reduction model of human motivation is as subject to criticism as Freud's. The concept of dynamism has an all-pervasive quality similar to Freudian sexuality and Adlerian inferiority, and has not enjoyed much popularity among modern psychologists. Also, Sullivan often fails to acknowledge his intellectual debts to his predecessors. He ignores obvious similarities between such concepts as actively maintained dissociations and actively maintained repressions, security operations and defense mechanisms, the malevolent transformation and Adler's theory of the neglected child, personifications and Adler's "fictions," and the self-system and the style of life.

Sullivan has also been criticized for attributing the formation of the self-system primarily to the appraisals of significant others, and for ignoring those distortions introduced by the child's own misperceptions and faulty cognitions. (See Arieti, 1974, p. 78; Ellenberger, 1970, p. 639.) Sullivan's theory, like those of Horney and Fromm, has not generated much empirical research. In comparison to Fromm, Sullivan's approach to dreams seems shallow and unconvincing. Finally, to an even greater extent than Fromm and Adler, Sullivan has been taken to task for overemphasizing the interpersonal aspects of personality.

Contributions

Perhaps Sullivan's greatest contributions concern the understanding and treatment of schizophrenia. Because of his emphasis on its nonorganic and interpersonal causes, and his many therapeutic successes with such patients, he has been credited as the first author to offer a convincing psychodynamic interpretation of this disorder (Arieti, 1974, p. 25). As with Horney and Fromm, Sullivan's rejection of libido theory finds favor with many modern psychologists.

Sullivan's conception of the important variable of anxiety is superior to that of Adler, and reflects a much better understanding of the pain and suffering that are involved. As Sullivan puts it, "Under no conceivable circumstances . . . has anyone sought and valued as desirable the experience of anxiety. . . . People who ride on roller coasters pay money for being afraid. But no one will ever pay money for anxiety in its own right. No one wants to experience it. Only one other experience—that of loneliness—is in this special class of being totally unwanted" (1954/1970, p. 100).

Sullivan devotes far more attention to the development of personality than either Horney or Fromm. His approach to important causes of psychopathology during adolescence appears preferable to Freud's and Adler's relative lack of concern with this stage of life. Finally, Sullivan's emphasis on observable behavior would be warmly endorsed by many modern behaviorists.

Sullivan's extensive neologisms are indeed troublesome, so much so that some students of human behavior prefer to avoid his ideas. This is highly unfortunate, for a careful study of his major writings will yield quite a few pearls of genuine wisdom.

Suggested Reading

The most complete discussion of Sullivanian theory is presented in *The Interpersonal Theory of Psychiatry* (1953/1968). Also well-regarded is his work on psychotherapeutic procedures, *The Psychiatric Interview* (1954/1970). For a biography of Sullivan, see Perry (1982).

■ SUMMARY

Like Horney and Fromm, Harry Stack Sullivan emphasizes the interpersonal nature of personality. However, Sullivan's theory devotes considerably more attention to the development of personality, and to the dynamics and treatment of schizophrenia.

1. THE BASIC NATURE OF HUMAN BEINGS. Sullivan is perhaps less optimistic about human nature than Horney and Fromm, but he does posit an inherent drive toward mental health. *The One-Genus Postulate:* To Sullivan, human personalities more closely resemble each other than anything else in the world. Therefore, unlike Adler, he prefers to emphasize the similarities among human beings rather than the differences. *The Need For Others:* Relationships with others are essential to proper personality development. In fact, Sullivan defines personality wholly in terms of interpersonal factors. *Tension Reduction:* Human beings are motivated to reduce various tensions, the most notable of which is anxiety. Others arise from the physicochemical needs, the need for sleep, and the arousal of maternal tenderness. *Dynamisms:* Sullivan rejects the construct of psychic energy, concluding instead that behavior can be explained wholly in terms of transformations of physical energy (dynamisms). *Other Factors:* Human experience occurs in one or more of three modalities: prototaxic, parataxic, and syntaxic. Like Jung and Adler, Sullivan concludes that behavior must be understood in terms of both causality and teleology.

2. THE STRUCTURE OF PERSONALITY. The growing child organizes its experience by forming mental conceptions (personifications) of other people and, most importantly, of itself. *The Self-System:* Personifications of oneself result from experiences with one's own body, and from the appraisals of significant others (particularly the parents). This self-system consists of the good-me and bad-me personifications, has the goal of reducing anxiety, and is remarkably resistant to change. *The Not-Me Personification:* Aspects of personality that occasion intense anxiety are dissociated from the self-system, and comprise the shadowy and dreadful not-me personification. This personification plays a significant role in schizophrenia. *Other Factors:* Sullivan regards much of personality as unconscious, but he attributes this to selective inattention rather than to repression. He interprets sublimation as an attempt to reduce anxiety, rather than as the diversion of illicit impulses.

3. THE DEVELOPMENT OF PERSONALITY. Sullivan regards developmental psychology as the key to understanding human behavior. He discusses in detail seven developmental epochs, each of which represents an optimal time for certain innate capacities to reach fruition. Infancy is highlighted by such oral events as crying and nursing, the beginnings of the self-system, and the beginning use of language. Childhood is a time for dealing with parental rewards and punishments, and may give rise to the malevolent transformation or loneliness. The juvenile era originates with the appearance of the need for playmates, and should ideally result in an

adequate orientation for living with other people. Preadolescence is highlighted by the need for an intimate relationship with a particular individual of the same sex, or chum. Early adolescence begins with puberty, and includes the desire for a close relationship with a member of the opposite sex. Late adolescence originates with the achievement of satisfying sexual activity, and involves increasing social responsibilities. Finally, adulthood—a stage of true maturity that is probably not attainable by most people—is denoted by the capacity for genuine love.

4. FURTHER APPLICATIONS. *Psychopathology:* Sullivan is particularly concerned with two forms of psychopathology. Obsessive-compulsive neurosis reflects an extreme vulnerability to anxiety and a profound loss of self-esteem, with ritualistic thoughts and actions used as security operations. Schizophrenia is caused by uncanny emotions that occur early in life, notably extreme anxiety, or by disastrous blows to one's self-esteem during such later stages as adolescence. It involves the dissociation of highly threatening aspects of one's personality. *Psychotherapy:* Sullivan regards psychotherapy primarily as a form of education, rather than as a medically-oriented "cure." The goals are to reintegrate dissociated aspects of personality and expand the self-system, thereby leading to a wider and more effective repertory of behavior. Sullivan has devoted considerable attention to the technique of psychiatric interviewing, and has published several articles on social change and international problems.

5. EVALUATION. Sullivan has been criticized for excessive neologisms, the use of a tension-reduction model of motivation, a shallow approach to dream interpretation, failing to acknowledge similarities between his constructs and those of Freud and Adler, and overemphasizing the importance of the interpersonal aspects of personality. Yet he has also been credited as the first to offer a convincing psychodynamic interpretation of schizophrenia, and he was a pioneer in advocating and using more humane treatment methods with such patients. He has furthered our understanding of personality development (including such stages as adolescence, which Freud ignored), of the important phenomenon of anxiety, and of psychiatric interviewing and psychotherapy. And he played a significant role in numerous international projects seeking the highly desirable, but elusive, goal of world peace.

STUDY QUESTIONS

1. Consider once again the case history described in the Appendix in Chapter 2, question 6; Chapter 4, questions 2 and 6a; and Chapter 5, question 1. (a) How would Sullivan explain the causes of this man's anxiety, given the following additional information? (1) His mother suffered from frequent anxiety, so much so that her hand often shook when she held his hand. (2) His mother often referred to relatives and friends in such negative terms as thoughtless, inconsiderate, and likely to hurt one's feelings. (3) He often feared his father's angry criticism and ridicule, but was not afraid of his

mother. (b) How would Sullivan explain this man's inability to alleviate his painful anxiety?

2. Both Sullivan and Jung were particularly interested in schizophrenia. How might Sullivan's concept of the parataxic mode be related to: (a) the lives of both theorists? (b) Jung's construct of synchronicity? (c) the kinds of constructs devised by both theorists?

3. How would Sullivan describe and explain the behavior of schizophrenic teenager Deborah Blau in the well-known autobiographical novel, *I Never Promised You a Rose Garden?*

4. (a) Sullivan rejects Freud's construct of libido on the grounds that "physical energy is the only kind of energy I know." Do you agree with Sullivan or Freud? Why? (b) Describe the purpose of dynamisms in a single sentence. (c) Give examples of behaviors that represent the same dynamism but differ in form and/or intensity.

5. Consider Sullivan's and Freud's definitions of sublimation. (a) How are they similar? (b) How do they differ? Illustrate with an example.

6. Freud contends that personality development is virtually complete by about age five or six. Sullivan argues that personality continues to develop through late childhood and adolescence, influenced by such factors as interactions with one's schoolmates, the preadolescent chum, and the emergence of the lust dynamism. Do you agree with Sullivan or Freud? Why?

7. Sullivan has been criticized for attributing the formation of the self-system primarily to the opinions of other people, and ignoring the distortions caused by the child's own misperceptions and incorrect thoughts. (a) Give a real-life example to illustrate how the child's own errors significantly affect the development of the self-system. (b) Why might the child want to blame any defects in its self-system entirely on the parents? (c) What personal reasons might Sullivan have had for developing this view of the self-system?

8

ERIK ERIKSON
Ego Psychology

Being rejected by one's professional colleagues is not among life's more pleasant experiences. Jung, Adler, Horney, Fromm, and Sullivan all chose to abandon Freud's psychic energy model, and they all incurred the wrath of the psychoanalytic establishment for doing so (as we have seen).

In contrast, some seminal thinkers have preferred to retain but modify libido theory. These psychologists readily accept such fundamental Freudian principles as infantile sexuality, unconscious processes and conflicts, and the structural model (id, ego, and superego). But they argue that Freud overemphasized the role of the irrational id and intrapsychic strife, while paying too little attention to more adaptive and peaceful mental functioning. Therefore, using some of Freud's own later writings as their point of departure (e.g., 1937/1963w; 1940/1969a), these theorists devote considerably more attention to the strengths and abilities of the ego. Accordingly, this modification of psychoanalysis has become known as **ego psychology.** The primary differences between ego psychology and basic Freudian (or "id") theory are shown in the accompanying Capsule Summary.

Although various theorists have contributed to the development of ego psychology, one exponent has achieved a singular degree of professional and popular acclaim. This unusual and creative man entered the Freudian circle in Vienna as a twenty-five-year-old itinerant artist, with no university degree at all, and emerged as a prominent child psychoanalyst. He contributed the term *identity crisis* to our everyday language, having first faced and resolved this difficult one of his own: Erik Homburger Erikson.

BIOGRAPHICAL SKETCH

Erik Homburger Erikson was born of Danish parents on June 15, 1902, in Frankfurt, Germany. His father, a Protestant, abandoned the family prior to Erik's birth. Some three years later his mother married Dr. Theodor Homburger, a pediatrician of the same Jewish faith as herself. Erik experienced considerable identity confusion because of this family upheaval, and because the contrast between his part-Jewish heritage and his Nordic features caused him to be rejected by childhood peers of both groups. Known as Erik Homburger during the first four decades of his life, he adopted the surname of Erikson upon becoming a naturalized American citizen in 1939, and he ultimately converted to Christianity. As he was to reflect many years later, "no doubt my best friends will insist that I needed to name [the identity] crisis and to see it in everybody else in order to really come to terms with it in myself" (Erikson, 1975, p. 26; see also Coles, 1970, pp. 180–181; Roazen, 1976a, pp. 93–99).

Erikson was a mediocre student, never earning a university degree of any kind. During his early twenties he became a wanderer, studied briefly at art schools, painted children's portraits, and struggled with psychological problems bordering between neurosis and psychosis. "I was an artist then, which can be a European euphemism for a young man with some talent, but nowhere to go." In the summer of 1927 he moved to Vienna, accepted a teaching position at a small school established for children of Freud's patients and friends, and enjoyed a "truly astounding adoption by the Freudian circle" (Erikson, 1964, p. 20; 1975, p. 29). Erikson now undertook training in child psychoanalysis, including a personal analysis by Anna Freud at the unusually low rate of seven dollars per month. He married Joan Serson on April 1, 1930, a successful and enduring union that has produced two sons and a daughter.

Erikson foresaw the coming Nazi menace and emigrated via Denmark to Boston in 1933. There he became the city's first practicing child analyst, and joined the staff of Henry Murray's clinic at Harvard. Like Jung, Erikson took a keen interest in cross-cultural studies and engaged in first-hand observation of two American Indian tribes: the Sioux of South Dakota in 1938, and the Yurok of northern California some five years later. His academic affiliations also included Yale University and the University of California at Berkeley, from which he resigned in 1950 rather than sign a loyalty oath. Although eventually declared "politically dependable," he nevertheless objected to the oath on principle: "Why not acquiesce in an empty gesture. . . . ? My answer is that of a psychologist. . . . My field includes the study of 'hysteria,' private and public, in 'personality' and 'culture.' It includes the study of the tremendous waste in human energy which proceeds from irrational fear and from the irrational gestures which are part of what we call 'history.' I would find it difficult to ask my subject of investigation (people) and my students to work with me, if I were to participate without protest in a vague, fearful, and somewhat vindictive gesture devised to ban an evil in some magic way—an evil which must be met with much more searching and concerted effort" (Erikson, 1951). During 1950 he also published his first book, *Childhood and Society,* which earned wide acclaim and was reissued in an enlarged edition in 1963. His subsequent study of Gandhi (1969) was honored with both the Pulitzer Prize and National Book Award.

Erikson's writings fill some dozen volumes. The high esteem accorded his work is evidenced by such prominent magazines as *Time* and *Newsweek,* which have referred to him as probably the most influential and outstanding of all psychoanalysts.

◼ CAPSULE SUMMARY
Ego Psychology Compared to Freudian Theory

	Freudian (id) Theory	Ego Psychology
The Id	The sole component of personality present at birth; entirely unconscious, amoral.	Similar, but less powerful.
The Ego	*Origin:* Begins to develop out of the id at age 6–8 months. *Characteristics:* A weak "rider" struggling desperately to control its instinctually energized "horse." Concerned solely with satisfying id impulses in a way that will also please its other two masters, the superego and external world. *Defense Mechanisms:* Used solely to ward off intrapsychic or external threats, primarily illicit id impulses and anxiety.	*Origin:* Begins to develop independently of the id very soon after birth. *Characteristics:* A relatively powerful and autonomous entity, which directs behavior toward such constructive goals as mastery of and adaptation to the environment. These ego functions are unrelated to the satisfaction of id impulses, yet are pleasurable in their own right. *Defense Mechanisms:* Are adaptive as well as defensive, as when fantasy leads to solutions to important problems.
The Superego	Includes introjected ideals and restrictions; may be overly harsh and oppressive.	Essentially similar.
Personality Development	Virtually complete by about age 5 years.	Continues throughout the whole life cycle from infancy to old age.
Society	An inevitable source of frustration and conflict, since illicit and irrational id impulses must be sublimated. An external burden imposed on the ego.	Not necessarily a source of frustration and conflict, since the ego functions are constructive and can therefore be expressed directly. Supports the ego by providing social roles and identities.
Libido	The psychic energy that fuels all mental activity.	Essentially similar; but accorded considerably less emphasis, so that greater attention can be devoted to ego and societal forces.
View of Human Nature	Pessimistic, because of the emphasis on powerful illicit id impulses.	More optimistic, because greater strength is attributed to the rational and adaptive ego.

THE BASIC NATURE OF HUMAN BEINGS

Biological Processes: Libido and Sexuality

Erikson remains true to Freudian psychoanalysis by including libido among his theoretical constructs, but not without some significant reservations. On the one hand, he expresses a marked appreciation for the "clear and unifying light . . . thrown into [the dark recesses of the mind] by the theory of a libido, of a mobile sexual energy which contributes to the 'highest' as well as to the 'lowest' forms of human endeavor—and often to both at the same time." Yet he also cautions against the literal acceptance of what Freud himself regarded as only a "working hypothesis," and warns that it makes little sense to speak of energies that cannot be demonstrated scientifically (Erikson, 1963, p. 63; see also Erikson, cited by Evans, 1967/1969, pp. 84, 86).

Erikson is similarly reserved about the importance of instinctual drives. He credits Freud for calling attention to the irrational aspects of personality, for discovering that sexuality begins with birth rather than at puberty, and for orienting psychoanalysis in a biological direction. But Erikson also regards our inborn sexual and aggressive instincts as vague drive fragments that are strongly influenced by parental training and cultural factors (such as school), and he argues that psychoanalysis must pay considerably more attention to innate adaptive forces. (See Erikson, 1963, pp. 44–46, 58–71, 95–97.)

Thus Erikson retains, but deemphasizes, the constructs of instinct and libido. He prefers instead to stress the role played by ego and societal forces in shaping the human personality.

Ego Processes: Identity and Mastery

Identity. To Erikson, the ego is far more than a sorely tried mediator among the insistent id, punitive superego, and forbidding environment. The ego not only defends against illicit instincts and anxiety, but serves important healthy functions as well.

One of these constructive ego functions is to preserve a sense of **identity** (**ego identity, psychosocial identity**). This complicated inner state includes four distinct aspects:

1. *Individuality.* A conscious sense of uniqueness and existence as a separate, distinct entity.
2. *Wholeness and synthesis.* A sense of inner wholeness and indivisibility, resulting from the unconscious synthesizing operations of the ego. The growing child forms a variety of fragmentary self-images: more or less lovable, talented, obedient, scholarly, athletic, independent, and so forth. The healthy ego integrates these images into a meaningful whole. (See Erikson, 1968, pp. 160–161, 165; 1974, p. 27.)

3. *Sameness and continuity.* An unconscious striving for a sense of inner sameness and continuity between who one has been in the past, and who one is likely to be in the future. A feeling that one's life has consistency, and is headed in a meaningful direction. (See Erikson, 1959, pp. 42, 102, 118; 1963, pp. 261–263; 1964, p. 91; 1968, pp. 19, 87; 1975, pp. 18–19.)

4. *Social solidarity.* A sense of inner solidarity with the ideals and values of some group; a feeling of social support and validation. A firm identity requires that the inner sense of sameness and continuity be meaningful to significant others, and correspond to their perceptions and expectations. This ensures recognition from people who are important to the individual. (See Erikson, 1959, p. 118; 1964, pp. 90–96; 1968, pp. 22, 165.)

While Erikson's construct of identity is more complicated than Fromm's, he agrees that it represents a vital need of every human being. "In the social jungle of human existence, there is no feeling of being alive without a sense of ego identity. Deprivation of identity, can lead to murder" (Erikson, 1963, p. 240; see also Erikson, 1959, p. 90). The state of **identity confusion** (or **role confusion,** also often referred to as an **identity crisis**) involves the converse of a firm identity: feelings of inner fragmentation, little or no sense of where one's life is headed, and an inability to gain the support provided by a satisfactory social role or vocation. The sufferer may feel very much like an outcast or wanderer, or not quite somebody—as did Erikson himself during his early twenties.

A sense of identity begins in infancy with recognition by such significant others as the mother, but does not reach full fruition until the trials of adolescence (as we will see). As with Sullivan's good-me and bad-me personifications, every identity includes aspects that are both positive (or consistent with what one has learned to regard as desirable) and negative (or similar to what one has been punished for, or warned against becoming). Developing a primarily positive identity is likely to be more difficult for certain segments of a given population, such as women in a patriarchal society or members of persecuted minority ethnic and religious groups. Since even a negative identity is likely to seem preferable to the inner turmoil of identity confusion, many such individuals adopt the debased role espoused for them by the majority. (See Erikson, 1958, p. 102; 1963, pp. 243–246; 1974; 1975, pp. 20–21.)

Mastery. In accordance with Adler and Fromm, Erikson concludes that we have a fundamental need to master our environment. Like identity, **mastery** is an ego function that affords pleasures unrelated to the satisfaction of id impulses, and its frustration also evokes intense rage. To Erikson, therefore, learning is not merely a form of sublimated sexual curiosity. It contains an energy of its own, and love of life can only win out over destructiveness and the love of death if we are given a chance to realize this important potential.

(See Erikson, 1963, p. 68; 1964, p. 50; Erikson, cited by Evans, 1967/1969, pp. 27, 68–69.)

As with identity, a sense of mastery depends on the expectations and support of one's society. A child is motivated to repeat and perfect such acts as walking not only to enjoy a sense of physical proficiency, or to locate objects that will satisfy libidinal drives, but also because the status of "one who can walk" is approved of by respected elders. In addition, the growing conviction that the ego can deal effectively with the external world helps promote a positive sense of identity. "Children cannot be fooled by empty praise and condescending encouragement. . . . [But] their ego identity [does gain] real strength . . . from wholehearted and consistent recognition of real accomplishment—i.e., of achievement that has meaning in the culture" (Erikson, 1963, pp. 235–236; 1968, p. 49).

Society and Culture

Besides adopting a more positive and rational view of human nature, Erikson rejects Freud's conception of society as necessarily inimical and frustrating:

> The greatest difficulty in the path of psychoanalysis as a general psychology probably consists in the remnants of its first conceptualization of the environment as [a hostile] "outer world." . . . Preoccupied with [symptoms and defenses,] . . . psychoanalysis had, at first, little to say about the way in which the ego's synthesis grows—or fails to grow—out of the soil of social organization. . . . [But psychoanalysis today is shifting its emphasis] to the study of the ego's roots in social organization. (Erikson, 1963, pp. 15–16, 282; 1975, p. 105. See also Erikson, cited by Evans, 1967/1969, p. 26.)

Thus a firm sense of identity or mastery requires the support of significant others, as we have seen. Society also helps lighten the inescapable conflicts of life by holding forth the promise of sanctioned roles, such as laborer, doctor, lawyer, mother, or father, which confirm that an individual has found a workable and effective life plan. In addition, the social affirmation provided by mutually enhancing relationships (**mutuality**) is a major human need in its own right. Such recognition provides us with the feeling that we exist in the eyes of others, while the denial of this need arouses intense hatred. (See Erikson, 1959, pp. 20–21; 1963, p. 277; 1968, pp. 87, 219; 1977, p. 88.)

Since Erikson believes that society plays a prominent role in molding the developing ego, he (unlike Freud) has devoted some time to studying the effects of different cultures on personality. Erikson observed first-hand two contrasting American Indian tribes: the trusting and generous Sioux, hunters of South Dakota; and the miserly and suspicious Yurok, salmon fishermen of northern California (Erikson, 1963, pp. 111–186). For example, the Sioux allow their children to breast-feed for several years, while the

Yurok prefer early weaning. The Sioux detest hoarders and insist upon sharing with others even when (as is often the case) their resources are meager, whereas the Yurok stress the importance of economic security. Thus the different identities of the typical Sioux and Yurok are due primarily to the respective societal values concerning the acquisition of money, and to the contrasting effects of the Sioux "paradise of the practically unlimited privilege of the mother's breast" and the Yurok "residue of infantile nostalgia for the mother from whom he has been disengaged so forcefully," rather than to some all-powerful instinct or character trait (Erikson, 1963, pp. 136, 176).

By helping individuals to find viable roles within the existing order, a culture also helps to enrich and perpetuate itself. However, social influences are not always beneficial. Cultures often confront an individual with contradictory values, as when our own society stresses both competition ("winning is the only thing") and cooperation ("do unto others . . ."), so that forming a consistent sense of identity can be difficult. Societies create oppressed minorities, whose members may find themselves compelled to adopt the negative identity imposed by the majority. A seriously pathogenic culture may even inflict this fate on a wide scale, as happened with the youths growing up in Nazi Germany (Erikson, 1963, pp. 326ff; Erikson, cited by Evans, 1967/1969, p. 32).

Zones and Modes

Like Freud and Sullivan, Erikson attributes some importance to the major bodily **zones** that interact with the environment: oral, anal, and genital. (See Erikson, 1963, pp. 52, 59, 72–97, 230.) He also enumerates seven **modes** of dealing with the external world:

Incorporative, type 1:	Passively receiving, "getting"
Incorporative, type 2:	Purposeful acquisition, "taking"
Retentive:	Holding fast to what one has
Eliminative:	Letting go of what one has
Intrusive:	Aggressively invading the environment; primarily masculine
Inclusive:	Inception and protection; primarily feminine
Generative:	Procreation

Erikson agrees with Freud as to the importance of fixations, but argues that they may occur with regard to either zones or modes. For example, a child may persist in thumb sucking well past the appropriate age (zone fixation, oral). Or an adult may expect always to get satisfaction without exerting much effort (mode fixation, incorporative type 1). In such instances, the excessive development of one mode or zone (and corresponding underdevelopment of the others) is indicative of a one-sided, immature personality.

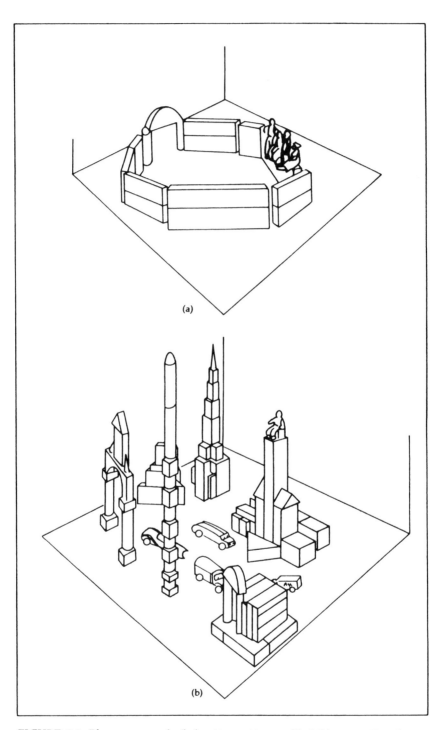

FIGURE 8.1. Play structures built by 10- to 12-year-old children. (a) Female inclusiveness. (b) Male intrusiveness.

Erikson regards the intrusive mode as more typical of boys, whereas girls sooner or later change to such milder forms as teasing, provoking, and making themselves attractive and endearing. He finds that the play of boys tends to emphasize the intrusive high-low dimension and the construction of tall objects, while girls concentrate on the inclusive mode of open versus closed and build toy structures that involve containment. (See Figure 8.1.) Erikson relates this difference, in part, to the physiological differences between the future inseminator and future child-bearer. (See Erikson, 1963, pp. 90–91, 102, 105.) However, like Fromm and Horney, Erikson is critical of the basic psychoanalytic approach to female sexuality. He shares Horney's belief that penis envy is symbolic of women's jealousy over the favored role of men in a patriarchal society, and agrees that men (consciously or unconsciously) envy women's capacity for motherhood. He also suggests that women are superior to men with regard to such capacities as touch and empathy, and he expresses the hope that emancipated women will help our nuclear age replace a masculine proclivity for war with new directions for peace and survival. (See Erikson, 1963, pp. 88, 411; 1964, pp. 113, 235; 1968, pp. 261–294; 1975, pp. 225–247; Erikson, cited by Evans, 1967/1969, pp. 43–47.)

The Unconscious

To Erikson, the unconscious ranks among Freud's greatest contributions—so much so that except for the implicit wisdom expressed in the Bible and Shakespeare, we have learned more in the past few decades about human motivation and development than during all of the preceding centuries. Erikson finds that even primitive cultures express an intuitive understanding of the unconscious, as indicated by rituals that attribute unusual dreams to supernatural visitations rather than to an individual's conscious motivation. (See Erikson, 1959, p. 99; 1963, pp. 153, 190, 216; 1964, pp. 78, 147, 243.)

THE STRUCTURE OF PERSONALITY

The Id

Except for the greater emphasis accorded the ego, Erikson's conception of personality structure is similar to Freud's. The **id** is entirely unconscious, amoral, and the sole component present at birth. It includes the whole of our evolutionary history, and all inherited instincts.

The Ego

The **ego** dwells between the id and the superego, and is largely unconscious. As in Freudian theory, the ego guards against illicit id impulses and excessive superego restrictions by using various defense mechanisms: repression, reaction formation, projection, denial of reality, identification with the aggressor, regression, fantasy, and so forth. Thus people often attribute to their neighbors those faults of which they themselves are most ashamed (projection), blithely ignore warnings of such impending catastrophes as nuclear war or death (denial of reality), or try to make a negative identity seem like an apparent virtue (reaction formation).

In contrast to Freud, however, Erikson argues that defense mechanisms may be used in adaptive as well as maladaptive ways. For example, fantasies may produce imaginative thoughts that help to solve important real-life problems. The capacities of the ego also include such essential constructive functions as identity and mastery, as we have seen. In fact, since Erikson's goal is to broaden Freudian psychoanalysis by explicating our more rational and conflict-free ego processes, nearly all of his work (and of the present chapter) could be subsumed under this heading.

The Superego

The **superego** includes introjected ideals and restrictions, and serves the essential function of keeping the id in check. But as in Freudian theory, the superego can also become oppressive and impose overly harsh standards of right and wrong upon the ego. Another drawback of the superego is that it perpetuates internally the relation of the superior, angry adult and the small, helpless child. Therefore, if parental training fails to reflect the standards of the society in which one lives, the rift between the ego and superego will deepen and lead to excessive intrapsychic conflict. "Man survives only where traditional child training provides him with a conscience which will guide him without crushing him, and which is firm and flexible enough to fit the vicissitudes of his historical era" (Erikson, 1963, p. 95; see also Erikson, 1963, pp. 60, 122, 192–194, 257, 311–312; 1964, pp. 223–224; 1968, p. 218).

Although Erikson retains Freud's structural model, he also cautions against the danger of reifying such concepts as id, ego, and superego. He stresses that these are abstract, tentative constructs designed to facilitate the discussion and understanding of personality, rather than concrete and universally established entities located somewhere within the psyche (Erikson, 1963, pp. 414–415; 1964, p. 77; 1975, p. 37).

THE DEVELOPMENT OF PERSONALITY

Like Freud, Erikson attributes considerable psychological importance to the unusually long period of human childhood. Our extensive early dependence facilitates the introjection of parental standards and development of the

■ CAPSULE SUMMARY
Some Important Eriksonian Terminology

Ego	A component of personality that dwells between the id and superego, and possesses significant constructive capacities (such as identity and mastery) as well as defenses against illicit id instincts and anxiety.
Ego psychology	A theory of personality that hews more closely to basic Freudian psychoanalysis than does the work of Jung, Adler, Horney, Fromm, and Sullivan, but stresses the strengths and capacities of the rational ego while deemphasizing the role of instincts and the irrational id.
Id	The sole component of personality present at birth, which includes all innate instincts; similar to Freud's use of the term.
Identity (ego identity)	A complicated inner state that includes conscious feelings of individuality and uniqueness, a sense of inner wholeness and indivisibility, an unconscious striving for inner sameness and continuity from past to future, and a sense of inner solidarity with the ideals and values of some group. Identity has both positive and negative aspects, with a preponderance of the former indicative of a healthy personality. But since there is no feeling of being alive without a sense of identity, even a negative one will seem preferable to none at all.
Identity confusion (identity diffusion, role confusion)	The inability to achieve a sense of identity. Involves painful feelings of inner fragmentation, little or no sense of where one's life is headed, and an inability to gain the support provided by a satisfactory social role.
Identity crisis	(1) A synonym for identity confusion. (2) A necessary, crucial turning point in the development of personality that commonly occurs during adolescence and young adulthood, wherein a decisive turn is taken either toward establishing a sense of identity or toward identity confusion.
Id psychology	A synonym for Freudian psychoanalysis.
Libido	The sexual psychic energy that powers mental activity. Similar to Freud's use of the term, but accorded less emphasis by Erikson because it is unobservable and undemonstrable.
Life cycle	The whole of personality development, from infancy through childhood and adolescence to old age.
Mastery	A sense of competence in dealing with the external environment; like identity, an ego function and vital human need.
Modes	Methods for dealing with the external world, including passively receiving or "getting" (incorporative type 1), purposeful acquisition or "taking" (incorporative type 2), retention, elimination, intrusiveness (primarily masculine), inclusiveness (primarily feminine), and generativity.

continued

247

Mutuality	The ideal form of human relationship, wherein the partners facilitate the development of each other's strengths and potentials.
Play therapy	A form of psychotherapy in which a child creates a scene or story with the aid of various toys; the "royal road" to a child's unconscious.
Repression	Unconsciously eliminating threatening material from awareness and being unable to recall it on demand. Similar to Freud's use of the term, as is Erikson's use of the other defense mechanisms.
Ritualizations	Repeated and socially sanctioned forms of interplay that facilitate the ego's adaptation to the environment. Ritualizations provide a sense of mutual affirmation, and familiarity with the mores of one's culture.
Role confusion	An often-used synonym for identity confusion.
Superego	The component of personality that includes introjected ideals and prohibitions; similar to Freud's use of the term.
Zones	The major bodily areas that interact with the external world: oral, anal, and genital.

superego, and it permits the substantial training that makes us far more technically and mentally capable than any other species. Erikson also agrees that childhood conflicts exert a significant influence on the adult personality, some of which concern the repressed issue of infantile sexuality. And he concludes that the prolonged inequality of adult and child leaves us with a lifelong residue of emotional immaturity, which inevitably conflicts with our more rational and ethical aims. (See Erikson, 1958, p. 18; 1963, p. 16; 1968, p. 82; 1969, p. 98; 1975, p. 160.)

Nevertheless, Erikson rejects Freud's "originological" efforts to explain personality wholly in terms of the first four or five years of life. Instead he stresses that personality development continues throughout the whole life cycle, and he posits eight stages that extend from infancy to old age.

The Epigenetic Psychosexual Stages, or "Eight Ages of Man"

Just as the development of our physical organs unfolds according to a predetermined genetic schedule, Erikson concludes that we inherit a psychological predisposition to adapt to an average expectable environment. All eight developmental stages are present in rudimentary form at birth and unfold according to an innate plan, with each stage making a new totality or ensemble out of the preceding ones. To Erikson, therefore, these stages are both psychosexual and **epigenetic** (*epi* = upon, *genesis* = emergence).

Every epigenetic psychosexual stage is characterized by a specific psychosocial problem or "crisis" (in the medical sense of a crucial turning point for better or worse, rather than in the political sense of imminent catastrophe). Each crisis is brought on by increasing physiological maturity and the resulting greater demands made by the parents and society, and should be resolved by the ego during the appropriate stage for personality development to proceed successfully. However, the outcome of any stage is by no means necessarily permanent. Any severe later crisis may revive earlier ones as well, and counteract previous successful or unsuccessful resolutions. (See Erikson, 1959, pp. 15, 52; 1963, pp. 248–274; 1964, pp. 138–142; 1968, p. 16; 1982.)

The Oral-Sensory Stage: Basic Trust Versus Mistrust. As in Freudian theory, the first epigenetic psychosexual stage centers around the oral zone and concerns the process of incorporation. The first thing the infant learns is to take in, not only with the mouth during feeding and sucking but also through the eyes and other senses. (See Erikson, 1963, pp. 72–80, 247–251; 1968, pp. 96–107.) Erikson also agrees that orality provides libidinal pleasure, and that passive incorporation ("getting") subsequently yields to a second, more aggressive mode (biting or "taking") when the teeth emerge. Like Sullivan, however, Erikson prefers to stress the psychosocial aspects of the oral-sensory stage—notably maternal nursing and cuddling, which represents the infant's first significant interactions with another person.

If the mother consistently responds to her baby's hunger with appropriate and affectionate feeding, the infant learns that there is some correspondence between its needs and the external world. This rudimentary sense of **trust** establishes the groundwork for mutuality and the capacity for giving to others, and is denoted by the infant's first social achievement: "[a] willingness to let the mother out of sight without undue anxiety or rage, because she has become an inner certainty as well as an outer predictability" (Erikson, 1963, p. 247). But if the painful state of hunger is often ignored, or if the mother is anxious and ineffective, the infant develops a profound sense of impending discomfort and danger (basic **mistrust**) and seeks to control others through duress or fantasy.

> The amount of trust derived from earliest infantile experience . . . [depends] on the quality of the maternal relationship. Mothers create a sense of trust in their children by . . . sensitive care of the baby's individual needs and a firm sense of personal trustworthiness. (Erikson, 1963, p. 249. See also Erikson, 1959, p. 63.)

Since not even the best of parents behave ideally on all occasions, every personality includes some degree of both trust and mistrust. This is by no means disadvantageous, for total optimism would be as maladaptive as unyielding pessimism. But if the psychosocial ratio between these two variables is weighted in favor of mistrust, the ego has been damaged and will be less likely to cope with the problems of the following stages. Conversely, to the extent that trust predominates, the infant learns to regard the world with an "enduring belief in the attainability of fervent wishes" (**hope**). The emergence of this positive and adaptive ego quality signifies that personality development has proceeded successfully past the crisis of the oral-sensory stage (Erikson, 1964, p. 118).

The Muscular-Anal Stage: Autonomy Versus Shame and Doubt. Just when the child begins to trust the nurturing mother and external world, its developing musculature makes possible some control over the environment. During the muscular-anal stage, therefore, the child must risk breaching the trustful relationship with the mother in order to progress beyond the incorporative mode and exert its **autonomy.** "The strength acquired at any stage is tested by the necessity to . . . take chances in the next stage with what was most vulnerably precious in the previous one" (Erikson, 1963, p. 263; see also Erikson, 1963, pp. 80–85, 178, 251–254; 1968, pp. 107–114).

Children in our culture soon learn that cleanliness and toilet-training are serious matters, and that they can now choose between the conflicting modes of retaining or eliminating bodily wastes. While Erikson readily accepts such basic psychoanalytic constructs as anal-retentive, anal-expulsive, and the anal personality (orderly, miserly, stubborn), he continues to emphasize the role of psychosocial influences on personality development. If parental control during this stage is firmly reassuring, the child develops a positive attitude about its displays of autonomy. But overly permissive parents may allow misguided attempts at independence that end in unnecessary and shattering failures. Or overprotective parents may impose rigid restrictions and methods of toilet-training, and respond to incontinence or stubborn retention with pronounced anxiety and disgust. The child's expressions of autonomy will then become associated with feelings of **shame** and **doubt.**

> This whole stage, then . . . becomes a battle for autonomy. . . . The infant must come to feel that his basic trust in himself and in the world (which is the lasting treasure saved from the conflicts of the oral stage) will not be jeopardized by this sudden violent wish to have a choice. (Erikson, 1963, pp. 82, 85. See also Erikson, 1959, p. 68; 1963, pp. 84, 254.)

As with basic trust and mistrust, both autonomy and shame are inevitable aspects of every personality. Successful development is denoted by a psychosocial ratio that favors the former characteristic, and results in an "unbroken determination to exercise free choice as well as self-restraint." This rudimentary ego quality of **will power** also depends on the successful resolution of the preceding oral-sensory stage. "Will cannot be trained until hope is secure . . . [and] no person can live, no ego remain intact without hope and will" (Erikson, 1964, pp. 115, 118, 119).

The Locomotor-Genital Stage: Initiative Versus Guilt. The third epigenetic psychosexual stage is highlighted by the development of such locomotor abilities as walking and running, which futher the ego's sense of mastery and make possible the intrusive mode. (See Erikson, 1963, pp. 85–92, 255–258; 1968, pp. 115–122.) During this stage, the child becomes aware of the difference between the sexes and begins to experience vague, rudimentary urges associated with the clitoris or penis. As in Freudian theory, these desires are at first associated with the nurturing mother; but they ultimately give way to "the boy's assurance that he will marry his mother and make her proud of him, and . . . the girl's that she will marry her father and take much better care of him" (Erikson, 1963, p. 90; see also Erikson, 1958, p. 73; 1963, pp. 87, 256, 410). Thus the parent of the same sex, to whom the child feels vastly inferior in genital capacity, is cast in the role of rival. However, the child soon realizes that its small stature effectively precludes any actual Oedipal satisfactions. Instead, he or she resorts to fantasies of sex and aggression. These illicit wishes arouse a deep sense of **guilt,** and a fear of punishment in the form of harm to the genitals.

Ideally, the child now learns to divert the threatening sexual drive into such acceptable goals as play. "Play is to the child what thinking, planning, and blueprinting are to the adult, a trial universe . . . [wherein] past failures can be thought through [and] expectations tested." If the child is able to abandon its Oedipal wishes and substitute play with toys, the relief from guilt and parental approval for new accomplishments contribute to a sense of **initiative.** A predominance of initiative over guilt results in the adaptive ego quality of **purpose,** or "the courage to envisage and pursue valued goals uninhibited by . . . the foiling fear of punishment" (Erikson, 1964, pp. 120, 122; see also Erikson, 1963, p. 255).

During the locomotor-genital stage, therefore, the child becomes divided between infantile desires to enjoy instinctual gratifications and a more mature self-guidance enforced by the superego. The emergence of a sense of purpose indicates that initiative has exceeded guilt, and that the crisis of this stage has been passed successfully.

The Latency Stage: Industry Versus Inferiority. As in Freudian theory, the fourth Erikson stage is a time of submerged sexuality and "lull before the storm of puberty" (Erikson, 1963, p. 260; see also Erikson, 1963, pp. 258–261; 1968, pp. 122–128). The latency stage is characterized by an intense curiosity and wish to learn, with the child now sublimating its intrusive tendencies and seeking to win recognition by producing things. Thus the child begins to learn the ethos of work; and all cultures assist this effort by providing some sort of systematic instruction, notably school.

The child's successes during this stage contribute to a positive sense of **industry,** while failures result in feelings of inadequacy and **inferiority.** Successful personality development is denoted by a psychosocial ratio that favors the former characteristic and is reflected in the ego quality of **competence,** or "the free exercise of dexterity and intelligence in the completion of tasks, unimpaired by infantile inferiority" (Erikson, 1964, p. 124).

Adolescence: Identity Versus Role Confusion. With the development of competence and the advent of puberty, childhood comes to an end. The fifth stage consists of adolescence, a period which Erikson (like Sullivan) regards as one of considerable importance. The adolescent must contend with the physiological revolution of genital maturity and the reemergence of latent sexual impulses, an inner turmoil that can only be resolved by gaining recognition and support from significant others:

> Like a trapeze artist, the young person in the middle of vigorous motion must let go of his safe hold on childhood and reach out for a firm grasp on adulthood, depending for a breathless interval on a relatedness between the past and the future, and on the reliability of those he must let go of, and those who will "receive" him. Whatever combination of drives and defenses, of sublimations and capacities has emerged from the young individual's childhood must now make sense in view of his concrete opportunities in work and love . . . [and] he must detect some meaningful resemblance between what he has come to see in himself and what his sharpened awareness tells him others judge and expect him to be. (Erikson, 1964, p. 90; 1958, p. 14. See also Erikson, 1958, p. 43; 1959, p. 161; 1963, pp. 261–263, 306–307; 1968, pp. 128–135.)

The crucial problem of this stage is the **identity crisis,** a fork in the developmental road that leads either to a pronounced sense of identity or to excessive inner fragmentation and role confusion (identity confusion). Adolescents are therefore particularly vulnerable to ideologies that offer the prospect of social acceptance and clearly defined roles, whether they be sinister doctrines that viciously deny equality to outsiders (such as the Nazi movements in Hitler's Germany), relatively benevolent movements (as with the Peace Corps in our own society), or clannish social in-groups. Even juvenile delinquents need a sense of identity; and they achieve it by conforming to group demands as rigid as those of the majority, a developmental failure for which Erikson blames society. He argues that if widespread criminality occurs, the entire adult generation must take the responsibility for failing the young by not providing other viable opportunities (Erikson, cited by Evans, 1967/1969, pp. 40, 66). Thus the potential dangers of adolescence include not only role confusion, but also the adoption of an ideologically supported negative identity.

A positive sense of identity depends partly on establishing an appropriate sexual role, and partly on achieving a satisfying occupation. If the identity crisis proves to be so troublesome that neither a primarily positive or negative identity can be achieved, the individual may reject the demands of adulthood and extend the adolescent stage well past the appropriate age. (This is particularly likely to happen if preceding developmental crises have not been successfully resolved.) Examples include "perennial students," dropouts who fail to complete their studies and adopt a vocation, and even Erikson himself up until the time he joined the Freuds in Vienna at age twenty-five. Conversely, the successful resolution of the adolescent identity

■ CAPSULE SUMMARY
The Epigenetic Psychosexual Stages (Erikson)

Stage	Developmental Crisis	Ego Quality That Denotes Successul Development
Oral-sensory	Basic trust versus mistrust	Hope: The enduring belief in the attainability of fervent wishes
Muscular-anal	Autonomy versus shame and doubt	Will power: The unbroken determination to exercise free choice as well as self-restraint
Locomotor-genital	Initiative versus guilt	Purpose: The courage to envisage and pursue valued goals, uninhibited by guilt or the fear of punishment
Latency	Industry versus inferiority	Competence: The free exercise of dexterity and intelligence in the completion of tasks, unimpaired by infantile inferiority
Adolescence	Identity versus role confusion (identity confusion)	Fidelity: The ability to sustain freely pledged loyalties, despite the inevitable contradictions of value systems
Young adulthood	Intimacy versus isolation	Love: The mutuality of devotion, which subdues the antagonisms inherent in divided functioning
Adulthood	Generativity versus stagnation	Care: The widening concern for others, overcoming the ambivalence to obligations
Maturity	Ego integrity versus despair	Wisdom: The detached concern with life in the face of death

Notes: (1) *Epigenetic* means "upon emergence," or unfolding according to an innate schedule. (2) Both the positive and negative characteristics of any stage (e.g., basic trust and mistrust) are present to some degree in every personality. A preponderance of the former denotes healthy adjustment, and results in the emergence of the corresponding ego quality. (3) A favorable or unfavorable resolution of each crisis is by no means permanent, but remains subject to future benign and pathogenic conditions. However, a given ego quality is unlikely to appear unless the preceding stages have developed satisfactorily.

crisis is reflected by a predominance of identity over role confusion and the emergence of the ego quality of **fidelity,** or "the ability to sustain loyalties freely pledged in spite of the inevitable contradictions of value systems" (Erikson, 1964, p. 125).

Young Adulthood: Intimacy Versus Isolation. The sixth epigenetic psychosexual stage represents the beginning of adulthood, and entails such responsibilities as work and marriage. (See Erikson, 1963, pp. 263–266; 1968, pp. 135–138.) During this period, the newly acquired sense of identity must be risked in order to make the compromises that permit close relationships with others. If a young adult suffers from the need to preserve a tenuous and fragile identity, profound **isolation** and self-absorption will appear preferable to meaningful contact with others. Conversely, a firm identity can be fused with that of another person without the fear of losing an essential aspect of oneself. Such **intimacy** is essential for the establishment of deep friendships and a meaningful marriage, and involves a sincere concern for the welfare of others.

Successful passage through the crisis of young adulthood is reflected by a preponderance of intimacy over isolation and the development of the ego quality of **love,** which is characterized by relationships that mutually enhance each individual's potentials for growth and development. "Love, then, is mutuality of devotion forever subduing the antagonisms inherent in divided function" (Erikson, 1964, p. 129; see also Erikson, 1968, p. 219).

Adulthood: Generativity Versus Stagnation. The stage of adulthood is ideally a time of **generativity,** which refers primarily to procreation and guiding the next generation. It also includes productivity and creativity. (See Erikson, 1963, pp. 266–268; 1968, pp. 138–139.) The corresponding danger is **stagnation,** an extreme state of self-indulgence similar to behaving as if one were one's own special child.

Merely having children is by no means sufficient evidence that the crisis of adulthood has been resolved. The true predominance of generativity over stagnation is reflected by the ego quality of **care,** or "the widening concern for what has been generated by love, necessity, or accident, [which] overcomes the ambivalence adhering to irreversible obligation" (Erikson, 1964, p. 131.)

Maturity: Ego Integrity Versus Despair. Only one who has successfully resolved the preceding seven developmental crises can achieve **ego integrity,** a feeling of affirmation concerning the life one has lived. (See Erikson, 1963, pp. 268–269; 1968, pp. 139–141.) The converse of ego integrity is **despair,** or fear that death will intervene before one can find alternative routes to a more meaningful life. Ideally, ego integrity prevails over despair; and this favorable psychosocial ratio results in the ego quality of **wisdom,** or "detached concern with life itself, in the face of death itself." Wisdom also exerts a positive influence on subsequent generations, for "healthy children will not fear life if their elders have integrity enough not to fear death" (Erikson, 1963, p. 269; 1964, p. 133).

Ritualizations

Erikson (1966; 1977) has devoted some attention to the ways in which personality development is influenced by **ritualizations,** or repeated and socially sanctioned forms of interplay that facilitate the ego's adaptations to the environment. Ritualizations help fulfill our inherent need for recognition and reassurance, as when the infant enjoys being picked up, cuddled, nursed, changed, and called by name. In addition, ritualizations provide a sense of familiarity with the mores of one's society. Among the miserly Yurok Indians, for example, the child is taught at mealtime "to put only a little food on the spoon, to take the spoon up to his mouth slowly, to put the spoon down again while chewing the food—and, above all, to think of becoming rich while he [enjoys and swallows] it" (Erikson, 1963, p. 177; 1977, p. 80). Such a ritual would be inconceivable among the generous and charitable Sioux—indicating once again the powerful influence of societal factors on the development of personality.

FURTHER APPLICATIONS OF ERIKSONIAN THEORY

Dream Interpretation

As with other aspects of his ego psychology, Erikson retains but modifies Freudian dream theory. He agrees that dreams provide important information about unconscious feelings and memories, that condensation produces dream symbols with more than one meaning, and that free association and day's residues are valuable aids to interpretation. To Erikson, however, the healthy ego remains relatively powerful even during sleep. It not only makes compromises with illicit id impulses, but also produces dreams of success and achievement that enable us to awaken with a sense of wholeness and competence.

Erikson also rejects Freud's contention that almost every dream fulfills some childhood sexual wish. Instead, dreams may deal with prior epigenetic crises. They may highlight current problems in the dreamer's life, such as an identity crisis, and suggest potential solutions. Or they may even be dreamed for the specific purpose of being interpreted by the dreamer, or the dreamer's psychoanalyst. "Once we set out to study our own dreams . . . we may well dream them in order to study them" (Erikson, 1977, p. 134). Thus Erikson agrees with Jung and Fromm that dreams are often teleological, and include asexual as well as sexual symbols. He also argues that some of Freud's own dreams, if properly reinterpreted, support psychosocial ego theory rather than instinctual id psychoanalysis. (See Erikson, 1954; 1958, p. 142; 1959, p. 154 n. 17; 1964, pp. 57–58, 177–201; 1968, pp. 197–204.)

One young male patient of Erikson's had a dream so traumatic that he feared the loss of his sanity: a horrible huge and empty face surrounded by slimy hair, that might perhaps have been his mother, sitting in a motionless horse and buggy. This patient suffered from grave doubts about his chosen religious vocation, and the empty face symbolized his profound lack of identity. The Medusa-like hair reflected bisexual confusion, and fears of women and heterosexuality. The horse and buggy called to mind his mother, whose longing for the rural locale of her childhood had intensified his feelings of being unable to progress in a modern and changing world. The face also represented his white-haired grandfather, against whom he had rebelled as a youth in his search for a sense of identity. Finally, the patient was concerned that Erikson (whose own hair is often quite unruly, and who had recently been compelled to interrupt therapy for an emergency operation) would desert him before he could achieve a coherent "face" or identity of his own (Erikson, 1964, pp. 57–76).

Another dream, reported by a young women patient of Erikson's, is perhaps the shortest on record: the single word S[E]INE lit up against a dark background, with the first "E" in brackets. She had first been overcome by her symptoms (agoraphobia) in Paris, near the river Seine. Her dream also suggested several German and Latin words, *sehen* (to see), *seine* (his), and *sine* (without), which brought back memories of having seen in Paris a frightening picture of Christ being circumsized. These thoughts led in turn to a traumatic incident in her childhood, being catheterized by her father (a pediatrician) because of a bladder condition during the locomotor-genital stage. "It will be obvious how traumatic at that stage an event was that both immobilized and exposed the little girl—in an 'oedipal' context." The bracketed first letter of Erikson's name suggested some transference resentment over the analytic requirement that such embarrassing ideas flow freely, like a river or urine, and a wish to turn the tables by exposing him instead. "This interpretation . . . led to some . . . shared laughter over the tricks of the unconscious, which can condense—and give away—all these meanings in one word" (Erikson, 1977, pp. 130–132).

Psychopathology

Although Erikson defines the course of healthy ego development in greater detail than Freud, he agrees that the well-adjusted individual is one who can do two things well: love and work. He also concurs that psychopathology represents a difference in degree, rather than in kind. And he shares Freud's belief that the study of analytic patients, and their unusually severe intrapsychic conflicts, helps to clarify important but generally concealed aspects of normal mental functioning (such as the defense mechanisms). However,

Erikson cautions that the conflict-free processes of the ego cannot be wholly understood from the behavior of pathological individuals:

> [We psychoanalysts] repeat for our own encouragement (and as an argument against others) that human nature can best be studied in a state of partial breakdown or, at any rate, of marked conflict. . . . As Freud himself put it, we see a crystal's structure only when it cracks. But a crystal, on the one hand, and an organism or personality, on the other, differ in the fact that one is inanimate and the other an organic whole which cannot be broken up without a withering of the parts. . . . [Thus] I do not believe that we can entirely reconstruct the ego's normal functions from an understanding of its dysfunctions . . . (Erikson, 1968, p. 276. See also Erikson, 1954; 1958, p. 16; 1963, pp. 45, 265, 308; 1968, p. 136.)

Origins of Psychopathology. Psychopathology occurs when the normally competent ego is seriously weakened by social trauma, physical ills, and (most importantly) by the failure to resolve prior epigenetic crises. For example, a young boy suffered from convulsions similar to epilepsy. His ego had been impaired by the failure to develop sufficient autonomy and will power during the muscular-anal stage, primarily because of profound guilt resulting from the (incorrect) belief that his aggressiveness had caused the death of his grandmother. The ego was further weakened by a cerebral disorder predisposing him to such attacks, and by the social difficulties of being the only Jewish family in a gentile town (Erikson, 1963, pp. 23–47).

Some social influences are pathogenic because they prevent effective resolutions of the various epigenetic crises. These include abrupt weaning or anxious and insensitive nursing during the oral-sensory stage, and overly severe or lenient toilet-training during the muscular-anal stage (as we have seen). The parents may overreact to the child's playing with its genitals, or break the child's spirit through domination and cruelty. However, the child is not without some influence of its own. "This weak and changing little being moves the whole family along. Babies control and bring up their families as much as they are controlled by them" (Erikson, 1963, p. 69; see also Erikson, 1958, p. 70; 1963, pp. 71, 207, 218, 257). For example, the child's negative response to a nervous and ineffective mother is likely to create a vicious circle by making her upset, guilty, and even less affectionate.

While social trauma and physical debilities play a role in the development of psychopathology, Erikson regards identity confusion as the major problem confronting modern psychotherapy. Patients in Freud's day had a fairly clear idea as to what kind of person they wanted to be, and suffered from inhibitions that prevented them from reaching this goal. In contrast, today's patients often do not know what to believe in and what personal goals to aim for. "The study of identity, then, becomes as strategic in our time as the study of sexuality was in Freud's time" (Erikson, 1963, p. 282; see also p. 279).

Varieties of Psychopathology. Erikson makes some use of the standard psychiatric nomenclature, but cautions that such labels may well become a self-fulfilling prophecy. That is, the sufferer may conform to official expectations by adopting the pathological classification (such as obsessive-compulsive, criminal, or even just "patient") as a firm negative identity. Erikson regards Freud's unsuccessful treatment of Dora as a typical example. She was unable to resolve her adolescent identity crisis because of the examples set by her perfidious elders, so she took great pride in being written up in scientific journals as a noted clinical case. "From Freud's early days onward, enlightened people have adapted to his insights by mouthing the names of their neuroses—and keeping the neuroses, too. . . . To be a famous, if uncured, patient had become for this woman one lasting . . . identity element" (Erikson, 1964, p. 173; 1968, p. 28; see also Erikson, 1963, pp. 307–308, 414; 1964, pp. 97, 166–174; 1968, pp. 77, 250–252).

Erikson shares Freud's belief that regression plays a major role in psychopathology, that all neurotics are in some way sexually handicapped, and that symptoms are usually overdetermined. One patient, a four-year-old-boy, was bloated virtually to the bursting point by a steadfast refusal to eliminate his feces. This extreme retentiveness was due partly to object-loss identification with a beloved nurse who had left his family upon becoming pregnant, with the boy concluding that babies were born through the bowels and that he himself was pregnant. It also reflected a desire to become a baby once again so that the nurse would take care of him, expressed through regression to behavior typical of the time when she was present. Fortunately, a simplified and friendly explanation of the facts of life produced a prompt cure. (See Erikson, 1963, pp. 53–58.)

However, Erikson's view of psychopathology differs from Freud's in several important respects. According to Erikson, pathological symptoms often represent a desperate attempt to develop and retain a sense of identity, rather than resulting from some instinctual force. He devotes considerably less attention to the unpleasant emotion of anxiety. And he attributes psychosis to an ego that has been so weakened by psychosocial disasters, and by profound mistrust, that even the individual and unique elements of one's identity are lost. Like Jung and Sullivan, Erikson concludes that the apparently bizarre speech of psychotics conveys important meanings. His writings provide some evidence of parataxic thought in schizophrenic children, as with a little girl's fear that she had caused her father to go away merely by touching him. (See Erikson, 1963, pp. 195–208; Erikson, cited by Evans, 1967/1969, pp. 55–57.)

Psychotherapy

Theoretical Foundation. Since Erikson regards himself primarily as a psychoanalyst, many of his therapeutic goals are similar to Freud's. Thus the patient strives to bring vital unconscious material to consciousness, and to achieve important insights on both an emotional and intellectual level. This strengthens the patient's capacity for rational, ego-directed choices. However, those symptoms that represent a desperate attempt to achieve a sense of identity can only be alleviated by helping the patient to complete this quest in more constructive ways.

In addition, Erikson differs from Freud by warning that standard psychoanalytic therapy contains hidden biasing elements. He even compares the analyst's sitting silently out of sight to "an exquisite deprivation experiment," one that may well evoke so much regression and transference as to obscure an understanding of the patient's behavior in more normal situations. He also warns that psychoanalysis is "a cure for which a patient must be relatively healthy in the first place and gifted," and that its use with people for whom it is unsuited may well make them even more disturbed (Erikson, 1977, p. 128; see also Erikson, 1958, pp. 17, 151–154; 1964, p. 50; Roazen, 1976a, pp. 67–72).

Therapeutic Procedures. Like Freud, Erikson regards free association as the best way to unravel the meaning of important unconscious material. However, most of his therapeutic procedures are designed to reduce the mystique and potential bias of Freudian psychoanalysis. For example, he adopts the more active Sullivanian role of participant-observer. Like Jung and Adler, Erikson stresses the equality of patient and therapist by often using face-to-face interviews. He also prefers to avoid a preoccupation with the patient's past, so as not to support such rationalizations as blaming a neurosis on one's parents and refusing to take responsibility for one's own behavior. (See Erikson, 1963, pp. 16, 33, 195; 1964, p. 58; Erikson, cited by Evans, 1967/1969, pp. 31, 97.)

To Erikson, it is play rather than dreams that represents the "royal road" to a child's unconscious. The aforementioned convulsive young boy was unable to verbalize his profound fear of being punished by death for his aggression toward his grandmother, but he readily expressed this threatening belief with the aid of **play therapy** by arranging a group of dominoes in the form of a coffin. A young girl revealed the Oedipal nature of her repressed anger by creating a play scene wherein a girl doll shuts the mother doll in the bathroom, and gives the father doll three shiny new cars:

> Children are apt to express in spatial configurations what they cannot or dare not say. . . . A child can be counted upon to bring into the solitary play arranged for him whatever aspect of his ego has been ruffled most . . . for to "play it out" is the most natural self-healing measure childhood affords. . . . As William Blake puts it: "The child's toys and the old man's reasons are the fruits of the two seasons." (Erikson, 1963, pp. 29, 222; see also pp. 98–99, 107–108, 186, 209.)

Resistance, Transference, and Countertransference. Erikson accepts the existence of unconscious resistances to therapy, such as pronounced silences and
avoiding important but unpleasant issues. But he attributes them to the
patient's fears that a weak identity will be shattered by the analyst's stronger
will, rather than to some sort of repetition compulsion.

Insofar as transference is concerned, Erikson takes a somewhat ambivalent position. He shares Freud's belief that it represents an essential
source of information and emotional attachment, and Jung's concern that
intensive levels (e.g., transference neurosis) will provoke excessive regressions and infantile wishes to depend on an omnipotent provider. Erikson
does concur that analysts are themselves capable of such damaging countertransferences as the desire to dominate or love the patient, and that a
personal analysis is therefore an indispensable part of psychoanalytic training. In addition, no therapeutic approach (Freudian, Eriksonian, Jungian, or
whatever) can possibly be effective unless it is compatible with the therapist's own identity (Erikson, 1963, pp. 190–191, 223; 1964, pp. 36–37, 43,
236; 1975, pp. 34, 105–106, 115–116; Erikson, cited by Evans, 1967/1969,
p. 95).

Psychotherapy and Social Reform. Since society plays an integral role in the
development of a firm sense of identity, the treatment of specific individuals
can accomplish only so much. Our technological culture is a common source
of discontent, for it destines all too many workers to be mere extensions of
complicated machines. Racial and other forms of prejudice contribute to
identity confusion, negative identities, and psychopathology. And the looming danger of nuclear war creates the pressing need to recognize our allegiance to the human species as a whole. "The only alternative to armed
competition seems to be the effort to *activate . . . what will strengthen
[another] in his historical development even as it strengthens the actor in his
own development.*" That is, mutuality may well be the only way to ward off
total atomic destruction (Erikson, 1964, p. 242; see also Erikson, 1963, pp.
155, 237, 241–246, 323; Erikson, cited by Evans, 1967/1969, pp. 108–110).

Work

In accordance with Adler, Erikson regards the inability to choose a vocation
during adolescence as indicative of psychopathology. Conversely, as we have
seen, the support afforded the ego by a satisfying career represents perhaps
the best way of avoiding identity confusion. Nevertheless, while Erikson
(1958, p. 17) regards work as probably the most neglected problem in
psychoanalysis, his own theory (like those of his predecessors) has relatively
little to say about this area of human endeavor.

Religion

Unlike Freud, Erikson does not dismiss religion as a collective neurosis. He
does agree that some forms of religious thought resemble psychopathology,

and seek to exploit our infantile wishes for safety by offering illusory promises that cannot be fulfilled. Erikson also shares Freud's belief that religion is not an innate need, and argues that many people prefer to derive faith from such secular activities as productive work, scientific pursuits, and artistic creation. However, religion does provide valuable support for such essential ego qualities as trust and hope. Thus there are millions who cannot afford to be without it, and whose apparent pride in not being religious is merely whistling in the dark. (See Erikson, 1958, p. 265; 1959, pp. 64–65; 1963, pp. 250–251, 277–278; 1964, pp. 153–155.)

In accordance with his theory, Erikson prefers to restate the "golden rule" in terms of mutuality. Doing unto others as we wish they would do unto us may well be unwise, for their needs and tastes may differ significantly from ours. Instead, ideal behavior is that which enhances both another's development and one's own. "Understood this way, the Rule would say that it is best to do to another what will strengthen you even as it will strengthen him—that is, what will develop his best potentials even as it develops your own" (Erikson, 1964, p. 233; see also Erikson, 1964, pp. 219–243; Erikson, cited by Evans, 1967/1969, pp. 72–73, 101–102). This revised golden rule applies even in psychotherapy, where the therapist seeks not only to cure the patient but to develop further as a practitioner and human being. Erikson (1969) also regards Mohandas Gandhi as a particularly good example, for his famous philosophy of nonviolent resistance ("Satyagraha") stresses the need for solutions that benefit both parties to a dispute.

Literature

To Erikson, the frequent allusions of some black writers to namelessness and facelessness reflect the identity confusion that typically befalls an exploited minority. The character Biff in *Death of a Salesman* also suffers from a similar problem, complaining that he can't get any sort of hold on life. However, Erikson cautions against always inferring pathology from such examples. He once discussed *Tom Sawyer* with a group of social workers, calling attention to Ben Rogers's playful imitation of a steamboat and its captain. Some members of the clinically oriented audience promptly decided that Ben was escaping from a tyrannical father with fantasies of being a bossy official, while others concluded that he was symbolically reliving some previous bedwetting or toilet trauma by imitating a boat displacing substantial quantities of water. In contrast, Erikson regards Ben as a healthy growing boy whose play symbolically makes a well-functioning whole out of such physiological processes as the brain (captain), the nerves and muscles of will (signal system and engine), and the body (boat). Tom does prove to be the better psychologist by inducing Ben to take over the tiresome job of whitewashing a fence, however, "which shows that psychology is at least the second-best thing to, and under some adverse circumstances may even prove superior to ordinary adjustment" (Erikson, 1963, p. 210; see also Erikson, 1963, pp. 211, 307; 1968, pp. 25, 131).

Psychohistory

Erikson has devoted considerable attention to the writings and lives of several noted historical figures, including Luther (1958), Hitler (1963, pp. 326–358), Gorky (1963, pp. 359–402), Gandhi (1969; 1975, pp. 113–189), and Jefferson (1974). While warning that autobiographies cannot be interpreted in the same way as free associations, and that the psychohistorian cannot avoid all countertransferential biases, Erikson seeks to illuminate the intrapsychic world of such personages with the aid of his theoretical principles. He has also used this technique in a conversation with Black Panther leader Huey Newton (Erikson, 1973).

EVALUATION

Criticisms and Controversies

Pro-Freudianism and Political Expediency. To some critics, Erikson's writings reflect a pronounced and disturbing schism. On the one hand, he professes a strong allegiance to Freudian theory, characterizes himself as a psychoanalyst, and retains the controversial construct of libido. He readily perpetuates some of the self-serving factual errors that surround Freud's life (such as the alleged ostracism by Vienna), and is overly charitable toward some of his mentor's more autocratic tendencies. Erikson goes so far as to attribute his own original construct of identity to his illustrious predecessor, repeatedly citing a single obscure speech in which Freud merely mentioned this term in passing. Yet despite these protestations, Erikson's theory often seems more like a radical departure from id psychology. His emphasis on positive ego and societal processes differs significantly from Freud's theoretical pessimism; and his actual references to libido are minimal and ambivalent, varying from a casual acceptance of this construct to virtual rejection because of its undemonstrable nature.

Erikson may simply be demonstrating an understandable loyalty to the group that took him in as a 25-year-old wanderer, and helped him to resolve his painful identity crisis. However, the gap between his self-proclaimed Freudianism and his revisionist constructs is so substantial as to give some critics (e.g., Roazen, 1976a) the impression of political expediency. That is, Erikson may well have feared the excommunication from psychoanalytic circles that befell those theorists who forthrightly rejected libido theory—a dire fate that even involved the total exclusion of their works from the reading lists given psychoanalytic trainees. But whatever the cause, Erikson's ambivalence has at least to some extent confused the nature and direction of his own theoretical contributions.

Social Conservatism and Optimism. Although Erikson explicitly denies any desire to advocate conformity, his theory is regarded by some as antipathetic to social change. His contention that healthy ego development requires the support of culturally sanctioned roles has been interpreted as an endorsement of such roles, and therefore of the status quo. Erikson's revised "golden rule" of mutuality has also been criticized as overly optimistic, in that many problems may not admit of solutions that allow all opposing parties to achieve some measure of benefit.

Other Criticisms. Like that of his predecessors, Erikson's work reflects a complete lack of quantification and statistical analyses. Some psychologists question the universality of the epigenetic psychosexual stages, finding little support in their own lives or those of their patients. Erikson fails to specify the influences that contribute to favorable or unfavorable psychosocial ratios in some of the later stages, such as industry versus inferiority. To those who regard anxiety as a construct of considerable importance, his rather superficial treatment suffers by comparison to the work of Horney and Sullivan. As we have seen, the construct of libido has been rejected by many modern psychologists. Finally, while overly appreciative of Freud's influence, Erikson fails to accord sufficient acknowledgment to such predecessors as Adler, Fromm, and Sullivan.

Empirical Research

Several studies have used an instrument devised by Marcia (1966) to measure identity strength. Some representative findings: women with a firm sense of identity are less likely to conform to group pressures to endorse an incorrect conclusion (Toder & Marcia, 1973). A strong identity tends to be related to the successful resolution of such previous psychosocial crises as basic trust, autonomy, and industry (C. K. Waterman et al., 1970). The expressive writing of poetry, but not the keeping of a diary, is helpful to college students in resolving identity crises (A. S. Waterman et al., 1977). And a firm sense of identity increases the likelihood of developing an intimate relationship during middle age (Schiedel & Marcia, 1985).

In general, however, there is relatively little empirical evidence to support the Eriksonian stages of personality development. This is due in part to the difficulty of testing such abstract concepts as hope and will in the research laboratory (Berzonsky, 1984).

Contributions

Perhaps Erikson's most notable contribution has been to broaden the scope of psychoanalytic theory. By rejecting Freud's contention that society must be a source of frustration and conflict, and by stressing the effects of social and cultural influences on personality development, he has helped to integrate psychoanalysis and sociology. His psychohistories represent an attempt to combine psychoanalysis and history. Furthermore, because of his emphasis on healthy and adaptive ego processes, psychoanalysis is no longer limited to the study of those characteristics that clinical cases and more normal individuals have in common.

For these reasons, some critics regard ego psychology as the most significant new direction to be taken by psychoanalytic theory since its inception. These psychologists emphatically reject the stereotype of the rigid and dogmatic psychoanalyst, who cannot accept even the slightest deviation from the verbatim writings of Freud. Instead they argue that psychoanalytic thinking is a continuing evolution of new ideas, as evidenced by ego psychology (and by such other relatively recent modifications as object relations theory, which stresses the influence on personality of relationships with the parents). (See for example Eagle, 1984; Polansky, 1982.)

In addition, the term *identity crisis* has become part of our everyday language. Erikson was one of the first analysts to treat children, including psychotics as well as neurotics, and to devise valuable techniques of play therapy. To those who do not regard personality as wholly determined during the first four or five years of life, Erikson's developmental stages and emphasis on adolescence offer an alternative to Freud's exclusive concern with childhood. Many modern psychologists accept the importance of establishing basic trust and hope during early infancy.

Erikson's study of Gandhi has been widely acclaimed as a major contribution. Like Adler and Sullivan, Erikson strongly opposes social prejudice and was one of the early defenders of the rights of minority groups. Similarly, his view of female sexuality is at least to some extent more equalitarian than Freud's. Finally, despite his pro-Freudianism, Erikson has called attention to some of the potential biases in basic psychoanalytic therapy that Freud preferred to overlook.

There remains some question as to whether Erikson deserves a far more illustrious reputation than theorists like Horney and Sullivan, who also stressed the importance of psychosocial variables while forthrightly rejecting the currently unpopular construct of libido. To many psychologists, however, Erikson's psychosocially oriented ego theory retains the considerable strengths of Freudian psychoanalysis while at the same time rectifying its most serious errors.

Suggested Reading

The best place to begin a first-hand study of Erikson's works is with his first book, *Childhood and Society* (1963). This eminently readable and comprehensive work includes most of his theoretical constructs, presents several interesting case histories, and describes his study of the Sioux and Yurok Indians. Also notable is his prizewinning biography, *Gandhi's Truth* (1969). Some important ideas are restated and expanded, albeit in a more dry and academic fashion, in *Insight and Responsibility* (1964) and *Identity: Youth and Crisis* (1968). Among the useful secondary sources are an interview reported by Evans (1967/1969), a laudatory biography by Coles (1970), and a much more critical effort by Roazen (1976a).

■ SUMMARY

Using some of Freud's own later writings as their point of departure, some theorists have sought to broaden psychoanalytic theory by deemphasizing the role of the irrational id and stressing instead the capacities of the rational ego. This approach has therefore become known as ego psychology, and one of its leading exponents is Erik Homburger Erikson.

1. THE BASIC NATURE OF HUMAN BEINGS. *Biological Processes:* Erikson retains, but deemphasizes, the Freudian constructs of libido and instinct. He prefers to stress the role played by the ego, and by societal forces, in shaping the human personality. *Ego Processes:* The ego not only defends against illicit instincts and anxiety, but serves important healthy functions as well. These constructive and adaptive ego functions are relatively independent of id instincts. Two of the most important are identity, a complicated inner state that includes feelings of individuality and uniqueness, wholeness and synthesis, sameness and continuity, and social solidarity; and a sense of mastery over the environment. Other essential ego qualities, such as hope and will power, are related to the various developmental stages. *Societal Processes:* Erikson regards society as a valuable source of support to the ego. A firm sense of identity or mastery is impossible without the approval of significant others, while society also holds forth the promise of fortifying, sanctioned roles. Erikson regards the social affirmation provided by mutually enhancing relationships (mutuality) as another human need, and concludes that different cultures exert differing effects on the development of the ego. *Other Considerations:* Erikson devotes some attention to various modes of dealing with the external world and bodily zones that interact with it, and regards the unconscious as of considerable importance.

2. THE STRUCTURE OF PERSONALITY. Erikson retains Freud's structural model of id, ego, and superego. He agrees that the id is the sole component of personality present at birth and includes all inherited instincts, and that the superego consists of introjected ideals and restrictions and is capable of becoming overly moral. But Erikson accords much greater emphasis to the capacities and strengths of the ego, so much so that nearly all of his work (and of the present chapter) could be subsumed under this heading.

3. THE DEVELOPMENT OF PERSONALITY. *The Epigenetic Psychosexual Stages:* Erikson regards childhood as a time of considerable importance, and readily accepts the Freudian belief in infantile sexualty. Unlike Freud, however, Erikson posits eight developmental stages that extend from infancy to old age. These stages are all present in rudimentary form at birth and unfold according to an innate plan,

with each stage making a new ensemble out of the preceding ones. Each stage is characterized by a specific psychosocial crisis brought on by increasing physiological maturity and external demands, which should ideally be resolved by the ego during that stage for personality development to proceed successfully. The outcome of any one stage is by no means permanent, however, for future benign or pathogenic conditions may counteract prior deficiencies or accomplishments. The various stages, associated crises, and ego qualities or strengths indicative of healthy development have been delineated in a preceding Capsule Summary. *Ritualizations:* The ego's adaptation to the environment is facilitated by repeated and socially sanctioned forms of interplay, which help fulfill our inherent need for mutual affirmation and provide a sense of familiarity with the mores of one's society.

4. FURTHER APPLICATIONS. *Dream Interpretation:* Erikson's approach to dream interpretation is similar in many respects to that of Freud. But he regards the ego as relatively powerful even during sleep, so that dreams are more likely to be constructive and teleological. *Psychopathology:* Neurosis and psychosis occur when the ego cannot maintain its usual adaptive and integrative functions because it has been seriously weakened by unresolved epigenetic crises, social trauma, and physical ills. Erikson shares Freud's view of psychopathology as a difference in degree rather than in kind, but concludes that the ego's normal functions cannot be entirely understood from the study of clinical cases. According to Erikson, identity confusion is the major problem confronting modern psychotherapists. *Psychotherapy:* Erikson regards himself primarily as a psychoanalyst, but cautions that this method is suitable only in some cases. He seeks to avoid some of the potential biases in Freudian therapy by using face-to-face interviews, rejecting transference neurosis, and avoiding a preoccupation with the patient's past. Erikson uses play therapy as the royal road to a child's unconscious. *Other Applications:* Unlike Freud, Erikson regards religion as a potentially valuable support for such essential ego qualities as trust and hope. He has also engaged in psychohistorical analyses of such noted figures as Luther, Gandhi, Hitler, Gorky, and Jefferson.

5. EVALUATION. Erikson has been criticized for professing a strong allegiance to Freud but espousing different theoretical constructs, a schism that may reflect excessive loyalty or a politically expedient attempt to avoid expulsion by the psychoanalytic establishment. He retains the currently unpopular construct of libido, gives some critics the impression of being overly conformist and optimistic, eschews any quantification or statistical analyses, and ignores important similarities between his constructs and those of Adler, Fromm, and Sullivan. Nevertheless, Erikson has significantly broadened the scope of psychoanalytic theory by stressing the role of healthy and adaptive ego processes, and by integrating psychoanalysis with such disciplines as sociology and history. The identity crisis, play therapy, the study of psychosocial influences on personality development and its continuation through adolescence and adulthood, and his prize-winning study of Gandhi are widely regarded as important contributions.

STUDY QUESTIONS

1. One striking indication of Erikson's own identity crisis is his eventual decision to change his name. Is some identity confusion likely to occur when: (a) an entertainer changes his or her name to something that will be more appealing to the public? (b) a woman changes her name because of marriage?

2. Of the four aspects of identity described by Erikson, are there any that you have found particularly difficult to achieve?

3. Give an example from real life or from fiction of a person who adopts a negative identity, rather than suffer the inner turmoil of identity confusion.

4. Erikson argues that a child finds mastery of the environment enjoyable for its own sake (and not just a means to the end of satisfying instinctual drives). Do you agree or disagree? Why?

5. (a) Give a real-life example to support Erikson's belief that our society creates difficulties for us by stressing contradictory values. (b) Give an example from your own life, from the life of someone you know well, or from fiction to illustrate the positive support provided by a socially sanctioned role.

6. Why is Erikson's direct investigation of different cultures, such as the Sioux and Yurok, a valuable departure from Freud's approach to the study of personality?

7. Using the case history discussed throughout the Appendix (e.g., Chapter 2, question 6; Chapter 4, questions 2 and 6a; Chapter 5, questions 1, 4b, and 5; Chapter 6, questions 3d and 4; Chapter 7, questions 1/a-1 and 7a), give an example to illustrate each of the following Eriksonian ideas: (a) The cause of basic mistrust, and the failure to satisfy the crisis of the oral-sensory stage. (b) The failure to satisfy the crises of the muscular-anal and locomotor-genital stages. (c) An identity crisis. (d) The failure to satisfy the crisis of young adulthood. (e) Parents who harm the child by using training that does not reflect the standards of the society in which they live. Also, (f) how might certain aspects of this case history be interpreted as *not* supporting Eriksonian theory?

8. (a) Give examples from two different stages to illustrate the following statement by Erikson: "The strength acquired at any stage is tested by the necessity to . . . take chances in the next stage with what was most vulnerably precious in the previous one." (b) What does this statement imply about the child's responsibility for any psychopathology that may develop from its relationship with the parents?

9. Does a healthy personality have no basic mistrust at all? Why or why not?

10. What important Freudian principles are supported by the "S[E]INE" dream?

PART III

RESEARCH-ORIENTED THEORIES OF PERSONALITY

PROLOGUE

The theories presented in the preceding chapters were based entirely on clinical observation. Although this method has produced many important insights about the human personality, it has some significant weaknesses as well. For example, as we noted in Chapter 1, such observations are subjective and uncontrolled. If a patient behaves in ways that support a particular theory, this might be due to subtle forms of influence by the therapist. Or the therapist's conclusions might be biased in favor of the theory, as by attributing any disagreement to the patient's resistances rather than to an incorrect interpretation.

It would therefore seem desirable to obtain more objective evidence by conducting experiments in the research laboratory. However, this approach also involves some important drawbacks.

Psychological Research and Statistical Inference

Psychological researchers must contend with an extremely troublesome problem: they can never measure all of the cases in which they are interested. Suppose that a personality theorist wishes to determine whether more introverted American adults are also more maladjusted (as Horney would argue), or if they are as mentally healthy as extraverts (as Jung would contend). Even in today's computer era, it would be much too expensive and time-consuming to obtain measurements on all of the millions of adults in this country, or even to study a substantial proportion of these cases.

What researchers normally do is to measure a relatively small number of cases drawn from the much larger group (population) of interest. A sample of (say) 100 people is small enough to interview, give written questionnaires, or use as subjects in a laboratory experiment. However, conclusions that apply only to the 100 people who happen to be included in the sample are unlikely to be of much interest. To advance our knowledge to any significant degree, a researcher must be able to draw much more general conclusions, such as: "Americans who are introverted tend to be no higher in psychopathology than Americans who are extraverted." A finding such as this is typically obtained from a research study that included no more than a few hundred subjects (and usually much less), yet it is stated in terms of the entire populations from which the samples were drawn—here, all adult Americans.

How is this possible? There are various mathematical procedures for drawing inferences about what is happening in a population, based on what is observed in a sample drawn from that population. These procedures, known as inferential statistics, are covered in courses and texts dealing with psychological statistics (e.g., Welkowitz, Ewen, & Cohen, 1991). The important point for our purposes is that there is *no* way to ensure that a sample is representative of the population from which it came. To be sure, a larger sample is more likely to be representative of the corresponding population. But no matter how carefully a researcher draws a sample, it is still possible that the data obtained from this sample will differ to a substantial extent from the true state of affairs in the population. The use of appropriate inferential statistics does make correct inferences about the population more likely, but not certain. Therefore, one or two studies never prove or disprove a theory or hypothesis; more substantial evidence must be collected before firm conclusions can be attempted.

Nor are the procedures of psychological research always as objective as might be imagined. A researcher faced with limited finances may be forced to draw a sample that is convenient but not very representative, as by studying only adults in his or her town (or university) when the results are supposed to apply to all American adults. Or it may prove extremely difficult to devise accurate measures of unconscious processes, such as intrapsychic conflicts and the defense mechanisms. The researcher may therefore avoid such important but methodologically troublesome areas, and focus instead on relatively trivial issues that can be measured more precisely.

Scientific research is superior to subjective opinion because it relies on hard data that can be verified and reproduced. Many things that people once "knew" to be true have been shown scientifically to be wholly incorrect, such as the notion that the earth is flat and that it is at the center of our universe. Psychological research has significant strengths as well as weaknesses, and has demonstrated that quite a few popular beliefs about human behavior have about as much validity as the flat-earth theory. But it is important to recognize that empirical research is no panacea insofar as personality theory is concerned.

Preview:
Allport, Murray, Cattell, and Kelly

Two of the first research-oriented personality theorists, Gordon Allport and Henry Murray, were colleagues at Harvard. They both share the clinician's concern for the intensive study of the individual, and both have devised well-known personality inventories to facilitate their experimental work. Interestingly, however, the theories of these physically proximate psychologists differ in almost every important respect. Murray is a neo-Freudian who strongly believes in the importance of unconscious processes, so his constructs and academic research probe deeply into the human personality.

Allport argues that Freud greatly overemphasized the unconscious, and focuses instead on the surface aspects of personality. "If you want to know something about a person," Allport says, "why not first ask him?" Thus, if a woman loves to entertain, this is her true and complete motive; there is no need to posit abstract and hidden goals, such as striving for superiority over her peers. This emphasis on the conscious and concrete aspects of human behavior leads Allport to some of the most unique and questionable conclusions in all of personality theory. Yet it is Allport's constructs, rather than Murray's, that have proved more popular among psychological researchers during the past three decades.

Raymond Cattell has sought to extend the scope of Allport's trait theory by using factor analysis, a complicated mathematical procedure. The resulting conceptual difficulties are so great that many psychologists prefer to ignore Cattell's work. Yet his ideas are based on an immense amount of empirical research; and some of his findings lead in surprising directions, as by supporting Freudian concepts that Allport specifically rejected.

Although an academician, George Kelly was primarily a clinician. His theory is included in this section because he argues that we all behave much like the research scientist, creating our own hypotheses and experimental tests for dealing with the world in which we live. For example, if you interpret (construe) a small bump on your wrist as "cancer," you will behave quite differently than if you construe it as a "harmless wart." It is your interpretation of reality that influences your behavior, at least until you decide to test your hypothesis by obtaining a doctor's opinion. Shakespeare had much the same idea when he had Hamlet say: "There is nothing either good or bad, but thinking makes it so." Thus Kelly concludes that every other personality theorist has followed the wrong strategy: rather than imposing a single set of scientific constructs on all humanity, the psychologist must try to understand the unique personal constructs created by each one of us.

GORDON W. ALLPORT,
HENRY A. MURRAY
Trait Theory/Personology

In 1920, one year after receiving his bachelor's degree from Harvard, Gordon Allport met Sigmund Freud for the only time—an event he was later to describe as "a traumatic developmental episode." Having written for and received an appointment "with a callow forwardness characteristic of age twenty-two," Allport was unprepared for the expectant silence with which Freud opened their meeting. Thinking to lighten the tension, he recounted an incident that had occurred on the tram car on the way to Freud's office: a four-year-old boy had displayed a pronounced phobia toward dirt, the cause of which clearly appeared to be the dominating and "well-starched" mother sitting beside him. Freud then fixed the rather prim and proper young Allport with a kindly therapeutic stare and asked, "And was that little boy you?"

While this question was by no means inappropriate, Allport's reaction was markedly negative. "Flabbergasted and feeling a bit guilty, I contrived to change the subject. . . . This experience taught me that depth psychology, for all its merits, may plunge too deep, and that psychologists would do well to give full recognition to manifest motives before probing the unconscious" (Allport, 1968, pp. 383–384).

BIOGRAPHICAL SKETCH: GORDON W. ALLPORT

Gordon W. Allport was born on November 11, 1897, in Montezuma, Indiana. His father was a country doctor, his mother a schoolteacher; and his home life was "marked by plain Protestant piety and hard work." Gordon's family included three older brothers, one of whom (Floyd) also was to become an academic psychologist. Most of his childhood and adolescence was spent in Cleveland, Ohio, where the Allports moved when he was six years old. Gordon was somewhat of a misfit as a child, quick with words but poor at games, and a schoolmate once observed sarcastically that "that guy swallowed a dictionary." Yet he nevertheless "contrived to be the 'star' for a small cluster of friends" (Allport, 1968, pp. 378–379).

Allport was an excellent and dedicated student, earning his B.A. from Harvard in 1919. During the following year he taught in Istanbul, traveled in Europe, and had his fateful meeting with Freud. He received his Ph.D. in psychology from Harvard in 1922. Save for two years of study in Europe immediately thereafter and a teaching position at Dartmouth College from 1926 to 1930, he was to spend the rest of his life at this renowned institution. Allport's personality course at Harvard is believed to be the first on this subject ever offered at an American college, and his initial book soon became a standard in the field (*Personality: A Psychological Interpretation,* 1937, later wholly revised as *Pattern and Growth in Personality,* 1961). Gordon married Ada Gould on June 30, 1925, a union that produced one son.

Allport's publications include some dozen books, numerous articles in psychological journals, and two personality inventories. Among his honors are being named president of the American Psychological Association in 1937 and the first Richard Cabot Professor of Social Ethics at Harvard in 1967, and receiving the APA Distinguished Scientific Contribution Award in 1964. But his most prized memento, reflecting his profound belief in the uniqueness of every personality, was a gift from fifty-five of his former psychology students: two handsomely bound volumes of their scientific publications, with the dedication: "From his students—in appreciation of his respect for their individuality" (Allport, 1968, p. 407). Gordon Allport died on October 9, 1967.

THE BASIC NATURE OF HUMAN BEINGS

In contrast to the interpersonal theories of Adler and Sullivan, Allport regards personality as something within the individual. "Of course the impression we make on others, and their response to us are important factors in the development of our personalities. . . . [But] what about the solitary hermit . . . or Robinson Crusoe before the advent of his man Friday? Do these isolates lack personality because they have no effect on others? [My] view is that such exceptional creatures have personal qualities that are no less fascinating than those of men living in human society. . . . [and that] we must have something inside our skins that constitutes our 'true' nature" (Allport, 1961, p. 24).

After reviewing some fifty definitions proposed by other theorists, Allport also reaches the following conclusions about personality: it is dynamic, growing and changing throughout one's life. It forms an organized pattern in the healthy person. It involves an inseparable union of both mental and physical functions. It consists of complicated systems of interacting elements. And it motivates or determines everything we do:

> There is, of course, no such thing as a correct or incorrect definition. Terms can only be defined in ways that are useful for a given purpose. For [our] purposes . . . *personality is the dynamic organization within the individual of those psychophysical systems that determine his characteristic behavior and thought.* (Allport, 1961, p. 28. See also Allport, 1937.)

Instinctual Drives

Allport is not wholly opposed to psychoanalysis, and even credits Freud with some brilliant discoveries. Allport agrees that we all strive to reduce such innate drives as hunger, thirst, sex, the need for oxygen, the need for sleep, and the necessity of eliminating bodily wastes. "All human beings in all the world do have drives. . . . If someone is very hungry, very much in need of oxygen, water, or rest, all other motives fade away until the drive is satisfied" (Allport, 1961, p. 205).

Instinctual drives are active to some degree throughout our lives and completely dominate the motivational scene of the very young child, whom Allport regards as an "unsocialized horror"—excessively demanding, pleasure-seeking, impatient, destructive, and conscienceless. In accordance with Freud and Fromm, therefore, he concludes that we must learn to overcome our inherent narcissism. "Self-love, it is obvious, remains always positive and active in our natures. [My] theory holds only that it need not remain dominant" (Allport, 1955, pp. 28, 30; 1961, p. 196; see also Allport, 1961, pp. xi–xii, 84–91, 197–257).

In most respects, however, Allport's conception of human nature differs radically from Freudian psychoanalysis. For example, Allport argues that we all possess the inherent potential to outgrow our self-centered beginnings. Failures are due primarily to disordered childhood relationships that impede the course of healthy development, rather than to an inability to sublimate illicit instincts. Most importantly (and most unlike Freud), Allport does not consider drive reduction to be a major determinant of *adult* behavior. Thus he is one of the few personality theorists who contend that the motives of children and adults differ significantly in kind, rather than merely in degree.

The Functional Autonomy of Adult Motives

According to Allport, adult motives differ from those of childhood in four significant ways.

Cognitions and Tension Increases. Instincts continue to operate during adulthood, and we all remain concerned with such pleasurable drive-reducing activities as eating, drinking, sleeping, and sexuality. But most adult motives consist of cognitive processes that are relatively independent of biological drives, differ from individual to individual, and often maintain or even increase levels of tension in order to achieve relatively distant goals.

For example, the Norwegian explorer Roald Amundsen pursued his chosen calling even at the cost of severe deprivations and drive increases— and, ultimately, the loss of his life. Some college students put aside such enjoyable activities as football or dating in order to undertake the burdensome studies required for a medical career. Kamikaze pilots during World

War II followed the manifestly unpleasurable course of sacrificing their lives for their country. Instances like these lead Allport to conclude that much of adult behavior cannot be explained in terms of drive reduction, or a Freudian pleasure principle:

> [Drive reduction is] only half the problem. While we certainly learn habitual modes of reducing tension, we also come to regard many of our past satisfactions to be as worthless as yesterday's ice cream soda. Though we want stability, we also want variety, . . . [and so] many things we are motivated to do merely increase our tensions, diminish our chances of pleasure, and commit us to a strenuous and risky course of life. (Allport, 1955, p. 66; 1961, p. 200. See also Allport, 1955, pp. 49, 57, 67; 1961, pp. 83, 90, 203.)

Thus, as in ego psychology, cognitive processes are no mere servants of instinctual drives but act as important motivators in their own right. Human nature includes both the need to reduce drives, which is most prominent in early childhood, and the tension-maintaining or -increasing "ambitions, interests, [and] outthrusts of the normally developing adult" (Allport, 1961, p. 221; see also pp. 89, 215, 222).[1]

Variety and Uniqueness. The preceding examples also indicate to Allport that cognitive motives vary considerably in kind from one individual to another, making it impossible to explain personality in terms of a few universal drives. "[There is an] extraordinary diversity of adult motives, unique in each particular personality" (Allport, 1961, p. 203; see also pp. 221, 226).

For this reason, Allport argues that personality theory must concern itself with the single case. As we observed in the prologue to this section, psychological research typically deals with groups of people (samples), and attempts to unearth general principles about human behavior (the **nomothetic** approach). Allport does not wholly reject the nomothetic approach, but he greatly prefers to study those idiosyncrasies that distinguish a particular individual from all others (the **idiographic** approach):

> Suppose you wish to select a roommate or a wife or a husband, or simply to pick out a suitable birthday gift for your mother. Your knowledge of mankind in general will not help you very much. . . . [Any given individual] is a unique creation of the forces of nature. There was never a person just like him, and there never will be again. . . . To develop a science of personality we must accept this fact. (Allport, 1961, pp. 4, 19, 21. See also Allport, 1955, pp. 19–28; 1961, pp. 11–16, 358; 1965, p. 159; 1968, pp. 81–102.)

Teleology. To Allport, the previous examples also imply that much of human behavior is *not* determined by prior causes. Instead, like Jung and Adler,

---

[1]Here Allport draws upon Maslow's dualistic theory of deficiency motives as opposed to growth motives, to be discussed in Chapter 13.

Allport concludes that we are often guided by **intentions.** This teleological form of motivation involves both an emotional want and a cognitive plan to satisfy it that is directed toward some future goal, such as exploring new lands, becoming a doctor, or even merely brushing off a fly. "To understand what a person is, it is necessary always to refer to what he may be in the future, for every state of the person is pointed in the direction of future possibilities" (Allport, 1955, p. 12; see also Allport, 1955, pp. 51, 76, 89, 92; 1961, pp. 85, 206, 221–225).

Functional Autonomy. Most theorists regard childhood and adult behavior as varying expressions of the same basic motives (such as sexuality and aggression in Freudian psychoanalysis, or striving for superiority in Adlerian theory). In contrast, Allport argues that adult motives often become independent in purpose (**functionally autonomous**) of their childhood or adolescent origins.[2]

To illustrate, a man who long ago earned his living as a sailor may feel a powerful urge to return to the sea, even though he has become financially independent and the original motive has disappeared. A college student who chose a medical career because of parental pressures may now pursue these studies because they have become very interesting and enjoyable. Or a miser who learned thrift because of an impoverished childhood may come to love the feel of gold or the size of a large bank account, and remain stingy despite having accumulated great wealth. In all of these examples, what was originally a means to an end becomes a functionally autonomous end in itself. (See Allport, 1961, pp. 277, 299, 364.)

Not all adult motives are functionally autonomous. Exceptions include the reduction of instinctual drives, and those neuroses and psychoses that are caused by unresolved childhood conflicts and can be cured by reliving the troublesome incidents from the past. There is no way to predict which motives will become functionally autonomous, however, nor does Allport consider it necessary to investigate the origins and history of such motives. "A functionally autonomous motive *is* the personality . . . [and we] need not, and cannot, look 'deeper' " (Allport, 1961, pp. 244; see also pp. 238–243).

Values

To Allport, as to Jung and Fromm, human beings need a unifying philosophy that gives meaning to one's life and affords some answer to such tragic problems as suffering and death. (See Allport, 1961, pp. 252, 294–304, 453–457.) Basing his ideas upon the work of a German philosopher, Eduard

---

[2]Technically, "perseverative functional autonomy" involves repeated movements and addictions (e.g., cigarettes, alcohol) related to some neurological or biochemical process. "Propriate functional autonomy" is of greater importance and includes more complicated acquired motives that do not depend on direct feedback, as in the following examples.

Spranger, Allport concludes that there are six particularly important types of
values (value-orientations):

Theoretical: An intellectual desire to discover truth and systematize
one's knowledge, as by becoming a scientist or philosopher.

Economic: A businesslike concern with the useful and practical.

Esthetic: An emphasis on the enjoyment of form, harmony, beauty,
and the artistic for its own sake.

Social: A concern for and love of other people.

Political: A love of power, not necessarily related to the field of politics per se.

Religious: A mystical desire for unity with some higher reality.

This classification is partly nomothetic, since it applies to people in
general. Yet it is also idiographic, since an individual's system of values
consists of a unique combination of the six possibilities. For example, one
person may be very interested in the theoretical and esthetic, but not in the
political or religious. Another individual may reflect much the reverse emphasis. Or a person may care about most or even all of the six values,
perhaps with one or two slightly more important than the others. There are
also those who lack any values or commitments, however depressed this may
make them (Allport, 1955, pp. 76–77). Allport is the first theorist discussed
thus far who has devised a written questionnaire to measure such constructs
as values, as we will see in a subsequent section.

Consciousness and Concreteness

Allport's approach to the unconscious is somewhat ambivalent, and unique
among the theorists discussed thus far. On the one hand, he shares the
psychoanalytic belief that "most of what goes on in our personalities belongs
in some way to a nonconscious stratum. . . . [Much motivation] is unconscious, infantile, and hidden from oneself." Yet he also concludes that the
healthy individual is motivated primarily by conscious impulses and conflicts, and he attributes the Freudian emphasis on unconscious processes to
an excessive concern with psychopathology. "Freud was a clinician who
worked year in and year out with disordered personalities. His insights are
more applicable to these cases than to personalities marked by healthy
functioning . . . [who] have a far more autonomous ego than [he] allows . . . [and whose motivation is] largely conscious" (Allport, 1961, pp.
140, 150, 152, 155, 217; see also Allport, 1961, pp. 139–164, 221–224;
Allport, cited by Evans, 1970, pp. 11–12).

In addition, Allport prefers to stress the concrete aspects of human
motivation. Human beings do not and cannot aim directly at the achievement of pleasure; we focus instead on such concrete goals as marrying a
particular person, obtaining a college degree, or earning a good living.

CAPSULE SUMMARY
Some Important Allportian Terminology

Common trait	A structural and motivational aspect of personality that initiates and guides consistent forms of behavior, such as friendliness, ambitiousness, and so forth. Common traits facilitate nomothetic comparisons among different people, but are only a rough approximation as to any individual, unique personality.
Functional autonomy	The independence in purpose of many adult motives from their childhood and adolescent counterparts; a means to an end becoming an end in itself, and continuing to influence behavior after the original motive has disappeared.
Idiographic approach	Studying the single case in order to discover those factors that make a given individual unique.
Intention	The fusion of an emotional want and a cognitive plan into an integral urge, directed toward some future goal.
Nomothetic approach	Studying (usually) groups of people in order to discover general principles and laws concerning human behavior.
Personal disposition (personal trait)	Similar in definition to common trait, but unique to a given individual and thus a reflection of one's true personality. On occasion, a single cardinal personal disposition influences virtually all of one's behavior. More often, some five to ten central personal dispositions are predominant. In addition, personality includes numerous less influential secondary personal dispositions.
Proprium	The unifying, distinctively personal core of personality. Somewhat similar to "self" or "ego" but more comprehensive, including the sense of bodily self, the sense of continuing self-identity, self-esteem, self-extension, the self-image, the self as rational coper, propriate striving, and the self as knower.
Value (value-orientation)	A unifying philosophy or orientation that gives meaning to one's life. Important values include the theoretical, economic, esthetic, social, political, and religious.

Similarly, Allport would consider a woman's love of entertaining to be her true and complete motive, rather than interpreting this behavior as the sublimation of some illicit wish or an overriding desire for superiority or mastery. "There are surely a million kinds of competence in life which do not interest [her] at all. Her motive is highly concrete. Entertaining, not abstract competence, is the bread of life to her; and any abstract scheme misses that point completely, and therefore sheds little or no light on her personality as it actually functions" (Allport, 1961, p. 226).

Because Allport regards healthy adult motives as primarily conscious and concrete, he argues that important aspects of personality can be ascertained by direct inquiry. His counterpart to Adler's "Question" would be to ask about what the individual expects to be doing in a few years, thereby tapping conscious intentions rather than seeking to unearth unconscious motives. "If you want to know something about a person, why not first ask him?" (Allport, 1942; see also Allport, 1961, pp. 224–225.)

THE STRUCTURE OF PERSONALITY

Unlike Freud and Jung, Allport does not draw a clear distinction between the motivational and structural aspects of personality. While the constructs to be discussed in this section are essentially structural, they also play a significant role in determining our behavior and thought.

Common Traits and Personal Dispositions

In accordance with his belief in the concreteness of human motives, Allport describes the structure of personality in terms of straightforward **traits** like friendliness, ambitiousness, cleanliness, enthusiasm, seclusiveness, punctuality, shyness, talkativeness, dominance, submissiveness, generosity, and so forth (with emphasis on the "and so forth," since he estimates that there are some 4,000–5,000 traits and 18,000 trait names!).

Definition of Traits. Allport does not claim that a shy or talkative person acts this way on every occasion. Any individual's behavior may become atypical because of changes in the surrounding environment, pressures from other people, and internal conflicts, so that *"no trait theory can be sound unless it allows for, and accounts for, the variability of a person's conduct."* Yet traits are nevertheless of considerable importance, since they direct the many constant aspects of one's personality:

> A trait is . . . a *neuropsychic structure having the capacity to render many stimuli functionally equivalent, and to initiate and guide equivalent (meaningfully consistent) forms of adaptive and expressive behavior.* (Allport, 1961, pp. 333, 347; see also Allport, 1960, pp. 131–135; 1961, pp. 332–375; 1968, pp. 43–66.)

A trait (such as cleanliness) is considerably more general than a habit (like regularly brushing one's teeth or washing one's hands). Traits are usually also broader in scope than attitudes, which involve an evaluation of specific objects (like communism, parsnips, or one's next-door neighbor). And they are often interrelated, as when outgoing individuals also tend to be talkative. Allport refers to traits as "neuropsychic" because, like Freud and Sullivan, he believes that it will ultimately be possible to relate the elements of personality to specific physiological processes.

Types of Traits. Although every personality is unique, a particular culture does tend to evoke roughly similar modes of adjustment. Thus **common traits** refer to *"those aspects of personality in respect to which most people within a given culture can be profitably compared . . .* [and are] indispensable whenever we undertake to study personality by scales, tests, ratings, or any other comparative method." But since common traits are nomothetic, they can provide no more than a rough approximation as to any particular personality. For example, many individuals are predominantly outgoing or shy, yet "there are endless varieties of dominators, leaders, aggressors, followers, yielders, and timid souls. . . . When we designate Tom and Ted both as *aggressive,* we do not mean that their aggressiveness is identical in kind. Common speech is a poor guide to psychological subtleties" (Allport, 1961, pp. 339–340, 355–356; compare also with the identical views of Adler, 1933/1964b, pp. 27, 148).

The true personality consists of **personal traits (personal dispositions),** which are defined similarly to traits in general but are unique to the individual and determine one's own style of behavior (Allport, 1961, p. 373).[3] Since personal dispositions reflect the subtle shadings that distinguish a particular individual from all others, they often must be described at length rather than with a single term. Thus we might say that "little Susan has a peculiar anxious helpfulness all her own," or a young man "will do anything for you if it doesn't cost him any effort" (Allport, 1961, p. 359).

A personality can be dominated by a single "cardinal personal disposition" that influences most of the individual's behavior. Examples include Scrooge's miserliness, Don Juan's seductiveness, de Sade's sexual cruelty, and Machiavelli's cleverness. But most personalities contain from five to ten important "central personal dispositions," as might be found in a carefully written letter of recommendation. There are also numerous, less influential "secondary personal dispositions" as well. (See Allport, 1961, p. 365; Allport, cited by Evans, 1970, pp. 27–28.) Thus, just as Adler claimed to understand an individual from a few manifestations of the style of life, Allport concludes that knowing a few central things about a person makes it possible to predict most of that individual's behavior.

Problems in Identifying Traits. Since personal dispositions cannot as yet be defined in terms of directly observable physiological processes, their existence must be inferred from overt actions. Allport concedes that this can be a difficult task.

First of all, no one act is ever the result of a single trait. For example, writing a letter to a relative may be due in part to the traits of responsibility, loyalty, and friendliness, as well as to various intentions (e.g., to receive a

---

[3]It is theoretically possible for an individual to be so typical of a given culture that common traits will adequately describe the true personality, but this occurs very rarely. There are also some extraordinary behaviors that are too infrequent ever to be classified as common traits but which can become important personal dispositions, such as treasonableness and kleptomania (Allport, 1961, pp. 342, 374).

reply) and external pressures (as from one's parents or spouse). Furthermore, apparently obvious inferences drawn from one particular situation may prove to be erroneous. A student who is in fact extremely punctual may arrive late to class on a given day because of an emergency. The giving of a gift may seem like an act of generosity, yet actually represent a self-seeking bribe. Or a professor who leaves the departmental library in total disorder may maintain an office or home that is fastidiously neat, with these contradictory (second-ary) personal dispositions governed by an underlying more central one of selfishness that demands orderliness for oneself but not for others (Allport, 1961, pp. 334, 337, 361–364).

Allport does suggest that a personal disposition is reflected in behaviors that occur with considerable frequency and intensity, and in a wide range of situations. For example, rejecting one invitation to a party may merely indicate a temporary mood (or a prior engagement). But a person who consistently refuses to attend parties, and who spends considerable amounts of time alone, would properly be described as seclusive. However, it remains unclear as to just how consistent and intense behaviors must be before the existence of a personal disposition can safely be inferred.

The Proprium

Although the healthy adult personality is complicated by the presence of numerous dispositions, intentions, and instincts, it is nevertheless organized around those matters that are most personal and important to oneself. Since terms like "self" and "ego" have been used by other theorists in a variety of ways, Allport refers to this unifying core of personality as the **proprium.** (See Allport, 1955, pp. 36–65; 1961, pp. 111–138). The proprium includes eight distinctively personal aspects of existence, which develop at different times of life.

The Sense of Bodily Self. The newborn infant cannot distinguish between self and others, and only gradually learns to separate internal from external events. While Allport (like Sullivan) cautions that we do not really know what the infant experiences, he shares Freud's belief that the first aspect of selfhood to emerge is related to the body. The sense of bodily self develops from organic sensations and external frustrations, for "a child who cannot eat when he wants to, who bumps his head, soon learns the limitations of his too, too solid flesh" (Allport, 1961, p. 113). And it remains important throughout life, for movements and sensations constantly make one aware that "I am I."

The Sense of Continuing Self-Identity. Like Erikson, Allport regards a feeling of inner sameness and continuity as essential to self-awareness. "Today I remember some of my thoughts of yesterday, and tomorrow I shall re-member some of my thoughts of both yesterday and today; and I am certain that they are the thoughts of the same person—of myself." The sense of self-identity also begins in early infancy and is aided by the development of language skills, notably having and hearing a name of one's own (Allport, 1961, pp. 114–117).

Self-Esteem (Ego-Enhancement). As we have seen, narcissism or self-love also originates very early in life. Self-seeking attempts to maintain pride and avoid embarrassment are so common that the most familiar forms of "self" and "ego" are "selfish" and "egotistical."

Self-Extension (Ego-Extension). At about age four to six years, the sense of self gradually extends to important external objects. This developing concept of "mine" includes the child's parents, siblings, and toys, and it establishes the foundation for such important later self-extensions as the love of one's country, religion, and career.

The Self-Image. The capacity for self-evaluation also originates at about age four to six. As in Sullivanian theory, the self-image includes a sense of "good-me" and "bad-me" that develops in response to parental expectations, rewards, and punishments. It also involves the perception of one's abilities and chosen goals. Ideally, this aspect of the proprium serves as an accurate guide to one's strengths and weaknesses. However, Allport (1955, p. 47) agrees with Horney that it may instead become a grossly exaggerated ideal*ized* image and establish unrealistic, unattainable standards.

The Self as Rational Coper (and Sometime User of Defense Mechanisms). Like the Freudian ego, the proprium must relate inner needs to outer reality. Thus the proprium forms rational plans for coping with biological impulses, environmental demands, and the prohibitions of one's conscience.

At times even a mature adult will choose to evade such difficulties rather than face them, behavior "brilliantly" explained by the various Freudian defense mechanisms. For example, a mother who unconsciously hates her offspring may be consciously solicitous and overly protest her love (reaction formation). A child who resents the birth of a sibling may keep repeating "no baby, no baby" (denial of reality). Or people given an uncomplimentary evaluation may argue that their critics don't really know them (rationalization). But since Allport does not regard illicit instincts as an integral part of human nature, he concludes that a personality dominated by defense mechanisms is abnormal. "Ego-defense mechanisms are present in all personalities. [But] when they have the upper hand we are dealing with a badly disordered life" (Allport, 1961, p. 164; 1968, p. 72).

The healthy individual usually confronts reality instead of seeking some measure of escape. The proprium is capable of achieving wholly satisfying solutions and adjustments, rather than having to settle for compromises and sublimations. Allport also differs from Freud by suggesting that rational coping begins to develop at about age six to twelve years. (See Allport, 1955, pp. 23, 46; 1961, pp. 155–163, 224.)

Propriate Striving. One particularly important function of the proprium is to form the teleological, cognitive, and tension-maintaining (or -increasing) intentions and goals that give purpose to one's life. This distinctively human characteristic first begins to develop in adolescence. "Mature [propriate] striving is linked to long-range goals . . . [which] are, strictly speaking, unattainable. . . . The devoted parent never loses concern for his child; the devotee of democracy adopts a lifelong assignment in his human relationships; [and] the scientist . . . creates more and more questions, never fewer. Indeed [one] measure of our intellectual maturity . . . is our capacity to feel less and less satisfied with our answers to better and better problems" (Allport, 1955, pp. 29, 67).

The Self as Knower. Finally, the proprium also observes its other seven functions and the remaining conscious aspects of personality. Thus we know that it is ourselves who have bodily sensations, self-identity, self-extension, and so forth.

Allport cautions that there is no sharp dividing line between the proprium and the rest of personality, nor is the proprium an entity or "little man" in the psyche ("homunculus") that manipulates whatever we do. "If we ask why this hospital patient is depressed, it is not helpful to say that 'the self has a wrong self-image.' To say that the self does this or that, wants this or that, [or] wills this or that, is to beg a series of difficult questions" (Allport, 1961, pp. 129–130; see also Allport, 1955, pp. 36–38, 54–56, 61).

Conscience

The various aspects of the proprium are not always separate and distinct, but often fuse together into a more complicated system. One such example is the conscience, which is virtually universal (save for a few psychopathic individuals) and represents a fusion of self-esteem, the self-image, and propriate striving.

Allport shares Freud's belief that a moral sense is not innate, and that the child introjects parental standards of right and wrong. But Allport argues that the adult conscience differs in kind from that of childhood, with the original fearful sense of what "must" and "must not" be done ultimately developing into a more mature "ought" based on one's own standards. "Conscience in maturity is rarely tied to the fear of punishment, whether external or self-administered. It is rather a feeling of obligation" (Allport, 1961, p. 136; see also Allport, 1955, pp. 68–74; 1961, pp. 134–137).

THE DEVELOPMENT OF PERSONALITY

Since Allport regards most adult motives as functionally autonomous of their childhood and adolescent origins, he sees little need to study the historical course of personality or to posit specific developmental stages. Similarly, he regards Freud's contention that personality is essentially determined by about age six as virtual nonsense (save perhaps for an occasional severe neurosis). Allport even concludes that "in a sense the first year is the least important year for personality, assuming that serious injuries to health do not occur" (1961, p. 78; see also Allport, 1961, p. 238; Allport, cited by Evans, 1970, p. 79).

To Allport, as to Horney, the unsocialized infant becomes a socially adjusted adult primarily because of innate healthy potentials. Unless the parents behave in highly pathogenic ways, such as erratic and inconsistent rewards and punishments, anxiety-provoking threats of castration, or failing to provide the essential minimum of security and love, personality development is free to pursue a course of unimpeded growth. (See Allport, 1955, pp. 26–35; 1961, pp. 102, 122–126, 288).

Criteria of Maturity

In accordance with his emphasis on studying the healthy adult personality, Allport (1960, pp. 155–168; 1961, pp. 275–307) has formulated criteria of mental health or maturity that are more extensive than Freud's "love and work." These include the possession of a *unifying philosophy* or set of values that gives purpose to one's life, and propriate *self-extension* to such meaningful spheres of human endeavor as one's marital partner, family, work, friends, hobbies, and political party.

The mature personality is also characterized by a capacity for *compassionate and loving relationships* that are free of crippling possessiveness and jealousy. Compassion also involves an appreciation of the considerable difficulties in living faced by all human beings. "No one knows for sure the meaning of life; everyone . . . sails to an unknown destination. All lives are pressed between two oblivions. No wonder the poet cries, 'Praise the Lord for every globule of human compassion.'" In contrast, the immature person feels that "he and his kind matter; no one else. His church, his lodge, his family, and his nation make a safe unit, but all else is alien, dangerous, [and] to be excluded from his petty formula for survival" (Allport, 1961, pp. 285–286).

Other criteria of maturity are *emotional security and self-acceptance,* or the capacity to endure the inevitable frustrations of life without losing one's poise and descending to childish rages or self-pity; *a realistic orientation* toward oneself and the external world, including the ability to meet the difficult task of economic survival without panic or defensiveness; and accurate *self-insight* as to one's disagreeable as well as desirable qualities. Like Freud and Jung, Allport cautions that true self-insight is deceptively difficult to achieve. "Since we think about ourselves so much of the time, it is comforting to assume . . . that we really know the score. . . . [But] this is not an easy assignment. [As] Santayana wrote, 'Nothing requires a rarer

intellectual heroism than willingness to see one's equation written out'"
(Allport, 1961, pp. 290–291).

The Style of Life

Because Allport regards every personality as unique, he rejects the use of
character typologies in favor of Adler's concept of the style of life. He argues
that there are so many respects by which a person could be categorized, (e.g.,
liberal, narcissistic, introverted, authoritarian, anal, and so forth) that any
individual would have to be located in literally hundreds of types, and that
nomothetically designed typologies cannot reflect the unique patterning of
any specific personality. "Typologies are convenient and seductive, but none
has ever been invented to account for the total individual. . . . [Instead,]
Adler's position . . . is essentially the same as the one [I advocate]" (Allport,
1955, p. 55; 1961, p. 17; see also Allport, 1955, pp. 39, 81–82; 1961, pp. 16–
18, 349–353; Allport, cited by Evans, 1970, pp. 7–9, 52–53).

FURTHER APPLICATIONS
OF ALLPORTIAN THEORY

Psychopathology, Psychotherapy, Social Reform

Allport is the first theorist discussed thus far who has virtually nothing to say
about dream interpretation, and who posits a difference in kind between
normality and psychopathology. The healthy individual usually confronts the
various difficulties imposed by life and is guided by motives that are primarily conscious, flexible, and functionally autonomous. But the neurotic or
psychotic, whose innate predisposition for normal development has been
blocked by pathogenic childhood influences, escapes important problems
through self-deceiving defense mechanisms and is dominated by motives
that are unconscious, compulsive, and childish. As a result, the pathological
individual is too self-centered and fearful to achieve the balanced give and
take required for meaningful interpersonal relationships. (See Allport, 1961,
pp. 150–152.)

   Not himself a practicing clinician, Allport finds some merit in various
kinds of psychotherapy. However, he does argue that delving into a patient's
childhood is useful only if the pathology has not become functionally autonomous. Conversely, if the neurosis or psychosis has become an integral part
of the sufferer's style of life, a more present-oriented therapy must be used to
facilitate the development of new goals and interests. But whatever the form,
the goal of psychotherapy should be to help the patient grow toward the six
criteria of maturity (Allport, 1961, pp. 239–240, 304–305; Allport, cited by
Evans, 1970, pp. 34–36).

   Like Fromm and Sullivan, Allport has taken some interest in social reform and international relations. He argues that even an infant discipline like psychology can and should offer properly cautious opinions concerning important world issues, notably that of facilitating peace. He also concludes that psychology and sociology are far more difficult sciences than physics or chemistry, and so merit considerably greater governmental research support. "It required years of labor and billions of dollars to gain the secret of the atom. It will take a still greater investment to gain the secrets of man's irrational nature" (Allport, 1954/1958, p. xi; see also Allport, 1960, pp. 169–180, 327–362; Allport, cited by Evans, 1970, pp. 105–111).

Religion

As we have seen, Allport differs from Freud by including religion among the six major adult value-orientations. He stresses that religion fortifies the individual against anxiety and despair, and makes it possible to relate to the totality of existence. Thus he is critical of personality theories that purport to be comprehensive, yet devote little or no attention to this important area. Allport shares Jung's belief that religion becomes most important during one's thirties and includes elements of wonder and mystery, but he cautions that a science such as psychology can neither prove nor disprove religious concepts.

Allport's view of religion is by no means entirely positive, however. He warns that the extrinsic use of religion as the means to an end (such as making business contacts or becoming an esteemed member of the community), as opposed to an intrinsic and sincere belief, is eminently undesirable and related to such abuses as prejudice. He also concludes that some two thousand years of religion have not had much success in improving human morality, and that it is essential to appeal in some way to each individual's own sense of responsibility. (See Allport, 1950; 1955, pp. 72–73, 93–98; 1961, pp. 299–303; 1968, pp. 55–59, 218–268; Allport, cited by Evans, 1970, pp. 67–74, 106.)

The Nature of Prejudice

Allport has taken a particular interest in the psychology of prejudice, which he defines as an irrational hostility toward others solely because of their presumed membership in a particular group. Because prejudice involves erroneous negative views about people or groups, "a wit defined [it] as 'being down on something you're not up on' " (Allport, 1954/1958, p. 8). But unlike most factual errors, prejudice is too rigid to be corrected merely by providing appropriate information. For example, some prejudiced hotel managers consistently rejected written requests for rooms from guests with Jewish-sounding names, and refused to be swayed by data indicating that Jews are by no means more disorderly or unsuitable guests than members of other ethnic groups. In contrast, an anthropologist refused to let his children play with a nearby tribe of American Indians because their village was rife with tuberculosis. He was not displaying prejudice, but responding to a real danger. Nor was a child's belief that residents of Minneapolis were evil "monopolists" indicative of prejudice, for his dislike vanished immediately upon discovering his confusion (Allport, 1954/1958, pp. 4–6, 9).

Allport regards prejudice as a complicated phenomenon, with multiple causes. As an illustration, consider prejudice against blacks in America. Such prejudice is due partly to the lingering effects of slavery, and the failure of reconstruction in the South following the civil war (historical factors). Some advertisements promote prejudice by encouraging contempt for those who are economically disadvantaged (sociocultural factors). Prejudice is more readily learned in areas where it is widely practiced and observed (situational factors). Some people who suffer major disappointments, such as losing a job or getting poor school grades, seek a scapegoat to hold responsible (psychodynamic factors). Some stereotypes depict all blacks as unintelligent and primitive (phenomenological factors). And dark skin (a characteristic of the stimulus object) may evoke irrational or, less frequently, justified fears and hostility (Allport, 1954/1958, p. 207; see also Allport, 1954/1958, pp. 28–67, 184–212, 271–322, 327; 1960, pp. 219–267; 1968, pp. 187–268).

Prejudice may be taught by parents who indicate (covertly or overtly) that groups to which the family belongs are superior and desirable, while other groups are inferior and hateful. Or prejudice may result from pressures to conform to national norms, as in Nazi Germany. Interestingly, those who are prejudiced against one minority are very often also highly intolerant of most others.

Like Adler, Allport regards prejudice as a cause of psychopathology. The effects of prejudice include the increased use of defense mechanisms, withdrawal and passivity, developing an equal prejudice against others, and/or identification with the aggressor that results in intense self-hate (Allport, 1954/1958, pp. 138–158). Prejudice may also lead to intergroup conflicts, or even to war. Thus, like Fromm and Sullivan, Allport concludes that we must pursue the difficult course of striving to reduce prejudice by developing a primary allegiance to humanity as a whole. "It seems today that the clash between the idea of race and of One World . . . is shaping into an issue that may well be the most decisive in human history. The important question is, Can a loyalty to mankind be fashioned before interracial warfare breaks out? Theoretically it can" (Allport, 1954/1958, pp. 42–43).

Personality Measurement

A Study of Values. Unlike the theorists discussed in preceding chapters, Allport has sought to evaluate his constructs by conducting empirical research. He and his associates have devised and validated two personality inventories, the A-S Reaction Study of ascendance-submission (Allport & Allport, 1928/1949) and the better-known Study of Values (Allport, Vernon,

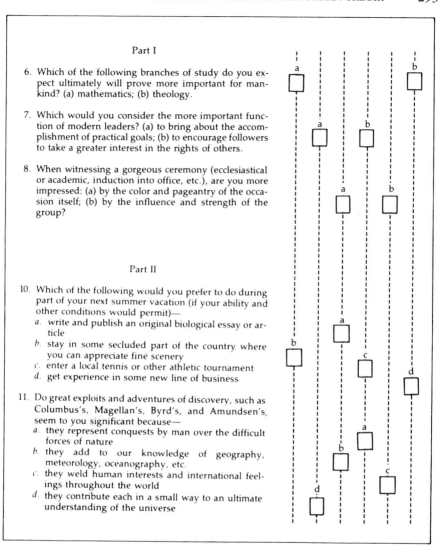

Part I

6. Which of the following branches of study do you expect ultimately will prove more important for mankind? (a) mathematics; (b) theology.

7. Which would you consider the more important function of modern leaders? (a) to bring about the accomplishment of practical goals; (b) to encourage followers to take a greater interest in the rights of others.

8. When witnessing a gorgeous ceremony (ecclesiastical or academic, induction into office, etc.), are you more impressed: (a) by the color and pageantry of the occasion itself; (b) by the influence and strength of the group?

Part II

10. Which of the following would you prefer to do during part of your next summer vacation (if your ability and other conditions would permit)—
   a. write and publish an original biological essay or article
   b. stay in some secluded part of the country where you can appreciate fine scenery
   c. enter a local tennis or other athletic tournament
   d. get experience in some new line of business

11. Do great exploits and adventures of discovery, such as Columbus's, Magellan's, Byrd's, and Amundsen's, seem to you significant because—
   a. they represent conquests by man over the difficult forces of nature
   b. they add to our knowledge of geography, meteorology, oceanography, etc.
   c. they weld human interests and international feelings throughout the world
   d. they contribute each in a small way to an ultimate understanding of the universe

FIGURE 9.1. Sample items from A Study of Values.

& Lindzey, 1931/1960; see also Allport, 1961, pp. 453–457; 1968, pp. 51–54). The latter instrument measures the relative extent to which an individual prefers the six major value-orientations (theoretical, economic, esthetic, social, political, religious), as follows: In Part I the respondent scores pairs of statements 3-0 or 2-1, depending on the degree to which one is favored over the other. In Part II, four choices must be ranked from 4 (most preferred) through 1. (See Figure 9.1.)

Notice that for each question, if you give a high score to one alternative (which represents one of the value-orientations), you must give lower scores to other values. So if you obtain a high total score on (say) the religious orientation, this means only that you value this orientation more than some of the others. It does *not* reveal *how much* you like religion: you may value the other orientations highly but religion even more, or you might not care much for religion but prefer the other orientations even less. Thus the Study of Values indicates the *relative* importance of the six value-orientations to a given individual. It is not designed to show the *absolute* strength of each value, or to facilitate comparisons among different people. The use of such self-oriented or "ipsative" scales remains a matter of some controversy for this reason, although the Study of Values is generally regarded as a viable instrument. (See for example Anastasi, 1976, pp. 539–540, 552–554.)

Letters from Jenny. Allport (1965) has also conducted a purely idiographic study into the writings of one neurotic elderly woman, Jenny Masterson (a pseudonym), based on a content analysis of some 301 letters she wrote to a young married couple over a twelve-year period (1926–1937, from age 58 to 70). After suggesting how her personality might be viewed by Freudians, Jungians, Adlerians, ego psychologists, and existential psychologists, Allport characterizes her in terms of eight central personal dispositions: paranoid suspiciousness, self-centeredness, independence, dramatic intensity, artistic appreciation, aggressiveness, cynical morbidity, and sentimentality. Although it proved impossible to delve deeply into Jenny's underlying motives, Allport concludes that the method demonstrates the capacity of psychological research to conduct careful quantitative work with the single case. (See Allport, 1961, pp. 59–62, 369.)

Other Research. Like Adler, Allport has taken considerable interest in overt expressive behavior (or "body language"). He concludes that behavior is not only directed toward a particular goal, but is also expressed in a stable and unique style that permits important inferences about an individual's personality. For example, some fairly accurate conclusions can be drawn from a person's gestures, facial expressions, vocal intonation, and posture (including one's bodily position while asleep). Even handwriting analysis predicts certain information at better than a chance level, although it is not nearly as flawless as some overenthusiastic graphologists would suggest and is best studied in combination with the other types of expressive behavior (Allport, 1961, pp. 460–494; Allport, cited by Evans, 1970, pp. 111–112; Allport & Vernon, 1933). Allport has also investigated the difference between intrinsic and extrinsic religious beliefs, the psychology of rumor, and the psychology of radio (Allport, 1960, pp. 311–326; Allport & Postman, 1947; Cantril & Allport, 1935).

Insofar as the general philosophy of research is concerned, Allport concludes that psychological journals contain all too many studies that are elegantly designed but have little bearing on truly important problems. He also warns research psychologists against an excessive commitment to any one method or theory. "Narrow systems, dogmatically held, tend to trivialize the mentality of the investigator. . . . No single brand of modern psychology is wholly adequate to the problem of man's individuality and growth. . . . [especially those] based largely upon the behavior of sick and anxious people or upon the antics of captive and desperate rats" (Allport, 1955, pp. 5, 17–18; see also Allport, cited by Evans, 1970, pp. 86–97).

EVALUATION

Criticisms and Controversies

Iconoclasms and Oversimplifications. Some of Allport's conclusions set him apart from virtually all other personality theorists. He denies the importance of the first few years of life to a degree that most modern psychologists would regard as excessive. His contention that all forms of psychopathology differ in kind from normality, rather than in degree, is also highly unusual and extremely questionable. The same is true of one of the cornerstones of Allport's theory, functional autonomy. He argues that adult motives differ radically in kind from those of childhood, yet his supporting anecdotal evidence does not rule out alternative explanations. For example, while Amundsen's explorations might have been examples of propriate striving, a Freudian or Eriksonian could undoubtedly explain such behavior at least partly in terms of childhood events and unresolved conflicts. Similarly, even though the retired sailor no longer earns his living from the sea, the concept of overdetermination suggests that other pressures from the past also influenced this behavior. Therefore, it might well be these same forces that continue to motivate his going to sea in the present.

In comparison to the meticulously detailed psychoanalytic theories, the explanatory power of trait theory appears at best somewhat incomplete when it leads to such statements as: a man likes blue because he likes blue (Allport, cited by Evans, 1970, p. 37). Therefore, Allport's emphasis on the conscious, concrete, and present aspects of personality has been criticized as a serious oversimplification.

Science and the Idiographic Approach. Allport is no more successful than Adler in trying to defend the uniqueness of every human personality. Valuable information can in fact be obtained by studying the single case, but investigating millions of individuals is an impossible task. Psychologists must be able to rely on at least some general principles, which permit information gleaned from patients or research subjects to be generalized to wider groups of people. Despite Allport's protestations that psychology not only must but can become far more idiographic, his profound emphasis on uniqueness seems to imply that psychology can never become a true science. The majority of current psychologists are as yet unwilling to accept this dire possibility, and even most of Allport's own research was primarily nomothetic in nature.

Circularity. It has been argued that trait theory depends far too heavily on circular reasoning, where the existence of a trait is inferred from certain behavior and then used to explain that behavior. For example, if we deduce that John is aggressive because he hit Mary, we cannot then turn the same definition around and say that John did so *because* he is aggressive. Such circular reasoning would explain nothing at all about the causes of aggressiveness. Yet it is all too easy to overlook the problem of circularity, and to conclude that traits actually explain the phenomena that they describe.

Other Criticisms. Some critics contend that human behavior is not sufficiently consistent to be described in terms of traits. They stress that considerably more attention must be devoted to environmental and other intrapersonal variables, and even Allport himself indicated a similar concern. (See for example Allport, 1968, p. 63; Mischel, 1973.) There also appear to be some contradictions in Allport's reasoning, as when he concludes that the unconscious constitutes most of personality yet also argues that it is only dominant in the abnormal individual.

Empirical Research

Trait theory has stimulated a vast amount of empirical research. A significant part of the psychological literature deals with such traits as introversion—extraversion, locus of control (the extent to which people believe that rewards and punishments depend on their own behavior, or on mere chance and the actions of others), shyness, cautiousness, rigidity, activity, and many others. However, these studies focus on the specific trait(s) of interest to the investigators; they are not intended as tests of Allport's theory of personality. Partly for this reason, a review of this voluminous literature is beyond the scope of the present text.

    Whereas Allport contends that there are some 4,000–5,000 different traits, some researchers have tried to clarify matters by reducing this extensive list to a much smaller number of presumably fundamental traits. Examples include Eysenck's (1967; 1970–1971) classification of extraversion, emotionality (or neuroticism), and psychotism; and the sixteen source traits obtained by Cattell via factor analysis, discussed in Chapter 10. At present, however, there is no widely agreed-upon list of basic human traits. Other theorists have questioned whether human behavior is as consistent as trait theory posits, since considerable variations tend to occur in different situations. For example, one may well be honest on some occasions (e.g., returning another person's property) but not others (filling out an income tax form). It appears reasonable to conclude that more research is needed regarding the relationship among traits, situations, and behavior; and that the primary contribution of trait research to our knowledge of personality has been in the areas of description and measurement. (See for example Mischel & Peake, 1982; Sundberg, 1984.)

Contributions

Allport's theory offers a possible alternative for those who share his reservations toward psychoanalysis. The concept of trait remains one of major importance, and has devoted defenders as well as critics (e.g., Bem & Allen, 1974; Wiggins, 1974). As in ego psychology, Allport's inclusion of drive-increasing, teleological, and innate healthy motives is widely regarded as preferable to the Freudian emphasis on illicit instincts, drive reduction, and causality. His generally positive approach to religion is also credited by some as superior to Freud's profound cynicism.

Allport is the first theorist discussed thus far to seek empirical support for his ideas by conducting formal experiments and statistical analyses, and the Study of Values is a respected personality inventory. He has elaborated upon the self or proprium, and the criteria of mental health, to a greater extent than any of his predecessors. *The Nature of Prejudice* (1954/1958) is regarded as a significant contribution to a most important area. Allport's study of expressive behavior anticipates modern work in nonverbal communication and "body language," while other ideas stimulated the thinking of such theorists as Rogers, Maslow, and May. Allport was also a gifted teacher, and his respect for each student's individuality and unique professional interests inspired many of them to become successful psychologists.

Gordon Allport's theory of personality does not seem sufficient to stand in its entirety as a viable alternative to those discussed in preceding chapters, and few current psychologists would characterize themselves as pure Allportians. Nevertheless, his ideas have been credited as exerting a considerable influence on the development of modern psychological thought.

Suggested Reading

The most comprehensive presentation of Allport's view is his textbook, *Pattern and Growth in Personality* (1961). A brief introduction to his theory is provided in *Becoming: Basic Considerations for a Psychology of Personality* (1955).

Whereas Allport's meeting with Freud left him rather skeptical about depth psychology, Henry Murray became a devotee of unconscious processes after conferring with Carl Jung. "I visited Dr. Jung in Zurich . . . in 1925 [at age 32] . . . We talked for hours, sailing down the lake and smoking before the hearth of his Faustian retreat. 'The great floodgates of the wonder-world swung open,' and I saw things that my philosophy had never dreamt of. . . . and I went off decided on depth psychology. I had *experienced* the unconscious" (Murray, 1940, pp. 152–153). In contrast to Allport, therefore, Murray's theoretical constructs, academic research, and measurement techniques probe deeply into the hidden recesses of the human personality.

BIOGRAPHICAL SKETCH:
HENRY A. MURRAY

Henry A. Murray was born on May 13, 1893, in New York City. His parents were affluent and his father even-tempered and jolly, though he recalls being weaned at an early age and feeling that his mother preferred his brother and sister. As a child Murray suffered from a vision defect and stuttering, which stimulated his desire to compensate by excelling in the classroom. Thus he became an outstanding and multifaceted student who earned a bachelor's degree from Harvard in 1915, graduated at the top of his class in the Columbia College of Physicians and Surgeons in 1919, performed research in embryology at the Rockefeller Institute in New York City a few years later, and received a Ph.D. in biochemistry from Cambridge University in England in 1927. (See Murray, 1940; 1959; 1967; Murray, cited by M. H. Hall, 1968b, p. 59.)

Murray married Josephine Rantoul after his first year of medical school, a successful union that produced one daughter. Josephine died in 1961, and Murray married Caroline Fish in 1969. During his surgical internship after graduating from Columbia, he had a memorable experience: helping to care for Franklin D. Roosevelt while the future president was undergoing his courageous struggle with polio (Smith & Anderson, 1989).

Influenced by his meeting with Jung in 1925 to pursue a career in psychology, Murray joined the Harvard Psychological Clinic in 1927 and completed formal psychoanalytic training by 1935. He also met Freud on one occasion, in 1937, at which time the founder of psychoanalysis inquired with some pique as to why Jung had recently received an honorary degree from Harvard rather than himself. Murray explained that Freud had in fact been the first choice of the conferring committee, but was passed over for fear that he would embarrass them by refusing the honor (Roazen, 1975/1976b, p. 296). During World War II, Murray (1948) aided in the screening of espionage agents for dangerous missions. He returned to Harvard in 1947, remaining there until his retirement in 1962.

Save for three books, Murray's writings are scattered throughout numerous journals and chapters in various anthologies. He is also the author (with Christiana Morgan) of a well-regarded projective measure of personality, the Thematic Apperception Test. Like Allport, Murray's honors include the Distinguished Scientific Contribution Award of the American Psychological Association. Henry Murray died of pneumonia on June 23, 1988.

THE BASIC NATURE OF HUMAN BEINGS

Murray's explorations into the depths of personality are guided by the same basic goal as ego psychology: to extend the scope of Freudian psychoanalysis to normal and healthy behavior.

> As I weigh it, Freud's contribution to man's conceptualized knowledge of himself is the greatest since the works of Aristotle; but that his view of human nature is exceptionally—perhaps projectively and inevitably—one-sided. . . . Were an analyst to be confronted by that much heralded but still missing specimen of the human race—the normal man—he would be struck dumb, for once, through lack of appropriate ideas. . . . [Thus my theory sets forth] a health-oriented extension of, and complement to, the illness-oriented Freudian system. (Murray, 1959, p. 37; 1968a, p. 6; 1951/1968b, p. 64. See Murray, 1959, pp. 38–45; 1962; Murray & Kluckhohn, 1953.)

Although Murray's theoretical goals differ radically from Allport's, he does agree that psychology must deal with the single case and has therefore named his theory **personology.** However, Murray regards personality as unique in only some respects. "There is no *elementary* variable which is not possessed and manifested, at least occasionally to a slight extent, by everyone" (Murray et al., 1938, p. 252; see also Murray et al., 1938, pp. 3–4; Kluckhohn & Murray, 1953, p. 53).

Needs

Like Freud, Murray concludes that human beings are motivated by the desire to satisfy tension-provoking drives (**needs**).

Definition of Needs. Murray shares Freud's belief that personality is related to as yet unknown physiological processes, which are located in the brain. He therefore defines need as a construct representing a force in the brain region that energizes and organizes our perceptions, thoughts, and actions, thereby transforming an existing unsatisfying situation in the direction of a particular goal. (See Murray et al., 1938, pp. 45–54, 76–84, 123–124; 1951, p. 267; Murray & Kluckhohn, 1953, p. 39.)

However, Murray argues that we are motivated primarily by the desire to achieve the pleasure that accompanies the reduction of needs. This pleasure is considerably more important to us than reaching some homeostatic or vegetative end state where no drives are active. Thus people readily learn to postpone eating or sex in order to develop greater levels of tension, and make the subsequent drive reduction more pleasurable. Even apparently distasteful activity is actually guided by the pleasure principle, a position that Allport fails to understand because he does not look deeply enough:

Most people do a great many things every day that they do not enjoy doing. "I don't do this for pleasure," a man will affirm, thinking that he has refuted the principle of hedonism. But in such cases, I believe . . . that the man is determined (consciously or unconsciously) by thoughts of something unpleasant (pain, criticism, blame, self-depreciation) that might occur if he does not do what he is doing. He goes to the dentist to avoid future pain or disfigurement, he answers his mail in order not to lose social status, and so forth. If it is not the thought of expected unpleasantness that prompts him, it is the thought of expected pleasure, possibly in the very distant future. Visions of heaven after death, for example, have often encouraged men to endure great suffering on earth. (Murray et al., 1938, p. 92.)

The Taxonomy of Human Needs. Like Jung and Erikson, Murray concludes that we possess both illicit instincts and innate positive potentials. He also posits many more specific human needs than does Freud. The list of biological needs includes hunger, thirst, sex, oxygen, the elimination of bodily wastes, and the avoidance of painful external conditions (such as harm, heat, and cold).

Murray also contends that human beings are motivated by mental needs, which are derived from the biological needs. Since the organic correlates of personality have not yet been identified, the existence of such needs must be inferred from more overt sources (as Allport does with traits). This is not an easy task, however, for human motivation is a complicated affair. Some needs are inhibited or repressed, because the individual regards them as unacceptable. A need may focus on one specific goal, such as the desire to affiliate with a particular boy or girl friend. Or it may be so diffuse as to permit satisfaction by many different objects in the environment, as with a general hunger for almost anything edible. Nevertheless, there are several good ways to infer the existence of a need: frequent and intense patterns of behavior, the results that the behavior achieves, expressions of satisfaction or dissatisfaction with these results, and significant accompanying emotions. (See Murray et al., 1938, pp. 251–262.)

For example, a person who consistently avoids the slightest risk of injury, takes considerable satisfaction in being safe and secure, and becomes profoundly anxious in the face of threats is reflecting a need to avoid harm ("n Harmavoidance"). Another individual who habitually seeks out opportunities to be with friends, expresses pleasure with sharing their company and loyalty, and is highly affectionate is demonstrating a need for others ("n Affiliation"). Murray's original taxonomy of twenty needs, typical questionnaire items used to measure them, and common related emotions are shown in the accompanying Capsule Summary.

Subsidation, Fusion, and Conflict. Human motivation is also complicated by the fact that needs often operate in combination. For example, one need may assist (become "subsidiary" to) another need. Thus a person may actively persuade a group to complete a challenging task (n Dominance subsidiary to n Achievement), argue passionately for freedom (n Dominance subsidiary to n Autonomy), or rule others through the use of force and punishment (n Aggression subsidiary to n Dominance). Subsidations may also be more extensive, as with an unscrupulous politician who befriends an informant in order to obtain scandalous facts about an opponent and win an election (n Affiliation subsidiary to n Aggression, which is in turn subsidiary to n Achievement).

Alternatively, needs may "fuse" into a more equally weighted composite. An individual may humbly serve a domineering master (n Deference fused with n Abasement), or become a prizefighter (n Aggression fused with n Exhibition). Finally, needs may instead conflict with one another (e.g., n Affiliation with n Dominance). "Even by restricting one's attention (as one inevitably must do and should do) to the most important properties, a personality cannot yet be adequately represented . . . in less than 5,000 words, let us say; certainly not by a short list of traits" (Murray, 1968a, p. 7; see also Murray et al., 1938, pp. 86–89, 111–115; Murray & Kluckhohn, 1953, pp. 13–15).

Press

Needs are often triggered by external as well as internal stimuli, so personality cannot be studied in isolation from environmental forces. "At every moment, an organism is within an environment which largely determines its behavior . . . [usually] in the guise of a *threat of harm* or *promise of benefit. . . .* The *press* of an object is what it can *do to the subject* or *for the subject*—the power it has to affect the well-being of the subject in one way or another" (Murray et al., 1938, pp. 39–41, 121; see also pp. 115–122). Thus **press** (which retains the same form for singular and plural) refers to those aspects of the environment that help or hinder a person's efforts to reach a given goal.

Since we do not always perceive the environment accurately, Murray distinguishes between an individual's interpretation of external events ("beta press") and actual reality as defined by objective inquiry ("alpha press"). In addition, a single need-press interaction is referred to as a **thema.** For example, if a person is rejected by someone else and responds in kind, the thema would consist of p Rejection (the environmental event) causing n Rejection (the need evoked). Alternatively, p Rejection might lead to n Abasement or n Aggression. The thema might be initiated by a need, as when an excessive n Affiliation causes inappropriate behavior that provokes disdain and p Rejection. Or other people may actually be favorably disposed toward oneself (p Affiliation, alpha press) but be misperceived as hostile and threatening (p Aggression, beta press). (See Murray, 1959, p. 31; Murray et al., 1938, p. 123.)

Teleology, Proceedings, and Serials

Like Jung, Murray concludes that human behavior is influenced by both causality and teleology. Thus he regards events during infancy and childhood as important determinants of adult behavior, but also stresses that we form plans and strategies that aim toward future goals.

To draw accurate inferences about personality, therefore, behavior must be studied in units that extend over a sufficient period of time. These may consist of relatively brief **proceedings,** such as talking to someone, reading a book, or having a violent argument. Or more extensive series of proceedings may be related to the same long-term goal (**serials**), as when one works for a college degree by attending classes, studying, taking examinations, and so forth. In either case, however, behavior can only be understood by referring to the events that have led up to it and the individual's designs for the future (Murray, 1951; 1959, p. 24; 1968a, p. 7; Murray & Kluckhohn, 1953).

The Unconscious

As we have seen, Murray attributes considerable importance to unconscious processes. He accepts the general idea of Jungian archetypes but adheres more closely to neo-Freudian theory, and he encourages prospective psychologists to experience the hidden aspects of their own personalities by undergoing psychoanalysis. "A personality is a full Congress of orators and pressure-groups, of children, demagogues, Communists, isolationists, warmongers, . . . Caesars and Christs, Machiavellis and Judases. . . . And a psychologist who does not know this in himself, whose mind is locked against the flux of images and feelings, should be encouraged to make friends, by being psychoanalyzed, with the various members of his household" (Murray, 1940, p. 161; see also Murray, 1959, pp. 36–38; Murray et al., 1938, pp. 49–53, 113–115).

THE STRUCTURE OF PERSONALITY

Murray expresses some misgivings about the use of structural constructs, fearing that they will understate the dynamic nature of personality. Nevertheless, he retains a revised version of Freud's tripartite model (Murray et al., 1938, pp. 134–141, 189–191; 1959, pp. 23–24, 38–45).

The Id

The **id** is present at birth, and is entirely unconscious. It includes not only our primitive and destructive instincts, but also such innate constructive forces as creativity and empathy. Murray also contends that the proportion of good and evil varies in different individuals, so that some will have more difficulty controlling the illicit aspects of the id than will others.

Murray's Original Taxonomy of Needs

Need	Description	Representative Questionnaire Item	Accompanying Emotion(s)
n Abasement	To submit passively to external force; to accept blame, surrender, admit inferiority or error	"My friends think I am too humble."	Resignation, shame, guilt
n Achievement	To accomplish something difficult; to master, manipulate, surpass others	"I set difficult goals for myself which I attempt to reach."	Ambition, zest
n Affiliation	To draw near and enjoyably cooperate or reciprocate with liked others; to win their affection, loyalty	"I become very attached to my friends."	Affection, love, trust
n Aggression	To overcome opposition forcefully; to fight, revenge an injury, oppose or attack others	"I treat a domineering person as rudely as he treats me."	Anger, rage, jealousy, revenge
n Autonomy	To get free of confinement or restraint; to resist coercion, be independent	"I go my own way regardless of the opinions of others."	Anger due to restraint; independence
n Counteraction	To master or make up for a failure by restriving. To overcome weakness, repress fear	"To me a difficulty is just a spur to greater effort."	Shame after failure, determination to overcome
n Defendance	To defend oneself against assault, criticism, blame; to vindicate the ego	"I can usually find plenty of reasons to explain my failures."	Guilt, inferiority
n Deference	To admire and support a superior; to praise, be subordinate, conform	"I often find myself imitating or agreeing with sombody I consider superior."	Respect, admiration

(Continued)

Need	Description	Representative Questionnaire Item	Accompanying Emotion(s)
n Dominance	To control one's human environment; to influence, persuade, command others	"I usually influence others more than they influence me."	Confidence
n Exhibition	To make an impression, be seen and heard; to excite, amaze, fascinate, shock others	"I am apt to show off in some way if I get a chance."	Vanity, exuberance
n Harmavoidance	To avoid pain, physical injury, illness, and death; to escape danger, take precautions	"I am afraid of physical pain."	Anxiety
n Infavoidance	To avoid humiliation; to quit or avoid embarrassing situations, refrain from acting due to the fear of failure	"I often shrink from a situation because of my sensitiveness to criticism and ridicule."	Inferiority, anxiety, shame
n Nurturance	To give sympathy and gratify the needs of someone helpless; to console, support others	"I am easily moved by the misfortunes of other people."	Pity, compassion, tenderness
n Order	To put things in order; to achieve neatness, organization, cleanliness	"I organize my daily activities so that there is little confusion."	Disgust at disorder
n Play	To act for fun without further purpose; to like to laugh, make jokes	"I cultivate an easygoing, humorous attitude toward life."	Jolliness
n Rejection	To separate oneself from disliked others; to exclude, expel, snub others	"I get annoyed when some fool takes up my time."	Scorn, disgust, indifference
n Sentience	To seek and enjoy sensuous impressions	"I search for sensations which shall at once be new and delightful."	Sensuousness
n Sex	To form and further an erotic relationship; to have sexual intercourse	"I spend a great deal of time thinking about sexual matters."	Erotic excitement, lust, love

Need	Description	Representative Questionnaire Item	Accompanying Emotion(s)
n Succorance	To have one's needs gratified by someone sympathetic; to be nursed, supported, protected, consoled	"I feel lonely and homesick when I am in a strange place."	Helplessness, insecurity
n Understanding	To ask or answer general questions. An interest in theory, analyzing events, logic, reason	"I think that *reason* is the best guide in solving the problems of life."	A liking for thinking

Note: Representative questionnaire items are intended to clarify the need in question. In practice, some 10–20 items were used to measure each need.

The Ego

As in Freudian theory, the **ego** is the rational and organizing component of personality. It stands between the id and superego as final arbiter and may side with one or the other, as by submitting to an id impulse or defending against it through repression or projection. But it is also capable of a certain degree of independent operation, and is likely to experience less intrapsychic conflict than in Freudian theory because the id is not wholly irrational. A strong ego is essential for a healthy personality.

The Superego

Murray also agrees with Freud that the **superego** is the moral component of personality, is largely unconscious, consists of standards introjected from the parents and (to a lesser degree) from later authority or even literary figures, and helps to perpetuate the cultural status quo. However, Murray believes that the superego continues to develop past early childhood under the influence of one's peer groups.

THE DEVELOPMENT OF PERSONALITY

As would be expected from his joint emphasis on causality and teleology, Murray differs from Allport by devoting considerable attention to infancy and childhood:

> Since every response is partially determined by the after-effects of previous experiences, the psychologist will never fully understand an episode if he abstracts it from . . . the developmental history of the individual. . . . "The

child is father to the man" . . . [and] the history of the personality *is* the personality. (Murray et al., 1938, pp. 3, 44; 1968a, p. 8. See also Murray, 1938, p. 39.)

Complexes

To Murray, as to Freud, infancy and childhood are fraught with pleasures and perils. First of all, there is the rude departure from the secure womb at birth. The sensuous joys of nursing culminate in the painful necessity of weaning. The pleasurable elimination of bodily wastes is eventually subjected to the rigors of toilet training. And gratifying genital self-stimulation may well evoke parental punishment. Every adult personality bears the (largely unconscious) effects of these crucial early events, and such **complexes** are considered abnormal only if extreme.

For example, natal frustrations may lead to a later "claustral complex" that includes passive dependency, the wish to return to a womblike state of security, and n Harmavoidance and n Succorance. An "oral complex" that originates when the child's nursing is frustrated, as by overly abrupt weaning, is likely to involve excessive dependency and n Succorance. As in Freudian theory, "anal complexes" usually result from toilet-training experiences and tend to involve retentiveness and n Order (including miserliness and stubbornness), or expulsiveness and n Aggression. However, the "castration complex" is limited to its literal meaning—anxiety concerning the loss of the penis—and is not regarded as the root of all neurotic anxiety (Murray et al., 1938, pp. 360–385; see also Murray, cited by M. H. Hall, 1968b, p. 59). Murray accepts the widespread existence of the Oedipus complex but does not believe it to be universal, and concludes that the child learns to prefer the parent who prefers him or her.

Childhood Press and Needs

Environmental press play a significant role in personality development. Some of these external events are primarily constructive, while others influence the growing child in the direction of psychopathology.

One particularly favorable childhood press is consistent and devoted family support, with happily united and secure parents providing tender care for their dependent offspring's needs. Conversely, pathogenic family insupport may take such forms as capricious and inconsistent discipline, discord and quarrels, an inability to appreciate the child's own unique interests, and extended parental absences or illness (especially neurosis, psychosis, or death). Other important childhood press include parental dominance, rejection, or neglect; losing valued possessions; sibling rivalry; dangers and misfortunes, such as accidents or getting lost; and the extent to which the child is afforded opportunities for affiliation and companionship.

■ CAPSULE SUMMARY
Some Important Murrayan Terminology

Complex	An enduring effect on adult behavior of such early experiences as birth, feeding and weaning, toilet training, or threats of castration.
Ego	The rational, organizing component of personality that represses illicit id impulses, but also promotes the id's constructive wishes and is capable of functioning independently.
Id	The component of personality present at birth, which includes both illicit impulses and such positive forces as creativity and empathy.
Need (n, drive)	A force in the brain that energizes and organizes behavior, thereby transforming an existing unsatisfying situation in the direction of a particular goal.
Personology	The name given by Murray to his theory of personality.
Press (p)	Aspect(s) of the environment that exert a significant effect on personality and behavior, usually by offering a promise of benefit or threat of harm.
Proceeding	A goal-directed activity whose duration, while brief, is sufficient to permit useful inferences about personality.
Serial	A series of proceedings related to the same long-term goal.
Superego	The component of personality introjected from parental standards, and from later authority and literary figures, that provides internal standards of right and wrong.
Thema	A single interaction between a need and a press, either of which may evoke the other.
Thematic Apperception Test (TAT)	A measure of personality that probes the unconscious through projection, by asking the subject to make up stories about relatively ambiguous pictures.

Murray stresses that the beta press is the crucial determinant of behavior, for the child acts on what it believes—which may well be quite different from what a psychologist thinks the situation should signify. (See Murray et al., 1938, pp. 289–314.)

Murray has also categorized the typical childhood needs evoked by the aforementioned press. For example, strict parental punishment may lead to n Abasement, or verbal abuse from peers may trigger n Infavoidance. The taxonomy is a lengthy one and includes many of the needs enumerated previously, and the interested reader is referred to Murray et al. (1938, pp. 314–360).

FURTHER APPLICATIONS
OF MURRAYAN THEORY

Psychopathology, Psychotherapy, Social Reform

Somewhat surprisingly for a depth psychologist, Murray has little to say about dream interpretation. His interest in studying relatively normal people also precludes much discussion of psychopathology and psychotherapy, though he does sound a dire note concerning the great probability of mankind committing suicide by nuclear warfare and stresses the need for social reform (Murray, cited by M. H. Hall, 1968b, p. 61).

Personality Measurement

The Thematic Apperception Test. To help ascertain the unconscious aspects of personality within the rigorous confines of the experimental laboratory, Murray (together with Christiana Morgan) has devised a personality inventory that ranks with the well-known Rorschach in current popularity. The **Thematic Apperception Test (TAT)** consists of twenty pictures, which are relatively ambiguous with regard to the events depicted and the emotions of the characters. (See Figure 9.2.) The pictures are presented one at a time, ten in each of two sessions separated by at least one day. Slightly different versions are used for men and women, and for boys and girls. The subject is advised that the TAT is a test of imagination and asked to make up a story that describes the events leading up to those shown in the picture, what is happening at the moment, and the outcome. The underlying rationale is that the subject will inevitably project important unconscious (and conscious) feelings, motives, and beliefs into the pictures and stories. (See Morgan & Murray, 1935; Murray, 1943; Murray et al., 1938, pp. 530–545, 673–680.)

For example, a picture of a man and woman might elicit a tale of a husband who is fired from his job, consoled by his wife, and sufficiently cheered to find another line of work. This story reveals the subject's belief that the failure to satisfy n Achievement leads to dejection, p Nurturance, nourishment, n Counteraction, n Achievement, and success. In contrast, a different individual with strong unconscious n Aggression might respond to the same picture by describing a terrible argument between a mother and son. Scoring a projective personality inventory like the TAT is a difficult task, however, and considerable training is required in order to administer it correctly. (See for example Rapaport, Gill, & Schafer, 1970, pp. 464–521.)

Other Research. Throughout his research, Murray strongly prefers the intensive study of a small group of subjects to the superficial examination of a large sample:

> The reason why the results of so many researches in personality have been misleading or trivial is that experimenters have failed to obtain enough perti-

FIGURE 9.2. Sample picture from the Thematic Apperception Test.

nent information about their subjects. . . . Academic men addicted to the methodology of science . . . [have limited] themselves to relatively unimportant fragments of the personality. . . . This may be regarded, perhaps, as one of many manifestations of a general disposition which is widespread in America, namely, to regard the peripheral personality—conduct rather than inner feeling and intention—as of prime importance. Thus we have . . . friendliness without friendship, the prestige of movie stars and Big Business, quantity as an index of worth . . . and behaviorism. (Murray et al., 1938, pp. ix, 9.)

Murray's first book (1938) probes deeply into the personalities of some fifty-one subjects (mostly college students), using numerous written, behavioral, and physiological measures (including, of course, the TAT). When asked to help select espionage agents with suitable personalities for perilous assignments during World War II, his unit devised appropriately intensive and stressful tasks. For example, a candidate was asked to demonstrate leadership by constructing a cube with the assistance of two "helpers," who were secretly instructed to sabotage the task through such devices as ridicule, passive disobedience, and "accidentally" blundering into and destroying the half-finished product. Another study of stressful interpersonal relations involved the effects of anger-provoking arguments on two samples of some twenty college students, whose reactions were studied in depth with the aid of motion pictures, tape recordings, physiological indices, and detailed reports by the subjects themselves (Murray, 1963).

Literature

Murray (1949; 1951/1968b) is also a devoted scholar of the works of Herman Melville and has authored a probing psychological analysis of *Moby Dick,* which he compares to a Beethoven symphony in words. He interprets Captain Ahab as the embodiment of a Jungian devil archetype and the Freudian id, albeit not without some redeeming qualities. "Ahab is at heart a noble being whose tragic wrong is that of battling against evil with 'power instead of love,' and so becoming 'the image of the thing he hates' " (Murray, 1951/1968b, p. 69). The first mate, Starbuck, represents the rational ego that is overwhelmed by the fanatical compulsiveness of the id. The great white whale, which Ahab characterizes as a wall that he cannot get past, stands for both a Jungian Godlike symbol and the restrictions of the superego (particularly with regard to puritanism and sexuality, crucial issues not only in Melville's era but in his own life as well). To Murray, therefore, one essential theme underlying Melville's dramatic epic is that of an insurgent id in mortal conflict with an oppressive cultural superego.

EVALUATION

Criticisms and Controversies

Murray's many neologisms and often dry, technical discussions are almost comparable in difficulty to the work of Jung. In addition, his neo-Freudian personology appears to lack the exciting, innovative constructs that might overcome such a handicap. Thus Murray's taxonomies have been criticized as making too many finicky distinctions, whereas other important details remain unclear (e.g., how mental needs are derived from biological ones). For a depth psychologist, Murray has devoted surprisingly little attention to such important applications as dream interpretation. And he scattered his writings throughout various journals and chapters in anthologies, rather than concentrating them in influential books of his own. As a result, personology has failed to generate a devoted school of followers or have an impact on modern psychology equal to some of the theories discussed previously.

Contributions

Murray's work at the Harvard Clinic represents the first major attempt to subject Freud's brilliant insights to the rigors of empirical research. As with ego psychology, personology retains many basic Freudian tenets while stressing normality rather than psychopathology, teleology as well as causality, and benign as well as illicit instincts. Murray's conception of motivation also appears preferable to anyone who has longed for the return of an increased appetite for food or sex, in order to gain the satisfaction of reducing such drives. The need for achievement, which Murray regards as probably the major mental need, has stimulated considerable research (notably by David McClelland). The TAT remains a highly respected projective measure of personality, while Murray's system of needs is also the basis for two other well-regarded inventories (the Edwards Personal Preference Schedule and the Jackson Personality Research Form). Finally, like Allport, Murray exerted a constructive influence on many colleagues and students.

Henry Murray was an outstanding scholar, with an unusually rich and diversified background. It would seem that he was not the best possible rallying point for academic neo-Freudian psychology, yet his approach to research remains timely and important. Two surveys of the field of personality, conducted some forty years after the publication of Murray's first book, conclude that modern psychological researchers seem to have lost touch with their subjects (Epstein, 1979; Phares & Lamiell, 1977). These reviewers are sharply critical of the current tendency to administer routine and superficial questionnaires or conduct unimaginative and trivial laboratory experiments, and they stress the need for more prolonged and intensive studies of human personality and behavior.

Henry Murray, and Gordon Allport, would be the first to agree.

Suggested Reading

A comprehensive discussion of Murrayan needs is presented in *Explorations in Personality* (1938). A brief overview of his theory is offered in an article by Murray and Kluckhohn (1953). A collection of Murray's papers is also available (Shneidman, 1981).

■ SUMMARY

Unlike the theorists discussed in preceding chapters, Gordon Allport and Henry Murray are academic researchers rather than clinicians. Colleagues at Harvard, their approach to personality is for the most part a striking study in contrasts.

1. GORDON W. ALLPORT. *The Basic Nature of Human Beings:* Allport is the first theorist discussed thus far who argues that the motives of children and adults differ in kind, rather than merely in degree. The child is an "unsocialized horror" governed by the need to reduce instinctual drives and gain immediate pleasure. The healthy adult is influenced primarily by motives that are cognitive, drive-maintaining or drive-increasing, teleological, and functionally autonomous of their prior counterparts. Allport also concludes that the healthy adult is motivated primarily by conscious and concrete impulses and conflicts, and that the unconscious predominates only in instances of psychopathology. Like Jung and Fromm, Allport believes that human beings need an underlying philosophy or set of values that gives meaning to one's life. Like Adler, he regards every personality as unique and recommends an essentially idiographic approach to the study of personality. *The Structure of Personality:* Allport does not clearly distinguish between motivational and structural constructs. Common traits refer to consistent aspects of personality on which different people can be meaningfully compared. Personal dispositions (personal traits) are similar, but describe the true (unique) personality of a given individual. The unifying core of personality is the proprium, a distinctively personal and private region that consists of eight important aspects. In contrast to the introjects of childhood, the adult conscience involves feelings of obligation rather than fears of punishment. *The Development of Personality:* Since Allport regards most adult motives as functionally autonomous of their childhood and adolescent origins, he sees little need to study the course of personality development. He has formulated six criteria of mental health or maturity, and prefers the Adlerian concept of a unique style of life to the use of character typologies. *Applications:* Allport has nothing to say about dream interpretation, regards psychopathology as different in kind from normality, and is essentially positive toward religion. He has devoted considerable attention to the psychology of prejudice, and to the measurement of personality through written inventories and case studies. *Evaluation:* Allport's theory has been criticized for denying the importance of childhood to an excessive degree, the idiosyncratic and questionable concept of functional autonomy, circular reasoning, a lack of explanatory power, an idiographic approach that seems fundamentally unscientific, and over-emphasizing the conscious and consistent aspects of personality. His contributions include gifted and devoted teaching, the currently popular construct of traits, attempts to evaluate his theory through formal experiments and statistical analyses, devising extensive criteria of mental health and of the nature of the self (proprium), and an important work on prejudice.

2. HENRY A. MURRAY. *The Basic Nature of Human Beings:* Murray is essentially a neo-Freudian, and concludes that human nature includes propensities for both good and evil. We are motivated to achieve the pleasure of reducing tension or drives, which extend beyond sex and aggression to include some twenty physiological and psychological needs. Personality is also significantly influenced by important environmental stimuli (press), which usually offer the promise of benefit or the threat of harm; by both causality and teleology; and by unconscious processes. *The Structure of Personality:* Murray retains a revised version of Freud's

structural model. The id is entirely unconscious and present at birth, but includes both illicit and benign impulses. The ego is the rational and organizing component of personality. The superego is the largely unconscious moral arm of personality and is introjected from parental standards, but it continues to develop past early childhood. *The Development of Personality:* To Murray, the history of the personality is the personality. Thus he devotes considerable attention to the effects of important early events on subsequent personality development, including complexes and childhood press and needs. *Applications:* Murray has devised a highly popular projective measure of personality, the Thematic Apperception Test. He strongly favors research that intensively studies a small group of subjects, rather than the superficial examination of a large sample. Murray is also a scholar of the works of Herman Melville. *Evaluation:* The neologistic, dry nature of Murray's writings has diminished their impact on modern psychology. Yet some of his ideas, including the TAT, n Achievement, and his approach to research remain important and timely.

STUDY QUESTIONS

1. Consider Allport's and Murray's theoretical differences regarding each of the following issues: (a) Stressing the conscious and concrete aspects of personality versus probing deeply into the unconscious. (b) Whether or not the pleasure principle applies to seemingly unenjoyable behavior, such as suffering intense cold in order to explore new lands or going to the dentist. (c) Whether childhood and adult motives are functionally autonomous, or expressions of the same basic motives. (d) The importance of studying personality development. (e) The importance of early childhood in the formation of personality and development of psychopathology. (f) Whether psychopathology and normality differ in kind or in degree. Which theorist do you agree with in each case?

2. (a) Why might Allport's reaction to Freud's statement during their meeting in 1920 be regarded as excessive? What might this imply about Allport's personality? About his theory? (b) Allport regards the very young child as an "unsocialized horror." What might this imply about his personality? About his theory?

3. A man who long ago earned his living as a sailor yearns to return to the sea, even though he is now financially independent. Allport regards this as an example of the functional autonomy of adult motives. How might Murray (or Freud) reply?

4. Suppose that you took Allport's personality inventory, A Study of Values. How would the results depict you with regard to the six value-orientations?

5. Allport argues that the adult conscience differs in kind from the conscience of childhood by stressing what "ought" to be done, rather than a fearful sense of what "must" and "must not" be done. Do you agree or disagree? Why?

6. Compare Allport's views of religion with those of Freud. Which do you prefer? Why?

7. Consider this statement by Allport: "Since we think about ourselves so much of the time, it is comforting to assume . . . that we really know the score. . . . [But] this is not an easy assignment. [As] Santayana wrote, 'Nothing requires a rarer intellectual heroism than willingness to see one's equation written out.'" Do you agree or disagree? Why?

8. (a) Consider the criticism of circularity regarding Allport's theory, and his statement that "a man likes blue because he likes blue." What does this imply about the ability of Allport's theory to *explain* human behavior? (b) Why might the idiographic approach favored by Allport imply that psychology can never become a true science?

9. Freud argues that we reduce drives in order to restore a previous state of equilibrium. Murray contends that we reduce drives in order to enjoy the pleasure that accompanies drive reduction. Which view do you prefer? Why?

10. Consider once again the case history discussed throughout the Appendix. (a) What traits are illustrated by this case history? (b) Which of Murray's 20 needs are illustrated by this case history? (c) Using this case history, give an example of one need becoming subsidiary to another need.

10

RAYMOND B. CATTELL
Factor-Analytic Theory

Even the most dedicated trait theorist would undoubtedly agree that Allport's list of 4,000—5,000 traits is unmanageable. It would seem reasonable to conclude that human nature cannot be this diverse, and that there must be a much smaller number of traits that represent the core of personality.

One such theorist is Raymond B. Cattell, who argues that psychology must become far more objective and mathematical if it is to be a mature science. Cattell bases his extensive research into the dimensions of personality on a complicated statistical technique known as **factor analysis.** The results do point toward a smaller number of fundamental human traits. But Allport might well be disconcerted to learn that some of Cattell's findings also lead in the direction of Freudian theory and depth psychology.

BIOGRAPHICAL SKETCH

Raymond B. Cattell was born in Staffordshire, England in 1905. He pursued an undergraduate degree in chemistry and physics at the University of London. But his interests soon shifted to more social concerns, and he shocked his friends and advisers by switching to psychology (then a field of rather dubious repute) upon graduating in 1924. Cattell earned his Ph.D. from the same university in 1929, with his graduate studies directed by the inventor of factor analysis, Charles Spearman. He married Monica Rogers in 1930, a union that ended partly because of the great depression and his preoccupation with his work. Cattell wed Alberta Schuettler in 1946. He has one son from the first marriage, and three daughters and a son from the second.

Cattell worked at various fringe jobs in psychology until 1937, when he came to the United States to accept a position at Columbia University. Shortly thereafter he moved on to Clark University in Massachusetts, and then to Harvard. He ultimately accepted a research professorship at the University of Illinois in 1945, where he was to remain for nearly thirty years.

Cattell is one of the most prolific of all personality theorists, and his writings include some 30 books and 350 journal articles. Cattell's honors include the Wenner-Gren Prize from the New York Academy of Sciences.

THE GENERAL LOGIC OF FACTOR ANALYSIS

Cattell's approach to personality is so abstruse that his writings are little understood by the majority of psychologists. A rough idea as to the conceptual difficulties presented by Cattell's theory may be gleaned from the following schematic and highly simplified example, which illustrates the general logic of one kind of factor analysis.

Illustrative Example

Step 1: The Correlation Matrix. Let us suppose that we wish to determine the dimensions that underlie human intellectual ability, a somewhat easier task than investigating the more abstract aspects of personality. We therefore obtain a sample of (say) 100 sixth-grade students, and administer six written tests: vocabulary, spelling, verbal analogies, addition, subtraction, and multiplication. The first step in this factor analysis is to compute the correlation coefficient[1] between each pair of variables, and we will assume that the results (listed for convenience in matrix form) are:

	Voc.	*Sp.*	*V.A.*	*Add.*	*Sub.*	*Mult.*
Vocabulary	—	.52	.46	.16	.18	.12
Spelling		—	.44	.15	.11	.13
Verbal Analogies			—	.10	.19	.15
Addition				—	.62	.57
Subtraction					—	.59
Multiplication						—

Thus the correlation between vocabulary and spelling is .52, that between vocabulary and verbal analogies is .46, and so on. (The correlation between spelling and vocabulary is of course also .52, since the same two variables are involved. So there is no need to list the values to the left of the diagonal, as these would merely duplicate the corresponding ones on the right.)

Step 2: Factor Analysis. The correlation matrix in this simplified example is small enough to be analyzed fairly well by mere inspection. The typical research study includes many variables, however, and hundreds or even thousands of correlation coefficients. Some method is needed to bring order out of chaos and render the data more comprehensible, and this is accomplished by subjecting the correlation matrix to the process of factor analysis. There are various ways to do so, and some thorny statistical issues to con-

---

[1]For an introduction to the correlation coefficient and related statistics, see Welkowitz, Ewen, and Cohen (1991), Chapter 12.

tend with (as we will see below). But for now, let us suppose that the results are as follows:

Variable (Test)	Factor 1	Factor 2
Vocabulary	.14	.67
Spelling	.16	.58
Verbal Analogies	.11	.61
Addition	.73	.12
Subtraction	.68	.09
Multiplication	.61	.15

Each of the numerical "factor loadings" shown above represents the correlation of one test with one **factor,** a hypothetical construct intended to simplify our understanding of the subject area under study. Addition, subtraction, and multiplication all correlate highly with one another, but not with the other three variables; so they all have high loadings on Factor 1, while the loadings of the remaining variables on this factor are far lower. Similarly, vocabulary, spelling, and verbal analogies form a cluster that defines Factor 2. Thus there are two main factors underlying these six tests, and it does not require great perspicacity to identify them as "mathematical ability" and "verbal ability," respectively. In this instance, therefore, we have simplified our understanding of the nature of human intellectual functioning by explaining six variables (tests) in terms of only two dimensions (factors).

It is also possible to factor analyze the results of a factor analysis and determine the underlying, "second-order" factors. If this were done in our schematic example, we might find that "general intelligence" is a second-order factor fundamental to both mathematical ability and verbal ability. Or the initial correlation coefficients might be computed between pairs of subjects or occasions (Cattell, 1952b).

Methodological Controversies

On the surface, factor analysis would seem to add a much-needed quantitative aspect to the study of personality. Appearances are often deceiving, however, and this technique is more controversial and less objective than its mathematical nature might imply.

Input Problems. The results of any factor analysis depend on the variables a researcher chooses to include in the correlation matrix. Our schematic example could not possibly have yielded a factor of spatial relations, even though this is widely regarded as one component of intellectual ability, because no such tests were administered to the students. Similarly, if only the addition, subtraction, and multiplication tests had been used, no verbal factor would have emerged. Thus factor analysis is not a route to some profound truth, but only a mathematical device for clarifying the co-relationships among the variables in a particular matrix. A researcher who unwittingly factor analyzes an unrepresentative set of variables, subjects, or occasions will emerge with a limited and misleading set of factors.

Mathematical Issues. There is more than one way to factor analyze an intercorrelation matrix, nor is it necessarily clear how many factors to extract in any given study. (The maximum possible number of factors is equal to the total number of variables, a highly undesirable outcome that would produce no simplification at all.) As a result, the factors extracted from even an apparently adequate input sample may represent only one of several possible sets of explanatory dimensions. For example, Overall (1964) factor analyzed a set of data based on the sizes of various books. Even in this instance, where it is clear that there should be precisely three dimensions, Overall did not obtain the expected factors of length, width, and depth. Instead his analysis indicated that books vary in terms of "general size" (a composite of the three physical dimensions), "obesity" (thickness relative to page size), and "departure from squareness."

Factor Naming. Although our schematic example offered little difficulty in identifying the two factors, matters would have been considerably more confused had one of them been characterized by high loadings with (say) spelling and multiplication. Despite the use of various technical aids (such as "marker variables" from previous factor analyses), such ambiguity is far from unusual in personality research, and factor naming can be a subjective and controversial issue.

Procedural Errors. With the advent of high-speed computers and packaged programs, it is relatively easy for even a mathematically naive researcher to obtain a factor analysis. Therefore it is by no means unusual to encounter studies that suffer from major procedural errors, such as generating a vast number of correlation coefficients and factor loadings from so small a sample of subjects that the results are hopelessly unreliable. (Such errors have been well enumerated and criticized by McNemar, 1951.)

   With the above overview of factor analysis in mind, let us now turn to some specifics of Cattellian theory.

THE BASIC NATURE OF HUMAN BEINGS

To Cattell (1946, p. 566; 1950, p. 2), personality is that which permits a prediction of what a person will do in a given situation. Cattell shares Allport's preference for describing these relatively stable and predictable characteristics in terms of **traits,** but differs in four significant respects. He concludes that the basic elements of personality (**source traits**) can be identified only through factor analysis. He regards only some traits as unique, with many genuine common traits shared to varying degrees by different individuals. He is more favorably disposed toward psychoanalytic theory. And he distinguishes more clearly between the motivational and structural aspects of personality.

Dynamic Traits

Ergs, Sentiments, and Attitudes. Human behavior is energized and directed toward specific goals by **dynamic traits,** some of which are innate and others learned through contact with the environment. Since the term "instinct" has been used in various ways by prior theorists, Cattell refers to our hereditary motives as **ergs** (after the Greek word "ergon" for work or energy). Environmentally-molded dynamic traits include general patterns of behavior (**sentiments**) and more specific tendencies and actions (**attitudes**), the ultimate objective of these being to reduce ergic tensions.

Cattell has sought to identify the number and nature of human ergs by measuring numerous attitudes, the basic unit of motivation, and conducting extensive factor analyses of the results. Attitudes may be measured by studying and rating the behavior of individuals in everyday life (**L data**), by using written or other tests (**T data**), or by obtaining self-reports on written questionnaires (**Q data**). (See Cattell, 1973, p. 3.) Ignoring for the moment such methodological differences, Cattell has identified some ten well-substantiated and six more tentative human ergs, which are relatively permanent but vary in strength from one person to the next.

For example, the erg of "security-seeking" is characterized by such attitudes as "I want my country to get more protection against the terror of the atom bomb," "I want to see any formidable militaristic power that actively threatens us attacked and destroyed," "I want to see the danger of death by accident and disease reduced," and "I want to take out more insurance against illness." Similarly, attitudes of "I want to fall in love with a beautiful woman," "I want to satisfy my sexual needs," "I like sexual attractiveness in a woman," "I like to enjoy smoking and drinking," and "I want to listen to music" denote the sex erg.[2] Each erg is characterized by a common emotion, indicated in parentheses below:

---

[2]This factor is relatively unambiguous, and includes other clearly sexual attitudes besides the ones cited above; yet it does illustrate the aforementioned issue of subjective naming. Cattell regards the last two attitudes as sexual on psychoanalytic grounds: smoking and drinking are forms of orality, while listening to music is a sublimation. A psychologist hostile to Freud's ideas might instead view these two items as asexual, consider their inclusion on this factor as indicative of some imperfection in the analysis, and object to Cattell's interpretation as an overly imaginative effort to identify the factor in a way consistent with his theory.

Well-Substantiated Ergic Goals	*More Tentative Ergic Goals*
Food (hunger)	Appeal (despair)
Mating (sex)	Rest (sleepiness)
Gregariousness (loneliness)	Constructiveness (creativity)
Parental protectiveness (pity)	Self-abasement (humility)
Exploration (curiosity)	Disgust (disgust)
Security (fear)	Laughter (amusement)
Self-assertion (pride)	
Narcissistic sex (sensuousness)	
Pugnacity (anger)	
Acquisitiveness (greed)	

According to Cattell, sentiments are also identified by factor analyzing sets of attitudes. For example, the religious sentiment is defined by attitudes like "I want to feel that I am in touch with God, or some principle in the universe that gives meaning and help in my struggles" and "I want to see the standards of organized religion maintained or increased throughout our lives." The sentiment for sports and games is characterized by such attitudes as "I like to watch and talk about athletic events," and "I like to take an active part in sports and athletics." Other important sentiments include one's profession, home, spouse, country, school, interests (mechanical, scientific, economic, clerical, outdoor, theoretical, philosophical, travel, household), clothes, and pets (Cattell & Child, 1975, p. 46; see also pp. 22–44).

Like ergs, sentiments vary in strength among different individuals. But sentiments are neither innate nor permanent, so it is quite possible to abandon a given profession, spouse, religion, or sport and substitute an alternative route to ergic satisfaction.

Subsidation Chains and the Dynamic Lattice. Cattell refers to the relationship between an attitude, sentiment, and erg as a **subsidation chain,** a term borrowed from Murray. For example, an attitude of covertly wishing or overtly voting for a stronger system of national defense may be subsidiary to the sentiment of patriotism and love of country, which is in turn subsidiary to the security erg:

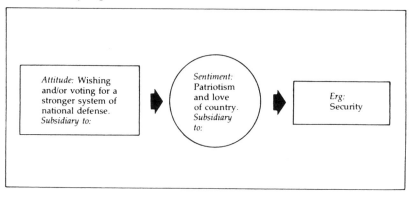

■ CAPSULE SUMMARY
Some Important Cattellian Terminology

Ability trait	A trait that determines how well one succeeds in reaching a particular goal.
Attitude	An overt or covert interest in pursuing a specific course of action, in response to a particular situation. A learned dynamic trait that represents the basic unit of motivation, and is subsidiary to the sentiments and ergs.
Common trait	A trait shared to varying degrees by different individuals.
Dynamic lattice	An individual's complete motivational structure, composed of a complicated network of interrelated subsidation chains and their component attitudes, sentiments, and ergs.
Dynamic trait	A trait that motivates and directs a person's behavior toward a particular goal; includes innate ergs, and learned sentiments and attitudes.
Erg	An innate and relatively permanent dynamic source trait; roughly similar to "instinct," but defined by factor analysis. There are some sixteen ergs, which differ in strength from one person to the next.
Factor (dimension)	A hypothetical construct designed to simplify our understanding of a larger set of variables, persons, or occasions.
Factor analysis	A mathematical technique for clarifying the co-relationships among a particular set of variables, persons, or occasions, and defining them in terms of a smaller number of factors.
L data	Personality data obtained by studying and rating the behavior of individuals in everyday life.
Q data	Personality data obtained through self-reports on written questionnaires.
Sentiment	A learned dynamic source trait that is more general than an attitude, and subsidiary to one or more ergs.
Sixteen Personality Factor Questionnaire (16 P.F.)	A measure of fifteen temperament source traits, and one ability source trait (intelligence).
Source trait	A basic element of personality, identifiable only through factor analysis. The converse of surface trait.
Specification equation	A weighted sum of an individual's various traits, used to predict what that person will do in a given situation.
Subsidation chain	The relationship between an attitude and a sentiment, and the erg they are intended to satisfy. The basic unit of a dynamic lattice.
Surface trait	A manifest personality characteristic resulting from the combination of two or more source traits; thus *not* a basic element

continued

	of personality, no matter how fundamental it may appear to the observer.
T data	Personality data obtained through written or other tests.
Temperament trait	A trait that determines the style with which one strives to reach a particular goal.
Traits	Psychological mental structures that are relatively stable and predictable, and characterize an individual's personality. Traits vary in function (dynamic traits, temperament traits, ability traits), origin (innate traits, learned traits), centrality (source traits, surface traits), and uniqueness (common traits, unique traits).
Unique trait	A trait characteristic of a particular individual, but not others.

Each individual's motivational structure (**dynamic lattice**) consists of an involved criss-cross of subsidation chains, some of which may "go underground" at some point and involve aspects that are unconscious. In Figure 10.1, for example, taxes are disliked (attitude) because they make it difficult to maintain a suitably large bank account (sentiment) and satisfy the ergs of hunger and security, but they are also somewhat desirable since they strengthen the sentiment for country and the security that it provides. Thus Cattell shares Freud's view of human motivation as highly complicated, and behavior as frequently overdetermined.

THE STRUCTURE OF PERSONALITY

Temperament and Ability Traits

Whereas dynamic traits determine *why* we do what we do, **temperament traits** and **ability traits** are concerned with the style and success of our actions—*how* we do what we do, and *how well.* Cattell has subjected All-port's list of some 4,000–5,000 traits to factor analysis and identified a far smaller number of structural source traits, which he defines with his own particular brand of neologisms. These are shown in the accompanying Capsule Summary, where the traits are listed in descending order of importance; Factor B is an ability trait, while the others are temperament traits. Each factor or trait is continuous, so an individual's score may fall anywhere from low through average to high. And "Q" factors appear only in factor analyses of Q data, while the others are derived from both L and Q data.

Cattell has devised a written personality inventory for measuring these source traits (the **Sixteen Personality Factor Questionnaire,** or **16 P.F.**), and has administered it to members of various work and diagnostic groups. To help clarify the meaning of each factor, some of these results are included in

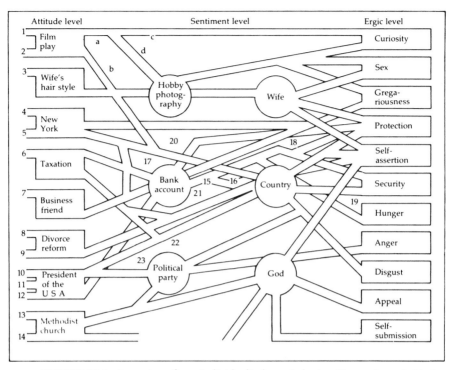

FIGURE 10.1. A portion of one individual's dynamic lattice, illustrating subsidation chains and their component attitudes, sentiments, and ergs (Cattell, 1965; Cattell & Child, 1975, p. 24; Cattell & Kline, 1976, p. 177).

the following discussion and Capsule Summary.[3] (See Cattell, 1973; Cattell & Child, 1975; Cattell, Eber, & Tatsuoka, 1970; Cattell & Kline, 1976.)

Factor A: Affectia-Sizia. The largest factor among the temperament and ability traits is related to Jungian extraversion-introversion. Affectics are outgoing, warmhearted, and easygoing. They enjoy dealing with people, as in the case of salespersons, social workers, successful psychotherapists, Shakespeare's Falstaff, and F. D. Roosevelt.[4] Conversely, sizics are reserved, detached, critical, and aloof. They are more comfortable with the world of ideas, as with scientists, writers, artists, musicians, creative people in general, and Calvin Coolidge. Attempted suicides, criminals, and paranoids tend to be sizic, whereas affectia is high in sociopaths. (See for example Cattell, 1965; 1973; Cattell & Kline, 1976.)

---

[3]These are not meant to imply that (say) every scientist is aloof, but rather that scientists as a group tend to be more aloof than the average. Undoubtedly, there are exceptions in all of the professional and clinical categories.

[4]In addition to those groups indicated by his research findings, Cattell includes well-known historical and fictitious personages as further illustrations of the structural traits.

Factor B: Intelligence. An ability trait, intelligence is related to the capacity for abstract thinking, breadth of intellectual interest, sound judgment, and perseverance. Its position as the second-largest structural factor attests to its importance, and accords well with the substantial attention that psychologists have long devoted to this human characteristic. (See also Cattell, 1971.)

Factor C: Ego Strength. This (temperament) trait concerns the capacity to control one's impulses, remain calm and emotionally stable, and deal realistically with one's problems. As posited by Freudian theory, low ego strength is characteristic of virtually all forms of psychopathology. It is also common among accountants, clerks, artists, professors, and Shakespeare's Hamlet. In contrast, high ego strength is more typical of airline pilots, flight attendants, researchers, administrators, nurses, and George Washington.

Factor E: Dominance—Submissiveness. Dominant people are primarily assertive, aggressive, competitive, and stubborn. Conversely, submissive individuals are typically humble, docile, and accommodating. Dominance is more common among males, competitive athletes, engineers, psychologists (notably Freud), writers, researchers, Richard Wagner, and Hitler. Submissiveness is exemplified by females, priests, farmers, clerks, Gandhi, and Buddha. Psychopaths are high in dominance, while neurotics and most psychotics are submissive.

Factor F: Surgency-Desurgency. Although this trait bears some apparent similarity to Factor A, Cattell regards it as a qualitatively different form of behavior. Surgency is denoted by a happy-go-lucky, gay, enthusiastic, and impulsive manner, including an ability to forget punishment easily. Desurgency is reflected by a sober, taciturn, and serious demeanor. Surgency is common among athletes, military personnel, airline pilots, flight attendants, psychopaths, delinquents, Voltaire, and H. G. Wells. Desurgency is more typical of accountants, administrators, artists, professors, writers, neurotics, alcoholics, Job, and Charles Darwin.

Factor G: Superego Strength. This trait resembles Freud's construct of the superego, and is accordingly low in criminals and psychopaths. Among those high in superego strength are airline pilots, flight attendants, priests, musicians, and Abraham Lincoln.

Factor H: Parmia-Threctia. Parmia, or venturesome boldness, is typified by brash salespersons, competitive athletes, musicians, and practicing psychologists. It is also very high in psychopaths. The converse, shy timidity (threctia), is characteristic of priests, farmers, obsessive-compulsive neurotics, and attempted suicides.

Factor I: Premsia-Harria. This factor was posited some 100 years ago by William James. Premsia, which stands for "protected emotional sensitivity,"

■ CAPSULE SUMMARY
The Structure of Personality (Cattell),
with Illustrative Examples from Various
Occupational and Diagnostic Groups

Factor	Characteristics of Individual with Low Score on Factor	Characteristics of Individual with High Score on Factor
A	*Sizia:* Reserved, detached, critical, aloof [scientists, writers, attempted suicides, paranoids]	*Affectia:* Outgoing, warmhearted, easygoing [salespersons, social workers, successful psychotherapists, sociopaths]
B	*Low Intelligence:* Dull	*High Intelligence:* Bright
C	*Lower Ego Strength:* Emotionally less stable, easily upset [artists, professors, virtually all forms of psychopathology]	*Higher Ego Strength:* Emotionally stable, calm, realistic [airline pilots and flight attendants, nurses, administrators]
E	*Submissiveness:* Humble, docile, accommodating [priests, clerks, neurotics, psychotics]	*Dominance:* Assertive, competitive, stubborn [psychologists, athletes, writers, psychopaths]
F	*Desurgency:* Sober, taciturn, serious [professors, writers, artists, neurotics]	*Surgency:* Happy-go-lucky, enthusiastic [athletes, airline pilots and flight attendants, psychopaths]
G	*Weaker Superego:* Expedient, disregards rules [artists, social workers, criminals, psychopaths]	*Stronger Superego:* Conscientious, moralistic [airline pilots and flight attendants, priests]
H	*Threctia:* Shy, timid [priests, attempted suicides, obsessive-compulsive neurotics]	*Parmia:* Venturesome, bold [salesperson, athletes, practicing psychologists, psychopaths]
I	*Harria:* Tough-minded, self-reliant [airline pilots, police officers]	*Premsia:* Tender-minded, sensitive, clinging [artists, professors, social workers, neurotics, attempted suicides]
L	*Alaxia:* Trusting, accepting [airline pilots and flight attendants, administrators]	*Protension:* Suspicious [artists, farmers, criminals, attempted suicides]
M	*Praxernia:* Practical, down-to-earth [police officers, airline pilots and flight attendants]	*Autia:* Imaginative, absent-minded [artists, "hippies," criminals, drug addicts]

(Continued)

Factor	Characteristics of Individual with Low Score on Factor	Characteristics of Individual with High Score on Factor
N	*Artlessness:* Forthright and genuine, but socially clumsy [artists, priests, manic depressives]	*Shrewdness:* Astute, socially aware [flight attendants, business executives, psychologists, salespersons]
O	*Untroubled Adequacy:* Secure, self-assured, serene [athletes, administrators, flight attendants, psychologists, ruthless dictators]	*Guilt Proneness:* Apprehensive, self-reproaching [religious leaders, artists, most forms of psychopathology]
Q$_1$	*Conservatism of Temperament:* Conservative, traditional [athletes, priests, police officers, obsessive-compulsive neurotics]	*Radicalism:* Experimenting, liberal, free-thinking [artists, writers, professors]
Q$_2$	*Group Adherence:* Joins and follows a group [football players, social workers, flight attendants]	*Self-Sufficiency:* Resourceful, self-reliant [writers, professors, research scientists]
Q$_3$	*Low Self-Sentiment Integration:* Lax, impulsive [artists, priests, neurotics, attempted suicides]	*High Strength of Self-Sentiment:* Controlled, compulsive [airline pilots, scientists, paranoids]
Q$_4$	*Low Ergic Tension:* Relaxed, tranquil, composed [airline pilots and flight attendants, social workers]	*High Ergic Tension:* Tense, frustrated, driven [writers, farmers, neurotics]

refers to tendermindedness and dependency. It is high in artists, professors, administrators, social workers, neurotics, attempted suicides, criminals, and Eleanor Roosevelt. Harria, or "hard realism," involves tough-mindedness and self-reliance. It is typical of physical scientists, airline pilots, foremen in industry, policemen, Mark Twain, and Napoleon.

Factor L: Protension-Alaxia. Protension resembles the Freudian concept of projected anger and introverted, paranoid suspiciousness. It is common among artists, farmers, criminals, homosexuals, attempted suicides, and Charles de Gaulle. The converse, a trusting and accepting approach to other people (alaxia), is more characteristic of accountants, administrators, airline pilots, flight attendants, musicians, and Dwight D. Eisenhower.

Factor M: Autia-Praxernia. Autia (derived from "autistic") involves disdain for the external world, absent-mindedness, unconventional behavior, and imaginativeness. It is exemplified by bohemians or "hippies," artists, drug addicts, criminals, homosexuals, Lewis Carroll, El Greco, and Picasso. In contrast, praxernia (derived from "practical concern") reflects a practical, down-to-earth approach to life. It is common among policemen, airline pilots, flight attendants, miners, those with psychosomatic illnesses, Herbert Hoover, and Calvin Coolidge.

Factor N: Shrewdness-Artlessness. Shrewdness, astuteness, and social awareness are more often found among business executives, flight attendants, psychologists, salespersons, and such worldly individuals as Casanova, Disraeli, and Voltaire. Behavior that is artless, forthright and genuine, but socially clumsy is common among artists, priests, miners, manic depressives, Diogenes, and Joan of Arc.

Factor O: Guilt Proneness-Untroubled Adequacy. Self-reproach, apprehensiveness and guilt are common in most instances of psychopathology, and among religious leaders (Christ, Buddha), artists, farmers, and Winston Churchill. A secure, self-assured sense of untroubled adequacy is characteristic of competitive athletes, administrators, physicists, flight attendants, psychologists, and ruthless leaders like Stalin.

Factor Q_1: Radicalism-Conservatism. This is the first of four factors that appear only in analyses of Q data. Radical, free-thinking behavior is typical of artists, writers, professors, Karl Marx, George Bernard Shaw, Leonardo DaVinci, and Napoleon. Conservative, traditional behavior is more common among athletes, priests, farmers, policemen, compulsives, Winston Churchill, and most popes.

Factor Q_2: Self-Sufficiency-Group Adherence. Self-reliant, resourceful behavior is exemplified by research scientists, creative writers, professors, artists, and conversion hysterics. In contrast, football players, nuns, social workers, flight attendants, domestic help, and those with psychosomatic illnesses more commonly prefer to join and follow the standards of some group.

Factor Q_3: Self-Sentiment Strength. The self-sentiment serves an organizing function, and is concerned primarily with integrating the personality and maintaining a sense of identity. Self-sentiment strengths is typically high among university administrators, airline pilots, scientists, and paranoids, who tend to be relatively controlled and compulsive. Low self-sentiment strength, reflected by laxity and impulsiveness, is common among artists, priests, delinquents, neurotics, and attempted suicides.

Factor Q_4: Ergic Tension. This trait bears some relationship to the concept of undischarged instinctual (id) energy in Freudian theory, but has not been found by Cattell to be related to any clinical disorders. Those high in ergic tension are tense, frustrated, and driven; while people low in ergic tension are relaxed, tranquil, and composed. Ergic tension tends to be high among farmers, writers, Shakespeare's Macbeth, neurotics, homosexuals, and alcoholics. Low ergic tension is more common in the case of airline pilots, flight attendants, physical scientists, and social workers.

Other Temperament Traits. Cattell (1973) also reports seven more recently discovered and less well-defined temperament traits. These include "insecure excitability" (Factor D), which is high in school dropouts, but low in neurotics; introverted reflectiveness (as with Hamlet) versus zestful and extraverted sociality ("coasthenia"—"zeppia," Factor J); polite behavior ("mature socialization") versus "boorishness" (Factor K); and casual self-assurance and a lack of ambition ("sanguine casualness," Factor P). In addition, Cattell has identified 21 primarily different structural traits that emerge from analyses of T data (Cattell & Kline, 1976). Thus it would seem that even his extensive research has not yet arrived at the final word concerning the structure of personality.

The Specification Equation

Having defined personality in terms of traits, Cattell proceeds to predict human behavior by means of **specification equations:**

$$P_j = b_1T_1 + b_2T_2 + \cdots + b_NT_N$$

where P_j is the performance j, the response predicted in a given situation; $T_1, T_2, \ldots, T_N$ are the traits of the individual for whom the prediction is being made (including dynamic, temperament, and/or ability traits); and $b_1, b_2, \ldots, b_N$ are the weights determined by factor analysis, reflecting the relevance of each trait to the predicted response.

For example, suppose that a young man considers asking out a sexually attractive girl who is rather uncongenial and disliked by his parents. Assuming for simplicity that the only traits involved in this behavior are the narcissistic sex erg (T_1), the gregariousness erg (T_2), and the parental sentiment (T_3), the specification equation for predicting whether or not he will actually do so (P_1) might prove to be:

$$P_1 = 0.5T_1 - 0.4T_2 - 0.1T_3$$

The negative signs preceding the weights for T_2 and T_3 indicate that parental disapproval and the girl's lack of congeniality count against asking her out, while the positive weight for T_1 shows that the sex erg operates in favor of this decision. The largest weight is b_1, so the sex erg (T_1) is the most important factor in this decision. If this trait is a powerful one, the young man is likely to pursue a date with this girl; but if it is relatively weak, and the gregariousness erg and parental sentiment are quite strong, he will tend to seek romantic gratification elsewhere. Measures of the strength of each trait are obtained from appropriate personality inventories and inserted into the specification equation, yielding a single numerical estimate as to the strength of response P_1.

To illustrate, suppose first that the young man's trait scores are 80 on T_1 (strong sex erg), 10 on T_2 (weak gregariousness erg), and 20 on T_3 (weak parental sentiment). We then have:

$$P_1 = (0.5)(80) - (0.4)(10) - (0.1)(20)$$
$$= 40 - 4 - 2$$
$$= 34$$

If instead the young man obtained trait scores of 40 on T_1 (moderate sex erg), 10 on T_2 (weak gregariousness erg), and 80 on T_3 (strong parental sentiment), we would have:

$$P_1 = (0.5)(40) - (0.4)(10) - (0.1)(80)$$
$$= 20 - 4 - 8$$
$$= 8$$

As the higher total score indicates, the young man is more likely to ask the girl out if his personality is characterized by the pattern of trait scores in the first example.

Measures of Conflict. The procedure described above also permits Cattell to quantify the degree of intrapsychic conflict experienced over this decision. One (simplified) method for doing so is the Conflict Index:

$$\text{Conflict Index} = \sqrt{\frac{\text{Sum of squared negative } b \text{ weights}}{\text{Sum of squared positive } b \text{ weights}}}$$
$$= \sqrt{\frac{(-0.4)^2 + (-0.1)^2}{+0.5^2}}$$
$$= \quad 0.8$$

The nearness of this ratio to 1.0 indicates a high degree of internal conflict, with the positive and negative influences on this decision being fairly equal. If instead the ratio were close to zero or infinity, the decision would be relatively clear-cut, and there would be little or no conflict. Thus Cattell claims not only to predict human behavior with mathematical precision, but to measure quantitatively the strength of inner conflicts described so vaguely and prescientifically by Freud, Horney, and others. (See for example Cattell & Child, 1975, pp. 88–89, 235, 247; Cattell & Kline, 1976, pp. 160, 194.)

THE DEVELOPMENT OF PERSONALITY

In contrast to some personality theorists, who draw their conclusions about childhood solely from the retrospections of adult patients or subjects, Cattell has factor analyzed large quantities of data obtained directly from children and adolescents. Measuring the same trait(s) at different age levels is a task fraught with methodological difficulties, since the surface behavior may well be considerably different. But Cattell has devised various statistical techniques that purport to resolve such problems, and he has drawn a variety of conclusions regarding the development of personality.

Influences on Personality Development

Heredity versus Environment. Cattell has attempted to measure the extent to which the various structural source traits are determined by heredity, as opposed to the environment. These studies involve analyses of data obtained from pairs of twins and siblings, some reared in the same home and others brought up in different homes due to adoption. (For example, if twins reared apart show great similarity in a particular trait, this would suggest a strong hereditary influence for that trait.) The degree of "heritability" is numerically indexed by dividing the amount of variability of scores on a trait that is due to heredity by the total variability of the scores, which includes the effects of both heredity and environment. (See for example Cattell, 1960; 1973, pp. 144–148; 1982.)

Not surprisingly, Cattell finds intelligence to be the structural trait most influenced by heredity. Such aspects of personality as a happy-go-lucky nature (surgency), introverted reflectiveness (coasthenia, one of the more recently discovered factors), outgoingness (affectia), tendermindedness (premsia), and suspiciousness (protension) are determined to a moderately large extent by heredity. Lowest in heritability, and thus most due to environmental influences, are radicalism-conservatism and ergic tension. This is a highly controversial area, however, and it is by no means generally accepted that Cattell's statistical procedures are in fact sufficient to resolve the age-old issue of heredity versus environment.

Learning. While stressing that some traits are more heritable than others, Cattell does not ignore the importance of environmental influences and learning on personality development. He concludes that emotional responses (such as attachments to other people and phobias) become associated with environmental stimuli through the well-known process of classical conditioning, whereas instrumental (operant) conditioning establishes the ways in which subsidations are formed and ergic goals are satisfied. (For a definition and discussion of conditioning, see Chapter 15.) Thus the dynamic lattice results largely from instrumental conditioning, and it is through such reward learning that we discover the behaviors that will satisfy our innate ergs. (See for example Cattell, 1965).

Parental Behaviors. Cattell agrees that parents exert a significant influence on the child's personality, but prefers to discuss this in terms of the structural source traits. He relates affectia to a warm home background where the father is cheerful, the mother is calm, and reasoning is used to control the child rather than punishment. Ego strength also tends to be higher among children whose parents prefer reasoning to punishment, but lower in families dominated by the mother.

Dominance is more common among children whose parents are authoritarian, enforce strict discipline, and criticize their offspring's sexual behavior. Superego strength is higher among children whose parents do not criticize their choice of friends and heterosexual companions, but do show greater warmth and prefer reasoning to punishment. Guilt proneness tends to be higher in children disciplined by physical punishment, and those with patriarchal families. High self-sufficiency is more common among children whose parents are happily married. Similarly, the formation of other structural source traits is related to various parental behaviors (Cattell, 1973, pp. 158–178).

Birth Order. Cattell has examined various other potential influences on personality development, one of which is the Adlerian issue of birth order. He finds that oldest children tend to be high in ego strength, dominance, and (as Adler would expect) conservatism, but low in self-sentiment strength. Only children tend to be more conservative and high in self-sentiment strength, whereas those who are not only children are more likely to be surgent. There is also a positive correlation between family size and ergic tension. (See Cattell, 1973.)

Development of the Structural Source Traits

Cattell has also studied the ways in which the structural source traits develop over time. Interestingly, many of these patterns appear to have logical and relatively straightforward explanations.

For example, people typically become higher in shrewdness as they grow older. This reflects their greater practice in, and skill at, human relationships. Ego strength shows a decrease in males during adolescence, a period that can indeed occasion considerable inner turmoil (as Erikson and Sullivan have stressed). Afterwards there is an increase in ego strength, as the individual discovers more successful outlets for ergic expression. Superego strength also drops more sharply in males during adolescence, presumably because they rebel more strongly against authority at this time than do females.

Males and females both become increasingly dominant up to about age 20, indicating that children are permitted a greater degree of assertiveness as they grow older. Young children become less affectic and surgent at approximately the time of entering school, a turning inward that Cattell attributes to the difficulties of leaving the safe and warm home environment and having to contend with the impersonal and competitive classroom. These traits increase in strength thereafter, indicating a return of socially outgoing behavior as the child adjusts to the new situation. For the same reasons, ergic tension shows a sharp increase at the time of entering school and then declines. Finally, radicalism-conservatism is the only trait that shows virtually no change in strength from childhood through adulthood and thereafter. (See for example Cattell, 1973, pp. 148–156.)

FURTHER APPLICATIONS OF CATTELLIAN THEORY

Psychopathology and Psychotherapy

Neurosis. Yet another way in which Cattell differs from most personality theorists is by defining psychopathology operationally. He argues that the meaning of neurosis must be determined by obtaining actual trait scores of neurotic individuals, and comparing them to the typical pattern obtained from more normal people. Thus he defines neurotics simply as people who seek (or are sent to) treatment because their feelings and behaviors are a burden to themselves or to others, and who are diagnosed accordingly. A more detailed description is drawn from his research findings: low ego strength (as Freud would predict), submissiveness, desurgency, low superego strength,[5] threctia, premsia, guilt proneness, high ergic tension, and high anxiety. (The different types of neuroses do differ from each other in some respects, but not a great deal.)

With these data-based observations at hand, it is then possible to investigate such issues as the causes of neurosis. For example, a high degree of premsia is typically fostered by parents who are overprotective and over-indulgent. (See for example Cattell & Kline, 1976, pp. 241–272; Cattell & Scheier, 1961.)

Psychosis. Neurosis and normality differ primarily in degree, so the structural source traits are to a large extent descriptive of both. In contrast, Cattell concludes that psychosis is quite a different matter—more a difference in kind than in degree—as evidenced by such extreme symptoms as thought disorders and a lack of contact with reality. Since he prefers an operational definition here also, he has found it necessary to expand upon the list of traits by factor analyzing data obtained from various clinical groups. He has thereby unearthed twelve additional "pathological primaries" on which psychotics (and neurotics) differ from more normal people.

For example, high "hypochondriasis" is evidenced by an overconcern with bodily functions and the possibility of becoming ill, while a low (more healthy) score on this trait is denoted by not finding ill health frightening. "Suicidal disgust" is reflected by disgust with life and thoughts of (or actual

---

[5]Although this is contrary to the psychoanalytic conception of an overly developed and tyrannical superego, Cattell notes that the characteristics of guilt proneness and high ergic tension do resemble the syndrome that Freud described.

attempts at) suicide, as contrasted with those who are content with life and harbor no death wishes ("zestfulness"). "High anxious depression" involves frequent disturbing dreams and becoming easily upset, while "low anxious depression" is denoted by calmness, poise, and confidence. "Low energy" consists of feelings of weariness and worry, whereas "high energy" involves enthusiasm for one's work and the ability to sleep soundly. "High guilt and resentment" is characterized by blaming oneself for everything that goes wrong, while those with "low guilt" are not troubled by such feelings. As with any Cattelian trait, the pathological primaries are continuous: an individual may score anywhere from low through moderate to high on any of them. (See for example Cattell, 1973, pp. 180–182; Cattell & Kline, 1976, pp. 53–57.)

Psychotherapy. Cattell sees merit in various kinds of psychotherapy. He cautions that research may well find some forms of therapy to be effective for certain disorders, and quite different methods preferable for others.

Cattell's research findings indicate that effective psychotherapists are high in affectia, superego strength, parmia, and shrewdness. But he warns that patients with certain trait patterns may do better with therapists who have similar (or opposite) patterns. Thus Cattell recommends that patients' traits be measured frequently during therapy, to determine the nature and extent of any changes in personality that result from the various interventions by the therapist. He concedes that this suggestion is unlikely to meet with widespread approval, however, since few therapists can afford the substantial amount of time needed to administer and interpret numerous written tests. (See Cattell & Kline, 1976, pp. 243, 269.)

Work

Some relationships between the structural source traits and various occupational groups were presented in a previous section. (For a more detailed discussion, see Cattell, Eber, & Tatsuoka, 1970; Cattell & Kline, 1976, pp. 293–312.) Also of interest are Cattell's findings that low ego strength is characteristic of people who are frequently unemployed, and that presidents of corporations tend to be low in superego strength (which supports the stereotype of the ruthless and conscienceless top executive).

Cattell also recommends that measures of the various traits be used in vocational guidance and selection, since a more thorough and accurate personality profile will make it easier to match a given individual's abilities and temperament with the demands of the job. He cautions that T-data are preferable to Q-data for purposes of selection, because applicants may falsify self-reports in order to have a better chance of being chosen by the organization. In vocational guidance, where the sole purpose is to assist the job seeker, it is reasonable to expect honest self-descriptions and to use Q-data. (See also Cattell, 1957; 1973; Cattell & Child, 1975.)

Education

The structural trait most highly related to success in school is intelligence, as would be expected. Next in importance is high superego strength. Some traits appear to be helpful in certain areas of study, but not others: premsia is positively correlated with performance in language courses, but negatively correlated with grades in mathematics. Low ego strength is characteristic of truants, while low self-sentiment strength is typical of college dropouts. Traits commonly found among good teachers include affectia, parmia, autia, high self-sentiment strength, and harria. (See Cattell, 1973; Cattell & Kline, 1976, pp. 273–291.)

Social Psychology

Cattell has devoted some of his research to the area of social psychology, which he also discusses in terms of the structural source traits.

Leadership. People who are officially chosen to lead a group tend to demonstrate affectia, surgency, parmia, high superego strength, high self-sentiment strength, praxernia, and low ergic tension. Conversely, dominant and guilt prone individuals are unlikely to be selected as leaders. Those who function as unofficial but effective group leaders are typically high in ego strength, self-sentiment strength, and parmia, and low in guilt proneness and ergic tension.

Marriage. Those who are affectic, surgent, and premsic are more likely to marry early in life (during their twenties), while those high in protension are less likely to do so. Better, more stable marriages are characterized by spouses who demonstrate ego strength, parmia, and self-sufficiency, but not dominance. An individual who is high in guilt proneness is less likely to enjoy sexual satisfaction in marriage.

Group and Religious Behavior. People who are characterized by affectia, dominance, surgency, and parmia make social contacts easily and more often. In contrast, those who are high in ergic tension and protension are likely to be socially unpopular, with the latter also acting as a detriment to group effectiveness. Frequent activity in church affairs is related to affectia and self-sufficiency, but is less common among those high in dominance and radicalism. (See for example Cattell, 1973; Cattell & Child, 1975; Cattell & Kline, 1976.) Cattell has also conducted research dealing with the personality of groups (*syntality*), and the prediction of group behavior through appropriate specification equations (e.g., 1948; 1964).

EVALUATION

Criticisms and Controversies

Although factor analysis is a valuable tool for simplifying large correlation matrices, its capacity for testing hypotheses and arriving at fundamental truths is far more debatable. In view of the limitations and controversies that beset this technique, some critics reject Cattell's contention that he has discovered the basic elements of personality and view his findings as no more than tentative (e.g., Anastasi, 1976, p. 509). Other theorists (such as Carl Rogers and Robert Oppenheimer) warn that quantification is no scientific panacea and argue that psychologists should devise methods more appropriate to their own unique subject matter, rather than trying to emulate the numerical precision of physics and chemistry. Unfortunately, those who wish to investigate the debate first-hand will find that Cattell's writings offer considerable difficulty because of their mathematical, neologistic nature.

Cattell's motivational model of ergic tension is essentially similar to drive or instinct reduction, and is subject to the same criticisms. As we have seen, numerous psychologists believe that psychopathology can be better explained by defining neurosis and psychosis on theoretical grounds, rather than operationally. Nor have Cattell's constructs and nomenclature been widely accepted: it is doubtful whether many psychologists would recognize such terms as praxernia and threctia, let alone be able to define them. If the worthiness of a theory is to be assessed by its impact on the field of psychology, rather than by critical reviews that politely praise the theorist's tireless research efforts and impressively complicated network of ideas, it would seem that Cattell's success has been at best minimal.

Contributions

Cattell has been commended for grounding his theory in empirical research, rather than subjective speculation. His extensive investigations have encompassed a wide variety of measurement techniques, areas of psychological inquiry, and cultures and nationalities, a breadth and diligence of effort that represents a staggering accomplishment. To many psychologists, the possibility of quantifying such abstruse issues as inner conflicts and trait strength does stand to make psychology a more scientific discipline. And Cattellian factors offer a potentially useful and well-researched set of dimensions for describing and studying the human personality. Thus it is difficult indeed to ignore Cattell's contributions to personality theory, even though his ideas and procedures would seem so idiosyncratic as ever to remain well outside the mainstream of psychological thought.

Suggested Reading

A more extensive discussion of Cattell's theory may be found in such relatively recent works as *Personality and Mood by Questionnaire* (Cattell, 1973), *Motivation and Dynamic Structure* (Cattell & Child, 1975), *The Scientific Analysis of Personality and Motivation* (Cattell & Kline, 1976), and the two-volume opus *Personality and Learning Theory* (Cattell, 1979; 1980).

■ SUMMARY

Raymond B. Cattell argues that psychology must become far more objective, and mathematical, if it is to be a mature science. He therefore bases his extensive research into the dimensions of personality on a complicated statistical technique known as factor analysis.

1. THE BASIC NATURE OF HUMAN BEINGS. Human behavior is organized and directed toward specific goals by dynamic traits, which include some sixteen innate ergs and numerous learned sentiments and attitudes. As with drives or instincts, our goal is to reduce the tension created by an activated innate need (erg). Attitudes and sentiments serve the objectives of the ergs, with human motivation involving a complicated dynamic lattice of interconnected erg-sentiment-attitude chains.

2. THE STRUCTURE OF PERSONALITY. Cattell defines personality structure in terms of temperament and ability traits, which determine the style and effectiveness of our actions. Sixteen of these have emerged clearly from his factor-analytic studies, as well as numerous additional and more tentative ones. Once numerical measures of each structural trait have been obtained for a given individual, appropriate specification equations are then used to predict that person's behavior.

3. THE DEVELOPMENT OF PERSONALITY. Cattell has factor analyzed large quantities of data obtained directly from children and adolescents, as well as from adults. He has attempted to measure the extent to which each structural trait is determined by heredity, as opposed to the environment. Much human learning takes the form of conditioning, with erg-sentiment-attitude chains and the dynamic lattice resulting primarily from instrumental conditioning. Parental behaviors also play a significant role in shaping the child's personality. The various structural traits follow different developmental patterns from childhood through adulthood.

4. FURTHER APPLICATIONS. Cattell defines neurosis and psychosis operationally, rather than theoretically. He has factor analyzed data from various clinical populations, and has discovered additional traits (pathological primaries) on which psychotics and neurotics differ from more normal individuals. Cattell is procedurally eclectic with regard to psychotherapy, and recommends the frequent measurement of patients' traits so as to best understand their progress. He has also

devoted considerable attention to the areas of work, education, and social psychology.

5. EVALUATION. Cattell's claims to have unearthed the basic elements of personality, and to measure and predict human behavior with mathematical precision, are doubtful in view of the controversies and limitations that beset the technique of factor analysis. His model of ergic tension is subject to much the same criticisms as drive reduction, and his constructs and nomenclature have not had much impact on the field of psychology. Yet the scope of his research represents a staggering accomplishment, and his factors represent a potentially valuable set of dimensions for describing and studying the human personality.

STUDY QUESTIONS

1. An inexperienced researcher administers a battery of tests to a sample of 12 college undergraduates. The tests chosen are: spelling, addition, vocabulary, spatial relations, verbal analogies, memory, and editing a manuscript to correct errors in grammar. The researcher performs a factor analysis and obtains these results: on Factor 1, spelling, vocabulary, verbal analogies, and editing have high loadings (between .50 and .65), and the other tests do not; on Factor 2, memory and spatial relations have moderate loadings (.38 and .40), and the other tests have negligible loadings. No other meaningful factors emerge from the analysis. The researcher labels the first factor as "verbal ability" and the second factor as "the ability to find and remember the correct classroom," and concludes that these are the only two abilities needed to succeed in college. What three serious errors did the researcher make?

2. Compare Cattell's list of ergs to Freud's "list" of instincts. Which do you prefer? Why?

3. Consider once again the case history discussed throughout the Appendix. (a) How would this man score on each of the structural traits measured by the 16 P.F.? (b) Does this profile agree with Cattell's findings regarding the pattern of traits typically found among neurotics? (c) Cattell relates affectia to a warm home background where the father is cheerful and the mother is calm, and premsia to parents who are overprotective. Are these ideas supported by this case history?

GEORGE A. KELLY
The Psychology
of Personal Constructs

To most people, the scientist is a breed apart: a trained professional preoccupied with abstruse thoughts, esoteric procedures, and the mysteries of the unknown. In contrast, George Kelly argues that we all behave much like the scientist. That is, each of us creates our own particular "hypotheses" and "experimental tests" for dealing with the world in which we live; and it is these unique personal constructs which psychologists must seek to understand, rather than trying to impose their own set of constructs on all humanity.

BIOGRAPHICAL SKETCH

George A. Kelly was born on April 28, 1905, on a farm in Kansas. He was the only child of devoutly religious parents, a doting mother and a father trained as a Presbyterian minister. Kelly's undergraduate degree was in physics and mathematics. Only after trying jobs as an aeronautical engineer and teacher of speech and drama, and winning an exchange scholarship to the University of Edinburgh in Scotland, did he decide on a career in psychology. Kelly received his Ph.D. in 1931 from Iowa State University, with his dissertation dealing with speech and reading disabilities. He married Gladys Thompson shortly thereafter, and the Kellys were to have one daughter and one son.

Kelly's first postdoctoral position was at Fort Hays Kansas State College, and included the establishment of traveling psychological clinics in the state of Kansas. At first he used Freudian theory with some success, then gradually evolved his own approach and abandoned psychoanalysis. Kelly served with the Navy during World War II as an aviation psychologist, had a brief postwar stint at the University of Maryland, and spent the next twenty years as professor of psychology and director of clinical psychology at Ohio State University. His magnum opus is a two-volume work, *The Psychology of Personal Constructs* (1955), and his honors include the presidency of the clinical and counseling divisions of the American Psychological Association. George Kelly died in March of 1966, shortly after accepting a position at Brandeis University.

THE BASIC NATURE OF HUMAN BEINGS

Most personality theorists tend to retain at least some established constructs. But Kelly prefers to leave virtually all familiar landmarks behind, including even the fundamental concept of motivation:

> [In our theory,] the term *learning* . . . scarcely appears at all. That is wholly intentional; we are for throwing it overboard altogether. There is no *ego,* no *emotion,* no *motivation,* no *reinforcement,* no *drive,* no *unconscious,* no *need.* . . . [Thus] the reader who takes us seriously will be an adventuresome soul who is not one bit afraid of thinking unorthodox thoughts about people. . . . (Kelly, 1955, pp. x–xi.)

Kelly defends these radical ideas by pointing out that psychology is as yet a young science, so we should not expect theories of personality to explain a wide variety of behavior. To be useful, any theory must be limited in scope to those aspects of human endeavor for which it is especially well suited (its **focus** and **range of convenience**). Kelly's own **psychology of personal constructs** is designed for the specific realm of clinical psychology, with emphasis on helping people overcome problems in their interpersonal relationships. "If the theory we construct works well within this limited range of convenience, we shall consider our efforts successful, and we shall not be too much disturbed if it proves to be less useful elsewhere" (Kelly, 1955, p. 23; see also pp. 9–11, 17–18).

Activity and Anticipation

Kelly's rationale for sidestepping the thorny issue of motivation (and constructs like instincts and psychic energy) is quite simple: he merely defines human nature as naturally active.

> By assuming that matter is composed basically of static units, it became immediately necessary to account for the obvious fact that what was observed was not always static, but often thoroughly active. . . . To [my] way of thinking . . . movement is the essence of human life itself . . . [and a person] is himself a form of motion. . . . Thus the whole controversy as to what prods an inert organism into action becomes a dead issue. (Kelly, 1955, pp. 35, 37, 48, 68. See also Kelly, 1955, p. 52; 1969, p. 77; 1970a, p. 8.)

Although Kelly explicitly rejects the use of motivational constructs, he does implicitly assume that we all seek a sense of order and predictability in our dealings with the external world. "Confirmation and disconfirmation of one's predictions [have] greater psychological significance than rewards, punishments, or . . . drive reduction" (Kelly, 1970a, p. 11). Thus human nature is basically teleological, and our inherent movement is directed solely toward the goal of anticipating the future.

THE STRUCTURE OF PERSONALITY

Personal Constructs

According to Kelly, we fulfill our goal of anticipating the future by behaving much like a research scientist. We make up theories about the environment in which we live, test these hypotheses against reality, and (if we are relatively healthy) retain or revise them depending on their predictive accuracy:

> *The scientist's ultimate aim is to predict and control.* This is a summary statement that psychologists frequently like to quote in characterizing their own aspirations. Yet, curiously enough, psychologists rarely credit the human subjects in their experiments with having similar aspirations. . . . [In contrast, I] propose that every man is, in his own particular way, a scientist. (Kelly, 1955, p. 5. See also Kelly, 1955, pp. 6–12, 49; 1970a, pp. 7–8; 1970b, p. 259.)

Thus each of us devises and "tries on for size" our own **personal constructs** for interpreting, predicting, and thereby controlling the environment. We not only respond to the external world, but actively construe (interpret) it and behave accordingly. Whether we do so accurately or inaccurately, it is our creative interpretation of reality that gives events their meaning and determines our subsequent behavior.

By "creative interpretation of reality," Kelly means that there are a great many alternative constructs from which each of us can choose. If Demosthenes had construed his childhood stuttering as an insurmountable obstacle, he undoubtedly would have succumbed to despair. But instead he interpreted it as a challenge to be overcome with effort and courage, and became a great orator. Similarly, a student who construes Kellyan (or any other) theory as an exciting new mode of thought is likely to approach it more successfully than one who interprets it as hopelessly confused jargon. "The events we face today are subject to as great a variety of constructions as our wits will enable us to contrive. . . . Even the most obvious occurrences of everyday life might appear utterly transformed if we were inventive enough to construe them differently." Such **constructive alternativism** is highly fortunate, for it enables us to overcome unpleasant present circumstances or unhappy and pathogenic childhood events (Kelly, 1970a, p. 1; see also Kelly, 1955, pp. 8–16; 1970a, pp. 11–13).

Characteristics of Personal Constructs: I. Postulates and Corollaries. Kelly's description of our "scientific" personality is couched in appropriately technical terms. He posits one **fundamental postulate,** or assumption so crucial that it underlies everything that follows, and eleven **corollaries** designed to clarify and elaborate upon the nature of personal constructs.

Fundamental Postulate: A person's processes are psychologically channelized by the ways in which he anticipates events (Kelly, 1955, p. 46). The

345

naturally active psychological processes that comprise our personality are shaped and directed into customary patterns ("channelized") by the ways in which we anticipate the future. We make these predictions by forming and using personal constructs, as explained in the following corollaries.

1. Construction Corollary: A person anticipates events by construing their replications (Kelly, 1955, p. 50). In order to predict the future, we must construe previous incidents in our lives and abstract the similarities and differences among them. "To construe is to hear the whisper of recurrent themes in the events that reverberate around us" (Kelly, 1955, p. 76).

For example, suppose that an individual must deal with two colleagues at work. This person will seek to bring order out of potential chaos by anticipating the nature of these relationships, basing such predictions on relevant prior experiences (replications). But since no two events are ever identical, merely recalling the replications will not suffice; it is necessary to devise a method that will bridge the gap between past and future. Thus the individual might construe the colleagues' past behaviors in terms of the abstract quality of friendliness (and, therefore, as clearly different from those acts which would be interpreted as unfriendly), use the personal construct of "friendly versus unfriendly" to predict that they will behave amiably on future occasions, and solicit their assistance and support. Alternatively, if this individual concludes from various replications that the future will be more accurately anticipated by using the personal construct of "demanding" (as opposed to "lenient"), he or she might well decide to tread gingerly and consult these colleagues only on rare occasions.

2. Individuality Corollary: Persons differ from each other in their construction of events (Kelly, 1955, p. 55). As implied by the personal nature of constructs, different people construe events differently. For example, the colleague viewed by one person as friendly might be construed by someone else as an opportunistic charmer.

Kelly does not go to Adler's and Allport's extreme of regarding every personality as wholly unique, for we can and do use constructs like "friendly versus unfriendly" in similar ways. (See Kelly, 1955, pp. 41–42, 113, 197, 455; 1969, p. 117; 1970a, p. 12; and the Commonality Corollary, below.) But two people's constructs are never identical and often differ considerably, making it essential to ascertain the particular ways in which any given individual construes the world.

3. Organization Corollary: Each person characteristically evolves, for his convenience in anticipating events, a construction system embracing ordinal relationships between constructs (Kelly, 1955, p. 56). Anticipating the future will be easier if our personal constructs are organized in some way. Therefore, we accord certain constructs a greater importance than others. The resulting hierarchical system may consist of several levels, is usually flexible enough so that different constructs may become prominent at differ-

Fundamental Postulate: The psychological processes that comprise our personality are naturally active, and are molded into customary patterns by the ways in which we anticipate the future.

COROLLARIES 1–9. INDIVIDUAL CHARACTERISTICS

1. Construction Corollary: We base our anticipations on our construction (interpretation) of prior events, abstracting the similarities and differences among them.

2. Individuality Corollary: Different individuals construe events differently.

3. Organization Corollary: To make anticipating events easier, we organize our personal constructs into a hierarchical system. Such hierarchies also differ among different individuals.

4. Dichotomy Corollary: Every personal construct is dichotomous (bipolar).

5. Choice Corollary: We value more highly that pole of a dichotomous personal construct that more readily enables us to achieve greater predictive accuracy. We strive to achieve such accuracy by choosing either the more secure course of further clarifying the constructs we already use, or the more adventurous path of exploring new realms and extending the range of convenience of our constructs.

6. Range Corollary: A personal construct is useful for anticipating only some types of events, a range of convenience that may be relatively narrow or wide.

7. Experience Corollary: We successively revise our system of personal constructs as we experience, and seek to improve, its ability to anticipate events.

8. Modulation Corollary: Some personal constructs less readily admit new elements to their range of convenience (are less "permeable") than others, limiting the extent to which the system can be revised.

9. Fragmentation Corollary: Contradictory subsystems of personal constructs may be used at different times by the same individual.

COROLLARIES 10–11. INTERPERSONAL CHARACTERISTICS

10. Commonality Corollary: We are psychologically more like those individuals whose personal constructs have much in common with our own.

11. Sociality Corollary: To relate effectively to another individual, it is necessary to understand how that person construes the world (but *not* to use the identical constructs oneself).

---

ent times, and characterizes one's personality to an even greater extent than the specific constructs that one uses.

Suppose that one person forms a major (**superordinate**) personal construct of "good versus bad" and includes two less influential (**subordinate**) constructs, "intelligent versus stupid" and "neat versus sloppy," among the things it abstracts (its **elements**). Since constructs are a personal matter, this

347

individual could decide that it is good to be stupid and sloppy. However, we will assume that the actual hierarchy follows a more traditional pattern:

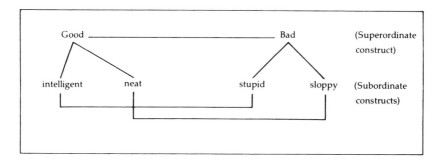

In contrast, a second person (or, conceivably, the same one at some other time) may accord superordinate status to the personal construct of "safe versus dangerous." On a more subordinate level are "good versus bad," and "friends versus strangers":

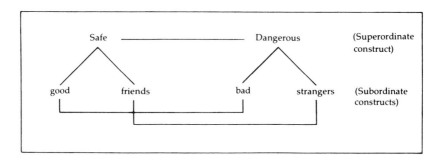

Both of these individuals make some use of the "good versus bad" construct. But their hierarchical organizations differ, and so does their behavior: the former person is extremely judgmental, while the latter consistently strives for security and adheres to familiar ground.

Since we create all of our personal constructs, superordinate and subordinate, we determine our own guidelines for living (Kelly, 1955, p. 78). However, some of our self-selected rules are much harder to change than others. For example, suppose that the latter individual eventually decides that seeking security is rather boring. It will be necessary to reconstruct the hierarchy in order to change this behavior, as by making "safe versus dangerous" subordinate to the construct of "interesting versus boring." This should not prove too difficult if "safe versus dangerous" is already subordinate to other constructs in the hierarchy. But if "safe versus dangerous" is so superordinate that it governs this individual's existence (a **core** construct), so that it cannot be altered or subordinated without creating the belief that the whole system is collapsing, change is likely to be impossible without the aid of psychotherapy.

4. Dichotomy Corollary: A person's construction system is composed of a finite number of dichotomous constructs (Kelly, 1955, p. 59). As the preceding examples imply, every personal construct is dichotomous (bipolar). Each one must be specified in terms of two opposite **poles,** which also often differ among different individuals. One person may form a personal construct of "gentle versus aggressive," while another construes the world in terms of "gentle versus abrasive" and "passive versus aggressive." "Masculinity" is meaningless without a converse, which is often "femininity" but might instead be "weakness" or "passivity." As a result, it is impossible to understand what is meant by any term without knowing what its user regards as relevantly opposed to it (Kelly, 1955, pp. 71, 116).

Furthermore, a construct must also specify a way in which at least two elements are alike. It would be redundant (and therefore useless) to describe Mary as the only gentle person in the world, since her unique qualities are already designated by "Mary." But it is meaningful to say that "Mary and Alice are gentle while Jane is aggressive," since "gentle" (versus "aggressive") now provides information over and above that conveyed by each individual's name.

While all personal constructs are dichotomous, they can be used in ways that allow for relative differences and scales with fine gradations. The construct of "black versus white" might be applied successively to several different elements, with X construed as black compared to Y and W as black compared to X. This would establish the relative scale of W (blackest), X, Y (whitest). Alternatively, several related constructs may be formed into an additive scale. Suppose that integrity consists of honesty (versus dishonesty), candor (versus deviousness), and objectivity (versus subjectivity). A person construed as honest, candid, and objective would reflect a higher degree of integrity than one construed as honest and objective but not candid, who would in turn be seen as having more integrity than one who was only honest (Kelly, 1955, pp. 66, 142–143; 1970a, pp. 12–14).

Only the tools that we use to interpret the world are necessarily dichotomous, not the end result. In fact, a person who stubbornly insists on construing relative differences in absolute terms (e.g., "people are either good or bad, and there is no middle ground") will suffer the fate that befalls any faulty construct system: consistently incorrect predictions.

5. Choice Corollary: A person chooses for himself that alternative in a dichotomized construct through which he anticipates the greater possibility for extension and definition [elaboration] of his system (Kelly, 1955, p. 64; 1970a, p. 15). Since personal constructs are our sole means of anticipating the future, we constantly strive to improve their usefulness. There are two quite different ways to do so. We may choose the more secure course of further clarifying those constructs we already use, and "trying to become more and more certain about fewer and fewer things." Or we may select the more adventurous path of exploring new aspects of life, extending the applicability of our system of constructs, and "trying to become vaguely aware of more and more things on the misty horizon" (Kelly, 1955, p. 67).

Having chosen either security or adventure (a decision that may well vary at different times), we value more highly that pole of any dichotomous personal construct that better enables us to achieve this end. Thus an individual who regards the world as hostile and decides upon security is likely to construe a stranger as "unfriendly," while an equally cynical but more adventurous person may elect to seek out new experiences by positing the newcomer as "friendly." Such decisions are by no means easy ones, however. Adhering to familiar constructs is more likely to result in immediate certainty, but leaves one without recourse when events fall outside the system's range of convenience. Yet a wider understanding of the world in which we live can only be achieved by sailing for a time in uncharted waters, risking uncertainty and incorrect predictions until we become more adept at anticipating the events in question. In the preceding example, therefore, the security-conscious and hostile individual may do a fine job of spotting the slightest threat but be wholly unable to cope with an attractive stranger who is romantically inclined, while the adventurous person is likely to make numerous blunders before being able to predict friendly behaviors accurately. "There is no such thing as adventure with safety guaranteed in advance" (Kelly, 1970a, p. 7).

6. Range Corollary: A construct is convenient for the anticipation of a finite range of events only (Kelly, 1955, p. 68). Like a good theory of personality, a personal construct has a finite focus and range of convenience: it helps anticipate some events, but is useless for others. For example, people and buildings are often construed as "tall" or "short". But one does not ordinarily refer to "tall weather" or "short fear," for these two elements lie outside the range of convenience of this construct and are therefore perceived as irrelevant. Some personal constructs have a relatively narrow range, while others encompass a wide variety of elements.

7. Experience Corollary: A person's construction system varies as he successively construes the replications of events (Kelly, 1955, p. 72). As with scientific constructs, no one has yet devised (or is likely to devise) a system of personal constructs "which will predict everything down to the last tiny flutter of a hummingbird's wing." Even the best construct system is imperfect, and must be frequently revised if we are to cope with an ever-changing reality. "Constructs are used for predictions of things to come, and the world keeps rolling along and revealing these predictions to be either correct or misleading. . . . [Thus] *all of our present interpretations of the universe are subject to revision or replacement"*—just as the psychology of personal constructs is a transient theory, ultimately to be discarded in the light of new developments (Kelly, 1955, pp. 14–15; see also p. 72).

It is not an easy task to profit from experience, for we can do so only by actively construing (or reconstruing) the events that confront us. Some individuals are so afraid that new information will "catch them with their constructs down," and shatter their guidelines for living, that they refuse to make any changes in their personal constructs. Thus parents may stubbornly insist that their spoiled and undisciplined child is a model of virtue, despite substantial evidence to the contrary. In fact, Kelly defines **hostility** as the continued effort to extort evidence in favor of a (social) prediction that has already proved to be a failure (1955, pp. 510–514, 879–884). Alternatively, as in any science, it is possible to design flawed experimental tests of personal constructs that yield fallacious conclusions. An individual who construes a neighbor's behavior as unfriendly may "test" this belief by building a fence that encroaches on the other's property, provoke an angry rebuke, and conclude that the personal construct has been confirmed.

Well-adjusted individuals proceed quite differently. They test their personal constructs against reality in logical ways, confirm or disconfirm the predictive accuracy of these constructs, and revise them more or less appropriately. This sequence often takes the form of the **C-P-C Cycle:** construing a situation in several different ways ("circumspection"), deciding upon a single construct for dealing with the issue in question ("preemption"), and selecting that pole of the construct that promises to improve one's predictions ("control," or "choice"). For example, a college student who does poorly on an exam may at first take a circumspect approach to the problem: he or she may be incompetent (as opposed to competent), the professor may have been unfair (as opposed to fair), the strategy for answering essay questions may have been inappropriate (as opposed to appropriate), and so forth. Ultimately the focus is narrowed to one crucial construct that preempts all others, which we will assume is the lattermost. The student therefore elects to consult the professor for advice on how best to take examinations, chooses a new strategy that appears more appropriate (such as writing lengthy and technical answers to the essay questions, rather than brief and informal ones), anticipates a high grade on the next test, receives it, and concludes from this confirming evidence that greater predictive accuracy has been achieved—at least insofar as this particular professor is concerned. (See Kelly, 1955, pp. 515–526; 1970a, p. 18.)

8. Modulation Corollary: The variation in a person's construction system is limited by the permeability of the constructs within whose range of convenience the variants lie (Kelly, 1955, p. 77). Some personal constructs less readily admit new elements to their range of convenience (are less **permeable**), thereby limiting the extent to which the system can be revised in the light of experience. To illustrate, "natural versus miraculous" would be a permeable construct to a believer willing to perceive at least some new events as miraculous, but impermeable to someone who concludes that the age of miracles is over (Kelly, 1955, p. 208).

Impermeability is not always undesirable, for a poorly designed construct (such as a psychotic delusion) should be closed off to new elements. It is usually preferable for superordinate constructs to be relatively permeable, however, so that new approaches to living may be more readily adopted. (See Kelly, 1955, pp. 81, 486–487.)

9. Fragmentation Corollary: A person may successively employ a variety of construction subsystems which are inferentially incompatible with each other (Kelly, 1955, p. 83). To allow for the illogical aspects of human behavior, Kelly assumes that contradictory subsystems of constructs may be used at different times by the same individual. Thus a person who usually subsumes "tolerance" under "good" may nevertheless take violent exception to an act of cowardice, because "coward" happens to be included under "hateful." For the most part, however, our anticipations form a consistent pattern. "One can tolerate some incompatibility [in one's system of personal constructs], but not too much" (Kelly, 1955, p. 496).

10. Commonality Corollary: To the extent that one person employs a construction of experience which is similar to that employed by another, his processes are psychologically similar to those of the other person (Kelly, 1970a, p. 20; see also Kelly, 1955, p. 90). As we have seen, the Individuality Corollary does not exclude the possibility of people sometimes construing events in similar ways. (Such commonality is by no means unusual, since members of a given culture are likely to find certain types of predictions more readily confirmed than others.) Psychologically, we more closely resemble those people whose personal constructs have much in common with our own.

11. Sociality Corollary: To the extent that one person construes the construction processes of another, he may play a role in a social process involving the other person (Kelly, 1955, p. 96). To anticipate and relate well to other people, it is essential to construe the ways in which they interpret the world. "The person who is to play a constructive role in a social process with another person need not so much construe things as the other person does, as he must effectively construe the other person's outlook" (Kelly, 1955, p. 95; see also pp. 96–102).

To facilitate this necessary but difficult task, Kelly recommends that we play readily understandable **roles.** "When one plays a *role,* he behaves according to what he believes another person thinks . . . [and puts] himself tentatively in the other person's shoes" (Kelly, 1955, pp. 177–178; 1970a, p. 26). Thus roles are determined by construing the constructs of people with whom one is socially engaged, rather than by the precepts of society. A person who can play such roles as spouse, parent, friend, leader, or subordi-

■ CAPSULE SUMMARY
Some Important Kellyan Terminology (II)

Anxiety

The awareness that important events lie mostly outside the range of convenience of every personal construct in one's system, making it virtually impossible to anticipate the future.

Channels

The customary ways in which a person's naturally active psychological processes operate; determined by how one anticipates the future.

Constellatory construct

A construct that rigidly determines the ways in which other constructs apply to its elements, as in stereotyped thinking: "A person who is 'Jewish' must also be 'miserly' and 'ruthless.'" A converse of propositional construct.

Construct system (construction system)

The hierarchically organized totality of personal constructs that an individual uses to anticipate the future.

Constructive alternativism

The principle that there are always alternative constructs that one can use to interpret the world, so that no one need be a victim of childhood events or current circumstances.

Core construct

A construct so superordinate that it governs one's identity and existence. The converse of peripheral construct.

Core role

A subsystem in which "self" is subordinated to constructs used to predict essential interactions with other people, as when a woman adopts the core role of nourishing mother and construes herself and her family accordingly.

C-P-C Cycle

A sequence wherein a decision is made by first construing a situation in various ways ("circumspection"), then focusing on one construct to the exclusion of all others ("preemption"), and then choosing the pole of this construct that appears more likely to predict accurately ("control," or "choice").

Elements

The things described (abstracted) by a construct; may be people, inanimate objects, events, or one or both poles of another construct.

Fixed-role therapy

A form of psychotherapy wherein the client tries to enact in everyday life a role carefully designed by a panel of therapists, with the goal of discovering and utilizing more effective personal constructs.

Focus and range of convenience

The particular aspects of human endeavor for which the typically limited scientific theory, or a personal construct, is maximally (focus) and generally (range) suited.

Guilt

Awareness that "self" has been dislodged from the core role, as when a woman who adopted the core role of nourishing mother can no longer construe herself in this way because her children have grown up and left home.

Hostility

Continued efforts to extort evidence in favor of a social prediction that has already proved to be a failure.

continued

353

Impermeable construct	A construct closed to new elements. The converse of permeable construct.
Loose construct	A construct that leads to varying, contradictory predictions. The converse of tight construct.
Peripheral construct	A construct that can be revised without greatly altering any core constructs.
Permeable construct	A construct that readily admits new elements to its range of convenience, and is therefore easily revised in the light of experience. The converse of impermeable construct.
Personal construct	A representation of the external world created by a particular individual, and tested against reality in terms of its predictive efficiency, in order to achieve control over the environment by anticipating events.
Poles	The two opposites that define a construct. A pole is an abstraction used to categorize concretely different elements that are in some way similar; e.g., " 'Mary' and 'Richard' [concrete elements] are 'friendly' [abstraction, or pole]."
Preemptive construct	A construct that prohibits any other constructs from applying to its elements; e.g., 'psychoanalysis' is nothing but 'magical thinking.' " A converse of propositional construct.
Preverbal construct	A construct that is not associated with a verbal label, usually because it was learned in infancy prior to the development of language skills, and is therefore difficult to identify and communicate.
Propositional construct	A construct that in no way limits other constructs from applying to its elements; e.g., " 'psychoanalysis' may be 'magical' or 'scientific,' 'good' or 'bad,' 'interesting' or 'boring,' and so forth." The converse of preemptive construct and constellatory construct.
Psychology of personal constructs	The name given by Kelly to his theory of personality.
Role	Specific patterns of behavior, determined by construing the constructs of people with whom one is engaged in a social task.
Role Construct Repertory Test (Rep Test)	A measure designed to provide preliminary information about a client's personal constructs and psychological problems. The client forms triads of significant people (mother, father, a favorite teacher, someone intelligent, and so forth), and devises constructs to describe how two members of each triad are alike yet different from the third.
Self-construct	The personal construct that distinguishes those elements that relate to oneself from those that concern other people.
Submergence	Difficulty in becoming aware of one pole of a personal construct, usually because it has intolerable implications.
Superordinate construct	A construct that includes another construct (called a *subordinate* construct) among its elements.

Suspension	Difficulty in becoming aware of some element, because revisions in one's construct system have excluded those constructs originally capable of interpreting it.
Threat	The awareness of imminent, widespread changes in one's core constructs.
Tight construct	A construct that leads to unvarying, clear-cut predictions. The converse of loose construct.

nate is more easily anticipated by other people, and is therefore more likely to develop effective interpersonal relations.

Characteristics of Personal Constructs: II. Preemptive, Constellatory, and Propositional Constructs. In addition to the issue of permeability, the variation in any construction system is limited by the relationships among the various constructs. Some constructs prohibit their elements from belonging to any other range of convenience, as when a critic contends that psychoanalysis is *nothing but* magical thinking—not (also) a potentially valuable and sometimes effective discovery, but *only* a superstition. Here the construct of "magical vs. scientific" is being used **preemptively** with regard to "psychoanalysis," making any revisions concerning this element extremely difficult (Kelly, 1955, pp. 154–155; see also pp. 156–157, 239).

Almost as rigid is the **constellatory** construct, which determines the ways in which other constructs apply to its elements. Stereotypes are a common illustration, as with a prejudiced individual who concludes that a person construed as Jewish *must also* be miserly and ruthless: once an element is classified according to the constellatory construct of "Jewish vs. non-Jewish," its membership in the ranges of other constructs ("miserly vs. generous," "ruthless vs. benevolent") is immediately determined.

A more open-minded approach is represented by the **propositional** construct, which in no way limits other constructs from applying to its elements. A person who uses the construct of "Jewish vs. non-Jewish" propositionally leaves open the possibility that an element construed as Jewish might be miserly or generous, ruthless or benevolent, friendly or unfriendly, and so forth, rather than regarding such issues as arbitrarily decided by the single attribute of Jewishness. "The propositional construct, therefore, represents one end of a continuum, the other end of which is represented by the preemptive and constellatory constructs" (Kelly, 1955, p. 155). The latter two do have some positive uses, as for example with the preemption stage of the C-P-C Cycle, but propositionality must ultimately be achieved for one's construct system to be open to change.

Characteristics of Personal Constructs: III. The Self-Construct and Core Role. To Kelly, there is one personal construct found in virtually every system: "self vs. others." However, this **self-construct** is often subordinated in different ways. One person may include "self" under "friendly" and "considerate," and act accordingly; while another subsumes "self" under "intelligent" and "others" under "stupid," and expects to be considerably more clever than most. (Since we do not necessarily construe ourselves as others do, someone else might well contend that the latter individual would be better described as "conceited.") The self-construct is excluded from those ranges of convenience for which it is deemed irrelevant, although even these apparently unrelated constructs must have some personal implications because they are of one's own creation. "One cannot call another person a bastard without making bastardy a dimension of his own life also . . . [and ordering] his world with respect to [this] dimension" (Kelly, 1955, p. 133, see also pp. 114, 131–135, 151).

When "self" is subordinated to constructs that concern essential interactions with other people, the resulting subsystem is referred to as the **core role.** For example, the core role of children typically involves their relations with the parents and membership in their own family. Some women subsume "self" under "nourishing mother" and devote themselves to their children. Others prefer to include the self element under "professional," opt for a career, and become distinctly annoyed at any implication that they ought to construe their core roles in terms of motherhood.

Any imminent change in the core aspects of one's construction system produces marked signs of disturbance. **Guilt** occurs when the self is perceived as dislodged from the core role, while **threat** is aroused by apparent widespread changes in the core constructs. To illustrate, the devoted mother whose children get married and leave home will feel guilty because she cannot maintain her core role. Clients entering psychotherapy are likely to be threatened by the prospect of making sweeping revisions in their core constructs (and may feel guilty as well), while the profound changes in one's construct system posed by the specter of imminent death are the most threatening of all (Kelly, 1955, pp. 166–167, 382–383, 489–495, 502–508).

Whereas threat and guilt result from perceived changes in one's core constructs, **anxiety** represents an inability to construe important events and anticipate the future. "The deeply anxious person has . . . [a] construction system [that] fails him. . . . He is confronted with a changing scene, but he has no guide to carry him through the transition" (Kelly, 1955, p. 496; see also pp. 495–502). Failing an examination would be threatening if it indicated the need to reconstrue drastically one's fundamental abilities and professional goals. But it would be anxiety-provoking if it fell mostly outside the range of convenience of every personal construct in the system, leaving the individual too confused to interpret this event and anticipate some sort of corrective action.[1] A certain amount of anxiety is inescapable because of the imperfect nature of every construct system, as with the momentary feeling of being at a total loss when one's checkbook fails to balance.

Characteristics of Personal Constructs: IV. Preverbality, Submergence, and Suspension. Although Kelly rejects the concept of an unconscious, he does conclude that some constructs are not readily accessible to awareness. **Pre-verbal** constructs are particularly difficult to identify because most of them originate prior to the use of language, and lack a convenient verbal label. Or one pole of a personal construct may be less available to awareness than its converse (**submerged**) because it has intolerable implications. A person who would regard hostility as highly probable (whether by oneself or others), but who prefers not to anticipate and deal with this possibility, may submerge the former pole of "aggressive vs. gentle" and conclude that the latter is true of everyone. As a third possibility, specific elements may be excluded from awareness (**suspended**) because revisions in one's construct system have excluded those constructs originally capable of interpreting them. Suspension bears some similarity to repression, for one may deliberately fail to devise the constructs that would enable certain experiences to be recalled. But it specifies that we remember what is structured and forget what is unstructured, rather than remembering what is pleasant and forgetting what is unpleasant.

Some personal constructs may create an impression of unconscious processes because they are somewhat ambiguous and lead to varying predictions (**loose**), like a rough sketch that is preliminary to a carefully drafted design. When such constructs are firmed up in order to generate unvarying predictions that can readily be tested (made **tight**), the appearance may be given of material gravitating from the depths of one's personality to consciousness. Or if subsuming "self" under one pole of a construct (e.g., "gentle") yields consistently erroneous predictions, it is far easier to switch it to the opposite pole ("aggressive") than to devise a new construct or reorganize the hierarchical system. Thus it is not unusual for a person's behaviors and interpretations of the world to be replaced by their opposites, giving the impression that reaction formation has taken place. To Kelly, therefore, apparently unconscious processes are actually due to limitations in one's construction system:

> If a client does not construe things in the way we [therapists] do, we assume that he construes them in some other way, not that he really must construe them the way we do but is unaware of it. If later he comes to construe them the way we do, that is a new construction for him, not a relevation of a subconscious construction which we have helped him bring to the fore. . . . [Thus,] if a client is today able to see hostility in his behavior whereas yesterday he could not see hostility, that does not necessarily mean that he . . . was unconsciously hostile all the time. . . . [Rather, he] came to construe [his behavior] as hostile. (Kelly, 1955, p. 467; see also p. 235, 483–485.)

---

[1]Events that fell entirely outside the range of the construct system would not be perceived at all, since the individual would lack any means of understanding them, and would therefore not create any anxiety.

THE DEVELOPMENT OF PERSONALITY

Like Murray, Kelly regards a temporal orientation as essential to the study of personality. "Life has to be seen in the perspective of time if it is to make any sense at all" (Kelly, 1955, p. 7; see also pp. 57, 401). However, his discussion of personality development is relatively superficial.

The all-important parents can impair the child's ability to anticipate the future by behaving in various pathogenic ways. Overindulgence teaches the child to predict that they will always satisfy its every need. Intense pressure or punishment leads the child to cling rigidly to a few familiar constructs, rather than seeking new ways to interpret the environment. Erratic and inconsistent behavior makes it virtually impossible for the child to predict the parents accurately. Or the parents may unwisely characterize the child in negative ways, such as "liar" or "cheater," with the result that the child readily forms the corresponding constructs and subordinates "self" to them.

Except for such maladaptive influences, personality development unfolds in a healthy and continuous way. The growing child gradually makes its constructs more permeable, less preemptive, and more propositional, as by abandoning its conception of the parents as only perfect and all-powerful and construing them as people who can be strong or weak, helpful or harmful, loving or inconsiderate, and so forth. (See Kelly, 1955, pp. 170, 365, 668–671, 710–711, 753, 841, 920.)

FURTHER APPLICATIONS OF KELLYAN THEORY

Dream Interpretation

Kelly regards dreams as potential clues to the less obvious aspects of personality, including submerged and preverbal constructs. However, he stresses that dream interpretation is primarily a technique for weaning a client from constructs that have become overly rigid and tight. Thus a dream may depict a parent or friend in such contradictory, loose ways as friendly and unfriendly, comforting and ominous, or happy and sad, with this wavering form of construction allowing the dreamer to explore various ways of classifying the person in question. Similarly, a client who tightly anticipates others as unfriendly may awaken one morning with vague memories of a satisfying dream-romance. Reporting this to the therapist serves to loosen the construct of "friendly vs. unfriendly" and bring the submerged former pole to light, after which the dreamer can tighten the new ideas and test the predictive accuracy of being liked or even loved by other people. A client who needs to loosen certain constructs, but who has great difficulty recalling any dreams, may be asked to keep a pad and pencil beside the bed and write them down immediately upon awakening. (See Kelly, 1955, pp. 133, 465, 470–472, 484–485, 1030–1031, 1037–1048.)

Since loosening is the major objective of dream interpretation, dreams that can be reported in a clear-cut and tightly construed manner are likely to be of little therapeutic value. Kelly also takes a particularly skeptical view of "gift dreams," which are designed to please the therapist by fitting his or her theoretical orientation (Oedipal, archetypal, or whatever). Such dreams indicate that the therapist's constructs have been imposed upon the client, at least to some extent, and that little progress is being made toward understanding the client's own system (Kelly, 1955, pp. 1040–1042).

Psychopathology

The mentally healthy person readily tests the predictive accuracy of his or her personal constructs, and makes appropriate revisions when necessary. In contrast, the pathological individual resembles an incompetent scientist who clings rigidly to outmoded hypotheses. Thus the sufferer may consistently expect to enjoy success, or make friends, or fall in love, yet never does so; and such inaccurate predictions turn daily living into an intolerable and nearly impossible task. *"From the standpoint of the psychology of personal constructs, we may define a disorder as any personal construction which is used repeatedly in spite of consistent invalidation"* (Kelly, 1955, p. 831).

Causes of Psychopathology. In accordance with the principle of constructive alternativism, Kelly takes an ahistorical approach to psychopathology. He attributes neurosis and psychosis to a construct system that is presently defective in some way, with the past important only to the extent that it helps explain the client's current methods for interpreting the environment.

Some personal constructs generate consistently inaccurate predictions because they fail to meet the minimum requirement: specifying a way in which at least two elements are alike, and different from a third. For example, the individual who escapes threatening hostility by submerging the pole of "aggressive" and construing everyone as "gentle" is certain to make many erroneous anticipations. Alternatively, properly formed constructs may fail to predict accurately because they are too impermeable, permeable, tight, loose, preemptive, and so forth. Thus a person may make the construct of "desirable versus undesirable" so impermeable to members of the opposite sex that no new element ever fits the former category, and every prediction of falling in love fails to be confirmed. Or one's self-construct may be too permeable, leading to the delusion that many irrelevant events have personal implications. The obsessive-compulsive uses overly tight constructs that produce rigid and trivial anticipations (e.g., that success will be achieved by wearing a red tie every day), whereas the psychotic devises bizarre constructs that are far too loose and seem capable of anticipating virtually anything. All such cases of psychopathology occur because one's personal constructs are too faulty to accomplish their primary objective of anticipating the future, an inability that typically evokes "that most common of all clinic commodities, anxiety" (Kelly, 1955, p. 58; see also pp. 62, 111–119, 468–469, 497).

Varieties of Psychopathology. Kelly shares Erikson's antipathy to formal diagnostic labels, warning that the client is all too likely to accept this official construct and adopt all of the corresponding symptoms. Instead, as with any role, the clinician must actively construe the particular constructions used by each client. Kelly even opposes the common trichotomous classification of normal, neurotic, and psychotic, preferring once again to establish a dichotomy (e.g., "normal versus pathological") rather than to exclude the possibility that a client might have in ways typical of both neurosis and psychosis. (See Kelly, 1955, pp. 185, 193, 198–200, 366, 453, 508, 595, 764, 770, 775, 866.)

Psychotherapy

Theoretical Foundation. The goal of Kellyan psychotherapy is to provide a setting in which the client can safely devise and experiment with new core constructs, escape the viselike grip of obsolescent ones, and reconstruct the system in ways that lead to more accurate anticipations. Such comprehensive changes require considerable effort, and involve more than a little threat. Therefore, Kelly prefers the designation of "client" to the more passive-sounding one of "patient." "Submitting *patiently* and unquestioningly to the manipulations of a clinician . . . is a badly misleading view of how a psychologically disturbed person recovers" (Kelly, 1955, p. 186; see also pp. 161–170).

The personal constructs of different individuals vary in many respects: hierarchical organization, poles, ranges of convenience, permeability, tightness and looseness, preemptiveness, and so forth. Therefore the therapist must maintain an open-minded approach, and experiment with tentative hypotheses about a client's particular way of viewing the world. To this end, the therapist should adopt a "credulous attitude" by accepting and exploring the meaning of whatever statements the client may make. And the therapist must use permeable and propositional constructs that allow for various theoretical possibilities, rather than relying solely on ones that are preemptive or constellatory (e.g., "this disorder must only involve Oedipal and childhood conflicts"). "[Therapy] is a matter of *construing* the [client's] experience, and not merely a matter of having him hand it to [the therapist] intact across the desk" (Kelly, 1955, p. 200; see also pp. 173–174, 196–198, 321, 595–596). Thus both client and therapist engage in various kinds of hypothesis testing, and psychotherapy is merely another instance of the individual as scientist rather than a special kind of application.

Therapeutic Procedures. Kellyan psychotherapy is conducted in 45-minute sessions, with the number of weekly appointments depending on the nature and severity of the client's problems. Kelly shares Sullivan's preference for having the client seated at right angles to the therapist, so either party can look at or away from the other. He also accepts the Freudian contention that most clients should avoid major life changes (such as marriage or quitting a job) until therapy has been concluded, but he differs by arguing in favor of taking written notes or (preferably) using tape recordings as an aid to the therapist's memory (Kelly, 1955, pp. 627–638, 646).

To provide some preliminary indications as to a client's personal constructs and psychological problems, Kelly (1955, pp. 219–318) has devised a measure called the **Role Construct Repertory Test (Rep Test).** The client is asked to indicate the names of significant people in his or her life, group these "role titles" into designated triads, and specify one important way in which two of the role titles in each triad are alike and different from the third. (Recall that this is the minimum requirement that a properly formed construct must meet.) For example, consider triad #7 shown in the accompanying Capsule Summary. Suppose that a client concludes that the liked teacher and current boy friend are friendly, whereas the previous boy friend is not. This reveals that "friendly" is one pole of a personal construct used to interpret other people (i.e., a role construct), whereupon the client is requested to designate the opposite extreme. If this should prove to be "critical," the therapist might well conclude that even the hint of a reproach will be interpreted by this client as antagonistic.

The Rep Test may be administered on a one-to-one basis, with each role title on a separate card that is sorted by the client, or as a written questionnaire suitable for use with groups. A complete analysis of the results is rather complicated, involving grid layouts of role titles versus constructs and the statistical procedure of factor analysis. Among the more straightforward conclusions are: A construct used to characterize numerous role titles is highly permeable and/or superordinate. A limited repertory of constructs suggests a lack of versatility in construing other people, and difficulty in assuming a variety of useful roles. Superficial and impersonal constructs, such as "mother and sister have blue eyes" or "father and employer are both men," also reflect an inability to construe the people in question and form suitable role relationships with them.

In addition to the Rep Test, Kelly (like Allport) advocates the use of more simple and direct self-reports. "The most useful clinical tool of the physician is the four-word question uttered audibly in the presence of the patient: 'How do you feel?' There is a similar golden rule for clinical psychologists. *If you don't know what's wrong with a client, ask him; he may tell you!*" (Kelly, 1955, p. 201). Thus Kelly has the client provide a personal character sketch, phrased in the third person as though written by an intimate and sympathetic friend. The information gleaned from this method sometimes suggests the desirability of **fixed-role therapy,** wherein a panel of clinicians devises a contrasting role for the client to enact in everyday life. For example, one client's self-characterization revealed a marked inability to construe other people accurately. The client was therefore asked to spend two weeks acting and living in the manner of "Kenneth Norton," a fictitious individual described in four carefully written paragraphs as having a knack for perceiving the viewpoints and subtle feelings of others (Kelly, 1955, pp. 374–375; see also Kelly, 1955, pp. 319–451; 1970b, pp. 265–267). Fixed-role therapy allows the client to experiment with radically new constructions and behaviors by pretending to be someone else, somewhat like trying on a new suit of clothes that can easily be removed if it does not fit very well. But this procedure involves considerable work for both therapist and client, and is suitable for only about one in fifteen cases.

More often, the Kellyan psychotherapist helps reconstruct the client's system in other ways. These include playing the roles of people to whom the client has difficulty relating in order to provide an opportunity to devise more effective constructs, and telling stories to introduce children to new constructs. Kelly even recommends that the therapist study the ways in which environmental influences validate a client's predictions, and he presents detailed guidelines for making firsthand inspections of schools and evaluating their effects on a child's construct system. (See Kelly, 1955, pp. 134–135, 162, 619, 687–731, 1029–1092, 1141–1155.)

Resistance, Transference, and Countertransference. Since the client relies on existing constructs in order to anticipate the future, attempts at reconstruction are likely to evoke anxiety and resistance. Thus a client may balk at the prospect of revising the core structure, vehemently protest that a prescribed fixed role is silly or impossible to enact, or retain faulty constructs in order to "show what a mess my parents made out of me" (Kelly, 1955, p. 572; see also pp. 58–59, 406, 492, 679). Like Horney, however, Kelly concludes that resistance can also protect the client from an overeager therapist who tries to induce change too quickly.

Each client anticipates the therapist by drawing on existing role constructs, which are derived from prior replications with other people. Therefore, transference is also an inevitable aspect of psychotherapy. Some ("secondary") transferences are helpful because they allow the client to experiment with various constructions of the therapist, such as parental authority figure or passive sibling, and because they enable the therapist to acquire a first-hand knowledge of the client's construction system. Other ("primary") transferences tend to impede therapeutic progress because they are preemptive. For example, the client may view the therapist as nothing but a savior and expect solutions to be provided on a silver platter. Or the client may become wholly involved with learning the therapist's theoretical terminology and fail to devise new *personal* constructs, possibly because the therapist is preoccupied with a countertransferential attempt to impose the same scientific system on every client "with all the intolerance of a father who persistently, though patiently, sets about 'larnin' his kids'" (Kelly, 1955, p. 673; see also pp. 575–581, 662–686, 1100).

Kelly also takes strong exception to the belief, so commonly espoused by psychoanalysts, that high fees benefit the client by motivating change or

The Role Construct Repertory Test (Rep Test), Group Form

PART A: ROLE TITLE LIST. The client is asked to give the name of each of the following persons. No name may be used more than once. If the client does not have a brother or sister or cannot remember a particular person, the most similar individual that can be recalled is substituted. (Some versions of the Rep Test also include "myself," neighbors, coworkers, and others.)

1. Mother
2. Father
3. Brother nearest client's age
4. Sister nearest client's age
5. Teacher client liked
6. Teacher client disliked
7. Previous, most recent boy or girl friend
8. Wife or husband, or present boy or girl friend
9. Employer or supervisor
10. Close associate who dislikes client
11. Person met in last six months whom client would most like to know better
12. Person client would most like to be of help to, feels most sorry for
13. Most intelligent person client knows personally
14. Most successful person client knows personally
15. Most interesting person client knows personally

PART B: CONSTRUCT SORTS. For each of the following fifteen triads in turn, the client specifies one important way in which two of the role titles in that triad are alike and different from the third. The client then states the opposite (contrast) of this construct.

Sort	Role Titles	Sort	Role Titles
1	10, 11, 12	9	1, 4, 7
2	6, 13, 14	10	3, 5, 13
3	6, 9, 12	11	8, 12, 14
4	3, 14, 15	12	4, 5, 15
5	4, 11, 13	13	1, 2, 8
6	2, 9, 10	14	2, 3, 7
7	5, 7, 8	15	1, 6, 10
8	9, 11, 15		

For example, if the client's liked teacher is Jane Smith, previous boy friend is John Jones, and current boyfriend is Richard Roe, the results of Sort #7 might be:

Client's Thoughts	Construct	Contrast
"Jane Smith and Richard Roe are friendly, but John Jones is not"	Friendly	Critical

A construct may be used with more than one triad, and/or with a different contrast in different triads.

regular attendance. "Because some of the necessities and conveniences of life are bound up with our economic system, it is necessary that a reasonable proportion of the clinician's services be financially rewarded. [But] fees assessed under this necessity are for the welfare of the clinician, not the client. Let us make no mistake about that!" (Kelly, 1955, p. 611; see also pp. 608–610, 671–674.)

Constructive Alternativism and Psychological Research

Kelly is keenly aware of the part played by theories in a science such as psychology, and of the difficulties in evaluating them through empirical research. He regards a good theory as one that provides a framework for organizing a multitude of facts, generates hypotheses and predictions about human behavior that can be tested experimentally, is in general supported by research results, and makes possible useful applications to important social problems. (Cf. with the criteria discussed in Chapter 1.)

Kelly emphasizes that it is far from an easy task to test out theories in the research laboratory. Among the many challenging problems are those of obtaining a representative sample of subjects, controlling for extraneous and biasing influences, and quantifying important abstract constructs (such as unconscious processes, or "mental health"). Thus the results of any research study are likely to be open to question, or admit to more than one interpretation. Even sound hypotheses are never substantiated with absolute finality, while a psychologist whose ideas appear to have been discredited can often find ways to dispute the findings and resurrect the theory in question. "Rarely does a scientific theory wholly stand or fall on the outcome of a single crucial experiment. . . . [Instead,] I have noted privately over the years that mostly they sort of lean, at about the .08 level of confidence . . . [and that] it is almost impossible to give any comprehensive theory the final coup de grâce" (Kelly, 1955, pp. 24–25; 1970b, p. 259; see also Kelly, 1955, pp. 22–43, 102–103; 1970a, p. 4).

In addition to having a limited focus and range of convenience, any theory is of only interim value. It must be regarded as ultimately expendable when sufficient new knowledge is obtained, an inevitable fate in view of the myriad possible ways of construing any personal or scientific event:

> A [scientist] who spends a great deal of his time hoarding facts is not likely to be happy at the prospect of seeing them converted into rubbish. He is more likely to want them bound and preserved, a memorial to his personal achievement. . . . [Thus our assumption that all facts] are wholly subject to alternative constructions looms up as culpably subjective and dangerously subversive to the scientific establishment. . . . [Nevertheless, we must] consider any scientific theory as an eventual candidate for the trash can. (Kelly, 1955, p. 31; 1970a, p. 2.)

EVALUATION

Criticisms and Controversies

All too often, Kelly's invitation to adventure seems more like a dull exercise in neologisms. His dryly scientific theory omits most of the characteristics that seem vitally and distinctively human: love and hate, passion and despair, achievement and failure, inferiority and arrogance, sexuality and aggression, and so forth. In view of the significance Kelly accords to experience and replications, his refusal to accept the construct of learning appears particularly arbitrary and unconvincing. Some critics regard Kelly's emphasis on cognition as excessive, and find it difficult to relate his ideas to actual human behavior. Psychoanalytically oriented theorists charge Kelly with insufficient attention to infancy and childhood, and view his contention that there is no such thing as latent or repressed hostility (but only a failure to construe one's behavior accordingly) as a gross oversimplification. For these reasons, it has been said that Kellyan theory fails to convey a convincing picture of the human personality.

Empirical Research

Like trait theory and factor-analytic theory, personal construct theory has generated a substantial amount of empirical research. Some investigators have tried to redress the great emphasis on cognitive issues by devoting more attention to the emotional aspects of personality. Other researchers have attempted to relate personal construct theory to established clinical concepts, such as schizophrenia and depression. Still others have sought to remedy its dry, technical nature by focusing more on a theory of persons than on abstract construct systems. (See for example Bannister, 1985; Epting, 1984; Neimeyer, 1985a; 1985b.)

Thus efforts are being made to address the criticisms described in the preceding section. But whether it is in fact possible to reconcile so idiosyncratic a theory as Kelly's with the mainstream of modern psychology remains open to question.

Contributions

Kelly's theory offers a possible alternative to those who share his reservations about psychoanalysis. In addition, the psychology of personal constructs effectively illustrates that the hallmark of a good theory is usefulness, not correctness. Even a theory that deliberately ignores (at least explicitly) the fundamental issue of motivation can facilitate successful psychotherapy, an advantage in view of the uncertainty that still pervades psychological attempts to define the basic nature of human beings. In contrast to the pompous claims of some psychoanalysts, who seek to enshrine untestable ideas as monuments to their unique insight and scathingly reject any attempts at innovation, Kelly's conception of a theory as a limited and ultimately expendable tool is particularly refreshing. He has called attention to the importance of subjective cognitions, and an empathy for the personal constructs of others, as aspects of personality and interpersonal relations. Unlike the extreme views of Adler and Allport, Kellyan theory allows for a considerable degree of personal uniqueness while providing logical and practicable guidelines for the nomothetic, scientific study of personality. Finally, to some psychologists (e.g., Fiske, 1978, p. 39), Kelly's approach represents the key to understanding all theories of personality; as personal constructs of their creators, albeit ones more systematic and explicit than those of most people.

Kelly himself (1955, p. 130) once expressed concern that his theory might be no more than the fulminations of his own unique construct system, and not readily usable by other psychologists. While it would not be surprising if his own reservations ultimately proved to be the most fitting judgment of his idiosyncratic theoretical constructs, his general approach and emphasis on personal cognitions represents an unusual and significant contribution to the field of personality theory.

Suggested Reading

Kelly's ideas are concentrated primarily in one two-volume work (1955). Also of interest are Kelly's articles (1969; 1970a; 1970b).

■ SUMMARY

1. THE BASIC NATURE OF HUMAN BEINGS. Among the most idiosyncratic of personality theorists, Kelly rejects the use of explicit motivational constructs. He assumes only that human beings are naturally active, and that our behavior is directed toward the goal of anticipating the future.

2. THE STRUCTURE OF PERSONALITY. Each of us forms our own personal constructs for predicting and thereby controlling the environment. Thus the psychologist must seek to understand the ways in which a particular individual views the world, rather than trying to impose a single set of scientific constructs on all humanity. Kellyan theory represents a system for understanding such personal constructs. *Postulates and Corollaries:* Kelly's description of our "scientific" personality is couched in terms of one fundamental postulate, and eleven corollaries. The former states that our psychological processes are channelized by the ways in which we anticipate the future, while the latter clarify and elaborate upon the nature of personal constructs (as delineated in a preceding Capsule Summary). *Other Characteristics of Personal Constructs:* Personal constructs may be preemptive, constellatory, or propositional. Every construct system includes that of "self versus others." This self-construct is typically subordinated to certain con-

structs that concern interactions with other people, a subsystem referred to as the "core role." Imminent changes in the core aspects of a person's construction system produce guilt or threat, while the inability to construe important events and anticipate the future results in anxiety. Some constructs are not readily accessible to one's awareness, but this is due to limitations in one's construction system rather than to supposedly unconscious processes.

3. THE DEVELOPMENT OF PERSONALITY. Like Murray, Kelly regards a temporal orientation as essential to the study of personality. Yet save for some discussion of pathogenic parental behaviors, he devotes little attention to personality development.

4. FURTHER APPLICATIONS. *Dream Interpretation:* Dreams offer potential clues to the less obvious aspects of personality, but are useful primarily for weaning a client from constructs that have become overly rigid and tight. *Psychopathology:* The pathological individual resembles an imcompetent scientist who clings rigidly to outmoded hypotheses, and whose predictions are therefore frequently incorrect. Thus the causes of psychopathology are in the present, and concern a personal construct system that is in some way defective. *Psychotherapy:* The goal of Kellyan psychotherapy is to enable the client to devise and safely experiment with new core constructs, escape the viselike grip of obsolescent ones, and reconstruct the system in ways that lead to more accurate predictions. Procedures include interviews, the Rep Test, self-reports, and fixed-role therapy. To Kelly, the primary purpose of personal construct theory is to facilitate effective psychotherapy.

5. EVALUATION. Kelly has been criticized for excessive and complicated neologisms, omission of most of the vital characteristics that make us distinctively human, arbitrary rejection of such established constructs as learning, and an oversimplified view of personality and human nature. Yet his theory has proved useful therapeutically, his conception of a theory as a limited and ultimately expendable tool offers a refreshing contrast to the pompous claims of certain psychologists, he has called attention to the importance of subjective cognitions and empathy as aspects of personality and interpersonal relations, his theory allows for much personal uniqueness while providing logical guidelines for nomothetic research, and his approach may well represent the key to understanding (and perhaps integrating) the myriad of personality theories.

STUDY QUESTIONS

1. Consider once again the case history discussed throughout the Appendix (e.g., Chapter 2, question 6; Chapter 4, questions 2 and 6a; Chapter 5, questions 1, 4b, and 5; Chapter 6, questions 3d and 4; Chapter 7, question 7a; Chapter 8, question 7; Chapter 9, question 10). Use this case history to illustrate each of the following Kellyan concepts: (a) A core construct that can be changed only with the aid of formal psychotherapy, because any

change creates the impression that the person's entire construct system is collapsing. (b) The conflict over whether to choose the safer course of further clarifying the constructs one already uses, or the more adventurous path of trying to use unfamiliar constructs. (c) A poorly designed "test" of a personal construct that yields an erroneous conclusion. (d) How anxiety results from the inability to construe important events and anticipate the future. (e) A preverbal construct. (f) The effects of parental pampering and overindulgence. (g) The effects of harsh parental criticism and punishment. (h) Using a personal construct repeatedly in spite of consistent invalidation.

2. Give an example from your own life, from the life of someone you know well, or from fiction to illustrate each of the following: (a) How the same event can be construed in alternative ways, and the different effects of these constructions. (b) Constructions based on relevant prior experiences. (c) The healthy use of the C-P-C cycle. (d) A construct becoming more permeable as one grows older. (e) The unhealthy use of a preemptive or constellatory construct. (f) The beneficial use of roles (as defined by Kelly).

3. According to Kelly, every construct is bipolar. How is it possible to establish a graded scale, such as: Restaurant A is my favorite; Restaurant B is my second choice; Restaurant C is third best; and I would never eat at Restaurant D again?

4. According to Kelly, "One cannot call another person a bastard without making bastardy a dimension of his own life also." How does this relate to Jung's contention that what we most dislike about other people is often what we most dislike about ourselves?

5. (a) How would Kelly interpret the "S[E]INE" dream discussed in Chapter 8 in the section on dream interpretation and in study question 10? (b) Who did Kelly have in mind when he wrote about the therapist who tries to impose his or her construct system on every client "with all the intolerance of a father who persistently, though patiently, sets about 'larnin' his kids,'" and the theorist who "is more likely to want [his theoretical constructs] bound and preserved, a memorial to his personal achievement. . . . [even though we must] consider any scientific theory as an eventual candidate for the trash can"? (c) Do you agree with Kelly's views in each case? Why or why not?

6. How would Kelly describe or explain each of the following: (a) The person in Sullivanian theory who conducts an endless quest for the ideal member of the opposite sex, and blames the inevitable failures on apparent defects in every candidate rather than on his or her own unconscious fears about heterosexuality. (b) The same person becomes aware of these fears of heterosexuality during psychotherapy, and concludes that they have emerged from his or her unconscious.

7. Why does Kelly conclude that "it is almost impossible to give any comprehensive theory the final coup de grace?"

PART IV

HUMANISTIC AND EXISTENTIAL PSYCHOLOGY

PROLOGUE

As the twentieth century progressed toward the halfway point, certain psychoanalysts and psychotherapists encountered a singularly puzzling phenomenon. Social standards had become far more permissive than in Freud's day, especially with regard to sexuality. In theory, this greater liberalism should have helped to alleviate troublesome id-superego conflicts and reduce the number of neuroses. Yet while hysterical neurosis and repression did seem to be less common than in Victorian times, more people than ever before were entering psychotherapy. And they suffered from such new and unusual problems as an inability to enjoy the new freedom of self-expression (or, for that matter, to feel much of anything), and an inner emptiness and self-estrangement. Rather than hoping to cure some manifest symptom, these patients desperately needed an answer to a more philosophical question: how to remedy the apparent meaninglessness of their lives.

As we have seen, some theorists tried to resolve this pressing issue within a more or less psychoanalytic framework (e.g., the Eriksonian identity crisis, Fromm's conception of escape from freedom). However, other noted psychologists called into question the basic rationale underlying analytic therapy. They pointed out that Freud's insights may well have applied brilliantly to the Victorian era, when an aura of repulsiveness surrounded the topic of sexuality and people suffered from the misconception that personality was wholly rational and conscious. But they argued that constructs like psychic determinism and the structural model, and Freud's pessimism about human nature, were now aggravating the modern patient's apathy and depersonalization by depicting personality as mechanical, fragmented, malignant, and totally preordained by prior causes.

Self-Actualization Theory

Among the most outspoken critics of Freudian pessimism are Carl Rogers and Abraham Maslow, both of whom contend that human nature is inherently healthy and constructive. Interestingly, these two theorists arrive at this optimistic conclusion from markedly different perspectives. Maslow, taking exception to the emphasis of so many personality theorists on abnormal behavior, concentrates his attention primarily on the study of notably well-adjusted individuals. Rogers is first and foremost a psychotherapist, one whose theory of personality represents somewhat of an afterthought to his clinical innovations.

The theories of Rogers and Maslow do differ in some respects. Maslow refers to the fulfillment of an individual's particular (and positive) innate potentials as *self-actualization*. Rogers calls this *actualization,* and reserves "self-actualization" for a special part of the actualizing tendency: our efforts to fulfill our learned, conscious conception of ourselves. Maslow is also more eclectic than Rogers, and is more accepting of at least some aspects of Freudian and neoanalytic theory. (Interestingly, despite Rogers's disclaimers, some of his major ideas very much resemble those of Karen Horney.) Yet both Rogers and Maslow agree that human nature is wholly positive, that we strive to fulfill these benign potentials unless we are deterred by pathogenic external forces—*and* that such pathogenic influences are very common and affect all of us, making actualization (or self-actualization) extremely difficult to achieve.

Existential Psychology

Other psychotherapists turned instead to a holistic and teleological philosophy of human nature, *existentialism,* as expressed in the writings of Albert Camus, Martin Heidegger, Sören Kierkegaard, Jean-Paul Sartre, Paul Tillich, and others. Existentialism is concerned with the science of being (*ontology*): what it means to exist as a distinctively human organism for one fleeting and random moment in an eternity of time, in one small and random corner of an infinitely vast universe. The existentialists regard personality as a unified whole, and as inseparable from the physical and social environment. They share Adler's view that we must choose our own course in life, Rogers's and Maslow's emphasis on the necessity (and difficulty) of discovering and fulfilling our own innate potentials, and Allport's conception of personality as a dynamic and ever-changing process of becoming. And, like Fromm, they stress the uniquely painful predicament of our singular species: to be sufficiently insightful to recognize the inevitability of death, yet obliged to gather our courage and assert our being despite the ultimate nothingness that awaits us—perhaps, even, at the very next moment.

The existential approach to psychotherapy was originated in part by two Swiss psychiatrists, Ludwig Binswanger and Medard Boss, whose complicated (and at times virtually untranslatable) constructs pose grave difficulties for American readers. We will therefore focus instead on an American existential psychologist who has achieved considerable professional and popular acclaim: Rollo May.

12

CARL R. ROGERS
Self-Actualization Theory (I)

Like Adler and some of the neo-Freudians, Carl Rogers is no stranger to the rancorous side of scientific inquiry. In 1939, some ten years after receiving his doctorate degree in psychology, Rogers's position as director of a child guidance clinic was strongly challenged by orthodox psychiatrists—not because of any question as to the quality of his work, but on the grounds that no nonmedical practitioner could be sufficiently qualified to head up a mental health operation. "It was a lonely battle, . . . a life-and-death struggle for me because it was the thing I was doing well, and the work I very much wanted to continue" (Rogers, 1974/1975, p. 129; see also Rogers, 1967, pp. 360, 364; 1977, pp. 144–145). A few years later he established a counseling center at the University of Chicago, and he again met with charges from psychiatrists that its members were practicing medicine without a license. Fortunately, Rogers won both of these confrontations; and his work has helped gain recognition and respect for the field of clinical psychology.

BIOGRAPHICAL SKETCH

Carl R. Rogers was born on January 8, 1902, in Oak Park, Illinois, a suburb of Chicago. His father was a successful civil engineer. His close-knit family, which included four brothers and one sister (three of them older), was committed to conservative Protestantism and the value of hard work. When Carl was twelve, the Rogerses decided to escape the evils and temptations of suburban life by moving to a farm west of Chicago. There he read extensively about scientific approaches to soils and feeds, reared lambs and calves, bred moths, and often rose before the crack of dawn to help with such chores as milking the cows. Thus Carl's childhood and adolescence were relatively solitary and scholarly, characterized by a love of books and little socializing outside the immediate family. (See Rogers, 1961, pp. 4–15; 1967.)

Carl's readings about farming generated a marked respect for the scientific method and led him to pursue an undergraduate degree in agriculture at the University of Wisconsin, but he soon became more interested in the helping professions. At first he considered joining the clergy and attended the Union Theological Seminary in New York, but his experiences at this liberal institution introduced him to a more enticing profession:

psychotherapy. He therefore transferred to Columbia University Teachers College, where he received his Ph.D. in 1928. Carl married Helen Elliott on August 28, 1924. The union proved to be a happy and successful one, and the Rogerses were to have one son and one daughter.

Rogers's first professional position was at a child guidance clinic in Rochester, New York, where he engaged in the aforementioned confrontation with orthodox psychiatry. Educated in Freudian theory among others, Rogers found that analytic insight often did not seem to benefit his clients and began to formulate his own approach to psychotherapy. In 1940 he accepted a full professorship at Ohio State University, about which he was later to observe: "I heartily recommend starting in the academic world at this level. I have often been grateful that I have never had to live through the frequently degrading competitive process of step-by-step promotion in university faculties, where individuals so frequently learn only one lesson—not to stick their necks out" (Rogers, 1961, p. 13; see also Rogers, 1967, p. 361).

Rogers moved to the University of Chicago in 1945 to establish a counseling center, and thence to the University of Wisconsin in 1957 to conduct research on psychotherapy and personality. The return to his alma mater proved to be a trying one, however. The doctoral program emphasized the memorization of trivial facts and rigid formal examinations, and many of his most able and creative graduate students either failed or left in disgust. Rogers also resigned in 1963 and joined the Western Behavioral Sciences Institute in La Jolla, California, where he devoted himself to the humanistic study of interpersonal relationships and ultimately founded the Center for Studies of the Person.

Throughout his career, Rogers devoted an average of some fifteen to twenty hours per week to the practice of client-centered therapy. He authored some ten books and numerous articles, and his honors include receiving the Distinguished Scientific Contribution Award of the American Psychological Association in 1956. Rogers was keenly interested in promoting world peace, organized the Vienna Peace Project that brought together leaders from thirteen nations in 1985, and conducted peace workshops in Moscow during 1986. Carl Rogers died on February 4, 1987, from cardiac arrest following surgery for a broken hip sustained in a fall.

THE BASIC NATURE OF HUMAN BEINGS

Rogers shares Kelly's disdain for the concept of a superior, prescient psychotherapist, on whom the "patient" passively depends for shrewd interpretations. Instead he emphasizes that only we ourselves can know, and choose, our proper directions in life. In accordance with this belief, Rogers originally named his approach "client-centered therapy." But since his ideas have subsequently been expanded to include such nonclinical areas as parenting, education, and interracial relations, he now prefers the broader designation of **person-centered theory.** (See Rogers, 1951, p. 7 n. 1; 1977, p. 5.)

Actualization

According to Rogers, human beings are motivated by a single positive force: an innate tendency to develop our constructive, healthy capacities. *"Persons have a basically positive direction* . . . [It is the urge] to expand, extend, become autonomous, develop, mature" (Rogers, 1961, pp. 26, 35; see also Rogers, 1951, pp. 487–491; 1959, p. 196; 1961, pp. 90–92, 105–106; 1977, pp. 7–8).

This inherent tendency to **actualize** our benign inner potentials includes both drive-reducing and drive-increasing behavior, as in the theories of Allport and Maslow. We seek to reduce such specific drives as hunger, thirst, sex, and oxygen deprivation, yet we also strive for pleasurable increases in tension and mastery over the environment. Among the growth-oriented aspects of the actualizing tendency are reproduction, creativity, curiosity, and the willingness to undergo even painful learning experiences in order to become more effective and independent:

> The first steps [of a child learning to walk] involve struggle, and usually pain. Often it is true that the immediate reward involved in taking a few steps is in no way commensurate with the pain of falls and bumps. . . . Yet, in the overwhelming majority of individuals, the forward direction of growth is more powerful than the satisfactions of remaining infantile. The child will actualize himself, in spite of the painful experiences in so doing. (Rogers, 1951, p. 490.)

Rogers's theoretical optimism does not prevent him from recognizing our great capacity for cruel and destructive behavior, but he attributes this primarily to external rather than innate forces. The most fundamental levels of personality are inherently positive, and the actualizing tendency will under ideal conditions select and develop only these constructive potentials. But there are many potential pitfalls along the path to actualization, and unfavorable circumstances may well cause us to behave in ways that belie our benign inner nature.

The Need for Positive Regard

All human beings need warmth, respect, and acceptance from other people, particularly such "significant others" as the parents. This need for **positive regard** remains active throughout life. But it also becomes partly independent of specific contacts with other people, leading to a secondary, learned need for **positive self-regard.** (See Rogers, 1951, p. 524; 1959, pp. 207–209, 223–224.) Interestingly, the quest to satisfy the powerful need for positive regard represents the single most serious impediment to the course of actualization—as we will see in a subsequent section.

Teleology

Rogers agrees that childhood events play a prominent role in forming the adult personality. But he prefers to emphasize teleology, currently active needs, and our purposeful striving toward the goal of actualization. "Behavior is not 'caused' by something which occurred in the past. Present tensions and present needs are the only ones which the organism endeavors to reduce or satisfy" (Rogers, 1951, p. 492; see also Rogers, 1942, p. 29; 1959, pp. 198–199; Rogers, cited by Evans, 1975, pp. 8, 75–76).

THE STRUCTURE OF PERSONALITY

Since actualization involves the total organism, Rogers sees little need to posit specific structural constructs. Yet his theory is not truly holistic, for he shares Horney's belief that we are all too often subject to painful intrapsychic conflicts. "The great puzzle that faces anyone who delves at all into the dynamics of human behavior . . . [is] that persons are often at war within themselves, estranged from their own organisms" (Rogers, 1977, p. 243).

Experience and The Organismic Valuing Process

Experience. Like Allport and Kelly, Rogers regards personality as a relatively unique process within the individual. Each of us exists at the center of our own private, ever-changing world of inner **experience** (**experiential field, phenomenal field**), one that can never be perfectly understood by anyone else. (See Rogers, 1951, pp. 483–484, 494–497; 1959, pp. 191, 197–198, 210.)

Experience comprises everything potentially available to awareness at a given moment: thoughts; perceptions, including those that are temporarily ignored (such as the pressure of the chair seat on which one is sitting); needs, some of which may also be momentarily overlooked (as when engrossed in work or play); and "feelings," or emotionally tinged events that also have a personal meaning (e.g., "I feel pleased with myself"). However, only a small portion of experience is conscious. The greatest part consists of stimuli and events that we perceive below the level of awareness ("subceptions," similar to subliminal perceptions in Jungian theory[1]):

> The individual's functioning [is like] a large pyramidal fountain. The very tip of the fountain is intermittently illuminated with the flickering light of consciousness, but the constant flow of life goes on in the darkness as well, in nonconscious as well as conscious ways. (Rogers, 1977, p. 244.)

The Organismic Valuing Process. According to Rogers, there is no need for us to learn what is or is not actualizing. Included among the primarily unconscious aspects of experience is an innate capacity to value positively

---

[1]Although Rogers (1959, p. 199) attributes the concept of subception to an article published by two psychologists in 1949, his usage of this term parallels Jung's discussion of some twenty years earlier (1927/1971b, p. 38).

whatever we perceive as actualizing, and to value negatively that which we perceive as nonactualizing (the **organismic valuing process**). Thus the infant values food when hungry but promptly becomes disgusted with it when satiated, enjoys the life-sustaining physical contact of being cuddled, and chooses a commendably balanced diet if given the freedom to eat whatever it wishes.

To Rogers, then, the nonconscious aspects of experience are an invaluable addition to our conscious thoughts and plans. It is at this deepest level of personality that we know what is good for us (actualizing) and what is not. And this implies that only we ourselves, rather than a parent or a psychotherapist, can identify our true organismic values and sense how best to actualize our own particular potentials:

> *Experience is, for me, the highest authority.* . . . When an activity *feels* as though it is valuable or worth doing, it *is* worth doing. . . . [Thus I trust] the totality of my experience, which I have learned to suspect is wiser than my intellect. It is fallible I am sure, but I believe it to be less fallible than my conscious mind alone. (Rogers, 1961, pp. 22–23. See also Rogers, 1951, pp. 498–499; 1959, pp. 210, 222; 1977, pp. 243–246.)

Experience and the External World. Although experience is subjective, it is not totally divorced from the external world. Like Kelly, Rogers concludes that we seek to evaluate our experiences by forming and testing appropriate hypotheses. If you perceive a white powder in a small dish as salt, investigate this possibility by tasting it, and find it to be sweet, the experience will promptly shift to that of sugar. However, the subjective aspects of experience are far more important than objective reality. An infant who is picked up by a friendly adult, but who perceives this situation as strange and frightening, will respond with cries of distress. Or a daughter who initially perceived her father as domineering and fearful, but who has learned through psychotherapy to regard him as a rather pathetic figure trying desperately to retain a shred of status and dignity, will experience him quite differently even though he himself has not changed. (See Rogers, 1951, pp. 484–486; 1959, pp. 199, 222–223.)

The Self-Concept (Self) and Self-Actualization

Definitions. Guided by the actualizing tendency, the growing infant expands its experiential field and learns to perceive itself as a separate and distinct entity. This **self-concept** (**self**) is entirely conscious, and thus represents part of the tip of the constantly flowing fountain of subjective experience.[2]

---

[2]Rogers defines the self-concept as wholly conscious on utilitarian rather than theoretical grounds. He argues that a theory of personality must be tested through empirical research, and the concept of a partially unconscious ego or self would offer grave difficulties in this regard because it cannot be operationally defined (Rogers, 1959, p. 202).

Some of the actualizing tendency now becomes directed toward an attempt to realize the goals and abilities represented by the self-concept. This important subsidiary tendency is referred to as **self-actualization,** after a term first popularized by Kurt Goldstein. (See Goldstein, 1939; 1940; Rogers, 1951, pp. 497–498; 1959, pp. 196–206, 223; Rogers, cited by Evans, 1975, pp. 6–7.)

How Conflict Develops Between the Actualizing and Self-Actualizing Tendencies. So long as the conscious, learned conception that we form of ourselves remains consistent (**congruent**) with our total experience, the actualizing and self-actualizing tendencies work in unison to fulfill our innate constructive potentials. Unfortunately, matters are rarely this simple.

For actualization to occur, the child must follow the inner guidelines provided by the organismic valuing process. However, self-actualization is achieved in a different way: the self-concept must be supported by positive regard from significant others, such as the parents. Therefore, the child must also pay close attention to parental requests and demands.

In the best of all possible worlds, parents would always treat the child's burgeoning self-concept with **unconditional positive regard** and limit their criticisms to specific undesirable behaviors. For example, if a little girl expresses hostility toward a sibling, her mother might ideally respond: "I can understand how satisfying it feels to you to hit your baby brother . . . and I love you and am quite willing for you to have those feelings. But I am quite willing for me to have my feelings, too, and I feel very distressed when your brother is hurt . . . and so I do not let you hit him. Both your feelings and my feelings are important, and each of us can freely have [our] own" (Rogers, 1959, p. 225; see also Rogers, 1951, pp. 498–503; 1959, pp. 208–210, 224). Thus the girl might well choose not to hit her brother in order to please her mother, rather than because of shame and guilt over her aggressive urges. Whatever her decision, her developing sense of positive self-regard would not be threatened and would also become unconditional. She would freely accept her aggressiveness into awareness as an aspect of her self-concept, which would therefore remain congruent with her experience and valuing process (that hitting baby brother is pleasant). And she would remain psychologically well-adjusted.

The favorable sequence of events described above is only a hypothetical, and unlikely, possibility. Instead, parents typically respond to the child with **conditional positive regard.** That is, they provide affection and respect only if the child's self-concept and feelings meet with their approval. They may indicate in direct or subtle ways that wishing to hit baby brother will result in the loss of their love, or that this urge "should" cause feelings of guilt and unhappiness instead of satisfaction. As a result, the child is confronted with a difficult and painful choice: to accept its true inner experience (i.e., that hitting baby brother is pleasurable), which risks the shattering possibility of becoming unloved; or to succumb to temptation, disown its

■ CAPSULE SUMMARY
Some Important Rogerian Terminology

Actualizing tendency	An innate tendency to develop our constructive capacities, and grow in ways that maintain or enhance our total organism; the fundamental motive underlying all human behavior.
Anxiety	A state of uneasiness and tension, resulting from experiences that are subceived as incongruent with the self-concept.
Awareness (consciousness)	That part of experience that is expressed in verbal or other convenient symbols.
Conditional positive regard	Liking and accepting another person only if that individual's feelings and self-concept meet one's own standards; the typical way in which parents behave toward the child.
Conditional positive self-regard	Liking and accepting oneself only if one satisfies the introjected standards of significant others (conditions of worth), even though these run counter to the actualizing tendency.
Condition of worth (introjected value)	A standard that must be satisfied to receive conditional positive regard from a significant other, which is therefore introjected into the self-concept and becomes a criterion for positive self-regard. Supersedes the organismic valuing process, and leads to behaviors that are not truly actualizing.
Congruence	A healthy state of unison between one's total organismic experience and a self-concept that is free of conditions of worth.
Defense	Responding to experiences that threaten the self-concept and evoke anxiety by perceptually distorting them, or (less frequently) by screening them out altogether from awareness.
Empathy (understanding)	A reasonably accurate understanding of someone else's experience; putting oneself in another person's shoes. One of the three essential characteristics of the successful therapeutic relationship.
Encounter group (T group)	A group of relatively well-adjusted individuals, who meet with a facilitator to pursue further personal growth.
Experience (experiential field, phenomenal field)	Everything going on within the individual that is presently within or potentially available to awareness, including thoughts, needs, perceptions, and feelings. A relatively small part of experience is conscious, while the greatest portion is subceived and nonconscious.
Fully functioning person	An optimally psychologically healthy individual.
Genuineness (realness)	The ability to achieve a state of congruence and openness to experience, and to express one's true beliefs and feelings when appropriate. One of the three essential characteristics of the successful therapeutic relationship.
Incongruence	A schism between one's total organismic experience and a self-concept burdened by conditions of worth (and, therefore,

continued

	between the actualizing and self-actualizing tendencies), resulting in a state of inner tension and confusion; the converse of congruence.
Introjection	Incorporating the standards of another person within one's own personality; similar to Freud's use of the term.
Openness to experience	A willingness to accept any and all experience into awareness, without distortion; the converse of defense.
Organismic valuing process	An innate capacity to value positively those experiences that are perceived as actualizing, and to value negatively those that are perceived as nonactualizing.
Perception	Apprehending stimuli at the level of awareness, and identifying them with appropriate symbols; the converse of subception.
Person-centered theory (client-centered therapy)	The name given by Rogers to his theory of personality.
Positive regard	Warmth, respect, and acceptance from another person; a universal, pervasive human need.
Positive self-regard	Liking and accepting oneself in the absence of specific contacts with others. A learned human need, derived from the need for positive regard.
Self-actualization	The tendency to actualize that portion of experience represented by the self-concept; a subsidiary of the actualizing tendency. To the extent that the learned self-actualizing tendency remains unified with the organismic actualizing tendency, the individual is psychologically well-adjusted.
Self-concept (self)	A learned, conscious sense of being separate and distinct from other people and things.
Significant other	An important source of positive regard, such as a parent.
Subception	Apprehending stimuli below the level of awareness, and thus not identifying them with appropriate symbols; the converse of perception.
Unconditional positive regard	Liking and accepting all of another person's feelings and self-concept; a nonjudgmental and nonpossessive caring for, and prizing of, another person. (Does *not* apply to specific behaviors, which may well be valued differentially.) One of the three essential characteristics of the successful therapeutic relationship.
Unconditional positive self-regard	An ideal state of total self-acceptance, or absence of any conditions of worth. Theoretically due to receiving unconditional positive regard from significant others, but probably never occurs in reality.

real feelings, and distort its experience in ways that will please others (as by concluding that hitting baby brother is distasteful).

Because the need for positive regard is so powerful, the child ultimately elects to abandon its true feelings at least to some extent (as in Horneyan theory). It incorporates the parental standards into the self-concept, a process for which Rogers borrows the Freudian term **introjection.** Its positive self-regard becomes conditional on satisfying these introjected **conditions of worth,** which supersede the organismic valuing process as an inner guide to behavior. Thus the self-concept clashes (becomes **incongruent**) with the totality of experience, the self-actualizing and actualizing tendencies become divided and work at cross-purposes, and the individual suffers from a state of confusion and anxiety:

> The accurate symbolization [of the child's experience] would be: "I perceive my parents as experiencing this behavior as unsatisfying to them." The [actual but] distorted symbolization, distorted to preserve the threatened concept of self, is: "*I* perceive this behavior as unsatisfying." . . . In this way the values which the infant attaches to experience become divorced from his own organismic functioning, and experience is valued in terms of the attitudes held by his [significant others]. . . . It is here, it seems, that the individual begins on a pathway which he later describes as "I don't really know myself." (Rogers, 1951, pp. 500–501. See also Rogers, 1959, pp. 203–205, 209–210, 224–226.)

At a later age, the journey away from self-knowledge is also encouraged by various social institutions and groups. For example, affluent members of society may reflect the belief that making large amounts of money is the most important goal of all. Or television and magazine advertisements may try to persuade us that certain products are essential to our well-being. Many of us introject these external standards and believe them to be our own, even though they may well run counter to our true organismic needs and values. (See Rogers, 1977, p. 247; Rogers & Stevens, 1967/1971, pp. 10–11.)

Defense

Any experiences that serve as a threatening reminder of the incongruence between the self-concept and organismic experience are likely to be **defended** against through distortion, or (less frequently) by screening them out altogether from awareness. For example, when the aforementioned little girl next sees her baby brother, she may decide that she feels nothing but love and would not dream of hurting him. Or a college student whose self-concept includes a strong belief in his academic competence, and who fails an examination, may rationalize this incongruent experience by attributing it to an inept grading system.

Even such positive feelings as love or success may be defended against if they fail to accord with the self-concept. A college undergraduate who thinks he is a poor student may attribute a high grade to luck or an error by the professor, while a woman whose self-concept is quite negative may refuse to believe that others regard her as intelligent or likable. (See Rogers, 1951, pp. 503–520; 1959, pp. 202–205, 227–228; Rogers & Wood, 1974, p. 218.)

A certain amount of incongruence and defense is probably inevitable, and does not necessarily indicate that one is neurotic. Yet any distortion or denial of experience and the organismic valuing process (including the mechanism of subception) represents less than ideal psychological adjustment, an unfortunate departure from our initial healthy inclinations.

THE DEVELOPMENT OF PERSONALITY

Rogers posits no specific developmental stages or criteria, preferring instead to stress the desirability of responding to the child with unconditional positive regard. This care and concern is best begun immediately upon the infant's exit from the womb, with the peaceful and soothing Leboyer technique of childbirth (soft lights, silence, stroking, immersion in warm water) far preferable to the usual traumatic method (loud noises, harsh lights, slaps):

> To come into the new life so gradually, with security and a caring, loving touch is much better for the child's psychological development than for him to be suddenly exposed to all sorts of terrifying stimuli and *forced* into a fearful new way of being. . . . The photographs of the screaming, terrified, blinded infants handled in [the] customary fashion are damning. (Rogers, 1977, pp. 32, 34. See also Leboyer, 1975.)

Thereafter, Rogers recommends that the growing child be treated as a person who is worthy of respect, with the right to evaluate its experience in its own way and to make the choices indicated by its organismic valuing process. (The parents are also entitled to respect, and to have rights that cannot be overridden by the child.) For example, in the all too common authoritarian family, the head (or heads) of the household makes all the decisions and issues various orders (e.g., "You *must* be neat! Clean up your room at once!"). The children must therefore resort to devious strategies for gaining some power of their own, such as sulking, pleading, setting one parent against the other, and complaining (e.g., "You're mean! Johnny's parents let *him* by sloppy!"). In contrast, the person-centered family emphasizes the sharing of nonjudgmental feelings. The mother may say, "I feel badly when the house is messy, and would really like some help resolving this"—and find to her amazement that her children devise some truly ingenious and effective ways of ensuring neatness, now that this is clearly and honestly defined as her problem rather than theirs. (See Rogers, 1977, pp. 29–41.)

Establishing a person-centered family is not an easy task, but Rogers argues that it is well worth the effort. It permits children to grow up with a minimum of pathogenic conditions of worth, and enables them freely to pursue their own path toward actualization.

The Fully Functioning Person

Like Allport, Rogers has formulated a rather extensive list of criteria that define mental health.

The **fully functioning person** is characterized by the *absence of any conditions of worth,* and therefore enjoys **unconditional positive self-regard.** This permits the self-concept to remain *congruent* with the totality of experience, and safe from threat or anxiety. Thus there is no need for defense, and all experiences can accurately enter awareness. Because of this **openness to experience,** the fully functioning person readily heeds the organismic valuing process rather than the "shoulds" and "oughts" of others. Any choices that do work out poorly are soon corrected, since these errors are perceived openly and accurately, and so the actualizing and self-actualizing tendencies work in unison toward the fulfillment of the person's own particular innate potentials.

For example, such highly creative individuals as El Greco, Hemingway, and Einstein knew full well that their work and thought were markedly idiosyncratic. Yet rather than misguidedly accepting the prevailing standards and hiding their true feelings behind a socially acceptable façade, they trusted their inner experience and persisted in the difficult but essential task of being truly and deeply themselves. "It was as though [El Greco] could say, 'good artists do not paint like this, but *I* paint like this" (Rogers, 1961, p. 175). Nor is this true only of artists or geniuses, for each of us is capable of living in accordance with our inner values and expressing ourselves in unique and satisfying ways.

Fully functioning persons also feel worthy of being liked by other people and capable of caring deeply for them, and satisfy their need for positive regard by *forming successful interpersonal relationships.* Thus they demonstrate unconditional positive regard for others, as well as toward themselves. Finally, such individuals *live wholly and freely in each moment.* They respond spontaneously to their experiences, and they regard happiness not as some fixed utopia but as an ever-changing journey. "The good life is a *process,* not a state of being. It is a direction, not a destination" (Rogers, 1961, p. 186; see also Rogers, 1959, pp. 234–235; 1961, pp. 163–196).

FURTHER APPLICATIONS OF ROGERIAN THEORY

Psychopathology

The fully functioning person represents an ideal that is rarely if ever achieved, for virtually every child encounters at least some conditional positive regard. Thus there is no sharp dividing line between normality and psychopathology, but rather a difference in degree.

The self-concept of the more neurotic individual includes more powerful conditions of worth, and is therefore more incongruent with the totality of experience. This results in a troublesome and painful schism: the sufferer's conscious efforts to achieve positive self-regard by satisfying the introjected standards (i.e., to self-actualize) fail to actualize the true inner needs, while the organismic needs and values become anxiety-provoking threats to the incongruent self-concept. The sufferer therefore attempts to protect the self through the aforementioned forms of defense. But this only increases the degree of inner confusion and alienation, and leads to such complaints as "I feel I'm not being my real self," "I wonder who I am, really," "I don't know what I want," and "I can't decide on anything" (Rogers, 1951, p. 511; 1959, p. 201; compare also with the similar views of Horney). The inability to recognize one's true needs also makes it extremely difficult for others to help satisfy them, thereby disrupting the sufferer's interpersonal relationships as well.

Psychosis is similar to neurosis but involves even more extreme forms of defense, such as dissociation (as in Sullivanian theory) and delusions. Thus a boy whose self-concept included highly puritanical conditions of worth was caught lifting the skirts of two little girls, yet insisted that he could not be blamed because he was "not himself" at the time (Rogers, 1951, pp. 509–510; 1977, p. 247).

For the most part, however, Rogers (like Erikson and Kelly) prefers to avoid formal diagnostic labels—even general ones like neurosis and psychosis. He regards such categories as pseudoscientific efforts to glorify the therapist's expertise and depict the client as a dependent object, whereas it is the client who must identify the nature of his or her inner conflicts and organismic values. "[If] the client perceives the locus of judgment and responsibility as clearly resting in the hands of the clinician, he is . . . further from therapeutic progress than when he came in" (Rogers, 1951, p. 223; see also Rogers, 1951, pp. 219–225; 1959, pp. 228–230; Rogers, cited by Evans, 1975, pp. 92–101). Even the so-called psychotic is simply an individual who has been badly hurt by life, and who desperately needs the corrective influence of a truly understanding and caring interpersonal relationship—the hallmark of Rogerian psychotherapy.

Psychotherapy

Theoretical Foundation. The client in person-centered psychotherapy first learns to abandon the defensive façades that protect the incongruent self-concept from threat, thereby bringing to light important material that had previously been blocked from awareness (e.g., anger, self-criticism, self-acceptance, a need for others, a need to fulfill specific inner potentials). As these newly recognized feelings and needs become more evident, so does their incongruence with the introjected conditions of worth. Ordinarily, the client would now resort to various distortions and denials. But in the safety of the therapeutic situation, he or she is able to accept these anxiety-provoking aspects of experience, realize that it is the self-concept that must be changed, and reorganize it appropriately. Thus the client brings the self-concept into congruence with the totality of experience, ends the estrangement between the actualizing and self-actualizing tendencies, and reclaims the innate ability to heed the organismic valuing process—in short, becomes a more fully functioning person.

For example, a client who has steadfastly claimed to have only positive feelings toward her mother and father may conclude: "I have thought I must feel only love for my parents, but I find that I experience both love and bitter resentment. Perhaps I can be that person who freely experiences both love *and* resentment." Or a client whose self-concept has been primarily negative, and who has therefore persistently blocked feelings of self-acceptance from awareness, may learn: "I have thought that in some deep way I was bad, that the most basic elements in me must be dire and awful. I don't experience that badness, but rather a positive desire to live and let live. Perhaps I can be that person who is, at heart, positive" (Rogers, 1961, p. 104).[3] Since the deepest levels of personality inevitably prove to be positive, the client does ultimately find true self-knowledge to be far more satisfying than painful. The resulting inner harmony is evidenced by feelings like "I've never been quite so close to myself," and by increased positive self-regard that is expressed through a quiet pleasure in being oneself (Rogers, 1961, p. 78; see also Rogers, 1951, pp. 72–83; 1959, pp. 212–221, 226–227; 1961, pp. 36, 63–64, 80, 85–87, 125–159, 185).

Except for the use of tape recordings and verbatim transcripts, aids to research that Rogers helped to pioneer, person-centered therapy differs from its predecessors by excluding formal procedures. There is no couch, no use of interpretation by the therapist, no investigation of the client's past, and no analysis of dreams. Positive therapeutic change is accomplished solely by establishing a constructive interpersonal relationship, which the client uses to recover the tendency toward actualization. For this to occur, the client must perceive the therapist as having three characteristics that Rogers regards as essential to any successful human relationship: genuineness, empathy, and unconditional positive regard.

Therapeutic Procedures. A constructive therapeutic relationship depends in part on the client perceiving the therapist as **genuine,** or in touch with his or her own inner experience and able to share it when appropriate. This does not mean that therapists should burden their clients with their own personal problems, or impulsively blurt out whatever may come to mind. It does imply that the therapist should reject defensive façades and professional jargon, maintain an openness to experience, and achieve congruence. This

---

[3]This bears some similarity to the Kellyan formulation of relaxing rigid personal constructs and adopting a more flexible view of oneself and others, as Rogers himself has noted (1961, pp. 132ff).

encourages a similar trusting genuineness on the part of the client, thereby helping to reduce the barriers to open and honest communication:

> To withhold one's self as a person and to deal with the [client] as an object does not have a high probability of being helpful. . . . It does not help to act calm and pleasant when actually I am angry and critical. It does not help to act as though I know the answers when I do not. It does not help . . . to try to maintain [any] façade, to act in one way on the surface when I am experiencing something quite different underneath. . . . [Instead,] I have found that the more that I can be genuine in the relationship, the more helpful it will be. This means that I need to be aware of my own feelings, in so far as possible . . . [and willing to express them]. (Rogers, 1961, pp. 16–17, 33, 47. See also Rogers, 1965; 1977, pp. 9–10; Rogers & Wood, 1974, pp. 226–229.)

In addition to genuineness, the therapist must also be perceived as **empathic** to the client's feelings and beliefs. Thus the therapist remains closely attuned to the client's verbal and nonverbal messages, including tones of voice and bodily movements, and concentrates on reflecting back the perceived meaning. For example, if a client observes that "for the first time in months I am not thinking about my problems, not actually working on them," the therapist might respond: "I get the impression you don't sort of sit down to work on 'my problems.' It isn't that feeling at all." If the therapist's view is accurate, the client is likely to reply: "Perhaps that *is* what I've been trying to say. I haven't realized it, but yes, that's how I *do* feel!" (Rogers, 1961, p. 78; 1977, p. 11). Conversely, disagreement by the client indicates a flaw in the therapist's understanding, rather than some form of resistance. Empathy serves as a powerful aid to healthy growth because it provides the client with a deep sense of being understood by a significant other, indicating that further self-exposure is very likely to be both safe and productive:

> In the emotional warmth of the relationship with the therapist, the client begins to experience a feeling of safety as he finds that whatever attitude he expresses is understood in almost the same way that he perceives it, and is accepted. . . . It is only as I *understand* the feelings and thoughts which seem so horrible to [the client,] or so weak, or so sentimental, or so bizarre . . . that [the client feels] really free to explore all the hidden nooks and frightening crannies of [his] inner and often buried experience. (Rogers, 1951, p. 41; 1961, p. 34. See also Rogers, 1959, pp. 210–211; 1961, pp. 18–19; 1965; 1980, pp. 137–163; Rogers & Wood, 1974, pp. 232–236.)

The therapist must also be perceived as demonstrating a nonjudgmental, nonpossessive respect and caring for the client's self-concept and feelings (the aforementioned quality of **unconditional positive regard**). "[This] is a caring enough about the person that you do not wish to interfere with his development, nor to use him for any self-aggrandizing goals of your own. Your satisfaction comes in having set him free to grow in his own fashion"

(Rogers, 1961, p. 84). Such unqualified acceptance enables the client to explore those feelings and values that were too threatening to admit to awareness, safe in the knowledge that they will not evoke criticism—or any form of judgment, for even "a positive evaluation is as threatening in the long run as a negative one, since to inform someone that he is good implies that you also have the right to tell him he is bad" (Rogers, 1961, p. 55). In one notable instance, Rogers sat quietly with a silent, schizophrenic client for long periods of time, indicating support and understanding through his physical presence yet not imposing any pressure to speak:

> To discover that it is *not* devastating to accept the positive feeling from another, that it does not necessarily end in hurt, that it actually "feels good" to have another person with you in your struggles to meet life—this may be one of the most profound learnings encountered by the individual, whether in therapy or not. (Rogers, 1961, p. 85. See also Rogers, Gendlin, Kiesler, & Truax, 1967, pp. 401–406; Rogers & Wood, 1974, pp. 229–232.)

Achieving unconditional positive regard, empathy, and genuineness is by no means an easy task, and the therapist is not expected to do so all of the time. But the frequent maintenance of these three qualities, duly perceived by the patient, is to Rogers necessary—and sufficient—for therapeutic progress to occur.

Encounter Groups. Becoming a fully functioning person is a lifelong quest. Therefore, even people who are relatively well-adjusted are likely to seek out ways of achieving further personal growth.

One popular method for meeting this need is the **encounter group** (or **T group**—for "training"), devised by Kurt Lewin and further developed by Rogers (1970/1973a). Perhaps a dozen people meet with one or two facilitators for a relatively brief period of time, often one weekend but sometimes a few weeks. The facilitator uses genuineness, empathy, and unconditional positive regard to establish a psychological climate of safety and trust (but no rules or planned procedures, hence the designation "facilitator" rather than "leader"). Thus the group members gradually reduce their defensive rigidities and distortions, bring out their true feelings toward each other and themselves, learn about their real impact on others, share deep emotional relationships with one another, and devise new goals and directions for themselves where appropriate. To Rogers, encounter groups fill a major void in our impersonal and technological society:

> The psychological need that draws people into encounter groups . . . is a hunger for something the person does not find in his work environment, in his church, certainly not in his school or college, and sadly enough, not even in modern family life. It is a hunger for relationships which are close and real; in which feelings and emotions can be spontaneously expressed without first being carefully censored or bottled up; where deep experiences—disappointments and joys—can be shared; where new ways of behaving can be risked

and tried out; where, in a word, he approaches the state where all is known and all accepted, and thus further growth becomes possible. (Rogers, 1970/1973a, p. 11. See also M. H. Hall, 1967c, p. 20; Rogers, 1977, pp. 143–185.)

While Rogers has found encounter groups to be generally successful in promoting personal growth, a cautionary note must be sounded regarding their use with relatively unskilled facilitators. Emotional sessions of such short duration may prove to be more than some members can handle, especially if there is little prior screening and more maladjusted persons are permitted to participate, resulting in psychological "casualties" of various kinds (Yalom & Lieberman, 1971).

Psychotherapy and Social Reform. As with several of the theorists discussed thus far, Rogers regards our society as very sick indeed. For example, he characterizes Watergate as blatant official contempt for the rights of the individual. The vast discrepancy in wealth between the "haves" and "have-nots" of the world sows the seeds of hatred, evidenced in part by terrorist groups who wreak their violence on innocent people. The resulting specter of nuclear war leaves humanity in mortal danger, teetering on the knife edge between survival and destruction. (See Rogers, 1961, pp. ix, 61; 1973b, p. 379; 1977, pp. 115–116, 255–260; Rogers, cited by Evans, 1975, p. 65.)

Rogers does conclude that we have achieved some significant social advances in just a few decades, such as improved civil rights and increased efforts toward population control. He also argues that the person-centered approach offers us the means for living together in harmony: rather than trying to seize and hold power and authority, the peoples of the world can treat one another with genuineness, empathy, and unconditional positive regard, and work together toward the common goal of helping to actualize humankind's benign potentials. (See Rogers, 1951, p. 224; 1972, pp. 71–72; 1977, pp. 115–140; 1982.)

Education

Since Rogers believes that genuineness, empathy, and unconditional positive regard are essential to any successful human relationship, he is highly critical of the authoritarian and coercive philosophy that pervades our educational system. All too often, the teacher assumes the mantle of power and directs the activities of passive, subservient students. Grading is based primarily on examinations, which require students to parrot back those specific facts that the teacher considers important. Pronounced distrust is evidenced by the teacher constantly checking up on the students' progress, and by the students' remaining on guard against trick exam questions and unfair grading practices. And there is a virtually total emphasis on thinking, with the emotional aspects of experience regarded as irrelevant and nonscholarly. The unfortunate result is that many potentially outstanding students develop negative attitudes toward further learning, which they perceive as an unpleasant obligation rather than as a golden opportunity. "Our schools are more damaging than helpful to personality development, and are a negative influence on creative thinking. They are primarily institutions for incarcerating or taking care of the young, to keep them out of the adult world" (Rogers, 1977, p. 256; see also Rogers, 1951, pp. 384–428; 1961, pp. 37, 273–313; 1969; 1977, pp. 69–89; 1980, pp. 263–335; Rogers, cited by Evans, 1975, pp. 38–48).

In contrast, the person-centered teacher (like the person-centered therapist) seeks to create a psychological climate that facilitates the students' inherent capacity to think and learn for themselves. Thus the teacher demonstrates empathy and unconditional positive regard for the students' feelings and interests, and genuineness concerning his or her own inner experience. Decision making is a shared process, with students helping to devise their own program of learning. Class periods are unstructured and devoted to free discussion, so that students may form and express their own opinions. The teacher serves as an optional resource, providing informed comments or suggested readings only when asked to do so. And grades are mutually agreed upon, with the student providing evidence as to the amount of personal and educational growth achieved during the course. This primarily self-directed approach enables students to discover and develop those directions that are truly rewarding to them, and to enjoy the process of learning, rather than forcing them to ingest irrelevant and uninteresting details prescribed by an externally imposed curriculum. (See Rogers, 1969; 1983.)

The person-centered approach to education often arouses initial resistance and hostility, since it threatens those who are used to being told what to do. "Students who have been clamoring for freedom are definitely frightened when they realize that it also means responsibility." However, Rogers concludes that this approach typically leads to more rapid and more pervasive learning at all educational levels—and to such positive student evaluations as "I was surprised to find out how well I can study and learn when I'm not forced to do it," "It was like I was an adult—not supervised and guided all the time," and "I've never read so much in my life" (Rogers, 1977, pp. 76–78).

Rogerian Theory and Empirical Research

Rogers is one of the few psychotherapists discussed thus far with a consuming interest in empirical research, which he attributes to his need to make sense and order out of psychological phenomena. He shares Allport's concern that psychologists are far too fearful and defensive about looking unscientific, so they concentrate on methodologically precise but trivial research topics. Instead he argues that a truly human science must deal with subjective experience, and willingly pursue intuitive hunches and innovative directions—especially a fledgling discipline like psychology, where careful observation and creative thought are as yet more feasible than the exact measurement typical of more mature sciences.

Like Kelly, therefore, Rogers cautions that any theory must be regarded as expendable in the light of new discoveries. "If a theory could be seen for what it is—a fallible, changing attempt to construct a network of gossamer threads which will contain the solid facts—then a theory would serve as it should, as a stimulus to further creative thinking" (Rogers, 1959, p. 191; see also M. H. Hall, 1967c, pp. 20–21; Rogers, 1959, pp. 188–190; Rogers, cited by Evans, 1975, pp. 88–90; Rogers & Skinner, 1956).

EVALUATION

Criticisms and Controversies

Like Adler, Rogers has been criticized for an overly optimistic and simplified view of human nature. Helping to actualize one's innermost potentials is desirable only if the deepest levels of personality are healthy and constructive. Yet it seems doubtful that an inherently peaceful and cooperative species would so frequently engage in war, crime, and other destructive behaviors solely because of introjected, pathological conditions of worth.

Psychotherapists of different theoretical persuasions do not agree that it is preferable to dispense with interpretations and rely wholly on genuineness, empathy, and unconditional positive regard. Others warn that genuineness might well be damaging in some instances, as by telling a narcissistic but vulnerable client that such constant self-preoccupation is causing the therapist to feel bored and angry (Kahn, 1985, p. 901). Save for a few brief references, Rogers ignores important similarities between his theory and those of Horney, Sullivan, and Jung. And in spite of Rogers's contention that theories are readily expendable in the light of new discoveries, his own approach has changed relatively little in the past twenty years—except perhaps for a greater acceptance of unconscious processes, which raises doubts as to the validity of defining the self-concept as entirely available to awareness and measuring it through the client's self-reports.

Empirical Research

A substantial amount of research on person-centered theory has dealt with the characteristics of genuineness, empathy, and unconditional positive regard. These studies have used rating scales of and by psychotherapists, and analyses of transcripts of tape-recorded therapy sessions (of course, with the client's prior permission). As is common in the challenging field of psychotherapy research, the results have been equivocal: numerous studies have found these variables to be significantly related to constructive change, while other findings have been negative. For example, some studies suggest that unconditional positive regard is *not* sufficient for people to become well-adjusted; specific training and modeling of the desired behaviors are also necessary. (See for example Barrett-Lennard, 1979; Bergin & Suinn, 1975, pp. 514–516; Epstein, 1980, pp. 122–127; Rogers, 1961, pp. 41–50; Rogers & Dymond, 1954; Rogers et al., 1967; Wexler & Rice, 1974.)

Another popular research topic is the self-concept, which can readily be investigated through direct inquiry since it is defined as entirely available to awareness. One finding of interest in this area is that improvement during psychotherapy is usually related to increased self-acceptance, and that this self-acceptance also facilitates a greater acceptance of other people. It also appears that the self-concept is a more complicated construct than might be apparent. For example, some self-descriptions may apply only under certain circumstances (e.g., "I'm a patient father except when I have a headache"). The social self-concept, or how we think others perceive us, may well differ from the personal self-concept, or how we see ourselves. Different social self-concepts may be used when dealing with different individuals or groups. And there are also ideal personal and social self-concepts, or what one wishes to be like and how one would like to be perceived by others. (See for example Rogers, 1961, pp. 199–270; Wylie, 1974; 1979; 1984.)

Contributions

Rogers was a sensitive and effective psychotherapist, and client-centered therapy has achieved considerable popularity. He was among the first to unveil the mysteries of the therapy session by using tape recordings and publishing verbatim transcripts, thereby stimulating a substantial amount of empirical research and statistical analyses. Rogers's conception of the psychotherapist as one who provides a psychological climate conducive to self-directed personal growth, rather than as an expert who offers profound interpretations, represents an innovative departure from neo-Freudian techniques. The self has proved to be an important, widely studied construct. In particular, Rogers's stress on healthy inner potentials stands as a major alternative (or "third force") to psychoanalysis (with its emphasis on illicit aspects of personality) and behaviorism (which concentrates on actual behaviors, as we will see in Chapter 15).

Finally, Rogers has offered a challenging and provocative extension of the democratic principles on which our society is based. Rather than being directed by some expert who presumes to know what is best for us (such as a teacher, parent, or psychotherapist), we are all better advised to treat one another as equals and derive our satisfactions from freeing others to pursue their own particular path toward actualization. Not surprisingly, this approach has proved more than a little threatening to those accustomed to striving for higher positions in the social pecking order and passing judgment on others. The expert authority is an idea that is deeply ingrained in most of us, and has advantages as well as disadvantages. And it may well be possible to carry the principle of equality too far, as when children need the security of dependency and inequality to their parents in order to explore and learn. Yet to those who believe in democracy in its truest sense, the emphasis of person-centered theory on self-direction and the legitimacy of one's own feelings may well represent Rogers's most significant contribution.

Suggested Reading

Rogerian theory is clearly described in *On Becoming a Person* (1961) and *Carl Rogers on Personal Power* (1977). A rather tedious but thorough discussion of person-centered definitions and theory may be found in an article (Rogers, 1959). Rogers's views on education are presented in *Freedom to Learn* (1969), and his thoughts on encounter groups in *Carl Rogers on Encounter Groups* (1970/1973a).

■ SUMMARY

1. THE BASIC NATURE OF HUMAN BEINGS. *Actualization:* The primary motive underlying all human behavior is an innate tendency to develop our constructive, healthy capacities (actualization). Among the growth-oriented aspects of the actualizing tendency are creativity, curiosity, and the willingness to undergo even painful learning experiences in order to become more effective and independent. *The Need for Positive Regard:* Pathogenic parental behaviors may cause us to behave in ways that belie our benign inner nature. This is likely to happen because we also have a powerful need for positive regard, especially from such significant others as our parents. Rogers also emphasizes that we are oriented toward future goals, rather than driven by prior causes.

2. THE STRUCTURE OF PERSONALITY. *Experience and the Organismic Valuing Process:* Each of us exists at the center of our own private, ever-changing world of inner experience. Experience is largely nonconscious, though it is potentially available to awareness. It includes an innate ability to value positively (or negatively) that which we perceive as actualizing (or nonactualizing), which is called the organismic valuing process. Thus the nonconscious aspects of experience are trustworthy and invaluable additions to our conscious thoughts and plans, and only we can know what is good for us (actualizing) and what is not. *The Self-Concept (Self) and Self-Actualization:* Personality also includes a conscious conception of oneself as a separate and distinct entity. Some of the actualizing tendency is directed toward an effort to realize the goals and abilities represented by this self-concept. If significant others make their positive regard conditional on meeting their standards, the child will try to preserve their love by introjecting these standards into the self-concept and behaving accordingly. Such introjected conditions of worth supersede the innate organismic valuing process as an inner guide to behavior. This results in a painful inner schism, since the conscious choices and goals fail to actualize the individual's true needs and potentials. *Defense:* This incongruence leads to defensive attempts to protect the self-concept by distorting

or denying the real needs and feelings, furthering the schism between the actualizing and self-actualizing tendencies.

3. THE DEVELOPMENT OF PERSONALITY. Rogers posits no specific developmental stages, criteria, or types. Instead he emphasizes the desirability of treating children with unconditional positive regard, and enumerates various characteristics that define the optimally adjusted ("fully functioning") person.

4. FURTHER APPLICATIONS. *Psychopathology:* The self-concept of the more neurotic person includes more powerful conditions of worth. So the sufferer makes greater efforts to achieve positive self-regard by satisfying these introjected standards (i.e., to self-actualize), resulting in greater failures to actualize the true inner needs. To make matters worse, the organismic needs and values become anxiety-provoking threats to the incongruent self-concept. Psychosis is similar to neurosis, but involves even more extreme forms of defense. For the most part, however, Rogers prefers to avoid formal diagnostic labels. *Psychotherapy:* Positive therapeutic change is accomplished solely by establishing a constructive interpersonal relationship between therapist and client. A climate conducive to self-directed personal growth is created through the use of genuineness, empathy, and unconditional positive regard. Genuineness encourages a similar trusting genuineness on the part of the client; empathy provides the client with a deep sense of being understood, indicating that further self-revelations are likely to be both safe and productive; and unconditional positive regard provides an unqualified acceptance that enables the client to explore those feelings and beliefs that were too threatening to admit to awareness. *Education:* Whatever the area of application, Rogerian principles remain essentially the same. Genuineness, empathy, and unconditional positive regard are also advisable in the educational setting, as by devising unstructured classes that involve shared decision making.

5. EVALUATION. Rogers has been criticized for an overly optimistic and simplified view of human nature, ignoring important similarities between his theoretical constructs and those of such predecessors as Horney and Sullivan, failing to update and revise his theory, relying solely on genuineness and empathy and unconditional positive regard to produce positive therapeutic change, and devoting insufficient attention to the unconscious aspects of the self-concept. Yet he is also credited with introducing an important form of psychotherapy, stimulating a great deal of empirical research, helping to establish a major theoretical alternative to psychoanalysis and behaviorism, and championing a truly democratic acceptance of each person's own inner feelings and direction in life.

STUDY QUESTIONS

1. Consider once again the case history discussed throughout the Appendix (e.g., Chapter 2, question 6; Chapter 4, questions 2 and 6a; Chapter 5, questions 1, 4b, and 5; Chapter 6, questions 3d and 4; Chapter 7, question

7a; Chapter 8, question 7; Chapter 9, question 10; Chapter 11, question 1). Use this case history to illustrate each of the following Rogerian concepts: (a) The need for positive regard. (b) Introjected conditions of worth. (c) Incongruence between the actualizing and self-actualizing tendencies. (d) Confusion and anxiety resulting from the feeling that "I don't really know myself."

2. Rogers argues that we are motivated to develop and mature by healthy innate tendencies. "The child will actualize himself [as by learning to walk], in spite of the painful experiences in so doing." Do you agree or disagree? Why?

3. (a) Why did Rogers define the self-concept as entirely conscious? (b) Do you agree or disagree? Why?

4. What is the difference between limiting criticism of a child to specific undesirable behaviors and using conditional positive regard? Illustrate with an example.

5. Rogers is sharply critical of typical methods of childbirth, preferring instead the Leboyer technique. Do you agree or disagree? Why?

6. Rogers points out that highly creative individuals trust their inner experience in spite of public criticism. "It was as though [El Greco] could say, 'good artists do not paint like this, but *I* paint like this'" How can one differentiate between healthy self-trust such as this and an unhealthy, stubborn refusal to accept criticism?

7. According to Rogers, genuineness, empathy, and unconditional positive regard are essential to any successful human relationship. How would you evaluate each of the following on these characteristics? (a) The parents of the man whose case history is discussed in question 1, above. (b) Your best friend. (c) Freud, during a therapy session.

8. According to Rogers, "[even] a positive evaluation is as threatening in the long run as a negative one, since to inform someone that he is good implies that you also have the right to tell him he is bad." Do you agree or disagree? Why?

9. Consider the following sentence, taken from the section dealing with Rogers's criticisms of our educational system: "There is a virtually total emphasis on thinking, with the emotional aspects of experience regarded as irrelevant and nonscholarly." Is this true of the study questions and Appendix in this book?

10. Who might Rogers have had in mind when he argued that any theory must be regarded as expendable in the light of new discoveries?

ABRAHAM H. MASLOW
Self-Actualization Theory (II)

One day shortly after the bombing of Pearl Harbor, at age thirty-three, Abe Maslow witnessed a pathetic and beggarly civilian parade—one that seemed only to emphasize the futility and tragic waste of war. With tears streaming down his face, he made a firm vow: to prove that the human race is capable of something grander than hate and destructiveness, and to do so by studying the psychologically healthiest people that he could find (M. H. Hall, 1968a, pp. 54–55).

BIOGRAPHICAL SKETCH

Abraham H. Maslow was born on April 1, 1908, in Brooklyn, New York. His parents were uneducated Jewish immigrants from Russia; his father owned a barrel manufacturing company. Maslow's childhood was both economically and socially deprived, and he was later to compare his position in a non-Jewish neighborhood to that of the first black in an all-white school (M. H. Hall, 1968a, p. 37). Isolated and unhappy, he grew up in the company of libraries and books rather than friends.

Maslow originally enrolled at Cornell University but soon transferred to the University of Wisconsin, primarily because its catalog advertised the presence of various prominent scientists. To his considerable disappointment, he found that these notables were only visiting professors who had long since departed. Yet he stayed to earn not only his bachelor's degree, but also his Ph.D. in psychology in 1934. Maslow's doctoral dissertation dealt with the sexual behavior of monkeys, under the supervision of Harry Harlow. His professors at Wisconsin also provided him with personal advice and instruction in the social amenities he had neglected, such as the fine art of buying a suit (M. H. Hall, 1968a, p. 37). Maslow married Bertha Goodman, his high school sweetheart, while still a twenty-year-old undergraduate. The marriage proved to be very happy and successful, and the Maslows were to have two daughters.

At first an ardent behaviorist, Maslow's firsthand experience with his children quickly convinced him to abandon this approach as inadequate. In 1937 he accepted a position at Brooklyn College, where he was to remain for some fifteen years. During this time he furthered his knowledge by obtaining personal interviews with such noted theorists as Adler, Fromm, and Horney, underwent psychoanalysis, and experienced the aforementioned

399

profound reaction to World War II. In 1951 Maslow moved to Brandeis University, and became perhaps the foremost exponent of humanistic personality theory. In addition to his academic endeavors, he also spent more than ten years practicing brief, nonanalytic psychotherapy.

Maslow's writings consist of some six books and numerous articles in psychological journals, and his honors include election to the presidency of the American Psychological Association in 1967. Long troubled by heart problems, Abe Maslow died of a heart attack on June 8, 1970.

THE BASIC NATURE OF HUMAN BEINGS

For the most part, Maslow shares Rogers's optimistic view of human nature. He regards our innate (**instinctoid**) tendencies as predominantly healthy and benign, and he emphatically affirms our inherent capacity for constructive growth, honesty, kindness, generosity, and love. Yet Maslow also agrees with Erikson that these "instinct-remnants" are only very weak fragments, easily overwhelmed by the far more powerful forces of learning and culture. "The human needs . . . are weak and feeble rather than unequivocal and unmistakable; they whisper rather than shout. And the whisper is easily drowned out" (Maslow, 1970b, p. 276; see also Maslow, 1965; 1968, pp. 164, 171, 191; 1970b, pp. ix, xvii–xix, 27–28, 77–95, 103).

As a result, a pathogenic environment can easily inhibit our positive potentials and evoke hatred, destructiveness, and self-defeating behavior. Thus Maslow prefers a more eclectic approach to personality, and advises psychologists to guard against excessive theoretical optimism by acquiring a thorough knowledge of Freudian psychoanalysis:

> [My goal is] to integrate into a single theoretical structure the partial truths I [see] in Freud, Adler, Jung, . . . Fromm, Horney, [and others]. . . . Freud is still required reading for the humanistic psychologist . . . [yet] it is as if [he] supplied to us the sick half of psychology, and we must now fill it out with the healthy half. . . . [Thus] it is already possible to reject firmly the despairing belief that human nature is ultimately and basically depraved and evil, . . . [and to conclude that the striving toward health] must by now be accepted beyond question as a widespread and perhaps universal human tendency. (Maslow, 1968, p. 5; 1970b, pp. xi–xiii. See also Maslow, 1968, pp. vii, 3–8, 48; 1966/1969; 1970b, pp. ix–xxvii, 117–129; 1971, pp. 4, 32.)

Deficiency and Growth Motives

Like Allport and Rogers, Maslow espouses a dualistic theory of motivation.

Deficiency Motives.   Some of our instinctoid impulses aim toward the reduction of such drives as hunger, thirst, safety, and obtaining love and esteem from others. These **deficiency motives** (**deficit motives, D-motives**) are possessed by all human beings, and involve crucial lacks within us that must be filled through appropriate external objects or people.

Growth Motives. In contrast to the deficiency motives, **growth motives (being motives, B-motives)** are relatively independent of the environment and are unique to the individual. These needs include pleasurable drive increases (e.g., curiosity), the unselfish and nonpossessive giving of love to others, and the development and fulfillment of one's own inner potentials and capacities. Whereas deficiency motives press toward their own elimination, growth motives actually gain in intensity through gratification:

> Growth is, *in itself,* a rewarding and exciting process. [Examples include] the fulfilling of yearnings and ambitions, like that of being a good doctor; the acquisition of admired skills, like playing the violin or being a good carpenter; the steady increase of understanding about people or about the universe, or about oneself; the development of creativeness in whatever field; or, most important, simply the ambition to be a good human being. . . . It is simply inaccurate to speak in such instances of tension-reduction, implying thereby the getting rid of an annoying state. For these states are not annoying. (Maslow, 1968, pp. 29–31. See also Maslow, 1968, pp. 21–43.)

Although deficiency needs serve such essential objectives as self-preservation, growth motives tend to represent a more pleasurable, higher, and healthier level of functioning. "Satisfying deficiencies avoids illness; growth satisfactions produce positive health . . . [like the] difference between fending off threat or attack, and positive triumph and achievement" (Maslow, 1968, p. 32). Thus Freud's emphasis on drive reduction is a direct consequence of studying only sick people, who have good reason to fear (and repress) their impulses because they handle them so poorly. In contrast, healthy individuals welcome drive increases because they signal potential satisfaction. As in Murray's theory, they may well protest that "the trouble with eating is that it kills my appetite" (Maslow, 1968, p. 28).

The Complexity of Human Motives. Unlike Murray, Maslow prefers not to list specific human needs. His reason is that our motives are so complicated and interrelated, and our behavior is so overdetermined, that it is usually impossible to explain personality in terms of separate and distinct drives.

For example, making love may be due to needs for sex, power, and to reaffirm one's masculinity or femininity. Or a hysterically paralyzed arm may fulfill simultaneous wishes for revenge, pity, and attention. Or eating may not only satisfy the hunger need, but also offer solace for an unrequited love. (See Maslow, 1970b, pp. 22–26, 35–58.) Furthermore, Maslow argues that the various human needs differ considerably in their level of prominence: some remain relatively unimportant, and unnoticed, until others have at least to some extent been satisfied. He therefore favors a general, **hierarchical** model of human motivation. (See Figure 13.1.)

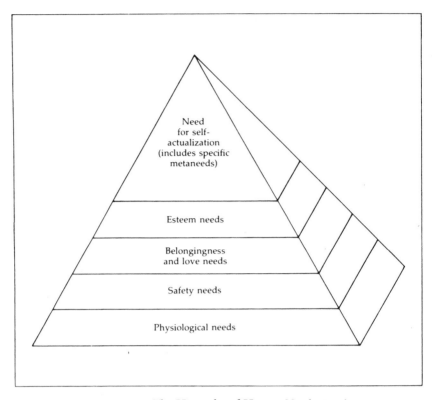

FIGURE 13.1. The Hierarchy of Human Needs (Maslow).

The Hierarchy of Human Needs

The Physiological Needs. If some unfortunate individual were unable to satisfy any of the basic human needs, he or she would be exclusively concerned with the bottom level of the hierarchy: the **physiological needs,** including hunger, thirst, sex, oxygen, sleep, and the elimination of bodily wastes. For example, a starving person cares very little about writing majestic poetry, buying an impressive-looking car, finding a sweetheart, or carefully avoiding the possibility of injury—or anything other than the overriding goal of obtaining food. Many of the physiological needs are deficiencies, but not all; among the exceptions are sexual arousal, elimination, and sleep. (See Maslow, 1968, p. 27; 1970b, pp. 35–38.)

The Safety Needs. As one's physiological needs become increasingly satisfied, the next level in the hierarchy gradually emerges as a motivator. These **safety needs** involve the quest for an environment that is stable, predictable, and free from anxiety and chaos.

For example, a young child may seek reassurance and protection after being frightened by a sudden loud noise (or an injury, illness, or parental quarrel). Or an adult in the grip of safety needs may pursue a tenured professorship, amass a substantial savings account, purchase extensive insurance against various potential disasters, or constantly prefer the familiar and routine to the unknown. Knowledge is often an effective way to satisfy these needs, as with the child who overcomes a fear of lightning by learning how unlikely it is to strike (and how to guard against it).

The safety needs help us avoid catastrophic pain and injury. But they can also become so powerful as to preclude further personal development, as when people willingly submit to dictatorial rule during periods of war or rampant crime in order to gain a measure of security. "In the choice between giving up safety or giving up growth, safety will ordinarily win out" (Maslow, 1968, p. 49; see also Maslow, 1968, pp. 46–47, 54; 1970b, pp. 39–43).

The Belongingness and Love Needs. Once the physiological and safety needs have been more or less satisfied, the **belongingness and love needs** come to the forefront as motivators. Thus the individual now hungers for affectionate relationships with friends, a sweetheart or spouse, and/or offspring.

To Maslow, love consists of feelings of tenderness, affection, and elation; yearnings for the loved one; and (often) intense sexual arousal. Our hunger to receive such love from others is a relatively selfish deficiency need (**D-love**), one that often involves anxious and manipulative efforts to win the loved one's affection. Yet this need must be satisfied in order for us to develop growth-oriented or "being" love (**B-love**), which is nonpossessive, unconditional, giving, and richer and more enjoyable than D-love. B-love is also denoted by honesty and naturalness, including a willingness to reveal one's weaknesses as well as strengths, and by cooperation and respect for the loved one's needs and individuality. (See Maslow, 1968, pp. 41–43; 1970b, pp. 43–45, 182–183, 250, 275–276.) Like Rogers, Maslow concludes that the common inability to satisfy the love and belongingness needs in our impersonal society is largely responsible for the widespread interest in encounter groups.

The Esteem Needs. In accordance with such theorists as Adler, Rogers, Fromm, and Erikson, Maslow attributes considerable importance to our need for superiority and respect. Virtually everyone strives for self-confidence and mastery, and to obtain recognition and appreciation from others. However, these **esteem needs** normally act as motivators only if the three lower types have been satisfied to some degree. Maslow cautions that true self-esteem is based on real competence and significant achievement, rather than external fame and unwarranted adulation (a theme well illustrated by Ayn Rand's classic novel *The Fountainhead*).

The Need for Self-Actualization. The highest form of need is **self-actualization,** which consists of discovering and fulfilling one's own innate potentials and capacities:

Self-actualization is idiosyncratic, since every person is different. . . . The individual [must do] what *he*, individually, is fitted for. A musician must make music, an artist must paint, a poet must write, if he is to be ultimately at peace with himself. What a man *can* be, he *must* be. (Maslow, 1968, p. 33; 1970b, p. 46. See also Maslow, 1968, pp. 7, 25; 1970b, pp. 47, 150.)

Thus self-actualization is a growth motive similar to actualization in Rogerian theory, except that it does not become important (or even noticeable) until the physiological, safety, love, and esteem needs have been at least partially satisfied. Like Jungian individuation, therefore, self-actualization is prominent only in older people. The young are more concerned with issues like education, identity, love, and work, which Maslow regards as only *"preparing* to live." In fact, the specific needs of those rare individuals who achieve this highest level differ considerably in quality from the lower needs. "It seems probable that we must construct a profoundly different psychology of motivation for self-actualizing people" (Maslow, 1970b, p. 159; see also Maslow, 1964/1970a, pp. 91–96; 1970b, pp. xx, 134–135; 1971, pp. 43–44, 192–195, 299–340).

Maslow therefore refers to the needs of self-actualizing individuals as **metaneeds (metamotives, B-values)**, among which are a love of beauty, truth, goodness, justice, and usefulness. And he devotes considerable attention to the characteristics of self-actualizing individuals, as we will see in a subsequent section.

Characteristics of Higher and Lower Needs. Maslow views the higher needs as distinctively human. "We share the need for food with all living things, the need for love with (perhaps) the higher apes, [and] the need for self-actualization with [no other species]" (Maslow, 1970b, p. 98; see also Maslow, 1968, p. 31; 1970b, pp. 67, 97–104).

The emergence of a higher need reflects a greater degree of psychological health, somewhat like reaching a more advanced developmental stage in Eriksonian or Freudian theory, and its satisfaction is valued far more highly by the individual than fulfilling a lower need. Yet the higher needs are also less urgent and tangible, they are not necessary for survival, and they are more easily blocked by a pathogenic environment. For these reasons, even recognizing the existence of these needs represents a considerable achievement. Maslow estimates that the average American citizen has satisfied perhaps 85 percent of the physiological needs and 70 percent of the safety needs, but only 50 percent of the love needs, 40 percent of the esteem needs, and 10 percent of the need for self-actualization (1970b, p. 54). Thus to Maslow, as to most personality theorists, achieving true self-knowledge is a difficult—albeit essential—undertaking.

The hierarchy of needs is presumed to apply to most people, though the specific form of satisfaction often varies in different cultures. Members of a primitive tribe may gain esteem by becoming great hunters, whereas those in a technological society are more likely to gratify these needs by

B-cognition	A special, and essentially indescribable, form of thinking common during peak experiences. B-cognition is nonjudgmental, does not aim toward the fulfillment of some motive, and emphasizes the unity of oneself and the cosmos.
B-love	An unselfish and nonpossessive giving of love and affection to another person. A growth motive, richer and more enjoyable than D-love.
D-cognition	A routine and self-preservative form of thinking oriented toward the satisfaction of deficiency motives. D-cognition is judgmental, and emphasizes the separateness of oneself and the various objects in the environment.
D-love	The selfish need to receive love and affection from others. A deficiency motive, prerequisite to the emergence of B-love.
Deficiency motive (deficit motive, D-motive)	The need to reduce a drive such as hunger, thirst, or D-love through appropriate external objects or individuals, thereby filling some crucial lack within the organism. Deficiency motives are common to all human beings.
Eupsychian	As psychologically healthful as possible.
Growth motive (being motive, B-motive)	The need to develop and fulfill one's inner potentials and capacities, including the enjoyment of pleasurable drive increases and the giving of B-love to others. Growth motives are relatively independent of the environment and unique to the individual.
Hierarchy of (instinctoid) needs	A model of motivation wherein certain human needs usually do not become important, or even noticeable, until other lower-order needs have to some extent been satisfied. Includes five levels of needs: physiological (lowest), safety, love, esteem, and self-actualization (highest).
Instinctoid need	An inborn but very weak instinctual impulse that represents the very essence of human nature, but is easily overwhelmed by the far more powerful forces of learning and culture. The frustration of an instinctoid need usually contributes to psychopathology, while its satisfaction normally facilitates healthy psychological development.
Metaneeds (metamotives, B-values)	The atypical, nonhierarchical needs of those rare individuals who have achieved self-actualization. Metaneeds include the love of beauty, truth, goodness, justice, and usefulness.
Metapathology	Occurs when an individual has largely gratified the four lowest need levels, but cannot satisfy his or her metamotives and achieve self-actualization. The highest form of psychopathology.

continued

Peak experience	A mystical, transcendent, awesome, episodic, and essentially indescribable experience that represents the highest and healthiest form of human functioning. Somewhat similar to numinosum in Jungian theory.
Self-actualization (full humanness)	The development and fulfillment of one's own inherent potentials and capacities; the highest and most pleasurable need of all, but also the most difficult to recognize and satisfy. A growth motive, similar to actualization in Rogerian theory.

advancing to an executive position. However, Maslow does allow for a variety of exceptions. Some people regard esteem as more important than love, while others accord creativity the highest status of all. Or the higher needs may sometimes emerge after the lower ones have been severely frustrated, rather than gratified (e.g., the displacement of sexual needs onto artistic endeavors). Nevertheless, the easiest way to release us from the dominance of our lower and more selfish needs (and to promote healthy psychological development) is by satisfying them. (See Maslow, 1970b, pp. 51–53, 59–60.)

The Unconscious and Teleology

Since our weak instinctoid needs are so easily obscured by environmental influences, they readily assume the status of unconscious processes. "[There is a] tremendous mass of evidence that indicates the crucial importance of unconscious motivation. . . . The basic needs are often largely unconscious. . . . [Thus a sound] theory cannot possibly afford to neglect the unconscious life" (Maslow, 1970b, pp. 22, 54; see also Maslow, 1968, pp. 5, 196; 1970b, pp. 27, 270, 273; 1971, pp. 114, 173). The unconscious also includes memories of our more shameful actions, and such important positive potentials as love, creativity, humor, goodness, and joy.

In contrast to Freud's emphasis on causality, Maslow stresses the teleological goals toward which we strive. "No theory of psychology will ever be complete which does not centrally incorporate the concept that man has his future within him, dynamically active at the present moment" (Maslow, 1968, p. 15).

THE STRUCTURE OF PERSONALITY

Maslow differs markedly from Freud, Sullivan, and Erikson by rejecting the idea of specific structural or zonal constructs, an approach he characterizes as immature and even mildly pathological. "There is no such entity as a need of the stomach or mouth, or a genital need. There is only a need of the individual" (Maslow, 1970b, p. 19; see also pp. ix, xi, 20). But Maslow does accept the existence of such Freudian defense mechanisms as repression, projection, reaction formation, and rationalization:

> Freud's greatest discovery is that *the* great cause of much psychological illness is the fear of knowledge of oneself—of one's emotions, impulses, memories, capacities, potentialities, of one's destiny. . . . If the psychoanalytic literature has taught us nothing else, it has taught us that repression is not a good way of solving problems. (Maslow, 1968, p. 60; 1971, p. 49. See also Maslow, 1968, pp. 66–67, 191; 1964/1970a, p. 41; 1970b, pp. 211, 220; 1971, pp. 29, 37.)

Maslow also favors an idea similar to one devised (albeit later abandoned) by Fromm, that of a humanistic as well as an introjected conscience. The former is intrinsic (innate), like the Rogerian organismic valuing process, and troubles us whenever we behave in ways that are contrary to our inner nature:

> The only way we can ever know what is right for us is that it feels better subjectively than any alternative. . . . The born painter who sells stockings instead, the intelligent man who lives a stupid life, the man who sees the truth and keeps his mouth shut, the coward who gives up his manliness, all these people perceive in a deep way that they have done wrong to themselves and despise themselves for it. (Maslow, 1968, pp. 7, 45. See also Maslow, 1968, pp. 121, 194–195; 1971, pp. 46–47, 184, 338–339.)

The latter form of conscience represents introjected parental standards, which may well clash with the individual's true organismic needs and values. Thus, like Horney and Rogers, Maslow concludes that every growing child faces a crucial fork in the developmental road: the healthy choice of heeding its own inner guidelines, or the pathological (yet probably inevitable) alternative of sacrificing its true potentials in order to conform to the standards of the all-important parents (Maslow, 1968, pp. 51–52).

THE DEVELOPMENT OF PERSONALITY

Whereas Freud contends that the child must be forced against its will toward maturity, Maslow argues that healthy children actively seek to gain new skills and satisfy their growth motives. Once they have received enough need satisfaction appropriate to a given developmental level or stage, they become bored with these old delights and eagerly proceed to higher and more complicated ones. "Given sufficient gratification, free choice, and lack of threat, [the child] 'grows' out of the oral stage and renounces it himself. He doesn't have to be 'kicked upstairs'" (Maslow, 1968, p. 56 n. 4; see also pp. 23–24, 46, 49–50, 55). For example, the infant ready to be weaned willingly and enthusiastically prefers solid to liquid food. Thus personality development will proceed normally so long as children are given the opportunity to heed their own inner guidelines and potentials, rather than having their judgment and self-trust undermined by excessive external pressures and controls:

> A priori plans for the child, ambitions for it, prepared roles, even hopes that it will become this or that . . . represent demands upon the child that it become what the parent has already decided it *should* become. Such a baby is born into an invisible straitjacket. (Maslow, 1970b, pp. xxiv–xxv. See also Maslow, 1970b, pp. 276–277.)

However, Maslow cautions that overpermissiveness also has undesirable consequences. The naïve and inexperienced child can hardly be expected to make the correct choice in every instance, and too much freedom may well be interpreted as neglect and lack of love. Some rules and training are necessary to help the child avoid costly errors in living, provide a welcome sense of safety and structure in an otherwise confusing world, and prevent the development of an overly selfish and (in Adlerian terms) pampered style of life. Furthermore, a certain amount of frustration serves to strengthen the growing personality. "The person who hasn't conquered, withstood, and overcome continues to feel doubtful that he *could.* . . . [Thus] grief and pain are sometimes necessary for the growth of the person" (Maslow, 1968, pp. 4, 8; see also Maslow, 1968, p. 119; 1970b, pp. 40–41, 71, 87, 121–122). For the most part, however, satisfying the child's various needs is the best way to promote healthy personality development.

The Self-Actualizing (Fully Human) Person

As we have seen, Maslow shares Allport's and Rogers's interest in defining optimal psychological adjustment. He has therefore studied those rare individuals whom he regards as having achieved the highest level of need gratification, self-actualization (or "full humanness"), using a relatively small sample of both living persons and such historical personages as Thomas Jefferson, Albert Einstein, Eleanor Roosevelt, Jane Addams, William James, Albert Schweitzer, and Baruch Spinoza. (See Maslow, 1968, pp. 26, 71–114, 135–145, 153–160; 1970b, pp. 149–180; 1971, pp. 28–30, 41–53, 183–184, 280, 299–340).

Although self-actualizers are unique in many ways, they also tend to share the following characteristics:

More Accurate Perception of Reality. Self-actualizing people are more free of unwarranted optimism, pessimism, and other defensive distortions of reality. They are able to evaluate people, events, ideas, and future trends more accurately.

Greater Acceptance of Self and Others. Self-actualizers are more tolerant of human frailty, and less judgmental of themselves and others. They are therefore relatively free of shame and anxiety, though they do feel guilty about any personal shortcomings that they could (but have not) overcome.

Greater Spontaneity and Self-Knowledge. Self-actualizing individuals are more spontaneous and natural in their behavior, and they better comprehend their true motives, emotions, abilities, and potentials. They are guided primarily by their own codes of ethics, often with the result that they feel much like aliens in a foreign land—and are difficult for most other people to understand.

Greater Problem Centering. Self-actualizers tend to be keenly interested in external problems, and relatively unconcerned with introspection. They normally have some consuming mission in life that occupies much of their energy, often involving philosophical or ethical issues. The corresponding lack of worry over minor details makes life easier not only for themselves, but for their associates as well. Yet they are also devoted to excellence, and seek to accomplish their goals as well as is humanly possible.

Greater Need for Privacy. Self-actualizers prefer a greater amount of privacy and solitude. This healthy detachment is due in part to their tendency to rely on their own feelings and values, resulting in less concern for the opinions of others. Yet it is often resented by those who mistake it for snobbishness, unfriendliness, or hostility.

Greater Autonomy and Resistance to Enculturation. Self-actualizers are motivated by the need to fulfill their own inner potentials, rather than by the desire for external rewards or possessions. They are therefore relatively independent of other people and the environment. Since their needs for love and esteem are largely satisfied, they are less likely to manipulate others for selfish purposes or to fear being disappointed by them. Self-actualizers are also less indoctrinated by the prevailing standards of the imperfect society in which they live, and they avoid any popular styles of dress or forms of entertainment that run counter to their personal criteria:

> [Self-actualizing individuals] taught me to see as profoundly sick, abnormal, or weak what I had always taken for granted as humanly normal: namely that too many people do not make up their own minds, but have their minds made up for them by salesmen, advertisers, parents, propagandists, TV, newspapers, and so on. (Maslow, 1970b, p. 161. See also Maslow, 1968, pp. 11–12, 34–37; 1970b, pp. 172, 177.)

Greater Freshness of Appreciation and Richness of Emotional Response. Need satisfactions and happiness are always episodic. Any goal that we may achieve, such as job success, marriage, children, or a new car, is all too easily taken for granted once the novelty has worn off. Self-actualizers live richer and more fulfilling lives because they cherish those blessings they have already received, and appreciate again and again the wonders of our existence:

> [There is a] widespread tendency to undervalue one's already achieved need-gratifications, or even to devalue them and throw them away. Self-actualizing persons are relatively exempted from this profound source of human unhappiness. . . . For such a person, any sunset may be as beautiful as the first one, any flower may be of breath-taking loveliness. . . . The thousandth baby he sees is just as miraculous a product as the first one he saw. He remains as convinced of his luck in marriage thirty years after [it], and is as surprised by his wife's beauty when she is sixty as he was forty years before. (Maslow, 1970b, pp. xxi, 163. See also Maslow, 1970b, pp. xv–xvi, xxi, 60–61, 72, 164.)

Greater Frequency of Peak Experiences. Most self-actualizing individuals have had mystical moments of absolute perfection, during which the self is lost or subsumed in feelings of sublime ecstasy, wonder, and awe. Like numinosum in Jungian theory, these **peak experiences** are difficult to describe to those who have not had them. They may ensue from love, sex, appreciating a great symphony or work of art, bursts of creativity, moments of profound insight or scientific discovery, or the full use of one's abilities and potentials. But whatever the form, their heavenly delight is the major reason why life is worth living.

Greater Frequency of B-cognition. Self-actualizing persons more often engage in a type of thinking called "being cognition" (**B-cognition**), which always accompanies a peak experience and may occur at other times as well. B-cognition is an essentially indescribable form of thought that is nonjudgmental, does not aim toward the fulfillment of some motive, and emphasizes the unity of oneself and the cosmos. In contrast, the more common "deficiency cognition" (**D-cognition**) is judgmental, concerns the necessary objective of satisfying deficiency motives, and stresses the separateness of oneself and the various objects in the environment. (See Maslow, 1968, pp. 71–102; 1971, pp. 251–266.)

Greater Social Interest. Like Adler, Maslow regards *Gemeinschaftsgefühl* as typical of the truly mature individual. Self-actualizers strongly identify with the human species, and have a genuine sympathy for and desire to help others. If they do in fact express hostility or anger, it is usually both well-deserved and for the good of some third party.

Deeper, More Loving Interpersonal Relationships. Self-actualizing people prefer intimate and loving relationships with a few close friends, rather than superficial contacts with a wide variety of associates. They are also more capable of achieving this goal, and of demonstrating nonpossessive B-love. Thus they have the rare ability to be proud of, rather than threatened by, the loved one's achievements. They regard sex as relatively meaningless without love, and may temporarily opt for chastity rather than accept opportunities that are devoid of genuine affection. And they are more attracted by such qualities as decency and considerateness than by physical characteristics.

More Democratic Character Structure. Self-actualizers have the ability to befriend people of all classes, races, and ethnic groups, and often seem virtually unaware of such differences. They strongly and effectively oppose injustice, inequality, cruelty, and the exploitation of others.

Greater Discrimination Between Good and Evil. Self-actualizing individuals have strong moral and ethical standards, and rarely vacillate as to the course of action they consider right or wrong. They typically accept the responsibility for their actions, rather than rationalizing or trying to blame their errors on others.

More Unusual Sense of Humor. Most self-actualizers dislike humor based on hostility or superiority, such as ethnic or "insult" jokes. Instead they prefer a form that is more philosophical and instructive (e.g., Abraham Lincoln's well-known anecdotes), which gives them the appearance of being unusually sober and studious.

Greater Creativity. Every self-actualizing person demonstrates a fresh and creative approach to life, a virtue by no means limited to the artist or genius. Thus a self-actualizing homemaker may devise novel ways of preparing and serving the family meals, thereby turning the dinner table into a visual and culinary delight. Or a creative psychotherapist may develop unorthodox but successful methods geared to the individual patient, rather than attempting to apply textbook methods indiscriminately.

Maslow cautions that self-actualization is a matter of degree, rather than an all-or-nothing affair. At times self-actualizing persons may display such weaknesses as ruthlessness, discourtesy, outbursts of temper, silliness, or bias. Or they may be overly irritating, boring, or softhearted. *"There are no perfect human beings!"* (Maslow, 1970b, p. 176; see also Maslow, 1968, pp. 97, 163; 1964/1970a, p. 37; 1971, p. 50). Conversely, the less healthy individual may on rare occasions achieve moments that approach peak experiences. The self-actualizer is distinguished by a much more frequent display of maturity, constructive behavior, creativity, happiness, and wisdom—so much so as to afford distinct hope for the prospects of our strife-torn species.

FURTHER APPLICATIONS
OF MASLOWIAN THEORY

Psychopathology

Causes of Psychopathology. According to Maslow, the primary cause of psychopathology is the failure to gratify one's fundamental needs: physiological, safety, love, esteem, and self-actualization. "[These needs] *must* be satisfied, or else we get sick" (Maslow, 1970b, p. 92; see also Maslow, 1968, pp. 4, 21; 1970b, pp. 62, 67, 102, 268–269, 279; 1971, p. 316).

The lower the level at which such need frustration occurs, the more severe the pathology. For example, an individual who has satisfied only the physiological needs and still strives desperately for safety (as in Horneyan theory) is more disturbed than one who has gratified the physiological, safety, and love needs, but cannot gain much esteem and respect. Similarly, the person who has satisfied all but the need for self-actualization is healthier than either of the preceding two individuals. Thus, like most of the theorists discussed thus far, Maslow regards psychopathology as a difference in degree rather than kind.

Since self-actualization cannot be achieved without first satisfying lower needs that involve other people (safety, belongingness and love, respect), Maslow accords considerable emphasis to the interpersonal determinants of psychopathology:

> Let people realize clearly that every time they threaten someone, or humiliate or hurt [someone] unnecessarily, or dominate or reject another human being, they become forces for the creation of psychopathology, even if these be small forces. Let them recognize also that every man who is kind, helpful, decent, psychologically democratic, affectionate, and warm is a psychotherapeutic force, even though a small one. (Maslow, 1970b, p. 254. See also Maslow, 1964/1970a, pp. xiii–xiv; 1970b, pp. 252–253.)

Characteristics of Psychopathology. Like Erikson and Kelly, Maslow objects to the use of formal diagnostic labels. "I hate all these words, and I hate the medical model that they imply because [it] suggests that the person who comes to the counselor is a sick person, beset by disease and illness, seeking a cure. Actually, of course, we hope that the counselor will . . . [help] foster the self-actualization of people" (Maslow, 1971, p. 51; see also pp. 30–36). He even prefers to substitute the term *human diminution* for *neurosis,* so as to emphasize that psychopathology involves the failure to fulfill one's true potentials.

Maslow does share Horney's belief that having conflicts may be a sign of health rather than pathology, as with the inner turmoil caused by an inability to accept the distorted standards of a disturbed parent or delinquent peer group. He also agrees that pathological needs differ from healthy ones in that they do not reflect the sufferer's true desires and potentials, and are therefore insatiable and unfulfilling. For example, a person with a vast hunger for power is unlikely ever to satisfy this drive because it is actually an unconscious substitute for some more fundamental need, such as love, esteem, or self-actualization. Unlike the healthy child, who selects a reasonably balanced diet when allowed to eat whatever it wishes, the pathological individual's choices are ultimately self-defeating and harmful. "A statement by Erich Fromm that has always impressed me very much [is:] 'Sickness consists essentially in wanting what is not good for us.' . . . Healthy people are better choosers than unhealthy people" (Maslow, 1968, p. 169; 1971, p. 211; see also Maslow, 1968, pp. 48, 150–152, 198–201; 1964/1970a, pp. 99–101; 1970b, pp. 78, 276–277).

Other pathological symptoms include: (1) Guilt, shame, and/or anxiety, at least one of which is present in every neurosis. (2) Apathy and hopelessness, as in Horneyan theory. (3) A faulty conception of oneself and the environment, as in Kellyan theory: "The neurotic is not [only] emotionally sick—he is cognitively *wrong!*" (Maslow, 1970b, p. 153; see also Maslow, 1968, pp. 7–8; 1970b, pp. xxii, 143–144, 155, 268, 274). (4) An excessive dependency on others for need satisfaction. (5) A fear of knowledge of oneself and others, resulting in the use of various defense mechanisms. (6) A steadfast adherence to the familiar and routine, especially in obsessive-compulsive neurosis: "The healthy taste for the novel and unknown is missing, or at a minimum, in the average neurotic" (Maslow, 1970b, p. 43; see also Maslow, 1968, pp. 60–67; 1970b, pp. 42, 68, 218–219, 232).

Maslow also contends that the person who has satisfied all but the need for self-actualization experiences symptoms of a higher form, albeit ones that are still quite painful. Such **metapathology** involves the repression or denial of one's true metamotives, a likely condition in a society that so often elevates material rewards above idealistic standards like truth and justice. It is typically denoted by such feelings as alienation, boredom, cynicism, joylessness, uselessness, and an inability to arrive at a satisfactory system of personal values. (See Maslow, 1970b, p. 71; 1971, pp. 316–322.)

Psychotherapy

Theoretical Foundation. Like Rogers, Maslow's therapeutic goal is to help patients regain the path toward self-actualization and fulfill their own particular potentials. But since he attributes psychopathology to the frustration of fundamental needs, he concludes that the most important function of psychotherapy is to bring about their gratification.[1] "For a child who hasn't been loved enough, obviously the treatment of first choice is to love him to death, to just slop it all over him" (Maslow, 1971, p. 34; see also Maslow,

---

[1]Not including the physiological needs, however; psychotherapy is hardly suitable for alleviating hunger and thirst (Maslow, 1970b, p. 100).

1970b, pp. 68–69, 93–95, 241–264, 270). The needs for safety, belongingness and love, and esteem can only be satisfied by other people. So the patient must learn to establish and maintain good human relationships, discover that they are in fact enjoyable, and ultimately replace formal psychotherapy with such sources of satisfaction as friends and marriage.

The preceding model does not apply to those patients who are lacking only in self-actualization, since they have fulfilled their interpersonal needs and are concerned solely with inner growth and self-direction. These individuals must be helped to overcome the social forces that have caused them to repress their metamotives, and discover those values toward which they truly wish to strive.

Therapeutic Procedures. Unlike Rogers, Maslow adopts an eclectic approach to psychotherapy. He does agree that the therapist should often be accepting, genuine, kind, and concerned, since these behaviors help satisfy the patient's needs for safety and belongingness. However, he cautions that there are too many patients who do not thrive in a warm and friendly atmosphere for this to become a universal procedure. For example, people with authoritarian personalities are likely to interpret kindness as weakness, while distrustful individuals may well regard friendliness as a dangerous trap. With such patients, Maslow recommends that the therapist assume the role of authority.

Maslow also differs from Rogers by favoring the use of Freudian psychoanalysis with seriously disturbed patients, notably those who are too enmeshed in infantile perceptions of themselves and others to accept those need satisfactions that may be offered. In less severe cases, however, briefer forms of psychotherapy may well suffice. This includes behavior therapy (see Chapter 15), so long as it does not uproot defenses and symptoms too quickly. "Change in *behavior* can produce personality change" (Maslow, 1970b, p. 311; see also pp. 44, 142, 257–264). Maslow does share Rogers's high regard for group therapy, however, and for the use of encounter groups to aid the development of relatively healthy people.

Whatever the form, Maslow strongly recommends psychotherapy as the best way to understand and treat psychopathology. "[Therapy] is the best technique we have ever had for laying bare men's deepest nature, as contrasted with their surface personalities. . . . The good professional psychotherapist has left the intuitive helper far behind" (Maslow, 1970b, pp. 241, 260).

Resistance, Transference, and Countertransference. Like Freud and Jung, Maslow argues that the psychotherapist must be sufficiently self-aware to avoid harmful countertransferences. Ideally, the therapist should be warm, sympathetic, emotionally secure, self-confident, happily married, financially successful, able to form satisfying interpersonal relationships, and capable of enjoying life.

Maslow also accepts the existence of resistance and transference. He agrees with Horney and Kelly that resistance may well represent a healthy and justified objection to therapeutic blunders, such as being arbitrarily assigned to a diagnostic category that neglects the patient's personal uniqueness and identity. (See Maslow, 1968, pp. 60, 126–130; 1970b, pp. 250–253, 260, 309.)

Work

Maslow is one of the few personality theorists discussed thus far who takes an active interest in the area of work. "If you are unhappy with your work, you have lost one of the most important means of self-fulfillment" (Maslow, 1971, p. 185; see also Maslow, 1965; 1966/1969; 1970b, pp. 277–278; 1971, pp. 208, 237–248, 306, 313).

At work, as elsewhere, those whose lower needs are satisfied will seek higher-level gratifications. Organizations should therefore be designed so that employees can satisfy their needs for belongingness, dignity, respect, and self-actualization, and grow to full psychological stature (an approach Maslow refers to as **Eupsychian** management). Maslow also contends that the ability of any organization to satisfy its workers' needs must be ascertained by studying the specific nature of employee complaints, rather than merely tabulating their frequency. For example, if many workers object to the physical conditions as unsafe, wet, and cold ("low grumbles"), even the lowest need levels are not being gratified. If instead numerous employees express dissatisfaction with their opportunities for belongingness or respect ("high grumbles"), the lower needs are reasonably well satisfied but the intermediate levels are not. And a preponderance of complaints about the inability to self-actualize ("metagrumbles") reflects a quite different state of affairs, for the emergence of these highest-level issues indicates that the four lowest need levels have at least to some extent been satisfied.

Thus management should not expect improving certain aspects of the organization to eliminate all worker complaints. A more likely outcome is the emergence of higher-level grumbles, indicating that the company has been largely successful in satisfying the employees' lower-level needs and that it is now time to turn to new and higher issues.

Religion

In accordance with his theoretical optimism, Maslow emphatically denies the existence of innate evil or original sin. He also shares Jung's opposition to unthinking faith, and Freud's contention that the dogma of religion must fall before the onslaught of science and truth:

> [Faith] in the hands of an anti-intellectual church [tends] to degenerate into blind belief . . . [which] tends to produce sheep rather than men . . . [When religion] was cut away from science, from knowledge, from further discovery, from the possibility of skeptical investigation, from confirming and discon-

firming, and therefore from the possibility of purifying and improving, such a . . . religion was doomed. (Maslow, 1964/1970a, pp. 13–14. See also Maslow, 1964/1970a, pp. 9–10; 1970b, pp. 83, 94, 122, 266.)

Maslow argues that the supposedly supernatural revelations claimed by prophets and seers are nothing more nor less than peak experiences, the potential for which is inherent in every human personality. It is these private, personal, unscheduled, and profoundly meaningful occurrences that constitute true religious experience, rather than rituals arbitrarily assigned to a particular building and day of the week. Thus most self-actualizers have enjoyed deep religious experiences, even though they often are not religious in any formal sense, while many people who regularly practice their religion have not. And only those who have had peak experiences can become effective religious leaders, for only they will be able to communicate the nature of such experiences to those who have not had them. (See Maslow, 1964/1970a, pp. viii, xi, 4, 11, 20, 24, 26, 29, 33; 1971, pp. 195, 339–340.)

Education

Like Rogers, Maslow advocates a nondirective and person-centered approach to education. He takes strong exception to the rigid formalities common to higher education: courses must all span precisely the same number of weeks, even though some subjects are more difficult and comprehensive than others. Academic departments are totally independent, as though human knowledge could be neatly divided into separate and distinct categories. The emphasis is on learning many specific facts, rather than on personal growth. And motivation is provided by such external rewards as grades, which often leads students to do only the work that is specifically required by the teacher. "The present school system is an extremely effective instrument for crushing peak experiences and forbidding their possibility" (Maslow, 1971, p. 188; see also Maslow, 1964/1970a, pp. 16–17, 48–58; 1970b, pp. 94, 177–178, 223; 1971, pp. 48, 168–195).

The ideal university would have no formal credits, required courses, or degrees. It would serve as an educational retreat where people could explore various subjects, discover their own true interests and identities, and appreciate the joys of learning and the preciousness of life. The teacher would show students how to hear the beauty of a great symphony, rather than merely having them repeat back the date of the composer's birth on an examination. He or she would be a self-actualizer, thereby serving as a model for the students' inevitable identifications, and would demonstrate unconditional positive regard for their particular interests. Thus education would achieve its proper goal: to help people become fully human and actualize their highest potentials.

Maslowian Theory and Empirical Research

Like Rogers, Maslow regards empirical research as a vital source of knowledge about the human personality. But he also agrees that all too many psychologists try to imitate the precision of the physical sciences by concentrating on experimentally simple but trivial issues:

> The besetting sin of the academicians [is] that they prefer to do what they are easily able rather than what they ought, like the not-so-bright kitchen helper I knew who opened every can in the hotel one day because he was so *very* good at opening cans. . . . The journals of science are full of instances that illustrate [this] point, that what is not worth doing, is not worth doing well. (Maslow, 1970b, pp. 18, 181. See also Maslow, 1968, pp. viii, 216; 1970b, pp. 1–17, 224; 1971, pp. 170–171.)

In contrast, the creative scientist avoids a rigid commitment to specific techniques or content areas. He or she dares to search for the truth in innovative and unusual ways, and to tackle such important but difficult research issues as unemployment, race prejudice, nationalism, and psychotherapy. Also, like Kelly, Maslow cautions that the psychologist must view any theory as applicable to only some aspects of human endeavor.

EVALUATION

Criticisms and Controversies

Maslow has been criticized for an overly optimistic view of human nature, although his greater acceptance of Freudian principles renders him less vulnerable to this charge than Rogers. However, Maslow's eclecticism does not seem sufficiently well thought out. For example, he fails to reconcile his professed holism with his acceptance of such processes as repression and reaction formation, constructs which necessarily imply that personality includes sufficient subparts to become a house divided. Similarly, he casually endorses Horney's construct of an idealized image (Maslow, 1971, p. 113) without considering the discrepancies between her inner conflict model and his holistic approach. Eclecticism requires more than merely accepting under one theoretical roof all those constructs of other theorists that one likes. The various ideas must also be integrated into a meaningful and non-contradictory whole, and this Maslow has not done.

Maslow's study of self-actualizing individuals defines such people subjectively, using his own personal criteria. It has been suggested that the behaviors he characterizes as ideal (and even the hierarchy of needs itself) represent not some fundamental truth, but his own idiosyncratic conception of what human values should be like. The sample is quite a small one on which to base such far-reaching findings, and Maslow's report lacks any statistical analyses and excludes such important biographical data as the intelligence, educational level, socioeconomic level, and ages of his subjects.

Maslow repeatedly refers to his theoretical ideas as empirically testable, yet many modern psychologists emphatically disagree. They criticize his constructs as vague and imprecise, and they raise the issue of how to measure the amount of satisfaction that must be achieved at a given level for the next higher need to become prominent. In addition, Maslow allows for so many theoretical exceptions (e.g., the possible emergence of a higher need after the *frustration* of a lower one) that his theory appears decidedly equivocal. In contrast to such theorists as Freud, Adler, and Erikson, Maslow's discussion of personality development and childrearing seems vague and ill-defined. Finally, his idiosyncratic writing style includes numerous extensive and rather dull lists, offhand and unexplained references to the work of other psychologists, and assertions that seem more philosophical than scientific and psychological.

Empirical Research

Save for the area of work, Maslow's theory has not generated a great deal of empirical research. This is partly because the hierarchical model implies that higher needs emerge over a period of time, as the lower ones are gradually satisfied, and longitudinal research studies are particularly difficult and costly to undertake. There does exist a validated instrument (the Personal Orientation Inventory) that can be used to measure the degree of self-actualization that one has achieved (Shostrom, 1963; 1965), and there is some evidence in favor of the need hierarchy (e.g., Graham & Balloun, 1973) as well as a survey indicating relatively little support for it (Wahba & Bridwell, 1976). On the whole, however, major research support for Maslow's theoretical contentions is still lacking.

Contributions

Maslow's emphasis on the study of healthy people offers a welcome contrast to those personality theories based solely on clinical data, and his model of deficiency and growth motives is preferred by many psychologists to Freud's preoccupation with drive reduction. Unlike many theorists, Maslow accords due credit to such predecessors as Freud, Jung, Adler, Horney, and Fromm. His ideas about religion are interesting and provocative, as is the general idea of a hierarchical model of human needs. Maslow is widely regarded as perhaps the foremost exponent of humanistic ("third force") psychology, which has gained widespread acceptance among those not favorably inclined toward either psychoanalysis or behaviorism, and his writings have proved quite popular with the general public. Although Maslow's theory seems too flawed to stand on its own as a viable alternative to its competitors, he has nevertheless made significant contributions toward a goal shared by Rogers and succinctly stated by Sören Kierkegaard: to help a person be that self which one truly is.

Suggested Reading

Of Maslow's various titles, there are two that represent the cornerstones of his theory: *Motivation and Personality* (1970b) and *Toward a Psychology of*

Being (1968). Also of interest are Maslow's memoirs and personal introspections (Lowry, 1979). For a biography of Maslow, see Hoffman (1988).

■ SUMMARY

1. THE BASIC NATURE OF HUMAN BEINGS. We are born with very weak instinctoid needs, which are essentially positive but are all too easily overwhelmed by the far more powerful forces of learning and culture. Maslow therefore advises psychologists to guard against excessive theoretical optimism by acquiring a thorough knowledge of Freudian psychoanalysis. *Deficiency and Growth Motives:* Our instinctoid needs include both deficiency motives and growth motives. The former involve drive reduction and filling lacks in the organism through some external source, while the latter include pleasurable increases in tension and the development of one's own potentials and capacites. Although deficiency motives serve essential purposes (such as self-preservation), growth motives tend to represent a higher, healthier, and more pleasurable level of functioning. *The Hierarchy of Human Needs:* Some needs do not become important, or even noticeable, until others have at least to some extent been satisfied. The hierarchy of human needs consists of five levels: physiological (lowest), safety, belongingness and love, esteem, and self-actualization (highest). The higher needs are less tangible, not necessary for survival, and more easily blocked by a pathogenic environment, so even recognizing their existence is a considerable achievement.

2. THE STRUCTURE OF PERSONALITY. Maslow professes a holistic approach and posits no specific structural constructs. He does accept the existence of Freudian defense mechanisms and two forms of conscience, one resembling the Rogerian organismic valuing process and one introjected from important others.

3. THE DEVELOPMENT OF PERSONALITY. Maslow has little to say about personality development. He does argue that the child should be given sufficient opportunities to heed its own inner guidelines, and have its fundamental needs satisfied. *The Self-Actualizing (Fully Human) Person:* Maslow devotes considerable attention to those people he regards as extremely psychologically healthy, and describes some fifteen characteristics typical of such self-actualizers.

4. FURTHER APPLICATIONS. *Psychopathology:* Psychopathology is caused primarily by the failure to satisfy one's fundamental needs. The lower the level at which such dissatisfaction occurs, the more pathological the individual. Psychopathology involves wanting what is not good for oneself, anxiety, hopelessness, being cognitively wrong, and other symptoms. Those who have satisfied all but the need for self-actualization experience symptoms of a higher and different form. *Psychotherapy:* Maslow finds merit in various types of psychotherapy, depending on the severity of the patient's problems. Except for self-actualization (and the physiological needs), the patient's unfulfilled needs can only be satisfied by other people, so

he or she must learn to establish and maintain effective interpersonal relationships. *Other Areas:* Maslow has also applied his theory to work, religion, and education.

5. EVALUATION. Maslow's eclecticism renders him less vulnerable to the criticism of excessive optimism than Rogers, but seems insufficiently thought out and includes too many confusions and contradictions. His study of self-actualizers has been criticized on methodological grounds, and his theoretical constructs have been characterized as vague, equivocal, and untestable. Yet Maslow is widely regarded as perhaps the most prominent exponent of humanistic psychology, his writings have gained widespread popularity, and his study of healthy people represents a welcome contrast to theories based solely on clinical observation.

STUDY QUESTIONS

1. Consider once again the case history discussed throughout the Appendix (e.g., Chapter 2, question 6; Chapter 4, questions 2 and 6a; Chapter 5, questions 1, 4b, and 5; Chapter 6, questions 3d and 4; Chapter 7, question 7a; Chapter 8, question 7; Chapter 9, question 10; Chapter 11, question 1; Chapter 12, question 1). Use this case history to illustrate each of the following statements by Maslow: (a) "People [who] perceive in a deep way that they have done wrong to themselves . . . despise themselves for it." (b) "[Excessive external pressures, and] demands upon the child that it become what the parent has already decided it *should* become, [are like being] born into an invisible straitjacket." (c) "The neurotic is not [only] emotionally sick—he is cognitively *wrong!*" (d) "The healthy taste for the novel and unknown is missing, or at a minimum, in the average neurotic."

2. Compare the views of human nature posited by Maslow, Rogers, and Freud. Which do you prefer? Why?

3. The following statements by Maslow express significant disagreements with Freud: (a) "Growth is, *in itself,* a rewarding and exciting process. . . . Given sufficient gratification, free choice, and lack of threat, [the child] renounces . . . [the oral stage] himself. He doesn't have to be 'kicked upstairs.'" (b) "Healthy people welcome drive *increases,* and may well complain that "the trouble with eating is that it kills my appetite." (c) "For the child who hasn't been loved enough, obviously the treatment of first choice [during psychotherapy] is to love him to death, to just slop it all over him." In each case, do you agree with Maslow or Freud? Why?

4. Maslow states that perhaps the most important growth motive is "simply the ambition to be a good human being." Do you agree or disagree? Why?

5. Where would each of the following be classified according to the hierarchy of human needs? (a) The person whose case history is discussed in question 1, above. (b) You.

6. By classifying self-actualization as the highest form of need (and thus the last to emerge), Maslow takes the position that discovering and fulfilling

one's own innate needs and potentials is extremely difficult. Do you agree or disagree? Why?

7. Consider the fifteen characteristics of self-actualizing (or "fully human") persons. (a) Would Maslow consider Freud to be a self-actualizer? (b) Does the person whose case history is discussed in question 1 fit any of these characteristics, or is he deficient in all of them?

8. According to Maslow, self-actualizing people taught him to see that too many people are "profoundly sick . . . [because they] have their minds made up for them by salesmen, advertisers, parents, propagandists, TV, newspapers, and so on." Do you agree or disagree? Why?

9. Maslow argues that there is a widespread tendency to undervalue need gratifications that one has already achieved, and that this is a profound source of human unhappiness. Do you agree or disagree? Why?

10. Is it possible for a job to be self-actualizing, yet have poor working conditions and not be esteemed by others? What would this imply about Maslow's theory?

ROLLO MAY
Existential Psychology

One former psychoanalyst contracted tuberculosis during his late thirties, and his fight against this formidable illness proved to be a decisive turning point in his life. At that time, effective medication had not yet been developed. So Rollo May waited hour by hour and day by day in an upstate New York sanitarium for the verdict that would spell either a return to health, lifelong invalidism, or death. May spent much of this suspenseful time reading, and he made a surprising discovery: his own profound anxiety had far more to do with the dread of nonbeing, as described by such existentialists as Kierkegaard, than with the mechanical and metaphysical construct of libido.

Fortunately, May recovered from his illness. But his psychoanalytic orientation did not, and his subsequent professional life has been devoted to the existential bases of personality.

BIOGRAPHICAL SKETCH

Rollo Reese May was born on April 21, 1909, in Ada, Ohio, but spent most of his childhood in Marine City, Michigan. May received his bachelor of arts degree from Oberlin College in 1930, after which he pursued an Eriksonian course by touring Europe as an itinerant artist and teacher. During this time he attended the summer school of Alfred Adler, whose work he admired but regarded as somewhat oversimplified. (See May, 1975, p. 37; Reeves, 1977, pp. 251–263.)

May returned to the United States to earn a divinity degree from the Union Theological Seminary in New York in 1938, where he first encountered existential thought, and later served in a parish in Montclair, New Jersey. However, his interest in psychology proved stronger than religion. So he proceeded to study psychoanalysis at the William Alanson White Institute, where he met and was influenced by Fromm and Sullivan. May opened his own private practice in 1946, and received the first Ph.D. in clinical psychology ever awarded by Columbia University in 1949. At about this time he underwent the aforementioned traumatic bout with tuberculosis, which did considerably more to influence him toward existentialism than his formal education. May married Florence deFrees in 1938; they have one son and two daughters.

May's published works include some dozen books, notably the best-selling *Love and Will* (1969c), and numerous articles. In addition to his work as a practicing psychotherapist, he has lectured at such institutions as Harvard, Yale, Princeton, Columbia, Dartmouth, Vassar, Oberlin, New York University, and the New School for Social Research.

THE BASIC NATURE OF HUMAN BEINGS

Being-In-The-World (Dasein)

Each of us has an inherent need to exist in the world into which we are born, and to achieve a conscious and unconscious sense of ourselves as an autonomous and distinct entity. The stronger this **being-in-the-world**[1] or **Dasein** (*sein* = to exist, or be alive; *da* = there), the healthier the personality.

To fulfill one's own innate potentials (that is, to develop Dasein) requires constant effort and courage. The only way to enjoy a meaningful life is by affirming and asserting our being-in-the-world—even (if need be) in the face of social pressures to conform, misguided parental standards, and the threat of death itself:

> The hallmark of courage in our age of conformity is the capacity to stand on one's own convictions—not obstinately or defiantly (these are expressions of defensiveness, not courage) nor as a gesture of retaliation, but simply because these are what one believes. It is as though one were saying through one's actions, "This is my self, my being." . . . [Thus it is through self-assertion and] will that the human being experiences his identity. "I" is the "I" of "I can." (May, 1969c, p. 243; 1953/1973, p. 236. See also May, 1958/1967b, pp. 37, 41–47, 55–61; 1958/1967c, pp. 31–32; 1969a, pp. 13, 19, 45; 1972, pp. 40–41; 1977b, pp. 303–304.)

Because Dasein is so personal a matter, no one else can tell an individual how or what to be-in-the-world. Each of us must discover our own potentials and values, and the best way to do so is by experiencing each moment actively and spontaneously. In fact, even such basic human drives as sexuality and aggression are of secondary importance to Dasein. Drives are an abstraction, and perceiving ourselves as "having" them is dehumanizing. We *are* our hunger, thirst, sexuality, feelings, ideas, and so forth, and it is this experiencing that is truly and distinctively human. (See May, 1958/1967b, pp. 42–44; 1969a, p. 14; 1969b, pp. 73, 78.)

Modes of Being-In-The-World. Our dynamic being-in-the-world comprises three simultaneous and interrelated modes (or "regions"): the world of

---

[1]As with Freudian theory, difficulties in translation have beset existential psychology. Here, for example, a compound word easily formed in German (the language used by Binswanger and Boss) must be expressed through hyphenation in English, an awkward method that does not quite convey the unity implied by the construct.

internal and external objects, which forms our physiological and physical environment (**Umwelt;** literally, "world around"); the social world of other people (**Mitwelt;** literally, "with-world"); and the psychological world of relationship to oneself, and to one's own potentials and values (**Eigenwelt;** literally, "own-world"). Whereas some personality theorists prefer to concentrate on only one of these modes, existential psychology holds that all three must be accorded equal emphasis in order to achieve a true understanding of the human personality. (See May, 1958/1967b, pp. 61–65.)

The Umwelt is the mode that so concerned Freud. In addition to our physical surroundings, it includes the state of need into which every person is cast by birth: hunger, thirst, sleep, and so forth. The factual conditions into which we are born, such as having instinctual needs, a genetically predetermined height, and a culture with certain expectations, represent the few aspects of existence we cannot control through our own choices. This circumstance is sometimes referred to as **thrownness,** or **facticity.**

The Mitwelt involves our inherent need to form personal relationships for their own sake, rather than to sublimate some instinctual drive. No one can achieve a meaningful existence in isolation, as stressed by such theorists as Adler, Fromm, Horney, and Sullivan.

The Eigenwelt is the uniquely human world of self-awareness (as in Rogerian theory), or knowing that we are the center of our existence and recognizing our own particular potentialities. This mode is evident when we judge accurately what we do or do not like or need, or personally evaluate an experience. Conversely, feelings of emptiness and self-estrangement reflect some distortion of Eigenwelt. (See May, 1958/1967b, p. 63; 1967d; 1981.)

In contrast to Erikson's construct of identity, Eigenwelt and Dasein do *not* depend on the opinions and expectations of other people. "If your self-esteem must rest in the long run on social validation, you have, not self-esteem, but a more sophisticated form of social conformity" (May, 1958/1967b, p. 45; see also pp. 46–47, 79). Nor is Dasein equivalent to the Freudian ego, for a knowledge of oneself as the being who can interact with the world is intrinsic—and thus exists prior to any actual contacts with the environment.

Nonbeing and Anxiety

Although the subjective and objective aspects of personality are inextricably intertwined, there is one absolute fact about being-in-the-world: death, which none of us ever escapes. Our tenuous existence may be terminated at any moment by such vagaries of fate as an automobile accident, criminal's bullet, earthquake, fire, flood, or heart attack. The awareness of an eventual end to our being, and the impending psychological destruction posed by rejections and insults, evoke the painful emotion of **anxiety:**[2]

[2]Another difficulty in translation: *anxiety* is actually a fairly weak rendition of the German word *Angst,* which has no English equivalent, wherefore some theorists prefer *dread* or *anguish.*

Anxiety is the apprehension cued off by a threat to some value that the individual holds essential to his existence as a personality. . . . [It] is the subjective state of the individual's becoming aware that his existence can become destroyed, that he can lose himself and his world, that he can become "nothing." (May, 1958/1967b, p. 50; 1977a, p. 205. See also May, 1953/1973, pp. 34–80; 1977a, pp. 204–239; Reeves, 1977, pp. 66–99, 176.)

Thus anxiety differs from fear in that it is **ontological,** or related to human existence or being. For example, suppose that a professor whom you know and respect passes by on the street without speaking. This snub may well strike at the very core of your self-esteem ("Am I not worth noticing? Am I nobody—nothing?"), thereby evoking anxiety that haunts you long after the event. Or if you conclude that survival is impossible without the love of a certain person (or a particular job, or some status symbol), the prospective loss of that love (or job, or symbol) will occasion considerable anxiety. In contrast, the fear caused by sitting in a dentist's chair does not attack Dasein—and is therefore soon forgotten once the incident is over. "Anxiety is ontological, fear is not. . . . Anxiety can be understood only as a threat to Dasein" (May, 1958/1967b, p. 51; 1977a, p. 205). Thus May attributes anxiety not to some divisive intrapsychic conflict or external danger, but rather to the fundamental clash between being and the threat of nonbeing. A certain amount of anxiety is therefore a normal, and inevitable, aspect of human nature.

Ontological anxiety confronts each of us with a major challenge. This unpleasant emotion intensifies whenever we choose to assert our Dasein and strive to fulfill our innate potentials, for emphatically affirming that we exist also brings a reminder that someday we will not. Therefore it is all too tempting to repress or intellectualize our understanding of death, deny our Dasein, and opt for the apparent safety of social conformity and apathy. That is, we may try to deprive nonbeing of its sting by (consciously or unconsciously) treating our being-in-the-world as meaningless. "The awareness of death is widely repressed in our day. . . . [In fact,] the ways we repress death and its symbolism are amazingly like the ways the Victorians repressed sex" (May, 1969c, p. 106). Nevertheless, the healthy course is to accept nonbeing as an inseparable part of being. This will enable us to live what life we have to the fullest:

To grasp what it means to exist, one needs to grasp the fact that he might not exist, that he treads at every moment on the sharp edge of possible annihilation and can never escape the fact that death will arrive at some unknown moment in the future. . . . Without this awareness of nonbeing . . . existence is vapid [and] unreal. . . . But with the confrontation of nonbeing, existence takes on vitality and immediacy, and the individual experiences a heightened consciousness of himself, his world, and others around him. . . . [Thus] the confronting of death gives the most positive reality to life itself. (May, 1958/1967b, pp. 47–49. See also Becker, 1973; May, 1969a, p. 30.)

Fallibility and Guilt

No one ever deals perfectly with the three modes of being-in-the-world. Try as we may, our choices inevitably fail to fulfill at least some of our innate potentials (a denial of Eigenwelt). Perfect empathy is impossible, so even the best-intentioned person sometimes relates to others in ways that are biased and dissatisfying (a denial of Mitwelt). And it is easy to overlook our communion with nature and the environment, and misperceive ourselves as separate and distinct from Umwelt.

Such inevitable failures evoke ontological **guilt,** another normal and necessary aspect of human nature. As with anxiety, the ideal course is to accept and use our guilt for constructive purposes—as by developing a healthy humility concerning the possibility of our own errors, and a readiness to forgive others their mistakes. (See May, 1958/1967b, pp. 52–55.)

Intentionality and Significance

In contrast to Freud, May attributes considerable importance to both psychic determinism and teleology. We are all to some extent impelled by forces from infancy and childhood, especially those of us who are more neurotic. Yet we also have the freedom, and the responsibility, to strive toward those goals that we select. Psychologically healthy people can readily imagine some desirable future state and then organize themselves to move in this direction, a capacity May refers to as **will** or **intentionality.**[3] (See May, 1939/1967a, pp. 45–53; 1958/1967b, pp. 41, 65–71; 1969c, pp. 92–94, 223–272; Reeves, 1977, pp. 147–221.)

According to May, a conscious and unconscious sense of purpose pervades all aspects of our existence—perceptions, memories, and so forth. For example, suppose that an individual perceives a house in the mountains. A prospective renter will look to see if it is well-constructed and gets enough sun, a real-estate speculator will regard it primarily in terms of probable profit or loss, and a person who encounters unpleasant hosts will more readily observe its flaws. In each case the house is the same, but the experience depends on the viewer's intentions; thus the future molds the present. And as in Adlerian theory, what we seek to become shapes what we remember of our childhood, so the future also determines the past (May, 1958/1967b, p. 69; 1969c, p. 232).

---

[3]In *Love and Will* (1969c), May uses both *intentionality* and *intention* to describe the way in which an individual anticipates the future. However, he now regards this as an error. Intentionality concerns the basic human capacity to behave teleologically, and is evident in the specific intentions that a person has (May, 1977b, p. 306). Also, technically, intentionality cuts across both conscious and unconscious and thus represents a deeper sense of purpose than will, which is conscious.

To May, the loss of intentionality represents the major psychopathology of our time. "The central core of modern man's 'neurosis' . . . is the undermining of his experience of himself as responsible, the sapping of his will and ability to make decisions" (May, 1969c, p. 184). May also concludes that the related feelings of intense powerlessness are likely to result in violence, a last-ditch attempt to prove that the sufferer can still affect someone significantly. Whereas Freud stressed psychic determinism in order to shatter the Victorian misconception that personality is wholly free of childhood influences and irrationalities, May argues that we now must emphasize intentionality in order to remedy our current self-estrangement and apathy:

> Everyone has a need for . . . significance; and if we can't make that possible, or even probable, in our society, then it will be obtained in destructive ways. The challenge before us is to find [healthy] ways that people can achieve significance and recognition . . . For no human being can stand the perpetually numbing experience of his own powerlessness. (May, 1969c, p. 14; 1972, p. 179. See also May, 1939/1967a, p. 216; 1969c, pp. 16, 31, 162, 182–183; 1972, pp. 21–23, 243.)

Love and Care

One particularly constructive way of affirming Dasein is through *love,* another important ontological characteristic. *"[Love is] a delight in the presence of the other person, and an affirming of his value and development as much as one's own"* (May, 1953/1973, p. 241; see also May, 1953/1973, pp. 227, 238–246; 1958/1967b, pp. 64–65, 75; 1969c, pp. 37–38, 72–79, 289–293, 302, 317–319; Reeves, 1977, pp. 100–146).

Love always involves a blending of four components, albeit in varying proportions. As in Freudian theory, our need for **sex** is satisfied through drive reduction and physical release. Another particularly important aspect of love is **eros,** a striving for fulfillment through union with significant others. In contrast to sex, eros includes such pleasurable tension increases as thinking of and yearning for the loved one. One noted example is the passion and vitality of Romeo, who compares his Juliet to rare jewels and the stars in heaven. Eros also involves the feeling that something in life does matter ("care"), as evidenced by the mother's compassionate concern for her child. The other two characteristics of love (to which May devotes considerably less attention) are friendship and liking (**philia**), as with the Sullivanian chum; and a nonpossessive devotion to the welfare of the other person (**agapé**), like Fromm's concept of love and Maslow's B-love. Thus love is a rich experience that encompasses all three modes of being-in-the-world: biological drives (Umwelt), relationship to others (Mitwelt), and the affirmation of one's self and values (Eigenwelt).

Not all aspects of love are pleasant. Love may also lead to increased anxiety, since it can bring disaster as well as joy—as one may well discover on becoming a parent for the first time, and realizing that the beloved child

■ CAPSULE SUMMARY
Some Important Existential Terminology

Anxiety	Apprehension caused by a threat to some value deemed essential to the existence of one's personality (i.e., a threat to Dasein); the awareness that one can be destroyed, physically or psychologically, and become nothing. Since death is the one absolute and inevitable aspect of existence, a certain amount of anxiety is a natural characteristic of being human (i.e., ontological).
Being-in-the-world (Dasein, existence)	A conscious and unconscious sense of oneself as a distinct, autonomous, and responsible entity who exists in the world of physiological and physical surroundings (Umwelt), other people (Mitwelt), and one's own self (Eigenwelt). A strong Dasein is essential to the healthy personality.
Care	The feeling that something in life does matter; an ontological characteristic.
Daimonic	Innate benign and illicit forces capable of dominating one's entire personality, such as sex, passion and eros, procreation, self-affirmation, destructiveness, rage, hostility, and the quest for power. As with the Jungian shadow, psychological health requires that the daimonic be accepted and integrated into consciousness.
Eigenwelt	The world of relationship to oneself, and to one's own potentials and values ("own-world"). One of the three simultaneous and interrelated modes of being-in-the-world.
Eros	A vital and passionate striving for self-fulfillment through union with significant others, including such pleasurable tension increases as thinking of and yearning for the loved one. One of the four components of love, and the one all too often denied or repressed in our society.
Existential psychology	A philosophy of human nature and psychotherapy that stresses the various ontological characteristics, and the necessity of asserting our Dasein despite the inevitable death that awaits us all.
Guilt	Regret resulting from the impossibility of fulfilling all of one's innate potentials (a denial of Eigenwelt), of relating perfectly to others (a denial of Mitwelt), and of always recognizing our communion with nature (a denial of Umwelt); an ontological characteristic.
Intentionality	The capacity of human beings to have a conscious and unconscious sense of purpose, and behave teleologically; an ontological characteristic.
Love	A delight in the presence of another person, and readiness to affirm that person's values and development as much as one's

continued

	own; an ontological characteristic. Love always involves a blending of four components, albeit in varying proportions: sex, eros, philia (friendship and liking), and agapé (non-possessive devotion).
Mitwelt	The world of relationship to other people ("with-world"). One of the three simultaneous and interrelated modes of being-in-the-world.
Ontological characteristics	Those qualities that are distinctively and definitively human, including Dasein, anxiety, guilt, intentionality, love, and care.
Ontology	The science of existence or being, notably of being human.
Repression	Excluding any of the various ontological characteristics from consciousness.
Thrownness (facticity)	A term referring to those few aspects of existence into which we are cast by birth and cannot control through our own choices, including such factual conditions as having instinctual needs and a culture with certain expectations.
Umwelt	The world of internal and external objects, which forms our physiological and physical environment ("around-world"). One of the three simultaneous and interrelated modes of being-in-the-world.
Will	The conscious capacity to move toward one's self-selected goals; thus, the more self-evident aspect of intentionality.

is all too vulnerable to potential nonbeing and the whims of fate. Therefore, the ability to love requires a strong being-in-the-world. Conversely, the widespread loss of Dasein and intentionality in our society has resulted in an inability to love. This is reflected in an emphasis on the mechanical and depersonalized aspects of sex, as evidenced by books on sexual technique and excessive concerns about performance, and the repression of eros:

> There is nothing *less* sexy than sheer nakedness, as a random hour at any nudist camp will prove. It requires the infusion of the imagination (which I . . . call intentionality) to transmute physiology and anatomy into [passion and eros]. . . . [Yet today,] elaborate accounting- and ledger-book lists—how often this week have we made love? did he (or she) pay the right amount of attention to me during the evening? was the foreplay long enough?—[hover] . . . in the stage wings of the drama of love-making the way Freud said one's parents used to . . . [and result in] alienation, feelings of loneliness, and depersonalization. . . . [In fact, whereas] the Victorian nice man or woman was guilty if he or she did experience sex, now we are guilty if we *don't.* (May, 1969c, pp. 40, 43–44; see also pp. 13–15, 30–33, 37–72, 102, 107, 111.)

Thus the solution to our inability to love is to rediscover our Dasein and will, and reunite sex with eros and passion.

The Daimonic

While destructiveness is due largely to the sense of powerlessness that results from the loss of Dasein, May (like Jung and Murray) does conclude that we are all driven by innate benign and illicit urges. Among the former are sex, passion and eros, and procreation; while the latter include hostility, rage, cruelty, and the quest for power. Any of these aspects has the potential to dominate one's entire personality. Therefore they are known as the **daimonic**, after an ancient Greek word for both the divine and diabolical. (See M. H. Hall, 1967b, p. 29; May, 1969c, pp. 122–177; 1977b, pp. 304–306.)

As with the Jungian shadow, the daimonic must be accepted and integrated into consciousness for psychological health to be achieved. Yet this is no easy task, for it is all too tempting to deal only with our virtues and repress the dark side of our personality. Such a denial of the daimonic produces a naive innocence that often has disastrous consequences, like the failure to understand and check a Hitler until it is too late or the misguided belief that one can walk safely through an armed confrontation like Kent State; to be unaware of evil is to be readily destroyed by it. Or a daimonic allowed to remain unconscious may be projected on members of other countries or ethnic groups, resulting in violence, assassination, and war.

THE STRUCTURE OF PERSONALITY

Since we are our Dasein, anxiety, guilt, love, and so forth, it would be misleading—and depersonalizing—to attribute these ontological characteristics to abstract structural constructs. Therefore, existential psychology adopts a holistic approach to personality. May does accept the importance of unconscious processes, however, and of such defense mechanisms as repression, intellectualization, projection, isolation, and reaction formation:

> The great contribution of Freud was his carrying of the Socratic injunction "know thyself" into new depths that comprise, in effect, a new continent, the continent of repressed, unconscious motives. . . . He uncovered the vast areas in which motives and behavior—whether in bringing up children, or making love, or running a business, or planning a war—are determined by unconscious urges [and] anxieties. . . . (May, 1969c, pp. 51, 182. See also May, 1958/1967c, pp. 22–23, 28; 1958/1967b, pp. 68, 79, 88–91; 1969a, p. 19; 1969c, pp. 132–133, 158, 174, 199, 205–206, 241, 260; 1953/1973, p. 52.)

When we repress anxiety, eros, or the daimonic (as we all too often do), it is not because one part of a fragmented personality is at war with some other part. It is the whole individual who lacks courage, chooses not to experience such threatening human characteristics, and (as in Fromm's theory) escapes from the freedom to know and be oneself—a misguided decision that inevitably results in the loss of Dasein.

THE DEVELOPMENT OF PERSONALITY

According to May, the development of a healthy personality may be impeded by various pathogenic parental behaviors. Rejection causes the child to deny Mitwelt and shy away from other people, especially when it is hypocritically disguised as loving concern. Stifling the child's natural expressions of will tends to result in a neurotic quest for safety, wherein Dasein is sacrificed in a desperate attempt to become obedient and angelic. Catering to children's every whim prevents them from establishing their individuality by rebelling against parental authority, with such pampering particularly likely in the case of the only child (as in Adlerian theory):

> There is great temptation to overprotect the [only child]. When he calls, the parents run; when he whimpers, they are abashed; when he is sick, they are guilty; when he doesn't sleep, they look as though *they* are going to have nervous breakdowns. The infant becomes a little dictator by virtue of the situation he is born into. . . . [Yet] all this attention actually amounts to a considerable *curtailing* of the child's freedom, and he must, like a prince born into a royal family, carry a weight for which children were never made. (May, 1969c, p. 120. See also May, 1969a, pp. 17–18; 1969c, pp. 119, 140, 278; 1972, pp. 113–114, 123–126, 144, 159, 176; 1953/1973, pp. 195–196; 1975, pp. 56–58.)

For the most part, however, existential psychology devotes relatively little attention to personality development.

FURTHER APPLICATIONS OF EXISTENTIAL PSYCHOLOGY

Dream Interpretation

Since intentionality and Dasein involve unconscious as well as conscious aspects, May often turns to dreams for information about an individual's being-in-the-world. Every dreamer uses various personal symbols in order to express particular ideas, so free association may be needed to unravel the meaning of this private language. But since May views personality as a unified whole, he rejects the idea of a Freudian dream-censoring component. Therefore, May's approach to dream interpretation tends to be more straightforward than Freud's.

For example, an impotent patient dreamed of having a metal pipe inserted in his head by his therapist, the end of which emerged below as an erect penis. This passive solution reflected his loss of Dasein and pathological dependence on other people, together with his misguided view of himself as a brainy but heartless sex machine. A college student who participated in violent protest movements proved to be compensating for unconscious feelings of intense powerlessness, as shown by recurrent nightmares wherein his parents and cousins did not know him and he disappeared, unmourned, into the Pacific Ocean. Another young man, who was just beginning to discover and accept his strength and Dasein, revealed this improvement through various dreams. In one of these he was a rabbit, chased by wolves, who ultimately turned on and attacked his pursuers. In another, he climbed a ladder with weak rungs by holding the sides together.

Some dreams cannot occur until the individual has made an appropriate decision in waking life. A dream that reveals the domineering nature of an employer (or a parent) may be possible only after choosing to quit the job in question (or to leave home). Thus dreams, like perceptions and memories, are a function of intentionality. (See May, 1958/1967b, pp. 77, 88; 1960; 1969b, p. 80; 1969c, pp. 56–57; 1972, pp. 36, 50, 133, 139; 1975, pp. 125ff.; May & Caligor, 1968.)

Psychopathology

Like Erikson and Maslow, May cautions that a complete theory of personality cannot be derived solely from the study of psychopathology. Yet clinical data are invaluable because they transcend our everyday defenses, and reveal vital aspects of human nature:

> It is one thing to discuss the hypothesis of aggression as resulting from frustration, but quite another to see the tenseness of a patient, his eyes flashing in anger or hatred, his posture clenched into paralysis, and to hear his half-stifled gasps of pain from reliving the time a score of years ago when his father whipped him because, through no fault of his own, his bicycle was stolen. . . . Such data are empirical in the deepest meaning of the term. (May, 1969c, p. 19.)

Psychopathology as Constricted Dasein. The healthy individual enjoys a strong Dasein, and lives actively and purposefully in Umwelt, Mitwelt, and Eigenwelt. In contrast, psychopathology involves a loss of will and the subjugation of one mode of being-in-the-world to another.

For example, the sufferer may reject interpersonal relationships (Mitwelt) as irreconcilable with his or her own needs and values (Eigenwelt). Or Eigenwelt may be sacrificed to Mitwelt, with the individual becoming a social chameleon and constantly trying to adapt to the wishes of others. (Compare these with moving away from people, and moving toward people, in Horneyan theory.) Or the sufferer may deny Umwelt, and an important drive like sexuality, in order to conform to parental demands. But whatever the form, such a constriction or loss of Dasein ultimately results in self-estrangement, apathy, and an inability to experience one's existence as real.

"The fundamental neurotic process in our day is the repression of the ontological sense, the loss of [one's] sense of being" (May, 1958/1967b, p. 86; see also May, 1969b, p. 75; 1969c, pp. 111, 212–218, 244).

Causes of Psychopathology. To May, as to Freud, psychopathology may be caused by trauma that occur early in life. For example, the child's love, trust, and will may be shattered by such pathogenic parental behaviors as overprotectiveness, overpermissiveness, domination, manipulativeness, rejection, and hypocrisy. Yet since May's goal is to free personality theory from the shackles of rigid psychic determinism, he prefers to stress the teleological aspects of psychopathology.

According to May, the sufferer's present inability to accept ontological anxiety and guilt leads to an extremely poor choice: namely, to neutralize the dread of nonbeing by sacrificing Dasein. But abandoning one's true innate potentials by desperately attempting to be what others want, by denying Mitwelt and living as a recluse, or by rejecting one's own biological drives is always to be on the verge of loneliness or frustration. Paradoxically, therefore, the sufferer's all-out quest for safety results in an existence so limited as to be all the more easily destroyed, and occasions considerably greater (neurotic) anxiety and guilt. (Conversely, the healthy person who asserts Dasein and readily accepts all three modes of being-in-the-world is far less vulnerable to threats in any one of them.) Thus May, like most of the theorists discussed thus far, regards psychopathology as a difference in degree rather than in kind. (See May, 1969c, pp. 16, 20–21, 25–26; Reeves, 1977, pp. 69–71, 87, 119.)

Varieties of Psychopathology. Existential psychologists look with disfavor on the standard psychiatric nomenclature, which they regard as yet another depersonalizing abstraction. Even psychosis is not an illness, but rather the living out of such personal truths as "I do not exist" or "My body is an empty shell, with no personality inside"—an extreme loss of Dasein that results in behavior that is totally subjective and seemingly bizarre, but actually quite meaningful. (Other theorists regard this view as oversimplified, however; see Arieti, 1974, pp. 126–128.)

May himself is not totally opposed to the use of diagnostic terminology, so long as it does not become dogma and preclude a true understanding of the patient. Thus he characterizes the majority of modern patients as suffering from obsessive-compulsive neurosis, and concludes that this typically represents a misguided effort to achieve some measure of personal significance. One young man suffered through a highly pathogenic childhood that included a pampering and seductive mother, a rejecting father who would hold grudges for weeks over trivial incidents, and belittlement by his peers. To survive in this virulent emotional climate, he denied his power to choose and became totally submissive. As a result, his assertive potentials emerged in an indirect and tortuous form: a daily compulsive ritual wherein he had to lift the bedsheets exactly the proper distance before arising, put his clothes on in precisely the right order, eat breakfast in a similarly rigid and predetermined manner, and so on, or else something terrible must surely happen to a member of his family. "What strikes us immediately in this complex system is the *tremendous power* it gives him. Any chance deed of his could decide whether someone lived or died" (May, 1972, p. 130; see also May, 1969a, pp. 22–23; 1969c, pp. 27, 196; 1972, pp. 126–137).

Psychotherapy

Theoretical Foundation. The goal of existential psychotherapy is to help patients recover their repressed Dasein, integrate their daimonic into consciousness, recapture their lost will, take responsibility for their own lives, and affirm those choices that lead to the fulfillment of their own innate potentials. "The aim of therapy is that the patient *experience his existence as real . . .* which includes becoming aware of his potentialities, and becoming able to act on the basis of them" (May, 1958/1967b, p. 85; see also pp. 37, 80, 86).

Although May retains the Freudian term *patient,* he shares Kelly's belief that it is misleadingly passive; changing one's personality requires considerable effort and courage. May also agrees that the therapist must be sufficiently flexible to understand and utilize each patient's constructs and language, rather than seeking to impose a single theoretical framework on all humanity. "The existential analysis movement is a protest against the tendency to see the patient in forms tailored to [the therapist's] own preconceptions" (May, 1958/1967c, p. 8; see also May, 1969a, pp. 22–23; 1969c, pp. 196–197).

Unlike Erikson, May warns that the therapist must *not* become an agent of social conformity. A patient who adapts to the prevailing mores does gain some temporary happiness and reduction in anxiety, but at a grave price: an abdication of Dasein and personal choice. Ultimately, therefore, this false cure results in still greater powerlessness and alienation, which may well emerge in the form of destructiveness against self and others. (See May, 1958/1967b, p. 87; 1969a, pp. 4, 39.)

Therapeutic Procedures. The existential psychotherapist strives to develop a genuine and empathic relationship with the patient, as in Rogerian psychotherapy. A variety of therapeutic procedures may be used, including face-to-face interviews and Rogerian unconditional positive regard, deducing vital information from the patient's bodily movements (as in Adlerian theory), and/or the Freudian couch and free association. But regardless of the specific methods, the therapist's primary goal is to engage the patient's will and capacity to choose. "[If] the intentionality of the patient is not reached, he . . . never fully commits himself, is never fully *in* the analysis" (May, 1969c, p. 248; see also May, 1958/1967b, pp. 45, 78, 84, 87; 1958/1967c, pp. 5, 27; 1969a, p. 21; 1969b, p. 76; 1969c, pp. 91, 231–232, 235, 241, 246–272).

According to May, the main purpose of free association is to reveal the patient's conscious and unconscious intentions. Other ways to raise the issue of intentionality include direct questions, such as "What do you wish from me today?" or "Why did you come today?" And any fledgling expressions of will by the patient, such as "perhaps I can try to do thus-and-so," are always focused upon by the therapist.

Resistance, Transference, and Countertransference. To a person who has surrendered Dasein and intentionality, the prospect of assuming responsibility and choosing a course in life is highly threatening. It is these fears, rather than some illicit instinct, that evoke the sort of resistances described by Freud. However, May does accept Freud's contention that paying for one's therapy helps to overcome such difficulties. "The whole meaning of resistance and repression testifies to the anxiety and pain accompanying [the] disclosures about one's self. That is one reason why it is good that the patient pay for his sessions; if he won't take too much when he pays for it, he will take scarcely a thing given him gratis!" (May, 1969c, p. 165; see also May, 1958/1967b, p. 79).

Existential psychologists are not overly concerned with the issue of countertransference, and regard an affection for the patient as a necessary and desirable aspect of therapy. May does credit transference as one of Freud's great contributions, and agrees that patients often unconsciously displace feelings and behaviors from previous significant others (such as the parents) to the therapist. But here again, he cautions that an excessive emphasis on the past can only erode the patient's sense of responsibility. Transference involves forces from the present as well, for the typical patient is so emotionally immature as to seek a beloved and omnipotent savior, and the therapist becomes a natural target for these current wishes and feelings. (See May, 1958/1967b, pp. 83–85, 89; 1969a, pp. 16–17.)

Psychotherapy and Social Reform. Like Fromm, May argues that our society is in many ways pathogenic. He contends that technology and technique have overwhelmed eros and passion, so that we are more concerned with functioning like well-oiled machines than with caring and loving. May is very critical of such inhuman behaviors as the Vietnam War, interracial strife, the cacophonous din and faceless hordes of the rush-hour subway, the assembly-line impersonality of giant corporations and universities, professors who write pointless books because they are more concerned with augmenting their list of publications than with pusuing any exciting truths, television advertising that uses subtle lies to sell various products, and government officials who show their contempt for us by "explaining" national policy in evasions and double-talk. Finally, looming above us all is the hideous prospect of nuclear war. (See May, 1969c, pp. 31, 96, 185; 1972, pp. 29–31, 53–54, 68–71, 243.)

May does not share Fromm's inclination to propose a radical remodeling of society. However, he does emphasize that we must achieve a more equitable distribution of authority and responsibility.

Religion

May rejects Freud's contention that religion is a form of neurosis, concluding instead that it may serve either constructive or destructive purposes. (See May, 1953/1973, pp. 193–208.) To be sure, any religion that tries to substitute dogma for personal freedom and responsibility is indeed pathogenic. Thus some religions try to alleviate the pain of ontological anxiety and guilt by teaching that blind faith will be rewarded by an omnipotent and protective deity, a reinforcement of infantile security wishes that inevitably inhibits Dasein and intentionality. One young girl was even instructed that her life was always to be directed by the will of God, as interpreted by her mother. Not surprisingly, she subsequently proved wholly unable to make such crucial personal decisions as whom to marry.

However, religion may instead be used to affirm the individual's dignity and power. Such constructive approaches stress the need to develop one's inherent capacities and responsibility to choose, thereby serving as a valuable aid to Dasein—and, therefore, to the emergence of a healthy personality.

Literature and Art

The relatively small number of people who enter psychotherapy are, for the most part, unusually sensitive and gifted. They suffer from conflicts that the average person has managed to repress or rationalize, but that typically become major social issues in subsequent years. Literature and art also represent communications from the unconscious of a person living on the psychological frontier of society, and illuminate vital human conflicts that have not as yet gained widespread recognition.

For example, novels like Camus's *The Stranger* and Kafka's *The Castle* offer a compelling picture of a man's estrangement from the world and from those he pretends to love. Playwrights such as Beckett, Pinter, Genêt, and Ionesco have dramatized our profound alienation and inability to communicate with one another on a truly human level. Melville's *Billy Budd* depicts the dangers of innocence, with the title character ultimately destroyed because of his blindness to the evil nature of a shipmate. Innocence is also a theme of the popular movie *The Last Picture Show,* wherein women deprived of any economic or political power resort to a guise of purity and devious sexual machinations in an effort to achieve some measure of personal significance. The cruelty of the daimonic is vividly portrayed by the mutual emotional butchery of the leading characters in *Who's Afraid of Virginia Woolf.* And artists like Cézanne, Picasso, and Van Gogh express our depersonalization visually, as by painting people who are literally in fragments. (See May, 1958/1967b, p. 57; 1958/1967c, pp. 16–17; 1969c, pp. 21–24, 110–111, 128, 148–149; 1972, pp. 49–50, 68, 116, 205–211, 253; 1953/1973, pp. 17–18, 58–59; 1985.)

EVALUATION

Criticisms and Controversies

Confusions and Contradictions. All too often, May fails to define and/or interrelate his constructs with sufficient clarity. For example, "intentionality" is used in four different ways. The opposite of apathy is sometimes defined as love, and sometimes as care. And neurosis is variously equated with the repression of one's ontological sense, and with a conflict between two different ways of not fulfilling oneself (May, 1969c, pp. 29, 89, 247; Reeves, 1977, pp. 57–60, 63, 135–136, 209–210).

Major constructs disappear completely from one of May's books to the next, leaving considerable doubt as to those that are essential to his theory. Even a fundamental concept like Dasein is virtually ignored in two of his major works, *Love and Will* (1969c) and *Power and Innocence* (1972). May's discussion of the causes and dynamics of neurosis appears quite vague in comparison with the theories of other humanistically oriented psychologists, such as Horney and Rogers. Also, like Maslow, May does not satisfactorily reconcile Freudian repression with his holistic conception of personality.

Lack of Originality. May has been criticized for presenting intentionality as a radically new addition to psychological thought in 1969, some ten to fifty years after the teleologically oriented theories of Adler, Jung, and Allport. In addition, May's treatment of power and innocence bears a marked similarity to the Adlerian concepts of striving for superiority and inferiority complex. Sacrificing Mitwelt to Eigenwelt (or vice versa), and the resulting increase in anxiety, is similar to Horney's conception of moving away from (or toward) people and the resulting vicious circle (Figure 5.1).

Some existential psychologists contend that their approach varies significantly from person-centered theory, primarily because Rogers argues that actualization unfolds smoothly and spontaneously in an ideal environment. Yet Rogers also states that no actual environment is ever ideal, for we all meet with conditional positive regard and introject some parental standards. This makes achieving true self-knowledge and self-affirmation a task requiring considerable effort and courage, just as in existential theory.

Lack of Scientific Rigor. The existential approach to science tends to rule out quantification and statistical analysis, a viewpoint most modern psychologists would reject. May makes sweeping statements (e.g., most Americans lack mercy) without any supporting data (1972, p. 53), giving his writing a distinctly sermonic, Frommian tone.

Empirical Research

Some existential psychologists have chosen to devise objective personality measures, and there exist inventories designed to measure such constructs as meaninglessness or "existential vacuum" (Crumbaugh, 1968) and existential morale and identity (Thorne & Pishkin, 1973). Other researchers have tried to determine whether we are motivated by powerful unconscious fears of death, as the existentialists claim. Unfortunately, this area is beset by methodological difficulties. It is not easy to study unobservable, unconscious processes in the research laboratory. Furthermore, the fear of death is a complicated and multidimensional variable: it is partly conscious as well as unconscious, and the fear of nonbeing is only one of several reasons for fearing death. (Others include the fear of physical suffering, fears about the psychological and economic impact that the death will have on loved ones, and being unable to achieve important goals.) Thus the results have been too equivocal for any definitive conclusions to be drawn. (See Schulz & Ewen, 1992, pp. 390–397.) In general, however, existential psychology has not generated much empirical research.

Contributions

To some psychologists, concepts such as being-in-the-world offer a valid and important new way of conceptualizing the human personality. The work of May and others led some clinicians to add a new category to the diagnostic list, "existential neurosis," which refers to chronic feelings of alienation and meaninglessness. The existentialists' emphasis on our repressed fear of death is generally regarded as a significant contribution, and their work with psychotics has furthered our understanding of (and compassion for) this apparently bizarre form of psychopathology. *Love and Will* (1969c) focused on such important issues as intentionality and personal responsibility, and became a national best-seller. And May's writings represent the thoughts of a compassionate and insightful psychotherapist.

As a commentary on our time, May's books include points of interest and importance. But as a theory of personality, his approach appears too flawed to stand on its own as a viable entity. Given these deficiencies, and the conceptual abstruseness of the major alternative approaches (Binswanger, Boss), existential psychology seems destined to occupy a secondary position to the similarly humanistic theories discussed in the preceding chapters.

Suggested Reading

May's existentialist constructs are most comprehensively presented in four articles (1958/1967b, 1958/1967c, 1969a, 1969b), while his readable and provocative books include *Man's Search for Himself* (1953/1973), *Love and Will* (1969c), *Power and Innocence* (1972), and *The Meaning of Anxiety* (1977a). Also useful is a comprehensive, if at times difficult, analysis of May's theory by Reeves (1977).

■ SUMMARY

Existential psychology is a philosophy of human nature and psychotherapy, devised to explain such modern forms of psychopathology as apathy and depersonalization. A leading exponent of this approach is Rollo May.

1. THE BASIC NATURE OF HUMAN BEINGS. *Being-in-the-world (Dasein):* Each of us has an inherent need to exist in the world into which we are born, and to achieve a conscious and unconscious sense of ourselves as an autonomous and distinct entity. This being-in-the-world (Dasein) comprises three simultaneous and interrelated modes: our physical and physiological surroundings (Umwelt), the social world of other people (Mitwelt), and the psychological world of relationship to oneself and one's innate potentials (Eigenwelt). Asserting Dasein and actualizing Eigenwelt is a task that requires constant effort, courage, and a willingness to accept the freedom and responsibility to choose one's own course in life. *Nonbeing and Anxiety:* Death is one aspect of being-in-the-world that none of us ever escapes, and it may terminate our existence at any moment. The prospect of eventual nonbeing evokes anxiety, a certain amount of which is a normal and inevitable aspect of human nature. *Guilt:* No one ever fulfills all of his or her innate potentials, or deals perfectly with the three modes of being-in-the-world. These failures evoke guilt, a certain amount of which is also a normal and inevitable aspect of human nature. *Intentionality:* We are our choices, and our plans for the future pervade all aspects of our personality—perceptions, memories, dreams, therapeutic insights, and so forth. To May, the main symptom of modern neurosis is the loss of will and personal responsibility. *Love:* Love is also an essential aspect of human nature. It always involves a blending of four components, albeit in varying proportions: sex, eros, philia, and agapé. Modern neurosis typically involves the repression of eros and passion, resulting in a mechanical and unsatisfactory sexuality. *The Daimonic:* Although human destructiveness is due in large part to the powerlessness resulting from the loss of Dasein, we also have innate urges that are both illicit and benign. This daimonic must be integrated into consciousness for psychological health to be achieved.

2. THE STRUCTURE OF PERSONALITY. May adopts an essentially holistic approach to personality, one that excludes any specific structural constructs. He does accept

the importance of the unconscious, however, and of repression and other Freudian defense mechanisms.

3. THE DEVELOPMENT OF PERSONALITY. May warns that such damaging parental errors as overprotection, overpermissiveness, domination, rejection, and hypocrisy are likely to shatter the child's independence and Dasein. For the most part, however, he devotes little attention to personality development.

4. FURTHER APPLICATIONS. *Dream Interpretation:* Since intentionality and Dasein involve unconscious as well as conscious aspects, May often turns to dreams for information about a person's being-in-the-world. In accordance with his conception of personality as a unified whole, he rejects the idea of a dream-censoring component in favor of a more commonsense approach to dream interpretation. *Psychopathology:* Neurosis is typified by an inability to accept ontological anxiety and guilt, which causes the sufferer to try and neutralize the dread of nonbeing by sacrificing Daesein. Thus one mode of being-in-the-world may be subjugated to another, as by rejecting interpersonal relationships in an attempt to preserve one's own needs and values (sacrificing Mitwelt to Eigenwelt). This abandonment of one's true needs and potentials results in self-estrangement, a loss of intentionality and will, increased anxiety, and an inability to experience one's existence as real. *Psychotherapy:* The goal of existential psychotherapy is to help patients recover their repressed Dasein, integrate their daimonic into consciousness, recapture their lost will, take responsibility for their own lives, and affirm those choices that lead to the fulfillment of their own innate potentials. The therapist is procedurally eclectic, and may use various techniques (e.g., Freudian, Rogerian). *Other Applications:* May concludes that religion may be either constructive or destructive, depending on how it is used. He finds many important examples of existential thought in literature and art, and refers to these sources frequently in his writings.

5. EVALUATION. May has been criticized for theoretical confusions and contradictions, failing to adhere to a relatively consistent set of constructs, an inadequate explanation of the causes and dynamics of neurosis, a lack of originality, and a lack of scientific rigor. His contributions include an emphasis on such important issues as intentionality, personal responsibility, anxiety, and our repressed fear of death, useful criticisms and insights concerning our present society, and books that have achieved widespread popularity.

STUDY QUESTIONS

1. According to May, a person who has surrendered Dasein and intentionality is threatened by the need to choose his or her own course in life. "The central core of modern man's 'neurosis' . . . [is] the sapping of his will and ability to make decisions." Does the case history discussed throughout the Appendix support this argument?

2. May's theory has been criticized as lacking in originality. Compare each of the following ideas to the related views of the theorist named in parentheses: (a) Feelings of intense powerlessness may be concealed behind violent attempts to act powerful. (Adler) (b) Repression is *not* caused by one part of personality banishing material to another part, since personality is unified and holistic. The whole individual lacks courage and chooses not to experience threatening material, such as anxiety or the daimonic. (Adler) (c) Neurosis may take the form of rejecting interpersonal relationships (Mitwelt) in order to protect one's own needs and values (Eigenwelt), or sacrificing Eigenwelt to Mitwelt and trying constantly to adapt to the wishes of others. These neuroses are caused by parental rejection and stifling the child's natural expression of will, and the constriction of Dasein leads to an increase in anxiety. (Horney) (d) One way to gain relief from the fear of nonbeing is through the apparent safety of social conformity. (Fromm) (e) Because Dasein is so personal, no one else can tell a person how or what to be-in-the-world; each of us must discover our own potentials and needs. (Rogers) Do these comparisons support the criticism? Why or why not?

3. May argues that Eigenwelt must be independent of the opinions and expectations of other people, because adapting to external customs will eventually result in a loss of Dasein and greater feelings of alienation. Erikson contends that identity requires social solidarity, or validation in the eyes of significant others. Do you agree with May or Erikson? Why?

4. (a) May contends that the primary cause of anxiety is the fear of nonbeing. Horney argues that anxiety results from repressing one's real self and wishes. How might these views be interpreted as supporting each other, rather than as contradictory? (b) Horney attributes anxiety to intrapsychic conflict, whereas May's conception of personality as a unified whole rules out the possibility of inner conflict. Which view do you prefer? Why?

5. Give an example from your own life, from the life of someone you know well, or from fiction to support May's argument that emphatically affirming our Dasein takes considerable courage.

6. (a) In addition to the fear of nonbeing, what other reasons might there be to fear death? What does this imply about May's theory? (b) According to May, the awareness of death is widely repressed in our society. Is this likely to be as true today as it was two decades ago, given the current emphasis on such issues as the "right to die" and concern about AIDS?

7. Give an example from your own life, from the life of someone you know well, or from fiction to show how several people viewing exactly the same object can see it quite differently because their intentions are different.

8. May concludes that the majority of today's patients are obsessive-compulsive, and shows how such behavior can provide the sufferer with "tremendous" feelings of power. (See the section on varieties of psychopathology.) Consider the following additional information from the case history discussed throughout the Appendix. What additional reasons might underlie this behavior?

Every night before going to bed, I feel compelled to check the alarm clock to be sure that it is set to go off the following morning. I do this not just once, but ten or fifteen times. I feel as though I want to stop this ritual; it's annoying and even embarrassing. But if I do stop, I worry about whether or not the clock is really set. Eventually I get so nervous that I have to examine the clock once again to be sure it's set properly—which, of course, it is.

PART V

THE BEHAVIORIST ALTERNATIVE

PROLOGUE

Throughout this book, we have seen that personality theorists seek to explain human behavior in terms of hypothesized inner causes: instincts, archetypes, feelings of inferiority, traits, needs, conditions of worth, intentions, conflicts between various components, and so forth. However, the validity of intrapsychic motives is by no means universally accepted.

At about the time Freud was introducing the death instinct and structural model, the noted American psychologist John B. Watson sought to discredit such theories by proving that a phobia could be induced solely through external forces. Watson had been favorably impressed by the work of Ivan Pavlov (1906; 1927; 1928), who first demonstrated the simple form of learning called *classical conditioning*. Pavlov placed a dog in restraint in a soundproof room, presented a neutral stimulus (such as a light or tone), and immediately followed it with food, which caused the dog to salivate. After numerous repetitions of this procedure, the dog salivated to the light alone. Thus the light was repeatedly paired with an *unconditioned stimulus* (food), which automatically elicited salivation (the *unconditioned response*). As a result, the light became a *conditioned stimulus* that could by itself evoke salivation (a response learned through conditioning, or *conditioned response*).

In accordance with Pavlov's procedure, Watson obtained an eleven-month-old infant (Albert) who feared nothing but loud noises. Watson presented Albert with a tame (and readily accepted) white rat, and then crashed a hammer against a steel bar held just behind Albert's head. After only seven repetitions of this traumatic sequence, Albert was conditioned: he now showed a strong fear of the rat alone, some of which not only lasted for a full month but also generalized to such other furry animals as rabbits. (See for example Harris, 1979; 1980; Samelson, 1980; Watson, 1913; 1919; 1924; Watson & Rayner, 1920; Watson & Watson, 1921.)

Watson therefore concluded that it was patently foolish (and dangerously misleading) to relate psychopathology to any inner cause, such as unresolved Oedipal strivings, id-ego conflicts, or even personality per se. Instead he argued that psychology should be redefined as the study of behavior—an approach that is anathematic to most personality theorists, but which has gained considerable acceptance among modern psychologists.

As is the case with personality theory, behaviorism is marked by lively disagreements rather than placid unity. In this section, therefore, we will consider several varieties.

Radical Behaviorism: B. F. Skinner

Undoubtedly the best known of current behaviorists, B. F. Skinner is an outspoken critic of any theory that attributes human behavior to inner causes. Skinner does *not* claim that inner states and unconscious processes do not exist. He argues that psychology can be scientific only if it restricts its attention to observable behaviors, and to visible operations performed on the organism from without. Skinner therefore discards such concepts as human nature, structural and developmental aspects of personality, and even personality itself. (Thus he is the only psychologist discussed in this book whose work cannot be organized according to our usual framework.)

Skinner's emphatic rejection of inner causes is accompanied by some sharp criticisms of theories discussed previously in this book, such as Freudian psychoanalysis and trait theory. His brand of behaviorism also leads to several radical and hotly debated conclusions. Thus Skinner contends that human beings do not and cannot plan for the future, or behave teleologically. Rather, all human behavior is determined by prior conditioning (although not necessarily classical conditioning). In fact, the controversy caused by Skinner's writings rivals the furor evoked by Freudian psychoanalysis.

More Eclectic Behaviorist Approaches

Although Skinner has made numerous important contributions to our knowledge of human behavior, the work of the theorists discussed in Chapters 2–14 is far too impressive to be replaced by his approach. In fact, an increasing number of behaviorists now accept the desirability of investigating at least some human inner states. It has even been argued that behaviorism cannot avoid paying some attention to introspections and thoughts, unobservable though they may be (e.g., Locke, 1971; Wachtel, 1977). Thus, Skinner's opinion notwithstanding, the most profitable future course for psychology may well involve some sort of rapprochement between personality theory and behaviorism.

One major effort to bridge the chasm between behaviorism and theories of personality is that of John Dollard and Neal E. Miller. Like Rogers, Dollard and Miller regard both clinical observation and experimental research as extremely important. Psychotherapy reveals deeply personal issues that the patient would be unlikely to discuss elsewhere, while the psychological laboratory has the advantage of greater scientific rigor. In marked contrast to Rogers, however, the goal of Dollard and Miller is to integrate the best features of psychoanalysis and behaviorism.

Dollard and Miller's theory is regarded by some as of primarily historical importance, in part because they have published little about it since 1950. Yet it represents an unusual and creative effort to merge two apparently irreconcilable schools of thought, and it has influenced the work of one well-known and highly regarded behaviorist. Albert Bandura has modified behaviorism in an even more eclectic direction, as by emphasizing the importance of cognitive and personal causes of behavior (e.g., expectations, beliefs, thoughts). He also devotes considerable attention to observational learning, which involves instruction and watching others perform tasks correctly. In fact, some critics would argue that Bandura's version of behaviorism is so eclectic that it actually represents more or less of a return to personality theory.

B. F. SKINNER
Radical Behaviorism

Like many of the theorists discussed in this book, B. F. Skinner experienced some painful moments of professional rejection. In Skinner's case, however, these problems involved a field other than psychology.

Skinner's initial professional goal was to become a novelist. He majored in English at Hamilton College and sent several of his short stories to the noted poet Robert Frost, who responded so favorably that Skinner spent some time after his graduation trying to write fiction. Yet one year later he abandoned his dream, having reached the unhappy conclusion that he had nothing literary to say and was only frittering away his time. Skinner also lacked the support of any peer or religious group, making this trying period much like an Eriksonian identity crisis (Elms, 1981; see also Mindess, 1988).

Interestingly, Skinner did not attribute his failure as a writer to some deficiency within himself. Instead, he regarded this failure as the inevitable result of the circumstances in which he found himself. When he later pursued a career in psychology, he followed a similar course: he concluded that all human behavior is determined not by any inner causes, but solely by the effects of the external environment.

BIOGRAPHICAL SKETCH

Burrhus Frederic Skinner was born on March 20, 1904, in Susquehanna, Pennsylvania. He remembers his father as a lawyer who gave the impression of conceit, yet hungered for praise. His mother was attractive and socially successful, but frigid and puritanical about sexual matters. The family also included a younger brother.

Skinner recalls growing up in a bountiful environment: enjoying a variety of fruits that grew in the back yard of his ramshackle home, driving to the country in the fall to gather hickory nuts, and catching turtles, mice, and chipmunks. He also built numerous toys and gadgets, one of which attached to a hook in his bedroom closet and confronted him with a sign whenever he failed to hang up his pajamas—a pet peeve of his mother's. (See Skinner, 1967; 1976/1977.)

Skinner received his A.B. from Hamilton College in 1926, where he was Phi Beta Kappa. After his failure to succeed as a novelist (described above), Skinner opted to pursue his interest in animal and human behavior through graduate work in psychology at Harvard University. Here he pursued a rigorous daily schedule: rising at six in the morning to study, going to classes, studying again until nine in the evening, and then going to bed, with virtually no time for movies or dates. (See Skinner, 1967, p. 398; 1976/1977, pp. 248–249, 263–265, 291–292.) It was here that Skinner became interested in the ideas of Pavlov and Watson, receiving his Ph.D. in 1931. Save for the years 1936–1948, when he was at the University of Minnesota and University of Indiana, Skinner spent his entire professional career at Harvard. He married Yvonne Blue on November 1, 1936, a union that produced two daughters.

Skinner's invention of the laboratory apparatus that bears his name was an interesting, and often amusing, process. Years later he recalled that having the animal's responses reinforce themselves was done primarily to make the experimenter's task easier, that intermittent reinforcement was originally a desperation measure when faced with a dwindling supply of food on a Saturday afternoon, and that the effects of extinction were first discovered when the food-delivering mechanism happened to jam (Skinner, 1972b, pp. 101–124). Skinner also devised a mechanical baby tender (or air crib), which he used with his second child. This spacious, temperature-controlled, soundproof, and germ-free enclosure is intended to provide an optimal environment for the growing baby. And it helps the parents as well, since it requires far less effort than changing bedding or clothing. However, his invention has not been widely accepted. (See M. H. Hall, 1967a, pp. 21–22; Skinner, 1972b, pp. 567–573; 1979.)

Skinner is the author of many journal articles and some dozen books, including a novel about an ideal behaviorist community (*Walden Two*, 1948)—one that has by now sold very well, although strongly attacked by critics and virtually ignored by the public for a dozen years following its publication. (See Skinner, 1969, pp. 29–30; 1978, p. 57.) His honors include the Distinguished Scientific Contribution Award of the American Psychological Association and various scientific medals.

Skinner's last public appearance was on August 10, 1990, when he gave the keynote address at the opening ceremony of the American Psychological Association's annual convention. He also received a special citation for his lifetime contributions to psychology. Skinner died eight days later of complications arising from leukemia.

CLASSICAL (RESPONDENT) VERSUS OPERANT CONDITIONING

Causality and Science

Skinner agrees that the goal of scientific psychology is to predict and control future behavior. (See Chapter 1.) However, he warns that this objective cannot be achieved by any theory that attributes our actions to inner causes.

Skinner likens all such approaches to the prescientific fallacies of the ancient physicists, who "explained" the laws of gravity by claiming that a falling body accelerated because it became happier on finding itself nearer home. To Skinner, the so-called inner causes of human behavior are nothing more than useless redundancies: to say that an organism eats *because* it is hungry, attacks *because* it feels angry, or looks into a mirror *because* it is narcissistic explains nothing whatsoever, for we are still left with the task of discovering why the organism happened to feel hungry, angry, or narcissistic. Even heredity does no more than set certain limits on the behaviors that a person can execute. "The doctrine of 'being born that way' has little to do with demonstrated facts. It is usually an appeal to ignorance" (Skinner, 1953/1965, p. 26). Thus psychology can only escape its own dark ages by rejecting the unscientific constructs that pervade personality theory, and studying actual behavior as a function of the external environment:

> A causal chain [consists] of three links: (1) an operation performed upon the organism from without—for example, water deprivation; (2) an inner condition—for example, physiological or psychic thirst; and (3) a kind of behavior—for example, drinking. . . . [Therefore,] we may avoid many tiresome and exhausting digressions by examining the third link as a function of the first. Valid information about the second link may throw light upon this relationship, but can in no way alter it. . . . [Thus my] objection to inner states is not that they do not exist, but that they are not relevant in a functional [i.e., causal] analysis. (Skinner, 1953/1965, pp. 34–35. See also Skinner, 1953/ 1965, pp. 6, 23–42, 143–144, 202–203, 257–282; 1969, pp. 242–243; 1971/1972a, pp. 5–13, 68; 1974–1976, pp. 39–40, 54–57, 174–183.)

Types of Conditioning

Skinner agrees with Pavlov and Watson that some behaviors are learned through classical (or "respondent") conditioning, as when the dentist's chair becomes a source of anxiety because it has been repeatedly paired with the painful drill. In Pavlovian conditioning, however, the conditioned stimulus (e.g., light) precedes and elicits the conditioned response (salivation). In contrast, Skinner argues that the vast majority of learning is due to what happens *after* the behavior occurs. "It is now clear that we must take into account what the environment does to an organism not only before but after it responds. Behavior is shaped and maintained by its consequences" (Skinner, 1971/1972a, p. 16; see also Skinner, 1953/1965, pp. 52–58, 66).

According to Skinner, behaviors that operate on the environment to produce effects that strengthen them (are **reinforced**) are more likely to occur in the future. He refers to such behaviors as **operants,** and to the process by which they are learned as **operant conditioning.**[1] Any stimulus

---

[1]Some psychologists use the term "instrumental conditioning" as a synonym for operant conditioning, but Skinner does not. (See Skinner, 1969, p. 109.)

that increases the probability of a response when presented (**positive reinforcer**), or when removed (**negative reinforcer**), is by definition a reinforcer. Thus Skinner makes no assumptions at all about inner satisfactions or drive reduction.

As an illustration, consider a person who has not consumed any liquids for several hours. This individual may well be positively reinforced by going to the kitchen and drinking a glass of water. If so, he or she will more frequently emit this response under similar conditions. If not, some other response is likely to prevail on a subsequent occasion (such as drinking a glass of juice or soda). We cannot assume that water is a reinforcer; we must determine this by studying its effects on the organism. Nor is there any need to deal with unobservable inner states, such as a thirst drive. Similarly, if taking off a tight shoe provides a reduction in pressure that proves to be negatively reinforcing, the probability of this behavior will be greater the next time a shoe pinches. (See Skinner, 1953/1965, pp. 72–75, 171–174, 185; 1969, pp. 5–7, 109; 1974/1976, pp. 44, 51.)

Beyond Freedom and Dignity

Perhaps Skinner's most controversial assertion is that we have no capacity for teleology, purpose, or will; *all* behavior is determined by prior conditioning, usually operant. We drink water or remove a troublesome shoe not as the result of some carefully formulated plan, but only because responses like these have previously been reinforced:

> Instead of saying that a man behaves because of the consequences which *are* to follow his behavior, [I] simply say that he behaves because of the consequences which *have* followed similar behavior in the past. . . . [Thus] no behavior is free. (Skinner, 1953/1965, pp. 87, 111. See also Skinner, 1971/1972a.)

Many people prefer to believe that they are free to choose their own course in life, especially insofar as their praiseworthy behaviors are concerned. To be sure, we may readily blame our failures and transgressions on external causes and "extenuating circumstances." Yet we cling to the myth of human freedom and dignity by refusing to surrender the credit for our achievements, even though these also are solely the result of conditioning— subtle and complicated though it may be. In fact, just as Freud did with psychoanalysis, Skinner compares behaviorism to the two great historical shocks to our self-esteem: the Copernican theory of the solar system, which displaced us from our preeminent position at the center of the universe; and the Darwinian theory of evolution, which challenged our presumed distinction from the animal kingdom (Skinner, 1953/1965, p. 7; 1971/1972a, p. 202).

Nevertheless, Skinner contends that the behaviorist rejection of free will has important advantages. The only way to resolve the potential catastrophes we face today, such as a world famine and nuclear holocaust, is by developing a true technology of behavior. This will enable us to understand the external forces that control our actions, and design them to ensure the survival and betterment of humankind:

> It is hard to imagine a world in which people live together without quarreling, maintain themselves by producing the food, shelter, and clothing they need, enjoy themselves and contribute to the enjoyment of others in art, music, literature, and games, consume only a reasonable part of the resources of the world and add as little as possible to its pollution, bear no more children than can be raised decently . . . and come to know themselves accurately and, therefore, manage themselves effectively. Yet all this is possible . . . [The behavioristic] view of man offers exciting possibilities. We have not yet seen what man can make of man. (Skinner, 1971/1972a, pp. 204–206. See also Skinner, 1978, pp. 29–30.)

PRINCIPLES OF OPERANT CONDITIONING

The Skinner Box

While Skinner is keenly interested in the prediction and control of human behavior, his extensive research deals mostly with animal subjects (primarily because they are more easily investigated under laboratory conditions). His main method for studying operant conditioning is the well-known piece of apparatus that he invented, and that is now widely referred to by others as the **Skinner box.** (He himself prefers the term *operant conditioning apparatus.*)

One version of Skinner's apparatus consists of a soundproof box approximately one foot square in which a pigeon is placed, with a lighted plastic key (disk) at one end that permits access to food when pecked. (See Figure 15.1a.) This is not a difficult operant for a pigeon to learn, especially since it is deprived of food for some time prior to the experimental session. The key is connected to an electronic recording system that automatically produces a graph of the pigeon's response rate (see Figure 15.1b), and the apparatus can be programmed so that reinforcement is available after every peck of the disk or only intermittently. (See M. H. Hall, 1967a, p. 22; Skinner, 1953/1965, pp. 37–38, 63–67; 1969, pp. 7, 109–113; 1972b, pp. 104–113, 259.)

Skinner has also created somewhat different versions of the box for use with animals not capable of pecking disks. For example, rats are positively reinforced by receiving food for pressing a bar. The Skinner box may also be used to study the effects of negative reinforcement, as by having a peck of the disk or press of the bar turn off or prevent an electric shock. Or complicated sequences of behavior may be conditioned, as when a pigeon is

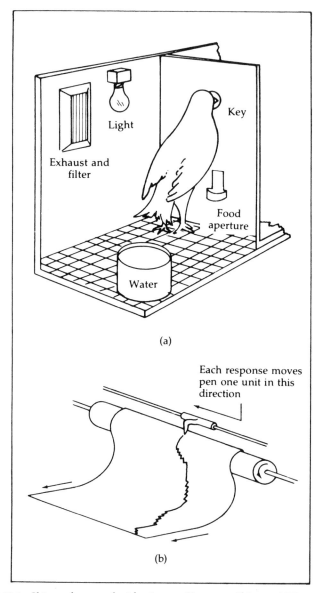

FIGURE 15.1. Skinner box used with pigeons (Ferster & Skinner, 1957, pp. 14, 24). (a) The experimental chamber (enclosed on all sides). (b) Diagram of the automatic cumulative recorder connected to the key.

reinforced for pecking a series of disks (with the order perhaps depending on their positions or colors). Thus Skinner's apparatus permits him to study the **contingencies of reinforcement** that he believes to control all behavior, namely the interrelationships among environmental stimuli (e.g., the disk), the response itself, and the reinforcing consequences.

Shaping

No pigeon or rat first placed in a Skinner box is acute enough to rush over and peck the disk, or press the bar; it wanders about, hesitates, and so forth. Rather than waiting a considerable length of time for the first correct response to be emitted and reinforced, the experimenter typically speeds up the learning process by **shaping** behavior in the desired direction.

For example, when the pigeon turns toward the disk, the experimenter presses a button that operates the reinforcement mechanism. (The pigeon has previously been acclimated to the Skinner box and food aperture, and so readily eats when given the opportunity.) This increases the probability that the pigeon will face the disk, and this behavior is reinforced until it is well learned. The experimenter then withholds reinforcement until the pigeon makes a slight movement toward the disk, then reinforces it only for moving still closer, and then only for touching the disk with its beak, thus leading it step by step to the desired response. (Such shaping usually takes no more than a few minutes.) "In this way we can build complicated operants which would never appear in the repertoire of the organism otherwise" (Skinner, 1953/1965, p. 92; see also pp. 91–93).

Shaping is by no means confined to the research laboratory; it plays an important role in the learning of virtually every operant. The growing child learns to walk and talk through a series of successive approximations, which are reinforced by success (e.g., becoming more nearly able to stand or speak) and by the approval of others.

Schedules of Reinforcement

Although the Skinner box can be programmed to provide reinforcement after every correct response (**continuous reinforcement**), this is not the most common form of learning. For example, the avid golfer does not sink every putt, and the gambling addict frequently fails to collect, yet both continue to pursue their respective avocations. Therefore, Skinner has conducted extensive studies of the ways in which behavior is affected by various schedules of **intermittent** (or **partial**) **reinforcement.**

Interval Schedules. In a **fixed-interval schedule** of (say) one minute ("FI 1"), reinforcement is given only for the first response that occurs at least one minute after the preceding reinforcement. This makes it impossible to obtain more than one feeding per minute, and so the pigeon eventually ceases pecking the disk after each reinforcement and gradually accelerates its responses to a high rate as the critical moment approaches.

Such pauses can be eliminated by varying the time interval randomly from trial to trial. A one-minute **variable-interval schedule** ("VI 1") includes some intervals of a few minutes and some of only a few seconds, with the average of all intervals being one minute. Variable-interval schedules produce learning that is extremely long-lasting, with some pigeons continuing to respond as many as 10,000 times after all reinforcement had ceased. (See Ferster & Skinner, 1957; Skinner, 1953/1965, pp. 70, 99–106; 1974/1976, pp. 64–67; 1978, p. 21.)

Ratio Schedules. Reinforcement may instead be given for every *n*th response (**fixed-ratio schedule**), or for an average of every *n*th response (**variable-ratio schedule**). Thus a fixed-ratio schedule of 50 ("FR 50") reinforces the fiftieth response following the preceding reinforcement, while a variable-ratio schedule of 50 ("VR 50") sometimes reinforces the fortieth subsequent response, sometimes the sixtieth, and so on.

Ratio schedules typically lead to very high response rates, since this produces more reinforcements. But the fixed-ratio schedule is less effective than the variable-ratio, and (like the fixed-interval schedule) tends to produce a pause following each reinforcement. Fixed-ratio schedules as high as 5,000 can be conditioned through shaping, as by giving reinforcement at first for every fifth response, then for every tenth response, and so on, but requiring so much effort may ultimately prove damaging to the organism.

Many complicated schedules of reinforcement have also been devised and studied by Skinner. Reinforcement may be given according to either a fixed-ratio or fixed-interval schedule, whichever is satisfied first. Both a fixed-ratio and a fixed-interval schedule may have to be satisfied in order to gain reinforcement. Or reinforcement may depend upon two or more schedules, which alternate at random. But whatever the form, Skinner regards the schedule of reinforcement as a far more important determinant of behavior than the amount or type. (See Ferster & Skinner, 1957; Skinner, 1953/1965, p. 101; 1968, p. 20; 1971/1972a, p. 32; 1978, p. 61.)

Conditioned Reinforcement (Secondary Reinforcement)

If a neutral stimulus is repeatedly paired with a reinforcer, it acquires the power to act as a reinforcer in its own right. Such **conditioned** (or **secondary**) **reinforcers** differ from the Pavlovian model in that they occur after a response, and thus serve to strengthen rather than elicit it.

To illustrate, suppose that a pigeon regularly receives its food together with a brief flash of light. It will learn to peck a key of a different color to produce the light alone, so the light has become a conditioned positive reinforcer. Or if the light has been repeatedly paired with an electric shock, a rat will learn to press the bar to turn off the light (which is now a conditioned negative reinforcer, or conditioned aversive stimulus). Or, since dark clouds have in the past been repeatedly followed by thunderstorms, a person is likely to "turn them off" by seeking shelter. (See Skinner, 1953/1965, pp. 76–81, 173–176; 1971/1972a, pp. 42, 115–117; 1978, pp. 22–23.)

Some conditioned reinforcers are commonly paired with several primary reinforcers, and are therefore particularly likely to be effective. For example, money (which is worthless in itself) can readily be exchanged for food, drink, shelter, and so forth.

Deprivation and Satiation

Reinforcement is not the only factor that affects the probability of an operant, for a pigeon that has undergone food **deprivation** for some time pecks the disk more frequently than does a satiated bird. Similarly, a child reluctant to drink its milk may have the probability of this response increased by restricting its water intake. "It is decidedly not true that a horse may be led to water but cannot be made to drink. By arranging a history of severe deprivation, we could be 'absolutely sure' that drinking would occur" (Skinner, 1953/1965, p. 32).

In accordance with his rejection of inner causes, Skinner defines such drives as hunger, thirst, sex, and sleep in terms of an external and precisely measurable set of operations: either the amount of time one has been without such reinforcements as food or water ("hours of deprivation"), or the reduction in weight resulting from food deprivation (measured as the percent of the weight achieved when allowed to eat freely):

> The net result of reinforcement is not simply to strengthen behavior, but to strengthen it *in a given state of deprivation.* . . . We [use] a *hungry* pigeon in our experiment[s], and we could not . . . [demonstrate] operant conditioning otherwise. (Skinner, 1953/1965, pp. 82, 149; see also pp. 68, 141–159.)

Whereas deprivation increases the probability of an operant, **satiation** may be used to decrease it. For example, a restaurant that charges a fixed price for dinner and wishes to get by with small portions may serve a large supply of good bread at the outset of the meal. Or bread lines and welfare programs may reduce the likelihood of aggressive behavior by the poorer members of society. (See Skinner, 1953/1965, p. 147.)

Stimulus and Response Induction (Generalization)

An operant tends to generalize to stimuli that resemble the conditioned stimulus, without any further conditioning. For example, a pigeon that has been reinforced for pecking a red key will respond when presented with one that is orange or yellow, albeit not as frequently. Such **stimulus induction** (or **stimulus generalization**) is also common with human beings, as when one is expecting an important telephone call and rushes to the phone at the faint sound of a doorbell. Stimulus induction is a *sine qua non* of learning, since no two situations are ever identical in every respect.

Conditioning also strengthens other responses that are similar to the operant (**response induction,** or **response generalization**). Thus training in one skilled behavior may improve performance in another, as when learning Latin facilitates one's proficiency in English. (See Skinner, 1953/1965, pp. 93–95, 132–134, 218).

Discrimination

If an organism can perceive a difference between two stimuli, or between the presence and absence of a stimulus, it can learn to respond to them in different ways (behavior known as **discrimination**). To illustrate, a rat will ultimately press the bar only when a light is on if reinforcement is withheld when the light is off. Or a pigeon presented with one red and one green key, only one of which produces reinforcement, will eventually peck only that one. Such "differential reinforcement" strengthens the control that the reinforced color has over the pigeon's behavior, while weakening that of the other color. Similarly, a child is taught by differential reinforcement to call red objects red ("That's right!") but not green ("That's wrong!"), and to discriminate other aspects of right from wrong.

Discrimination is also essential to learning, as otherwise we would respond to every situation in much the same way. It plays a particularly important role in the learning of skilled behaviors: the expert pianist or golfer becomes able to recognize and correct subtle physical errors that the novice cannot identify, and is reinforced for doing so with better performances. (See Skinner, 1953/1965, pp. 107–110, 134–136, 258–261; 1974/1976, p. 116.)

Extinction

If a pigeon that has learned to peck the key should subsequently receive no food for doing so, and this lack of reinforcement is repeated numerous times, the response frequency will decrease—and ultimately cease. Such **extinction** occurs more slowly if learning has occurred under intermittent reinforcement, or if the prior reinforcement has been prolonged. For example, a veteran writer with many previous publications may persistently submit a new manuscript to one uninterested publisher after another, whereas the near-beginner who has been reinforced with only one prior acceptance gives up after the first rejection. Thus operant conditioning is concerned not only with the learning of behavior but also its maintenance, for an operant will eventually extinguish if it is no longer followed by reinforcement. "One who readily engages in a given activity is not showing an interest, he is showing the effect of reinforcement. . . . [Conversely,] to become discouraged is simply to fail to respond because reinforcement has not been forthcoming" (Skinner, 1953/1965, p. 72; see also pp. 69–71, 98).

A response undergoing extinction does sometimes increase in frequency at the beginning of a new experimental session, without any additional reinforcement. This phenomenon is known as **spontaneous recovery,** and is

CAPSULE SUMMARY
Some Important Behaviorist Terminology (I)

Behaviorism	An approach to psychology that regards only actual behavior as suitable to scientific study.
Classical conditioning (respondent conditioning)	A simple form of learning first demonstrated by Pavlov, wherein a conditioned stimulus (e.g., light) becomes capable of eliciting a particular conditioned response (salivation) by being repeatedly paired with an unconditioned stimulus (food).
Conditioned reinforcement (secondary reinforcement)	Reinforcement that is provided by a conditioned stimulus.
Conditioned response	A response to a conditioned stimulus; thus, one learned through conditioning.
Conditioned stimulus	A previously neutral stimulus that acquires positive or aversive properties through conditioning.
Contingencies of reinforcement	The interrelationships between stimuli in the external environment, a particular response, and the reinforcement that follows that response.
Continuous reinforcement	Reinforcement given after every correct response. The converse of intermittent reinforcement.
Deprivation	Withholding a primary reinforcer (such as food or water) for some time, so that it may be used to reinforce and condition an operant.
Discrimination	(1) Reinforcing an organism for responding to some difference between two or more stimuli. (2) The resulting increase in the probability of responding to the reinforced stimulus.
Extinction	(1) Consistently following an operant with no reinforcement at all, thereby decreasing or eliminating its probability of occurrence. (2) The resulting decrease in frequency, or cessation, of the operant in question.
Fixed-interval schedule (FI)	Reinforcing the first correct response that occurs after a specified interval of time, measured from the preceding reinforcement. A schedule of intermittent reinforcement.
Fixed-ratio schedule (FR)	Reinforcing the last of a specified number of correct responses, counted from the preceding reinforcement. A schedule of intermittent reinforcement.
Intermittent reinforcement (partial reinforcement)	Reinforcement given after some correct responses, but not all. The converse of continuous reinforcement.

continued

Negative reinforcer (aversive stimulus)	A stimulus that increases the probability of a response when removed following that response, such as an electric shock or disapproval.
Operant	A type or class of behavior on which reinforcement is contingent, such as pecking the key in a Skinner box.
Operant conditioning	A form of learning wherein a response emitted by the organism operates on the environment to produce a positive reinforcer or to remove a negative reinforcer, and is therefore more likely to recur.
Positive reinforcer	A stimulus that increases the probability of a response when presented following that response, such as food or approval.
Probability of a response	The likelihood that a response will be emitted within a specified period of time; usually inferred from changes in its rate or frequency.
Punishment	A procedure designed to reduce the probability of an operant, wherein the behavior in question is followed by the presentation of a negative reinforcer or the removal of a positive reinforcer; thus, the converse of reinforcement.
Reinforcement	(1) In operant conditioning: following a response with the presentation of a positive reinforcer (positive reinforcement), or with the removal of a negative reinforcer (negative reinforcement), thereby increasing its probability of occurrence. (2) In classical conditioning: presenting a conditioned and an unconditioned stimulus at approximately the same time.
Response	(1) A single instance of an operant, such as one peck of the disk in a Skinner box. (2) A synonym for operant.
Response induction (response generalization)	A change in the probability of a response that has not itself been conditioned, because it is similar to one that has.
Satiation	(1) Decreasing the probability of an operant by providing reinforcement without requiring the correct response to be made. (2) The resulting decrease in the probability of the operant in question.
Schedules of reinforcement	Programs of continuous or (more frequently) intermittent reinforcement, including interval schedules, ratio schedules, and various combinations thereof.
Shaping (response shaping)	Facilitating learning by reinforcing increasingly more accurate approximations of the desired response.
Spontaneous recovery	A temporary increase in the probability of an operant that is undergoing extinction, which occurs at the beginning of a new experimental session without any additional reinforcement.
Stimulus induction (stimulus generalization)	The occurrence of a conditioned response to a stimulus that resembles the conditioned stimulus, without any further conditioning.
Unconditioned response	An automatic, unlearned response elicited by an unconditioned stimulus.

Capsule Summary, continued

Unconditioned stimulus	A stimulus that automatically elicits a particular (unconditioned) response, without any learning or conditioning being necessary.
Variable-interval schedule (VI)	Reinforcing the first correct response that occurs after a varying interval of time, measured from the preceding reinforcement, with the series of intervals having a specified mean. A schedule of intermittent reinforcement.
Variable-ratio schedule (VR)	Reinforcing the last of a varying number of correct responses, counted from the preceding reinforcement, with the series of ratios having a specified mean. A schedule of intermittent reinforcement.

attributed by Skinner to the fact that extinction is not yet complete (Ferster & Skinner, 1957, p. 733).

Complicated Sequences of Behavior

According to Skinner, even the most complicated sequence of behavior—driving a car, building a home, talking, and so on—can be explained in terms of conditioning. As a laboratory illustration, he has conditioned rats to pull a string that produces a marble from a rack, pick up the marble with the forepaws, carry it to a tube, and drop it inside. Such learning is accomplished by beginning with the lattermost response (here, dropping the marble into the tube), which is reinforced by food. When this behavior has been well learned, the next prior response (carrying the marble) is conditioned by using the tube as a secondary reinforcer, and so forth. Skinner has also used this approach to teach pigeons to peck out a few tunes on the piano and even to play a sort of ping-pong, although this latter experiment caused more notoriety than he would have liked. (See M. H. Hall, 1967a, pp. 22, 72; Hilgard & Bower, 1975, pp. 206, 231; Skinner, 1953/1965, p. 224; 1972b, pp. 533–535, 574–591.)

THE OPERANT EXPLANATION OF CONCEPTS RELATED TO PERSONALITY THEORY

Emotion

Skinner readily accepts the *existence* of private as well as overt behaviors, such as emotions and thinking; it is their purported *causal* function to which he objects. He defines emotion as a particular strength or weakness of one or more responses, or a predisposition to behave in certain ways, which is due to some external event (Skinner, 1953/1965, p. 166; see also Skinner,

1953/1965, pp. 69–70, 160–170, 178–181, 259, 361; 1974/1976, pp. 25–28, 35, 52–54, 241–243).

For example, an "angry" individual is more likely to turn red and act aggressively. This is due to a specifiable event, like a stuck desk drawer that stubbornly refuses to budge. A "frightened" person has a greater probability of running away because of some aversive stimulus, such as a mugger wielding a knife. And an "anxious" individual is more likely to behave in distressed and inefficient ways due to a conditioned aversive stimulus, such as a parent's contorted facial expression that typically precedes a spanking or ridicule. In each case, the emotion is real (and internal), but is caused by clearly identifiable external stimuli.

It is possible to ask people how they feel, and to gain some useful information from these self-reports, because humans can sense such internal stimuli. But Skinner warns that the language of emotion is far from scientifically precise: we learn to label our feelings by using words taught to us by other people, yet no one else can truly know one's own inner world. Therefore, emotion is best studied behavioristically. "Men do not work to maximize pleasure and minimize pain, as the hedonists have insisted; they work to produce pleasant things and to avoid painful things" (Skinner, 1971/1972a, p. 102; see also Skinner, 1971/1972a, pp. 100–101; 1974/1976, p. 242).

Thinking

Making decisions, recalling something that has been forgotten, and solving problems are also primarily private behaviors that Skinner explains in behaviorist terms. "Thinking is behaving. The mistake is in allocating the behavior to the mind" (Skinner, 1974/1976, p. 115; see also Skinner, 1953/1965, pp. 213–216, 242–256; 1957; 1969, pp. 133–171; 1971/1972a, pp. 184–186; 1974/1976, pp. 113–131, 245–246).

Decision-Making. Indecision occurs when a response cannot be emitted because it is interfered with by another one of equal strength, and is aversive because it precludes gaining reinforcement. Conversely, making a decision occurs when the strength of one alternative increases sufficiently for it to prevail over the other(s), and is negatively reinforcing.

To illustrate, suppose that a person who is ready to take a vacation finds that the responses of going to the seashore and to the mountains are equally powerful. Thus no decision is made, and no reinforcement is obtained. The prospective vacationer may therefore pore through various travel magazines until one response gains considerably in strength, emit the words "I am going to the seashore," and thereby escape from the aversive state of indecision. Skinner regards decision-making as a deficient form of behavior that has been misguidedly reinforced by others (e.g., "Look before you leap!"), for conditioning that produced more immediate responses would yield reinforcement far more quickly (1953/1965, p. 244).

Recall. Some of our behaviors help us to emit other behaviors, thereby allowing recall to take place. For example, suppose you see an acquaintance whose name you have forgotten. You may ask yourself whether the name begins with the letter "a," "b," and so on, with this "self-probe" increasing the probability that the name will be recalled and emitted. Similarly, a student preparing for an examination may use mnemonic codes to prompt the recall of important facts during the test.

Problem-Solving. A problem occurs when a response with a high probability cannot be emitted because of some external impediment, thereby making reinforcement impossible. Conversely, solving the problem involves behavior that alters the external situation so that the response in question can be made.

To illustrate, a person who wishes to drive home may find that the car refuses to start. The immobilized driver may then use self-probes to review such possible solutions as looking under the hood and checking the gas gauge, decide on the latter, find that the gauge reads "empty," and have gas put in the tank. The problem is now solved, and the response of driving home is promptly emitted. To Skinner, this operant approach to thinking and problem-solving offers considerable advantages:

> So long as originality is identified with spontaneity, or [with] an absence of lawfulness in behavior, it appears to be a hopeless task to teach a man to be original or to influence his process of thinking in any important way. . . . [But if my] account of thinking is essentially correct, there is no reason why we cannot teach a man how to think. (Skinner, 1953/1965, p. 256. See also Skinner, 1968, pp. 115–144.)

Punishment

Punishment is a procedure designed to reduce the probability of an operant, and is thus the opposite of reinforcement. It consists of following behavior with the *presentation* of a negative reinforcer (such as a spanking), or with the *removal* of a positive reinforcer (as by taking candy from a baby). Conditioned reinforcers may also be used for purposes of punishment, as when one issues a verbal reprimand or cuts off a dependent without a cent. (See Skinner, 1938; 1953/1965, pp. 71, 73, 182–193, 318–319, 342–344; 1971/1972a, pp. 56–95; 1974/1976, pp. 68–71.)

Punishment does tend to produce an immediate decrease in the behavior that it follows, a consequence that is reinforcing to the punisher. Nevertheless, Skinner regards punishment as an inherently defective technique. "Punishment does not permanently reduce a tendency to respond, [which] is in agreement with Freud's discovery of the surviving activity of what he called repressed wishes" (Skinner, 1953/1965, p. 184; see also p. 361). Furthermore, the effects of punishment may interfere with later healthy behaviors. For example, if adolescents are severely punished for a sexual act, they may subsequently have difficulty engaging in marital sex because their own preliminary actions generate sights and sensations that have become conditioned aversive stimuli—ones that make doing virtually anything else reinforcing.

A better way to reduce the probability of an operant is by reinforcing acceptable behaviors that are incompatible with the undesirable ones. Thus parents may pay no attention to a child's temper tantrums, and respond only to more quiet and orderly behavior. Since the child gets what it wants only after being calm, such behavior is more likely to be emitted in the future. Unfortunately, "we are still a long way from exploiting the alternatives [to punishment]" (Skinner, 1953/1965, p. 192; see also Skinner, cited by Evans, 1968, p. 35).

Freudian Concepts

Since Skinner attributes all behavior to prior conditioning, his approach is as deterministic as Freudian psychoanalysis. "[Freud's great achievement] was to apply the principle of cause and effect to human behavior. Aspects of behavior which had hitherto been regarded as whimsical, aimless, or accidental, Freud traced to relevant variables" (Skinner, 1953/1965, p. 375; see also Skinner, 1972b, p. 239). Skinner has found that the effects of conditioning can last as long as half the life of a pigeon, which tends to support Freud's contention that childhood events can influence behavior in ways that persist into adulthood. "If, because of early childhood experiences, a man marries a woman who resembles his mother, the effect of certain reinforcements must have survived for a long time" (Skinner, 1953/1965, p. 71).

Skinner also agrees with Freud that guilt can be even more aversive than punishment (and can lead to self-inflicted injuries), and that behavior is often overdetermined (albeit by external causes). For example, a young woman was once asked to speak in favor of the repeal of Prohibition. She became extremely ill at ease about appearing before a large audience, and sought to throw herself on the mercy of her listeners by saying: "This is the first time I have ever faced a speakeasy." Skinner attributes this "Freudian slip" to the subject of her talk (which concerned the evils of the speakeasy), the presence of the microphone before her (a device which helps one to speak more easily), and her thoughts about whether or not she could in fact speak easily, all of which greatly increased the probability of emitting the word "speakeasy" (Skinner, 1953/1965, p. 212; see also pp. 209–216, 238–239, 366–367).

For the most part, however, Skinner regards Freudian theory as an elaborate set of explanatory fictions. Repression occurs because it is reinforcing to avoid an aversive stimulus, such as the thought of behavior that has previously led to punishment. Other processes that seem to be unconscious actually represent a lack of discrimination, for we will not discriminate among and identify our own behaviors unless we have been reinforced for doing so. A person who seems to be dominated by an id impulse has been reinforced for behavior that is aversive to others, as with the conqueror's spoils of war or the child who grabs a toy from another. And since the same individual has undoubtedly also been reinforced for other behaviors that benefit people, any contingencies that produce these cooperative actions give the appearance that a superego has taken control. "We do not need to say that [the id, ego, and superego] are the actors in an internal drama. The actor is the organism, which has become a person with different, possibly conflicting repertoires [of behavior] as the result of different, possibly conflicting contingencies [of reinforcement]" (Skinner, 1974/1976, p. 167; see also Skinner, 1953/1965, pp. 189, 216–217, 222–223, 284–294, 375–378; 1971/1972a, pp. 58–59; 1974/1976, pp. 166, 169–174).

Traits

Skinner agrees that traits like "learned," "ignorant," "enthusiastic," "discouraged," "intelligent," and "narcissistic" convey important information about a person. However, he argues that such concepts do not in any way explain the behavior that they describe. "[The trait theorist begins] by observing a preoccupation with a mirror which recalls the legend of Narcissus, [invents] the adjective 'narcissistic' and then the noun 'narcissism,' and finally [asserts] that the thing presumably referred to by the noun is the cause of [this] behavior. . . . But at no point in such a series [does he] make contact with any event outside the behavior itself which justifies the claim of a causal connection" (Skinner, 1953/1965, p. 202; see also pp. 194–203).

Instead, as always, Skinner stresses that a causal analysis must be based on contingencies of reinforcement. The "learned" individual has been reinforced for acquiring knowledge that the "ignorant" one has not, the "enthusiastic" person has been reinforced more effectively than the "discouraged" one, an "intelligent" individual becomes conditioned more quickly than an "unintelligent" one, and so forth.

Intentions and Teleology

As we have seen, Skinner argues that human beings have no purpose or will. What we mistakenly believe to be intentions are actually responses to internal stimuli.

For example, saying that you plan to go home is the equivalent of "I observe events in myself which characteristically precede or accompany my going home." Similarly, "I feel like playing cards" may be translated as "I feel as I often feel when I have started to play cards." "A person disposed to act because he has been reinforced for acting may feel the condition of his body at such a time and call it 'felt purpose,' but what behaviorism rejects is the causal efficacy of that feeling" (Skinner, 1974/1976, p. 246; see also Skinner, 1953/1965, p. 262; 1969, pp. 105–109; 1971/1972a, p. 112; 1974/1976, pp. 31–32, 61–63, 180; 1978, pp. 38, 103).

FURTHER APPLICATIONS
OF SKINNERIAN PSYCHOLOGY

Psychopathology

Skinner dismisses neurosis as yet another explanatory fiction, one that suggests the existence of mythical inner causes. Instead, he defines psychopathology as behavior that is disadvantageous or dangerous to the individual and/or to other people. Such behavior can result from poorly designed contingencies of reinforcement, but is more often due to punishment. The more frequent the punishment, the greater the number of behaviors that generate conditioned aversive stimuli, and the more inhibited the individual.

Alternatively, a child may engage in temper tantrums because the parents have reinforced such behavior with attention and concern. Or a busy parent may fail to respond to the child's polite requests and answer only louder and louder calls, thereby shaping the child in the direction of becoming irritatingly noisy. "[Such] differential reinforcement supplied by a preoccupied or negligent parent is very close to the procedure we should adopt if we were given the task of conditioning a child to be annoying" (Skinner, 1953/1965, p. 98; see also Skinner, 1953/1965, pp. 166–167, 361–366, 372–374, 381; 1972b, pp. 565–566).

Compulsions are likely to be caused by particularly inept schedules of reinforcement. Suppose that a hungry pigeon is given a small amount of food every fifteen seconds. Whatever the pigeon may be doing at that moment is reinforced, even though this behavior does not operate to produce food. Eventually, therefore, some wholly irrelevant ("superstitious") behavior becomes conditioned, such as hopping from one foot to another or bowing and scraping. Such "noncontingent reinforcement" is generally harmful, as when a person given unconditional welfare payments demonstrates a reduced probability of engaging in constructive work. (See M. H. Hall, 1967a, pp. 68–69; Skinner, 1953/1965, pp. 55, 84–87, 350–351; 1972b, pp. 524–532; 1978, pp. 12–13.)

Psychotherapy

Rationale. The goal of Skinnerian **behavior modification** (or **behavior therapy**[2]) is to remove or replace the client's pathological behaviors by establishing more effective contingencies of reinforcement. These new contingencies may extinguish the disadvantageous behaviors, or they may reinforce incompatible and more acceptable responses. "It is not an inner cause of behavior but the behavior itself which [must be changed] . . . [and be-

---

[2]Skinner uses *behavior modification* to refer to the change of behavior through changes in the relevant contingencies of reinforcement, notably positive reinforcement (1978, pp. 10, 40–41). But probably the majority of psychologists use this term synonymously with *behavior therapy,* a general term that includes both operant and nonoperant techniques.

472

havior is] changed by changing the conditions of which it is a function" (Skinner, 1953/1965, p. 373; 1971/1972a, p. 143; see also Skinner, 1953/1965, pp. 367–383).

Behavior therapy typically begins with an initial interview, which enables the therapist to learn about the client's problems and to decide upon the specific procedures most likely to resolve them. Warmth and concern are important characteristics for the behavior therapist, since they encourage the client to remain in therapy and to discuss painful and embarrassing issues. But behavior change is achieved primarily through the treatment methods chosen and imposed by the therapist, several of which may well be used with a given client.

Skinnerian Procedures. Skinner has not written extensively about therapeutic applications, primarily because he sees little conceptual difference between psychotherapy and other areas of behavior modification. As a result, the operant procedures used by behavior therapists are essentially the same as those discussed previously in this chapter.

For example, *positive reinforcement* and *shaping* may be used to help an autistic child or psychotic adult speak in coherent sentences. The client is first reinforced for sounds that approximate real words, then for simple words, then for simple phrases, and so on, while reinforcement is withheld following bizarre utterances or silence. Typical reinforcers include candy, praise, smiles, or an opportunity to play freely. But as always, whether or not any of these are reinforcing for a particular client must be determined by actual test.

Conditioned positive reinforcers play an important role in the **token economy,** a detailed and complicated procedure that has many applications (e.g., with hospitalized psychotics, juvenile delinquents, and mentally retarded and normal schoolchildren). The first step is to clearly specify desirable behaviors, such as spelling a word correctly, keeping oneself or one's room clean, or proceeding in an orderly fashion to the dining room at mealtime. These behaviors are then reinforced with plastic tokens or points, a sufficient number of which can later be exchanged for some special treat chosen by the client (such as candy, watching television, or a private room). While a token economy by no means cures psychosis, it is capable of producing marked improvements in behavior. (See for example Ayllon & Azrin, 1968; Kazdin, 1977.)

The *extinction* of undesirable behaviors may be facilitated by placing an unruly delinquent child in a comfortable but uninteresting room until more quiet behavior is emitted, which is then reinforced by allowing the child to leave the room and pursue other activities. Or alcoholics may be shown pictures of liquor that are followed by an electric shock, so that avoiding alcoholic beverages will become negatively reinforcing. The use of **aversive control** is controversial, however, since inflicting pain is objectionable to many people even when this is done for the client's own good. Some psychologists share Skinner's belief that aversive control is inferior to positive reinforcement, and that its effects are usually only temporary, while others regard this technique more favorably. (See for example Bower & Hilgard, 1981, p. 292; Skinner, 1953/1965, p. 56.)

Modern behavior therapists also use a variety of other techniques. Some of these involve certain of Skinner's suggestions, such as replacing a disadvantageous response with a more desirable one, shaping, or following desired behaviors with reinforcement. Three of these behaviorist procedures are discussed in the following section.

Related Procedures. **Reciprocal inhibition** is an essentially Pavlovian approach originated by Mary Cover Jones (1924a; 1924b) and Joseph Wolpe (1958). In this procedure, the behavior therapist uses a positive stimulus to elicit responses that will inhibit the client's anxiety.

For example, suppose that little Albert were known to be fond of gumdrops. His animal phobia could then be treated by presenting the feared tame rat at a considerable distance, while at the same time allowing him to eat a piece of this candy. Since the rat is far away, the anxiety that it elicits is very weak and is overwhelmed by the more powerful positive responses evoked by the candy. The process is then repeated with the rat a bit closer, with eating again inhibiting the anxiety. The distance between Albert and the rat is gradually reduced until he can eat the candy with one hand and pet the rat with the other, whereupon his anxiety is gone and the phobia is cured. (This illustration is only hypothetical, however, for poor Albert never was deconditioned by Watson. See Harris, 1979.)

A second technique devised by Joseph Wolpe (1973; Wolpe & Lazarus, 1966), **systematic desensitization,** differs from reciprocal inhibition in two respects. The client merely imagines the feared stimuli (in most cases), and inhibits the resulting anxiety by relaxation rather than by eating.

As an illustration, consider a capable college student who frequently fails examinations because of intense anxiety. This student would be a poor candidate for reciprocal inhibition, since he or she could hardly be confronted with a genuine testing situation during the therapy sessions. Instead, the student is first taught techniques of deep muscular relaxation, which consist of successively tensing and relaxing the various muscles of the body in a sequence predetermined by the therapist. The client then constructs an "anxiety hierarchy," which lists the fearful stimuli in order of the amount of anxiety evoked. For example, the student may specify the most anxiety-provoking item (#1) as going to the university on the day of the exam, the next most feared item (#2) as actually answering the exam questions, #3 as the moment just before the doors to the exam room open, and so on down to a fourteenth and least anxiety-provoking stimulus, having an exam a month away (Wolpe, 1973, p. 116). As this actual example illustrates, anxiety hierarchies must be constructed primarily by the client because they are an individual matter: many students might well find item #2 the most anxiety-provoking, but this particular client does not. The third step is to imagine the bottom stimulus in the hierarchy (here, an exam a month away) while relaxing deeply, thereby replacing the response of anxiety with a far less painful and disadvantageous one. After this has been well learned, the client practices relaxing while imagining stimulus #13, and gradually proceeds up the hierarchy until the topmost situation no longer elicits any anxiety. This usually requires some thirty therapy sessions and suffices to resolve the client's difficulties, although *in vivo* desensitization may be necessary for those who cannot imagine themselves in the relevant situations vividly enough to feel anxious. (And still other methods will be needed for clients who cannot learn to relax.)

A third technique due largely to Wolpe and to Andrew Salter, **assertive training,** helps the client to become less anxious and gain reinforcements by expressing feelings in an honest, personally satisfying, and socially appropriate manner (Salter, 1949; Wolpe, 1958; 1973; Wolpe & Lazarus, 1966). The therapist first ascertains those areas in which the client is overly inhibited, such as asking for a date, expressing anger, or correcting a waiter who has given the incorrect change. The client then role-plays his or her typical behavior in such situations (e.g., "You don't really want to go out with me, do you?") and strives to adopt changes suggested or actually enacted by the therapist ("There's a good movie playing Saturday night, and I'd very much like to take you if you're free"). The therapist uses praise to reinforce any improvement, a form of shaping called "behavior rehearsal."

Effective assertiveness is not rude or destructive. It includes empathy for the other person's position, and excludes personal attacks. Offensive behavior may be challenged ("There seems to be an error in this bill, won't you check it again?") but *not* an individual's worth or ability ("You moron, can't you add!?"). Thus assertive training may also be useful with clients who are unnecessarily aggressive in particular situations, as well as with those who are excessively timid.

Various other procedures are used by behavior therapists, some of which will be discussed in the following chapter. In general, behavior therapy differs from many of the forms of psychotherapy devised by personality theorists in the following ways: (1) Its goals are to change clearly specified target behaviors and/or symptoms, rather than some unobservable inner state. (2) Active and overt control is exercised by the therapist, who chooses and imposes specific procedures designed to bring about the desired changes in behavior. (Of course, some cooperation by the client is still essential.) (3) It emphasizes the present nature of the client's difficulties, and may well succeed even when the original causes are completely unknown. (4) Different techniques are used with those problems for which they are especially well suited (e.g., desensitization for a fear of examinations, assertive training for a client inhibited with members of the opposite sex, or various procedures in combination), rather than applying a single approach with virtually all clients (as in Freudian psychoanalysis and Rogerian person-centered therapy). (5) Therapy is typically of shorter duration, and may well last as little as a few months. (6) Perhaps most importantly, the techniques of behavior therapy are based on empirical research, rather than on a psycho-therapist's theoretical speculations and subjective judgments.

Behavior Modification and Social Reform. In a rare moment of agreement with certain personality theorists, Skinner warns that our present existence on earth is quite precarious. Haphazard contingencies of reinforcement are strengthening behaviors that jeopardize our very survival, notably over-population and pollution. "Unless something is done, and soon, there will be too many people in the world, and they will ever more rapidly exhaust its resources and pollute its air, land, and water, until in one last violent struggle for what is left, some madman will release a stockpile of nuclear missiles" (Skinner, 1978, p. 17; see also Skinner, 1969, pp. 37, 40, 46, 98; 1978, pp. 6–7, 21, 46, 112; 1986; 1987).

To avoid such a catastrophe, Skinner advocates the design of con-tingencies that will strengthen appropriate behaviors without wasting essen-tial reinforcers (as by using more intermittent schedules). This concern for the future will require us to undergo certain deprivations, the *sine qua non* of operant conditioning. But since schedules of reinforcement are a more important determinant of behavior than the amount, it is possible that skillfully designed survival-oriented contingencies will make us happier even while receiving less (Skinner, 1978, pp. 41, 61).

Work

Skinnerian principles have also been applied to the area of work. For exam-ple, one group of employees created a serious hazard by hurrying down a narrow corridor at the close of each workday. They were readily induced to substitute safer incompatible responses, such as stopping to adjust their clothing, by the simple expedient of installing mirrors on the walls (Skinner, 1953/1965, p. 316).

Pay is a conditioned positive reinforcer (as we have seen). It has no value in and of itself, but can easily be exchanged for many primary reinfor-cers. Piecework pay is a form of fixed-ratio schedule, since the employee receives a specified amount of money for producing or selling a given number of items. Such schedules are likely to be effective so long as the ratio is not too high, and the workers do not have to produce a large number of units just to gain a minimal wage. However, the weekly or monthly paycheck is *not* a true fixed-interval schedule. The appearance of this reinforcer is *not* necessarily contingent on immediately preceding work-oriented responses, for the employee might collect the check just after a break or from the home mailbox after watching television on a Saturday afternoon. To prevent laxity during those periods well in advance of payday, this method is typically supplemented by undesirable forms of behavior control—such as a watchful supervisor who uses the threat of suspension or dismissal as punishments. (See Skinner, 1953/1965, pp. 384–391.)

Some Important Behaviorist Terminology (II)

Assertive training	Helping a client who is overly inhibited in certain situations to reduce anxiety, and gain reinforcements, by expressing feelings in an honest and socially appropriate way. May also be useful with clients who are overly aggressive and derogatory. A form of behavior therapy devised by Andrew Salter and Joseph Wolpe.
Aversive control (aversion therapy)	Using an aversive stimulus, such as an electric shock, to reduce the probability of pathological behaviors (such as alcoholism). A relatively controversial form of behavior therapy.
Behavior modification	(1) A synonym for behavior therapy. (2) A term referring specifically to Skinnerian methods for changing behavior, ones that need not necessarily involve psychopathology.
Behavior therapy	An approach to psychotherapy that seeks to change particular "target" behaviors and/or symptoms of the client, rather than trying to alter some unobservable or unconscious inner state.
Programmed instruction	A Skinnerian approach to education wherein specific correct responses are reinforced, often by a teaching machine, in a sequence designed to produce optimal learning.
Reciprocal inhibition	Using a powerful positive stimulus to inhibit the anxiety caused by an aversive stimulus, with the latter first presented at a considerable distance and then gradually brought closer until it can be handled without anxiety. A form of behavior therapy devised by Mary Cover Jones and Joseph Wolpe.
Systematic desensitization	A form of behavior therapy, devised by Joseph Wolpe, wherein the client imagines a hierarchical sequence of feared stimuli and inhibits the resulting anxiety by practicing previously taught techniques of muscular relaxation. Alternatively, *in vivo* desensitization may be used with clients who are unable to imagine the feared situations vividly enough to feel anxious.
Token economy	A detailed and complicated form of behavior therapy, based on Skinnerian operant conditioning, wherein desirable behaviors are followed with conditioned positive reinforcers (such as plastic tokens) that can later be exchanged for more primary reinforcers chosen by the client.

Skinner is also critical of the usual contingencies of reinforcement found in the workplace. He argues that these contingencies do not induce many people to work hard or carefully, or enjoy what they are doing. Economic incentives have become less effective in our well-to-do society, for affluence makes money less reinforcing (Skinner, 1978, pp. 25, 27).

Religion

Skinner attributes religious belief primarily to an accident of birth, namely the conditioning imposed by one's parents (or by the religious school to which they send the child). Many religions try to control behavior by claiming some connection with supernatural forces, which presumably punish behaviors defined by the religion as immoral (as with the threat of Hell) and reward behaviors defined as moral (as with the promise of Heaven). When "sinful" behavior is in fact emitted, these religions offer powerful reinforcement in the form of absolution. Other religions do not appeal to the supernatural, and simply reinforce with approval those behaviors that they deem to be virtuous (e.g., the "Golden Rule.") But whatever the form, religion is to Skinner merely another example—and by no means a special or necessary one—of behavior control through conditioning. "A person does not support a religion because he is devout; he supports it because of the contingencies [of reinforcement] arranged by the religious agency" (Skinner, 1971/1972a, p. 111; see also M. H. Hall, 1967a, p. 23; Skinner, 1953/1965, pp. 9, 310, 345, 350–358; 1971/1972a, pp. 60, 108–110).

Education

Education seeks to establish behaviors that will benefit the student and other people at some later time, using such conditioned reinforcers as grades, promotions, scholastic honors, and diplomas. Here again, however, Skinner regards most existing contingencies of reinforcement as markedly inferior.

Some teachers excuse students from additional homework as a form of reward—a procedure exactly the opposite of proper behavior modification, which would make extra schoolwork positively reinforcing and the inability to study punishing. Crowded classrooms make it virtually impossible for even the most dedicated teacher to meet every pupil's needs, for lectures and other group methods inevitably proceed too quickly for some students and too slowly for others. Although the birch rod has generally been abandoned, teachers still employ such forms of punishment as sharp criticism, failing grades, and keeping students after school or sending them to the principal's office. And those positive reinforcements that are provided typically occur minutes or even hours after a correct response, rather than immediately thereafter, which destroys most of their effectiveness. Small wonder, then, that more and more young people fail to learn, develop intense anxiety at the sight of a column of figures, resort to vandalism, or drop out of school. They have not "lost their love of learning," but have been victimized by educational contingencies of reinforcement that are not very compelling. (See Skinner, 1953/1965, pp. 402–412; 1968; 1972b, pp. 171–235; 1978, pp. 129–159; 1984; Skinner, cited by Evans, 1968, p. 70.)

The solution advocated by Skinner is **programmed instruction,** a method wherein specific correct responses are promptly reinforced in a carefully prepared sequence designed to produce optimal learning. This is typically accomplished by using a "teaching machine" (originally an idea of Sidney Pressey), one simple form of which works as follows: certain information together with a question based on that information appear in an opening on the front of the machine, and the student writes an answer in a separate space. The student then advances the program, revealing the correct answer and the next question. (In some versions, the program cannot be advanced until the correct response has been made.) Alternatively, programmed instruction can be presented on the printed page or via electronic computer. The latter method makes it possible to provide helpful hints following an incorrect response, or even to switch automatically to a program of remedial instruction after a certain predetermined number of errors. (See Figure 15.2a & b.)

To Skinner, properly executed programmed instruction has numerous advantages. Students gain immediate (and thus more powerful) reinforcement for correct answers, can proceed at their own pace, and are presented with material in a maximally effective order. The teacher is freed from many tedious chores, such as grading vast numbers of specific responses, and has more time to give individual assistance to those who most need it. And since the behaviors in question are to be of later advantage to the student, natural reinforcers will eventually take over and make the teaching machine no longer necessary.

As one dramatic illustration of the potentialities of programmed instruction, Skinner cites the case of a forty-year-old microcephalic idiot who had never been able to do much more than dress himself without help. With suitable programming, this man learned to press a panel to get a candy reward, then to press only a panel on which a circle appeared, then to discriminate the circular panel from ones with ellipses of a nearly similar shape, and then even to pick up a pencil and trace letters faintly projected on a piece of paper:

> The intellectual accomplishments of this microcephalic idiot in the forty-first year of his life have exceeded all those of his first forty years. They were possible only because he has lived a few hours of each week of that year in a well programmed environment. No very bright future beckons [for him, but] . . . bright futures [do] belong to the normal and exceptional children who will be fortunate enough to live in environments which have been designed to maximize *their* development, and of whose potential achievements we have now scarcely any conception. (Skinner, 1968, pp. 77–78; see also pp. 74–76.)

Literature

Skinner is one of the few psychologists to author a novel, one that depicts a society designed in accordance with operant principles. Contrary to what some skeptics might expect, *Walden Two* (Skinner, 1948) does *not* consist of

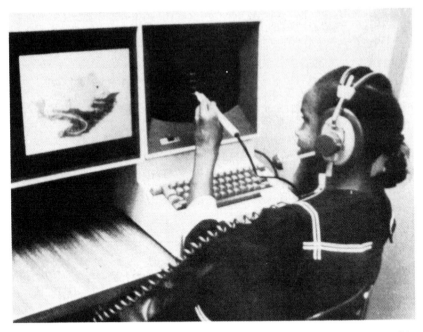

FIGURE 15.2. Examples of programmed instruction. (a) An electronic teaching machine using multiple-choice questions. The right-hand screen presents several words ("bat," "cat," "rat"), and the student must touch the one that matches the picture on the screen at the left.

a group of people frantically pressing bars in Skinner-type boxes. It is a satisfied and largely self-sufficient community, characterized by such psychological, organizational, and mechanical innovations as:

—A pleasant rural setting, free from such modern "advances" as long lines and rush-hour traffic.

—Skillfully designed work schedules that require only four hours per person per day, avoid the ills resulting from overwork, and afford ample time for avocations.

—Education that uses shaping and positive reinforcement rather than punishment, allows students to proceed at a pace best suited to their own particular abilities, and is a source of enjoyment rather than anxiety.

—More efficient devices and procedures of various kinds, such as tea glasses that fit inside grass carrying jackets (and are thus easily transported without spillage) and lawns kept trim by grazing sheep (which also serve as a source of food) rather than by lawnmowers.

—Comfortable clothing that accentuates the more attractive physical

Sentence to Be Completed	Word to Be Supplied
1. The important parts of a flashlight are the battery and the bulb. When we "turn on" a flashlight, we close a switch which connects the battery with the _____.	bulb
2. When we turn on a flashlight, an electric current flows through the fine wire in the _____ and causes it to grow hot.	bulb
3. When the hot wire glows brightly, we say that it gives off or sends out heat and _____.	light
4. The fine wire in the bulb is called a filament. The bulb "lights up" when the filament is heated by the passage of a(n) _____ current.	electric
5. When a weak battery produces little current, the fine wire, or _____, does not get very hot.	filament
6. A filament which is *less* hot sends out or gives off _____ light.	less
7. "Emit" means "send out." The amount of light sent out, or "emitted," by a filament depends on how _____ the filament is.	hot
8. The higher the temperature of the filament, the _____ the light emitted by it.	brighter, stronger

FIGURE 15.2. (b) The first eight items of a thirty-five-item sentence completion program in high school physics (Skinner, 1968, p. 45). The machine presents one item at a time, and the student completes the item and then uncovers the corresponding word shown at the right. Or such a program might instead be printed in a textbook, with the student instructed to cover the answers with a sheet of paper.

attributes of each individual, rather than universal conformity to some externally imposed and artificially created style of dress.

—Excellent sanitation and medical care.

Interestingly, the least satisfied individual in *Walden Two* is its designer. He has found that his goal of creating the ideal society can be achieved only by assuring other people of positive reinforcement, a totally effective yet also wholly unselfish method of behavior control, so he does not have (or seek) any particular power or prestige. Nevertheless, the idea of a planned community such as *Walden Two* has evoked considerable criticism from those who regard it as a grave threat to fundamental and essential human freedoms. (See Skinner, 1948; 1969, pp. 29–30; 1972b, p. 123; Skinner, cited by Evans, 1968, p. 49.)

Social Psychology

According to Skinner, the operant principles that explain an individual's responses are equally applicable to group behavior. As we have seen, pigeons can be conditioned to "compete" at a sort of ping-pong. Or operant techniques can be used to facilitate cooperation, as by requiring two hungry pigeons to peck two different disks simultaneously in order to receive food.

Human interactions tend to be considerably more complicated. They involve such "social reinforcers" as attention, approval, smiles, and hugs (that is, reinforcers that require the presence of other people). Yet these interactions are also are due solely to conditioning. For example, suppose that a loquacious individual keeps talking much too long. It may well be that the listener is unwittingly providing such reinforcements as attention, eye contact, and polite smiles—and that the removal of these reinforcers will help to extinguish this unwanted behavior. (See Skinner, 1953/1965, pp. 297–349; 1971/1972a, pp. 102–111; 1972b, pp. 533–537.)

Verbal Behavior

Skinner has devoted considerable attention to an operant explanation of speech, which he regards as similar in principle to other forms of behavior. For example, a *mand* is a verbal operant that makes some demand on the hearer. It is reinforced by a characteristic consequence, as when "Stop that!" is applied to an external action and is strengthened by its cessation. *Tacts* refer to the discrimination and naming of different stimuli, as illustrated by the child who correctly refers to objects of a particular color as "red" and is reinforced by parental approval. This aspect of Skinner's work is particularly controversial, however, with some psychologists regarding it as a major contribution and others (perhaps the majority) dismissing it as largely fallacious. (See for example Chomsky, 1959; 1971; Bower & Hilgard, 1981, pp. 192–194, 206–209; MacCorquodale, 1969; 1970; Skinner, 1957; 1969, pp. 10–13; 1972b, pp. 359–417; 1974/1976, pp. 98–112.)

Aging and Memory

Old age tends to bring lapses in memory, as Skinner himself found on reaching age 80. As could be expected, he proposes various behavioristic techniques for overcoming such problems.

Suppose that a half hour before an elderly person is to leave the house, the television weather report predicts rain. The obvious response is to take an umbrella. But this behavior cannot yet be emitted, and it may well be forgotten when the time comes to leave. The solution is to hang the umbrella on the doorknob at that moment, so that the individual cannot leave without seeing it. Similarly, when Skinner got a good scientific idea in the middle of the night, he immediately recorded it on a notepad or tape recorder kept by the side of his bed. Thus, by appropriate manipulation of the environment, it is possible to guard against forgetting. "In place of memories, memoranda" (Skinner, 1983, p. 240; see also Skinner & Vaughan, 1983).

EVALUATION

Criticisms and Controversies

Skinner's writings have provoked a professional uproar rivaling that caused by Freudian psychoanalysis. Some scathing criticisms reflect a regrettable ignorance of the points discussed in the preceding pages, as when opponents contend that he totally denies the existence of cognitions, emotions, self-knowledge, or any sort of "unconscious" behavior. And some have been generally refuted by research on behavior therapy, notably the common psychoanalytic contention that eliminating a pathological symptom without unearthing the underlying causes must always result in yet another troublesome symptom appearing in its place ("symptom substitution"). However, there are attacks on Skinnerian psychology that merit serious consideration.

Fascism in the Guise of Science. To some critics, behaviorism raises the specter of fascism in the more socially acceptable guise of scientific endeavor. These psychologists are extremely concerned about the abuses that can occur when behavior is controlled by external forces. Such behaviorist procedures as the token economy have been likened to the philosophy of Mussolini, the ruthless dictator to whom the end of efficiency justified any means whatsoever (Singer, 1970, pp. xviii–xix).

Skinner agrees that behavior change can be induced destructively as well as constructively, as in the case of punishment. But he argues that dictatorial forms of behavior control are far *less* likely if we become aware of the contingencies of reinforcement that regulate our actions, design them more effectively, and arrange for appropriate methods of countercontrolling the controllers. He also stresses that the most effective form of behavior control is a benign one, namely positive reinforcement. However, this argument glosses over an important fact: operant conditioning is impossible without deprivation, a state that many would consider aversive. For example, to control certain of a child's behaviors with candy, the child must be made hungry and prevented from obtaining this reinforcer at other times. (See Skinner, 1953/1965, pp. 32, 82, 149, 319, 443–445; 1971/1972a, p. 163; 1972b, pp. 122–123; 1974/1976, pp. 267–268.)

The comparison of behavior modification to fascism seems rather silly in light of the many clients helped by this form of therapy. Nevertheless, it is by no means clear that effective behavior control is as inevitably benevolent as Skinner would have us believe.

People and Pigeons. Skinner has also been accused of basing his conclusions too heavily on studies of pigeons and rats, and denying the unique qualities of human beings. Here his defense is that human behavior is perhaps the most difficult of all subjects to study scientifically, so the best course is to begin with the simplest and most easily revealed principles (a procedure followed by virtually all other sciences). In respect to such basics, Skinner believes that humans do not differ appreciably from other species. He therefore sees little reason not to use animal subjects, which are far more easily studied under laboratory conditions. And he argues that even if human beings are unique in some respects, a full understanding of these characteristics may not be necessary to achieve important results—as indicated by the various successful applications of operant principles to human life. (See Skinner, 1953/1965, pp. 12, 38, 41, 204; 1969, pp. 109–113; 1971/1972a, pp. 150–152; 1972b, pp. 101, 120–122.)

Nevertheless, the possibility remains that psychology does need to understand certain human qualities not found in lower organisms. For example, cognitions might have causal aspects that are beyond the capacity of rats and pigeons. To some critics, ruling inner and unconscious causes out of psychology because they cannot be measured scientifically resembles the ludicrous "solution" offered by some cynics to the Vietnam war: define your way out of the problem by declaring a victory and withdrawing, even though you actually have achieved no victory at all.

People as Puppets. Since Skinner's conception of behavior is as deterministic as that of Freud, he is open to similar criticisms by those who attribute considerable importance to intentions and teleology. Skinner contends that it is the Pavlovian model which conceptualizes people as puppets, since it posits that responses are *elicited* by external stimuli, whereas operant conditioning holds that we *emit* behaviors whose strength is contingent upon their consequences. However, certain modern learning theorists have concluded that there is much less of a distinction between classical and operant conditioning than Skinner believes (e.g., Bower & Hilgard, 1981, pp. 199–203).

Despite Skinner's various references to emitted behaviors and countercontrol, environmental rule is clearly his reigning principle. This raises the paradox of how supposedly controlled organisms can ever be sufficiently free to change the prevailing contingencies of reinforcement. (See Bandura, 1978, p. 344.)

Other Criticisms. Skinner is not overly concerned with the issue of why a reinforcer is reinforcing, which gives his definitions a distinctly circular quality: a reinforcer is whatever strengthens a response, and this increased frequency of responding is what proves that the item in question is a reinforcer. He does suggest that reinforcers facilitate survival, and that their existence is thus due to a sort of Darwinian evolutionary process. (See Skinner, 1953/1965, p. 55; 1969, p. 46; 1971/1972a, p. 99; 1974/1976, pp. 41, 51; 1978, p. 19.)

Punishment is regarded by some modern psychologists as a valuable technique when properly used, as by administering the punishment immediately after the undesirable response, making it as intense as possible, preventing any escape, and providing an acceptable alternative way to obtain reinforcement. (See Bower & Hilgard, 1981, pp. 187–188.) Other theorists question whether a series of simple conditioned operants can in fact be shown to cause extremely complicated behaviors, such as writing a book or human speech.

Contributions

As we have seen, behavior modification has proved to be of considerable value in many areas. The various innovations in psychotherapeutic methodology, Skinnerian and otherwise, have gained widespread acceptance during the past three decades. Many educational institutions have utilized programmed learning, or other varieties of personalized instruction. And behaviorism is based on a vast amount of empirical research, rather than on the subjective and frequently untestable speculations that pervade personality theory.

Skinner's status as a major learning theorist is unquestioned. One need not be a behaviorist to appreciate his concepts, or to agree that there are some very poorly designed contingencies of reinforcement in our present society. The Skinner box is probably the single form of apparatus most widely used by psychologists studying animal behavior, his work on schedules of reinforcement has been praised for calling attention to an important determinant of behavior, and some of the internally oriented "explanations" of behavior of which he is so critical do seem distinctly redundant. Whether one attributes Skinner's remarkable performance to particularly effective conditioning (as he would), or to an unusually brilliant and inventive mind (as would a personality theorist), there is no denying his profound contributions to psychology—or the desirability of acquiring a first-hand knowledge of his writings.

Suggested Reading

The most comprehensive statement of Skinner's position is provided in *Science and Human Behavior* (1953/1965). *Beyond Freedom and Dignity* (1971/1972a) is both readable and provocative, as is his novel *Walden Two* (1948), while *About Behaviorism* (1974/1976) represents an attempt to answer some twenty common specific criticisms of his position. Papers concerning his invention of the Skinner box and the air crib, and his studies of ping-pong-playing pigeons, are included in *Cumulative Record* (1972b), and his views on education are presented in *The Technology of Teaching* (1968).

■ SUMMARY

Whereas personality theorists seek to explain behavior in terms of hypothesized inner causes, certain psychologists prefer to redefine their field as the study of behavior itself. Undoubtedly the best known of the modern behaviorists is B. F. Skinner, who strongly opposes the idea of any intrapsychic causes of behavior.

1. CLASSICAL (RESPONDENT) VERSUS OPERANT CONDITIONING. Skinner agrees with Pavlov and Watson that some behaviors are learned through classical conditioning. However, Skinner contends that the vast majority of learning is due to the consequences of our actions ("operant conditioning"): those responses that operate on the environment to produce effects that strengthen them (are reinforced) are more likely to occur in the future, whereas those that do not do so are less likely to recur. A positive reinforcer increases the probability of a response when presented, while a negative reinforcer does so when removed. According to Skinner, human beings have no capacity for teleology, purpose, or will; all behavior is determined by prior conditioning.

2. PRINCIPLES OF OPERANT CONDITIONING. Skinner uses a laboratory apparatus of his own invention (commonly referred to as the Skinner box), and pigeons and rats, to study principles of operant conditioning. These include learning, shaping, schedules of reinforcement (which he regards as extremely important determinants of behavior), conditioned reinforcers, deprivation (a *sine qua non* of operant conditioning, since a satiated organism will not learn), satiation, generalization, discrimination, extinction (which shows that reinforcement is necessary for the maintenance of behavior, as well as for learning), and complicated sequences of behavior.

3. THE OPERANT EXPLANATION OF CONCEPTS RELATED TO PERSONALITY THEORY. Skinner accepts the existence of such internal stimuli as emotions and thinking; it is their causal status to which he objects. Thus he has attempted to explain these phenomena, and various concepts proposed by Freud and other personality theorists, in terms of operant conditioning and environmental control. Skinner is also opposed to the use of punishment, which he regards as far less effective than the positive reinforcement of alternative acceptable behaviors.

4. FURTHER APPLICATIONS. Skinner defines psychopathology as behavior that is disadvantageous or dangerous to the individual, and results from punishment or faulty reinforcement procedures. Thus the goal of psychotherapy is not to bring unconscious material to consciousness, but rather to remove or replace the client's pathological behaviors and symptoms. Skinner has not written extensively about psychotherapy, since he sees little conceptual difference between this area and other applications of behavior modification. For example, positive reinforcement and shaping may be used to help an autistic child speak in coherent sentences. But many other behaviorists have devoted considerable attention to such forms of therapy, including the token economy, reciprocal inhibition, systematic desensitization, and assertiveness training. Skinner also advocates the use of programmed instruction, and has related operant conditioning principles to work, religion, social psychology, verbal behavior, and aging and memory.

5. EVALUATION. Skinner has been severely criticized for contending that the environment wholly controls our behavior, and for denying the importance of cognitive and other personal causes. He is also accused of overstating the benign nature of behavior control, basing his conclusions too heavily on research with animal subjects, failing to resolve the paradox of how totally controlled organisms can make the changes in their environment that he recommends, exaggerating the differences between classical and operant conditioning, circular definitions, an overly negative view of punishment, and failing to provide a satisfactory explanation of the more complicated forms of human behavior. Yet his status as a major learning theorist is unquestioned, he has devised many valuable concepts and the noted Skinner box, his work is grounded in empirical research rather than subjective speculation, and he has given considerable impetus to a currently popular approach to psychology.

STUDY QUESTIONS

1. Disappointment is an inevitable aspect of life, and many people learn to take it more or less in stride. Why, then, do some critics argue that Skinner's psychological ideas were unduly influenced by his failure as a writer?

2. Skinner argues that operant conditioning is an unselfish and benign form of behavior control, because others must be assured of reinforcement. Yet some critics contend that his ideas represent a serious threat to individual freedom. Which view do you prefer? Why?

3. Give an example from real life, or from fiction, to illustrate each of the following Skinnerian concepts: (a) Response shaping. (b) Partial reinforcement. (c) Stimulus generalization. (d) Discrimination. (e) Extinction.

4. I wish to decide whether to include more or fewer study questions in this section. I decide that I feel like adding a few questions, and I do. I then claim that this shows I have free will, since I did what I felt like doing; I could just as easily have chosen to delete a few questions. (a) How would Skinner reply? (b) Do you agree or disagree with Skinner? Why?

5. Rats in a Skinner box learn by what is called "trial and error": they try out various responses (e.g., rearing up on their hind paws, crouching, moving to the rear of the box) until they hit on the one that produces reinforcement (pressing the bar). Why do some critics regard Skinner's approach as *not* applicable to many areas of human endeavor?

6. According to Skinner, emotion is a predisposition to behave in certain ways that is caused by some external event (such as anger over a drawer that is stuck). Can an emotion such as anger be caused by an event within the individual?

7. How would Skinner explain the indecisiveness of the patient described in the comment in the Appendix to Chapter 14, question 4b?

8. Give an example from real life, or from fiction, to support Skinner's contention that a good way to reduce the probability of an undesirable operant is by reinforcing acceptable behaviors that are incompatible with the undesirable ones.

9. Skinner argues that apparently unconscious processes actually reflect a lack of discrimination. (a) How does this idea compare to the quote by Kelly at the very end of the section on the structure of personality in Chapter 11? (b) Do you agree or disagree with Skinner? Why?

10. Consider the following clinical cases: (a) A woman with no prior history of mental disorder is involved in a traumatic automobile accident. She develops a phobia about cars and cannot even get into one that is standing still, let alone ride in one. (b) The case history discussed throughout the Appendix (e.g., Chapter 2, question 6; Chapter 4, question 2). Would you advocate behavior therapy for either of these cases? If so, which procedures would you recommend?

16

JOHN DOLLARD
AND NEAL E. MILLER,
ALBERT BANDURA
More Eclectic
Behaviorist Approaches

Are such behaviorist concepts as reinforcement wholly incompatible with the inner causes favored by personality theorists? John Dollard and Neal E. Miller do not think so. In marked contrast to Skinner, Dollard and Miller's primary goal is to synthesize the major contributions of two seemingly irreconcilable theorists: Freud and Pavlov.

BIOGRAPHICAL SKETCH: JOHN DOLLARD AND NEAL E. MILLER

John Dollard was born in Menasha, Wisconsin on August 29, 1900. His mother was a schoolteacher, his father a railroad engineer who was killed in a train wreck during John's childhood. Dollard was an excellent student, receiving his B.A. from the University of Wisconsin in 1922 and his Ph.D. in sociology from the University of Chicago in 1931. Dollard's unusually wide range of professional skills and interests was reflected by his training in Freudian psychoanalysis at the Berlin Institute, and holding academic appointments at Yale University in no fewer than three fields: anthropology, sociology, and psychology.

In 1937 Dollard authored a well-regarded study of the exploitation of blacks in the American South, an undertaking that required considerable courage at that time. During World War II, he and Miller conducted studies of the reaction of infantrymen to fear in battle. Dollard was ultimately to write some ten books, and numerous journal articles. Yet he paid a price for his unusual interdisciplinary interests: academic departments tend to look with disfavor on those who depart from the common mold, and he did not become a voting full professor in the Department of Psychology at Yale until age 52. (See Miller, 1982.) John Dollard died on October 8, 1980.

Neal E. Miller was born in Milwaukee, Wisconsin on August 3, 1909. He received his B.S. from the University of Washington in 1931, and his Ph.D. in psychology from Yale University in 1935. He also studied psychoanalysis, albeit at the Vienna Institute, thereby paving the way for his eventual collaboration with Dollard. Most of Miller's professional career was spent at Yale, which he left in 1966 to accept an appointment as professor of psychology and head of the Laboratory of Physiological Psychology at

Rockefeller University. He remained in this position until 1980, at which time he accepted emeritus status.

Miller's experimental work on learned drives, reinforcement, and conflict has been published primarily in psychological journals. It has earned him such honors as election to the presidency of the American Psychological Association in 1959 and various scientific medals—one of which, the U.S. President's Medal of Science, has been awarded to only two other behavioral scientists.

THE BASIC NATURE OF HUMAN BEINGS

Dollard and Miller regard the clinical setting as an unusually rich source of data. "Outside of psychotherapy, how many subjects have been studied for an hour a day, for five days a week, [and] for from one to three years . . . [and in a] life situation [which] is vital, [where] the alternatives are years of misery or years of relative peace and success?" (Dollard & Miller, 1950, p. 4; see also pp. 3–11). Yet Dollard & Miller are also experimentalists who value the greater scientific rigor of the research laboratory. They agree with Skinner that basic principles of human behavior can be discovered through animal studies, and that the use of behaviorist terminology eliminates ambiguous constructs and produces testable hypotheses.

Primary and Secondary Drives

In essence, Dollard and Miller share Freud's belief that our basic motivation is to reduce various drives. However, they differ from Freud by positing two distinct types of drives.

Primary Drives. Much of our behavior is due to such **primary** (or **innate**) **drives** as hunger, thirst, sex (in part), and the avoidance of pain. All of these drives can be satiated, but never extinguished. Thus it is possible to keep a person from ever being very hungry, but quite impossible to eliminate altogether the need for food. In accordance with Skinner, Dollard and Miller define the strength of drives like hunger and thirst in such objective terms as hours of deprivation (1950, p. 30 n. 6).

Secondary Drives. Also of considerable importance are drives that are learned, and can in theory be extinguished (**secondary drives,** or **learned drives**). Included in this category are anger, guilt, sexual preferences for various physical characteristics, the need for money or power, conformity, nonconformity, and many others.

To Dollard and Miller, by far the most important learned drive is the

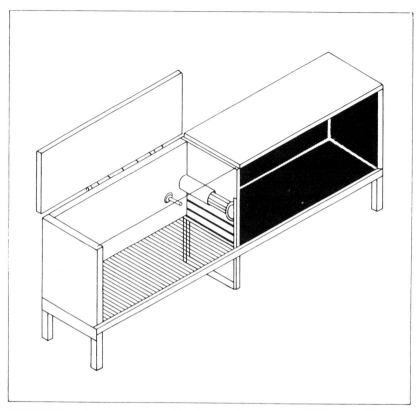

FIGURE 16.1. Apparatus for studying fear as a learned drive (slightly modified from Dollard & Miller, 1950, p. 64).

fear or anxiety elicited by a previously neutral stimulus.[1] In a famous experiment, Miller showed that a rat who readily accepted the white side of an apparatus with two compartments learned to fear it when electric shocks were administered there. (See Figure 16.1.) The rat persistently escaped into the safe (black) compartment long after all shocks were discontinued, and showed obvious signs of fear (e.g., urination, crouching) if prevented from doing so. It also learned new responses, such as turning a wheel or pressing a bar, in order to open a door to the black side. Thus its fear of the white compartment represented not only a *response* elicited by the conditioned aversive stimulus, but also a learned *drive* capable of motivating new behaviors. (See Dollard & Miller, 1950, pp. 30–32, 62–94, 211.)

Skinner would argue that the rat's behavior in this experiment is *emitted,* and is negatively reinforced by the consequence of escaping from

---

[1]Dollard and Miller state that *fear* refers to a stimulus that is known and *anxiety* to one that is vague or repressed (1950, p. 63), but do not emphasize this distinction.

the aversive white compartment. In contrast, Dollard and Miller contend that this stimulus *elicits* both the escape response *and a resulting fear drive.* (This is precisely the sort of inner causal concept that Skinner abhors.) The conflict between such learned fears and other important drives plays a crucial role in the etiology of neurosis, as we will see in a subsequent section.

How Drives Are Reduced

The Strengthening of Stimulus-Response Connections through Reinforcement. Dollard and Miller prefer to replace the vague psychoanalytic pleasure principle with the more exact and rigorous behaviorist concept of reinforcement. They define reinforcement as any event that strengthens the tendency for a response to be repeated (i.e., elicited by a particular stimulus).

The most important form of reinforcement is drive reduction. Unlike Freud, however, Dollard and Miller allow for the possibility of other varieties as well. "[We assume only] that a sudden reduction in a strong drive acts as a reinforcement; we do not need to make the more controversial assumption that all reinforcement is produced in that way" (Dollard & Miller, 1950, p. 42; see also pp. 39–41, 54–55, 214). Reinforcement exerts its effects automatically, without the individual's conscious knowledge, and should immediately follow the response in question in order to be most effective (as in Skinner's formulation).

According to Dollard and Miller, we learn to reduce our drives by responding to stimuli in the environment that serve as signals (**cues**). For example, suppose that a hungry little girl is told that candy is hidden somewhere in the room. If she sees a bowl, she may look inside it for the candy. Or she may ask the experimenter where the candy is. These are responses that she already knows how to perform, which are elicited by environmental cues (the bowl or the experimenter).

Any response that leads to the reduction of the hunger drive is more likely to occur again to that cue. Let us assume that the girl removes a book from the bookcase, discovers the candy, and promptly and happily eats it. She is likely to return to that book more quickly on the next trial, although she might guess (based on previous experiences with hiding games) that the experimenter will try to fool her by moving the candy. But if it is always concealed in the same place, the connection between seeing that book and removing it will be most strongly strengthened because it occurs immediately prior to the reinforcement. Other behaviors more remote in time (such as looking in the wrong place two minutes earlier) are much more weakly reinforced and tend *not* to recur, enabling her behavior to become more efficient. To Dollard and Miller, then, learning consists of the strengthening of connections between particular stimuli or cues (e.g., the correct book) and certain responses that they elicit (removing it from the shelf) through reinforcement (finding and eating the candy). Therefore, their approach is commonly referred to as **stimulus-response theory.**

The learning process in this experiment could have been speeded up by telling the girl that the candy was somewhere in the bookcase, making it more likely that she would attend to important cues (a step that was taken by the experimenter). What if she were so young as never to have removed a book from a bookcase, making it virtually impossible for her to respond correctly? She could be helped to behave in this way by watching while another child did so and found the candy, a form of **social learning** that Miller and Dollard (1941) were among the first to recommend. Conversely, if a child touches a hot stove, the reinforcing reduction in pain achieved by withdrawing its hand decreases the strength of the connection between the sight of the stove and touching it. Therefore, the child is less likely to touch the stove in the future. (See Dollard & Miller, 1950, pp. 25–47.)

Behavior may be motivated by more than one drive, as with the Freudian concept of overdetermination. For example, the little girl may have sought the candy not only to satisfy her hunger (primary drive reduction), but also to please the experimenter (secondary drive reduction). The stronger the drive(s), the greater the extent to which reinforcement strengthens the stimulus-response connections in question. If no drives are active, reinforcement—and learning—are impossible. "Completely self-satisfied people are poor learners" (Dollard & Miller, 1950, p. 32).

Extinction and Other Behaviorist Concepts. Like Pavlov and Skinner, Dollard and Miller conclude that most learned responses (and learned drives) that are repeatedly *not* followed by reinforcement will decrease in frequency (extinguish). Thus reinforcement is essential not only for the acquisition of behavior, but also its maintenance.

Extinction can be highly advantageous. It enables inappropriate and maladaptive responses to drop out, and be replaced by ones that are drive-reducing. Unfortunately for the patient in psychotherapy, however, fears and anxieties are typically learned very quickly but are highly resistant to extinction. Dollard and Miller agree with Skinner that partial reinforcement produces greater resistance to extinction; but they disagree on other specifics, as by contending that the amount of reinforcement per trial during learning is equally important. (See Dollard & Miller, 1950, pp. 49–51, 72–73, 162–163.)

Dollard and Miller also use various other behaviorist concepts discussed in the preceding chapter, including conditioned or learned reinforcers (e.g., money), generalization, and discrimination. Their definition of these terms is essentially the same as was given in Chapter 15.

Higher Mental Processes. Human behavior is not always a matter of automatic responses to external stimuli. It often involves important internal phenomena, such as trains of thought.

For example, the little girl's discovery of the candy did more than strengthen the connections between the book cue and certain overt responses. It also reinforced some of her covert thoughts, such as "Maybe the candy is under that book." Dollard and Miller regard the latter as a **cue-producing response:** one that does not itself cause an immediate change in the external world, but serves as a cue that elicits yet another response that does (such as removing the book from the shelf). Other examples include counting one's change after making a cash purchase, which cues such other responses as either putting the money in one's pocket or asking for more, and writing down numbers while performing long division. (See Dollard & Miller, 1950, pp. 97–124.)

Cue-producing responses may be overt (out loud) as well as covert (silent), and verbal or nonverbal (as with mental images). Most importantly, and in marked contrast to Skinnerian psychology, such cognitions can indeed be causal. Misguidedly naming (**labeling**) one's own illness as "cancer" will undoubtedly evoke the powerful learned drive of fear, whereas deciding that it is "only a cold" will provide fear-reducing reinforcement. If a student thinks, "That test I have tomorrow will be very tough," this may well cause fear (and perhaps some additional studying). But if the student reflects that "I've done well on similar exams in the past," this is likely to produce calmness and confidence. A professor not invited to a party given by a long-term associate may arouse the learned drive of anger by concluding that "He's insulting me." Or she may resolve this troublesome problem by noting that all the guests were from a field other than her own, and labeling the event as a "departmental party." Notice that here Dollard and Miller are solidly within the realm of personality theory, for this model closely resembles Kelly's concept of constructive alternativism.

Higher mental processes also enable us to behave more effectively by reasoning and planning ahead, as when parents decide how to provide for their children's future education. Thus Dollard and Miller differ from Skinner by regarding stopping to think as highly advantageous. They also stress that any severe impairment of our invaluable higher mental processes must have grave consequences—as happens with the repressions so prominent in neurosis.

THE STRUCTURE AND DEVELOPMENT OF PERSONALITY

In accordance with their preference for behaviorist terminology, Dollard and Miller reject the use of abstract structural constructs. Thus they attribute worry and guilt not to a superego, but rather to unlabeled fear responses that become attached to stimuli during childhood and are then elicited whenever these stimuli recur (Dollard & Miller, 1950, p. 141). Also, like Horney, Dollard and Miller couch their discussion of personality development primarily in terms of the causes and dynamics of psychopathology.

FURTHER APPLICATIONS
OF DOLLARD AND MILLER'S THEORY

Psychopathology

How Fear Is Learned. To Dollard and Miller, as to Freud, neurosis is usually due to powerful unconscious conflicts that originate during childhood. Rather than concentrating on intrapsychic structures and energies, however, they argue that such neurotic conflicts are taught by the parents and learned by the child. Four stressful childhood situations are particularly likely to cause such pathogenic learning: feeding, toilet training, sex training, and the child's displays of anger. "The idealization of childhood in the 'myth of the happy child' has prevented candid discussion of the strains of family life and the frequent misery and conflict of children. . . . Thanks much to Freud's work we all now seem ready to tell the truth, . . . and admit that growing up in a family is a strenuous affair" (Dollard & Miller, 1950, p. 129; see also pp. 127–197).

Suppose that an infant is often not fed until it is very hungry, and crying very loudly. The infant is strongly reinforced for its extreme outbursts, since these occur closest in time to the feeding. It will also generalize its fear of intensely painful hunger to the preceding state of more normal hunger. The unfortunate result is that the infant learns to overreact to increases in its drives, possibly in the form of tantrums. It also learns to fear being alone, the cue associated with the powerful hunger pangs. The well-timed feeding and tender care provided by a loving mother will help to prevent such pathogenic learning, and will also make her later appearance a positive secondary reinforcer.

Toilet training is also likely to become a source of fear and conflict. The powerful connection between the bowel stimulus and evulsion response must be weakened, and replaced by a complicated series of preliminary actions that are difficult for a child to learn (such as going into the bathroom, unbuttoning its clothes, and so on). Some anxiety must therefore be attached to the child's incontinence through punishment. But if the parents react with excessive anger and disgust, not an unlikely occurrence in this emotional area, strong fears may instead become associated with the bathroom—and even with the parents themselves.

In contrast to Freud, Dollard and Miller conclude that extreme hunger or thirst (or even ambition) may well become more powerful drives than sexuality. However, they do agree that sex is particularly likely to become a troublesome and painful issue. This drive is more easily inhibited (as by fear) than are the other primary drives: we can survive without sex, but not without food or drink. Dollard and Miller also accept the existence of childhood sexuality, concluding that "erection of the penis can be observed in male infants" (1950, p. 141), and they concur with Freud about the Oedipus complex. Thus they warn that a father who treats his son as a rival, and/or a mother who seeks emotional gratification from her son in order to compensate for sexual frustrations with her husband, may well cause the boy's penis and sexual drive to become cues that elicit an intense fear response (i.e., castration anxiety). "The uninstructed boy may assume that the girl once had an external genital but has been deprived of it, perhaps as a punishment. There is no doubt that this inference is often made" (Dollard & Miller, 1950, p. 146; see also pp. 144–147, 210). This fear is likely to generalize to later adult heterosexual relationships, leaving the sufferer impotent. Sexual fears and conflicts may also be caused by parental anger and disgust at the child playing with its genitals, or by parents who very much wanted a child of the opposite sex and who therefore teach their son (daughter) to be overly effeminate (masculine).

A fourth common source of fear and conflict concerns the child's angry responses to the inevitable frustrations that it faces. To Dollard and Miller, this is probably the most frequent cause of severe punishment. The resulting anxiety may then generalize to healthy assertiveness as well, with the sufferer becoming overly meek and able to express anger only in such indirect ways as habitual deceit. "Robbing a person of his anger completely may be a dangerous thing, since some capacity for anger seems to be needed in the affirmative personality" (Dollard & Miller, 1950, p. 149; see also Dollard, Doob, Miller, Mowrer, & Sears, 1939).

Whatever the specific issue, the fear and conflicts learned in infancy and early childhood automatically become unconscious—and thus extremely difficult to resolve—because of the inability to use language to identify them properly. "*Early conflicts [are] unlabeled, [and] therefore unconscious. . . .* What was not verbalized at the time cannot well be reported later" (Dollard & Miller, 1950, p. 136; see also pp. 140–141, 198, 209).

The Effects of Fear: I. Unconscious Conflicts and Unreduced Drives. Like Horney, Dollard and Miller draw a sharp distinction between conscious and unconscious conflicts. Both result from two or more drives that cause incompatible responses. But the former are an inevitable aspect of living and are by no means pathological, while the latter play a primary role in neurosis. (See Dollard & Miller, 1950, pp. 13–14, 352–368.)

Suppose that you must make a conscious choice between two positive alternatives (**approach-approach competition**), such as whether to enjoy an ice cream soda or milk shake. This is usually an easy problem to resolve, because any movement toward one of these desirable goals strengthens the tendency to approach still further (and ultimately choose that one).

Greater difficulty is presented by the need to decide between two negative possibilities (**avoidance-avoidance competition**), as when you must either do a great deal of studying or fail an examination. You may find this issue fairly easy to resolve if one of these alternatives is considerably less aversive than the other. But if they are of about equal strength, you will probably spend a considerable amount of time vacillating between them.

■ CAPSULE SUMMARY
Some Important Dollard-Miller Terminology

Anxiety	See *fear*.
Approach-approach competition	A situation wherein an organism must choose between two desirable goals; usually easily resolved by moving toward one of them.
Approach-avoidance conflict	A conflict caused by a goal that has both desirable and undesirable qualities. Moving toward it eventually evokes fear; moving away from it prevents satisfaction. To Dollard and Miller, unconscious approach-avoidance conflicts which involve fear play a prominent role in neurosis.
Avoidance-avoidance competition	A situation wherein an organism must choose between two negative possibilities. May be resolved fairly readily if one alternative is considerably less aversive than the other, but will result in vacillating between them (or escaping the situation altogether if possible) if they are of about equal strength.
Cue	A stimulus that serves as a discriminative signal, rather than as a motivator. May be external (e.g., an object or person) or internal (as with thoughts).
Cue-producing response	A response that does not itself produce an immediate change in the external world, but serves as a cue that elicits yet another response that does. One of the important human higher mental processes.
Drive	A strong stimulus that impels an organism to behave; may be primary (innate) or secondary (learned).
Fear	A learned response of apprehension, elicited by a previously neutral stimulus, which also functions as a learned drive capable of motivating behavior. Technically, fear refers to a stimulus that is known and anxiety to one that is vague or repressed; but in practice, the terms are used interchangeably.
Labeling	Attaching a verbal name to some event, stimulus, response, person, and so on. To Dollard and Miller, fears and conflicts that occur during infancy and early childhood automatically become unconscious because of the inability to label them.
Primary drive (innate drive)	A drive that can be satiated but never eliminated, such as hunger, thirst, sex (in part), and the avoidance of pain.
Repression	Similar to Freud's use of the term, but attributed by Dollard and Miller to an automatic and fear-reducing response of stopping thinking rather than to some intrapsychic component of personality. Contributes to neurosis by incapacitating the higher mental processes.
Secondary drive (learned drive)	A drive that is learned and can in theory be extinguished, such as fear (anxiety), anger, guilt, the need for money or power,

continued

	and many others. Unfortunately, fear has proved to be highly resistant to extinction.
Social learning	Learning based on the observation and imitation of others; essentially similar to Bandura's concept of modeling.
Stimulus	A term that includes both drives and cues.
Stimulus-response theory	The name commonly given to Dollard and Miller's theory, because of its definition of learning as the strengthening of connections between specific stimuli and certain responses that they elicit through reinforcement.

(Or you might instead escape the situation altogether if possible, as by dropping the course in question).

A still more troublesome conflict occurs when one goal has both positive and negative qualities (**approach-avoidance conflict**), such as a prospective date with a physically attractive but rather unpleasant person. So long as this conflict remains conscious, you can apply higher mental processes to the problem and achieve some reasonably effective solution. But the unconscious conflicts caused by strong fears (or, less frequently, by such other learned drives as guilt) are very likely to be insoluble without the aid of psychotherapy:

> Conflict itself is no novelty. Emotional conflicts are the constant accompaniment of life at every age and social level. . . . [But] where conflicts are strong and unconscious, the individuals afflicted keep on making the same old mistakes and getting punished in the same old way. (Dollard & Miller, 1950, p. 154.)

To illustrate, suppose that fear has become a learned response to sexual stimuli. This is precisely what happened to one attractive and intelligent female patient ("Mrs. A"), who suffered from such childhood trauma as seduction by a younger brother and a mother who preached that sex was dirty and wrong. (See Dollard & Miller, 1950, pp. 16–22, 222–226.) Since the sexual drive is innate and inescapable, the unfortunate result was an unconscious approach-avoidance conflict about this important issue: Mrs. A had both a powerful drive to enjoy sex, and a strong need to reduce the associated fears by escaping from sexual situations. According to Dollard and Miller, the strength of the avoidance tendency increases more rapidly than that of approach. (See Figure 16.2.) Sexuality therefore seems attractive from a distance, so the sufferer makes some moves in this direction (as by deciding to get married). But fear dominates when close to the goal, whereupon the individual reduces this drive by moving away (as by rejecting every invitation to engage in marital intercourse). Thus the sex drive is sacrificed

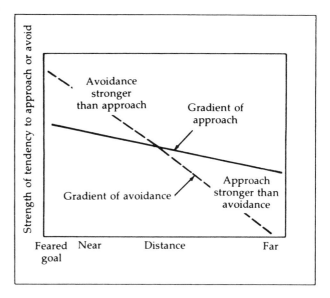

FIGURE 16.2. Simple graphic representation of an approach-avoidance conflict (Dollard & Miller, 1950, p. 356).

to the reduction of the fear drive and remains unreduced and nagging, the hallmark of neurotic misery.

Fear may instead block the reduction of some other important drive with which it has become associated, such as anger. But whatever the specific issue, the sufferer cannot understand and attack the problem effectively because the higher mental processes have been incapacitated—either by the inability to label those fears and conflicts that are learned during the preverbal childhood years (and which therefore automatically become unconscious), or by such defense mechanisms as repression.

The Effects of Fear: II. Repression. It is not only actions that are inhibited by the need to reduce the learned fear drive, but thoughts as well. For example, the fear associated with punished behaviors (e.g., masturbation, anger) tends to generalize to thoughts about them. Therefore, avoiding such cognitions is reinforcing.

A conscious decision to stop thinking about an anxiety-provoking issue need not be harmful, since it remains within one's control. But **repression,** while also a response of stopping thinking that is reinforced by a reduction of the fear drive, is usually harmful because it cannot be controlled by the individual. It incapacitates the all-important higher mental processes, thereby preventing the sufferer from using reasoning and planning to solve the painful issues. The unfortunate result of this automatic thought-stopping is strikingly inept behavior in those areas related to the neurosis:

> [The neurotic] is not able to solve his conflict even with the passage of time.
> Though obviously intelligent in some ways, he is stupid insofar as his neurotic
> conflict is concerned. This stupidity is not an overall affair, however. It is really
> a stupid area in the mind of a person who is quite intelligent in other respects.
> (Dollard & Miller, 1950, p. 14.)

Thus Mrs. A misguidedly concluded that she either had no interest in
sex, or was the victim of an organic disease. She could not recognize the
relationship between her mother's distorted teachings and her current difficulties, nor was she consciously aware of any hostility toward her mother.
She was unable to discriminate between illicit forms of sex and her right to
enjoy intercourse with her husband. And she was incapable of forming any
coherent plans for resolving the severe neurotic misery caused by her unreduced sexual drive. (See Dollard & Miller, 1950, pp. 14–22, 147, 198–221.)

The Effects of Fear: III. Pathological Symptoms. According to Dollard and
Miller, most pathological symptoms serve to reduce the sufferer's conflicts
and fears. For example, a soldier torn between a fear of combat and guilt
over the possibility of letting his comrades down developed hysterical paralysis of an arm, thereby alleviating his problem without having to face it
consciously. And Mrs. A became preoccupied with a compulsion to count
her heartbeats, an (unconscious) way of avoiding thoughts about her sexual
conflict and reducing her fears. (See Dollard & Miller, 1950, pp. 15–16,
157–170). Pathological symptoms evade rather than resolve the true problem, so the neurotic will continue to suffer the intense misery of unreduced
drives—at least until he or she seeks help from formal psychotherapy.

Psychotherapy

Theoretical Foundation. In contrast to virtually all behaviorists, Dollard and
Miller argue that removing a pathological symptom without treating the
underlying causes will *not* produce any improvement. Instead they stress
that psychotherapy must enable patients to reduce their irrational fears,
begin abandoning the harmful response of repression, and start applying
their higher mental processes to their emotional problems. Because of this
emphasis on bringing unconscious material to consciousness, Dollard and
Miller advocate an approach to psychotherapy that is essentially Freudian in
nature. (See Dollard & Miller, 1950, pp. 15, 168, 221, 229–238.)

Therapeutic Procedures. According to Dollard and Miller, free association
enables the patient to reveal feared issues in an atmosphere that is permissive and free of criticism. As one painful problem is discussed and

experienced emotionally, the associated anxiety is extinguished by the therapist's accepting attitude. This in turn generalizes to the next most threatening issue, which can then be brought to light and have the related anxiety extinguished in the same way. Therapeutic progress is typically slow and irregular, since it is hard work for the patient to confront and deal with anxiety. Therefore the therapist should concentrate on fear reduction ("lowering the avoidance gradient") and put off urgings to approach the feared goal ("raising the approach gradient"), for the latter is all too likely to evoke such intense anxiety as to drive the patient out of therapy. "The patient likes a [therapist] who takes his time" (Dollard & Miller, 1950, p. 248; see also pp. 240–259, 359).

Because of the powerful tendency to repress feared material, the patient is likely to engage in various resistances. These include avoiding certain crucial topics, concentrating on unimportant details, trying (unconsciously) to confuse the issue, and engaging in long silences. "The patient who has been starved for years for a chance to speak, and who has his whole life behind him, suddenly cannot think of anything else to say. Since the therapist knows that this is impossible in a free mind, he assumes that repression is at work, *i.e.,* that the patient has something to say but unconsciously dares not say it" (Dollard & Miller, 1950, p. 255; see also pp. 270–271). One way to overcome such resistances is by teaching the patient to label repressed material, and to discriminate the past from the present. Mrs. A's therapist therefore suggested that she might well be very angry with her mother, and pointed out the difference between blindly accepting her mother's puritanical teachings and pursuing her own legitimate wishes to enjoy sex with her husband. Thus, as in Freudian theory, therapeutic interpretations typically involve childhood issues. "Without understanding the past, the future cannot be changed" (Dollard & Miller, 1950, p. 246; see also pp. 254–256, 266–267, 281–320).

Transference occurs when the patient generalizes previously learned responses from (say) the parents to the therapist because the latter is a similar stimulus in many respects, as by also being an authority figure. Thus therapy is facilitated by the patient's desire to please the therapist, as one would a parent, and slowed by the transfer of dependent behavior and wishes for an omnipotent provider. It is particularly important for the irrational fears to be transferred to the therapeutic situation, however, so that they can be extinguished. "The patient must pronounce the forbidden sentences *while being afraid*" (Dollard & Miller, 1950, p. 249; see also pp. 109, 260–280, 303–304). Thus Dollard and Miller agree with Freud and Horney that insight must be both intellectual and emotional to be effective, and that intellectualization is antithetic to therapeutic progress. They also concur that the patient must work through in real life the insights gained in therapy, and that the interpretation of dreams and parapraxes affords valuable information about the patient's unconscious mental life. (See Dollard & Miller, 1950, pp. 10, 256–257, 331–351.)

EVALUATION

Criticisms and Controversies

Dollard and Miller's theory has been criticized for certain technical short-comings: whether simple stimulus-response connections are sufficient to explain complicated behaviors, their stress on drive reduction, and whether the results of their crucial animal studies can be accurately generalized to human beings. However, two considerations loom above all others. Dollard and Miller failed to follow their therapeutic application of learning theory to its logical conclusion, retaining Freudian techniques rather than achieving the methodological breakthroughs later accomplished by Wolpe and others. And they presented their views as tentative suggestions in 1950 but published nothing further in this area thereafter, hardly the best way to synthesize such bitterly opposed theoretical camps as behaviorism and psychoanalysis. Thus their theory is widely regarded as primarily of historical interest, and has even been accused of delaying the advent of true behavior therapy.

Contributions

To some psychologists, Dollard and Miller's attempted rapprochement between behaviorism and psychoanalysis contains much of interest and importance. They have been praised for emphasizing and clarifying two particularly important variables, anxiety and conflict, and for their non-metaphysical definition of repression. And there is also some indication that they may actually have been ahead of their time, for their ideas have helped to inspire at least one significant similar modern attempt (Wachtel, 1977).

Suggested Reading

Dollard and Miller's psychoanalytic-behaviorist synthesis is presented in a single book, *Personality and Psychotherapy* (1950).

One aspect of Miller and Dollard's work has been accepted and expanded upon by some modern behaviorists: their earlier writings on social learning (1941). Perhaps the leading exponent of this approach is Albert Bandura, who emphatically rejects Skinner's radical behaviorism. Instead, Bandura's theory stresses the mutual interrelationships among behavior, internal causes, and environmental factors.

BIOGRAPHICAL SKETCH: ALBERT BANDURA

Albert Bandura was born on December 4, 1925, in Mundara, a small town in Alberta, Canada. He received his B.A. from the University of British Columbia in 1949 and his Ph.D. in psychology from the University of Iowa in 1952, and has been on the faculty of Stanford University since 1953. Bandura married Virginia Varns; they have two children. He is the author or editor of some six books and numerous journal articles, and his honors include several distinguished scientist awards and election to the presidency of the American Psychological Association in 1974.

THE BASIC NATURE OF HUMAN BEINGS

Reciprocal Determinism

Bandura is highly critical of Skinner's emphasis on a totally controlling environment, and the apparent paradoxes to which this conception leads:

> [To contend] that people are [wholly] controlled by external forces, and then to advocate that they redesign society by applying psychotechnology, under-mines the basic premise of the argument. If humans were in fact incapable of influencing their own actions, they might describe and predict environmental events but they could hardly exercise any intentional control over them. When it comes to advocacy of social change, however, [Skinnerians nevertheless] become ardent advocates of people's power to transform environments in pursuit of a better life. (Bandura, 1977, pp. 205–206. See also Bandura, 1978, p. 344; 1986.)

Bandura argues that behavior, environmental influences, and internal personal factors (including beliefs, thoughts, preferences, expectations, and self-perceptions) all operate as interlocking regulators of each other (**reciprocal determinism**). For example, the behavior of watching a particular television program is dictated in part by your personal preferences. Both of these factors exert an effect on the environment, since producers cancel shows that do not attract enough viewers. And external forces also help to shape preferences and behaviors, for you cannot like or select a program that is not televised:

> In the social learning view, people are neither driven [solely] by inner forces nor buffeted by environmental stimuli. Rather, psychological functioning is explained in terms of a continuous reciprocal interaction of personal and environmental determinants. . . . [Therefore,] to the oft-repeated [Skinner-ian] dictum "change contingencies and you change behavior," should be add-ed the reciprocal side "change behavior and you change the contingencies." In

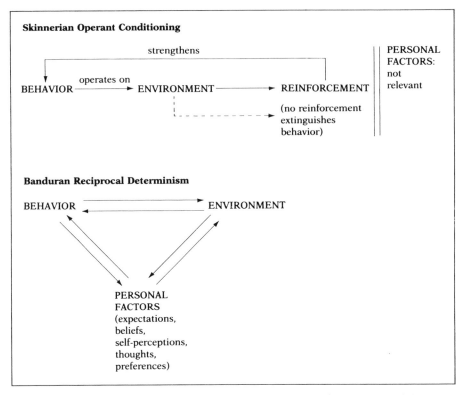

FIGURE 16.3. Skinnerian operant conditioning and Banduran reciprocal determinism compared.

the regress of prior causes, for every chicken discovered by a unidirectional environmentalist, a social learning theorist can identify a prior egg. (Bandura, 1977, pp. 11–12, 203. See also Bandura, 1973, p. 43; 1977, pp. vii, 108–109, 194–213; 1978, pp. 345–346.)

Reciprocal determinism implies that we do enjoy some freedom to act. But the number of options open to us is limited by external constraints, and by our own inability or unwillingness to behave in certain ways. (See Figure 16.3.)

Cognitive Causes

Bandura agrees with Skinner that some so-called inner causes of behavior are merely redundant descriptions. Yet his position on this issue is much closer to that of Dollard and Miller, for he readily accepts the existence of causal cognitions.

For example, anxiety may be generated by thoughts about sustaining a probable injury. People can make themselves sick by imagining nauseating situations, angry by thinking of purported insults, or sexually aroused by conjuring up erotic fantasies. And some innovators or unpublished authors think so strongly of being right that they labor for years'to achieve their ends, with these cognitive self-inducements substituting for the lack of any reinforcing recognition. "Because some of the inner causes invoked by theorists over the years have been ill-founded does not justify excluding all internal determinants from scientific inquiry. . . . [There is] growing evidence that cognition has causal influence on behavior . . . [and that any theory which] denies that thoughts can regulate actions does not lend itself readily to the explanation of complex human behavior" (Bandura, 1977, p. 10; see also Bandura, 1969, pp. 49, 364; 1973, pp. 39–53; 1977, pp. 2–3, 61, 68, 207–208). Cognitions therefore play a crucial role in Bandura's definition of reinforcement, as we will see in the next section.

Reinforcement

Pavlov, Skinner, and Dollard and Miller all conclude that reinforcement operates without our awareness. Bandura disagrees, and argues that we must be aware of reinforcement in order for it to be effective. In particular, reinforcement involves a change in our conscious anticipations: we are more likely to act in ways which we *expect* to produce rewards, and/or to avoid punishments:

> The notion of "response strengthening" is, at best, a metaphor. . . . Outcomes change behavior in humans largely through the intervening influence of thought . . . [while] consequences generally produce little change in complex behavior when there is no awareness of what is being reinforced. Even if certain responses have been positively reinforced, they will not increase [in probability] if individuals believe, from other information, that the same actions will not be rewarded on future occasions. (Bandura, 1977, pp. 18, 21; see also pp. 17–22, 67, 96–97, 109.)

Partial reinforcement produces greater resistance to extinction because we expect that our efforts will eventually be successful, as with the slot machine player who continues to invest quarters despite frequent losses. Secondary reinforcers, such as money, approval, or criticism, are previously neutral stimuli that we now expect to be associated with primary reinforcers. And irrational fears are extremely difficult to eliminate because we keep away from whatever causes them, which confirms our expectation of avoiding harm and prevents us from learning that there is no real danger. "Humans do not simply respond to stimuli; they interpret them" (Bandura, 1977, p. 59; see also pp. 58–62, 102, 116).

THE STRUCTURE OF PERSONALITY

Like Dollard and Miller, Bandura sees little value in abstract structural constructs. But he does devote substantial attention to the ways in which people regulate and reinforce their own behavior, and to the effects of an individual's perceived self-effectiveness on his or her behavior.

Self-Regulated and Self-Reinforced Behavior

According to Bandura, our behavior is also influenced by learned criteria that we establish for ourselves. "If actions were determined solely by external rewards and punishments, people would behave like weathervanes, constantly shifting in different directions to conform to the momentary influences impinging upon them. . . . [In actuality, people also] set certain standards of behavior for themselves, and respond to their own actions in self-rewarding or self-punishing ways" (Bandura, 1977, pp. 128–129; see also Bandura, 1973, pp. 48–49; 1977, pp. 130–158; 1978).

For example, authors do not need someone hovering over their shoulders and reinforcing each well-phrased sentence with praise (or a piece of candy). They are guided by an inner standard of what constitutes acceptable work. They rewrite each page numerous times until this criterion is met, and then reinforce themselves with self-satisfaction and pride. The more exacting the author's standards, the more effort spent in revision—perhaps even to the extent of doing much more editing than is necessary, or becoming so self-critical as to be unable to complete the manuscript.

We are more likely to set higher standards for ourselves if an activity seems particularly important, if we are in the habit of comparing ourselves to capable people (e.g., highly skilled parents or friends), or if we have achieved a significant amount in the past (since attaining a previous level of performance is no longer challenging). A child frequently praised by lenient parents is more likely to engage in self-praise, however, which may result in lower self-standards. Or frequent self-approval may be learned by watching a model (such as a sibling) being rewarded for easy tasks. (See Bandura, 1977, pp. 129–138, 161.)

Some rare individuals appear to be totally guided by self-standards, as when Thomas More was beheaded rather than renounce his beliefs. Most often, however, self-standards are related to external ones. Thus praising oneself for inept or mediocre behavior is usually avoided, because it is likely to evoke painful criticism from other people. "Individuals who regard their behavior so highly that the reactions of their associates have no effect are rare indeed" (Bandura, 1977, p. 149; see also pp. 153–155). Nevertheless, self-standards and self-reinforcement play an extremely important role in determining human behavior. "Self-rewarded behavior tends to be maintained more effectively than if it has been externally reinforced. . . . Including self-reinforcement processes in learning theory thus greatly increases the explanatory power of reinforcement principles as applied to human functioning" (Bandura, 1977, pp. 129, 144).

■ CAPSULE SUMMARY
Some Important Banduran Terminology

Learning	Acquiring the capacity to perform new behaviors, albeit not necessarily executing them.
Modeling	(1) A synonym for observational learning. (2) A form of behavior therapy wherein the client observes one or more people demonstrating desirable behaviors, either live or on film, and is then reinforced for imitating them.
Observational learning (modeling, social learning)	Learning by observing other people's behavior, and its consequences for them. Reinforcement is *not* necessary for observational learning to occur; but it may well facilitate paying attention to the model and remembering the relevant information, or it may be essential to make the subject perform what has been learned.
Perceived self-efficacy	The perception that an individual has of his or her potential effectiveness in coping with the demands of the environment.
Performance	Actually executing particular behaviors.
Reciprocal determinism	The continuous mutual interrelationship of behavior, internal personal factors (e.g., thoughts, beliefs, expectations), and environmental influences, any one of which may regulate any of the others.
Reinforcement	An increase in the frequency of certain behaviors, based on one's conscious expectations that they will gain rewards or avoid punishments.
Self-reinforcement	Establishing certain standards of behavior for oneself, and praising or criticizing oneself accordingly. Self-standards are determined by such factors as one's prior levels of achievement, and direct and observational learning from parents and other models.
Social learning theory	The name given by Bandura to his psychological theory.
Vicarious punishment	A decrease in the frequency of certain behaviors, which occurs as the result of seeing others punished for the same actions (i.e., through observational learning).
Vicarious reinforcement	An increase in the frequency of certain behaviors, which occurs as the result of seeing others rewarded for the same actions (i.e., through observational learning).

Perceived Self-Efficacy

People tend to undertake those tasks that they judge themselves to be capable of performing, while avoiding activities that they regard as beyond their abilities. Thus human behavior is also strongly influenced by how we perceive our potential effectiveness in coping with the demands of the environment (our **perceived self-efficacy**).

A person who is high in perceived self-efficacy is more likely to persist in the face of obstacles or aversive experiences. People low in perceived self-efficacy tend to view their problems as more formidable than they actually are, and to slacken their efforts or quit altogether in the face of adversity. (A modest degree of uncertainty may prove advantageous, however, by preventing inadequate preparation through overconfidence.) Furthermore, perceived collective efficacy is rooted in perceived self-efficacy: those who believe more (less) highly in their own effectiveness are more (less) likely to conclude that appropriate group action will succeed in making needed changes in society, and to mobilize their efforts and resources accordingly. (See Bandura, 1981; 1982a; 1982b.)

Perceived self-efficacy is closely related to the Rogerian self-concept. However, Bandura differs from Rogers by arguing that a single global self-image cannot possibly account for the vastly different behaviors of people in different situations. Instead he concludes that the strength of one's self-concept varies in different areas (e.g., scholastics, athletics, social situations, solitary creative endeavors), and that these aspects must therefore be studied separately.

THE DEVELOPMENT OF PERSONALITY

Observational Learning (Modeling)

In contrast to Skinner, Bandura argues that behavior need not be performed and reinforced for learning to occur. **Modeling** (or **observational learning,** or **social learning**) involves learning by observing other people's behavior and its consequences for them, and is responsible for the vast majority of human learning.

For example, the novice does *not* learn to drive an automobile or perform brain surgery by emitting various random behaviors, and having the unsuccessful ones negatively reinforced by the resulting carnage. He or she learns through instruction, and by watching others perform these important tasks correctly. Bandura argues that if the pigeons and rats in operant conditioning experiments had faced such real dangers as drowning or electrocution, the limitations of this form of learning would have been forcefully revealed. "Observational learning is vital for both development and survival. Because mistakes can produce costly or even fatal consequences, the prospects for survival would be slim indeed if one could learn only by suffering the consequences of trial and error" (Bandura, 1977, p. 12; see also Bandura, 1969; 1971, pp. 2–3; 1977, pp. 58, 91).

The responses learned through observation may be novel ones. Or rewarding a model may increase the probability of a previously learned response (**vicarious reinforcement**), while punishing the model may decrease the frequency of such a response (**vicarious punishment**). In one experiment, observers learned to fear a buzzer by watching a model who supposedly received intensely painful electric shocks immediately after hearing it (actually only a simulation, with the model a convincing—and unshocked—actor). In other studies, observers who watched highly destructive or self-critical models became much more aggressive or self-punitive. Similarly, the probability of illicit or criminal behavior is increased by seeing others perform such actions without incurring any punishment. Thus Bandura shares the belief of certain theorists (e.g., Fromm, Rogers) that human destructiveness is typically due to learning, notably observational learning, rather than to some innate instinct. Conversely, socially acceptable behavior is often learned by watching conformist models get along well with others— as with the dictum "When in Rome, do as the Romans do" (Bandura, 1977, pp. 87–88; see also Bandura, 1973; 1977, pp. 65–67, 117–128, 151; Bandura & Walters, 1963).

How does observational learning occur? Bandura concludes that cognitions play a vital role: we imagine ourselves in the same situation, and incurring similar consequences. Observational learning can therefore change the effectiveness of certain reinforcers, as when a modest amount of money (or praise) produces little behavior change because an underpaid employee has seen other workers getting much more for the same responses.

Observational learning often occurs without either the model or the subject being reinforced. However, behavior change is unlikely to occur if the subject fails to observe the relevant activities (perhaps because they are too boring or painful to watch), does not try to remember this information, or does not want to perform the desired responses. Thus reinforcement may prove helpful by motivating the subject to pay attention and remember, or it may be necessary to make the subject *perform* the learned responses. The effectiveness of observational learning also depends on certain characteristics of the model and learner: better results are likely to be achieved if the model is attractive and similar to the learner in age and sex, and if the learner is particularly dependent or perceptive. (See Bandura, 1971, pp. 16–26; 1977, pp. 22–29, 38, 88–90.)

Chance Encounters

Bandura (1982c) also observes that a person's course in life may be strongly influenced by unintended meetings with previously unknown persons. For example, Paul Watkins was an excellent and model student until he decided to visit an acquaintance. Unbeknownst to Watkins, his friend had previously moved elsewhere. The new residents of the cabin in question proved to be the Manson "family," who diverted Paul into highly illicit activities. A young female actress began to receive in the mail announcements of communist meetings, which were actually intended for another person of the same name. Her quest for help led to a meeting with the then president of the Screen Actors Guild, and it was not too long before Nancy Davis married Ronald Reagan. Herbert Brown, a Nobel laureate, embarked on his chosen career in the rare field of boron hydrides because his girlfriend wished to give him a graduation present, and a book on that subject was the cheapest one available in the university bookstore. Thus "the most important determinants of life paths often arise through the most trivial of circumstances" (Bandura, 1982c, p. 749).

Psychology cannot be expected to predict the occurrence of chance encounters. But it can assess the probable impact of such events, as if people high in perceived self-efficacy should prove more likely to resist social traps that will lead them down detrimental paths.

FURTHER APPLICATIONS OF BANDURAN THEORY

Psychopathology

Bandura attributes psychopathology to faulty learning, and to the resulting incorrect anticipations. Thus a man may mistakenly conclude from one or two unpleasant experiences that all blondes are gold-diggers, and become hostile or fearful toward blondes. These defensive behaviors are likely to evoke true negative reactions from the next blonde that he meets, thereby perpetuating the faulty belief. Or a phobia may be due to inappropriate generalizations, such as little Albert's fear of rabbits.

Children may develop pathological behaviors because these actions are rewarded, as when a well-meaning but misguided teacher pays close attention to shy pupils only when they isolate themselves from their classmates and sulk. Or parents may inadvertently teach their children to be annoying by responding only to their loudest requests, as Skinner has also pointed out. Perhaps the most painful of all problems is an overly severe set of self-standards, and the resulting attempts to avoid guilt or external punishments through excessive self-criticism. "There is no more devastating punishment than self-contempt. . . . Linus, the security-blanketed member of the 'Peanuts' clan, also alluded to this phenomenon when he observed, 'There is no heavier burden than a great potential' " (Bandura, 1977, pp. 141, 154).

As the last example indicates, Bandura differs from Skinner by attributing considerable importance to inner, cognitive causes of psychopathology. "Many human dysfunctions and ensuing torments stem from problems of thought. This is because, in their thoughts, people often dwell on painful pasts and on perturbing futures of their own invention. . . . They drive themselves to despondency by harsh self-evaluation . . . And they often act on misconceptions that get them into trouble." (Bandura, 1986, p. 515.)

Psychotherapy

Theoretical Foundation. Whatever the specific form, pathological individuals suffer from a similar problem: they cannot behave in ways that they expect to gain rewards or avoid punishments. This feeling of powerlessness may well result in depression, paranoia, frequent fantasies of success, or suicide.

The psychotherapist's primary goal is therefore to help clients restore their sense of self-efficacy, or belief that they can master a situation and bring about desirable outcomes through their own efforts. This increased self-efficacy makes it more likely that the client will confront irrational fears, instead of avoiding them. "[Clients] who persist in performing activities that are [frightening but safe] will gain corrective experiences that further reinforce their sense of efficacy, thereby eventually eliminating their fears and defensive behavior. [But] those who give up prematurely will retain their self-debilitating expectations and fears for a long time" (Bandura, 1977, p. 80).

Bandura therefore advocates forms of behavior therapy that involve actual performance of the feared tasks. "Conversation is not an especially effective way of altering human behavior. In order to change, people need corrective learning experiences" (Bandura, 1977, p. 78; see also Bandura, 1969; 1977, pp. 5, 79–85). Bandura is also critical of insight therapies because, like Kelly, he believes that clients' thoughts are all too often molded in the direction of the therapist's particular theory of personality.

Therapeutic Procedures. A client who is too anxious or unskilled to behave in certain desirable ways may be shown one or more people demonstrating these behaviors, either live or on film, and then be reinforced for imitating them (the technique of **modeling**). For example, a child afraid of dogs may see and then imitate a peer who first observes a dog from a distance, then moves somewhat closer, then still closer, and then pets it, being reinforced by the therapist at each point (a form of shaping called "graduated modeling"). Modeling is also useful in changing undesirable behaviors, as when unruly and uncooperative children watch a film of children playing together enjoyably and are then reinforced for behaving similarly.

According to Bandura, treatments that combine modeling with guided participation are particularly effective in eliminating dysfunctional fears and inhibitions. "Through this form of treatment, incapacitated clients lose their fears, become able to engage in activities they formerly inhibited, and develop more favorable attitudes toward the things they abhorred" (Bandura, 1977, p. 84).

Psychotherapy and Social Reform. In accordance with some personality theorists, Bandura strongly recommends certain social reforms. He is highly critical of the extent to which television and other media portray violent behaviors, since these are all too likely to serve as models (especially in the case of children). Thus he urges such controls as a privately funded board that would try to sway public opinion against media violence, and in favor of programs that are nonviolent and informative (such as the well-known "Sesame Street"). (See Bandura, 1973.)

EVALUATION

Criticisms and Controversies

Bandura has been criticized for ignoring such important and complicated aspects of human behavior as conflicts, both conscious and unconscious, and for an excessive bias against psychoanalysis (Wachtel, 1977, pp. 98–101, 118–119). He all too readily accepts the negative findings of outdated and outmoded laboratory studies of the defense mechanisms, and he rejects the value of clinical data without considering the other side of the story (Bandura, 1986, pp. 3–4). In addition, there would seem to be some pronounced (yet largely ignored) similarities between Bandura's ideas and those of other theorists: Kelly's emphasis on the importance of interpreting (construing) our environment, and of our expectations and predictions; the stress of Adler, Erikson, Fromm, and May on a sense of mastery, and the debilitating effects of intense feelings of powerlessness and inferiority; Freud's concept of an overly severe superego; and Horney's emphasis on self-contempt. Thus it would appear that Bandura has achieved more of a rapprochement with personality theory than his writings indicate.

Contributions

Social learning theory has been praised for its grounding in empirical research, for emphasizing studies with human rather than animal subjects, for promulgating such significant new forms of psychotherapy as modeling, and for providing behaviorism with a far more convicing rationale than either Skinner or Dollard and Miller. As an indication of the esteem currently accorded Bandura, leading books on behavior therapy typically refer to his work even more often than that of Skinner.

Suggested Reading

A more detailed discussion of Bandura's views may be found in *Social Learning Theory* (1977) and the rather dry and technical *Social Foundations of Thought and Action* (1986), while a comparison of various alternative explanations of modeling is presented in *Psychological Modeling: Conflicting Theories* (1971). In addition, he has authored a social learning analysis of aggression (Bandura, 1973).

■ SUMMARY

In an effort to retain the advantages of behaviorism, yet redress its more serious defects, some psychologists have (overtly or covertly) sought to effect some sort of rapprochement with personality theory.

1. JOHN DOLLARD AND NEAL E. MILLER. Basing their ideas on both clinical observation and laboratory research, Dollard and Miller seek to synthesize psychoanalysis and behaviorism. *The Basic Nature of Human Beings:* We are motivated by the desire to reduce primary (innate) and secondary (learned) drives. This is accomplished via the strengthening of stimulus-response connections through reinforcement, the extinction of behavior that is not reinforced, and the use of higher mental processes (including cue-producing responses and labeling). *The Structure and Development of Personality:* Dollard and Miller prefer behaviorist terminology to structural constructs, and couch their discussion of personality development primarily in terms of the causes and dynamics of psychopathology. *Further Applications:* Neurosis occurs when a learned drive (most often fear) conflicts with one or more other drives and prevents their reduction, with this dammed-up state representing the hallmark of neurotic misery. Neurotic fears are typically learned from such difficult childhood experiences as feeding, toilet training, sex training, and parental responses to anger, and become unconscious because the child cannot use language well enough to label them. Since neurosis involves powerful unconscious conflicts between competing drives, Dollard and Miller advocate the use of Freudian therapeutic techniques to bring these repressed issues to consciousness. *Evaluation:* Dollard and Miller have been criticized for their emphasis on drive reduction, basing their theory on simple stimulus-response connections, using primarily animal subjects, and retaining Freudian therapeutic techniques rather than achieving the methodological breakthroughs of the later behaviorists. Yet their approach contains much of interest and importance, notably their analyses of fear and conflict.

2. ALBERT BANDURA. One aspect of Dollard and Miller's work has been accepted and expanded upon by some modern behaviorists, namely their earlier writings on social learning. *The Basic Nature of Human Beings:* Bandura is highly critical of Skinnerian behaviorism. He argues that psychological functioning involves a continuous reciprocal interrelationship among behavior, environmental influences, and internal personal factors (including expectations, beliefs, thoughts, preferences, and self-perceptions). He accepts the existence of cognitive causes, and explains reinforcement in terms of an expectation that certain behaviors will gain rewards or avoid punishments. *The Structure of Personality:* Bandura also prefers behaviorist terminology to structural constructs. He concludes that we can and do set standards of behavior for ourselves, and praise or criticize ourselves accordingly. In fact, self-regulated and self-reinforced behavior tends to be maintained more effectively than if it had been externally reinforced. Our behavior and performance are also affected by the way in which we perceive our potential effectiveness in coping with the demands of the environment (perceived self-efficacy). *The*

Development of Personality: The majority of human learning occurs through observation ("modeling"), rather than through performing the response in question. Bandura regards aggression and destructiveness as due primarily to such observational learning, rather than to some innate instinct. Chance encounters also play a role in shaping a person's course in life. *Further Applications:* Bandura attributes psychopathology to faulty learning, and to the resulting incorrect anticipations. Defensive avoidance behaviors serve to confirm one's prediction of evading harm, and thus prevent the self-defeating fearful expectations from being unlearned. He therefore advocates the use of behavior therapy to provide the necessary disconfirming experiences, preferably procedures wherein the client actually performs the feared tasks. *Evaluation:* Bandura has been criticized for ignoring such important issues as conscious and unconscious conflicts, and for an excessive bias against psychoanalysis. He has been credited with grounding his work in empirical research, emphasizing studies with human rather than animal subjects, and providing behaviorism with a far more convincing rationale than his predecessors. Yet in view of the similarities between his ideas and those of such psychologists as Kelly, Adler, Erikson, Fromm, May, Freud, and Horney, it would seem that Bandura's success derives from achieving a rapprochement with (rather than an alternative to) personality theory.

STUDY QUESTIONS

1. (a) Use the case of "Mrs. A" to illustrate Dollard and Miller's contention that fear is a learned drive. How did Mrs. A learn this fear? In what way is it a drive, rather than merely a response? (b) Could this case be interpreted instead as supporting Skinnerian operant conditioning? Why or why not?

2. Give a real-life example to support Dollard and Miller's argument that fears and conflicts learned in infancy and early childhood become unconscious (and therefore difficult to resolve) because the child cannot use language to label them properly.

3. Compare the views of Dollard and Miller with those of Skinner regarding the advantages of stopping to think before you act. Which do you prefer? Why?

4. Give an example from your own life, from the life of someone you know well, or from fiction to illustrate each of the following: (a) An approach–approach competition. (b) An avoidance–avoidance competition. (c) An approach–avoidance conflict.

5. In contrast to Skinner, Dollard and Miller and Bandura argue that cognitions are valid causes of behavior. Give an example from real life, or from fiction, to illustrate each of the following: (a) Labeling an event in different ways can cause quite different behaviors. (b) Thoughts alone can cause a person to become angry or depressed.

6. (a) Give an example from your own life to support Bandura's argument that self-regulation and self-reinforcement have a major influence on behav-

ior. (b) According to Bandura, self-standards are usually related to external standards. Is this wise, or should a person's self-standards be entirely independent of environmental influences? Why?

7. Give a real-life example to show that a person who is low in perceived self-efficacy is less likely to persist in the face of obstacles or aversive experiences.

8. Give a real-life example to support the following arguments by Bandura: (a) The effectiveness of a reinforcer depends on our conscious expectations. (b) Observational learning can change the effectiveness of a reinforcer, such as the amount of money that one earns.

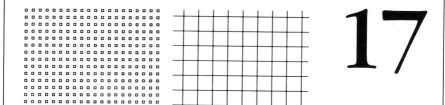

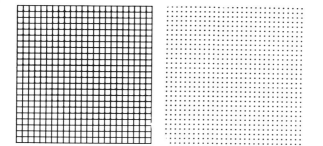

17

CONCLUSION
Perspectives and Postscript

Our journey into the realm of personality theory has featured a formidable array of constructs and principles, many contradictory ideas and heated disputes, and some islands of general agreement. Therefore, let us try to conclude on a more orderly note by returning to our organizing framework one last time. Our goal will be to summarize the major issues discussed previously, and to determine the conclusions most justified by the wealth of information that we have surveyed.

THE BASIC NATURE OF HUMAN BEINGS

The Quality of Human Nature

Many personality theorists have been intimately concerned with the quality of human nature: is it inherently malignant or benign?

At the most negative extreme is Freudian psychoanalysis, with its emphasis on innate incestuous and destructive drives. This implies that we must sublimate our true wishes into less satisfying but more socially acceptable outlets, and that conflict must occur with society and within one's own psyche. At the other extreme are such theorists as Horney and Rogers, who assume that our innate potentialities and desires are wholly positive (and thus need not be compromised through sublimation). Fromm and Maslow are relatively optimistic: they conclude that we have a positive innate nature, but one that is rather easily subverted by a pathogenic environment. So too is Adler, who rejects the importance of heredity but does posit an inherent potential for healthy social interest. Finally, some theorists adopt a more moderate position by attributing to us both malignant and benign drives. Included in this category are Jung, Erikson, Allport, Murray, May, and Cattell. (See Figure 17.1.)[1]

All personality theorists are well aware that human beings behave in both good and evil ways; it is our innate nature that is at issue. In fact, pessimistic Freudian theory has little trouble explaining healthy behavior: proper parenting urges the reluctant child along the path to effective sub-

[1]The numerical scales in this figure (and those following) are intended only as approximations, designed to facilitate an overall comparison, and not as mathematically precise measures. They also reflect only the opinions and judgments of this author; others might disagree with the ratings in some instances.

The Quality of Human Nature				
Malignant				Benign
1	2	3	4	5
Freud		Jung	Adler	Horney
		Erikson	Fromm	Rogers
		Allport	Sullivan	
		Murray	Maslow	
		May		
		Cattell		

Note: Theorists not included do not take a strong stand on or interest in this issue.

FIGURE 17.1. The quality of human nature as viewed by various personality theorists and behaviorists.

limations, and socially acceptable satisfactions. Conversely, those who posit a partly or wholly optimistic view of human nature can readily explain psychopathology: misguided parental behaviors cause the child to surrender its true (healthy) desires and potentials, and to replace them with the quest to be safe or to satisfy the standards of other people. To these theorists, destructiveness and self-hate are not innate but learned—"the outcome of unlived life."

This theoretical adroitness, plus the virtual impossibility of measuring the quality of human nature empirically, might lead you to question the importance of this issue. However, such assumptions significantly affect other aspects of a theory. For example, Freud recommends not allowing the child too much (or too little) gratification at any stage of development, so as to prevent innate illicit wishes from becoming dominant. He also regards psychotherapy as a long and difficult struggle against the patient's efforts to retain forbidden wishes (resistances), which the therapist must be careful not to encourage. But Maslow stresses that the child's needs must be fully satisfied, recommends a similar course for patients in therapy, and interprets resistance more positively (e.g., as protection against a therapist who is moving too quickly). Thus important conclusions and practical recommendations depend to a considerable extent on the theorist's particular view of human nature. (See also Ewen, 1984.)

Although it is valuable to know where a given theorist stands on this issue, it appears impossible to draw any definitive conclusions about our innate predisposition for good or evil. We may reasonably speculate that Freud's idiosyncratic position at the pessimistic end of the spectrum is overly negative, and that human beings do seem to have at least some innate capacity for (and enjoyment of) constructive growth. But the extreme optimism of a Horney or Rogers also seems unwarranted when we consider the frequency of war, crime, and other human evils. Perhaps, then, those theorists who have opted for the middle ground on this issue have come closest to an appropriate characterization of human nature.

The Dynamics of Human Nature

Drive Reduction. Freud, Sullivan, and Cattell conclude that our sole motivation is to reduce various drives, eliminate the accompanying unpleasant tensions, and achieve a state of inner equilibrium. Other theorists, such as Maslow and Allport, take exception to this exclusive emphasis on drive reduction. They argue that our behavior must also be explained in terms of pleasurable tension-maintaining and tension-increasing activities, including curious exploration, acquiring an admired skill or level of competence, and increasing one's understanding of the world or of oneself.

Here the available evidence supports the latter view. That is, human beings are motivated both by drive reduction and by pleasurable drive increases.

Causality versus Teleology. Freud also posits, as does Skinner, that all mental and physical behavior is determined by prior causes. But many theorists conclude that our behavior must also be understood in terms of its purposes or goals, while some attribute virtually all motivation to teleology. (See Figure 17.2.)

The debate concerning this issue has been lengthy and involved. It appears justified to conclude that we are motivated both by prior causes, and by our intentions and expectations of the future. One interesting possibility is that relatively healthier individuals may be more influenced by teleology, and less limited by the effects of earlier experiences. However, the past can never be entirely circumvented: Allport's idiosyncratic concept of

		Human Motivation		
Causality				*Teleology*
1	2	3	4	5
Freud	Horney	Jung	Rogers	Adler
Skinner	Erikson	Sullivan	Maslow	Allport
	Cattell	Murray	May	Kelly
	Dollard &	Fromm		
	Miller	Bandura		

FIGURE 17.2. The issue of causality versus teleology as viewed by various personality theorists and behaviorists.

	The Importance of Unconscious Motivation			
Low				*High*
1	2	3	4	5
	Adler	Rogers	Maslow	Freud
	Allport	Cattell	May	Jung
	Kelly			Horney
	Skinner			Fromm
	Bandura			Sullivan
				Erikson
				Murray
				Dollard & Miller

FIGURE 17.3. The importance of unconscious motivation as viewed by various personality theorists and behaviorists.

functional autonomy leads to statements that lack any explanatory power whatsoever ("a man likes blue because he likes blue"), and is best rejected in favor of the majority view that traces adult motives back to childhood and adolescent origins.

Unconscious Motivation. Most personality theorists agree about the substantial importance of unconscious motivation, and regard true self-knowledge as a difficult goal to achieve. (See Figure 17.3.) Thus we may conclude that significant, influential aspects of every personality are concealed from awareness in some way. Conceivably, relatively healthier people may be less influenced by unconscious processes; but no personality is ever entirely (or even mostly) conscious.

What material is most likely to become unconscious? Likely candidates include threats to major aspects of one's personality (Freud, Adler, Horney, and others), events that would otherwise evoke strong anxiety (Freud, Horney, Sullivan, May), subliminal perceptions (Jung, Rogers), and that which occurs at too early an age to be labeled properly (Dollard and Miller). Whatever the exact processes and dynamics may be, anyone who wishes to understand his or her own personality—or to devise a satisfactory theory of human behavior—must devote considerable attention to unconscious motivation.

The Catalog of Human Motives

Yet another controversy concerns the number and specific nature of human motives. Some theorists prefer to emphasize one or two overriding drives or goals:

      Freud: sexuality, destructiveness

      Adler: striving for superiority, social interest[2]

   Horney: self-realization

     Kelly: anticipating the future

   Rogers: actualization, positive regard

      May: to exist in the world into which we are born

Other theorists espouse a list of motives that is somewhat, or considerably, larger:

   Erikson: sexuality, destructiveness, identity, mastery of the environment, mutually enhancing relationships

    Fromm: hunger, thirst, sex, defense through fight or flight, other people, mastery of the environment, identity, meaning to one's life

      Jung: hunger, thirst, sex, power, activity, creativity, individuation, meaning to one's life, religion, others

   Sullivan: hunger, thirst, sex, respiration, elimination of bodily wastes, sleep, reducing anxiety, other people, expressing tenderness to one's offspring

   Dollard   hunger, thirst, sex, avoiding pain, numerous motives
and Miller: that are learned rather than innate (anxiety, anger, guilt, power, conformity, others)

   Maslow: hunger, thirst, safety, obtaining love from others, curiosity, creativity, competence, belongingness, esteem, metamotives of self-actualizing individuals

    Cattell: food, mating, gregariousness, parental protectiveness, curious exploration, security, self-assertion, narcissistic sex, pugnacity, acquisitiveness; perhaps also appeal, rest, constructiveness and creativity, self-abasement, disgust, laughter

    Murray: abasement, achievement, affiliation, aggression, autonomy, counteraction, defendance, deference, dominance, exhibition, harmavoidance, infavoidance, nurturance, order, play, rejection, sentience, sex, succorance, understanding

And still more extreme is the position of Allport, who contends that human motives are unique to each individual—so much so that no list of drives or needs, however lengthy, will suffice.

[2]Although Adler stresses that every personality is unique, this applies to the style (of life) in which our behaviors are expressed. He regards all people as having the same fundamental motives, as indicated by his emphasis on the issue of inferiority.

Except for Freud, who chose to regard hunger and thirst as manifestations of sexuality, we may assume that there is no real dispute about these motives: any theorists who failed to list them undoubtedly regarded them as self-evident. The same may be said of our needs for sex, respiration, and eliminating bodily wastes. We can also discern a few motives on which some theorists agree: identity (Erikson and Fromm), mastering the environment (Adler, Erikson, Fromm, and Cattell's self-assertion erg), individuation and self-actualization (Jung, Horney, Rogers, and Maslow), the need for other people (Adler, Erikson, Fromm, and Sullivan, and Cattell's gregariousness erg); creativity (Jung, Maslow, and Cattell), and meaning to one's life (Jung and Fromm). For the most part, however, the various personality theorists disagree as to the specific prime movers of human behavior. Therefore, as much as we might like to end this section on a more definitive note, we can only conclude that this particular issue is as yet unresolved.

THE STRUCTURE OF PERSONALITY

Structural Constructs: Pro and Con

Some theorists have sought to depict the complicated, often contradictory aspects of personality by devising appropriate structural constructs. Others regard such constructs as unnecessary, or even misleading. (See Figure 17.4.) In all, there are four distinct positions on this issue:

1. Structural constructs and intrapsychic conflicts are both important. The theorists in this camp regard personality as a house that is often divided against itself, and believe that structural constructs are the best way to summarize and describe such conflicts. Typical of this approach is Freud's tripartite classification of id, ego, and superego. Erikson and Murray also use these three constructs but define them somewhat differently, in order to convey their belief that human beings possess both malignant and benign instincts. Jung's discussion of inner conflicts utilizes such constructs as ego, shadow, persona, attitudes, and functions. Rogers focuses on the self as the structural construct best suited to explain intrapsychic conflicts. And Cattell uses structural source traits to devise various indices, which purport to measure our inner conflicts numerically.

2. Intrapsychic conflicts are important; structural constructs are not. Some theorists attribute great importance to intrapsychic conflicts, but do *not* regard structural constructs as necessary or desirable. Perhaps the leading exponent of this approach is Horney; others include Fromm and Maslow. These theorists warn that structural constructs are all too likely to become reified: continuous usage of such terms may result in the belief that there is (say) an id, ego, and superego lurking somewhere within every personality.

In actuality, of course, such constructs are not undeniable truths. Nor

		Structural Constructs	
		Important	Unimportant
		Freud	Horney
		Jung	Fromm
	Important	Erikson	Maslow
		Murray	Dollard and Miller
		Rogers	
		Cattell	
Intrapsychic Conflicts			
		Allport	Adler
	Unimportant	Kelly	May
		Sullivan	Bandura

FIGURE 17.4. The importance of structural constructs and intrapsychic conflicts as viewed by various personality theorists and behaviorists.

are they concrete entities that exist somewhere within the psyche. They are only concepts that have been created (or adopted) by a personality theorist, in order to better describe and explain human behavior. Nevertheless, repeated discussions of "the ego doing this" and "the id doing that" are likely to create the impression that these constructs are real and undeniable. This is not only misleading (and, to some theorists, depersonalizing), but will also make it more difficult to dispense with constructs that lose their utility in light of subsequent discoveries—a not unlikely occurrence, considering our relatively limited knowledge about the human personality.

3. Structural constructs are important: intrapsychic conflicts are not. Still other theorists make use of structural constructs, but devote little attention to intrapsychic conflicts. Examples include Allport's traits and proprium, and Kelly's personal constructs.

4. Neither structural constructs nor intrapsychic conflicts are important. Finally, it may be argued that structural constructs are unnecessary because personality is a unified, indivisible whole—never in conflict with itself. Adler is the main advocate of this position.

Once again we have an area that is marked more by controversy than agreement. However, the evidence discussed throughout this book supports the existence and importance of intrapsychic conflicts. Therefore, those theorists who reject or minimize this issue must be charged with neglecting a vital aspect of human behavior.

Anxiety and the Defense Mechanisms

One major contribution of personality theory has been to improve our understanding of (and concern about) anxiety. The discovery that psycho-

The Importance of Anxiety				
Low				*High*
1	2	3	4	5
Adler	Jung	Murray	Fromm	Freud
	Erikson	Kelly	Rogers	Horney
	Allport	Cattell		Sullivan
	Maslow	Skinner		May
		Bandura		Dollard & Miller

FIGURE 17.5. The importance of anxiety as viewed by various personality theorists and behaviorists.

logical pain is real despite the lack of observable wounds, and that such anxiety can be a problem that is even more serious than physical pain, ranks among the truly important additions to our knowledge. The extent to which the various personality theorists have emphasized anxiety is shown in Figure 17.5.

Whether or not one accepts Freud's theory of anxiety and defense, the importance of such behaviors as reaction formation, projection, displacement, denial of reality, rationalization, identification, and fantasy has been firmly established. These concepts have been accepted and incorporated into virtually every theory of personality, if at times with some changes in terminology and underlying rationale. While more healthy people probably rely less on such defense mechanisms, all of us have undoubtedly used most (or all) of them at some time in our lives. Thus we may consider this as yet another major contribution to our knowledge that has been provided by personality theory.

THE DEVELOPMENT OF PERSONALITY

Stages of Development

Only a few theorists posit specific developmental stages, and they do not agree with one another. There are five psychosexual stages in Freudian theory, with personality development assumed to be virtually complete by about age five years. Sullivan argues that there are seven developmental epochs, ranging from infancy to adulthood. And Erikson discusses eight epigenetic psychosexual stages, which extend into middle age.

Although some of these theorists' ideas about the development of personality have been generally accepted, no one set of stages is currently regarded as correct. Most modern psychologists do prefer Sullivan's and

		The Importance of Events *in Infancy and Early Childhood*		
Low				*High*
1	2	3	4	5
Allport		Jung Fromm Kelly Maslow May Cattell Skinner Bandura	Adler Sullivan Erikson Murray Rogers Dollard & Miller	Freud Horney

FIGURE 17.6. The importance of events in infancy and early childhood as viewed by various personality theorists and behaviorists.

Erikson's view that personality development continues through late childhood and adolescence. But it now appears that personality does tend to remain relatively stable during adulthood, barring such special efforts to change as formal psychotherapy. (See for example Schulz & Ewen, 1992, Chapter 7.)

The Importance of Early Childhood

While events during infancy and early childhood do not totally determine one's personality, virtually all theorists agree that they are extremely important. (See Figure 17.6.)[3] Another major contribution of personality theory has been to identify the ways in which parents cause their children to become neurotic: pampering, neglect, overpermissiveness, overprotectiveness, frequent anxiety, perfectionism, domination, rejection, ridicule, hypocrisy, inconsistent standards, a lack of tenderness and warm affection, brutality, rigidity, pessimism, narcissism, conditional positive regard, and others. This not only provides useful guidelines for those who seek to become better parents, but also is a source of reassurance to anyone who does suffer from neurosis. That is, since neurotic self-defeating behaviors and attitudes were typically learned during childhood, they have a logical cause. And this implies that there is also a logical remedy, in that relief can be gained by unlearning them (as through psychotherapy).

---

[3]Note that this is *not* the same as the issue of causality versus teleology. For example, Adler is not an exponent of causality, but he does stress the importance of such influences as pampering and neglect during early childhood.

The Importance of Adolescence

As noted above, such theorists as Sullivan and Erikson deserve credit for emphasizing the importance of adolescence. This is indeed a time of turmoil and potential change—one that can have a corrective effect on a troubled personality, or exert a pathogenic influence of its own. However, events during infancy and childhood undoubtedly do play a greater role in shaping one's personality. A person who emerges from childhood with a faulty view of self and others is more likely to behave in misguided and self-defeating ways during adolescence, bringing on disapproval and rejection from others and intensifying the sufferer's problems. Conversely, a psychologically healthier child is more likely to handle the rigors of adolescence successfully.

The Outcome of Personality Development

Character Typologies. Several theorists, including Freud, Jung, and Fromm, have devoted some attention to personality types. In contrast, Adler and Allport strongly oppose the use of character typologies. They argue that every individual develops his or her own unique style of life, making it impossible for any typology to describe the total personality.

The importance of certain typological constructs has been supported to at least some extent by research evidence: the oral personality, the anal personality, introversion, extraversion. But here again, no one theory is currently regarded as correct in all (or even most) aspects.

Criteria of Mental Health. Freud's well-known definition of mental health consists of two characteristics, the ability to love and to work. Allport, Rogers, and Maslow prefer to expand upon the ideal personality. These theorists tend to agree that mental health is denoted by greater emotional security and self acceptance; successful, loving, and nonpossessive interpersonal relationships; greater spontaneity; greater self-knowledge (self-insight); and a greater reliance on one's own needs and values, rather than on external standards. Yet they disagree in various other respects, indicating that it is not yet possible to define the criteria of mental health in universally acceptable terms.

FURTHER APPLICATIONS
OF PERSONALITY THEORY

As we have seen throughout this book, personality theory has made profoundly important contributions to our understanding of dreams, psychopathology, and psychotherapy. Thanks to such theorists as Freud and Fromm, we are much better able to interpret the information conveyed by our dreams. It is now generally accepted that psychopathology differs from normality in degree, rather than in kind; and that neurotic (and psychotic) behaviors have logical causes and meanings, strange though they may seem on the surface. And the potential benefits of psychotherapy have become widely recognized, with countless numbers of people obtaining relief from serious and painful problems and discovering how to make their lives more rewarding.

Here again, however, the controversies that beset personality theory have taken their toll. No one method of psychotherapy is currently accepted as best, nor is there agreement as to which varieties (e.g., Freudian, Rogerian, behaviorist) should be used with which kinds of disorders. Thus it has been argued that considerably more effort must be devoted to understanding therapeutic principles, and improving therapeutic procedures. And many unanswered questions also remain with regard to dream interpretation and psychopathology.

Other areas to which personality theorists have contributed include work, religion, education, and literature. A summary of the interests of each theorist, including the question of psychological laboratory research, is shown in Figure 17.7.

EVALUATION

Whither Personality Theory?

Personality theory has a distinguished past. However, its future is more uncertain.

Most modern psychologists do not ally themselves with any theory of personality. They prefer to identify their professional interests in terms of specific content areas, such as motivation, personality development, child psychology, adolescent psychology, psychopathology, psychotherapy, or more narrowly defined issues (e.g., the interaction of traits and situations). In fact, of the forty-odd divisions of the American Psychological Association that are organized by subject matter, not one is devoted solely (or even primarily) to personality theory. Thus it is most unlikely that any new, comprehensive, and widely accepted theory of personality will emerge in the foreseeable future.

Those psychologists who do regard themselves as personality theorists tend to choose among three approaches. The least desirable is to remain true to every tenet of one original theory, since no theorist has been wholly (or even largely) correct. A second alternative is to build upon a particular theory by revising it as necessary. For example, some psychoanalysts have sought to retain basic Freudian principles while discarding such metaphysical constructs as libido, id, ego, and superego. A third possibility is to try and integrate the major ideas of several theories, seeking to retain the most useful aspects of each. This last alternative appears most likely to benefit the discipline of psychology, since all of the theorists whose work we

Applications

Theorists	Dream Interpretation	Psychopathology	Psychotherapy	Work	Religion	Education	Literature	Laboratory Research
Freud	+	+	+	−	√	−	√	−
Jung	+	+	+	−	+	√	+	−
Adler	√	+	+	+	√	+	−	−
Horney	√	+	+	√	√	−	−	−
Fromm	+	+	+	−	√	−	+	−
Sullivan	√	+	+	−	−	−	−	−
Erikson	√	+	+	−	√	−	√	−
Allport	−	−	−	−	√	−	−	+
Murray	−	−	−	−	−	−	√	+
Kelly	√	+	+	−	−	√	−	+
Rogers	−	+	+	−	−	+	−	+
Maslow	−	+	+	+	√	√	−	+
May	+	+	+	−	√	−	√	−
Cattell	−	+	−	+	−	+	−	+
Skinner	−	√	√	√	√	+	√	+
Dollard & Miller	−	+	+	−	−	−	−	+
Bandura	−	+	+	−	−	−	−	+

FIGURE 17.7. Applied interests of various personality theorists and behaviorists. + = substantial interest; √ = some interest; − = little or no interest.

have examined have made at least some valuable contributions. But it is also the most difficult and time-consuming, so we can only hope that an effective integration of the various theories of personality will someday be achieved.

Personality Theory and Cultural Perspectives

Some psychologists argue that personality theory must necessarily include a cross-cultural perspective. They point out that many peoples throughout the world interpret concepts like responsibility, morality, identity, and achievement much differently from Western Europeans and North Americans, who developed the theories that we have examined.

A personality theorist's culture may indeed influence, and limit, the constructs and principles of that theorist. You should therefore be aware that the theories presented in this book may not apply very well (or even at all) to Oriental, third world, and other non-Occidental peoples. In fact (as we have seen), it has even been argued that a theory may hold true only for those whose personal background resembles that of the theorist. (Recall Adler's contention that children become Oedipal only if they have been as pampered as Freud himself.) Thus the cultural issue may be regarded as an extension—albeit an important one—of this type of criticism.

We have also seen that a theory need not be universal in scope to be useful. There are ample challenges and rewards for those who seek better ways to describe, understand, predict, and control our own complicated and far-from-perfect society. Consequently, as in other areas of psychology, the pursuit of cross-cultural information is *not* a *sine qua non*. It is a matter of personal preference. In this book, our preference has been to keep the quantity of material within reasonable bounds by discussing the most prominent theories since Freud. Having concluded this introduction to personality theory, those of you who wish to go on and acquire an understanding of different cultures (or study in detail the specific cultural factors that influenced the development of a particular theory) should now have a sufficiently strong background to do so.

POSTSCRIPT:
SOME PERSONAL PERSPECTIVES

Now that we have reached the end of our journey into the realm of personality theory, let me relinquish the scholarly form of narrative and close with some personal perspectives and comments.

On the one hand, I am extremely impressed by the many profound insights which personality theorists have gained into the mysteries of human behavior (notably those derived from clinical observation). Yet I am also disappointed by their inability to resolve the most fundamental of issues, indicating that psychology is still far from a mature science. And I fear that the capacity of humans to think, to lie to others, and to deceive themselves will prevent psychology from ever achieving the precision of physics and chemistry unless some major methodological breakthrough is made, such as discovering a direct (and perhaps physiological) measure of covert and unconscious behaviors. Like Maslow, I believe that some form of psychological therapy is unquestionably the best choice for those suffering from the torments of psychopathology. But I also now agree with Allport that the social sciences are inherently far more difficult than the physical ones—a view quite different from the one I held when I first chose to study psychology, some 35 years ago.

Since the unconscious aspects of behavior are so difficult to measure, it is understandable that many psychologists prefer to turn their attention elsewhere. I agree with Kelly that a theory may serve a valuable purpose even if it ignores, or rejects, certain major aspects of human behavior. Yet since virtually every theory discussed in this book accepts the existence of some sort of unconscious processes (even Skinner's), those who claim that psychology can study only overt or conscious forces and still be comprehensive (and/or who pursue safely objective but trivial research topics) strike me as substituting expediency for scientific integrity.

I can empathize with the frustrations of my readers, who have had to learn virtually a new language in every chapter (or subchapter). Personality theorists have been far too free with neologisms, and have often duplicated one another's efforts without any apparent knowledge of having done so. Perhaps these theorists genuinely believed that their own ideas were different. Perhaps they were not aware of, or did not understand, the ideas of other theorists. Or they may have been influenced by an academic system that penalizes agreement while rewarding controversy, since the latter is far more likely to generate large quantities of scholarly publications (a view shared by Fiske, 1978, p. 63). The issue here is *not* necessarily to arrive at one "right" theory, which could all too easily prove to be stultifying; lively debate is healthy for a science. But too many theorists have created too many supposedly new constructs instead of relating their work to that of other psychologists, a serious waste of time and effort—and a potentially lethal one, in a nuclear age when time may very well be of the essence.

In my opinion, however, there is another more positive reason for the great diversity of personality theories: people think differently, and some of these individuals are psychologists who have formulated their personal construct systems in more detail than most. (See also Fiske, 1978, p. 39.) Thus, while my respect for a genius like Freud remains profound, I am now less impressed by any approach that regards a single construct system as applicable to all humanity. No doubt Oedipal complexes do exist; yet I wonder how much time has been lost in psychoanalytic therapy because some "resistant" patients conceptualized their childhood problems differently, in terms the therapist could not understand psychoanalytically, and would not adopt the analyst's construct system. (In fairness to Freud, a similar criticism could be made of almost every personality theory.) Psychologists have made substantial efforts to eliminate prejudice in many areas, yet all too many still advocate a form of constructual tyranny: any way but their own of conceptualizing behavior (and/or the philosophy of psychology) is wrong, or "prescientific."

For this reason, I believe that the study of personality theory offers considerable benefits. If you truly understand the various theories, you will have a more versatile and openminded approach to psychology, as well as a better understanding of human behavior. This will help to safeguard against becoming a constructual tyrant. And since I also believe that the most profitable future course for psychology is to integrate the various personality and behaviorist theories, I regard such a broad background as the best possible preparation for those who wish to participate in this challenging, frustrating, difficult, but deeply rewarding field.

■ SUMMARY

1. THE BASIC NATURE OF HUMAN BEINGS. *The Quality of Human Nature:* Personality theorists disagree about our innate predisposition for good or evil. At the most negative extreme is Freudian psychoanalysis, with its emphasis on innate incestuous and destructive drives. At the other extreme are such theorists as Horney and Rogers, who assume that our innate desires and potentialities are wholly positive. Other theorists adopt a more moderate (and perhaps more justifiable) position by attributing to us both malignant and benign drives. *The Dynamics of Human Nature:* It appears justified to conclude that human beings are motivated by both drive reduction and pleasurable drive increases, and by both causality and teleology. Nearly all personality theorists agree about the substantial importance of unconscious motivation. *The Catalog of Human Motives:* Some theorists prefer to emphasize one or two overriding drives or goals, while others espouse a list of motives that is substantially larger. There are a few points on which there is a modicum of agreement; but for the most part, the various theorists disagree as to the specific prime movers of human behavior.

2. THE STRUCTURE OF PERSONALITY. *Structural Constructs:* Some theorists have sought to depict the complicated, often contradictory aspects of personality by devising appropriate structural constructs. Others regard such constructs as unnecessary, or even misleading. Although this issue remains controversial, the evidence does support the existence and importance of intrapsychic conflicts. *Anxiety and the Defense Mechanisms:* The discovery that psychological pain is real despite the lack of observable wounds, and that such anxiety can be a problem that is even more serious than physical pain, ranks among the truly important contributions to our knowledge. The same is true of such defense mechanisms as reaction formation, projection, displacement, denial of reality, rationalization, identification, fantasy, and others, which have been accepted and incorporated into virtually every theory of personality (if at times with some changes in terminology and underlying rationale).

3. THE DEVELOPMENT OF PERSONALITY. *Stages of Development:* Only a few theorists posit specific developmental stages, and they do not agree with one another. No one set of stages is currently accepted as correct. *The Importance of Early Childhood:* Events during infancy and early childhood do not totally determine one's personality, but are extremely important. Yet another major contribution of personality theory has been to identify the parental influences that cause children to become neurotic. *The Importance of Adolescence:* Most modern psychologists agree that personality development continues through late childhood and adolescence. Such theorists as Sullivan and Erikson deserve credit for emphasizing the importance of adolescence, though events during infancy and childhood undoubtedly do play a greater role in shaping one's personality. *The Outcome of Personality Development:* Several theorists, including Freud, Jung, and Fromm, have devoted some attention to personality types. Others strongly oppose the use of character typologies, arguing instead that every individual develops his or her own unique style of life. Some theorists have expanded upon the ideal personality; their criteria of mental health agree in some respects, and disagree in others.

4. FURTHER APPLICATIONS. Personality theory has made profoundly important contributions to our understanding of dreams, psychopathology, and psychotherapy. Other areas to which personality theorists have contributed include work, religion, education, and literature.

5. EVALUATION. Although personality theory has a distinguished past, its future is uncertain. Most modern psychologists identify their professional interests in terms of specific content areas. Because of this specialization, it is unlikely that any new, comprehensive personality theory will emerge in the foreseeable future. An integration of the various theories of personality appears most likely to benefit the discipline of psychology, since all of the theorists discussed in this book have made at least some valuable contributions. However, achieving such an integration will be difficult and time-consuming.

6. POSTSCRIPT: SOME PERSONAL PERSPECTIVES. The present writer is most impressed by the many profound insights that personality theorists have gained into the mysteries of human behavior, disappointed by their inability to resolve the most fundamental of issues, and concerned that psychology may never achieve scientific precision unless some direct (and perhaps physiological) measure of covert behavior is discovered. Since virtually every theory discussed in this book accepts the existence of some sort of unconscious processes, those who claim that psychology can study only overt or conscious forces and still be comprehensive (and/or who pursue safely objective but trivial research topics) would seem to be substituting expediency for scientific integrity. Many supposedly new constructs only duplicate the work of other psychologists, so some integration of the various personality and behaviorist approaches is desirable. But the multiplicity of theories is also due to the fact that people think differently, some of whom are psychologists who have formulated their personal construct systems in more detail than most. Thus a true understanding of the various theories of personality will facili-

tate a better understanding of human behavior, help to safeguard against constructual tyranny (attempting to apply a single construct system to all humanity), and provide an excellent foundation for those interested in the challenging, frustrating, difficult, controversial, but deeply rewarding field of psychology.

APPENDIX:
Comments, Notes, and Hints about the Study Questions

Before using this Appendix, see the note preceding the study questions at the end of Chapter 2. The views expressed herein are those of this author; others might disagree in some instances.

CHAPTER 2. FREUD

1. Suppose the theorist's introspections reveal that he or she has some highly undesirable (perhaps even shocking) personality characteristics. Suppose further that the theorist is a moral, ethical person. How might the theorist feel if these characteristics were possessed by very few people? If these characteristics could be attributed to human nature?

2. (a) Recall the family situation in which Freud grew up, and compare this with Jung's family situation (biographical sketch, Chapter 3). (b) If a person wishes to startle the world and achieve fame as an unraveler of great mysteries, what better way than to discover an immense, vitally important, but largely unexplored realm within every human being?

3. (a) Recall the discussion of Freud's "creative illness" in the biographical sketch. Also consider how a highly intelligent and sensitive person would feel if he or she suffered from painful psychological problems for which no good methods of treatment existed. (b) I don't think so. I concede that there are relatively well-adjusted psychologists who are interested in studying personality, possibly including their own. But insofar as the deep and intense self-analysis of a Freud or Jung is concerned, my views are well summarized by the following case history, written by a middle-aged former psychologist:

> I suffered from a variety of psychological problems in my early twenties, including frequent anxiety and difficulty relating to other people. At that time I was fascinated by books on personality theory and abnormal psychology, especially those that seemed to be related to my own problems. I spent a great deal of time in self-study, trying to determine the reasons for my difficulties. I even became a psychologist, with hopes of correcting the errors of Freud and other predecessors and devising a brilliant new theory. Now, in my forties, I have resolved many of my problems with the aid of formal psychotherapy. My

anxiety level is much lower; I have a good marriage and a family. And I no longer want to read about personality theory or abnormal psychology, or to analyze myself; I'm burned out. I feel as though I have pretty much finished with a painful and difficult war—namely, the battle to overcome my own pathology—and it's time to move on to other things.

4. (a) Consider Freud's statements about the merits of Oedipal theory and dream interpretation, and his harsh treatment of people (e.g., Jung, Adler) who disagreed with certain aspects of his theory. (b) Why is it necessary for a theorist to create constructs? (c) In Chapter 11, we see that George Kelly regards any scientific theory and its constructs as an "eventual candidate for the trash can."

5. I am angry at my wife or six-year-old daughter, and thinking quite unhusbandly or unfatherly thoughts. A few moments later I accidentally collide with a piece of furniture and sustain a painful bruise. Freud would argue that this is no accident; I am relieving my guilt over my illicit thoughts by punishing myself. He would also contend that this parapraxis indicates an underlying conflict, possibly the obvious one between love and anger toward my family and perhaps some deeper and more complicated ones as well. (Recall that the causes of important psychic phenomena and behavior are usually overdetermined.) In this case, I'd be inclined to agree with him.

6. The following case history was written by a person who gained valuable insights from formal psychotherapy, and who is reflecting on how it felt to be highly anxious.

It is fairly late at night, and I am walking in a large city on the way home from a friend's house. I am only a few blocks away from my apartment, and the area is not especially dangerous. Yet my hands are sweaty, my stomach churns, and I feel that something very bad is about to happen. I'm afraid! So I start to walk faster. Soon I'm running. I reach my apartment building and safety, and I turn to look back. The street is almost empty, except for a few harmless-looking individuals who are strolling casually and enjoying the night air. The area is well lit.

There is no danger. It's all been in my imagination.

It isn't only city streets that I fear. When I am with other people, especially those I don't know well, I often get the same reaction: sweaty palms, butterflies, and a desire to escape as soon as possible. So I shy away from other people and spend lots of time alone in my room. I don't know why I feel this way, which only makes matters worse. I'm confused and even guilty about feeling afraid with no apparent reason, so I hide my true feelings from everyone else. I keep my thoughts, emotions, and perceptions in a narrow shell around me, like a cocoon, because I don't see any hope for me in the outside world and I just want to avoid hurting any more than I do now. I feel as though my interactions with other people and the outside world are like a game I'm playing and observing with a small part of my mind, while most of my attention is tied up by the emotional pain and turmoil going on inside me. In fact, I usually feel like an empty shell going through the motions of talking, listening,

or behaving. I suspect that something is desperately wrong with me, but that something seems so strange and frightening that I don't dare look for it.
I'm so tired of being afraid.

7. (a) The preceding case history can serve as an illustration of projection. The person fears aggression from other people when walking in the street; yet it is he who has powerful repressed feelings of anger, due partly to parents who were very perfectionistic and demanding and partly to his own inability to deal with them. Since it is highly threatening to be so angry at one's own parents, he unconsciously projects these feelings onto others. (b) The defense mechanisms achieve a temporary reduction in anxiety by concealing the person's true but threatening feelings and beliefs from himself or herself. (c) But since the defense mechanisms hide the true problem, they make any successful resolution impossible, so the sufferer's difficulties and anxieties will continue (and perhaps even increase). (d) Consider a patient in psychotherapy who gradually realizes that an anxiety-provoking situation (such as walking in a safe street) is actually not dangerous, and then tries to discover the true source of the anxiety.

8. I don't like waiting in long lines at the supermarket or bank (or even short lines). I tell myself that I have many more important things to do, and I don't want any delays in gratification. The checkout clerk or teller is working hard to satisfy everyone, and my ego should develop an anticathexis against these id impulses. But all too often the id impulses win out, and I become childishly impatient.

9. A young teacher is speaking in front of a large class. Most of what the teacher says is well thought out, instructive, even entertaining. But a few statements and attempts at humor are inept and fall flat. Later, the teacher focuses on these failures, is very self-critical for not preparing more thoroughly, and is upset at how silly these remarks were, thereby depriving himself or herself of the legitimate gratification that should have been derived from a good and effective presentation.

10. Suppose that this person has considerable difficulty confronting other people (even when absolutely necessary) and expressing anger, especially to authority figures, and prefers instead to sulk and punish others by not talking to them.

11. During much of the time in which Freud lived, women in the United States were not allowed to smoke or vote. Should a theorist be able to rise above such prevailing standards?

12. You could argue that she actually didn't want to go where the train would take her; perhaps her spouse insisted on vacationing in a place that she didn't like. I would look more deeply, however, and posit an underlying conflict. Suppose that the train trip represents her journey to psychological maturity. She partly wants to grow up and be her own woman (and catch the train), but is also afraid of surrendering her dependence on her parents and the protection that they provide. The latter wish is the stronger one at this

moment, so she arranges in her dream to miss the train. Freud would presumably see an Oedipal conflict somewhere, perhaps with the train as a phallic symbol.

13. (a) I don't. Science relies on objective observation and hard data that can be verified and reproduced by other people. Recall that Freud did not take notes during the psychoanalytic session or allow the presence of outside observers (understandably, in view of the sensitive material being discussed), and that it is virtually impossible to have a legitimate argument about sexuality with a Freudian (evaluation section). (b) I do. We all use defense mechanisms and experience anxiety to some extent, and these ideas (like all of Freud's) were derived from his analytic work. Modern psychologists generally agree that at least some forms of psychopathology represent differences in degree from healthy adjustment, rather than differences in kind.

14. How does a resistance enable a patient to avoid having to confront his or her threatening feelings, beliefs, emotions, and memories? How might the concept of resistance enable Freud to find fault with those attacking psychoanalytic theory?

15. Freud argued that prohibitions against questioning religious doctrines are a clear sign of weakness, designed to protect those ideas from critical examination. Does this bear any similarity to some of the criticisms of psychoanalytic theory? What might this imply about Freud's personal reasons for rejecting religion?

CHAPTER 3. JUNG

1. See the discussion of the autonomy of the psyche in the evaluation section.

2. Recall that Jung saw a luminous figure with a detached head emanating from his mother's bedroom, and that he conversed with voices in his head that he believed to be souls returning from the dead. Apparently Jung experienced psychotic ideation firsthand, whereas Freud did not.

3. I think so. The first sentence aptly represents Freud's views of Oedipal theory, while the remainder of the quote fits Freud's self-perception as an unraveler of great mysteries. Since Jung saw himself in much the same way, it is hardly surprising that he ultimately broke with Freud; it was essential to find new mysteries and new explanations.

4. Ask a psychoanalyst and an analytical psychologist and you'll get two different answers. However, I prefer Jung's list. All too often I am reluctant to risk trying something new, preferring instead the safety of the familiar. So I have found that it is quite possible to be sexually satisfied, but dissatisfied with regard to what Jung calls activity (which includes the love of change, the urge to travel, and play). I therefore share Jung's belief that activity and sexuality are separate needs.

5. When I see a television evangelist crusading with great intensity and passion against sexual behavior (usually because I have accidentally tuned to the wrong channel), I suspect that these extremely negative conscious attitudes about sexuality conceal powerful repressed sexual urges, and that the crusade is a form of reaction formation. (Of course, there are other possibilities. But there are many other ways to make a living, yet the evangelist chose this one.) So I am not surprised when a scandal erupts because the evangelist is caught in a sexually compromising situation, as actually happened not long ago.

6. (a) In my teens, I became an avid bridge player. For some 25 years thereafter I participated in tournaments, read voraciously about bridge, discussed bridge with friends for hours on end, and even wrote numerous bridge books and articles. I also had no interest in religion. Some ten years ago, however, enantiodromia set in. My interest in bridge yielded to almost complete disinterest; I hardly ever play, and I no longer read or write about it. (Some might say that I "burned out.") Also, I have become very involved with religion; I enjoy working actively with my religious organization and studying religion from the point of view of modern psychology. This also supports Jung's belief that middle age is highlighted by a shift in one's strongest convictions and interests. I find all this particularly striking because I'm not a Jungian. (b) It's probably unfair to analyze a noted person whom I have never met, but I suspect that Howard Cosell fits the description rather well.

7. My late father detested Richard Nixon, even to the point of becoming red-faced with anger when talking about him. Unlike Nixon, my father was scrupulously honest. But he would not have been pleased to hear that he shared one of Nixon's prominent characteristics, namely becoming furiously and unreasonably angry at people who violated his standards of acceptable behavior. I now believe that my father disliked this aspect of himself (perhaps unconsciously), but did not know how to deal with it.

8. If you disagree because you have always known who you are and what you wanted, I envy you (though I'm a bit suspicious that you may not know yourself as well as you think). Having spent too much of my time obeying the dictates of introjected parental demands (or what I thought were parental demands), I have experienced more than a little difficulty untangling my own wishes from these introjected standards and figuring out what I really want (as by finding work that I genuinely like). So I agree with Jung's statement. See also the quote that appears at the end of the section on criteria of maturity in the chapter on Allport, and Freud's quote at the very end of the section on the ego in Chapter 2.

9. My answers: (a) Introversion. I am introspective, usually more comfortable being by myself than with other people, and not wildly enthusiastic about seeking out new situations. (b) Thinking. I emphasize rationality and trying to solve problems by thinking out good answers. (c) Extraversion: yes. (See above.) Feeling: I usually don't have much difficulty evaluating the

desirability of what I perceive, so here I disagree with Jung. But if this term were meant more literally (namely, the experiencing of emotion), I would agree. (d) A writer of textbooks on psychology.

10. I have never experienced an archetypal symbol emerging into consciousness, which makes it more difficult for me to appreciate Jung's theory. However, I have had one dream in my life that might well fit the description of a "big dream:"

> I dreamed that I was a physiological psychologist studying cell mechanisms. I was on the track of something unbelievably important, for I was going to be the first person to discover the true meaning of life. But then some invisible super-being put a message in my head: "They kill you if you find out too much. The secret of life is DEATH!" So I gave up my research and decided that it was safer not to know what life really meant. This was not a nightmare; the dream had an awesome quality, as though I were experiencing rare and profound wonders.

This dream may indicate that there were unpleasant aspects of my life that I was on the verge of discovering, but ultimately preferred not to know about. Or I could have been placing too much emphasis on raising my self-esteem by making brilliant discoveries and achieving lasting fame (like a Freud or Jung), and the dream might have been warning me that this was psychological suicide; I should instead be working on other issues, such as my relationships with important people in my life. (See also the section on dream interpretation in Chapter 6 and the dream of a writer driving up a mountain peak.) Jung might well see an emerging archetype somewhere.

11. How might placing all the blame on the parents enable the patient to see himself or herself as a relatively helpless individual? What necessary but painful tasks might this self-perception enable the patient to avoid?

12. (a) Consider Freud's views about secondary gains, managing the transference correctly in order to create a transference neurosis, and religion. (b) Consider Jung's views about transference neurosis, religion, and the purpose of the third stage of psychotherapy.

13. I find something useful in each approach. I agree with Freud that some people focus too heavily on a hereafter, and misguidedly sacrifice their maturity and responsibility for making decisions by conceiving of an all-powerful Being who will direct their behavior and solve their problems. Certainly many evils, such as wars, have been committed in the name of religion. But I also share Jung's belief that many people (including myself) need to believe that there is some greater meaning to life, and that it is not "a tale told by an idiot." Surely many evils have been committed because of a failure to follow important moral and ethical principles that are found in religion. And it has been shown that people who are religious are more likely to survive certain serious illnesses because they are reassured by a real and valuable faith.

14. Science emphasizes the importance of using predictions to verify a theory; after-the-fact reasoning is suspect. Consider that a great many other coincidences might have occurred at the time of the person's death: his clock might have stopped (as in Jung's example), his house might have been damaged by a storm, a stock he owned might have fallen, a friend might have had an accident. There are countless possibilities—so many, in fact, that it might be more surprising if nothing coincidental happened at the moment of the person's death. Also, we tend to forget the many times when no coincidence occurred. To find one specific coincidence like the falling picture and then argue after the fact that this event somehow shows the existence of "synchronicity" is unscientific—and, in my opinion, incorrect.

CHAPTER 4. ADLER

1. Consider Adler's painful parting with Freud and desire to develop his own theory. Recall that Freud emphasized the importance of instinctual drives, the unconscious, and intrapsychic conflicts, and was himself introspective (e.g., his self-analysis). And note that "cheap tricks" and "easy way of escape" imply that unhealthy character traits and neurosis are largely within our conscious control.

One might ask why Adler did not deviate from Freud by devising a theory that stressed the unconscious in a different way, as did Jung. A possible answer is that Jung (like Freud) suffered from painful inner conflicts and anxiety, whereas Adler apparently did not. (See the corresponding biographical sketches.)

2. I disagree. Anyone who has actually experienced severe neurotic anxiety knows that it is far too painful to be only a conscious "trick" for gaining sympathy and attention, though this may indeed be one of the resulting secondary gains. Nor is there anything "easy" about a severe neurosis, even though it may well enable the patient to avoid necessary but frightening tasks. Consider that Freud found his own anxiety and neurosis so painful that he was driven to devise appropriate methods of treatment. Also recall the case history described in Chapter 2, question 6 in this Appendix, from which the following quote is also taken:

> Anxiety and inner conflict: that's the story of my life. I want friendship, affection, and love. But I'm afraid! When I'm in a room with several people I don't know, my hands sweat so much that I'm ashamed to shake hands with anyone. I keep mostly to myself, and when I do talk to someone I stumble over my words and embarrass myself. I feel the pain and confusion of being pulled in two different directions at the same time: wanting close relationships, yet also constantly trying to avoid other people.

I therefore prefer Karen Horney's approach to anxiety and intrapsychic conflicts (see the following chapter).

3. (a) Which is more common in our society: people who stress charity and caring for others, or people who are individualistic and highly competitive (as with the well-known sentiment, "winning isn't everything, it's the only thing")? (b) Consider corporate raiders and dishonest stock brokers, as exemplified by the insider trading scandals of not long ago and movies such as *Wall Street*.

4. A fictional example of fictions: there are many instances in James Clavell's *Shogun* where a belief in some sort of reincarnation influences the behavior of samurai warriors, notably their willingness to "die gloriously" in this life. A real-life parallel is that of Kamikaze pilots during World War II. Of course, social pressures as well as fictions are involved in both examples. Some samurai or Kamikaze pilots might well have doubted the desirability (let alone the glory) of dying for their liege lord or country, but feared the reaction of their leaders and peers.

5. (a) Consider the effects of pampering, neglect, and organ inferiorities, and the resulting life goals chosen by the individual. (b) Weakness can be overcome by building up one's strength, as through appropriate training or learning. Conversely, attributing one's problems to inherited influences may make them seem much more difficult or even insuperable. (c) Consider the behaviors that the person avoids because of these traits. How might it be more comforting not to try these behaviors, rather than to try and fail?

6. (a) Following is more of the case history discussed in Chapter 2, question 6 in this Appendix, and question 2.

> My parents were always nervous about the possibility of something happening to me. In fact, when I was very young, they told me never to walk through the kitchen. This seemed pretty silly to me; the quickest way to get from the dining room to my room was through the kitchen, and I saw every day that nothing bad ever happened there. So one day I broke the rule while they were watching, to show them what I thought. I was proud of myself for a minute, but then my parents said how disappointed they were in me and turned their backs on me in disgust. I was shattered; I felt all alone, like I'd been kicked out of my own family. [The patient had previously suffered an extremely painful separation from one parent for nearly a year, which may well have left him particularly sensitive to rejection.] Recently, when I asked my parents about this, they explained that they had read a newspaper story about a kitchen stove blowing up in an apartment down the street. "What else could we do? It was our responsibility to protect you."
>
> Thinking back over my life, I found many other instances when my parents were pampering and overprotective. It often seemed like they were trying to satisfy my needs even before I expressed them (or even knew I had them!). So I learned never to show any initiative, and that the most important thing in life is to be safe. I decided that I had no right to take any chances at all, even if I really wanted to. And avoiding risk wasn't easy, what with unexplained danger lurking even in my own kitchen.

As noted in question 2, however, this patient reaches different conclusions about the results of such pampering than would Adler:

> I was too young to put these rules of life that I had learned into words. So they became unconscious, and have been directing my behavior ever since. Only recently have I become aware that my conflict between wanting to try new things and needing to be safe represents a conflict between my true desires and a need to keep my parents' love—love that I felt was taken away when I walked through the kitchen.

(b) and (c) One of my favorite fictional examples, albeit not one that is well known, is that of Clark Fries in Robert Heinlein's *Podkayne of Mars.* Clark is a precocious, unemotional, and highly intelligent eleven-year-old who has been neglected by parents busy following their careers. He develops a style of life characterized by a distrust of other people and constant attempts to demonstrate his superiority, which are usually successful. For example, when a woman passenger on a spaceship acts snobbish and sarcastic toward his family, he soaks her washcloth in an undetectable chemical that causes her face to turn bright red for a few days, forcing her to confine herself to her quarters. He grudgingly tolerates his sister, a likable and apparently normal teenager, and takes pleasure in writing critical comments in her diary in invisible ink. Only at the end of the book is there a hint that Clark may some day be able to break through to his feelings and ability to care for other people. (d) Two fictional examples: Ebenezer Scrooge, for obvious reasons; and Gail Wynand in Ayn Rand's *The Fountainhead,* who detests common people because they are so fallible and keeps a secret cellar containing precious works of art that only he can enjoy. (e) At the risk of sounding cynical, I don't know of many such examples. I hope you do.

7. I once heard a mother (not someone I knew) bawl out a child of about age five with words like the following: "What's wrong with you? You're bad! Nobody good would do something like that! You'll never amount to anything! You're stupid!" Incidents like this are usually not isolated ones; they represent typical patterns of behavior between parent and child. As Adler points out, such attacks on the child's personality can have extremely harmful consequences, including profound resentment and the development of an inferiority complex. Like any parent, I sometimes overreact to my six-year-old daughter's misbehaviors, but I am careful to criticize her actions and not her personality. I might say: "Don't make so much noise! That's not a good thing to do when mommy is trying to rest. Please be more quiet and more considerate."

8. I agree that only children tend to be pampered, to expect to be the center of attention, and to exaggerate their own importance. But I doubt that accurate predictions about any one person's specific behavior can be made solely from his or her birth order, even though there are some books that claim to be able to do so.

9. Consider Adler's painful parting with Freud, the great emphasis placed by Freud on dreams, and the purpose of the dream of the lawyer who had once been a classmate of Freud's (see the section on dream interpretation in Chapter 2).

10. (a) What emotions might result on awakening from this dream, and how might these emotions influence the dreamer's behavior? (b) What warning might this dream convey about the dreamer's personality?

11. Consider Adler's views about women and his therapeutic procedures.

12. (a) Recall that Adler was not a particularly good student, whereas Freud was. (b) If our society desperately needs more capable people, should we risk slowing the progress of gifted children by placing them in regular classes, where the teacher must proceed in ways that will meet the needs of the majority of students? Conversely, in a democratic society, should the needs of slower learners matter just as much as the needs of gifted children?

CHAPTER 5. HORNEY

1. Consider the case history described in this Appendix in Chapter 2, question 6 and Chapter 4, questions 2 and 6a. The patient suffers from a severe inner conflict between moving toward people and moving away from people, with the latter having been chosen as the neurotic solution. (He is able to describe his own conflict because he has made progress in bringing it to consciousness through formal psychotherapy; otherwise it would be too deeply repressed.) The idealized image sets unattainable standards, such as never needing other people, which are diametrically opposed to (and thus in conflict with) his needs for love and affection. When he does occasionally try to relate to other people, his efforts are awkward and unsuccessful because he is unpracticed in social skills. These failures are threatening reminders that the idealized image is a fiction, and that the real self is all too capable of error. So the failures (and the real self and wishes) are concealed by emphasizing the idealized image even more, which leads to more unrealistic and unattainable standards, which lead to more failure, and so on. (See Figure A.1.)

2. Consider the movie *Patton,* and the well-known scene where the general slaps a soldier who is suffering from battle fatigue. This is rather extreme behavior even for a hardened military leader, and Patton is subsequently disciplined. Might this behavior indicate that Patton unconsciously detested weakness in himself? Is his love for war sufficient evidence to classify him as "moving against people," an orientation where the person's own helplessness is repressed because it is incompatible with the desire for mastery? Patton's ill-advised clashes with his superiors invariably did him more harm than good; might this suggest the lack of flexibility that is typical of the neurotic solutions, namely an inability to abandon the "moving against" orientation even when it would have been to his advantage to do so?

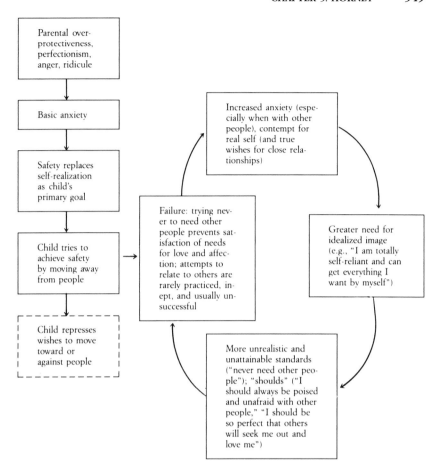

FIGURE A.1. Summary of the case history described in question 1.

3. The standards set by the idealized image are far more demanding than simply trying to do your best, or having your reach exceed your grasp. They are perfectionistic demands that are virtually impossible to satisfy. Even if there is some temporary "success" (e.g., the person writes a novel that becomes world famous or wins an Academy Award), any satisfaction does not last very long because the real problem has not been resolved: the person hates his or her real self, and has abandoned his or her true desires in order to satisfy the demands of the idealized image for glorious triumphs. In all probability, this person does not enjoy writing or acting, but represses these feelings because they are threatening reminders of the painful inner conflict between the real self and idealized image. So the person concludes instead that the fame or award simply isn't enough, and compulsively pursues still greater triumphs—a course that must eventually end in failure.

Consider also the following example, taken from the case history we have been discussing throughout (as in question 1):

Once I had to drive to an address in an unfamiliar city. I took the usual expressway and got off at the indicated exit. Now I was in unknown territory. I decided to make a right turn. Three blocks later, I chose to turn left. And four blocks later, I arrived at my destination! I had followed the best possible route without having any idea where I was going. (I still don't understand how I did this.)

At the time, this seemed like a great success. Since I was uncomfortable with people, especially strangers, I didn't want to stop and ask for directions. As it happened, I didn't have to. But in retrospect, I can see that all I accomplished was to strengthen my belief that I didn't need other people. And that made it still harder for me to gain the love and affection that I really wanted.

Moral: even an apparent "success" may not be.

4. (a) Without consciously realizing it, a young man tried to obligate his friends by working hard on a joint project. He didn't particularly like this task, but felt that the only way to keep his friends was by spending considerable effort to help them out. His friends had not asked for his help, so they assumed that he was participating because he was enjoying himself. He later asked one of these friends for a favor, expecting prompt agreement because he had worked so hard. The friend was of course unaware of the young man's imaginary claim, and turned him down because the favor was a rather unreasonable one. Needless to say, the young man felt very hurt and victimized. (b) The following example is from the case history discussed in questions 1 and 3:

Because I learned during childhood to fear any attempts at showing initiative and to dread the possibility of making mistakes, I approached my college work with extreme anxiety. I never took any courses just for the fun of it, even though I had room in my schedule for electives; I felt that I had to limit myself to only those courses that I needed for my future profession. When I realized after the first week of a course in advanced chemistry that I was in way over my head, I felt that I had no choice but to stick it out, even though dropping a course was clearly permitted by college regulations. So I suffered a great deal, learned nothing, and wound up with a D. It was like that all the time; there were always commands that I simply had to follow.

I never realized that these orders came from my own mind, and that the misguided purpose that they served was to conceal some very threatening aspects of reality. I had been ignoring my own wishes and seeking safety for so long that I no longer had any idea what I really wanted. By always having things that I "should" do, I was able to avoid facing up to the fact that I was free—but too weak and helpless to take advantage of it.

Notice that these shoulds are related to the patient's idealized image (e.g., "I'm so capable that I can do well in an advanced chemistry course, even though I lack the necessary prerequisites and enrolled in it by mistake"). They drive him to follow a course of action that can only end in failure. They also help the idealized image to conceal the fallible and hated real self.

5. Using the same case history as an illustration: (a) The patient behaves inconsistently by expressing a desire for love and affection (which reflects the dimly sensed wishes of the real self), but usually avoiding other people (this being the chosen neurotic solution to the problem of basic anxiety). (b) He has great difficulty making such decisions as whether or not to go to a party, which reflects the conflict between the desires of the real self and the usual course of moving away from people. (Since this decision is typically made when he is alone, his anxiety about being with people is not as great, and his true wishes are somewhat more accessible.) (c) His ineffectual attempts to relate to others are due partly to his lack of practice and failure to develop adequate social skills, and partly to the inability to satisfy the contradictory wishes of his real self and idealized image. As Horney points out, trying to simultaneously reach out to people and avoid them is like driving a car with one foot pressing the gas pedal and the other foot pressing the brake. (d) His social failures are all too unpleasant reminders of his fallible real self, which he is trying so hard (albeit unconsciously) to conceal with the idealized image.

6. When I was younger, I believed that other people could raise or lower my self-esteem. Praise or a favorable book review made me feel as though I were a worthwhile person, while criticism or an unfavorable review suggested that there was something significantly wrong with me. However, I now know that Horney is correct. I have worked at establishing inner guidelines for measuring my personal worth, with some success. I know when I have done something well, and I enjoy that. I know when I have done something poorly, which I regret—and then I put the regrets aside and go on to figure out how to improve matters. I still care about the opinions of other people, because I can learn from them, but I am usually able to prevent these opinions from manipulating my self-esteem. Praise is nice, but it's like the cherry on the hot fudge sundae; it adds a little something, but it isn't essential. Criticism is momentarily disconcerting, but then I try to look at it objectively: it may offer some worthwhile ideas, or my critic may be having a bad day and be upset for reasons that have nothing to do with me. It's not easy to strike a good balance between giving proper consideration to the opinions of others and taking these opinions too seriously, and I'm not always successful. But often I am—and it helps to keep Horney's statement in mind.

7. Consider that the patient truly believes that the neurotic solution is life-saving, no matter how obviously self-defeating it appears to someone else.

8. It is difficult to arrive at a valid interpretation from a single dream, let alone dream fragments such as these, especially without knowing anything about the dreamer. But I suspect Horney would argue as follows: (a) The dream reflects the loss of the dreamer's real self. (b) The dreamer wishes to maintain the basic orientation of moving away from people, as expressed by the considerable distance between the dreamer and the therapist. (c) As in Adlerian theory, this dream of falling expresses the insecurity that underlies the dreamer's conscious conceit. (d) The dreamer uses externalization to blame other people, here the taxi driver, for her problems.

9. I would consider this a valid criticism of theories derived primarily by male psychotherapists treating male patients (e.g., Freud's).

10. Consider the common complaint of a person who has committed a crime or done something wrong and then says, "You're only against me because I'm _____." (Fill in the name of any minority group.)

CHAPTER 6. FROMM

1. One reason: Fromm devotes considerable emphasis to changing society. Since we do not have any innate illicit tendencies, the causes of psychopathology must be external, namely society (and its agents, the parents). In contrast, Freud devotes considerable emphasis to changing the individual (as through psychoanalytic therapy). Since we have powerful illicit instincts that always remain part of our personality, it is we who must change by sublimating these instincts in order to reduce the inevitable conflicts between ourselves and society.

In my opinion, there is merit in both of these views. Surely, we should all try to improve our society (which is in need of considerable improvement). Surely, we should all strive for self-improvement, and to replace our self-defeating and pathological behaviors with healthy ones. (Recall that we are all at least a little neurotic—some of us more than a little.) However, I suspect that Freud's view is likely to yield more immediate dividends. It is extremely difficult to change society; those in power have a vested interest in maintaining the status quo, since it has worked well for them. Even if Fromm's recommended social changes are desirable, and even if we do try to implement some of them, these changes are so sweeping that it may well take several lifetimes before any real progress is made. Changing oneself is also difficult, but experience with formal psychotherapy has shown that significant progress is quite possible—and in less than one lifetime.

2. I don't think so. Fromm's conception of love is virtually identical to Adler's construct of social interest, since it involves a caring for all humanity rather than an infatuation with a specific person, and (secondary) narcissism is the same as exaggerated self-interest. So I regard this as yet another example of Adler's ideas being subsumed into other theories of personality, albeit using a different terminology.

3. (a) and (b) Although everyone needs to feel that "I am I," this is not easy to achieve. Life has many dangers, such as accidents, earthquakes, floods, illness, crime, and death. Much as we might like to have it both ways, we cannot simultaneously be directed by an all-powerful protector and free to follow our own choices, as the growing child discovers when given more freedom to do what he or she wants. We must choose between independence and being protected (perhaps making a different choice at different times, as when the child who has gone off to play independently sustains a minor injury and runs back to the parents for sympathy and support). Since

the world is a difficult and dangerous place, it is all too tempting to sacrifice our independence and identity, escape from the freedom to make our own choices, and seek out a powerful protector who will provide security by telling us what to do. (c) If we only had organic drives, we would be more like lower organisms whose behavior is totally determined by innate instincts. Without reason, self-awareness, and imagination, there would be fewer (or perhaps even no) choices for us to make, and little or no freedom from which to escape. (d) Freedom is frightening to this person because he is too weak and conflicted to take advantage of it. He has repressed his real self so well that he usually does not know what he wants, and freedom is a threatening reminder of this painful situation. So he would rather not be free, and he unconsciously creates inner commands for himself ("shoulds") that make it seem as though he has no free choice. (Other ways of escaping from freedom that he might have chosen, but did not, include becoming a conformist or an underling who blindly follows the orders of a dictator or religious zealot.)

4. See the case history discussed in this Appendix, Chapter 4, questions 2 and 6a. Because of such pathogenic parental behaviors as overprotectiveness and destructive criticism of the child's personality, and his own inability to deal with these behaviors, he developed basic anxiety (in Horney's terminology) and surrendered his real self. Yet his parents always said how much they loved him (which, in their way, they did). So he equates love with being overprotected, dominated, criticized, and having to abandon his real wishes. These beliefs are largely unconscious; he is aware only of considerable anxiety concerning the prospect of intimate relationships and love.

5. Possible examples: (a) Horney's description of "Cinderella bereft of her fairy godmother." (b) The movie *Wall Street;* a novel popular many years ago, *What Makes Sammy Run;* the character of Sheldon Grossbart in Philip Roth's short story, "Defender of the Faith." (c) See the answer in this Appendix to Chapter 4, question 6d; the hoarding orientation is much the same as Adler's description of the person who "guards his wretched treasures." The case history discussed throughout this Appendix is also appropriate; the patient not only moved away from people but also overemphasized the importance of material possessions, was disinclined to share with others, and was particularly orderly, compulsive, and stubborn. (d) See the answer in this Appendix to Chapter 4, question 6e.

6. Recall that to Fromm, every dream is an important communication from the dreamer to himself or herself. How might Fromm's interpretation vary according to the following additional information? (a) Her husband hates the comics. (b) Her husband loves the comics. (c) At a party on the evening prior to this dream, her husband accused her of being too silly and comical. (d) Her husband likes to talk during breakfast; she prefers to read the paper. (e) She likes to talk during breakfast; her husband prefers to read the paper. (f) On the day prior to this dream, she read a comic strip wherein a presumably happy husband and wife were revealed as having serious marital diffi-

culties. (g) She wants to have cosmetic surgery; her husband argues that it is too expensive. On the day prior to this dream, she read a comic strip wherein a woman had a successful facelift. (Do you see why it is usually necessary to know more about the dreamer, and perhaps obtain the dreamer's free associations, in order to interpret a dream accurately?)

7. (a) Are advertisements illogical? Is this likely to impair the ability to use reason of those who see them? (b) How often do you actually meet those who represent you in government? Do they usually tell the truth in their speeches and statements? (c) and (d) Starvation is a serious problem in "have-not" countries, as is the possibility that they might start a nuclear war. So too is the problem of the homeless in this country. But where is the money to come from? (e) Why is this harmful? Why, then, is this country respected for allowing freedom of religion? (f) How serious is this threat in view of the major changes within the USSR? Might it get worse in the not too distant future? (g) What are the dangers of following our present course? What changes should be made?

CHAPTER 7. SULLIVAN

1. (a-1) "The tension of anxiety, when present in the mothering one, induces anxiety in the infant." Here, the means by which anxiety is communicated is physical. (a-2) "If you have to maintain self-esteem by pulling down the standing of others, you are extraordinarily unfortunate. . . . The doctrine that if you are a molehill, then, by God, there shall be no mountains . . . is probably the most vicious of the [inappropriate] performances of parents with juveniles." The patient accepted his mother's views as accurate, which strengthened his resolve to move away from people. He failed to realize that her beliefs were due in large part to her own inability to relate well to others. (a-3) The child need not be afraid of its mother to become anxious; anxiety in the mothering one is sufficient. Nevertheless, this is more difficult for Sullivan to explain. His theory focuses on the child's relationship with a single "mothering one" (usually the mother), and has virtually nothing to say about the behavior of a second parent (i.e., the father). (b) What does Sullivan regard as the best way to reduce anxiety? Is a person who moves away from people likely to obtain safe relationships with nonanxious others?

2. (a) Recall that both men had firsthand experiences with psychotic thoughts or episodes, and that the parataxic mode is common in schizophrenia. (b) Recall that the parataxic mode involves a lack of understanding about causality, and see the comment in this Appendix concerning Chapter 3, question 14. (c) Consider that the parataxic mode is also characterized by the use of private symbols, and that the theories of Sullivan and Jung contain unusually difficult neologisms.

3. Deborah's private world of Yr, with gods who speak in words that only

she can understand, illustrates the parataxic mode. Several childhood incidents are described that caused Deborah intense anxiety. (Recall Sullivan's views concerning the causes of schizophrenia.) In accordance with Sullivan's definition of psychopathology, Deborah's behaviors are often inappropriate and inadequate. And you may well be able to find other examples. (If you have not read this book, I strongly recommend it.)

4. (a) Consider the following arguments: "If libido is *not* the same as physical energy, a person could be physically exhausted yet still have a great deal of sexual energy. That doesn't seem likely." "Physical energy can be measured, but the amount of libido invested in a particular mental event cannot be measured. So the concept of physical energy has scientific value, but the construct of libido does not." (b) To convert physical energy into behavior that will satisfy the person's needs and reduce tension. (c) For the guilt dynamism: Saying "I made a mistake, and I'm sorry" (which involves relatively small amounts of physical energy), agonizing for days over a mistake (which involves considerably more energy), daydreaming about having avoided a mistake by doing the right thing, forming powerful unconscious beliefs that one is a bad person.

5. (a) Both involve substituting a less desirable activity for one that would be more desirable, but would create more anxiety. (b) Freudian sublimation represents ideal behavior; it is helpful to the person, and to society, because it redirects illicit instincts into healthy outlets. In contrast, Sullivanian sublimation can be wholly disadvantageous to the person who uses it. For example, suppose the parents overreact with horror or harsh criticism when the child toys with its genitals. The child responds by becoming anxious, and associates this anxiety with sexuality. As an adult, this person rejects all sexual relationships because they evoke too much anxiety, and substitutes such behaviors as daydreaming about making love. This is in no way beneficial, since the person is deprived of healthy and socially acceptable gratification.

6. The case history discussed throughout this Appendix doesn't provide much support for this aspect of Sullivanian theory. The patient's characteristic behavior of moving away from people was well established by early childhood, and was not changed by his subsequent interactions with schoolmates, a relationship with a preadolescent chum, or the need to satisfy the lust dynamism during adolescence. He did have casual and superficial relationships with some of his peers, but no close or intimate relationships. How might a Sullivanian respond to this negative evidence? What evidence might be provided in support of Sullivan's position?

7. (a) Consider the case history described in this Appendix in Chapter 4, question 6a, from which the following quote is also taken:

> Even today, I still think about the time when I walked through my kitchen and my parents said how disappointed they were in me. Maybe this wasn't such a terrible rejection. I vaguely recall my parents saying something about my

behavior being "cute," and perhaps even trying to hide a chuckle or two. Maybe my conclusion that they were very angry because there was great danger in my own kitchen (and in the world), and that I should seek safety at all costs, was based on a faulty interpretation of what happened.

At the time, I didn't discuss my feelings about this incident with my parents for two reasons: I was very young and had trouble putting my feelings into words, and I was afraid. If I criticized my parents, as by arguing that they were wrong or had overreacted, I thought my father would go into one of his angry outbursts and really wipe me out. But that may also have been a misperception on my part. I was hurt and confused; I should have let them know.

See also my comment to question 1, part a-2. (b) and (c) See my comment in this Appendix concerning Chapter 3, question 11, and recall Sullivan's negative recollections of his mother (biographical sketch).

CHAPTER 8. ERIKSON

1. (a) I think so. A name is extremely personal; each of us has associated our own name with the concept of "I" or "myself" since early childhood. The entertainer will now have to equate a new and unfamiliar label with "I," and may well associate different personality characteristics with the new name (e.g., behaving like a celebrity). Though there are undoubtedly exceptions, at least some identity confusion would seem to be involved in such cases. (b) The same reasoning applies in this situation, but the amount of identity confusion may well be less for three reasons: the woman is gaining the socially sanctioned role of "wife," she is following a procedure that is accepted by the majority of married women in our society, and only her last name is changed. Even so, this still strikes me as a sacrifice, and I'm not at all sure that I would be willing to do it if this social custom were reversed. I am pleased that my wife took my name, partly because this is the prevailing custom and partly because this makes it easier to explain to our daughter what her last name is.

2. I have often had trouble achieving a sense of social solidarity. During my years as a college professor, I enjoyed teaching but didn't like research. This put me at odds with my colleagues, who regarded research as the most important task of an academic psychologist, and the resulting lack of social support and validation contributed to more than a little identity confusion on my part.

More recently, I have achieved some social solidarity through my affiliation with my religious organization, whose procedures and goals I find compatible with my personal and psychological beliefs. This has helped me to establish one aspect of my identity as a "moderately religious person." Since my religion permits the questioning of established beliefs and allows choices as to the rituals I wish to follow, rather than demanding blind faith,

Erikson (and Jung) would probably agree that it is a desirable source of personal support.

3. Possible fictional examples: Shakespeare's Richard III (see the section on neglect during personality development in Chapter 4), Darth Vader. Possible real-life examples: members of any persecuted minority group who accept the second-class status and deferential role prescribed by the majority.

4. I agree. My six-year-old daughter has often seemed to enjoy her accomplishments for their own sake, such as sitting up for the first time in her crib during infancy, learning to walk, and operating the VCR by herself. As Erikson points out, parental expectations do play a part; I'm sure she knows that both of her parents value achievement. But we take a fairly relaxed approach to her performance, and her enjoyment doesn't depend on words of approval from us. (I cringe when I read about parents who put a child of age two or three through rigorous training in order to improve his or her intelligence. Childhood should be a time to be a child.) What I have seen during the past six years is contrary to Freud's view that a child must always be "kicked upstairs" to the next stage of development, and supports Erikson's contention that mastery affords pleasure over and apart from the satisfaction of instinctual impulses.

5. (a) Consider the contradiction between "winning isn't everything, it's the only thing" and "do unto others as you wish they would do unto you." How does one reconcile the desire for personal success, which may well involve defeating other people, with the need to be caring and considerate? Who should be our role model: the collegiate coach who carefully follows every rule about recruiting high school athletes and loses the important game (and perhaps the job as well), or the coach who defeated him or her by bending or breaking the regulations in order to acquire some first-class talent? (b) See the second half of my answer to question 2, above. My identity is also supported in part by such roles as "husband" and "father."

6. How might comparisons provide crucial evidence about the psychosocial determinants of personality that could *not* be obtained by studying only those patients who happen to come to the therapist for treatment?

7. (a) Consider the anxiety shown by the patient's mother during the oral-sensory stage (and later), and his basic mistrust of people (e.g., Chapter 7, study question 1, part a-1; this Appendix, Chapter 4, question 2). (b) Consider his self-doubts, absence of will power, and lack of purpose; and the "kitchen" episode, which occurred during one of these stages (see this Appendix, Chapter 4, questions 2 and 6a; Chapter 5, questions 4b and 5). (c) This is evident throughout; he has repressed his real self and true desires. (d) This is clearly shown by his preference for isolation. (e) Our society stresses initiative and independence, especially (albeit unfairly) with regard to men; yet his parents consistently approved of submissiveness, while reacting harshly to many of his attempts at independence. (f) Some of these events did not occur at the ages, or in the order, predicted by Erikson. The

tendency toward isolation was well established long before young adulthood, while signs of an identity crisis were visible before adolescence.

8. (a) Is it possible to exert one's autonomy, yet always do what is approved of by others (e.g., the parents)? (See also the comment in this Appendix to Chapter 6, questions 3a and 3b.) Is it possible to have an intimate relationship without making any changes in one's identity? (b) See the comments in this Appendix to Chapter 7, question 7a; and Chapter 3, question 11.

9. How would parents have to behave for this to happen? What would happen to a person who trusted everyone?

10. Some possibilities: repressed memories, condensation, displacement and/or transference, childhood sexuality and Oedipality, the importance of childhood causes of psychopathology, and perhaps others. And all this in a dream consisting of a single word! What better example could there be of how deceptively complicated our personalities are?

CHAPTER 9. ALLPORT, MURRAY

1. My answers: (a) Murray. Note particularly Chapter 8, study question 10, and the corresponding comment in the Appendix (and most of the rest of the Appendix as well). (b) Murray. See his quote in the section on definition of needs. (c) Murray. See question 3. (d) Murray. See the preceding chapters on Sullivan and Erikson, among others. (e) Murray. See all of the preceding (and most of the subsequent) material in this book, and the Appendix. (f) Murray, at least with regard to neurosis and certain other forms of psychopathology. (You might surmise from the preceding that I am rather unhappy about the fact that it is Allport's theory, rather than Murray's, that has proved more popular among psychological researchers during the past few decades. Why might this have happened?)

2. (a) Why didn't Allport reply calmly (and perhaps with a friendly smile), "No, it was a boy I saw on the tram car on the way to your office"? What does extremely defensive behavior suggest about that individual's personality? How might these personality characteristics have influenced Allport to devise a theory that stresses the conscious and concrete aspects of personality? (b) Although young children can certainly behave in highly unsocialized ways (and provoke considerable parental irritation), it would never occur to me to describe my daughter in this way. What might Allport's statement imply concerning his feelings about children in general? How might these feelings have influenced him to devise a theory of personality that rejects the importance of events in infancy and early childhood?

3. Consider that behavior is often overdetermined, and other motives might also have caused him to seek the sea as a youth (e.g., a fondness for being on the water, friendly interactions with other sailors, deriving feelings of achievement from helping to sail a ship safely).

4. Keep in mind that the Study of Values shows only the relative standings of each of the six values, and not how much you like each one. Even though I am now particularly interested in religion, it would probably rank no better than second in my profile because I value the theoretical orientation even more. Yet religion might also rank second (and score about the same) in the profile of a person who values it much less than I do—namely, an individual who doesn't particularly value any of the six orientations but dislikes religion somewhat less than most of the others.

5. I'm inclined to agree that this is the ideal. I like to think that my present conscience is based on a sense of what is right (and wrong) for myself, my family, my friends, my religious organization, my country, and so on, rather than on the fear that some authority will punish me severely if I do something wrong (even though this might happen). But I also agree with Erikson that it is difficult to outgrow the childlike conscience because the superego perpetuates internally the relationship between the superior, angry adult and the small, helpless child.

6. I prefer Allport's. His analysis of the strengths and weaknesses of religion accords very well with my own views.

7. See Chapter 3, study question 8, and the corresponding comment in the Appendix.

8. (a) If we say that a person is shy because she constantly avoids other people, can we then say that she avoids other people because she is shy? Does this explain the cause of her behavior? (b) Why does psychological research rely on such techniques as drawing samples from populations and inferential statistics? (See the Prologue to this section.)

9. I prefer Murray's. Some eight years ago, I was hospitalized (for the only time in my life) with severe pneumonia. Normally, I love to eat; I even go into a mild depression when what I order in a restaurant proves to be dissatisfying, because this means that there will be one less meal that I will enjoy in my lifetime. Because of this illness, I lost my appetite (and about 15 pounds, which I could not afford; I'm slightly underweight even when healthy). Food tasted like cardboard, and chewing and swallowing it was a miserable experience. I only ate because I was threatened with the alternative of intravenous feeding, and I'm not fond of needles. Needless to say, I was delighted when I eventually regained my appetite.

I enjoy the pleasures that accompany drive reduction. I'm not particularly enthusiastic about vegetative states of equilibrium.

10. (a) Keep in mind that common traits, such as "shyness" and "seclusiveness," provide only a rough description of one's personality. Try to use more descriptive personal dispositions that may take one or two sentences, such as: "seeks out relatively impersonal contacts with a very small number of trusted friends, but is highly anxious with strangers and avoids large groups." (b) Clearly, n Infavoidance and n Harmavoidance; also n Autonomy, n Order, n Achievement (he saw his quest for glorious triumphs as the way to get love and affection from others), n Deference, and perhaps

others. (c) One example would be n Deference subsidiary to n Infavoidance, as when he often (though not always) was deferential to others so that they would not criticize or ridicule him.

CHAPTER 10. CATTELL

1. First, the sample is much too small. (Recall that the smaller the sample, the less likely it is to be representative of the population from which it was drawn.) This makes it all too likely that the resulting correlation coefficients and factor loadings will be considerably different from those in the population (here, all college students), leading to incorrect conclusions. Second, the researcher's naming of the second factor is subjective (and suspect). Something like "abstract reasoning" might be more appropriate, though the presence of only two tests with appreciable loadings makes naming the factor difficult. Finally, the researcher's choice of tests made it impossible to obtain such factors as mathematical ability, spatial relations, and memory. There is no way to obtain any high correlations between pairs of tests of (say) mathematical ability, since there is only one test of mathematical ability, so no such factor could ever emerge from this study.

2. I prefer Jung's. Freud's list is too brief, and Cattell's is too neologistic. (See Chapter 3, study question 4, and the corresponding comment in the Appendix.)

3. (a) My answers: Very sizic, very intelligent, very low in ego strength, neither dominant nor submissive (he is stubborn but not assertive), very desurgent, very high in superego strength, very threctic, neither premsic nor harric (he is self-reliant but also sensitive), very high in protension, high in autia, artless (especially with regard to social clumsiness), very high in guilt proneness, somewhat conservative, very self-sufficient, very high in self-sentiment strength and very high in ergic tension. (No doubt you had to consult the definition of most of these terms in order to understand this. So did I. This is a good indication as to why Cattell's theory has not had much of an impact on modern psychology—and why there are relatively few study questions in this chapter.) (b) Yes, with regard to low ego strength, desurgency, threctia, guilt proneness, ergic tension, and anxiety. No, with regard to submissiveness, low superego strength, and premsia. (c) Yes, in that his mother was anxious (rather than calm), his father was demanding and critical (and not overly cheerful), and he became sizic (rather than affect). No, in that his parents were overprotective yet he did not become clinging and dependent.

CHAPTER 11. KELLY

1. (a) Consider the construct of "safe–dangerous." (b) Recall Kelly's description of the security-conscious and hostile individual who always uses

the construct of "unfriendly" and does a fine job of detecting threats, but cannot cope with an attractive stranger who is romantically inclined. (c) He meets someone new at a party and decides to test the possibility that this person is "friendly" (as opposed to "unfriendly"). But his social skills suffer from a lack of practice, his opening remarks are awkward, his hands perspire, and he is more concerned with his own anxiety than learning about his new acquaintance. The other person is somewhat disconcerted by all this and responds cautiously, whereupon the patient concludes that this person is clearly "unfriendly." (d) Note the confusion that this man often experiences (e.g., this Appendix, Chapter 2, question 6), and that his predictions are very often incorrect: he is fearful but no real danger appears, he expects someone else to be friendly but they act distant and unfriendly, and so on. (e) Consider the following additional information from this case history:

> I've always known that one of the most traumatic incidents in my life was when my father was drafted into the army; I was only three at the time, and we were very close. [The patient did not experience severe difficulties with his father until some time later, when independence became an issue.] My parents tried to explain what was happening, but the concept of the draft was incomprehensible to me. So when my father said goodbye to me at the door, I only sensed dimly that this was very different from other occasions. Maybe because I wanted to believe it, I decided that he was just going shopping at a nearby store and would be back soon. So I didn't run to him for a goodbye hug, and I didn't tell him that I loved him very much and was sorry that he was going. (Even now, I can feel how much I wanted that hug!) But it was many months—a period that seemed like an eternity—before I saw him again.
>
> My failure to realize that he would be gone for a long time, and that this was my last chance to get a hug, made me feel stupid. Not showing my emotions made me feel like a coward. But words like "stupid" and "coward" were beyond me at that age, so I felt only a strong and long-lasting self-hate that I never really understood.

(f) He learned to predict that his parents would satisfy his every need, and he now expects to get love and affection from others without having to make the considerable effort to improve his social skills. (g) According to Kelly, such parental behavior causes the child to cling rigidly to a few familiar constructs, rather than seeking new ways to interpret the environment. (h) Consider that he consistently chooses the "unfriendly" pole of the "friendly–unfriendly" personal construct, in spite of the fact that this never brings him the love and affection that he wants.

2. (a) Recall the example that if you construe Kellyan theory as an exciting new mode of thought, you are likely to learn more and enjoy it more than if you construe it as hopelessly confused jargon. I used this principle to good advantage when I first wrote this chapter; it helped me to avoid being overwhelmed by Kelly's many neologisms, and to become very interested in what he was saying. (b) A student must decide whether a forthcoming examination is likely to be "difficult" (as opposed to "easy"). The student

makes this decision by construing previous exams in this course (or this school) as "difficult" or "easy." (c) I am preparing these study questions, and I predict that I will like what I see when I review what I have written. However, my examination of one particular question fails to confirm this prediction. I consider various possibilities (circumspection): the example I have chosen may be "inappropriate" (as opposed to "appropriate"), the question may be "poorly written" (as opposed to "well written"), and so forth. I decide to use the construct of "poorly written–well written" to deal with this problem (preemption), and I choose the "poorly written" pole as most likely to improve my predictions (control, or choice). So I thoroughly revise the wording, and I predict that I will like it when I read it over. This prediction is confirmed, so I conclude that the problem is solved (and that I made the right decision by not substituting a different example). (d) My construct of "good" (versus "bad") has become much more permeable to the construct of "religious" (as opposed to "agnostic") as I have grown older. (See the comment in this Appendix to Chapter 3, question 6a.) Or you could say that my construct of "religious" (versus "agnostic") has become more permeable to my self-construct. (e) All too many authors seem to assume that a textbook is nothing but "scholarly," and not also "entertaining." (f) My six-year-old daughter's efforts to construe my behavior are aided by her taking the role of daughter while I take the role of father, which makes our behaviors more predictable (most of the time, anyway).

3. Suppose I first apply the personal construct of "delicious–ordinary" (or "good–bad") to Restaurant A and Restaurant B, then to Restaurant B and Restaurant C, and so on.

4. Remember that personal constructs are of our own creation. Also see Chapter 3, study question 7, and the corresponding comment in the Appendix.

5. (a) He would probably conclude that the client has become preoccupied with learning Erikson's theoretical constructs (such as repression, condensation, and Oedipality), is offering this dream as a gift to show how well she is doing, and is not devising the new personal constructs that she needs to solve her problems. (b) Surely, Freud. (Recall that Kelly used psychoanalytic theory at one time.) These comments could also be applied to other theorists whose work we have discussed, however. (c) My answer: Yes and no. I'm particularly impressed by Erikson's interpretation of the "S[E]INE" dream, and what this indicates about the complexity of the human personality. But I also think that Kelly's views have considerable merit. As noted in Chapter 17, I suspect that a considerable amount of time has been lost in psychoanalytic therapy because some "resistant" patients conceptualized their problems differently, in terms the therapist could not understand psychoanalytically, and were either unable or unwilling to adopt the analyst's construct system. (Of course, Freudians would say that I have not been sufficiently psychoanalyzed. I suppose they might even be right.)

6. (a) The person's construct of "desirable–undesirable" is too imperme-

able to members of the opposite sex. (b) Nothing has emerged from an "unconscious." The person previously construed this behavior in terms of "desirable–undesirable" (as applied to members of the opposite sex), and has learned to substitute the construct of "afraid–unafraid" (as applied to the patient). How can one decide whether a belief such as "I am afraid of heterosexuality" actually existed in the patient's psyche but was repressed, or whether the person simply learned to use this terminology to describe his or her behavior?

7. Consider the difficulties in conducting research described in the Prologue to this section. Why might it almost always be possible to find plausible ways to reject the findings of a research study that claims to disprove one's theory? Might some of the personality theorists who tried and rejected various other jobs have decided on psychology because they realized (consciously or unconsciously) how difficult it would be for anyone to prove that their theories were incorrect?

CHAPTER 12. ROGERS

1. (a) The man in this case history tries extremely hard to win approval from his parents. He is also sensitive to the opinions of other people, even relative strangers. (b) This is clearly illustrated by the "kitchen" episode (this Appendix, Chapter 4, question 6a). (c) Actualization involves satisfying his real needs and wishes, including those for love and affection. But because of his introjected conditions of worth, his self-concept is strengthened by remaining totally independent, avoiding rejection, and not needing other people. (Compare with the comment in this Appendix concerning Chapter 5, question 1.) (d) See the comments in this Appendix concerning Chapter 2, question 6 and Chapter 4, question 2.

2. See Chapter 8, question 4, and the corresponding comment in this Appendix.

3. (a) Recall footnote 2 in the section dealing with the self-concept. (b) See Chapter 3, study question 8, and the corresponding comment in this Appendix; and Chapter 9, study question 7.

4. See Chapter 4, study question 7, and the corresponding comment in this Appendix. When relating to my six-year-old daughter, I also follow Rogers's advice to accept the responsibility for my own feelings—as by saying that I don't like it if the family room is messy, rather than trying to convince her that she shouldn't like it. This doesn't always succeed in getting her to clean up the family room; but she usually helps, and it does seem to save a lot of wear and tear on everyone's feelings.

5. I can't comment on the Leboyer technique, since I have never seen it firsthand. But I was present in the delivery room when my daughter was born, using relatively standard procedures that have been updated in certain

ways. (For example, the baby is held by both the mother and the father soon after birth to encourage bonding with both parents.) The moment of birth does seem difficult for the baby and does involve crying, but I don't think the whole procedure is nearly as traumatic as Rogers implies.

6. It isn't easy. Some years ago, my writing style had certain idiosyncrasies that I strongly defended ("*I* write like this"). Now I no longer agree about some of them, and have changed them so my writing will be more clear. (If possible, compare the first edition of this text with this edition and see if you agree.) However, I still trust my inner experience insofar as my writing is concerned. See also the comment in this Appendix to Chapter 5, question 6.

7. (a) My answers: Extremely low in genuineness; both parents were very defensive, especially when he tried to argue that they had made mistakes. Very low in empathy; they could understand obvious displays of anger or unhappiness, but had very little idea as to how he really felt about most things. Extremely low in unconditional positive regard; they judged him almost entirely on whether or not he satisfied their standards. (b) Based on my experiences with friends, I'm inclined to agree with Rogers. But I have never met anyone who is very high on all three characteristics. (c) Did Freud express his true beliefs and feelings during therapy? Can a therapist of any theoretical persuasion be effective without at least some openness to experience and empathy? Was Freud empathic in the case of Dora? Could a person as opinionated as Freud practice unconditional positive regard? Would he want to?

8. What kind of relationship exists between two people when one of them evaluates the other? Does it matter whether this evaluation is positive or negative? Is it possible for a psychologically healthy person to care when others give a positive evaluation, but not care when they give a negative evaluation?

9. I hope not. Certainly these questions are designed to stimulate thinking. But I hope that the case histories, practical examples, and personal comments have also touched your emotions.

10. See Chapter 11, study question 5b, and the corresponding comment in this Appendix.

CHAPTER 13. MASLOW

1. (a) Some of the origins of his self-hate are revealed in the comment to Chapter 11, question 1e. The vicious circle involving his increasing self-hate is shown in the comment to Chapter 5, question 1. (b) Some of these pressures and demands are illustrated in the comment to Chapter 4, question 6a. Consider also the following additional information from this case history:

> My father was very perfectionistic. Once I gave him a paper I had written for
> my high school geography class, expecting a few comments and helpful sug-

gestions. But when he returned it, he never said a word. I opened the paper, and every page was covered with corrections in glaring red pencil. I was crushed; I really felt stupid.

Nothing I ever did seemed to be good enough for him. When I told him that I had made the honor roll for my first semester in high school, I expected something like a cheery smile and a warm hug. I thought this was a significant accomplishment; it isn't easy to adjust to a new school. But all I got was an expressionless nod.

My parents had my intelligence tested when I was eight years old, and I scored extremely high. After that, I guess the only thing that might have satisfied my father would have been some truly earthshaking achievement, like winning the Nobel Prize. (Or maybe even that wouldn't have been enough.)

(c) He is wrong about safety always being the best choice, and to expect that his father will be rewarding and affectionate in spite of ample evidence to the contrary. See also Chapter 11, study question 1h, and the corresponding comment in this Appendix; and Chapter 7, question 7a, and the corresponding comment in this Appendix. (d) This is evident throughout; see for example the comment in this Appendix to Chapter 4, question 6a.

2. All of these theorists are able to explain our propensity for both healthy and destructive behavior, but I prefer Maslow's position because it is neither wholly pessimistic nor wholly optimistic.

3. My answers: (a) Maslow. See Chapter 8, study question 4, and the corresponding comment in this Appendix. (b) Maslow. See Chapter 9, study question 9, and the corresponding comment in this Appendix. (c) Freud would undoubtedly regard this procedure as all too likely to reinforce the patient's secondary gains, and I'm inclined to agree. This goes far beyond the therapist being empathic and caring—much too far, in my opinion.

4. Would our society (and the world) be a better place if more people pursued this particular ambition?

5. (a) He is clearly preoccupied with the safety needs, which overwhelm his needs for belongingness and love. But he is at least somewhat aware of his belongingness needs and also recognizes some esteem needs, which does not accord well with Maslow's hierarchy. (b) I have trouble classifying myself according to the hierarchy, because Maslow never specifies the amount of satisfaction that must be achieved at any given level for the next higher need to become prominent. My safety needs are fairly well satisfied, but are stronger than I would like. My belongingness/love and esteem needs are also fairly well satisfied. And I believe I am aware to some extent of my need for self-actualization, but I'm not sure. I seem to be working on some of these levels simultaneously, rather than in succession as Maslow would argue.

6. I agree. See Chapter 3, study question 8, and the corresponding comment in this Appendix.

7. (a) Consider some of the following characteristics of self-actualizers: They are relatively unconcerned with introspection, more tolerant of human

frailty, less judgmental of themselves and others, guided by strong moral and ethical standards, able to evaluate people more accurately, consumed by some mission in life that occupies much of their energy, and creative. (b) He is clearly lacking in many of these characteristics. He does not perceive reality very accurately, does not accept himself and others, worries over minor details, lacks much emotional response, lacks social interest, and does not have deep and loving interpersonal relationships. But he is autonomous (albeit excessively so), has strong moral and ethical standards, and is creative. This is yet another illustration that pathology often differs from healthy behavior in degree, rather than in kind.

8. I'm inclined to agree with the statement, but I don't agree that this belief can only be ascertained from the study of healthy individuals; Fromm and Rogers reached the same conclusion from their clinical work. See Chapter 6, study question 7a, and Rogers's discussion of how the journey away from self-knowledge is encouraged by certain social institutions.

9. Consider the professional athlete who is receiving an extremely large salary but becomes so unhappy about not earning more that he (or, less often in our society, she) sits out part of the season, sulks, and perhaps even damages his career. (As I write this, one of our local professional basketball players is doing exactly that.)

10. Consider an artist who loves to paint and values his or her own work, but who is not appreciated by the public and lives in squalor. Does this suggest that it is possible to complain about physical conditions, or not satisfy the need for esteem from others, yet still be able to self-actualize? (See also Chapter 5, study question 6, and the corresponding comment in this Appendix.)

CHAPTER 14. MAY

1. I think so. See for example Chapter 5, study question 5b, and the corresponding comment in this Appendix.

2. (a) See the discussion of inferiority and superiority complexes in the section on psychopathology in Chapter 4. (b) See the discussion of the structure of personality in Chapter 4. (c) See the discussion of neurosis in Chapter 5. (d) See the discussion of mechanisms of escape and defense in Chapter 6. (e) See the discussion of experience and the organismic valuing process in Chapter 12.

I think so. May does devote more emphasis to gaining superiority through explicit violence than does Adler; he is somewhat more specific about the parental behaviors that cause each form of neurosis than is Horney; and he differs from Fromm by stressing our dread of nonbeing, rather than our need to escape from the frightening choices that we must make because our behavior is not preordained by innate instincts. But I don't regard these as major differences.

3. I find merit in both of these views, even though they are contradictory. I agree with May that it is highly inadvisable to base Eigenwelt on the opinions of other people. (See the comment in this Appendix to Chapter 5, question 6.) But I also think that social solidarity can support one's identity without overwhelming it. (See the comment in this Appendix to Chapter 8, question 2.) What harm might befall the individual from carrying either of these views to an extreme—that is, depending too heavily on social solidarity or never paying any attention to the opinions of others?

4. (a) Is death the only form of nonbeing? Is there any great difference between "nonbeing" and the loss of one's real self, or between physical destruction and psychological destruction? (b) Consider the following additional information from the case history discussed in question 1: when this man did finally take the risk of going to a party, he spent much of his time wandering back and forth between the door and the room where the people were, unable to decide whether to stay or leave. What two simultaneous opposing wishes might be reflected by this behavior?

5. Ayn Rand's novel *Atlas Shrugged* contrasts a small group of people who love life and are willing to take considerable risks to affirm their Dasein (e.g., John Galt) with the large majority who are afraid to affirm their being-in-the-world and merely go through the motions of living. Her characters are rather one-dimensional and unrealistic, but her argument is a cogent one. The man in the case history described throughout this Appendix is desperately afraid to affirm his Dasein. And there have been times in my own life when I preferred to back down and not be noticed, rather than assert my beliefs and/or existence and risk physical or psychological destruction.

6. (a) Consider the fear of failing to achieve important goals, such as seeing one's children grow up or finishing a book that one is writing; the fear that one's children will lack financial and emotional support; and perhaps others as well. Are these reasons for fearing death as likely to be repressed? (b) Is it possible to be aware of something on an intellectual level, yet not experience the corresponding emotions?

7. Three people are watching a college basketball player during an important game. A pro scout who is considering drafting this player looks to see if his skills match up well with those required in the NBA, a coed evaluates his desirability as a romantic interest, and a professor whose course he is flunking sees him as a symbol of what is wrong with the priorities in higher education.

8. Might a person sometimes express in physical actions what he or she is unable or unwilling to put into words, such as: "I am inept. I feel so ineffectual that I can't even trust an inert object like an alarm clock to stay set after I pull the lever. This is what my parents wanted, and what I must be to keep their love"? Might these repeated actions keep him too busy to focus on highly threatening feelings, such as his sadness over his inability to obtain love and affection? Might reaction formation be taking place (as if he is

concealing strong feelings of depression, so much so that he might be considering never waking up again)?

CHAPTER 15. SKINNER

1. How might the belief that there are no inner causes, and that there is no free will, have helped Skinner to rationalize his failure as a writer? Do extreme theoretical positions suggest that the theorist has been overly influenced by personal issues? (See also Chapter 2, study questions 1, 2, and 3, and the corresponding comments in this Appendix; and Chapter 3, study question 1, and the corresponding comment in this Appendix.) Consider Skinner's statement that "to become discouraged is simply to fail to respond because reinforcement has not been forthcoming [and therefore does not show a 'lack of interest']." Is one year a long time to try without success, especially where one's heartfelt dream is concerned?

2. Who is more subject to external control: A person using a programmed instruction machine, or an individual who browses through various books in the library? A behaviorist who prepares complicated schedules of reinforcement that a hungry animal must satisfy to obtain a food reward, or the animal that causes food to appear by making the correct responses? An individual who is deprived, or one who is satiated? (Recall that deprivation must exist for operant conditioning to be possible.) If Skinnerian ideas are a threat to individual freedom, how then has behavior therapy been able to help so many clients?

3. (a) A disturbed child who must wear eyeglasses to see properly keeps taking them off and throwing them on the ground. An acceptable reinforcer is found (say, the child likes a particular kind of candy). When hungry, the child is given a piece of this candy for touching the eyeglasses gently as they rest on a table. When this response has been well learned, the child is reinforced for picking up the eyeglasses carefully, then for bringing them nearer to his face, then for trying them on, and so on until he routinely wears the eyeglasses without incident. The reinforcement provided by his improved vision eventually replaces that provided by the candy. (b) A gambler continues to play a slot machine, even though it only pays off once in a great many trials. (c) I go to the bakery to buy a loaf of my favorite bread. The loaf I see on the shelf is not exactly the same as the bread I bought yesterday; no two loaves are identical. But it is very similar, so I am able to emit the behavior of asking the salesperson for it. (d) During a bridge tournament, I make a play that works out badly and fails to provide any reinforcement. On another occasion, the same play succeeds brilliantly. So I decide that the first situation is actually different from the second one and requires a different strategy. When I next encounter the former situation, I regard it as different from the latter one and elect to use my new strategy. My plan succeeds, and this reinforcement increases the probability that I will continue to behave

differently in these two situations. (e) Consider the comment in this Appendix concerning Chapter 3, question 6a. Skinner would argue that I did not lose interest in bridge, but rather that external contingencies of reinforcement were too poorly designed for me to continue to emit the behavior of playing.

4. (a) Skinner would argue that I detected feelings within myself similar to those that I experienced on prior occasions when I was about to behave in the same way, but these feelings didn't cause anything. (Recall that Skinner does not deny the existence of inner thoughts and feelings; it is their causal status to which he objects.) What I might have done instead is irrelevant. (b) I disagree. Psychologists and philosophers have debated the issue of free will at great length, and I'm not about to resolve it in a few sentences. But I believe that being human means the freedom to choose, and that who we are is defined to a great extent by the choices that we make.

5. Consider what would happen to a person who knew nothing at all about each of the following tasks, and tried to learn them by trial and error: brain surgery, driving a bus, flying an airplane, acupuncture, defusing a bomb, being a parent. (On second thought, perhaps that last example does support Skinner . . .)

6. I am alone in my room. My thoughts wander to a person who treated me badly in the past. As I think about this incident, I become increasingly angry. Does such an example contradict Skinner's ideas, or would he be able to point to some external event that caused this behavior?

7. What two responses are incompatible and about equal in strength? How might they have been learned? Why is this situation aversive? What might happen to increase the strength of one response so that it can be emitted?

8. My six-year-old daughter is making a great deal of noise at a time when I would prefer quiet. I may react by saying "stop that!", which works some of the time. (If it doesn't work, and I try still stronger commands, the situation may well become unpleasant for both of us.) I am much more successful on those occasions when I can distract her by suggesting an alternative that is incompatible with making noise, such as doing crafts work that she likes (which requires too much attention for shouting).

9. (a) Both theorists argue that supposedly unconscious processes actually reflect a failure to identify or name (construe) the behaviors in question. (b) I disagree, as you may well have gathered from many of the preceding study questions in this book (e.g., the comment in this Appendix to Chapter 8, question 10). But it can be difficult to decide whether an apparently new idea previously existed in one's unconscious and gravitated to consciousness, or whether the person simply learned to identify previously unlabeled behavior. So I suppose Skinner could be right.

10. (a) This woman is an excellent candidate for behavior therapy, since her phobia concerns a specific external object and situation. Such techniques as systematic desensitization have been successful with cases like this one. (b) I think behavior therapy is less likely to help in this case, since his anxiety is

involved with his self-concept and unconscious beliefs and feelings. Given his tendency to distrust others, it is doubtful that he would submit to the control (however benign) of a behaviorist who would choose and impose various treatments, and there is no evidence that he ever tried behavior therapy. However, changes in behavior can produce personality change (as Maslow points out). If behavior therapy were able to help him become less anxious with other people and gain more affection and love, such successes might well lead to increased self-esteem and a more healthy personality.

CHAPTER 16. DOLLARD AND MILLER, BANDURA

1. (a) Consider Mrs. A's childhood experiences, and the behavior that this fear motivates regarding marital relations with her husband. (b) Might Mrs. A's husband have become a conditioned aversive stimulus?

2. See the comment in this Appendix to Chapter 11, question 1e.

3. How do Dollard and Miller define repression? How is repression harmful to the individual? Why do Dollard and Miller conclude that "[the neurotic] is stupid insofar as his neurotic conflict is concerned. . . . [But this] is really a stupid area in the mind of a person who is quite intelligent in other respects"? How can this "selective stupidity" be overcome?

4. (a) I cannot decide whether to cook spaghetti or make a tuna salad for dinner. Spaghetti is my favorite dish, but tuna salad is attractive because I have not had it for some time. (Although moving toward one of these goals is supposed to help resolve this competition, I sometimes find that approaching the spaghetti makes matters worse because it arouses stronger regrets about not having the tuna salad. Nevertheless, I would agree that this is the easiest of the three conflicts to resolve.) (b) Consider the dilemma faced some years ago by men who opposed the Vietnam war: whether to risk their lives for a cause they disapproved of, or become draft dodgers and go to jail. (Some resolved this painful conflict by leaving the field and going to Canada.) (c) A shy person wants love and affection, but has learned to fear intimate relationships (as in the case history discussed throughout this Appendix; see for example Chapter 14, question 4b). He can plan to go to a singles party without evoking great anxiety, since the avoidance gradient is lower than the approach gradient when he is distant from the goal. But since the avoidance gradient is higher than the approach gradient when he is close to the goal, he avoids talking to anyone at the party and leaves early.

5. (a) I like the example given previously in this chapter: labeling one's own illness as "cancer" will evoke intense fear, whereas deciding that it is "only a cold" will cause a much calmer journey to the medicine cabinet. A similar example occurs in the movie *Hannah and Her Sisters,* when Woody Allen decides that he has a brain tumor and becomes rather upset; he feels better when the "tumor" turns out to be a smudge on the X-ray. As an example from real life, consider the case history discussed in the comment in this

Appendix to Chapter 11, question 1e: how different might this man's self-concept have turned out had he regarded himself as "fallible," rather than as a "coward" and "stupid"? (b) See Chapter 15, study question 6, and the corresponding comment in this Appendix. Or consider a patient in psychotherapy who enters the day's session in a relatively placid mood, begins to work on his or her problems, thinks about distressing material, and becomes depressed and even tearful (a painful experience that may well be conducive, or even necessary, to the success of the treatment and personal growth).

6. (a) Here again, I like one of the examples given previously in this chapter: authors do not need someone hovering over their shoulders and reinforcing each well-phrased sentence with praise (or a piece of candy); they are guided by inner standards of what constitutes acceptable work, and they reinforce themselves for meeting this criterion with self-satisfaction and pride. Perhaps Skinner could also explain such behavior in terms of a complicated sequence of operant conditioning, but I doubt it; I prefer Bandura's approach. (b) See Chapter 14, study question 3, and the corresponding comment in this Appendix (and the related comments to Chapter 5, study question 6, and Chapter 8, study question 2).

7. The man whose case history is discussed throughout this Appendix is clearly low in perceived self-efficacy; he does not expect his own actions to produce important rewards, such as love and affection from others. See for example the comments in this Appendix to Chapter 2, question 6, and Chapter 4, question 2.

8. (a) A man tells two young boys that he will "pay them well" for shoveling the snow off his walk. Unwisely, they do not negotiate a specific amount. After an hour's hard work, the walk is clear. The first boy expects to be paid $3, while the second boy expects $15. The man gives each boy $5. The amount of the reinforcer is identical, but its effect on each boy is quite different. (b) A professional athlete is quite happy making $2 million per year; he enjoys his sport and his affluence. He then sees the contracts of two other players, whose performance and statistics he regards as very inferior to his own, and finds that they are making $3 and $4 million per year. So he becomes extremely unhappy, sulks, and holds out for half the season. The reinforcer (his salary) has not changed; but the effect has, due to observational learning.

REFERENCES

Abraham, K. A short study of the development of the libido. Original publication: 1924. In *Selected Papers.* London: Hogarth Press, 1927.

Adler, A. *The neurotic constitution: Outline of a comparative individualistic psychology and psychotherapy.* Original publication: 1912. Hardcover English edition: New York: Moffat, 1917a.

Adler, A. *Study of organ inferiority and its psychical compensation: A contribution to clinical medicine.* Original publication: 1907. Hardcover English edition: New York: Nervous and Mental Disease Publishing Co., 1917b.

Adler, A. *Understanding human nature.* Original publication: 1927. Hardcover English edition: New York: Greenberg, 1927. Paperback reprint: Greenwich, Conn.: Fawcett, 1957.

Adler, A. *What life should mean to you.* Original publication: 1931. Hardcover English edition: Boston: Little Brown, 1931. Paperback reprint: New York: Capricorn Books, 1958.

Adler, A. *The problem child: The life style of the difficult child as analyzed in specific cases.* Original publication: 1930. Paperback English edition: New York: Capricorn Books, 1963.

Adler, A. *Problems of neurosis.* Original publication: 1929. Hardcover English edition: London: Routledge & Kegan Paul, 1929. Paperback reprint: New York: Harper Torchbooks, 1964a.

Adler, A. *Social interest: A Challenge to mankind.* Original publication: 1933. Hardcover English edition: London: Faber & Faber, 1938. Paperback reprint: New York: Capricorn Books, 1964b.

Adler, A. *The science of living.* Original publication: 1929. Hardcover English edition: New York: Greenberg, 1929. Paperback reprint: New York: Anchor Books, 1969.

Adler, A. *The practice and theory of individual psychology.* Original publication: 1920. Hardcover English edition: London: Routledge & Kegan Paul, 1925. Paperback reprint: Totowa, N.J.: Littlefield, Adams & Co., 1973.

Adler, A. Advantages and disadvantages of the inferiority feeling. Original publication: 1933. In H. L. Ansbacher & R. R. Ansbacher (Eds.), *Superiority and social interest: A collection of Alfred Adler's later writings.* New York: Norton, 1979a, pp. 50–58.

Adler, A. Complex compulsion as part of personality and neurosis. Original publication: 1935. In H. L. Ansbacher & R. R. Ansbacher (Eds.), *Superiority and social interest: A collection of Alfred Adler's later writings.* New York: Norton, 1979b, pp. 71–80.

Adler, A. Compulsion neurosis. Original publication: 1931. In H. L. Ansbacher & R. R. Ansbacher (Eds.), *Superiority and social interest: A collection of Alfred Adler's later writings.* New York: Norton, 1979c, pp. 112–138.

Adler, A. The death problem in neurosis. Original publication: 1936. In H. L. Ansbacher & R. R. Ansbacher (Eds.), *Superiority and social interest: A collection of Alfred Adler's later writings.* New York: Norton, 1979d, pp. 239–247.

Adler, A. The differences between individual psychology and psychoanalysis. Original publication: 1931. In H. L. Ansbacher & R. R. Ansbacher (Eds.), *Superiority and social interest: A collection of Alfred Adler's later writings.* New York: Norton, 1979e, pp. 205–218.

Adler, A. The neurotic's picture of the world: A case study. Original publication: 1936. In H. L. Ansbacher & R. R. Ansbacher (Eds.), *Superiority and social interest: A collection of Alfred Adler's later writings.* New York: Norton, 1979f, pp. 96–111.

Adler, A. On the origin of the striving for superiority and of social interest. Original publication: 1933. In H. L. Ansbacher & R. R. Ansbacher (Eds.), *Superiority and social interest: A collection of Alfred Adler's later writings.* New York: Norton, 1979g, pp. 29–40.

Adler, A. Religion and individual psychology. Original publication: 1933. In H. L. Ansbacher & R. R. Ansbacher (Eds.), *Superiority and social interest: A collection of Alfred Alder's later writings.* New York: Norton, 1979h, pp. 271–308.

Adler, A. The structure of neurosis. Original publication: 1932. In H. L. Ansbacher & R. R. Ansbacher (Eds.), *Superiority and social interest: A collection of Alfred Adler's later writings.* New York: Norton, 1979i, pp. 83–95.

Adler, A. Typology of meeting life problems. Original publication: 1935. In H. L. Ansbacher & R. R. Ansbacher (Eds.), *Superiority and social interest: A collection of Alfred Adler's later writings.* New York: Norton, 1979j, pp. 66–70.

Allport, G. W. *Personality: A psychological interpretation.* New York: Holt, 1937.

Allport, G. W. *The use of personal documents in psychological science* (Bull. 49). New York: Social Science Research Council, 1942.

Allport, G. W. *The individual and his religion.* New York: Macmillan. 1950.

Allport, G. W. *Becoming: Basic considerations for a psychology of personality.* New Haven: Yale University Press, 1955.

Allport, G. W. *The nature of prejudice.* Reading, Mass.: Addison-Wesley, 1954. Paperback reprint [abridged]: New York: Anchor Books, 1958.

Allport, G. W. *Personality and social encounter.* Boston: Beacon Press, 1960.

Allport, G. W. *Pattern and growth in personality.* New York: Holt, Rinehart and Winston, 1961.

Allport, G. W. *Letters from Jenny.* New York: Harcourt, Brace and World, 1965.

Allport, G. W. *The person in psychology: Selected essays.* Boston: Beacon Press, 1968.

Allport, G. W., & Allport, F. H. *The A-S reaction study.* Original publication: 1928. Revised edition: Boston: Houghton Mifflin, 1949.

Allport, G. W., & Postman, L. *The psychology of rumor.* New York: Holt, 1947.

Allport, G. W., & Vernon, P. E. *Studies in expressive movement.* New York: Macmillan, 1933.

Allport, G. W., Vernon, P. E., & Lindzey, G. *A study of values.* Original publication [Allport & Vernon]: 1931. Third edition: Boston: Houghton Mifflin, 1960.

American Psychological Association. *Cumulative subject index to Psychological Abstracts 1981–1983.* Washington, D.C.: APA, 1984.

Anastasi, A. *Psychological testing* (4th ed.). New York: Macmillan, 1976.

Arieti, S. *Interpretation of schizophrenia* (Rev. ed.). New York: Basic Books, 1974.

Ayllon, T., & Azrin, N. H. *The token economy: A motivational system for therapy and rehabilitation.* New York: Appleton-Century-Crofts, 1968.

Bandura, A. *Principles of behavior modification.* New York: Holt, Rinehart and Winston, 1969.

Bandura, A. (Ed.). *Psychological modeling: Conflicting theories.* Chicago: Aldine Atherton, 1971.

Bandura, A. *Aggression: A social learning analysis.* Englewood Cliffs, N.J.: Prentice-Hall, 1973.

Bandura, A. *A social learning theory.* Englewood Cliffs, N.J.: Prentice-Hall, 1977.

Bandura, A. The self system in reciprocal determinism. *American Psychologist,* 1978, *33:* 344–358.

Bandura, A. Self-referent thought: A developmental analysis of self-efficacy. In J. H. Flavell & L. Ross (Eds.), *Social cognitive development: Frontiers and possible futures.* Cambridge, England: Cambridge University Press, 1981.

Bandura, A. Self-efficacy mechanism in human agency. *American Psychologist,* 1982a, *37:* 122–147.

Bandura, A. The self and mechanisms of agency. In J. Suls (Ed.), *Psychological perspectives of the self* (Vol. 1). Hillsdale, N.J.: Erlbaum, 1982b.

Bandura, A. The psychology of chance encounters and life paths. *American Psychologist,* 1982c, *37:* 747–755.

Bandura, A. *Social foundations of thought and action: A social cognitive theory.* Englewood Cliffs, N.J.: Prentice-Hall, 1986.

Bandura, A., & Walters, R. *Social learning and personality development.* New York: Holt, Rinehart and Winston, 1963.

Bannister, D. (Ed.) *Issues and approaches in personal construct theory.* Orlando, Florida: Academic Press, 1985.

Barrett-Lennard, G. T. The client-centered system unfolding. In F. J. Turner (Ed.), *Social work treatment: Interlocking theoretical approaches* (2nd ed.). New York: Free Press, 1979.

Becker, E. *The denial of death.* New York: Free Press, 1973.

Bem, D. J., & Allen, A. On predicting some of the people some of the time: The search for cross-situational consistencies in behavior. *Psychological Review,* 1974, *81:* 506–520.

Bergin, A. E. The evaluation of therapeutic outcomes. In A. E. Bergin & S. L. Garfield (Eds.), *Handbook of psychotherapy and behavior change: An empirical analysis.* New York: Wiley, 1971.

Bergin, A. E., & Strupp, H. H. *Changing frontiers in the science of psychotherapy.* Chicago: Aldine Atherton, 1972.

Bergin, A. E., & Suinn, R. M. Individual psychotherapy and behavior therapy. *Annual Review of Psychology,* 1975, *26:* 509–556.

Berzonsky, M. D. Eriksonian developmental stages. In R. Corsini (Ed.), *Encyclopedia of Psychology.* New York: Wiley, 1984, pp. 447–448.

Bieber, I. *Cognitive psychoanalysis.* New York: Aronson, 1980.

Blumenthal, R. Scholars seek the hidden Freud in newly emerging letters. *The New York Times,* 18 August 1981, pp. 15–16. (a)

Blumenthal, R. Did Freud's isolation, peer rejection prompt key theory reversal? *The New York Times,* 25 August 1981, pp. 13, 16. (b)

Bottome, P. *Alfred Adler: A portrait from life* (3rd ed.). New York: Vanguard Press, 1957.

Bower, G. H., & Hilgard, E. R. *Theories of learning* (5th ed.). Englewood Cliffs, N.J.: Prentice-Hall, 1981.

Breger, L. *Freud's unfinished journey: Conventional and critical perspectives in psychoanalytic theory.* London: Routledge & Kegan Paul, 1981.

Brenner, C. *An elementary textbook of psychoanalysis* (Rev. ed.). New York: International Universities Press, 1973. Paperback reprint: New York: Anchor Books, 1974.

Brome, V. *Jung: Man and myth.* New York: Atheneum, 1978.

Cantril, H., & Allport, G. W. *The psychology of radio.* New York: Harper, 1935.

Carlson, R. Personality. *Annual Review of Psychology,* 1975, *26:* 393–414.

Carlson, R., & Levy, N. Studies of Jungian typology: I. Memory, social perception, and social action. *Journal of Personality.* 1973, *41:* 559–576.

Cattell, R. B. *Description and measurement of personality.* New York: World Book Co., 1946.

Cattell, R. B. Concepts and methods in the measurement of group syntality. *Psychological Review,* 1948, *55:* 48–63.

Cattell, R. B. *Personality: A systematic, theoretical, and factual study.* New York: McGraw-Hill, 1950.

Cattell, R. B. *Factor analysis: An introduction and manual for psychologist and social scientist.* New York: Harper, 1952a.

Cattell, R. B. The three basic factor-analytic research designs—their interrelations and derivatives. *Psychological Bulletin,* 1952b, *49:* 499–520.

Cattell, R. B. *Personality and motivation structure and measurement.* New York: World Book Co., 1957.

Cattell, R. B. Personality theory growing from multivariate quantitative research. In S. Koch (Ed.), *Psychology: A study of a science* (Vol. 3). New York: McGraw-Hill, 1959, pp. 257–327.

Cattell, R. B. The multiple abstract variance analysis equations and solutions for nature-nurture research on continuous variables. *Psychological review,* 1960, *67:* 353–372.

Cattell, R. B. *Personality and social psychology.* San Diego: Knapp, 1964.

Cattell, R. B. *The scientific analysis of personality.* London: Penguin, 1965.

Cattell, R. B. (Ed.). *Handbook of multivariate experimental psychology.* Chicago: Rand McNally, 1966.

Cattell, R. B. *Abilities: Their structure, growth, and action.* Boston: Houghton Mifflin, 1971.

Cattell, R. B. *Personality and mood by questionnaire.* San Francisco: Jossey-Bass, 1973.

Cattell, R. B. *Personality and learning theory,* Vol. 1, *The structure of personality in its environment.* New York: Springer, 1979.

Cattell, R. B. *Personality and learning theory,* Vol. 2, *A systems theory of maturation and structured learning.* New York: Springer, 1980.

Cattell, R. B. *The inheritance of personality and ability: Research methods and findings.* New York: Academic Press, 1982.

Cattell, R. B., & Child, D. *Motivation and dynamic structure.* New York: Wiley, 1975.

Cattell, R. B., & Dreger, R. N. (Eds.). *Handbook of modern personality theory.* New York: Appleton-Century-Crofts, 1975.

Cattell, R. B., Eber, H. W., & Tatsuoka, M. M. *Handbook for the sixteen personality factor questionnaire.* Champaign, Ill.: Institute for Personality and Ability Testing, 1970.

Cattell, R. B., & Kline, P. *The scientific analysis of personality and motivation.* New York: Academic Press, 1976.

Cattell, R. B., & Scheier, I. H. *The meaning and measurement of neuroticism and anxiety.* New York: Ronald, 1961.

Chomsky, N. Review of Skinner's *Verbal Behavior. Language,* 1959, *35:* 26–58.

Chomsky, N. The case against B. F. Skinner. *New York Review of Books,* 1971, *12/20:* 18–24.

Clark, R. W. *Freud: The man and the cause.* New York: Random House, 1980.

Coles, R. *Erik H. Erikson: The growth of his work.* Boston: Little, Brown, 1970.

Corsini, R. (Ed.). *Current psychotherapies.* Itasca, Ill.: F. E. Peacock, 1973.

Crumbaugh, J. C. Cross-validation of purposes-in-life test based on Frankl's concept. *Journal of Individual Psychology,* 1968, *24:* 74–81.

Dement, W. Experimental dream studies. In J. Masserman (Ed.), *Science and psycho-*

analysis: Scientific proceedings of the academy of psychoanalysis (Vol. 7). New York: Grune & Stratton, 1964.

Dement, W. *Some must watch while some must sleep.* San Francisco: Freeman, 1974.

Dinkmeyer, D. C., Dinkmeyer, D. C., Jr., & Sperry, L. *Adlerian counseling and psychotherpy* (2nd Ed.). Columbus, Oh: Merrill, 1987.

Dollard, J., Doob, L. W., Miller, N. E., Mowrer, O. H., & Sears, R. R. *Frustration and aggression.* New Haven: Yale University Press, 1939.

Dollard, J., & Miller, N. E. *Personality and psychotherapy: An analysis in terms of learning, thinking, and culture.* New York: McGraw-Hill, 1950.

Dunnette, M. D. Fads, fashions, and folderol in psychology. *American Psychologist,* 1966, *21:* 343–352.

Eagle, M. N. *Recent developments in psychoanalysis: A critical evaluation.* New York: McGraw-Hill, 1984.

Eagle, M. N. Review of P. I. Mahony: *Freud and the Rat Man. Contemporary Psychology,* 1988, *33:* 205–206.

Ellenberger, H. F. *The discovery of the unconscious.* New York: Basic Books, 1970.

Ellenberger, H. F. The story of "Anna O.": A critical review with new data. *The Journal of the History of the Behavior Sciences,* 1972, *8:* 267–279.

Elms, A. C. Skinner's dark year and *Walden Two. American Psychologist,* 1981, *36:* 470–479.

Epstein, S. Explorations in personality today and tomorrow: A tribute to Henry A. Murray. *American Psychologist,* 1979, *34:* 649–653.

Epstein, S. The self-concept: A review and the proposal of an integrated theory of personality. In E. Staub (Ed.), *Personality: Basic aspects and current research.* Englewood Cliffs, N.J.: Prentice-Hall, 1980.

Epting, F. R. *Personal construct counseling and psychotherapy.* Chichester, England: Wiley, 1984.

Erikson, E. H. Statement to the committee on privilege and tenure of the University of California concerning the California loyalty oath. *Psychiatry,* 1951, *14:* 243–245.

Erikson, E. H. The dream specimen of psychoanalysis. *Journal of the American Psychoanalytic Association,* 1954, *2:* 5–56.

Erikson, E. H. *Young man Luther: A study in psychoanalysis and history.* New York: Norton, 1958.

Erikson, E. H. *Identity and the life cycle: Selected papers.* New York: International Universities Press, 1959.

Erikson, E. H. *Childhood and society.* (2nd ed.). New York: Norton, 1963.

Erikson, E. H. *Insight and responsibility: Lectures on the ethical implications of psychoanalytic insight.* New York: Norton, 1964.

Erikson, E. H. The ontogeny of ritualization. In R. Loewenstein et al. (Eds.), *Psychoanalysis—a general psychology.* New York: International Universities Press, 1966.

Erikson, E. H. *Identity: Youth and crisis.* New York: Norton, 1968.

Erikson, E. H. *Gandhi's truth: On the origins of militant nonviolence.* New York: Norton, 1969.

Erikson, E. H. *In search of common ground: Conversations with Erik H. Erikson and Huey P. Newton.* New York: Norton, 1973.

Erikson, E. H. *Dimensions of a new identity: The 1973 Jefferson lectures in the humanities.* New York: Norton, 1974.

Erikson, E. H. *Life history and the historical moment.* New York: Norton, 1975.

Erikson, E. H. *Toys and reasons.* New York: Norton, 1977.

Erikson, E. H. *The life cycle completed: A review.* New York: Norton, 1982.

Erwin, E. Psychoanalytic therapy: The Eysenck argument. *American Psychologist,* 1980, *35:* 435–443.

Evans, R. I. *Dialogue with Erich Fromm.* New York: Harper & Row, 1966.

Evans, R. I. *B. F. Skinner: The man and his ideas.* New York: E. P. Dutton, 1968.

Evans, R. I. *Dialogue with Erik Erikson.* New York: Harper & Row, 1967. Paperback reprint: New York: E. P. Dutton, 1969.

Evans, R. I. *Gordon Allport: The man and his ideas.* New York: E. P. Dutton, 1970.

Evans, R. I. *Carl Rogers: The man and his ideas.* New York: E. P. Dutton, 1975.

Evans, R. I. *Jung on elementary psychology: A discussion between C. G. Jung and Richard I. Evans* (2nd ed.). New York: E. P. Dutton, 1976.

Ewen, R. B. *An introduction to theories of personality.* (1st ed.). New York: Academic Press, 1980.

Ewen, R. B. Personality theories. In R. Corsini (Ed.), *Encyclopedia of Psychology.* New York: Wiley, 1984, pp. 19–23.

Eysenck, H. J. *Dimensions of personality.* London: Routledge & Kegan Paul, 1947.

Eysenck, H. J. The effects of psychotherapy: An evaluation. *Journal of Consulting Psychology,* 1952, *16:* 319–324.

Eysenck, H. J. The effects of psychotherapy. *International Journal of Psychiatry,* 1965, *1:* 99–142.

Eysenck, H. J. *The effects of psychotherapy.* New York: International Science Press, 1966.

Eysenck, H. J. *The biological basis of personality.* Springfield, Ill.: Thomas, 1967.

Eysenck, H. J. (Ed.). *Readings in extraversion–introversion* (Vols. 1–3). London: Staples, 1970–1971.

Fenichel, O. *The psychoanalytic theory of neurosis.* New York: Norton, 1945.

Ferster, C. B., & Skinner, B. F. *Schedules of reinforcement.* New York: Appleton-Century-Crofts, 1957.

Fiedler, F. E. A comparison of therapeutic relationships in psychoanalytic, nondirective, and Adlerian therapy. *Journal of Consulting Psychology,* 1950, *14:* 436–445.

Fine, R. Psychoanalysis. In R. Corsini (Ed.), *Current Psychotherapies.* Itasca, Ill.: F. E. Peacock, 1973, pp. 1–33.

Fisher, S., & Greenberg, R. P. *The scientific credibility of Freud's theories and therapy.* New York: Basic Books, 1977.

Fiske, D. W. *Strategies for personality research.* San Francisco: Jossey-Bass, 1978.

Fordham, F. *An introduction to Jung's psychology.* Great Britain: Pelican Books, 1966.

Foulkes, D. *The psychology of sleep.* New York: Charles Scribner's Sons, 1966.

Freud, A. *The ego and the mechanisms of defense.* Original publication: 1936. Revised edition: New York: International Universities Press, 1966.

Freud, S. Character and anal erotism. Original publication: 1908a. Standard edition: London: Hogarth Press, Vol. 9.

Freud, S. "Civilized" sexual morality and modern nervous illness. Original publication: 1908b. Standard edition: London: Hogarth Press, Vol. 9.

Freud, S. Analysis of a phobia in a five-year-old boy. Original publication: 1909. Standard edition: London: Hogarth Press, Vol. 10.

Freud, S. A difficulty in the path of psychoanalysis. Original publication: 1917a. Standard edition: London: Hogarth Press, Vol. 17.

Freud, S. On the transformation of instincts with special reference to anal erotism. Original publication: 1917b. Standard edition: London: Hogarth Press, Vol. 17.

Freud, S. *Why war?* Original publication: 1933. Standard edition: London: Hogarth Press, Vol. 22.

Freud, S. *Moses and monotheism.* Original publication: 1939. Standard edition: London: Hogarth Press, Vol. 23.

Freud, S. *Totem and taboo.* Original publication: 1912–1913. Standard edition: London: Hogarth Press, Vol. 13. Paperback reprint: New York: Norton, 1950.

Freud, S. *On dreams.* Original publication: 1901. Standard edition: London: Hogarth Press, Vol. 5. Paperback reprint: New York: Norton, 1952.

Freud, S. *Group psychology and the analysis of the ego.* Original publication: 1921. Standard edition: London: Hogarth Press, Vol. 18. Paperback reprint: New York: Norton, 1959.

Freud, S. *Beyond the pleasure principle.* Original publication: 1920. Standard edition: London: Hogarth Press, Vol. 18. Paperback reprint: New York: Norton, 1961a.

Freud, S. *Civilization and its discontents.* Original publication: 1930. Standard edition: London: Hogarth Press, Vol. 21. Paperback reprint: New York: Norton, 1961b.

Freud, S. *The future of an illusion.* Original publication: 1927. Standard edition: London: Hogarth Press, Vol. 21. Paperback reprint: New York: Norton, 1961c.

Freud, S. *The ego and the id.* Original publication: 1923. Standard edition: London: Hogarth Press, Vol. 19. Paperback reprint: New York: Norton, 1962.

Freud, S. *An autobiographical study.* Original publication: 1925. Standard edition: London: Hogarth Press, Vol. 20. Paperback reprint: New York: Norton, 1963a.

Freud, S. Fragment of an analysis of a case of hysteria. Original publication: 1905. Standard edition: London: Hogarth Press, Vol. 7. Paperback reprint: *Dora: An analysis of a case of hysteria.* New York: Collier, 1963b, pp. 21–144.

Freud, S. Formulations on the two principles of mental functioning. Original publication: 1911. Standard edition: London: Hogarth Press, Vol. 12. Paperback reprint: *General psychological theory.* New York: Collier, 1963c, pp. 21–28.

Freud, S. On narcissism: An introduction. Original publication: 1914. Standard edition: London: Hogarth Press, Vol. 14. Paperback reprint: *General psychological theory.* New York: Collier, 1963d, pp. 56–82.

Freud, S. Instincts and their vicissitudes. Original publication: 1915. Standard edition: London: Hogarth Press, Vol. 14. Paperback reprint: *General psychological theory.* New York: Collier, 1963e, pp. 56–82.

Freud, S. Repression. Original publication: 1915. Standard edition: London: Hogarth Press, Vol. 14. Paperback reprint: *General psychological theory.* New York: Collier, 1963f, pp. 104–115.

Freud, S. The unconscious. Original publication: 1915. Standard Edition: London: Hogarth Press, Vol. 14. Paperback reprint: *General psychological theory.* New York: Collier, 1963g, pp. 116–150.

Freud, S. The economic problem of masochism. Original publication: 1924. Standard edition: London: Hogarth Press, Vol. 19. Paperback reprint: *General psychological theory.* New York: Collier, 1963h, pp. 190–201.

Freud, S. *Jokes and their relation to the unconscious.* Original publication: 1905. Standard edition: London: Hogarth Press, Vol. 8. Paperback reprint: New York: Norton, 1963i.

Freud, S. *Inhibitions, symptoms, and anxiety.* Original publication: 1926. Standard edition: London: Hogarth Press, Vol. 20. Paperback reprint: *The problems of anxiety.* New York: Norton, 1963j.

Freud, S. My views on the part played by sexuality in the etiology of the neuroses. Original publication: 1906. Standard edition: London: Hogarth Press, Vol. 7. Paperback reprint: *Sexuality and the psychology of love.* New York: Collier, 1963k, pp. 11–19.

Freud, S. The psychogenesis of a case of female homosexuality. Original publication: 1920.

Standard edition: London: Hogarth Press, Vol. 18. Paperback reprint: *Sexuality and the psychology of love*. New York: Collier, 1963l, pp. 133–159.

Freud, S. Some neurotic mechanisms in jealousy, paranoia, and homosexuality. Original publication: 1922. Standard edition: London: Hogarth Press, Vol. 18. Paperback reprint: *Sexuality and the psychology of love*. New York: Collier, 1963m, pp. 160–170.

Freud, S. The infantile genital organization of the libido: A supplement to the theory of sexuality. Original publication: 1923. Standard edition: London: Hogarth Press, Vol. 19. Paperback reprint: *Sexuality and the psychology of love*. New York: Collier, 1963n, pp. 171–175.

Freud, S. The dissolution of the Oedipus complex. Original publication: 1924. Standard edition: London: Hogarth Press, Vol. 19. Paperback reprint: *Sexuality and the psychology of love*. New York: Collier, 1963o, pp. 183–193.

Freud, S. Some psychological consequences of the anatomical distinction between the sexes. Original publication: 1925. Standard edition: London: Hogarth Press, Vol. 19. Paperback reprint: *Sexuality and the psychology of love*. New York: Collier, 1963p, pp. 183–193.

Freud, S. Female sexuality. Original publication: 1931. Standard edition: London: Hogarth Press, Vol. 21. Paperback reprint: *Sexuality and the psychology of love*. New York: Collier, 1963q, pp. 194–211.

Freud, S. On psychotherapy. Original publication: 1905. Standard edition: London: Hogarth Press, Vol. 7. Paperback reprint: *Therapy and technique*. New York: Collier, 1963r, pp. 63–75.

Freud, S. The future prospects of psychoanalytic therapy. Original publication: 1910. Standard edition: London: Hogarth Press, Vol. 11. Paperback reprint: *Therapy and technique*. New York: Collier, 1963s, pp. 77–87.

Freud, S. Further recommendations on the technique of psychoanalysis. I. On beginning the treatment. Original publication: 1913. Standard edition: London: Hogarth Press, Vol. 12. Paperback reprint: *Therapy and technique*. New York: Collier, 1963t, pp. 135–156.

Freud, S. Further recommendations on the technique of psychoanalysis. II. Recollection, repetition and working through. Original publication: 1914. Standard edition: London: Hogarth Press, Vol. 12. Paperback reprint: *Therapy and technique*. New York: Collier, 1963u, pp. 157–166.

Freud, S. Further recommendations on the technique of psychoanalysis. III. Observations on transference-love. Original publication: 1915. Standard edition: London: Hogarth Press, Vol. 12. Paperback reprint: *Therapy and technique*. New York: Collier, 1963v, pp. 167–179.

Freud, S. Analysis terminable and interminable. Original publication: 1937. Standard edition: London: Hogarth Press, Vol. 23. Paperback reprint: *Therapy and technique*. New York: Collier, 1963w, pp. 233–271.

Freud, S. Constructions in analysis. Original publication: 1937. Standard edition: London: Hogarth Press, Vol. 23. Paperback reprint: *Therapy and technique*. New York: Collier, 1963x, pp. 273–286.

Freud, S. Notes on a case of obsessional neurosis. Original publication: 1909. Standard edition: London, Hogarth Press, Vol. 10. Paperback reprint: *Three case histories*. New York: Collier, 1963y, pp. 15–102.

Freud, S. Psychoanalytic notes on an autobiographical account of a case of paranoia (dementia paranoides). Original publication: 1911. Standard edition: London: Hogarth Press, Vol. 12. Paperback reprint: *Three case histories*. New York: Collier, 1963z, pp. 103–186.

Freud, S. From the history of an infantile neurosis. Original publication: 1918. Standard edition: London: Hogarth Press, Vol. 17. Paperback reprint: *Three case histories.* New York: Collier, 1963aa, pp. 103–316.

Freud, S. *The interpretation of dreams.* Original publication: 1900. Standard edition: London: Hogarth Press, Vol. 4–5. Paperback reprint: New York: Avon Books, 1965a.

Freud, S. *New introductory lectures on psychoanalysis.* Original publication: 1933. Standard edition: London: Hogarth Press, Vol. 22. Paperback reprint: New York: Norton, 1965b.

Freud, S. *The psychopathology of everyday life.* Original publication: 1901. Standard edition: London: Hogarth Press, Vol. 6. Paperback reprint: New York: Norton, 1965c.

Freud, S. *Three essays on the theory of sexuality.* Original publication: 1905. Standard edition: London: Hogarth Press, Vol. 7. Paperback reprint: New York: Avon Books, 1965d.

Freud, S. *Introductory lectures on psychoanalysis* (Rev. ed.). Original publication: 1916–1917. Standard edition: London: Hogarth Press, Vol. 15–16. Paperback reprint: New York: Norton, 1966.

Freud, S. *On the history of the psychoanalytic movement.* Original publication: 1914. Standard edition: London: Hogarth Press, Vol. 14. Paperback reprint: New York: Norton, 1967.

Freud, S. *An outline of psychoanalysis* (Rev. ed.). Original publication: 1940. Standard edition: London: Hogarth Press, Vol. 23. Paperback reprint: New York: Norton, 1969a.

Freud, S. *The question of lay analysis.* Original publication: 1926. Standard edition: London: Hogarth Press, Vol. 20. Paperback reprint: New York: Norton, 1969b.

Freud, S., & Breuer, J. *Studies on hysteria.* Original publication: 1895. Standard edition: London: Hogarth Press, Vol. 2. Paperback reprint: New York: Avon Books, 1966.

Fromm, E. *The forgotten language: An introduction to the understanding of dreams, fairy tales, and myths.* New York: Holt, Rinehart, & Winston, 1951. Paperback reprint: New York: Grove Press, 1957.

Fromm, E. *Marx's concept of man.* New York: Frederick Ungar, 1961.

Fromm, E. *Beyond the chains of illusion: My encounter with Marx and Freud.* New York: Simon & Schuster, 1962a.

Fromm, E. Interview in *The New York Post,* 22 April 1962b.

Fromm, E. *Escape from freedom.* New York: Holt, Rinehart & Winston, 1941. Paperback reprint: New York: Avon Books, 1965.

Fromm, E. *Psychoanalysis and religion.* New Haven: Yale University Press, 1950. Paperback reprint: New York: Bantam Books, 1967.

Fromm, E. *The crisis of psychoanalysis: Essays on Freud, Marx, and social psychology.* New York: Holt, Rinehart, & Winston, 1970. Paperback reprint: New York: Fawcett, 1971a.

Fromm, E. *The heart of man: Its genius for good or evil.* New York: Harper & Row, 1964. Paperback reprint: New York: Perennial, 1971b.

Fromm, E. *The anatomy of human destructiveness.* New York: Holt, Rinehart, & Winston, 1973.

Fromm, E. *The art of loving.* New York: Harper & Row, 1956. Paperback reprint: New York: Perennial, 1974a.

Fromm, E. *The revolution of hope.* New York: Harper & Row, 1968. Paperback reprint: New York: Perennial, 1974b.

Fromm, E. *Man for himself: An inquiry into the psychology of ethics.* New York: Holt, Rinehart & Winston, 1947. Paperback reprint: New York: Fawcett, 1976a.

Fromm, E. *The sane society.* New York: Holt, Rinehart & Winston, 1955. Paperback reprint: New York: Fawcett, 1976b.

Fromm, E. *To have or to be?* New York: Harper & Row, 1976c.

Fromm, E. *Greatness and limitations of Freud's thought.* New York: Harper & Row, 1980.

Fromm, E. *On disobedience: And other essays.* New York: Seabury Press, 1981.

Fromm-Reichmann, F. *Principles of intensive psychotherapy.* Chicago: University of Chicago Press, 1950.

Furtmüller, C. Alfred Adler: A biographical essay. Originally prepared: 1946. In H. L. Ansbacher & R. R. Ansbacher (Eds.), *Superiority and social interest* (3rd ed.). New York: Norton, 1979, pp. 311–394.

Garfield, S. Psychotherapy: A 40-year appraisal. *American Psychologist,* 1981, *36:* 174–183.

Gay, P. *Freud: A life for our time.* New York: Norton, 1988.

Gelman, D. Finding the hidden Freud. *Newsweek,* 30 November 1981, pp. 64–70.

Gelman, D. Revival sessions: A resurgence of interest in classic psychoanalysis. *Newsweek,* 25 November 1991, pp. 60–61.

Goldfried, M. R. Toward the delineation of therapeutic change principles. *American Psychologist,* 1980, *35:* 991–999.

Goldstein, K. *The organism.* New York: American Book Co., 1939.

Goldstein, K. *Human nature in the light of psychopathology.* Cambridge, Mass.: Harvard University Press, 1940.

Goleman, D. As a therapist, Freud fell short, scholars find. *The New York Times,* 6 March 1990, pp. B5, B9.

Gomes-Schwartz, B., Hadley, S. W., & Strupp, H. H. Individual psychotherapy and behavior therapy. *Annual Review of Psychology,* 1978, *29:* 435–471.

Graham, W., & Balloun, J. An empirical test of Maslow's need hierarchy theory. *Journal of Humanistic Psychology,* 1973, *13:* 97–108.

Hall, C. S. *The meaning of dreams.* New York: McGraw-Hill, 1966.

Hall, M. H. An interview with B. F. Skinner. *Psychology Today,* 1967a, *1*(5): 21–23; 68–71.

Hall, M. H. An interview with Rollo May. *Psychology Today,* 1967b, *1*(5): 25–29; 72–73.

Hall, M. H. A conversation with Carl Rogers. *Psychology Today,* 1967c, *1*(7): 19–21; 62–66.

Hall, M. H. A conversation with Abraham H. Maslow. *Psychology Today,* 1968a, *2*(2): 35–37; 54–57.

Hall, M. H. A conversation with Henry A. Murray. *Psychology Today,* 1968b, *2*(4): 57–63.

Harris, B. Whatever happened to little Albert? *American Psychologist,* 1979, *34:* 151–160.

Harris, B. Ceremonial versus critical history of psychology. *American Psychologist,* 1980, *35:* 218–219.

Heine, R. W. A comparison of patients' reports on psychotherapeutic experiences with psychoanalytic, nondirective, and Adlerian therapists. *American Journal of Psychotherapy,* 1953, *7:* 16–23.

Hetherington, E. M., & McIntyre, C. W. Developmental psychology. *Annual Review of Psychology,* 1975, *26:* 97–136.

Hilgard, E. R., & Bower, G. H. *Theories of learning* (4th Ed.). Englewood Cliffs, N.J.: Prentice-Hall, 1975.

Hoffman, E. *The right to be human: A biography of Abraham Maslow.* Los Angeles: Tarcher, 1988.

Horney, K. *The neurotic personality of our time.* New York: Norton, 1937.

Horney, K. *New ways in psychoanalysis.* New York: Norton, 1939.

Horney, K. *Self-analysis.* New York: Norton, 1942.

Horney, K. *Our inner conflicts: A constructive theory of neurosis.* New York: Norton, 1945.

Horney, K. *Neurosis and human growth: The struggle toward self-realization.* New York: Norton, 1950.

Horney, K. *Feminine psychology.* Original publication: 1923–1937. Paperback English edition: New York: Norton, 1967.

Hunt, J. M. Psychological development: Early experience. *Annual Review of Psychology,* 1979, *30:* 103–143.

Jackson, D. N., & Paunonen, S. V. Personality structure and assessment. *Annual Review of Psychology,* 1980, *31:* 503–551.

Jaffé, A. *The myth of meaning: Jung and the expansion of consciousness.* New York: G. P. Putnam's Sons, 1971. Paperback reprint: New York: Penguin Books, 1975.

Jones, E. Rationalization in everyday life. *Journal of Abnormal Psychology,* 1908, *3:* 161.

Jones, E. *The life and work of Sigmund Freud.* New York: Basic Books, Vol. 1, 1953. Paperback reprint (abridged): New York: Anchor Books, 1963a.

Jones, E. *The life and work of Sigmund Freud.* New York: Basic Books, Vol. 2, 1955. Paperback reprint (abridged): New York: Anchor Books, 1963b.

Jones. E. *The life and work of Sigmund Freud.* New York: Basic Books, Vol. 3, 1957. Paperback reprint (abridged): New York: Anchor Books, 1963c.

Jones, M. C. The elimination of children's fears. *Journal of Experimental Psychology,* 1924a, *7:* 382–390.

Jones, M. C. A laboratory study of fear: the case of Peter. *Journal of Genetic Psychology,* 1924b, *31:* 308–315.

Jung, C. G. The association method. Original publication: 1910. Standard edition: Princeton, N.J.: Princeton University Press, Vol. 2.

Jung, C. G. *Symbols of transformation.* Original publication: 1911–1912. Standard edition: Princeton, N.J.: Princeton University Press, Vol. 5.

Jung, C. G. Commentary on *The Secret of the golden flower.* Original publication: 1929. Standard edition: Princeton, N.J.: Princeton University Press, Vol. 13.

Jung, C. G. Some aspects of modern psychotherapy. Original publication: 1930. Standard edition: Princeton, N.J.: Princeton University Press, Vol. 16.

Jung, C. G. Problems of modern psychotherapy. Original publication: 1929. Standard edition: Princeton, N.J.: Princeton University Press, Vol. 16. Paperback reprint (slightly different translation): *Modern man in search of a soul.* New York: Harcourt, Brace & World, 1933a, pp. 28–54.

Jung, C. G. The aims of psychotherapy. Original publication: 1931. Standard edition: Princeton, N.J.: Princeton University Press, Vol. 16. Paperback reprint (slightly different translation): *Modern man in search of a soul.* New York: Harcourt, Brace & World, 1933b, pp. 55–73.

Jung, C. G. Archaic man. Original publication: 1931. Standard edition: Princeton, N.J.: Princeton University Press, Vol. 10. Paperback reprint (slightly different translation): *Modern man in search of a soul.* New York: Harcourt, Brace & World, 1933c, pp. 125–151.

Jung, C. G. Psychotherapists or the clergy. Original publication: 1932. Standard edition: Princeton, N.J.: Princeton University Press, Vol. 11. Paperback reprint (slightly different translation): *Modern man in search of a soul.* New York: Harcourt, Brace & World, 1933d, pp. 221–244.

Jung, C. G. A review of the complex theory. Original publication: 1934a. Standard edition: Princeton, N.J.: Princeton University Press, Vol. 8.

Jung, C. G. Archetypes of the collective unconscious. Original publication: 1934b. Standard edition: Princeton, N.J.: Princeton University Press, Vol. 9, Part 1.

Jung, C. G. The state of psychotherapy today. Original publication: 1934c. Standard edition: Princeton, N.J.: Princeton University Press, Vol. 10.

Jung, C. G. Principles of practical psychotherapy. Original publication: 1935a. Standard edition: Princeton, N.J.: Princeton University Press, Vol. 16.

Jung, C. G. What is psychotherapy? Original publication: 1935b. Standard edition: Princeton, N.J.: Princeton University Press, Vol. 16.

Jung, C. G. Psychological factors determining human behavior. Original publication: 1937. Standard edition: Princeton, N.J.: Princeton University Press, Vol. 8.

Jung, C. G. Psychology and religion (the Terry lectures). Original publication: 1938. Standard edition: Princeton, N.J.: Princeton University Press, Vol. 11. Paperback reprint: New Haven, Conn.: Yale University Press, 1938.

Jung, C. G. The psychology of the child archetype. Original publication: 1940. Standard edition: Princeton, N.J.: Princeton University Press, Vol. 9, Part 1.

Jung, C. G. *Psychology and alchemy.* Original publication: 1944. Standard edition: Princeton, N.J.: Princeton University Press, Vol. 12.

Jung, C. G. *Aion: Researches into the phenomenology of the self.* Original publication: 1951. Standard edition: Princeton, N.J.: Princeton University Press, Vol. 9, Part 2.

Jung, C. G. *Mysterium coniunctionis.* Original publication: 1955–1956. Standard edition: Princeton, N.J.: Princeton University Press, Vol. 14.

Jung, C. G. Flying saucers: A modern myth. Original publication: 1958a. Standard edition: Princeton, N.J.: Princeton University Press, Vol. 10.

Jung, C. G. The undiscovered self (present and future). Original publication: 1957. Standard edition: Princeton, N.J.: Princeton University Press, Vol. 10. Paperback reprint: *The undiscovered self.* New York: Mentor, 1958b.

Jung, C. G. *Memories, dreams, reflections.* New York: Random House, 1961. Paperback reprint: New York: Vintage Books, 1965.

Jung, C. G. (Ed.) *Man and his symbols.* London: Aldus Books, 1964. Paperback reprint: New York: Dell, 1968.

Jung, C. G. On psychic energy. Original publication: 1928. Standard edition: Princeton, N.J.: Princeton University Press, Vol. 8. Paperback reprint: *On the nature of the psyche.* Princeton, N.J.: Princeton University Press, 1969a, pp. 3–66.

Jung, C. G. On the nature of the psyche. Original publication. 1947. Standard edition: Princeton, N.J.: Princeton University Press, Vol. 8. Paperback reprint: *On the nature of the psyche.* Princeton, N.J.: Princeton University Press, 1969b, pp. 69–144.

Jung, C. G. Analytical psychology and education: Three lectures. Original publication: 1926. Standard edition: Princeton, N.J.: Princeton University Press, Vol. 17. Paperback reprint: *Psychology and education.* Princeton, N.J.: Princeton University Press, 1969c, pp. 55–122.

Jung, C. G. Child development and education. Original publication: 1928. Standard edition: Princeton, N.J.: Princeton University Press, Vol. 17. Paperback reprint: *Psychology and education.* Princeton, N.J.: Princeton University Press, 1969d, pp. 39–52.

Jung, C. G. The gifted child. Original publication: 1943. Standard edition: Princeton, N.J.: Princeton University Press, Vol. 17. Paperback reprint: *Psychology and education.* Princeton, N.J.: Princeton University Press, 1969e, pp. 125–135.

Jung, C. G. *The psychology of the transference.* Original publication: 1946. Standard edition: Princeton, N.J.: Princeton University Press, Vol. 16. Paperback reprint: Princeton, N.J.: Princeton University Press, 1969f.

Jung, C. G. Psychological aspects of the mother archetype. Original publication: 1938. Standard edition: Princeton, N.J.: Princeton University Press, Vol. 9, Part 1. Paperback reprint: *Four archetypes.* Princeton, N.J.: Princeton University Press, 1970a, pp. 9–44.

Jung, C. G. Concerning rebirth. Original publication: 1940. Standard edition: Princeton, N.J.: Princeton University Press, Vol. 9, Part 1. Paperback reprint: *Four archetypes.* Princeton, N.J.: Princeton University Press, 1970b, pp. 45–81.

Jung, C. G. The phenomenology of the spirit in fairytales. Original publication: 1945. Standard edition: Princeton, N.J.: Princeton University Press, Vol. 9, Part 1. Paperback reprint: *Four archetypes.* Princeton, N.J.: Princeton University Press, 1970c, pp. 85–132.

Jung, C. G. On the psychology of the trickster-figure. Original publication: 1954. Standard edition: Princeton, N.J.: Princeton University Press, Vol. 9, Part 1. Paperback reprint: *Four archetypes.* Princeton, N.J.: Princeton University Press, 1970d, pp. 135–152.

Jung, C. G. The stages of life. Original publication: 1930–1931. Standard edition: Princeton, N.J.: Princeton University Press, Vol. 8. Paperback reprint: *The portable Jung.* New York: Viking Press, 1971a, pp. 3–22.

Jung, C. G. The structure of the psyche. Original publication: 1927. Standard edition: Princeton, N.J.: Princeton University Press, Vol. 8. Paperback reprint: *The portable Jung.* New York: Viking Press, 1971b, pp. 23–46.

Jung, C. G. Instinct and the unconscious. Original publication: 1919. Standard edition: Princeton, N.J.: Princeton University Press, Vol. 8. Paperback reprint: *The portable Jung.* New York: Viking Press, 1971c, pp. 47–58.

Jung, C. G. Marriage as a psychological relationship. Original publication: 1925. Standard edition: Princeton, N.J.: Princeton University Press, Vol. 17. Paperback reprint: *The portable Jung.* New York: Viking Press, 1971d, pp. 163–177.

Jung, C. G. The transcendent function. Original publication: 1916. Standard edition: Princeton, N.J.: Princeton University Press, Vol. 8. Paperback reprint: *The portable Jung.* New York: Viking Press, 1971e, pp. 273–300.

Jung, C. G. On the relation of analytical psychology to poetry. Original publication: 1922. Standard edition: Princeton, N.J.: Princeton University Press, Vol. 15. Paperback reprint: *The spirit in man, art, and literature.* Princeton, N.J.: Princeton University Press, 1971f, pp. 65–83.

Jung, C. G. Psychology and literature. Original publication: 1930. Standard edition: Princeton, N.J.: Princeton University Press, Vol. 15. Paperback reprint: *The spirit in man, art, and literature.* Princeton, N.J.: Princeton University Press, 1971g, pp. 84–105.

Jung, C. G. Mandalas. Original publication: 1955. Standard edition: Princeton, N.J.: Princeton University Press, Vol. 9, Part 1. Paperback reprint: *Mandala symbolism.* Princeton, N.J.: Princeton University Press, 1972a, pp. 3–5.

Jung, C. G. A study in the process of individuation. Original publication: 1934. Standard edition: Princeton, N.J.: Princeton University Press, Vol. 9, Part 1. Paperback reprint: *Mandala symbolism.* Princeton, N.J.: Princeton University Press, 1972b, pp. 6–70.

Jung, C. G. Concerning mandala symbolism. Original publication: 1950. Standard edition: Princeton, N.J.: Princeton University Press, Vol. 9, Part 1. Paperback reprint: *Mandala symbolism.* Princeton, N.J.: Princeton University Press, 1972c, pp. 71–100.

Jung, C. G. On the psychology of the unconscious. Original publication: 1917. Standard edition: Princeton, N.J.: Princeton University Press, Vol. 7. Paperback reprint: *Two essays on analytical psychology.* Princeton, N.J.: Princeton University Press, 1972d, pp. 3–119.

Jung, C. G. The relations between the ego and the unconscious. Original publication: 1928. Standard edition: Princeton, N.J.: Princeton University Press, Vol. 7. Paperback reprint: *Two essays on analytical psychology.* Princeton, N.J.: Princeton University Press, 1972e, pp. 123–241.

Jung, C. G. New paths in psychology. Original publication: 1912. Standard edition: Princeton, N.J.: Princeton University Press, Vol. 7. Paperback reprint: *Two essays on analytical psychology.* Princeton, N.J.: Princeton University Press, 1972f, pp. 245–268.

Jung, C. G. Answer to Job. Original publication: 1952. Standard edition: Princeton, N.J.: Princeton University Press, Vol. 11. Paperback reprint: *Answer to Job.* Princeton, N.J.: Princeton University Press, 1973a.

Jung, C. G. Synchronicity: An acausal connecting principle. Original publication: 1952. Standard edition: Princeton, N.J.: Princeton University Press, Vol. 8. Paperback reprint: *Synchronicity.* Princeton, N.J.: Princeton University Press, 1973b, pp. 3–103.

Jung, C. G. On synchronicity. Original publication: 1951. Standard edition: Princeton, N.J.: Princeton University Press, Vol. 8. Paperback reprint: *Synchronicity.* Princeton, N.J.: Princeton University Press, 1973c, pp. 104–115.

Jung, C. G. General aspects of dream psychology. Original publication: 1916. Standard edition: Princeton, N.J.: Princeton University Press, Vol. 8. Paperback reprint: *Dreams.* Princeton, N.J.: Princeton University Press, 1974a, pp. 23–66.

Jung, C. G. On the nature of dreams. Original publication: 1945. Standard edition: Princeton, N.J.: Princeton University Press, Vol. 8. Paperback reprint: *Dreams.* Princeton, N.J.: Princeton University Press, 1974b, pp. 67–83.

Jung, C. G. The practical use of dream-analysis. Original publication: 1934. Standard edition: Princeton, N.J.: Princeton University Press, Vol. 16. Paperback reprint: *Dreams.* Princeton, N.J.: Princeton University Press, 1974c, pp. 87–109.

Jung, C. G. Individual dream symbolism in relation to alchemy. Original publication: 1936. Standard edition: Princeton, N.J.: Princeton University Press, Vol. 12. Paperback reprint: *Dreams.* Princeton, N.J.: Princeton University Press, 1974d, pp. 115–297.

Jung, C. G. Psychoanalysis and association experiments. Original publication: 1905. Standard edition: Princeton, N.J.: Princeton University Press, Vol. 2. Paperback reprint: *The psychoanalytic years.* Princeton, N.J.: Princeton University Press, 1974e, pp. 3–32.

Jung, C. G. *The psychology of dementia praecox.* Original publication: 1907. Standard edition: Princeton, N.J.: Princeton University Press, Vol. 3. Paperback reprint: Princeton, N.J.: Princeton University Press, 1974f, pp. 3–151.

Jung, C. G. On the psychogenesis of schizophrenia. Original publication: 1939. Standard edition: Princeton, N.J.: Princeton University Press, Vol. 3. Paperback reprint: *The psychology of dementia praecox.* Princeton, N.J.: Princeton University Press, 1974g, pp. 155–171.

Jung, C. G. The theory of psychoanalysis. Original publication: 1913. Standard edition: Princeton, N.J.: Princeton University Press, Vol. 4. Paperback reprint: *Critique of psychoanalysis.* Princeton, N.J.: Princeton University Press, 1975a, pp. 3–144.

Jung, C. G. General aspects of psychoanalysis. Original publication: 1913. Standard edition: Princeton, N.J.: Princeton University Press, Vol. 4. Paperback reprint: *Critique of psychoanalysis.* Princeton, N.J.: Princeton University Press, 1975b, pp. 147–160.

Jung, C. G. Freud and Jung: Contrasts. Original publication: 1929. Standard edition: Princeton, N.J.: Princeton University Press, Vol. 4. Paperback reprint: *Critique of psychoanalysis.* Princeton, N.J.: Princeton University Press, 1975c, pp. 225–232.

Jung, C. G. *Psychological types.* Original publication: 1921. Standard edition: Princeton, N.J.: Princeton University Press, Vol. 6. Paperback reprint: Princeton, N.J.: Princeton University Press, 1976.

Kahn, E. Heinz Kohut and Carl Rogers: A timely comparison. *American Psychologist,* 1985, *40:* 893–904.

Kaufmann, W. *Discovering the mind,* Vol. 3, *Freud versus Adler and Jung.* New York: McGraw-Hill, 1980.

Kazdin, A. E. *The token economy: A review and evaluation.* New York: Plenum Press, 1977.

Kelly, G. A. *The psychology of personal constructs* (2 vols.). New York: Norton, 1955. Paperback reprint [chapters 1–3 only]: *A theory of personality: The psychology of personal constructs.* New York: Norton, 1963.

Kelly, G. A. *Clinical psychology and personality: Selected papers.* (B. Maher, Ed.) New York: Wiley, 1969.

Kelly, G. A. A brief introduction to personal construct theory. In D. Bannister (Ed.), *Perspectives in personal construct theory.* New York: Academic Press, 1970a, pp. 1–29.

Kelly, G. A. Behavior is an experiment. In D. Bannister (Ed.), *Perspectives in personal construct theory.* New York: Academic Press, 1970b, pp. 255–269.

Kelman, H. C. Introduction. In K. Horney, *Feminine psychology.* New York: Norton, 1967.

Kilmann, R. H., & Taylor, V. A contingency approach to laboratory learning: Psychological types versus experimental norms. *Human Relations,* 1974, *27:* 891–909.

Kluckhohn, C., & Murray, H. A. Personality formation: The determinants. In C. Kluckhohn, H. A. Murray, & D. M. Schneider, (Eds.), *Personality in nature, society, and culture* (2nd ed.). New York: Knopf, 1953, pp. 53–67.

Lazarus, A. A. Where do behavior therapists take their troubles? *Psychological Reports,* 1971, *28:* 349–350.

Leboyer, F. *Birth without violence.* New York: Knopf, 1975.

Lewis, H. B. *Freud and modern psychology, Vol. 1: The emotional basis of mental illness.* New York: Plenum Press, 1981.

Locke, E. L. Is "behavior therapy" behavioristic? (An analysis of Wolpe's psycho-therapeutic methods). *Psychological Bulletin,* 1971, *76:* 318–327.

Lowry, R. J. (Ed.). *The Journals of A. H. Maslow.* (2 Vols.). Monterey, Ca.: Brooks/Cole, 1979.

Luborsky, L., Singer, B., & Luborsky, L. Comparative studies of psychotherapies: Is it true that "Everyone has won and all must have prizes?" *Archives of General Psychiatry,* 1975, *32:* 995–1008.

MacCorquodale, K. Skinner's *Verbal behavior:* A retrospective appreciation. *Journal of the Experimental Analysis of Behavior,* 1969, *12:* 831–841.

MacCorquodale, K. On Chomsky's review of Skinner's *Verbal behavior. Journal of the Experimental Analysis of Behavior,* 1970, *13:* 83–100.

Maher, B. (Ed.) *See* Kelly, 1969.

Mahony, P. J. *Freud and the Rat Man.* New Haven, Conn.: Yale University Press, 1986.

Manaster, G. J., & Corsini, R. J. *Individual psychology: Theory and practice.* Itasca, Ill.: F. E. Peacock, 1982.

Marcia, J. E. Development and validation of ego-identity status. *Journal of Personality and Social Psychology,* 1966, *3:* 551–558.

Marmor, J., & Woods, S. M. (Eds.). *The interface between the psychodynamic and behavioral therapies.* New York: Plenum, 1980.

Maslow, A. H. *Eupsychian management: A journal.* Homewood, Ill.: Irwin-Dorsey, 1965.

Maslow, A. H. *Toward a psychology of being* (2nd ed.). New York: Van Nostrand Reinhold, 1968.

Maslow, A. H. *The psychology of science: A reconnaissance.* New York: Harper & Row, 1966. Paperback reprint: Chicago: Regnery, 1969.

Maslow, A. H. *Religions, values, and peak-experiences.* Columbus: Ohio State University Press, 1964. Paperback reprint: New York: Viking, 1970a.

Maslow, A. H. *Motivation and personality* (2nd ed.). New York: Harper & Row, 1970b.

Maslow, A. H. *The farther reaches of human nature.* New York: Viking, 1971.

Masters, W. H., & Johnson, V. E. *Human sexual response.* Boston: Little, Brown, 1966.

May, R. (Ed.). Symbolism in religion and literature. New York: Braziller, 1960.

May, R. *The art of counseling.* Nashville: Abingdon-Cokesbury, 1939. Paperback reprint: Nashville: Apex Books, 1967a.

May, R. Contributions of existential psychotherapy. In R. May, E. Angel, & H. F. Ellen-berger (Eds.), *Existence: A new dimension in psychiatry and psychology.* New York: Basic Books, 1958. Paperback reprint: New York: Touchstone Books, 1967b, pp. 37–91.

May, R. The origins and significance of the existential movement in psychology. In R. May, E. Angel, & H. F. Ellenberger (Eds.), *Existence: A new dimension in psychiatry and psychology.* New York: Basic Books, 1958. Paperback reprint: New York: Touchstone Books, 1967c, pp. 3–36.

May, R. *Psychology and the human dilemma.* New York: Van Nostrand-Reinhold, 1967d.

May, R. The emergence of existential psychology. In R. May (Ed.), *Existential psychology* (2nd ed.). New York: Random House, 1969a.

May, R. Existential bases of psychotherapy. In R. May (Ed.), *Existential psychology* (2nd ed.). New York: Random House, 1969b.

May, R. *Love and will.* New York: Norton, 1969c.

May, R. *Power and innocence: A search for the sources of violence.* New York: Norton, 1972.

May, R. *Man's search for himself.* New York: Norton, 1953. Paperback reprint: New York: Delta, 1973.

May, R. *The courage to create.* New York: Norton, 1975.

May, R. *The meaning of anxiety* (Rev. ed.). New York: Norton, 1977a.

May, R. Reflections and commentary. In C. Reeves, *The psychology of Rollo May.* San Francisco: Jossey-Bass, 1977b, pp. 295–309.

May, R. *Freedom and destiny.* New York: Norton, 1981.

May, R. *My quest for beauty.* Dallas, Texas: Saybrook, 1985.

May, R., & Caligor, L. *Dreams and symbols: Man's unconscious language.* New York: Basic Books, 1968.

McGuire, W. (Ed.). *The Freud/Jung letters.* Princeton, N.J.: Princeton University Press, 1974.

McNemar, Q. The factors in factoring behavior. *Psychometrika,* 1951, *16:* 353–359.

Meltzoff, J., & Kornreich, M. *Research in psychotherapy.* New York: Atherton, 1970.

Menninger, K. A., & Holzman, P. S. *Theory of psychoanalytic technique* (2nd ed.). New York: Basic Books, 1973.

Miller, N. E. Obituary: John Dollard (1900–1980). *American Psychologist,* 1982, *37:* 587–588.

Miller, N. E., & Dollard, J. *Social learning and imitation.* New Haven: Yale University Press, 1941.

Mindess, H. *Makers of psychology: The personal factor.* New York: Human Sciences Press, 1988.

Mischel, W. Toward a cognitive social learning reconceptualization of personality. *Psychological Review,* 1973, *80:* 252–283.

Mischel, W., & Peake, P. K. Beyond deja vu in the search for cross-situational consistency. *Psychological Review,* 1982, *89:* 730–755.

Morgan, C. D., & Murray, H. A. A method for investigating fantasies. *Archives of Neurological Psychiatry,* 1935, *34:* 289–306.

Mosak, H. H., & Dreikurs, R. Adlerian psychotherapy. In R. Corsini (Ed.), *Current psychotherapies.* Itasca, Ill.: F. E. Peacock, 1973, pp. 35–83.

Mullahy, P. A theory of interpersonal relations and the evolution of personality. Original publication: 1945. In H. S. Sullivan, *Conceptions of modern psychiatry.* New York: Norton, 1953, pp. 239–294.

Murray, H. A. What should psychologists do about psychoanalysis? *Journal of Abnormal and Social Psychology,* 1940, *35:* 150–175.

Murray, H. A. *Thematic Apperception Test manual.* Cambridge, Mass.: Harvard University Press, 1943.

Murray, H. A. (Office of Strategic Services Assessment Staff). *Assessment of men.* New York: Rinehart, 1948.

Murray, H. A. Introduction. In H. Melville, *Pierre, or the ambiguities.* New York: Farrar Straus, 1949.

Murray, H. A. Some basic psychological assumptions and conceptions. *Dialectica,* 1951, *5:* 266–292.

Murray, H. A. Preparations for the scaffold of a comprehensive system. In S. Koch (Ed.), *Psychology: A study of a science* (Vol. 3). New York: McGraw-Hill, 1959, pp. 7–54.

Murray, H. A. The personality and career of Satan. *Journal of Social Issues,* 1962, *28:* 36–54.

Murray, H. A. Studies of stressful interpersonal disputations. *American Psychologist,* 1963, *18:* 28–36.

Murray, H. A. Autobiography. In E. G. Boring & G. Lindzey (Eds.), *A history of psychology in autobiography* (Vol. 5). New York: Appleton-Century-Crofts, 1967, pp. 283–310.

Murray, H. A. Components of an evolving personological system. In D. L. Sills (Ed.), *International encyclopedia of the social sciences* (Vol. 12). New York: Macmillan and Free Press, 1968a, 5–13.

Murray, H. A. In nomine diaboli. *New England Quarterly,* 1951, *24:* 435–452. Reprinted in *Psychology Today,* 1968b, *2*(4): 64–69.

Murray, H. A., & Kluckhohn, C. Outline of a conception of personality. In C. Kluckhohn, H. A. Murray, & D. M. Schneider (Eds.), *Personality in nature, society, and culture* (2nd ed.). New York: Knopf, 1953, pp. 3–52.

Murray, H. A. et al. *Explorations in personality.* New York: Oxford University Press, 1938.

Myers, I. B. *The Myers-Briggs Type Indicator.* Princeton, N.J.: Educational Testing Service, 1962.

Neimeyer, R. A. *The development of personal construct psychology.* Lincoln: University of Nebraska Press, 1985a.

Neimeyer, R. A. Personal constructs in clinical practice. In P. C. Kendall (Ed.), *Advances in cognitive-behavioral research and therapy* (Vol. IV). Orlando, Florida: Academic Press, 1985b, pp. 275–339.

Olson, H. A. (Ed.). *Early recollections: Their use in diagnosis and psychotherapy.* Springfield, Ill.: Charles C Thomas, 1979.

Oppenheimer, R. Analogy in science. *American Psychologist,* 1956, *11:* 127–135.

Orgler, H. *Alfred Adler: The man and his work.* New York: Liveright, 1963. Paperback reprint: New York: Mentor Books, 1972.

Overall, J. E. Note on the scientific status of factors. *Psychological Bulletin,* 1964, *61:* 270–276.

Pavlov, I. P. The scientific investigations of the psychical faculties or processes in the higher animals. *Science,* 1906, *24:* 613–619.

Pavlov, I. P. *Conditional reflexes: An investigation of the physiological activity of the cerebral cortex.* New York: Oxford University Press, 1927.

Pavlov, I. P. *Lectures on conditioned reflexes.* New York: International Publishers, 1928.

Perry, H. S. *Psychiatrist of America: The life of Harry Stack Sullivan.* Cambridge, Mass.: Belknap/Harvard University Press, 1982.

Phares, E. J., & Lamiell, J. T. Personality. *Annual Review of Psychology,* 1977, *28:* 113–140.

Polansky, N. A. *Integrated ego psychology.* New York: Aldine, 1982.

Progoff, I. *Jung's psychology and its social meaning.* New York: Julian Press, 1953. Paperback reprint (2nd ed.): New York: Anchor Books, 1973.

Rapaport, D., Gill, M. M., & Schafer, R. *Diagnostic psychological testing* (Rev. ed., edited by R. R. Holt). London: University of London Press, 1970.

Reeves, C. *The psychology of Rollo May.* San Francisco: Jossey–Bass, 1977.

Reik, T. *Listening with the third ear.* New York: Farrar, Straus and Co., 1948. Paperback reprint: New York: Pyramid, 1964.

Rieff, P. *Freud: The mind of the moralist.* New York: Viking, 1959. Paperback reprint: New York: Anchor Books, 1961.

Rieff, P. Introduction. In S. Freud, *Dora: An analysis of a case of hysteria.* New York: Collier, 1963.

Roazen, P. (Ed.). *Sigmund Freud.* Englewood Cliffs, N.J.: Prentice-Hall, 1973.

Roazen, P. *Erik H. Erikson: The power and limits of a vision.* New York: Free Press, 1976a.

Roazen, P. *Freud and his followers.* New York: Knopf, 1975. Paperback reprint: New York: Meridian, 1976b.

Rogers, C. R. *Counseling and psychotherapy: Newer concepts in practice.* Boston: Houghton Mifflin, 1942.

Rogers, C. R. *Client-centered therapy: Its current practice, implications, and theory.* Boston: Houghton Mifflin, 1951.

Rogers, C. R. A theory of therapy, personality, and interpersonal relationships, as developed in the client-centered framework. In S. Koch (Ed.), *Psychology: A study of a science* (Vol. 3). New York: McGraw-Hill, 1959, pp. 184–256.

Rogers, C. R. *On becoming a person: A therapist's view of psychotherapy.* Boston: Houghton Mifflin, 1961.

Rogers, C. R. Client-centered therapy. In E. Shostrom (Ed.), *Three approaches to psychotherapy* (Film No. 1). Orange, California: Psychological Films, 1965 (Transcript reprinted in Rogers & Wood, 1974, pp. 237–253.)

Rogers, C. R. Autobiography. In E. G. Boring & G. Lindzey (Eds.), *A history of psychology in autobiography* (Vol. 5). New York: Appleton-Century-Crofts, 1967, pp. 341–384.

Rogers, C. R. *Freedom to learn: A view of what education might become.* Columbus, Ohio: Charles E. Merrill, 1969.

Rogers, C. R. *Becoming partners: Marriage and its alternatives.* New York: Delta, 1972.

Rogers, C. R. *Carl Rogers on encounter groups.* New York: Harper & Row, 1970. Paperback reprint: New York: Perennial, 1973a.

Rogers, C. R. Some new challenges. *American Psychologist,* 1973b, *28:* 379–387.

Rogers, C. R. In retrospect: Forty-six years. *American Psychologist,* 1974, *29:* 115–123. (Reprinted in Evans, 1975, pp. 121–146.)

Rogers, C. R. *Carl Rogers on personal power.* New York: Delacorte, 1977.

Rogers, C. R. *A way of being.* Boston: Houghton-Mifflin, 1980.

Rogers, C. R. Nuclear war: A personal response. *American Psychological Association Monitor,* 1982, *13*(8): 6–7.

Rogers, C. R. *Freedom to learn for the 80s.* Columbus, Ohio: Merrill, 1983.

Rogers, C. R., & Dymond, R. F. (Eds.). *Psychotherapy and personality change.* Chicago: University of Chicago Press, 1954.

Rogers, C. R., Gendlin, E. T., Kiesler, D. J., & Truax, C. B. *The therapeutic relationship and its impact: A study of psychotherapy with schizophrenics.* Madison: University of Wisconsin Press, 1967.

Rogers, C. R., & Skinner, B. F. Some issues concerning the control of human behavior: A symposium. *Science,* 1956, *124:* 1057–1066. (Reprinted in Evans, 1975, pp. xliv–lxxxviii.)

Rogers, C. R., & Stevens, B. *Person to person: The problem of being human.* Moab, Utah: Real People Press, 1967. Paperback reprint: New York: Pocket Books, 1971.

Rogers, C. R., & Wood, J. K. Client-centered theory: Carl R. Rogers. In A. Burton (Ed.), *Operational theories of personality.* New York: Brunner/Mazel, 1974, pp. 211–258.

Rosenhan, D. L. On being sane in insane places. *Science,* 1973, *179:* 250–258.

Rubins, J. L. *Karen Horney: Gentle rebel of psychoanalysis.* New York: Dial, 1978.

Salter, A. *Conditioned reflex therapy.* New York: Farrar Straus, 1949.

Samelson, F. J. B. Watson's Little Albert, Cyril Burt's twins, and the need for a critical science. *American Psychologist,* 1980, *35:* 619–625.

Schiedel, D. G., & Marcia, J. E. Ego identity, intimacy, sex role orientation, and gender. *Journal of Personality and Social Psychology,* 1985, 21, 149–160.

Schulz, R., & Ewen, R. B. *Adult development and aging: Myths and emerging realities.* (2nd ed.) New York: Macmillan, 1992.

Schur, M. *Freud: Living and dying.* New York: International Universities Press, 1972.

Searles, H. F. *Collected papers on schizophrenia and related subjects.* New York: International Universities Press, 1965.

Sechrest, L. Personality. *Annual Review of Psychology,* 1976, *27:* 1–27.

Shevrin, H., & Dickman, S. The psychological unconscious: A necessary assumption for all psychological theory? *American Psychologist,* 1980, *35:* 421–434.

Shlien, J. M., Mosak, H. H., & Dreikurs, R. Effect of time limits: A comparison of two psychotherapies. *Journal of Counseling Psychology,* 1962, *9:* 31–34.

Shneidman, E. S. (Ed.). *Endeavors in psychology: Selections from the personology of Henry A. Murray.* New York: Harper & Row, 1981.

Shostrom, E. *Personal Orientation Inventory (POI): A test of self-actualization.* San Diego, Calif. Educational and Industrial Testing Service, 1963.

Shostrom, E. An inventory for the measurement of self-actualization. *Educational and Psychological Measurement,* 1965, *24:* 207–218.

Silverman, L. H. On the role of data from laboratory experiments in the development of the clinical theory of psychoanalysis. *International Review of Psycho-Analysis,* 1975, *2:* 1–22.

Silverman, L. H. Psychoanalytic theory: "The reports of my death are greatly exaggerated." *American Psychologist,* 1976, *31:* 621–637.

Singer, E. *Key concepts in psychotherapy* (2nd ed.). New York: Basic Books, 1970.

Skinner, B. F. *The behavior of organisms: An experimental analysis.* New York: Appleton-Century-Crofts, 1938.

Skinner, B. F. *Walden Two.* New York: Macmillan, 1948.

Skinner, B. F. *Verbal behavior.* New York: Appleton-Century-Crofts, 1957.

Skinner, B. F. *Science and human behavior.* New York: Macmillan, 1953. Paperback reprint: New York: Free Press, 1965.

Skinner, B. F. Autobiography. In E. G. Boring & G. Lindzey (Eds.), *A history of psychology in autobiography* (Vol. 5). New York: Appleton-Century-Crofts, 1967, pp. 385–413.

Skinner, B. F. *The technology of teaching.* Englewood Cliffs, N.J.: Prentice-Hall, 1968.

Skinner, B. F. *Contingencies of reinforcement: A theoretical analysis.* Englewood Cliffs, N.J.: Prentice-Hall, 1969.

Skinner, B. F. *Beyond freedom and dignity.* New York: Knopf, 1971. Paperback reprint: New York: Bantam, 1972a.

Skinner, B. F. *Cumulative Record: A selection of papers* (3rd ed.). New York: Appleton-Century-Crofts, 1972b.

Skinner, B. F. *About behaviorism.* New York: Knopf, 1974. Paperback reprint: New York: Vintage Books, 1976.

Skinner, B. F. *Particulars of my life.* New York: McGraw-Hill, 1976. Paperback reprint: New York: McGraw-Hill, 1977.

Skinner, B. F. *Reflections on behaviorism and society.* Englewood Cliffs, N.J.: Prentice-Hall, 1978.

Skinner, B. F. *The shaping of a behaviorist: Part two of an autobiography.* New York: Knopf, 1979.

Skinner, B. F. Intellectual self-management in old age. *American Psychologist,* 1983, *38:* 239–244.

Skinner, B. F. The shame of American education. *American Psychologist,* 1984, *39:* 947–954.

Skinner, B. F. What is wrong with daily life in the western world? *American Psychologist,* 1986, *41:* 568–574.

Skinner, B. F. *Upon further reflection.* Englewood Cliffs, N.J.: Prentice-Hall, 1987.

Skinner, B. F., & Vaughan, M. E. *Enjoy old age: A program of self-management.* New York: Norton, 1983.

Sloane, R. B., Staples, F. R., Cristol, A. H., Yorkston, N. J., & Whipple, K. *Psychotherapy versus behavior therapy.* Cambridge, Mass.: Harvard University Press, 1975.

Smith, M. B., & Anderson, J. W. Henry A. Murray (1893–1988). *American Psychologist,* 1989, 44, 1153–1154.

Stern, P. J. *C. G. Jung: The haunted prophet.* New York: Braziller, 1976. Paperback reprint: New York: Delta Books, 1977.

Strupp, H. H. Some comments on the future of psychoanalysis. *Journal of Contemporary Psychotherapy,* 1971, *3:* 117–120.

Strupp, H. H. On the technology of psychotherapy. *Archives of General Psychiatry,* 1972, *26:* 270–278.

Strupp, H. H. On the basic ingredients of psychotherapy. *Journal of Consulting and Clinical Psychology,* 1973, *41:* 1–8.

Strupp, H. H., & Bergin, A. E. Some empirical and conceptual bases for coordinated research in psychotherapy: A critical review of issues, trends, and evidence. *International Journal of Psychiatry,* 1969, *7:* 18–90.

Sullivan, H. S. Entry in *Current Biography,* 1942.

Sullivan, H. S. *Conceptions of modern psychiatry.* Original publication: 1947. Paperback reprint: New York: Norton, 1953.

Sullivan, H. S. *The interpersonal theory of psychiatry.* Original publication: 1953. Paperback reprint: New York, Norton, 1968.

Sullivan, H. S. *The psychiatric interview.* Original publication: 1954. Paperback reprint: New York: Norton, 1970.

Sullivan, H. S. *The fusion of psychiatry and social science.* Original publication: 1964. Paperback reprint: New York: Norton, 1971.

Sullivan, H. S. *Personal psychopathology.* Originally prepared: 1932–33. New York: Norton, 1972.

Sullivan, H. S. *Clinical studies in psychiatry.* Original publication: 1956. Paperback reprint: New York: Norton, 1973.

Sullivan, H. S. *Schizophrenia as a human process.* Original publication: 1962. Paperback reprint: New York: Norton, 1974.

Sulloway, F. J. *Freud, biologist of the mind: Beyond the psychoanalytic legend.* New York: Basic Books, 1979.

Sundberg, N. Trait psychology. In R. Corsini (Ed.), *Encyclopedia of psychology.* New York: Wiley, 1984, pp. 436–437.

Thorne, F. C., & Pishkin, V. The existential study. *Journal of Clinical Psychology,* 1973, *29:* 387–410.

Toder, N. L., & Marcia, J. E. Ego identity status and response to conformity pressure in women. *Journal of Personality and Social Psychology,* 1973, *26:* 287–294.

VandenBos, G. R. (Ed.) Special issue: Psychotherapy research. *American Psychologist,* 1986, *41:* 111–214.

VandenBos, G. R., & Pino, C. D. Research on the outcome of psychotherapy. In G. R. VandenBos (Ed.), *Psychotherapy: practice, research, policy.* Beverly Hills, Calif.: Sage, 1980, pp. 23–69.

Wachtel, P. L. *Psychoanalysis and behavior therapy: Toward an integration.* New York: Basic Books, 1977.

Wachtel, P. L. Investigation and its discontents: Some constraints on progress in psychological research. *American Psychologist,* 1980, *35:* 399–408.

Wachtel, P. L. *Action and insight.* New York: Guilford Press, 1987.

Wahba, M. A., & Bridwell, L. G. Maslow reconsidered: A review of research on the need hierarchy theory. *Organizational Behavior and Human Performance,* 1976, *15:* 212–240.

Wallerstein, R. S., & Sampson, H. Issues in research in the psychoanalytic process. *International Journal of Psychoanalysis,* 1971, *52:* 11–50.

Waterman, A. S., Kohutis, E., & Pulone, J. The role of expressive writing in ego identity formation. *Developmental Psychology,* 1977, *13:* 286–287.

Waterman, C. K., Buebel, M. E. & Waterman, A. S. Relationship between resolution of the identity crisis and outcomes of previous psychosocial crises. *Proceedings of the Annual Convention of the American Psychological Association,* 1970, *5:* 467–468.

Watson, J. B. Psychology as the behaviorist views it. *Psychological Review,* 1913, *20:* 158–177.

Watson, J. B. *Behavior from the standpoint of a behaviorist.* Philadelphia: Lippincott, 1919.

Watson, J. B. *Behaviorism.* New York: Norton, 1924.

Watson, J. B., & Rayner, R. Conditioned emotional reactions. *Journal of Experimental Psychology,* 1920, *3:* 1–14.

Watson, J. B., & Watson, R. R. Studies on infant psychology. *Scientific Monthly,* 1921, *13:* 493–515.

Welkowitz, J., Ewen, R. B., & Cohen, J. *Introductory statistics for the behavioral sciences* (4th ed.). San Diego, Calif.: Harcourt Brace Jovanovich, 1991.

Wexler, D. A., & Rice, L. N. *Innovations in client-centered therapy.* New York: Wiley, 1974.

White, M. J. Sullivan and treatment. In P. Mullahy (Ed.), *The contributions of Harry Stack Sullivan.* New York: Hermitage House, 1952, pp. 117–150.

Whitmont, E. C., & Kaufmann, Y. *Analytical psychotherapy.* In R. Corsini (Ed.), *Current psychotherapies.* Itasca, Ill.: F. E. Peacock, 1973, pp. 85–117.

Wiggins, J. S. *In defense of traits.* Paper presented at the 9th annual symposium on the use of the MMPI, Los Angeles, 1974.

Williams, J. B. W., & Spitzer, R. L. (Eds.) *Psychotherapy research: Where are we and where should we go?* New York: Guilford, 1984.

Wolpe, J. *Psychotherapy by reciprocal inhibition.* Stanford, Ca.: Stanford University Press, 1958.

Wolpe, J. *The practice of behavior therapy* (2nd ed.). New York: Pergamon, 1973.

Wolpe, J., & Lazarus, A. A. *Behavior therapy techniques: A guide to the treatment of neuroses.* New York: Pergamon, 1966.

Wolpe, J., & Rachman, S. Psychoanalytic "evidence": A critique based on Freud's case of Little Hans. *Journal of Nervous and Mental Diseases,* 1960, *131:* 135–148.

Wylie, R. C. *The self-concept* (Vol. 1). Lincoln: University of Nebraska Press, 1974.

Wylie, R. C. *The self-concept* (Vol. 2). Lincoln: University of Nebraska Press, 1979.

Wylie, R. C. Self-concept. In R. Corsini (Ed.), *Encyclopedia of psychology.* New York: Wiley, 1984, pp. 282–285.

Yalom, I. D., & Lieberman, M. A. A study of encounter group casualties. *Archives of General Psychiatry,* 1971, *25:* 16–30.

CREDITS

Photos

Chapter 2
p. 17, The Bettmann Archive, Inc.

Chapter 3
p. 79, The Bettmann Archive, Inc.

Chapter 4
p. 123, The Bettmann Archive, Inc.

Chapter 5
p. 163, The Bettmann Archive, Inc.

Chapter 6
p. 187, UPI/The Bettmann Archive, Inc.

Chapter 7
p. 203, The Bettmann Archive, Inc.

Chapter 8
p. 233, UPI/The Bettmann Archive, Inc.

Chapter 9
p. 273, The Bettmann Archive, Inc. (Gordon Allport)
AP Wide World Photos (Henry A. Murray)

Chapter 10
p. 313, Courtesy Raymond B. Cattell

Chapter 11
p. 339, Ohio State University Photo Archives

Chapter 12
p. 371, The Bettmann Archive, Inc.

Chapter 13
p. 395, Brandeis University Photo

Chapter 14
p. 419, Courtesy Rollo May

Chapter 15
p. 447, The Bettmann Archive, Inc.

Chapter 16
p. 485, Yale University Archives, Yale University Library (John Dollard)
AP Wide World Photos (Neal E. Miller)
Courtesy Albert Bandura

Figures

8.1. Slightly modified from Children and Society, Second Edition, by Erik H. Erikson, by permission of W.W. Norton & Company, Inc. Copyright 1950, © 1963 by W.W. Norton & Company, Inc. Copyright renewed 1978 by Erik H. Erikson.

9.1. This publication is based on *Study of Values,* Allport, G.W., Vernon, P.E., and Lindzey, G.A., Copyright © 1960. Reprinted with permission of the Publisher, The Riverside Publishing Company, 8420 W. Bryn Mawr Avenue, Chicago, IL 60631. All rights reserved.

9.2. Murray, H.A. Thematic Apperception Test Manual, Harvard University Press, Copyright © 1943 by the President and Fellows of Harvard College, 1971 by Henry H. Murray. Adapted from Plate 12-F.

10.1. Cattell, R.B. The Scientific Analysis of Personality, Penguin, 1965. Adapted from Cattell, R.B. and Kline, P. *The Scientific Analysis of Personality and Motivation,* Academic Press, 1976, Fig. 9-1, p. 177.

15.1. Courtesy B.F. Skinner.

16.1. Adapted from *Personality and Psychotherapy: An Analysis in Terms of Learning, Thinking, and Culture* by J. Dollard and N. Miller. Copyright © 1950, McGraw-Hill Book Company. Used by permission.

INDEX

(Note: Page numbers in *italics* refer to definitions in Capsule Summaries.)

597